S0-CNC-474

THE BEST PLAYS OF 1928-29

THE BEST PLAYS OF 1928-29

AND THE

YEAR BOOK OF THE DRAMA IN AMERICA

Edited by

BURNS MANTLE

LIBRARY
SEMINOLE JR. COLLEGE

FEB 19 1975

SANFORD, FLORIDA

DODD, MEAD AND COMPANY
NEW YORK - - - - - 1969

"Street Scene," copyright, 1928, 1929, by Elmer Rice.
Copyright and published, 1929, by Samuel French, New York.

"Journey's End," copyright, 1929, by R. C. Sherriff.
Copyright, and published, 1929, by Brentano's.

"Wings Over Europe," copyright, 1928, 1929, by Robert Nichols and Maurice Browne.
Copyright and published, 1929, by Covici-Friede, New York.

"Holiday," copyright, 1928, by Philip Barry.
Copyright and published, 1929, by Samuel French.

"The Front Page," copyright, 1928, by Ben Hecht and Charles MacArthur.
Copyright and published, 1928, by Covici-Friede, New York.

"Let Us Be Gay," copyright, 1928, 1929, by Rachel Crothers.
Copyright and published, 1929, by Samuel French.

"Machinal," copyright, 1928, by Sophie Treadwell.

"Little Accident," copyright, 1928, by Floyd Dell and Thomas Mitchell.

"Gypsy," copyright, 1928, by Maxwell Anderson.

"The Kingdom of God," copyright, 1923, 1929, by G. Martinez Sierra.
Copyright and published, 1929, by E. P. Dutton & Co., New York.

Copyright, 1929,
By DODD, MEAD AND COMPANY, Inc.

PRINTED IN THE U. S. A.

INTRODUCTION

THIS is the tenth anniversary volume of "The Best Plays" series. No particular significance attaches to it for that reason, save that it does round out a ten-year history of what we are already beginning to speak of in America as the *living* theatre to differentiate it from the on-rushing and terribly named *talkies* and their mechanical reproduction of new dramas and old.

Unquestionably the next ten years will see vast changes in the theatre entertainment offered American playgoers. The living theatre will either meet the opposition and grow greater year by year, strengthening its position of superiority as a medium of dramatic expression, as we believe it will, or it will be gradually relegated to a position of secondary importance and be passed in popularity by its younger and cheaper screen rival, as many bolder visionaries are courageous enough at the moment to contend.

This tenth year in our own book history of the native theatre has been one, I am not at all pleased to report, that has given some comfort to the opposition. Its productions have been fewer, its successes scarcer than usual. Its fine plays have been quite up to standards formerly established, but there were not many of them. I found it extremely difficult to make a selection of ten that should prove both readable and fairly representative of this most unusual season for inclusion in this book.

Not only have I been puzzled, but my usually dependable collaborateur, the playgoing public, has been distressfully uncertain of its own changing tastes. No more than two of the ten plays I have selected enjoyed extended runs such as have been scored by at least six of each ten chosen in other years. In fact several of the plays I have taken this year, from the public's viewpoint, have been entitled to no more than quite limited engagements. Notably Robert Nichols' and Maurice Browne's "Wings Over Europe" and Maxwell Anderson's "Gypsy."

"Wings Over Europe" is an extremely well written and, to me, fascinatingly imaginative drama. "Gypsy" is also well written and is, again to me, important in that it represents another American writer's attempt to expose, and thereby help to clear, certain accepted phases of a new feminine psychology that will stand a considerable amount of observation and discussion. It follows a course charted by Sidney Howard in "The Silver Cord" in revealing certain handicaps of birth and training that the romantic drama has long suppressed.

"Street Scene," with which Elmer Rice won this year's Pulitzer award, is worthy of the honor conferred. The popularity of this vibrant drama will, I feel, be greater in those theatre centers familiar with congested tenement life and the consequent juxtaposition of families of mixed blood, but its strongly humanized story should win supporters for it anywhere.

"Journey's End" is an English boy's simple statement of adventures and reactions experienced in the World War. Because of its simplicity and its convincing truth this play achieves drama that is human and fine beyond that of any other war play I know. It probably is not as big a play, as it is neither as steadily moving nor as exciting emotionally, as our own "What Price Glory?" But I feel a reason for this is found in the fact that it is a story exclusively of an officer group as contrasted with the Stallings-Anderson study of the human run of a marine battalion.

Philip Barry's "Holiday" and Rachel Crothers' "Let Us Be Gay" are observant social comedies revealing recognizable American characters in action. Mr. Barry, writing with an eye to fitting the peculiarities of an actress who herself has sprung from the social strata with which his play deals, has managed also to focus attention upon characteristic reactions of our monied aristocracy that are revealing and interesting. Miss Crothers, one feels, has written largely with the idea of furnishing no more than an evening's light entertainment, but there is also back of her little comedy enough intelligent observation to give it some purpose.

"The Front Page" is the most vivid and in certain aspects the truest of newspaper plays. Its profanities and vulgarities are, I feel, a bit overdone in the cause of an exposure that shall hew ruthlessly to the last oath, and many people have foolishly accepted its personnel as representing all newspaper men in place of that segregated group devoted to the police and criminal court assignments in the larger cities. But it is true to its theme and vibrantly thrilling as drama.

Floyd Dell's and Thomas Mitchell's "Little Accident" was the only light comedy success of the year, and the first American play I recall that has taken even semi-serious account of a paternal instinct that reasonably parallels that of the maternal.

Sierra's "The Kingdom of God" is confessedly episodic, but achieves moments of fine eloquence. Its underlying theme also serves to draw attention to such human injustice as needs correction the world over and it represents Ethel Barrymore's choice of a play with which she hopes to begin the establishment of a repertory.

I debated long as to whether I should use Frederick Lonsdale's "The High Road" or Sophie Treadwell's "Machinal." The Lonsdale piece is about the only romantic drama in the season's list, and there is, I know, a considerable public that still demands romance in the theatre. It was also approved by a considerable public through its run of a hundred and forty-seven performances.

On the other hand "Machinal" is a stronger and more original work, and failed of popular endorsement largely, I felt at the time of its playing, because it was generally accepted as merely one more retelling of a sordid murder trial such as clutter our court dockets—such a trial as that of Ruth Snyder and Judd Gray which admittedly inspired its writing. Also it is true that "Machinal" is dependent to a considerable extent upon the effectiveness of its presentation, upon its visualization as well as its statement. In the production these features were admirably emphasized by the direction of Arthur Hopkins and the mise-en-scène furnished by Robert Edmund Jones.

However, when I came to compare the two scripts Miss Treadwell's drama seemed so much more significant as a character study that I promptly determined to give it preference.

Among other plays I considered were Somerset Maugham's "The Sacred Flame," a strong and well written drama that was, unfortunately, a two-week failure, indicating that its unpleasant theme (that of a mother's justification for murdering a cripple son to save him the discovery of his wife's unfaithfulness) is not to the liking of our public; Maxwell Anderson and Harold Hickerson's "Gods of the Lightning," which was an excellent job of special pleading for the Sacco-Vanzetti sympathizers, and naturally, limited in appeal, and Sil-Vara's continental comedy, "Caprice," which I feel, so far as our theatre is concerned, was carried to success very largely by the personal appeal of its chief players, Alfred Lunt and Lynn Fontanne, of the Theatre Guild's first acting company. None of these plays seemed to me to possess stronger claims for inclusion than those I used.

"The Best Plays of 1928-29" contains also, you will find if you are interested, such statistical and other information as has featured previous volumes. I hope you like it.

B. M.

Forest Hills, L. I., June 15, 1929.

CONTENTS

	PAGE
Introduction	v
The Season in New York	3
The Season in Chicago	11
The Season in San Francisco	17
The Season in Southern California	21
Street Scene, by Elmer Rice	26
Journey's End, by R. C. Sherriff	54
Wings Over Europe, by Robert Nichols and Maurice Browne	88
Holiday, by Philip Barry	120
The Front Page, by Ben Hecht and Charles MacArthur	152
Let Us Be Gay, by Rachel Crothers	195
Machinal, by Sophie Treadwell	225
Little Accident, by Floyd Dell and Thomas Mitchell	252
Gypsy, by Maxwell Anderson	283
The Kingdom of God, by G. Martinez Sierra	316
The Plays and Their Authors	347
Plays Produced in New York, 1928-29	352
Little Theatre Tournament	500
Statistical Summary	513
Plays That Have Run Over 500 Performances on Broadway	514
Birth Places and Birth Dates of Prominent Actors	515
Necrology	524
Index of Authors	529
Index of Plays and Casts	533

THE BEST PLAYS OF 1928-29

THE BEST PLAYS OF 1928-29

THE SEASON IN NEW YORK

THE impression is fairly general that the legitimate theatre came a cropper this last season. I am without record of the number of times the report has been sent out from New York that such was the case—that the season of 1928-29 was, in very fact, the worst theatre season the Broadway stage has suffered within the memory of living playgoers—but I have good reason to believe that that statement was repeated in print a good hundred times and out of print thousands of times the last six months.

Normally all things in the theatre are weighed in the scales of comparison. A season, a play, a producer, an actor—these are either good or bad as they, singly or collectively, may be compared with a standard set by a better season, a better play, a more successful producer, or a more popular actor gone before.

This year, however, for the first time in many years, the cries of pain and protest from the camps of the showmen have been inspired by more tangible causes than those of active imaginations and comparative misfortunes.

It *has* been a bad season. Even, as it most frequently is described in the selecter showman circles, a rotten season.

It started being a bad season, in fact, as far back as February of last year, before the previous season closed. About that time the season of 1927-28 broke sharply. Suddenly managers and producers found themselves forced to admit a state of great confusion, both mental and financial. Something had happened. They did not know just what, but they were glad when June came.

When activities were resumed in August the more hopeful of them were whistling bravely and hoping for the best. During September, October and November they came forward courageously with the pick of their new stock—and not more than a half dozen of the first hundred plays produced paid the costs of their production.

Alibis, explanations, excuses were numerous. The most popular of these centered about the menace of the talkies. With this great novelty added to the previously established fascinations of the screen, and sold at prices one-half of those charged by the living theatre, it was not to be wondered that the legitimate theatre suffered.

But there were also many contributing causes admitted. These included a boast of prophecies come true by those of high standards of taste and decency in public exhibits. Had they not said if the theatre continued to be given over to those profane and lascivious exhibitions that had characterized it the last few years it would soon lose the support of its most dependable patrons?

Those who hate the speculators blamed the speculators. Those who have had trouble with impudent or irritable box-office attachés traced the growing unpopularity of the playhouse to them. The high cost of playgoing was frequently cited.

About everything that could be blamed was blamed—except the bad plays. The fact that there were many, many more ill-advised and poorly directed productions of short-weight and extravagantly priced entertainments than in any other single season in the history of the theatre escaped general comment.

The theatre has been and is still suffering from a period of too great in place of too little prosperity. Sensational post-war profits attracted a choice assortment of speculative, inexperienced and incompetent producers to what is called show business. The overproduction that followed cheapened the theatre's output and disgusted its patrons.

Being naturally an optimistic person, particularly after all the shooting is over, I can find cheering events enough in last season's record to make it seem worth while.

It was the season, for instance, in which the Theatre Guild completed its first ten years of intelligent play producing and was able to call attention to a record that included seventy dramas presented, nine thousand performances given and thirty-two thousand subscribers signed as supporters in New York alone. All this from bankrupt beginnings and through a period in which other and less intelligent ventures were failing and falling on every hand.

Moreover this same Theatre Guild was able to report the spread of its activities to other cities—to Chicago, Philadelphia, Boston, Cleveland, Pittsburgh, Baltimore, Detroit, Cincinnati, St. Louis and Washington to be specific—and to the support of several thousand subscribers in each of these centers. Here, then, are playgoers with faith in the living theatre and a confidence in its better play producers that not only augurs well for the theatre's future but actually guarantees its more important enterprises.

The fact that the Theatre Guild repertory is frequently distasteful to one public and as frequently entirely beyond the comprehension of another is beside the point. The fact remains that it is a constructive and soundly visioned enterprise of great value to the drama and to all believers in the theatre.

Last season was also the season that Eva Le Gallienne's Civic Repertory Theatre, organized for the good of those who may be poor in purse but rich in the artistic urge, enjoyed its most prosperous year without a single new popular hit to bless its box office with. Its most generally supported productions were revivals of Tchekov's "The Cherry Orchard" and Barrie's "Peter Pan."

It was, on its discouraging side, the season that Eugene O'Neill failed with "Dynamo" to top or equal the success of "Strange Interlude" or live up to the hopes and expectations of his too-expectant critics. The fact that he plainly said, in explanation of this particular discussion drama, that it was the first of a trilogy and therefore could not be fairly judged save as a sort of prologue, did not save him. I don't know that it should have saved him. "Dynamo," preceding the plays to follow by a season or two, had to be judged on its values and meaning as independent entertainment. As such it failed to interest all save those who are themselves given to fascinated and puzzled contemplation of the eternal mysteries which religion attempts to explain.

Future historians of the theatre will be able to extract the better part of a chapter from this troubled season of 1928-29 from the adventure of Christopher Morley and associates in Hoboken drama.

Mr. Morley, being a scholar and a gentleman by birth and training and a showman by instinct, thought that to play with a stock company on the Jersey side of the Hudson would furnish a good season's fun. With three others, Cleon Throckmorton, a scene designer; Harry Wagstaffe Gribble, an author and director, and Conrad Milliken, a writer, he leased the old Rialto Theatre, engaged a group of players and began the presentation of a typical present-day resident stock company repertory.

For some weeks business was neither very good nor very bad. There were enough good weeks to keep the partners ininterested, but hoped-for profits were lacking and discouragement dogged the heels of enterprise. Then one week, Throckmorton having acquired a script of that old Boucicault melodrama in which William A. Brady used to be an actor, a piece called "After Dark," he proposed that they try a revival of that play set, costumed and acted as it was forty years ago. They did. For a week or two there was not much response. Jersey audiences were pleased to jeer politely at the crudities of the old drama, but nothing resembling a hit developed until the play had been running ten days or two weeks.

Then some one discovered that here was a new adventure in playgoing. The Broadway Theatre at the time was wallowing in the doldrums. Plenty of new plays were being tried but nothing interesting was being revealed. Why not take the tubes or the ferry to Hoboken, test the reports that real beer could be had with one's meals and stay for a look at Mr. Morley's dramatic curio?

Within a fortnight such adventuring had literally become the fad of the hour. Seats for the performances of "After Dark" were booked weeks ahead at the speculators' libraries and at speculators' prices. Places at table in the Hoboken restaurants were reserved days in advance. At Meyers' hotel, a famous German hofbrau before the war, tables were set up in the lobby where bookkeepers formerly kept the brass-tagged keys and the guests' mail, in the old-fashioned barroom, in the reading rooms and in the cellar. And all these were filled with diners from Manhattan and its surrounding boroughs. Mr. Morley began the circulation of advertisements describing Hoboken as "The Last Seacoast of Bohemia" and business grew apace.

The last report I had of it "After Dark" was still running strong through its thirty-second week with no visible indication of distress. It gave every prospect of continuing through the summer, even though a group of the snoopier prohibition agents had taken steps to stop the flow of hops and hilarity at the neighboring bars.

Following the success of "After Dark" the Morleys leased a second theatre and revived "The Black Crook," with a feminine chorus that, broadly speaking, had never heard of the Hollywood diet nor would be interested if it had. This, too, proved a popular success for several weeks, but never attained the favor of "After Dark," and was withdrawn at the end of the season, after a run of twelve weeks.

Last season was also the season that saw the dedication of a theatre named to honor Ethel Barrymore, an event of no great significance in one way, seeing that practically every second person in the theatre has had a theatre named for him at one time or another, but a fitting tribute to the reigning head of America's best beloved stage family.

It was the season that saw great preparation made to welcome the ex-champion of the prize ring, Mr. John Dempsey, to the drama. And it is to the season's credit that it rejected Mr. Dempsey as both artist and entertainer, for all he proved a better actor than most of his predecessors sprung from the same calling.

Finally it was a season that, starting with the brazenly profane "Front Page," grew gradually less and less profane through its nine months until at the end stage cursing had practically returned to normal. Playwrights are still given to plain and fancy swearing, but the need must now justify the use of such words as were formerly either forbidden by managers or deleted by good taste.

Picking up the sequence of events where we left it in the previous volume of this series, the last half of June, 1928, saw two plays produced and neither successfully. One was the importation of the Play-Arts Guild of Baltimore, a revival of the Gilbert-Sullivan "Patience" that had been successfully presented at home.

July was distinguished by the arrival of Mr. George White's "Scandals" and by nothing else. August brought the first outstanding success in Charles MacArthur's and Ben Hecht's "The Front Page," previously mentioned.

Mr. Carroll's "Vanities" also began in August, being average as to merit. A dramatization of the Sinclair Lewis' novel, "Elmer Gantry," failed in August, or shortly thereafter, and so did a promisingly atmospheric story of negroes in the great war written by Ransom Rideout and entitled "Goin' Home." A second newspaper play, "Gentlemen of the Press," was less colorful and less profane than "The Front Page" and likewise less successful.

The September group included Sophie Treadwell's impressive idealization of the Snyder murder trial, and scored two definite musical successes, the first Arthur Hammerstein's production of "Good Boy," filled with imported trick scenery, and the other "The New Moon," an operetta destined to annex the season's popularity prize in its division of entertainment.

Included in this September group were Philip Dunning's melodrama "Night Hostess"; Frederick Lonsdale's "The High Road," a comedy of an actress who could have married into the peerage but didn't; a piece called "This Thing Called Love," which stayed on for four months; and "Jarnegan," a rough drama concerned with life in Hollywood as Jim Tully saw it and Richard Bennett played it. "Jarnegan" lasted for 136 performances, which surprised several persons.

October's contributions are frequently the most important of the year. In one respect they proved so this year. There were thirty-eight of them altogether, and of the thirty-eight I count eight that lingered for more than a hundred performances.

These eight were George Cohan's clean little musical comedy, "Billie"; Irene Bordoni's not so clean little French comedy, "Paris"; Tom Barry's "Courage," which ran on and on for months with Janet Beecher playing the lead; Floyd Dell's and Thomas Mitchell's "Little Accident," which ran the season out; a sweeping musical comedy success called "Hold Everything"; the annual Fred Stone show, "Three Cheers," with the amiable Will Rogers nobly substituting for Fred, who had smashed himself up in an airplane accident; the two-charactered melodrama, "Jealousy," in which Fay Bainter and John Halliday played, and George Kaufman's "Animal Crackers," written to fit several Marx brothers.

The police closed Mae West's "Pleasure Man" in October. Channing Pollock tried to awaken a distrust of our wasteful ways and slipping moral standards with a Broadway allegory called "Mr. Moneypenny," and there was a splendidly enthusiastic production of a drama called "Gods of the Lightning," written by Maxwell Anderson and Harold Hickerson with the Sacco-Vanzetti trial as background and the injustice of a certain commonwealth's courts as a theme. But these were all financially unsuccessful.

November was also normally active. The imported "This Year of Grace," with Noel Coward, its author, and Beatrice Lillie in the chief parts, was an early entrant; Philip Barry's "Holiday" came late, as also did Margaret Barnes' dramatization of "The Age of Innocence" and A. A. Milne's "The Perfect Alibi." All these ran through the season.

George Tyler's revival of "Macbeth," with Lyn Harding and Florence Reed; the Coburn's revival of "The Yellow Jacket"; the Guild's revival of Bernard Shaw's "Major Barbara"; the production of "A Most Immoral Young Lady," which Alice Brady carried through several months; the regretted failure of a powerful but unpleasant drama, "The Sacred Flame," by Somerset Maugham, and the production of a showy melodrama of the South Seas called "Congai," with Helen Menken, were incidents of the month before the holidays.

The season was near its peak by now. Florenz Ziegfeld, continuing a five-year record of successes, brought Eddie Cantor, "Whoopee" and five Lady Godivas to the New Amsterdam stage early in December and they were popular until the following midsummer. The Guild produced and stunned even its intellectuals with the Browne-Nichols "Wings Over Europe"; David Belasco converted the Belasco Theatre into a steel-sheeted hades for "Mima" and Lenore Ulric, Miss Barrymore opened her theatre with Sierra's "Kingdom of God" and the Alfred Lunts returned to the Guild Theatre with "Caprice."

Otherwise the holidays may be recalled by those who enjoy recalling such things as the time of Walter Hampden's revival of "Cyrano de Bergerac," the arrival of Bert Lytell from the cinema pastures with a double-exposure melodrama called "Brothers," which he played successfully through the winter and into hot weather, and Lew Fields' return to the stage in a piece put together mostly by his son Herbert and his daughter Dorothy and called "Hello, Daddy!"

Now the producers began noticeably to falter. Of twenty-six plays produced in January only two were successful. One of these, fortunately for us, was Elmer Rice's "Street Scene." The other was a lively musical comedy about golf called "Follow Thru," which developed into a tremendous favorite. Otherwise there was nothing, save Lewis Beach's comedy called "Merry Andrew," which deserved a better fate than it won, and S. N. Behrman's oversophisticated study in fantastic satire, "Serena Blandish."

There were only sixteen plays produced in February, and none of them successfully. "Fioretta," being clean and costly, did threaten to disturb the jazz producers, but could do no more than threaten and was withdrawn when Earl Carroll's backers padlocked the bankroll that had made the production possible.

O'Neill's "Dynamo" was the oustanding failure of the month and Rachel Crothers' "Let Us Be Gay" the single outstanding success. A Jewish character comedy, "Kibitzer," did fairly well and a colored piece called "Harlem" brought a picture of a negro "rent party" to Broadway that caused a mild sensation because of its orgiastic dances. Basil Sidney and Mary Ellis tried a second Milne comedy, a fluffy bit called "Meet the Prince," in February, and carried it through three months on the strength of their personal popularity. They were married a month after the play closed.

March was another month of few productions and a single hit.

Gilbert Miller sent over "Journey's End" from London and this splendid war play, written by R. C. Sherriff an English amateur, did much to revive a faith in the drama that was slowly but surely expiring.

The first musical comedy for which Owen Davis has written the book, one called "Spring Is Here," with Glenn Hunter playing its chief adolescent, had a March opening and did well for twelve weeks. More than that was expected of it, but much was expected of a lot of plays last season that failed of realization.

The Theatre Guild suffered one of its few failures with a well-intentioned but slightly dated comedy by Bruce Gould and Beatrice Blackmer called "Man's Estate" and recovered with a quasi-success, "The Camel Through the Needle's Eye," adapted by Philip Moeller from a Czechoslovakian original in April. Ethel Barrymore, through temporarily with "The Kingdom of God," produced "The Love Duel" with some success, but not a great deal. Morris Gest excitedly introduced the Freiburg "Passion Play" in a repainted Hippodrome and less excitedly removed it six weeks later. New York was not interested. Nor at all scandalized by the introduction of Adolph Fassnacht as a living Christ.

Late April saw "The Little Show" annex the spring revue honors, watched "The Grand Street Follies" slip into an unexpected failure, and took more interest than usual in Walter Hartwig's annual Little Theatre tournament which was won by the Gardens Players of Forest Hills, L. I., with their production of Barrie's "Shall We Join the Ladies?" There was nothing in May worth mentioning and less in early June.

There were, if you are interested in figures, 224 productions during the season, which is only thirty below last year's record and twenty-five below that of the year before. Of these one hundred and fifty odd were dramatic and the rest musical. We will agree that, by and large, it was a bad season and get it over with.

THE SEASON IN CHICAGO

By Virginia Dale
Dramatic Critic, *Chicago Journal*

THE Chicago season of 1928-1929 felt that much press-agented depression rather by the scarcity of entertainment supplied from the fountainhead of Manhattan than by lack of support vouchsafed such plays as arrived worthy of attention.

The established homes of the drama were ofttimes with a sorrier tale to tell than the drama itself. The Princess was only lighted once, and that was for the deservedly short life there of Garland Anderson's "Appearances." The Studebaker had but two attractions and The Playhouse, returned hopefully to the usage of the Dramatic Muse after two years as a cinema, had but one. That house of long tradition, the LaSalle, is turned definitely into a rendezvous for those devoted to the leaping lithographs (it is one of the few remaining within the confines of the Loop not to install sound equipment), and the old Olympic, renovated, with its façade washed and its interior posts removed, took up fresh life as the New Apollo—the Shuberts thus reinstating the name given a former theatre which went film and disdained identification with the famous god.

The first palatial home of vaudeville in this mid-west, the Majestic, after six years' occupation with the small time, also snuggled under the ever-expanding wing of Shubert; musical shows have populated it with two briefly-enduring exceptions. The Woods alternated from September (1928) almost painstakingly between plays and pictures, bridging "the silly season" with "After Dark" for whose sake hisses became as sibilant and happy as ever they could have been in Hoboken. The decision at the end of the season was to keep the so-called twin theatres—the Harris and Selwyn—for dramatic attractions in the future, thus robbing the musical didos of two occasional locales.

The Goodman Theatre, our local pride and joy, made not only further inroads into civic favor but showed the less abstract proof of a sixty percent financial advance over its former year. This fourth season of its life saw such productions as Sheridan's "The

Critic," Barrie's "Dear Brutus," Sean O'Casey's first American exhibition of "Shadow of a Gunman," Pirandello's "Six Characters in Search of an Author" and a translation of Leibick's "The Golem" (previously done here by the Moscow Art Theatre in Russian), added to its repertoire. It saw B. Iden Payne become a standing co-director with Thomas Wood Stevens, and Whitford Kane rejoining the repertory company as sometime director and actor following his affiliation with the New York Theatre Guild Acting Company. The resumption of activities at the Goodman will see an added theatre nestling at the foot of the one so well fixed, and to be christened the Studio Theatre; it will be used for more intimate productions generally, but at least a part of its first season will be spent with a second company acting the identical plays being done simultaneously in its mother house—an experiment to be undertaken in the interests of the overflow, and interesting enough in its singularity.

The Goodman is important in that it is the first of the numerous attempts to establish a resident repertoire organization that has met with success. A long list of leaders, many with more ambition than ability, has settled on this lakeside momentarily with the intention of Bringing Art to the Masses, and vanished like the magician's rabbits. We knew Maurice Browne when!—when he used a dishpan from Mr. Woolworth's emporium to hold his cluster of lights in the wings, and long before he discovered prosperity and "Journey's End." The Goodman has eschewed the esoteric and never thumbed its admittedly artistic (but not arty) nose at commercialism. Its ever-increasing promise and current fulfillment provides nice evidence that Chicago, with its bit more than 3,000,000 souls, not only can, but will, support a theatre meriting it.

The season's tragedy followed close on the opening in May of the comedy, "Your Uncle Dudley," which took possession of the long dark Illinois. The piece had gone into rehearsal under George C. Tyler with Hilda Moore whose death, three days before the première, caused the excellent Beatrice Terry to arrive here with the star, Raymond Hitchcock, and Mrs. Jacques Martin. The play (by Howard Lindsay and Bertrand Robinson) was a rich bit of fun, admirably plotted to develop the character of title reference—a small-towner given to promoting his town's welfare at the expense of his own. "Your Uncle Dudley" clicked instantly and seemed set for a summer run. Hitchcock had given three performances under the stress of horrible pain, leaving his bed at St. Luke's Hospital to be on hand at curtain time. But with the arrival of the first mid-week matinée he was unable to raise his head and the show was closed. (Hitchcock remained in the Chicago hospital for several weeks in a serious condition.)

Otis Skinner presented our metropolis with another notable première, "A Hundred Years Old," translated from the Quinteros' original by the Granville-Barkers. Supported by Fred Tiden, Katherine Grey, Octavia Kenmore and others, the expectation was to play but three weeks; however, the successful box office was responsible for its remaining thrice that. "A Hundred Years Old" is assuredly the most placid piece of playmaking ever done, fastening for its interest on the centenarian whose birthday approaches, and so amazingly minus situation or incident as to foster the opinion it was solely by the fine acting of Mr. Skinner and his large personal following, that not only survival but success, attended it.

The Theatre Guild provided another première—"Arms and the Man"—done later in New York. It was the only offering of the Guild season here to contain Lynn Fontanne and Alfred Lunt, a circumstance that caused some discontent. "Volpone," "Marco Millions" and "Porgy" followed, all splendidly acted, but the names of Fontanne and Lunt have a glamour to the natives of this inland who felt the absence of these white-headed children meant Chicago was being slighted. It is worthy of notice, however, that the Guild has leased the Blackstone for its next season here from Sept. 23 to March 22 (1930) and so early as June its subscriptions nearly equalled the total at the time of its last opening. As the bookings stand at this writing, we are promised "Caprice," "Major Barbara," "Wings Over Europe," "R.U.R." and "Strange Interlude."

Shakespeare found much attention during the late winter and early spring, no less than three companies presenting the great poetic works within four weeks, while Genevieve Hamper (Mrs. Robert Mantell) stole along in late April and in an outlying house went into her repertoire.

George Arliss was the first to arrive; his gentlemanly performance of "The Merchant of Venice" was being well received when "Macbeth" opened, so heralded and linked with the name of Gordon Craig as to cause some confusion in the minds of the naïve who were almost ready to believe some one called Craig had written a new tragedy called "Macbeth." The two-week engagement was at the Auditorium (the only other attraction there during the season outside of opera was the return run of "Rio Rita"), and though there was a $2.50 top, business was not such as to promote unrestrained joy on the part of the revival's producer, George C. Tyler.

The Stratford-Upon-Avon players slipped rather inauspiciously into the Studebaker on the not too-firmly planted heels of Scotland's king; in two weeks no less than a quartet of plays was given: "The Taming of the Shrew," "Hamlet," "Julius Cæsar" and "The Merry Wives of Windsor." All of them found considerable admiration on the part of the critics and support—that less altruistic quality—on the part of the public.

Repertoire was further represented here by the D'Oyley Carte Opera company which in a fortnight presented five of the delightful Savoyard works: "The Gondoliers," "The Mikado," "Trial by Jury," "The Pirates of Penzance" and "Iolanthe," and while the company was accepted as the reigning survival of the original, its "business" with the famous works so frequently departed from recognized tradition to fall to a somewhat music 'all level, those taking their Gilbert and Sullivan without a grain of salt felt as children might who see Santa Claus without his whiskers.

Jed Harris added materially to his substantial bank account with his three synchronically-running productions: "The Front Page," "The Royal Family" and "Coquette." They were high in the list of the season's successes. James B. Fagin's "And So To Bed" had a nice run, stimulated by the instant recognition of the fine talents of Eugenie Leontovitch, a fact which was immediately exploited with the result that this capable Russian's name went up in lights. "The Queen's Husband" jogged comfortably along for fifteen weeks at the Cort with Roland Young, and "Jealousy" found fond response at the Adelphi for nine.

"The Trial of Mary Dugan" quickly clicked with its original company headed by Ann Harding and Robert Williams, and was eventually supplanted by a second and then a third group, slipped in without causing a decline in business. "The High Road," with Edna Best and Herbert Marshall and an entirely British supporting cast, was first listed for two weeks, later granted four and ended with three to its credit—which tells its own story. "Paris Bound" never hit. Mae West met with much patronage for eighteen weeks with her "Diamond Lil." The tail-end of the season brought along Frank Kirkland's laborious effort to be dramatically obscene by using the old ballad, "Frankie and Johnnie," for the basis of a play and which resulted in the unforgivable sin: stupidity. A palpable intention to out-

Lil "Diamond Lil," "Frankie and Johnnie" was less an example of a woman done wrong than a play. It was in its third poor week at the Adelphi when the police rushed in where its angel (A. H. Woods) feared to tread, and closed it. No one mourned the passing.

Richard Bennett built a good box office for Jim Tully's dramatized novel, "Jarnegan," perhaps less because of the quality and interest in the mud-slinging play itself, than by his curtain speeches. Crowds hastened to hear Mr. Bennett chastize the critics, and came away ruminating on his voluminous (and very vocal) arguments for Truth in the drama; there was less concern with whatever truth was encountered in the drama in question. However, reasons appear to have less importance than results in the business of the theatre, and Bennett's expert showmanship, equalling his ability as an actor, was responsible for one of the season's most profitable engagements.

The excellent acting of "Burlesque" suffered lack of attention to a degree, due, it seemed, to the title. Our seat and center of mid-west culture is peppered with burlesque houses, and our natives and their friends appeared to regard a name as a description. "The Command to Love" and "The Bachelor Father" had better than a fair success. "Dracula" was another hit. Unlike the previous season, crime pieces achieved scant approval. Such tries as "Gang War" and "Trapped" speedily gave up their local ghosts and sought sympathy in towns perhaps less furnished with the spectacle of gun play on the part of their own citizenry.

Chicago's polyglot population has always been the target for such alien-tongued actors as any impresario is fathering. Few twelve months pass without either the Hebrew or Yiddish companies settling here briefly, and the last year was no exception. Maurice Schwartz appeared with his Yiddish Art Theatre acting Sholom Asch's "Kiddus Hashem" for four weeks. The teutonic touch was sponsored by Morris Gest who presented Moissi in August Scholz' German translation of "Redemption." But the high hopes of the buoyant Gest were dashed by a not too profitable two weeks' run.

It was the first season within recent memory to see all-colored companies in the drama; revue has been containing such negroes as are framed by our prosceniums. The flourishing six-weeks' engagement of "Porgy" found "In Abraham's Bosom" taking up residence almost around the corner, but the latter's combination of Pulitzer prize award and suggestion of Being Worth

While was perhaps too terrifying for amusement seekers generally. It was short lived. "Harlem" arrived in late spring and magnetized immediate attention. The negro denizens denounced it through their own two newspapers and but for a small trickle, refused to buy seats. After eight weeks our alert police awoke—or was prodded—into taking action against it and "Harlem" was saved for an increase of patronage by the deletion of a few scenes.

As always, musical comedies, operettas and revues added their glint to the fiscal returns; Thurston came with his hanky-panky and the Isadora Duncan Dancers sent a chosen few into throes of enthusiasm. The newspaper reporters and special interviewers were kept on the hop, skip and jump meeting trains filled with deserting Broadway players trekking for the gold in them thar mountains of celluloid and sound on the western frontier.

The attendance upon the so-called "talkies" unmistakably stole something from the legitimate theatre, but by no means left it to languish, and in proportion to the depression reported elsewhere, business was about as usual beside the sweet waters of Lake Michigan—as usual, that is, for such attractions as found their way here. If their numbers were diminished Chicago's interest was not.

THE SEASON IN SAN FRANCISCO

By George C. Warren

THE theatrical year ending June 1 has been without much novelty, but has been interesting because it has moved Broadway nearer to San Francisco in the matter of plays and players. A number of the successes, most of them, in fact, of the New York season have been seen here with capable casts, often with several of the New York actors who played in them in the metropolis; occasionally as in the cases of "The Bachelor Father," "Coquette" and "The Silent House," the casts intact.

Earlier in the season plays of last year in New York came with casts almost complete. Some of them were "The Command to Love," with everybody but Ferdinand Gottschalk, who didn't want to travel so far; "The Spider" with William Courtenay; "The Road to Rome" including Jane Cowl and Sir Guy Standing, and Frank Craven in "The Nineteenth Hole" with nine of the principal people that had acted with him in the comedy in New York.

Two developments of the year have been the advancing power and prestige of Henry Duffy, and the formation of a producing firm made up of Edward Belasco and Homer Curran, who are taking the Broadway plays and presenting them with strong casts. During the year Duffy has had built for him and has opened the Dufwin Theatre in Oakland, California, a modern theatre in every way, where with casts of as much strength as he employs in Los Angeles and San Francisco, he is able to put plays on for runs of three to five weeks.

He also leased for a long term the old Baker Theatre in Portland, Ore., completely reconstructed it, called it the Dufwin—a combination of the first syllables of his name and that of his wife, Dale Winter—and is presenting plays there for from one to five weeks, the latter unprecedented run being accomplished by Leo Carrillo in a revival of "Lombardi, Ltd."

Duffy has also developed a guest star system and finds many of the prominent actors are anxious to come out to the Pacific Coast and act for him. During the year his casts have been headed by Berton Churchill, Sidney Toler, Edmund Breese, May

Robson, Robert McWade, Clara Blandick, Emma Dunn, Leo Carrillo, Walker Whiteside and Guy Bates Post, as well as some other well known actors.

Surprises of the year were the great success of the Stratford-upon-Avon Festival Players in repertoire of Shakespeare's plays, and a three weeks' engagement of the D'Oyley Carte Opera company in the comic operas of Gilbert and Sullivan. The Stratford players, coming the week before Christmas, packed the Geary Theatre for two weeks doing six plays in that time, and turning away hundreds with "Hamlet" and "Richard III."

The company gives good smooth performances of Shakespeare, and nothing more. They are a versatile lot of actors, entirely competent, but in no case brilliant. George Hayes, the best known actor among them, is a fair Hamlet and an interesting Richard—they use the Shakespeare text in "Richard III." Roy Byford, a corpulent gentleman, played Falstaff in "The Merry Wives of Windsor" and in "King Henry IV, Part One," and is an excellent interpreter of the Fat Knight, but does not obliterate memories of William F. Owen in the rôle.

D'Oyley Carte's son brought the London group of Gilbert and Sullivan singers with Henry Lytton playing and singing the comedy rôles. They were seen in "The Mikado," "The Pirates of Penzance," sung with "Trial by Jury"; "The Gondoliers," "Iolanthe" and "Ruddigore," dividing the weeks with these productions. Their success was enormous, their performances filling the big Columbia Theatre for the entire engagement.

Both of these English companies came across Canada, through British Columbia, and down the Pacific Coast by way of Seattle and Portland.

One of the high spots of the year was the reopening of the Capitol Theatre for almost an entire performance of "The Captive," which was stopped just before the final curtain when the police leaped over the footlights and in somewhat dramatic fashion arrested the players.

This theatre has had a checkered career of late years. It had been remodeled and refurnished for the opening with "The Captive." It was built some years ago by John Cort and was known for several seasons as the Cort Theatre. Homer Curran took it to establish a playhouse here, and called it the Curran.

Under his management it was for many years the home of the Shubert attractions in San Francisco. On the building of the new Curran Theatre, it became the Century, and subsequently was named the Capitol.

At the present moment Oliver Morosco, hoping to stage a comeback, has taken a lease on the house and proposes to open it June 15 with the production of a play dealing with night club life called "Some One in White." The play is by Mrs. Fremont Older, wife of a distinguished citizen of the State, long time editor of the *San Francisco Call.*

Of the few original productions in the bay region, one of the chief plays is "The Maniac," by Tom Barry, produced by Henry Duffy at his President Theatre, San Francisco, with Edmund Breese in the title rôle.

Duffy had made a tentative production of the play in his Portland house, where it was done by the regular stock company for trial purposes. It is a play of the terror school with something of mystery in its plot. The story is logical, with all the strange happenings accounted for at the end of the play. There are moments of suspense and generally good character drawing. It will probably have a Broadway hearing next season.

Another play headed for the Big Street is "Romance, Inc.," written by Crane Wilbur and H. H. Van Loan. It was tried at the Fulton Theatre, Oakland, with Wilbur and his wife, Beatrice Blinn, in the cast. The play deals with motion picture making and is original in its use of the entire audience as part of the plot. Much of the action takes place in the auditorium and finally the audience is engaged as a body of extras for a theatre scene in the picture that is being made.

A third play, that may have a New York production, is "What a Woman Wants," which Marjorie Rambeau hopes to use as her reintroduction to Broadway next season. It is by DeWitt Newing, and is concerned with the rebellion of a forty-year-old spinster against her domineering sister, twenty years her elder. The comedy has good material but needs tightening and some rewriting. Miss Rambeau tried it May 5 at the Fulton Theatre, Oakland.

A phenomenon of the season is the run of "Easy for Zee Zee," a farce adapted from French sources, and purposely salacious, which has been running for forty-one weeks at the present time and is still going. It was written by a San Franciscan, Sam Dickson, using the pen name of Pierre Dijon. Sid Goldtree produced it at the Green Street Theatre, a small house in the Bohemian North Beach district.

The dramatic departments of Stanford University and the University of California have kept up their records of production, each presenting ten or a dozen plays during the year. One of the novelties of the season at the University of California was a performance of Oliver Goldsmith's "The Good Natured Man," a play that has had few representations in America—a few performances at the old Park Theatre, New York, under Price; a performance or two by Charles Matthews, and a production by Augustin Daly at his Fifth Avenue Theatre in 1874 when Fanny Davenport was his leading lady, constituting its recorded professional productions.

Amateur performances have been few, excepting the four programs of one act plays given by the Playmakers of Berkeley, and the regular performances, two a week, of the Playhouse Association, also of Berkeley. The Playmakers are in their sixth season. The members write the plays, stage them, direct them and act them. The Playhouse Association, which is housed in an old church, has presented plays by Chiarelli, Shakespeare, Shaw and other high class dramatists, and made an experiment with a revival of "Hazel Kirke," which showed itself to be very faded, but still had vivid dramatic moments.

A group of San Francisco men and women interested in the theatre is planning the building of an intimate playhouse to seat 500 persons, of which Irving Pichel will be director, for the purpose of producing plays not seen in the commercial theatres, and also the presentation of original plays, if any worth production can be found. A sum of $150,000 is sought for purposes of buying land and erecting the theatre, and most of this money has been subscribed at the present time. Also a subscription guarantee of $30,000 yearly for three years is asked.

Henry Duffy, finding it difficult to get the plays he wants for his chain of theatres, has announced a play contest, with a prize of $1,000, the contest being open to dramatists all over America, and the $1,000 to be considered advance royalties if the play is produced. The contest closes October 1. The critics of the Pacific Coast are to be the judges, men on the newspapers of British Columbia, Washington, Oregon, Nevada and California having consented to act. They are to elect three of their number as final judges, and award is to be made November 1. Duffy hopes to find several available manuscripts in this contest.

André Ferrier continues his French Theatre, now in its ninth season. He produced several Paris successes during the year, "La Souriante Madame Bendet," "Le Marche Indienne" and "Les Vignes du Seigneur," among them.

Theatre Arts, Inc., has been the most consistent of the amateur groups in San Francisco. It has kept up its policy of monthly performances, usually programs of one-act plays, and one of them the presentation of four such small dramas found in a contest. Three full length plays were given during the year, each having two performances. They were "Hedda Gabler," "Mr. Pim Passes By" and Galsworthy's "The Elder Son." The last two were acted by different casts on the two nights of performance. Talma-Zetta Wilbur has been the director of this group since its formation six years ago.

As the year ends two companies sent out by the New York Theatre Guild are playing here, the Repertory company, headed by Elisabeth Risdon, Peg Entwistle, Warburton Gamble, Brandon Evans, Neal Caldwell, Lawrence Leslie and Edwin Maxwell, and the special "Strange Interlude" company, with Judith Anderson sent on from New York for the San Francisco run.

THE SEASON IN SOUTHERN CALIFORNIA

By Monroe Lathrop

Drama-Editor of the *Los Angeles Express*

HOLLYWOOD, that blazing comet in the theatrical sky, with its new and mysterious portent in the world of the drama and player, must be mentioned before anything else in a review of the past year in the theatre of Southern California.

This El Dorado of the actor, with its glamorous repute, promise of world-wide fame, and realization of riches, has profoundly affected the entire situation here, as it bids fair to do at the fountain-head of supply for the stage, the Metropolis.

Its reflection has been cast over all phases of the situation. Last year's annual review found everything that Hollywood stood for at the lowest ebb, and the theatre was profiting by it. Public interest in the silent movie had waned so rapidly that its sponsors were alarmed for their investments.

The picture-play had calcified into a set form so monotonous that its old devotees were flocking to the better dramas and living players of the stage. Suddenly appeared the talkie comet, and the face of all things took on a new aspect. For the better all around, because, whatever the effect may be elsewhere, the Coast now swarms with the best of American actors.

Many of these have found their way to the footlights, with the result that the year has been the most interesting and of the highest standard in the history of western theatricals. Estimates of the number of "legitimate" actors, directors, authors and musicians drawn west by the talkie boom vary from 800 to 1,800. At any rate the number is enormous, and the native theatre is bound to profit from it.

Many people would put first in importance, if not in order, among the year's playhouse experiences, the visit of two companies of the New York Theatre Guild and the organization of the Los Angeles Repertory Theatre, which has become its working ally.

The Guild companies brought Eugene O'Neill's "Strange Interlude" for a stay of nine weeks in Los Angeles and its Hollywood suburb, and a brace of revivals at another theatre including Bernard Shaw's "The Doctor's Dilemma," Sidney Howard's "Ned McCobb's Daughter," Behrman's "The Second Man," and St. John Irvine's "John Ferguson."

The new Repertory Theatre, with its 2,500 sustaining subscribers (whose number is expected to be doubled this year), produced or sponsored in order "The Silver Cord," "The Beggars' Opera" (from London), "The Guardsman," Galsworthy's "Escape," "Mr. Pim Passes By," and, as its crowning work, the Capek brothers' spectacular satire, "The World We Live In." The last named was given its second American production. It is significant of this, as also of other plays of the year, that several members of the original eastern cast were at hand to assume their rôles.

The primacy in interest of these remote theatrical allies and their activities will be challenged by many who will put first in importance the visits of two English companies, whose marvelous talent, team-work and resultant "authority" made them veritable "smashes."

One was the company from the Shakespeare Memorial Theatre at Stratford-on-Avon, in a repertory of the Bard's plays so splendidly given without the exploitation of any star that they were acclaimed by packed houses. The same thing was true of the other troupe, which took the Coast by storm as well as by surprise.

It was the D'Oyley Carte Opera company from the Savoy Theatre in London. Neither of these organizations reached the eastern coast, but returned by way of Canada. Misgivings concerning the opera company were swept away by surprised enthusiasm as it gave, one after another, the Gilbert and Sullivan pieces in brilliant style.

The repute of the original D'Oyley Carte was known, but the long absence of the name from American stages led many to suspect that what his name stood for was now little more than a memory. What they found was a troupe with several of the original company and long-trained accretions, steeped in the Savoyard traditions and up to its highest standards.

American companies, with seldom more than one or two good singers, were put to blush by this one with a score of thrilling vocalists—so plenteous, indeed, and so well trained that a member of the chorus in one performance would be found shining in the next in a principal rôle.

Both companies have promised return visits. The avaricious maw of Hollywood, by the by, did not fail to skim some of the cream off of these as well as other visiting companies.

The London troupe came in a season singularly bereft of musical attractions. With the exception of "The Desert Song," which returned for a visit of 22 weeks (part of a tour of exceptional prosperity all over the Pacific Slope), there has been no worthy musical production.

"The Wishing Well," by Peter Gawthorn, an Australian actor who played in it, was one of the swift and signal failures of the season. Another, "Lupino Lane's Revue," staged by the English comedian bearing its name, and starring him, had six weeks of fair prosperity in the Hollywood Music Box. "The Beggars' Opera," in its third visit, did three weeks of good business. "Gay Paree," with inferior talent, did three weeks and passed on unmourned. "A Pair O' Docs," with Kolb and Dill, failed.

The plays of most favor, judged by their tenure, were "The Desert Song," with 22 weeks; "The Shannons of Broadway," with the Gleasons, 12; "Strange Interlude," 9; "The Marriage Bed," 6; "Dracula," 11; "The Baby Cyclone," 8; "The Front Page," 11; "The Spider," 7; "The Royal Family," 7; "Her Cardboard Lover," 8; "The Swan," 11; "The Skull," 8; "The Mission Play," 15; "Why Men Leave Home," 8; "So This Is London" (repeat), 7; "The Bad Man," 7; "The Streets of New York," 6; "The 19th Hole," with Frank Craven, 7; "Burlesque," 7; "Let Us Be Gay," 7.

The figures perhaps do scant justice to such plays as "The Merchant of Venice," with George Arliss; "The Road to Rome," with Jane Cowl; "Burlesque," with Hal Skelly; "Straight Thru the Door," with William Hodge, and some other touring attractions which came for a short visit, and the limited engagements of the New York Theatre Guild and Los Angeles Repertory company.

New productions of the year bore little fruit. One of the most pretentious, "The Pirate," registered the effort of Doris Keane to find a worthy successor to her long success, "Romance." A lavish investiture and well-picked cast failed to give the breath of reality to "The Pirate," a pseudo-historical romantic comedy by William Dubois, and it went down with all on board in a fortnight.

"The Marriage Bed," by Ernest Pascal, later shown in New York, was one fresh essay to approach real favor; "What a Man," a farce-comedy by Seymour Hicks, with John T. Murray, had a run of five weeks. "Little Orchid Annie," a comedy of flappers by Harley Waters and Charles Beahan, achieved several weeks, helped by cut-rates, but has a doubtful future.

"Osceola," by John Steven McGroarty, author of the Mission Play, based upon the life of the Seminole Indian chief, was found to be wanting at its première. Something like the stamp of real success rests upon "Danger," a new mystery comedy by Tom Barry, which is still running to good business at this writing, in its fourth week. "Squawk," a farce by John McDermott based upon local politics, staggered through four weeks and collapsed from inanition. "Window Panes," revised by its author, Olga Printzlau, had another chance but failed.

It has been a year of many revivals. In addition to those above that will be recognized by all who know their theatre, Edward Everett Horton found a real hit in going farthest back for Boucicault's "The Streets of New York." The Pasadena Community Theatre also dug deeply into the archives and brought out "East Lynne" and "Ten Nights in a Barroom."

From more recent theatrical history came "The Bad Man," "The Ghost Train," "Dancing Mothers," "The Guardsman," "The Swan," plays of Ibsen, Dostoievsky, Barrie and Shaw at Pasadena, "The Torchbearers," Pinero's "Mid-Channel" (With Conway Tearle), "Clarence," Pirandello's "Right You Are If You Think So," and some others of less significance.

As usual Gilmor Brown's Pasadena institution made itself felt, most signally by an elaborate production of Ansky's "The Dybbuk," with a guest director and player from the Habima Players of Moscow, and a presentation of high color; Romaine Rolland's "The Wolves," dealing with passions of the French Revolution. Brown also repeated "Lazarus Laughed," at tremendous labor.

With three houses Henry Duffy has been the most active of

the local producers, with a large variety of plays savory enough for his clientele, including recent New York successes and revivals, with guest stars including Guy Bates Post, May Robson, Robert McWade, Leo Carrillo, Hal Skelly, the Gleasons, Taylor Holmes, Emma Dunn, Belle Bennett and Edmund Breese regaling patrons of eight Duffy theatres along the coast.

Edward Everett Horton has been almost uniformly successful as a producer of handsomely mounted plays with strong casts. His theatre has been most conspicuous in drawing upon talent from the motion picture field which had previously earned its spurs in the "legitimate."

Franklin Pangborn has also joined the local producers, opening a succession of comedies with a revival of "Broadway." A third new entrepreneur to enter the field is O. D. Woodward, a veteran of theatrical life in the Middle West, who has made an auspicious bow by giving the public "Dracula," Lonsdale's "The High Road" and Barry's "Paris Bound," with "Holiday" to come.

"The Mission Play," John S. McGroarty's pageant-play of early California days, passed through its eighteenth year and added 15 more weeks to its thousands of performances.

"The Pilgrimage Play," outdoor drama based upon the life of Christ, had its annual brief season, and a production of "Joseph and His Brethren" in the Hollywood Bowl gave another sacred tinge to the theatrical year.

Little Theatre activity has been slight. The Cordova Play Shop did its best work with "Hamlet" in modern clothes. The Theatre Mart, in Hollywood, presented several plays by new authors but disclosed nothing promising.

STREET SCENE

Drama in Three Acts

By Elmer L. Rice

THERE had not been much to distinguish the theatre year up till holiday time. Nor was there great promise in the announcement that William A. Brady, Sr., had decided to produce a play by Elmer Rice called "Street Scene," and that Mr. Rice had not only selected the cast but was also conducting the rehearsals.

The Rice output of dramas has been consistently interesting, from the year he wrote "On Trial" to that in which he experimented with an expressionistic drama reflecting a phase of the American scene called "The Adding Machine." But because he is a writer who favors the extremists and has a passion for new forms, the chances that he would produce a salable and popular success seemed slightly remote. Also it was known that this particular play had been in many managers' offices and failed of sale.

"Street Scene," offered at the Playhouse January 10, 1929, proved another of those exciting exceptions that make play production the fascinating gamble that it is. Critical opinion was favorable but qualified and often restrained. The play, being another depressing study of tenement life, did not impress this writer, for one, as an entertainment likely to achieve wide appeal.

And yet the response of playgoers was immediate and consistently sustained through the season. The Playhouse is not a large theatre, and keeping it packed is easier than is the case with many others. But there is reason to believe that Mr. Rice's vivid drama would have proved popular in New York wherever it had been presented. In March the play was awarded the Pulitzer prize as the best drama of the year.

As "Street Scene" opens it is a hot June evening. In front of a New York walkup apartment—an ancient town house of the brownstone front variety now become one of the cheaper tenements in a mean quarter of the city—the residents of the building are variously disposed.

In the window of the right-hand first floor apartment Abraham Kaplan, Russian Jew, 60, is reading his Yiddish newspaper. On the opposite side of the four-step porch, in the window of the corresponding apartment, Greta Fiorentino, a blonde German, 40, ruddy-faced and stout, leans comfortably out of the window, her elbows resting upon an ample pillow. She is fanning herself languidly and a little hopelessly. A sign in the window of the Fiorentino apartment announces Lippo Fiorentino as musician and teacher.

The upper part of the windows letting into the janitor's basement apartment, seen through the iron grating of the areaway down which the basement steps descend, are also lighted. The two second floor apartments are dark. An arc light on the corner, beyond the range of vision from our side of the street, shines steadily upon the face of the tenement house. From the distance the various night noises of the city roll in—"the distant roar of 'L' trains, automobile sirens, and the whistle of boats on the river; the rattle of trucks and the indeterminate clanking of metals; fire engines, ambulances, musical instruments, a radio, dogs barking and human voices calling, quarelling and screaming with laughter. The noises are subdued and in the background but they never wholly cease."

Emma Jones, "middle aged, tall and rather bony," returned from an errand, pauses at the foot of the stoop to agree with Mrs. Fiorentino that the heat is at least terrific. Mrs. Jones hasn't what she would consider a dry stitch on her and Mrs. Fiorentino is frankly without shoes or corsets, if the truth were revealed.

Mrs. Olsen, "a thin, anemic Scandinavian with untidy fair hair," mounts the basement stairs with some effort to remind Mrs. Fiorentino that she has failed to put her garbage on the dumb-waiter and is therefore at the moment blocking the orderly procedure of Mr. Olsen's collections.

Willie Maurrant, "a disorderly boy of 12," arriving on roller skates to yell a demand for a sight of his "ma," brings Mrs. Maurrant, "a fair woman of 40 who looks her age but is by no means unattractive," to the window of the Maurrant's second floor apartment to tell Willie that he has already had too many ice cream cones and that if she does give him another dime it certainly will be the last.

With Willie skating in chase of his cone and Mrs. Maurrant disappeared from the window, the half-whispered exchange of confidences between Mrs. Jones and Mrs. Fiorentino go far to indicate that Mrs. Maurrant is one who is very foolishly tempting fate by carrying on, as practically every one in the house knows she is carrying on, with a person named Sankey— A woman of her age! With a grown-up daughter and all— Two times already this week Sankey has—

Mrs. Maurrant's appearance in the vestibule forces a change of subject. If it had not been so hot, Mrs. Maurrant agrees, confirming the weather, she would have gone to the park concert. Mrs. Maurrant is just crazy about music, she says, and so is Rose, her daughter, but Frank Maurrant, her husband, doesn't care for anything like that. . . .

From a third-story window Mr. Buchanan is calling. Mrs. Buchanan, it seems, is expecting her baby any time now, and Mr. Buchanan is sticking around in case he may be needed to go for the doctor or something. He is grateful to the neighbors for their interest but he hasn't been able to get Mrs. Buchanan to eat a thing—even though, as Mrs. Jones suggests, he knows she ought to keep up her stren'th, now that she has two to feed.

"You'd think it was him that was havin' the baby," ventures Mrs. Jones, when Mr. Buchanan has returned to his vigil.

"She's such a puny thing," sighs Mrs. Maurrant.

"Well, that's the way it goes," insists Mrs. Fiorentino; "the little skinny ones have them and the big, strong ones don't."

"Don't take it that way," encourages Mrs. Maurrant; "you're a young woman yet."

Frank Maurrant, his coat on his arm, walks into the group. "He is a tall, powerfully built man of 45, with a rugged, grim face." Maurrant is a little peevish at the moment, having been "rehearsing with lights" since 12 o'clock. To make it worse he will have to go to Stamford to-morrow for a try-out—an announcement that to a close observer plainly interests Mrs. Maurrant.

Frank Maurrant is also anxious about his daughter, Rose. Where is she? Why isn't she home? Workin' overtime? In a real-estate office? Frank never heard of nothing like that. Anyway, a girl should let her people know where she is and a girl's mother should make it her business to know what her daughter's doin'. . . .

Mr. Maurrant has stormed back upstairs and Mrs. Maurrant has just been explaining that she thinks it is a shame people can't make allowances for a lot of things—("After all, we're all human, and we can't just go along by ourselves, all the time, without ever getting a kind word," she says)—when Steve Sankey appears. "He is in the early thirties and is prematurely bald. He is rather flashily dressed in a patently cheap, light gray suit and a straw hat with a plaid band."

Mrs. Jones and Mrs. Fiorentino exchange significant glances, and it is plain that both Mrs. Maurrant and Sankey are making a conscious effort to avoid looking at each other. Sankey is just passing by, he says, on his way to the drugstore to get Mrs. Sankey some cooling ginger ale and is soon gone.

Sankey, Mrs. Jones explains, is the collector for the milk company. And when Mrs. Maurrant says she is going to look for Willie and takes the same direction Sankey took Mrs. Jones is convinced that any one who doesn't think there is something between them two is silly.

"The way he stands there and looks and looks at her," chimes in Mrs. Fiorentino.

"And what about the looks she was givin' him?" demands Mrs. Jones. "You'd think he was the Prince of Wales instead of a milk collector. And didja get the crack about not seein' him for two weeks?"

"And just to-day he was upstairs, Mrs. Olsen says."

"Someday her hoosban' is killing him," predicts Olsen, the janitor, who, being occupied with the disposal of a garbage can at the head of the areaway, had not previously taken part in the conversation.

MRS. FIORENTINO—Dot would be terrible!

JONES—He's li'ble to, at that. You know, he's got a wicked look in his eye, dat baby has.

MRS. JONES—Well, it's no more than he deserves, the little rabbit—goin' around breakin' up people's homes. (*Mockingly.*) "Good evenin', folks!" Jes' like Whozis on the radio.

JONES—D'ya think Maurrant is wise to what's going on?

MRS. JONES—Well, if he ain't, there must be somethin' the matter with him. But you never can tell about men. They're as blind as bats. An' what I always say is, in a case like that, the husband or the wife is always the last one to find out. (MISS CUSHING, *carrying a small paper bag, hurries on, at the left, in a state of great excitement.*)

MISS CUSHING (*breathlessly, as she comes up the left of the stoop*)—Say, what do you think! I just saw them together—the two of them!

MRS. JONES (*rising excitedly*)—What did I tell you?

MRS. FIORENTINO—Where did you see them, Miss Cushing?

MISS CUSHING—Why, right next door, in the entrance to the

warehouse. They were standing right close together. And he had his hands up on her shoulders. It's awful, isn't it?

JONES—Looks to me like this thing is getting pretty serious.

MRS. JONES—You didn't notice if they was kissin' or anythin', did you?

MISS CUSHING—Well, to tell you the truth, Mrs. Jones, I was so ashamed for her, that I hardly looked at all.

JONES—Maurrant's comin'.

"A conspirators' silence falls upon them as Maurrant, pipe in mouth, comes out of the house." Mrs. Maurrant has gone to look for Willie, they tell him, explaining with some particularity that boys of Willie's age are pretty sure to need a lot of lookin' after. . . .

Shirley Kaplan, daughter of Isadore, has brought her father a cup of tea and he quits his Yiddish newspaper to drink it. . . . Lippo Fiorentino, "a fat Italian with thick black hair and mustache, clutching a violin in his left arm and balancing five ice cream cones in his right hand," comes to treat the crowd and cool 'em off. . . . Miss Simpson, from the charities, is looking for Mrs. Hildebrand—poor little Mrs. Hildebrand, who, with her two children, is about to be dispossessed. Mrs. Hildebrand, who happens in at the moment, is a "small, rather young woman with a manner of perpetual bewilderment." How should she be expected to realize that it was wrong to take the 75 cents Miss Simpson had given her to buy groceries with and take the children to a moving picture show?

"We always went Thursday nights to the pictures when my husband was home," Mrs. Hildebrand explains.

"Yes, but your husband isn't home. And as far as anybody knows, he has no intention of coming home," counters Miss Simpson.

Kaplan, the Jew, would like to argue the subject of charity with Miss Simpson. In fact Mr. Kaplan would be pleased to argue with anybody, being something of a radical and with rather positive views.

Miss Simpson is of no mind to argue but she knows one thing, and that is that nobody is going to give anybody money to spend on moving picture shows. . . . The great trouble with Miss Simpson, Mr. Fiorentino is convinced, is that she is still a spinster. . . .

Mrs. Maurrant is back from looking for Willie, and anxious about Rose. Mr. Maurrant is anxious about the lot of them.

. . . Miss Simpson has got the Hildebrands temporarily set and is ready to leave. . . . Mr. Kaplan would like to tell her a little something more about the economic weaknesses of organized charity.

MISS SIMPSON (*turning, angrily*)—Nobody's asking your opinion.

KAPLAN—Dot's oll right. I'm taling you wit'out esking. You hoid maybe already dot poem:

> "Orgenzied cherity, measured and iced,
> In der name of a kushus, stetistical Christ."

MISS SIMPSON (*fiercely*)—All the same, you Jews are the first to run to the Charities. (*She strides angrily off at the right.* LIPPO, *affecting a mincing gait, pretends to follow her.*)

KAPLAN (*leaning out of the window*)—Come back and I'll tal you somet'ing will maybe do good your kerecter.

MRS. FIORENTINO—Lippo!

MRS. JONES (*highly amused*)—Look at him, will ya?

LIPPO (*laughing and waving his hand*)—Gooda-bye, lady! (*He comes back to the stoop.*)

KAPLAN (*to the others*)—Dey toin out in de street a mudder vit' two children, and dis female comes and preaches to her bourgeois morelity.

MRS. JONES (*to* MRS. FIORENTINO)—He's shootin' off his face again.

SHIRLEY—Papa, it's time to go to bed!

KAPLAN (*irritably*)—Lat me alone, Shoiley. (*Rising and addressing the others.*) Dees cherities are notting but anudder dewise for popperizing de verking-klesses. W'en de lendlords steal from de verkers a million dollars, dey give to de Cherities a t'ousand.

MAURRANT—Yeah? Well, who's puttin' her out on the street? What about the lan'lord here? He's a Jew, ain't he?

MRS. JONES—I'll say he's a Jew. Isaac Cohen!

KAPLAN—Jews oder not Jews—wot has dis got to do vit' de quastion? I'm not toking releegion, I'm toking economics. So long as de kepitalist klesses—

MAURRANT (*interrupting*)—I'm talkin' about if you don't pay your rent, you gotta move.

MRS. MAURRANT—It doesn't seem right, though, to put a poor woman out of her home.

MRS. FIORENTINO—And for her husband to run away—dot vos not right either.

LIPPO—I betcha 'e's got 'nudder woman. He find a nice blonda chicken, 'e run away.

MRS. JONES—There ought to be a law against women goin' around, stealin' other women's husbands.

MRS. FIORENTINO—Yes, dot's right, Mrs. Jones.

MAURRANT—Well, what I'm sayin' is, it ain't the landlord's fault.

KAPLAN—Eet's de folt of our economic system. So long as de institution of priwate property exeests, de verkers vill be at de moicy of de property-owning klesses.

MAURRANT—That's a lot o' bushwa! I'm a woikin' man, see? I been payin' dues for twenty-two years in the Stage-Hands Union. If we're not gettin' what we want, we call a strike, see?—and then we get it.

LIPPO—Sure! Ees same wit' me. We gotta Musician Union. We getta pay for da rehears', we getta pay for da overtime—

SHIRLEY—That's all right when you belong to a strong union. But when a union is weak, like the Teachers' Union, it doesn't do you any good.

MRS. JONES (*to* MRS. FIORENTINO)—can y' imagine that?—teachers belongin' to a union!

KAPLAN (*impatiently*)—Oll dese unions eccomplish notting wotever. Oll dis does not toch de fondamental problem. So long as de tuls of industry are in de hands of de kepitalist klesses, ve vill hev exploitation and sloms and—

MAURRANT—T' hell wit' all dat hooey! I'm makin' a good livin' an' I'm not doin' any kickin'.

OLSEN (*removing his pipe from his mouth*)—Ve got prosperity, dis coontry.

JONES—You said something!

KAPLAN—Sure, for de reech is planty prosperity! Mister Morgan rides in his yacht and upstairs dey toin a voman vit' two children in de street.

MAURRANT—And if you was to elect a Socialist president tomorrow, it would be the same thing.

MRS. FIORENTINO—Yes, dot's right, Mr. Maurrant.

JONES—You're right!

KAPLAN—Who's toking about electing presidents? Ye must put de tuls of industry in de hands of de vorking-klesses and dis ken be accomplished only by a sushal revolution!

MAURRANT—Yeah? Well, we don't want no revolutions in this country, see? (*General chorus of assent.*)

MRS. JONES—I know all about that stuff—teachin' kids there ain't no Gawd an' that their gran'fathers was monkeys.

JONES (*rising, angrily*)—Free love, like they got in Russia, huh? (KAPLAN *makes a gesture of impatient disgust, and sinks back into his chair.*)

MAURRANT—There's too goddam many o' you Bolshevikis runnin' aroun' loose. If you don't like the way things is run here, why in hell don't you go back where you came from?

The argument waxes hot and hotter. Shirley Kaplan tries to drag her father away. Mrs. Maurrant anxiously urges her pugnacious husband to quit. But the men are full of fight, Mr. Kaplan insisting on a reconstructed social order, Mr. Maurrant standing for the old-fashioned home and family honor.

"No reason to exist, huh?" Maurrant repeats. "Well, it's gonna exist, see? Children respectin' their parents an' doin' what they're told, get me? An' husbands an' wives, lovin' an' honorin' each other, like they said they would, when they was spliced—an' any dirty sheeny that says different is li'ble to get his head busted open, see?"

Now the neighbors take a hand, and with some difficulty keep the belligerents apart. It is Mr. Lippo's conviction that Mussolini would be giving them both a dose of castor oil. . . .

Sam Kaplan has arrived home. "He is twenty-one, slender, with dark, unruly hair and a fine, sensitive, mobile face." Sam is more interested in a book he is reading as he walks along than he is in any of his neighbors. Neither is he in easy agreement with them in other matters.

He doesn't like the kind of music Lippo likes. Sam likes the soulful music of the Russians. Lippo prefers the Italian music that makes you want to dance—in illustration of which he grabs Mrs. Maurrant and is dancing with her across the sidewalk as Sankey returns. The milkman stops again awkwardly in passing. Frank Maurrant stares pointedly at him.

"Look out! You're blockin' traffic!" warns Mrs. Jones. Nor is the tension relieved greatly when Willie Maurrant comes in scratched and torn and sobs an explanation that he wouldn't have been fighting if a big bum hadn't said something to him—something he refuses to tell his father.

Frank Maurrant has gone down to Callahan's to get a drink.

. . . Sam Kaplan, disgusted with the gossip of the stoop, has dashed protestingly into the house. . . . Mrs. Jones and Mrs. Olsen have disappeared. . . . The Fiorentinos have gone to bed, Mr. Fiorentino issuing a final warning to Mrs. Fiorentino that if he ever catches any milkman in his house there is going to be a lot of neck breaking.

Then Rose Maurrant and Harry Easter appear. "Rose is a pretty girl of 20, cheaply but rather tastefully dressed. Easter is about 35, good looking and obviously prosperous."

Mr. Easter is reluctant to bid Rose good-night without some definite demonstration that she considers the evening has been a success. In fact Mr. Easter is rather persistent. He begs a kiss. He even suggests that he has time to go into the house with Rose for a minute. Anyway he is sure Rose is old enough to do what she pleases. Furthermore, even if he is married, Mr. Easter insists he is quite off his nut about Rose. And he thinks she is very foolish living the way she does.

"Why not snap out of it all?" suggests Mr. Easter.

"Out of what?"

EASTER (*indicating the house*)—This! The whole business. Living in a dirty old tenement like this; working all day in a real-estate office, for a measly twenty-five a week. You're not going to try to tell me you like living this way, are you?

ROSE—No, I can't say that I like it, especially. But maybe it won't always be this way. Anyhow, I guess I'm not so much better than anybody else.

EASTER (*taking her hand*)—Do you know what's the matter with you? You're not wise to yourself. Why, you've got just about everything, you have. You've got looks and personality and a bean on your shoulders—there's nothing you haven't got. You've got It, I tell you.

ROSE—You shouldn't keep looking at me, all the time, at the office. The other girls are beginning to pass hints about it.

EASTER (*releasing her hand, genuinely perturbed*)—Is that a fact? You see, that shows you! I never even knew I was looking at you. I guess I just can't keep my eyes off you. Well, we've got to do something about it.

ROSE (*nervously snapping the clasp of her hand-bag*)—I guess the only thing for me to do is to look for another job.

EASTER—Yes, that's what I've been thinking, too. (*As she is about to demur.*) Wait a minute, honey! I've been doing a little thinking and I've got it all doped out. The first thing you do is throw up your job, see?

ROSE—But—

EASTER—Then you find yourself a nice, cozy little apartment somewhere. (*As she is about to interrupt again.*) Just a minute, now! Then you get yourself a job on the stage?

ROSE—How could I get a job on the stage?

EASTER—Why, as easy as walking around the block. I've got three or four friends in the show-business. Ever hear of Harry Porkins?

ROSE—No.

EASTER—Well, he's the boy that put on "Mademoiselle Marie" last year. He's an old pal of mine, and all I'd have to say to him is: (*putting his arm around her shoulder.*) "Harry, here's a little girl I'm interested in," and he'd sign you up in a minute.

ROSE—I don't think I'd be any good on the stage.

EASTER—Why, what are you talking about, sweetheart? There's a dozen girls, right now, with their names up in electric lights, that haven't got half your stuff. All you got to do is go about in the right way—put up a little front, see? Why, half the game is nothing but bluff. Get yourself a classy little apartment, and fill it with trick furniture, see? Then you doll yourself up in a flock of Paris clothes and you throw a couple or three parties and you're all set. (*Taking her arm.*) Wouldn't you like to be on Broadway?

ROSE—I don't believe I ever could be.

EASTER—Isn't it worth trying? What have you got here, hm? This is no kind of a racket for a girl like you. (*Taking her hand.*) You do like me a little, don't you?

ROSE—I don't know if I do or not.

EASTER—Why, sure you do. And once you get to know me better, you'd like me even more. I'm no Valentino, but I'm not a bad scout. Why, think of all the good times we could have together—you with a little apartment and all. And maybe we could get us a little car—

ROSE—And what about your wife?

EASTER (*letting go her hand*)—The way I figure it is, she doesn't have to know anything about it. She stays up there in Bronxville, and there are lots of times when business keeps me in New York. Then, in the summer, she goes to the mountains. Matter of fact, she's going next week and won't be back until September.

ROSE (*shaking her head and going towards the stoop*)—I don't think it's the way I'd want things to be.

EASTER—Why, there's nothing really wrong about it.

ROSE—Maybe there isn't. But it's just the way I feel about it, I guess.

EASTER—Why, you'd get over that in no time. There's lots of girls—

ROSE—Yes, I know there are. But you've been telling me all along that I'm different.

EASTER—Sure, you're different. You're in a class by yourself. Why, sweetheart— (*He tries to take her in his arms.*)

ROSE (*pushing him away*)—No. And you mustn't call me sweetheart.

EASTER—Why not?

ROSE—Because I'm not your sweetheart.

EASTER—I want you to be—

An unearthly yell of pain issues from the Buchanan apartment. Mrs. Buchanan's expectations are evidently about to bc realized. . . . Down the street Rose sees her father approaching. Mr. Easter decides that under the circumstances his further hopes can wait.

Mr. Maurrant is rough and suspicious. Where has Rose been? Who was that she was talkin' to? Out on a pettin' party, eh? Well, there ain't goin' to be any of that in Mr. Maurrant's family—

Rose has little success answering him. She hasn't been petting. She's been to dinner with Mr. Easter. He is the manager of her office. After dinner they went some place and danced. . . .

The Buchanan situation is again acute. Mr. Buchanan must get the doctor right away. If Rose will do the telephoning he can stay with Mrs. Buchanan. She's got terrible pains— The screaming from upstairs bears out that statement. . . .

Mae Jones and Dick McGann, she "a vulgar shopgirl of 21," he "a vacuous youth of about the same age," arrive at the stoop. Mae wears Dick's straw hat. They are both quite drunk. They do not stay long. A swig or two out of Dick's flask and they are gone—to Fred Hennessy's apartment. Dick has the key. . . .

Rose Maurrant is back from telephoning. The Buchanan doctor is on his way. . . . Vincent Jones, "a typical New York taxicab driver," stops Rose as she starts to enter the house. He, too, is a neighbor. . . . He, too, is interested in Rose. Why won't she come take a ride in his hack? Rose is trying to get away from Vincent when Sam Kaplan interferes.

"Take your hands off her!" shouts Sam, climbing out of the window of the Kaplan apartment.

"Well, look who's here!" mockingly answers Vincent. "Haster gesehn de fish in de Bowery? (*Menacingly*). "What de hell do you want?"

"You keep your hands off her!" repeats Sam.

In answer to which Vincent reaches suddenly up and pulls Sam down before him. After that he deliberately puts the flat of his hand against Sam's face and pushes him until he sprawls on the walk.

"You big coward!" explodes Rose. "If you hit him again I'll call my father!"

"Gee! Don't frighten me like dat. I got a weak heart!" sneers Vincent.

The arrival of Mrs. Jones, who has had her dog out for a walk, helps to clear the situation. Vincent is willing to call it an incident and go in with his mother to eat the stew she has saved for him.

"You seem to have plenty of admirers, Miss Maurrant," Mrs. Jones flings back of her. "But I guess you come by it natural."

Sam Kaplan is hysterical. He wants to kill Vincent. He wants to sob out his disgust of his own weakness. Rose's sympathy is but cold comfort. . . . Gradually Rose's troubles take precedence in their thoughts. The problem of her mother, now that everybody knows what's going on, worries Rose. And yet it is natural enough with her mother being sort of gay and happy and her father being the way he is; meaning well, and all, but sort of making you freeze up when you really want to be nice and loving.

SAM—I wish I could help you, Rose.

ROSE—You do help me, Sam—just by being nice and sympathetic and talking things over with me. There's so few people you can really talk to, do you know what I mean? Sometimes I get the feeling that I'm all alone in the world and that—(*A scream of pain from* MRS. BUCHANAN.)

ROSE (*springing to her feet*)—Oh, just listen to her!

SAM—Oh, God!

ROSE—The poor thing! She must be having terrible pains.

SAM—That's all there is in life—nothing but pain. From

before we're born, until we die! Everywhere you look, oppression and cruelty! If it doesn't come from Nature, it comes from humanity—humanity trampling on itself and tearing at its own throat. The whole world is nothing but a blood-stained arena, filled with misery and suffering. It's too high a price to pay for life—life isn't worth it! (*He seats himself despairingly on the stoop.*)

ROSE (*putting her hand on his shoulder*)—Oh, I don't know, Sam. I feel blue and discouraged, sometimes, too. And I get a sort of feeling of, oh, what's the use. Like last night. I hardly slept all night, on account of the heat and on account of thinking about—well, all sorts of things. And this morning, when I got up, I felt so miserable. Well, all of a sudden, I decided I'd walk to the office. And when I got to the Park, everything looked so green and fresh, that I got a kind of feeling of, well, maybe it's not so bad, after all. And then, what do you think?—all of a sudden, I saw a big lilac-bush, with some flowers still on it. It made me think about the poem you said for me—remember?—the one about the lilacs.

SAM (*quoting*)—

"When lilacs last in the dooryard bloom'd
And the great star early droop'd in the western sky in the night,
I mourn'd and yet shall mourn, with ever-returning spring."

(*He repeats the last line*):

I mourn'd and yet shall mourn, with ever-returning spring? Yes!

ROSE—No, not that part. I mean the part about the farm-house. Say it for me Sam. (*She sits at his feet.*)

SAM—"In the door-yard, fronting an old farm-house, near the whitewashed palings,
Stands the lilac-bush, tall-growing, with heart-shaped leaves of rich green,
With many a pointed blossom, rising delicate, with the perfume strong I love,
With every leaf a miracle—and from this bush in the door-yard,
With delicate-color'd blossoms and heart-shaped leaves of rich green,
A sprig with its flower I break."

ROSE (*eagerly*)—Yes, that's it! That's just what I felt like doing—breaking off a little bunch of the flowers. But then I thought maybe a policeman or somebody would see me, and then I'd get into trouble, so I didn't.

BUCHANAN'S VOICE—Miss Maurrant! Miss Maurrant! (SAM *and* ROSE *spring to their feet and look up.*)

ROSE—Yes?

BUCHANAN'S VOICE—Do you mind phoning to the doctor again? She's getting worse.

ROSE—Yes, sure I will. (*She starts to go.*) Wait! Maybe this is the doctor now.

BUCHANAN'S VOICE (*excitedly as* DR. WILSON *appears at the left*)—Yes, that's him. Mrs. Maurrant! Tell her the doctor's here! Doctor, I guess you're none too soon.

DR. WILSON (*a seedy, middle-aged man in a crumpled Panama*)—Plenty of time. Just don't get excited. (*He throws away his cigarette and enters the vestibule. The mechanical clicking of the door-latch is heard as* DR. WILSON *goes into the house.*)

ROSE—I hope she won't have to suffer much longer.

MAURRANT (*appearing at the window, in his under-shirt*)—Rose!

ROSE (*rather startled*)—Yes, pop, I'll be right up.

MAURRANT—Well, don't be makin' me call you again, d'ya hear?

ROSE—I'm coming right away. (MAURRANT *leaves the window.*)

ROSE—I'd better go up now, Sam.

SAM—Do you have to go to bed, when you're told, like a child?

ROSE—I know, Sam, but there's so much wrangling goes on, all the time, as it is, what's the use of having any more? Good night, Sam. There was something I wanted to talk to you about, but it will have to be another time. (*She holds out her hand.* SAM *takes it and holds it in his.*)

SAM (*trembling and rising to his feet*)—Rose, will you kiss me?

ROSE (*simply*)—Why, of course I will, Sam. (*She offers him her lips. He clasps her in a fervent embrace, to which she submits but does not respond.*)

ROSE (*freeing herself gently*)—Don't be discouraged about things, Sam. You wait and see—you're going to do big things, some day. I've got lots of confidence in you.

SAM (*turning away his head*)—I wonder if you really have, Rose?

ROSE—Why, of course I have! And don't forget it! Good night. I hope it won't be too hot to sleep.

SAM—Good night, Rose. (*He watches her, as she opens the door with her latchkey and goes into the house. Then he goes to the stoop and seating himself, falls into a reverie. A Policeman appears at the right and strolls across, but* SAM *is oblivious to him. In the distance a home-comer sings drunkenly. A light appears in the* MAURRANT *hall-bedroom, and a moment later Rose comes to the window and leans out.*)

ROSE (*calling softly*)—Hoo-hoo! Sam! (SAM *looks up, then rises.*) Good night, Sam. (*She wafts him a kiss.*)

SAM (*with deep feeling*)—Good night, Rose, dear. (*She smiles at him. Then she pulls down the shade.* SAM *looks up for a moment, then resumes his seat. A scream from* MRS. BUCHANAN *makes him shudder. A deep rhythmic snoring emanates from the Fiorentino apartment. A steamboat whistle is heard. The snoring in the Fiorentino apartment continues.* SAM *raises his clenched hands to heaven. A distant clock begins to strike twelve.* SAM's *arms and head drop forward. The curtain falls.*)

ACT II

It is daybreak the following morning. Slowly the tenement is coming to life and getting to bed. Mr. Jones is returning a bit dazed from a neighboring speakeasy. . . . The Olsen baby is voicing a demand for food. . . . Through their windows the Fiorentinos are heard snoring, frequently in concert. . . . Dr. Wilson, after a wakeful night at the Buchanans', now on his way home, pauses on the stoop to light a cigarette. . . . Mae Jones and Dick McGann, back from the Hennessy apartment, are exchanging early morning insults. . . . A milkman and a policeman, meeting at the curb, exchange the day's greetings. . . .

Rose Maurrant is at the window of the Maurrant apartment looking for Willie. . . . There can be no breakfast until Willie gets back with the bread. . . . Sam Kaplan is out on the stoop reading. . . . Shirley Kaplan notes the greeting of the two and is worried.

SHIRLEY—Sam, breakfast is ready.

SAM—I don't want any breakfast.

SHIRLEY—What do you mean, you don't want any breakfast? What kind of a business is that, not to eat breakfast?

SAM—Do I have to eat breakfast, if I don't want to?

SHIRLEY—You've got your head so full of that Rose Maurrant

upstairs that you don't want to eat or sleep or anything any more.

SAM—If I don't feel like eating, why should I eat? (*Bursting out.*) You're always telling me: "Eat!" "Don't eat!" "Get up!" "Go to bed!" I know what I want to do, without being told.

SHIRLEY—I don't see, just when you're graduating from college, why you want to get mixed up with a little batzimer like that!

SAM—It's always the same thing over again with you. You never can get over your race prejudice. I've told you a hundred times that the Jews are no better than anybody else.

SHIRLEY—I'm not talking about that! Look at the kind of family she comes from. What's her father? Nothing but an illiterate rough-neck. And her mother—

SAM (*indignantly*)—Are you starting, too?

KAPLAN'S VOICE—Shoi-ley!

SHIRLEY—Wait a minute, papa's calling. (*Into the room.*) All right, papa! (*To* SAM.) Come in, Sam, or papa will be making long speeches again.

SAM (*impatiently*)—All right!

The Buchanan baby is a girl. . . . At 3.30 A.M. she came and Mrs. Buchanan's yelling should have waked the neighborhood, according to Mr. Buchanan. . . . The letter carrier is not impressed by Mr. Buchanan's pride of paternity. . . . The letter carrier has six children and is still carrying a mail-bag at 62.

Lippo Fiorentino is both delighted and saddened by the Buchanan achievement. . . . Lippo is delighted for the Buchanans but saddened that Mrs. Fiorentino cannot do as well by him. . . . Lippo is also saddened for Rose. . . . It is too bad that Rose should not be happy, that she should not marry a ver' reech man and travel and know these Eetaly, these Sorrent'—La Belle Sorrent'—these Baia di Napoli! . . . No, Rose is not in love with "da leetla kike." Rose, so far as she knows, is not in love with any one. But Sam Kaplan's being a Jew wouldn't stop her loving him. . . .

Mrs. Jones, back with the dog, is glad to hear of Mrs. Maurrant's night's vigil with Mrs. Buchanan. . . . Havin' children's terrible, but no mother would ever give hers up, especially if they turn out all right, says Mrs. Jones. . . . Still, she'd think twice before she ever let one of hers bring a Jew into the family. . . . The nerve of Mrs. Jones stuns Rose, but Mrs. Maurrant is convinced it is best never to pay attention to such things. . . .

Frank Maurrant is ready to go to work, but before he goes he would like to know a few things. . . . Where's Mrs. Maurrant been all night? . . . With the Buchanans? . . . Yeah? . . . Well, where's she goin' now? . . . "Just around to Kraus's to get a chicken," answers Mrs. Maurrant. "I thought I'd make her some chicken soup to give her strength."

MAURRANT—Say, how about lookin' after your own home an' lettin' the Buchanans look after theirs.

MRS. MAURRANT—All I'm trying to do is to be a little neighborly. It's the least anybody can do, with the poor thing hardly able to lift her hand.

MAURRANT—That's all right about that! (*Coming down the steps.*) A woman's got a right to stay in her own home, lookin' after her husband an' children.

MRS. MAURRANT (*going towards him*)—What else have I been doing all these years, I'd like to know?

MAURRANT—Well, just see that you don't forget it, that's all —or there's li'ble to be trouble.

MRS. MAURRANT (*putting her hand on his arm*)—All right, Frank. Don't say any more, please. When will you be back—to-morrow?

MAURRANT—I don' know when I'll be back. Whenever I'm t'roo wit' me work—that's when. What are you so anxious to know for, huh?

MRS. MAURRANT—Why, I just asked, that's all.

MAURRANT—Oh, you just asked, huh? Just in case somebody wanted to come aroun' callin', is that it?

MRS. MAURRANT—No, it isn't. It isn't anything of the kind. You got no right to talk to me like that, in front of my own daughter. You got no right. No, you haven't! (*She turns away and hurries off, abruptly, at the left.*)

ROSE—Ma! (*She starts to run after her mother.*)

MAURRANT (*imperiously*)—Come back here, you! (ROSE *hesitates.*) Come back, hear me? (ROSE *turns and comes back.*) You stay right here. (*He puts down his satchel and takes a flask from his pocket.*)

ROSE—Why do you talk to her like that?

MAURRANT—Nobody's askin' you.

ROSE—If you were only a little nicer to her, maybe everything would be different.

MAURRANT—Yeah? Where's she got any kick comin'. Ain't

I always been a good husband to her? Ain't I always looked after her? (*He takes a drink.*)

ROSE—It's not that, pop. It's somebody to be sort of nice to her that she wants—sort of nice and gentle, the way she is to you. That's all it is.

MAURRANT (*turning to her*)—So she's got you headed the same way, has she? Goin' out nights with married men, huh?

ROSE—You don't need to worry about me, pop. I can take care of myself, all right.

MAURRANT—No daughter o' mine ain't gonna go that way. I seen too many o' those kind around the theaytre.

ROSE—Things are different, nowadays, pop. I guess maybe you don't realize that. Girls aren't the way they used to be—sort of soft and helpless. A girl nowadays knows how to look out for herself. But not her, pop; she needs somebody to look after her.

MAURRANT—Aw, can all that talk! You been listenin' to them bolshevikis, that's the trouble. But I'm gonna keep you straight, by God, or I'll know the reason why.

ROSE—I guess I've got a right to think about things for myself.

MAURRANT—Yeah? Well, don't let me ketch that other bozo comin' around here, either—that's all I got to say.

ROSE (*hesitantly, going up to him*)—Pop, listen—couldn't we get a little house somewhere—Queens or somewhere like that?

MAURRANT—What's the idea?

ROSE—Well, I don't know. I sort of thought it would be nice for all of us. And maybe if ma had a nice little home and some real nice neighbors—do you see what I mean?

MAURRANT—This place suits me all right.

ROSE—You can get some real nice little houses, that don't cost such an awful lot. And I wouldn't mind helping to pay for it. And once we had it all fixed up—

MAURRANT—Forget it! I don' know when I'll be back. (*As he starts to go right.*) An' remember what I told you, hear?

The Hildebrand children have gone cheerily to school. . . . Later they are to be dispossessed, they report, gleefully, and Miss Simpson of the Charities is going to find them a new place to live. . . . It's quite exciting. . . . Mrs. Maurrant is back from her marketing, relieved to find Mr. Maurrant gone. . . . She's always tried to be a good wife to Maurrant, Mrs. Maurrant explains to her daughter, but it never has seemed to make any difference to him. . . . She's always tried to be a good mother, too, and to make a home. . . . But what's the use? . . . "What's the good of being alive if you can't get a little something out of life? You might just as well be dead," sobs Mrs. Maurrant.

Rose understands her mother, but she can see things differently, too. "What I was thinking was, if he didn't come around here so much, maybe," she suggests. "Do you see what I mean, ma?"

"Yes, Rose."

"It's on account of all that's going around—everybody in the whole house. You see what I mean, don't you, ma?"

"Every person in the world has to have somebody to talk to," sighs Mrs. Maurrant. "You can't live without somebody to talk to. I'm not saying that I can't talk to you, Rose, but you're only a young girl and it's not the same thing."

"It's only on account of pop. I'm scared of what he's likely to do if he starts drinking."

"Well, I'll see, Rose. Sometimes I think I'd be better off if I was dead." . . .

Shirley Kaplan is ready to start for school. . . . Not a pleasant prospect, she admits to Rose Maurrant, trying to keep forty children quiet another hot day. . . . Vacation in two weeks? . . . Vacations don't mean much when you're taking summer courses at Teachers College.

SHIRLEY—Miss Maurrant, if you don't mind, I want to talk to you about my brother, Sam.

ROSE—Why certainly, Miss Kaplan.

SHIRLEY—I guess you know he's only finishing college, this month—

ROSE—Yes, of course I do.

SHIRLEY—Then he has to go three years to law-school and pass the bar examinations, before he can be a full-fledged lawyer.

ROSE—Yes, it takes a long time.

SHIRLEY—A long time and lots of money. And before a young lawyer begins to make his own living, takes a long time, too. It will be ten years, maybe, before he's making enough to support himself and a family. (*Looking away.*) Then, it's time enough for him to think about marriage.

ROSE—You don't mean me and Sam, Miss Kaplan?

SHIRLEY—Yes, that's just what I mean.

ROSE—Why, we're just good friends, that's all.

SHIRLEY—I know how it is with a boy like Sam, Miss Maurrant. He thinks he's a man, already; but he's nothing but a boy. If you're such a good friend, you shouldn't take his mind away from his work.

ROSE—But I haven't meant to, Miss Kaplan—honest I haven't.

SHIRLEY—I've had to work hard enough to get him as far as he is. And I have my father to take care of, too. The few dollars he makes, writing for the radical papers, don't even pay the rent. Believe me, every dollar I make goes.

ROSE—I know. Sam's often told me how much he owes to you.

SHIRLEY—He doesn't owe me anything. I don't care about the money. Only he should be thinking about his work and not about other things.

ROSE—Yes, he should be thinking about his work. But don't you think there are other things in the world, too, besides just work?

SHIRLEY—Don't you think I know that? I know that just as well as you do. Maybe, you think I'm an old-maid school-teacher, without any feelings.

ROSE—Oh, I don't—really I don't!

SHIRLEY (*turning her head away*)—Maybe I'm not a movie vamp, with dimples—but I could have had my chances, too. Only, I wanted to give Sam an education.

ROSE—I haven't tried to vamp Sam, honestly I haven't. We just seemed sort of naturally to like each other.

SHIRLEY—Why must you pick out Sam? You could get other fellows. Anyhow, it's much better to marry with your own kind. When you marry outside your own people, nothing good ever comes of it. You can't mix oil and water.

ROSE—I don't know. I think if people really care about each other—

SHIRLEY—He's nothing but a baby. He sees a pretty face and, right away, he forgets about everything else.

ROSE (*with a flash of temper*)—I know I haven't as much brains as Sam, or as you, either, if that's what you mean.

SHIRLEY (*contritely, going towards her*)—I didn't mean to hurt your feelings. I haven't got anything against you. Only, he's all I've got in the world. What else have I got to live for?

Sam Kaplan's arrival stops them. . . . Sam is even more unhappy this morning than he was last night. . . . Rose is going to a synagogue to her boss's funeral and the thought of it depresses Sam. . . . He has never been inside a synagogue himself, his people being rationalists. . . . Nor has he any funny idea about the God people tell themselves lies about because reality is too terrible for them to face. . . . Even the happiness that people strive so hard for is nothing but an illusion to Sam this morning. . . . What's the use of anything? What's the use of living? Why not, with 10 cents worth of carbolic acid, have it all over with? . . . But Rose wants to live.

"Why?" shouts Sam. "Why? What is there in life to compensate for the pain of living?"

"There's a lot," answers Rose. "Just being alive—breathing and walking around. Just looking at the faces of people you like and hearing them laugh. And seeing the pretty things in the store-windows. And rough-housing with your kid brother. And—oh, I don't know—listening to a good band, and dancing—Oh, I'd hate to die!"

Rose tries earnestly to get Sam's promise that he will not talk about killing himself any more. . . . Soon, worrying about her problem, he has forgotten his own. . . . There is a man in her office who wants to put Rose on the stage, she reports; there is the chance that she could get away from the tenement and make a lot of money and perhaps help her whole family. . . . Even if she did have to pay the price men expect. . . .

The reappearance of the freshly insulting Vincent Jones intensifies Rose's disgust with her surroundings. . . . It also convinces Sam that perhaps he and Rose had better run away together. . . .

Mr. Easter, from the office, stops in passing to take Rose to the boss's funeral. . . . A skinny pupil arrives for Mr. Fiorentino's instruction. . . . A strawberry huckster down the street calls his wares. . . . Sankey, the milk collector, appears nonchalantly at the stoop. . . . From her window above Mrs. Maurrant invites him in. . . . Maurrant is in Stamford, she reports, and Rose won't be home for an hour. . . .

The City Marshal and his assistant are there to dispossess the Hildebrands. . . . Olsen, the janitor, directs them to the fourth floor. . . . The strawberry salesman draws nearer. . . . An ol' clos' merchant shares the air with him. . . . Mae Jones gets started sleepily toward her job. . . .

Frank Maurrant suddenly appears. . . . The Maurrant window shades are drawn. . . . Sam Kaplan tries to stop Maurrant as he rushes up the stairs! . . . Sam Kaplan tries to yell a warning! . . . "Mrs. Maurrant! Mrs. Maurrant!" . . .

There are two shots and then a heavy fall. . . . Suddenly one of the Maurrant shades shoots up . . . Sankey, coatless, his face deformed by terror, tries to open the window. . . . His elbow shatters a pane. . . . Maurrant drags him back into the room. . . . Another shot is heard!

"For Chris' sake what's happenin'? Get an ambulance, you!" . . . The City Marshal is excited. . . . A crowd begins to gather. . . . The Marshal's assistant leans out the Maurrant window. . . . "Grab dat boid! He's comin' down!"

Maurrant appears in the doorway. . . . "His coat is open and his shirt is torn almost to shreds. His face, hands and clothing are covered with blood." . . .

As the crowd closes in Maurrant whips out a revolver and forces them back. . . . Now, having them cowed, he has dashed down the cellar stairs. . . .

A woman calls from above: "Hurry up! Get an ambulance!" . . . No one hears her. . . . A cop arrives. . . . Despite the warnings of the crowd the cop and two men dash into the cellar. . . .

"It's a moider," reports Fred, the Marshal's assistant, to the pushing crowd. "Dis boid's wife and some other guy! Jesus, you oughta see de blood!" . . .

A second policeman pushes his way through the crowd and into the hall. . . . From the Maurrant window the second policeman yells to the Marshal to call the "resoives" . . . There's a phone next door.

Clanging bells and the ambulance. . . . "Hurry up, Doc, she's still breathin'!" urges the policeman from the window. . . . They get the stretcher through the crowd and into the house. . . .

Suddenly there is a cry from Sam Kaplan. . . . He has seen Rose Maurrant coming down the street. . . . He rushes to her.

ROSE—What's the matter, Sam? What's the ambulance for? Did anybody get hurt?

SAM—Go away, Rose. Go away.

ROSE—Who is it? What's the matter? Is it my mother? It's not my mother, is it? (*Clinging to him.*) Sam, is it?

SAM—There's been an accident. Go away, Rose. (*He tries to force her away.*)

ROSE—Tell me what's happened! Tell me!

MISS CUSHING (*appearing at the window*)—They're bringing her down!

ROSE (*with a cry*)—It is my mother!

MISS CUSHING (*seeing her*)—Oh, my God, there's Rose! (MRS. FIORENTINO, MRS. JONES, MRS. HILDEBRAND, LIPPO *and* BUCHANAN *crowd to the* MAURRANT *windows.*)

SAM—Rose! Go away! (*She pays no attention to him, but stands watching the door, transfixed.* THE INTERNE *comes briskly out of the house.*)

THE INTERNE (*to the* MARSHAL)—Hold the door open, will you? (*He comes down the steps.*)

THE MARSHAL—Sure, doc! (*He hurries into the vestibule.*)

THE INTERNE (*to the crowd*)—Keep back, now!

ROSE (*seizing* THE INTERNE'S *arm*)—Doctor! Is she dead?

THE INTERNE—Who are you? Her daughter?

ROSE—Yes, sir. I'm her daughter.

THE INTERNE—She's pretty badly hurt. Step aside, now! (*They step aside, as* THE AMBULANCE-DRIVER *and* THE POLICEMAN *come out of the house, carrying* MRS. MAURRANT *on the stretcher. There is a low murmur from the crowd.*)

THE AMBULANCE-DRIVER—Easy, now.

THE POLICEMAN—All right. (*They come down the steps and go towards the left.*)

ROSE (*running forward and gripping the side of the stretcher.*) —Mother! Mother!

MRS. MAURRANT (*opening her eyes, feebly*)—Rose! (*She tries to lift her hand, but it falls back.*)

THE INTERNE (*pulling* ROSE *back*)—You mustn't talk to her now. (SAM *takes her about the shoulders. They and* THE INTERNE *follow the stretcher off, at the left. The crowd swarms after them.* FRED *comes out of the house, carrying one end of an iron bedstead. The curtain falls.*)

ACT III

It is mid-afternoon of the same day. Movers are just taking away the last of the Hildebrand furniture. Policemen in charge of the Maurrant case have gathered together the blood-stained dress of Mrs. Maurrant and the coat, cap and bill-holder belonging to Sankey.

Two nurse maids have wheeled their perambulators into the street to have a look at the scene of the murder so graphically described on an afternoon tabloid, which they read wonderingly: "Composograph showing Sankey, scantily clad, in a last vain attempt to escape the vengeance of the jealousy-crazed husband, whose home he had destroyed."

Harry Easter is looking for Rose Maurrant, but the policeman on guard has seen nothing of her since she went to the horspital that morning. Maurrant? No they ain't caught 'im yet, but they'll git 'im.

Mrs. Jones is back from Police Headquarters. . . . And the things they asked her down there! . . .

Rose Maurrant is back from a shopping trip. . . . She has a bow of crape for the door. . . . She has a white dress and white stockings for her mother. . . . She is grateful for all that both Mrs. Jones and Mr. Easter want to do for her, but there isn't anything anybody can do, now. . . . She will manage some way. . . . She will have to find a place where she and Willie can live and perhaps if it is away from all they have been used to it will be better. . . . But she couldn't let Mr. Easter help her find it, even if his intentions and ideas have all been changed by the tragedy. . . . She just doesn't want to be under obligations to anybody. . . .

Shirley Kaplan is sympathetic. . . . It is Shirley who goes with Rose back into the Maurrant apartment to help her change her dress and pick up such things as she and Willie will need. . . . Willie is at his aunt's. He thinks there has been some kind of accident. . . .

Isadore Kaplan is back in the window with his newspaper. . . . Mr. Buchanan is on his way to the drug store.

"Dees is a terrible t'ing vich hes heppened," ventures Mr. Kaplan.

"I'll say it is," replies Mr. Buchanan. "You know the way I look at it, he didn't have a right to kill the both of them like that. Of course I'm not saying what she did was right, either."

"How ken ve call ourselves ciwilized, ven ve see thet sax jealousy hes de power to awaken in us de primitive pessions of de sevege?"

"Yes, that is true, too," agrees Buchanan, a little bewildered. "Of course you can't expect a man to stand by and see his home broken up. But murdering them, like that, is going a little too far. Well, I got to go and phone the doctor. This thing's given my wife a kind of a relapse. She thought a lot of Mrs. Maurrant."

From down the street come the sound of shots being fired. . . . Excited voices cry out. . . . "They got 'im!" . . . The neighbors rush out of the house, Rose Maurrant with them. . . . They try to keep Rose back, but she will not stay. . . . She wants to see her father.

The crowd bellows in, Maurrant between two policemen in front; a second policeman holding the crowd back behind them. . . . "Maurrant's clothes are torn, and his right arm is in a crude sling. Sweat, blood and grime have made him almost unrecognizable."

ROSE (*running forward*)—Pop! Are you hurt?

MAURRANT (*seeing her for the first time*)—Rose!

ONE OF THE POLICEMEN (*to whom* MAURRANT *is manacled*)—Keep back, miss!

MAURRANT—It's me daughter! Fer Chris' sake, boys, lemme talk to me daughter! Maybe I'll never be seein' her again!

FIRST POLICEMAN—Give 'im a woid wit' her. (*He is the Officer who was on duty in the Maurrant apartment.*)

SECOND POLICEMAN (*after a moment's hesitation*)—Well, all right. (*Savagely to* MAURRANT.) But don't try to pull nothin', hear? (*There is a forward movement in the crowd.*)

FIRST POLICEMAN (*to the crowd*)—Keep back, youse!

MAURRANT—Rose! You're wearin' a black dress, Rose!

ROSE—Oh, pop, why did you do it? Why did you?

MAURRANT—I must o' been out o' me head, Rose. Did she say anythin'?

ROSE—She never opened her eyes again.

MAURRANT—I'd been drinkin', Rose—see what I mean?—an' all the talk that was goin' around, I just went clean off me nut, that's all.

ROSE—What'll they do to you, pop?

MAURRANT—It's the chair for me, I guess. But I don't care—let 'em give me the chair. I deserve it all right. But it's her, I'm thinkin' of, Rose—the way she looked at me. I oughtn't to done it, Rose.

ROSE—She was always so good and sweet.

MAURRANT—Don't I know it? I ain't no murderer—you ought to be the one to know that, Rose. I just went out o' me head, that's all it was.

SECOND POLICEMAN—All right, that's all now. Come on!

MAURRANT—Gimme a minute, can't you? She's me daughter. Gimme a chance, can't you? What's gonna happen to you, Rose?

ROSE—I'll be all right, pop. You don't need to worry about me.

MAURRANT—I ain't been a very good father, have I?

ROSE—Don't worry about that, pop.

MAURRANT—It ain't that I ain't meant to be. It's just the

way things happened to turn out, that's all. Keep your eye on Willie, Rose. Don't let Willie grow up to be a murderer, like his pop.

ROSE—I'm going to do all I can for him, pop.

MAURRANT—You're a good girl, Rose. You was always a good girl.

ROSE (*breaking down*)—Oh, pop!

Rose has thrown her arms around her father's neck. . . . Maurrant is sobbing hoarsely. . . . The policeman tries to be gentle but firm in separating them. . . . The procession is resumed. . . . The crowd falls in and follows after. . . . Sam and Rose are left behind.

SAM—I must talk to you! What are you going to do, Rose?

ROSE—Well, I haven't really had any time to do much thinking. But I really think the best thing I could do would be to get out of New York. You know, like we were saying, this morning—how things might be different, if you only had a chance to breathe and spread out a little. Only when I said it, I never dreamt it would be this way.

SAM—If you go, I'll go with you.

ROSE—But, Sam dear—

SAM—I don't care anything about my career. It's you—you —I care about. Do you think I can stay here, stifling to death, in this slum, and never seeing you? Do you think my life means anything to me, without you?

ROSE—But, Sam, we've got to be practical about it. How would we manage?

SAM—I don't care what I do. I'll be a day-laborer; I'll dig sewers—anything. (*Taking her passionately in his arms.*) Rose, don't leave me!

ROSE—I like you so much, Sam. I like you better than anybody I know.

SAM—I love you, Rose. Let me go with you!

ROSE—It would be so nice to be with you. You're different from anybody I know. But I'm just wondering how it would work out.

SAM—If we have each other, that's the vital thing, isn't it? What else matters but that?

ROSE—Lots of things, Sam. There's lots of things to be considered. Suppose something was to happen—well, suppose I was to have a baby, say. That sometimes happens, even when you don't want it to. What would we do, then? We'd be tied down then, for life, just like all the other people around here. They all start out loving each other and thinking that everything is going to be fine—and before you know it, they find out they haven't got anything and they wish they could do it all over again—only it's too late.

SAM—It's to escape all that that we must be together. It's only because we love each other and belong to each other, that we can find the strength to escape.

ROSE (*shaking her head*)—No, Sam.

SAM—Why do you say no?

ROSE—It's what you said just now—about people belonging to each other. I don't think people ought to belong to anybody but themselves. I was thinking, that if my mother had really belonged to herself, and that if my father had really belonged to himself, it never would have happened. It was only because they were always depending on somebody else, for what they ought to have had inside themselves. Do you see what I mean, Sam? That's why I don't want to belong to anybody, and why I don't want anybody to belong to me.

SAM—You want to go through life alone?—never loving any one, never having any one love you?

ROSE—Why, of course not, Sam! I want love more than anything else in the world. But loving and belonging aren't the same thing. (*Putting her arms about him.*) Sam, dear, listen. If we say good-bye, now, it doesn't mean that it has to be forever. Maybe some day, when we're older and wiser, things will be different. Don't look as if it was the end of the world, Sam!

SAM—It is the end of my world.

ROSE—It isn't, Sam! If you'd only believe in yourself, a little more, things wouldn't look nearly so bad. Because once you're sure of yourself, the things that happen to you, aren't so important. The way I look at it, it's not what you do that matters so much; it's what you are. (*Warmly.*) I'm so fond of you, Sam. And I've got such a lot of confidence in you. (*Impulsively.*) Give me a nice kiss! (SAM *takes her in his arms and kisses her, passionately. A gawky Girl of seventeen—one of* LIPPO'S *pupils, appears at the left, and looks at them, scandalized. Then she goes into the vestibule and rings the bell. The door clicks and she enters the house, as* SHIRLEY *comes out, carrying a wicker suit-case.* SHIRLEY *looks at* SAM *and* ROSE.)

ROSE (*to* SHIRLEY)—I was just telling Sam, that I think I'll soon be going away from New York. (SAM *looks at her, for a moment, in agony, then goes abruptly into the house.*)

SHIRLEY—I put your things in this suit-case. (*She comes down to the pavement. The Girl, in the Fiorentino apartment, begins tuning her violin.*)

ROSE (*taking the suit-case*)—You've been awfully nice to me. Don't worry about Sam, Miss Kaplan. Everything will be all right with him.

SHIRLEY—I hope so. (*From the Fiorentino apartment, come the strains of Dvorák's Humoresque, jerkily played on a violin.*)

ROSE—Oh, I just know it will! (*Extending her hand.*) Good-bye, Miss Kaplan.

SHIRLEY—Good-bye, Rose (*impulsively*). You're a sweet girl! (*She hugs and kisses her.*)

ROSE—I hope I'll see you again.

SHIRLEY (*crying*)—I hope so, Rose. (ROSE *takes up the suit-case and goes off at the left.* SHIRLEY *stands watching her.*)

KAPLAN (*re-appearing at his window*)—Shoiley, vot's de metter again vit Sem? He's crying on de bed.

SHIRLEY—Let him alone, papa, can't you? (*She turns and enters the house.* KAPLAN *sighs and, seating himself at the window, opens a newspaper. A shabby, middle-aged couple appear at the right, and approach the stoop.*)

THE MAN (*reading the To-Let sign*)—Here's a place. Six rooms. Want to take a look at it? (*A group of children off-stage left, begin singing The Farmer in the Dell. This continues until after the curtain is down.*)

THE WOMAN—All right. No harm lookin'. Ring for the janitor. (THE MAN *goes up the stoop and rings the janitor's bell.*) Somebody must o' just died.

THE MAN—Yeah, maybe that's why they're movin' out. (*Wiping his face with a handkerchief.*) Phoo! Seems to be gettin' hotter every minute. (MRS. FIORENTINO seats herself, at *her window, a sewing-basket in her lap.* MRS. JONES *and* MISS CUSHING *appear at the right, busily engaged in conversation.*)

MISS CUSHING—The poor little thing!

MRS. JONES (*as they go up the steps*)—Well, you never can tell with them quiet ones. It wouldn't surprise me a bit, if she turned out the same way as her mother. She's got a gentleman friend, that I guess ain't hangin' around for nothin'. I seen him, late last night, and this afternoon, when I come home from the police— (*She is still talking, as they enter the house.*) MRS. OLSEN *comes up from the cellar steps. A Sailor appears at the left, with two girls, an arm about the waist of each. They stroll slowly across. The curtain falls.*)

JOURNEY'S END

Drama in Three Acts

By R. C. Sherriff

THE importation of the then current success of the London theatre season, which was the war play, "Journey's End," served the New York theatre a particularly good turn in late March of 1929.

That lack of confidence in the theatre which invariably follows the production of a series of disappointing plays and the resulting refusal of playgoers to support them had greatly discouraged native producers. Critics of the drama and upholders of what generally is termed the legitimate theatre were beginning also to doubt.

Perhaps, people agreed, the so-called "talkies" were sounding the death-knell of spoken drama! Perhaps the drama, as represented by the better plays and the better players for some hundreds of years, was doomed, as the hucksters of a cheaper and shoddier entertainment had insisted!

And then came "Journey's End" to revive hope and cheer the spirits of the drama's defenders. Within a week the Miller Theatre in which it was played had been practically bought out for the three months following, which would carry the drama into hot weather, and there was every prospect that the war play could continue successfully so long as the English cast brought over to play it could stand the strain.

Something of the history of "Journey's End" is told elsewhere in this volume. This is an account of the play itself. The setting is an officers' dugout in the British trenches before St. Quentin. The time in March, 1918. Looking into the dugout you see a few rough steps that lead to the trench at the rear. There is a table occupying a good part of the floor space, two or three crude chairs, a bench, and a bunk or two. From left and right tunnels lead to other and, you feel, much less roomy sleeping holes. The light is furnished by candles stuck in bottles, or empty beef tins. There are a few cutout pictures of girls wearing nothing much in the way of clothes stuck to the walls.

"The earth walls deaden the sounds of war, making them faint and far away, although the front line is only fifty yards ahead. The flames of the candles that burn day and night are steady in the still, damp air.

"Through the doorway can be seen the misty grey parapet of a trench and a narrow strip of starlit sky. A bottle of whiskey, a jug of water and a mug stand on the table amongst a litter of papers and magazines."

Save for the presence of Captain Hardy, red-faced and cheerful, the dugout at the moment is unoccupied. Captain Hardy is trying to dry a sock over a candle flame that he may complete an otherwise satisfactory toilet. He sings as he dries, or at least hums so many of the words of an army song as he can recall.

Presently Hardy is joined by First Lieutenant Osborne, a tall, thin man with a fine head and close-cropped, iron grey hair. Osborne has come up with the new outfit that is taking over this section of the line. His Captain, Stanhope, is behind with the men.

Hardy is quite happy at turning the place over. It's been rather nerve-racking the last several days. Quiet as death for hours, and then a sudden attack that just literally blows everything up. Something's happening over in the Boche country, less than a hundred yards away. Hardy is satisfied of that. Probably the big German attack long promised can be expected any day now.

Otherwise the situation is about as usual. Quarters not so good. There's room in the dugout for five officers and four men, but they can't be too particular. Two or three of the beds are bottomless and when you try to sleep in them by hanging your legs and arms over the sides if your legs get too low the rats gnaw your boots.

"You got many rats here?" idly inquires Osborne.

"I should say—roughly—about two million," Hardy estimates: "but then, of course, I don't see them all."

Trench stores are all right, considering everything, and Hardy is soon ready to adjust his pack and get out. He thinks he won't stay and meet Stanhope. He is a little sensitive about Stanhope.

"He's a good chap, I know," admits Hardy, in reply to Osborne's quick defense of his captain. "But I never *did* see a youngster put away the whiskey he does. D'you know, the last time we were out resting at Valennes he came to supper with us and drank a whole bottle in one hour fourteen minutes—we timed him.

OSBORNE—I suppose it amused everybody: I suppose everybody cheered him on, and said what a splendid achievement it was.

HARDY—He didn't want any "cheering" on—

OSBORNE—No, but everybody thought it was a big thing to do. (*There is pause.*) Didn't they?

HARDY—Well, you can't help, somehow, admiring a fellow who can do that—and then pick out his own hat all by himself and walk home—

OSBORNE—When a boy like Stanhope gets a reputation out here for drinking, he turns into a kind of freak show exhibit. People pay with a bottle of whiskey for the morbid curiosity of seeing him drink it.

HARDY—Well, naturally, you're biased. You have to put him to bed when he gets home.

OSBORNE—It rather reminds you of bear-baiting—or cock-fighting—to sit and watch a boy drink himself unconscious.

HARDY—Well, damn it, it's pretty dull without something to liven people up. I mean, after all—Stanhope really is a sort of freak: I mean it is jolly fascinating to see a fellow drink like he does—glass after glass. He didn't go home on his last leave, did he?

OSBORNE—No.

HARDY—I suppose he didn't think he was fit to meet papa. (*A pause.*) You know his father's vicar of a country village?

OSBORNE—I know.

HARDY (*laughing*)—Imagine Stanhope spending his leave in a country vicarage tea! He spent his last leave in Paris, didn't he?

OSBORNE—Yes.

HARDY—I bet it was some leave!

OSBORNE—Do you know how long he's been out here?

HARDY—A good time, I know.

OSBORNE—Nearly three years. He came out straight from school—when he was eighteen. He's commanded this company for a year—in and out of the front line. He's never had a rest. Other men come over here and go home again ill, and young Stanhope goes on sticking it, month in, month out.

HARDY—Oh, I know he's a jolly good fellow—

OSBORNE—I've seen him on his back all day with trench fever —then on duty all night—

HARDY—Oh, I know: he's a splendid chap!

OSBORNE—And because he's stuck it till his nerves have got battered to bits, he's called a drunkard.

HARDY—Not a drunkard: just a—just a hard drinker: but you're quite right about his nerves. They are all to blazes. Last time out resting we were playing bridge and something happened —I don't remember what it was: some silly little argument—and all of a sudden he jumped up and knocked all the glasses off the table! Lost control of himself: and then he—sort of—come to—and cried—

OSBORNE—Yes, I know.

HARDY—You heard about it?

OSBORNE—He told me.

HARDY—Did he? We tried to hush it up. It just shows the state he's in. (*He rises and puts on his pack. There is a pause.*) You know, Osborne, you ought to be commanding this company.

OSBORNE—I?

HARDY—Of course you ought. It sticks out a mile. I know he's got pluck and all that, but, damn it, man, you're twice his age—and think what a dear, level-headed old thing you are.

OSBORNE—Don't be an ass. He was out here before I joined up. His experience alone makes him worth a dozen people like me.

HARDY—You know as well as I do, you ought to be in command.

OSBORNE—There isn't a man to touch him as a commander of men. He'll command the battalion one day if—

HARDY—Yes, if!

Now the taking over is completed and Hardy departs with enough impediment to make him fearfully frightening to a German, Osborne thinks, if he should meet one suddenly coming around a corner.

Mason, the cockney soldier servant, is in to lay the table for supper. A very good supper, Mason thinks, considering.

"What are you going to tempt us with to-night, Mason?" the First Lieutenant inquires.

"Soup, sir—cutlets—and pineapple."

"Cutlets?"

"Well, sir—well, yes, sir—cutlets," persisted Mason.

"What sort of cutlets?"

"Now, sir, you've got me. I shouldn't like to commit meself too deep, sir."

"Ordinary ration meat?"

"Yes, sir. Ordinary ration meat, but a noo shape, sir. Smells like liver, sir, but it 'asn't got that smooth, wet look like liver's got."

Stanhope's company is short an officer. Now one arrives in the person of Second Lieutenant Raleigh, sent up from Battalion Headquarters. "He is a well-built, healthy looking boy of about eighteen" with a very new uniform. To Osborne he makes report of his assignment and his adventures since having been sent out almost direct from school the summer before.

Raleigh has had, he thinks, a "frightful bit of luck" in being assigned to Stanhope's company. He had known Stanhope at school. Raleigh was only a kid then, and Stanhope, three years his senior, was one of the big fellows, but their fathers had been friends and away from school they managed to be terrific pals. One summer Stanhope had spent a part of his vacation at the Raleighs'. Met Raleigh's sister. She was just a kid then, too, but by the time war came she had grown up and there was a sort of understanding between them. Stanhope was her hero, too. Now Raleigh has brought his captain a message from her.

The story rather worries Osborne. Delicately he tries to prepare Raleigh for the change he may notice in Stanhope. Three years of fighting, three years of such service as Stanhope has known, is likely to change a man a lot, make him a bit quick-tempered and that sort of thing—

But Raleigh is prepared for that. "I know old Dennis's temper," he laughs. "I remember once at school he caught some chaps in a study with a bottle of whiskey. Lord! the roof nearly blew off. He gave them a dozen each with a cricket stump. (*Osborne laughs.*) He was so keen on the fellows in the house keeping fit. He was frightfully down on smoking—and that sort of thing."

"You must remember he's commanded this company for a long time—through all sorts of rotten times. It's—it's a big strain on a man."

"Oh, it must be!"

"If you notice a—a difference in Stanhope—you'll know it's only the strain?"

"Oh, yes!"

Osborne is very gentle, rather paternal, in fact, about acquainting the younger man with his duties and what are likely to be his experiences during his six days in line. The dugout, the boy learns, lets in from the support trench; the front line's about fifty yards farther on. He'll probably be sent on duty with one of the older men at first, until he gets used to it; after that he will stand his three hours on and six hours off with the rest of them.

It is a little hard for Raleigh to imagine that he is at last in the very thick of everything. The occasional spells of quiet are confusing, with nothing but the distant booming of the guns up Wipers way to remind him of the war. And to think—Osborne suggests—a hundred yards away the Germans are sitting in their dugouts wondering about the quiet, too!

There's something romantic about it all, Osborne has concluded. At least it is best always to think of it as being romantic. That helps. . . .

Now Captain Stanhope and Second-Lieutenant Trotter have come down the dugout steps and thrown their packs on the floor. "Despite his stars of rank Stanhope is no more than a boy; tall, slimly built but broad-shouldered. His dark hair is carefully brushed; his uniform, though old and war-stained, is well cut and cared for. He is good-looking, rather from attractive features than the healthy good looks of Raleigh. Although tanned by months in the open air, there is a pallor under his skin and dark shadows under his eyes. His short and fat companion—Second Lieutenant Trotter—is middle-aged and homely looking. His face is red, fat, and round; apparently he has put on weight during his war service, for his tunic appears to be on the verge of bursting at the waist."

Free of his pack burdens and his mind freed of his opinion of the way Hardy has permitted his men to leave the trenches; having refused Mason's suggestion that he have some soup and called rather peremptorily for whiskey, Stanhope is made aware of his new officer's presence. He is properly apologetic, his face all smiles, his hand haltingly half extended and then dropped suddenly to his side as Raleigh moves into the light.

Stanhope stares at Raleigh as though dazed. Nor are Osborne's efforts at relieving the tension by calling attention to the forthcoming food completely successful.

In fact the tension continues all through the supper, though there is now the food to talk about, the explanations of Mason to question, and the general discouragement of Trotter with the whole mess of war to ponder—the mess war creates when it comes to upsetting meals. . . .

Supper is over, finally. Trotter and Raleigh have gone to relieve Hibbert, who comes in complaining of his neuralgia. He gets precious little sympathy from his captain. It is Stanhope's private opinion, he tells Osborne, as soon as Hibbert goes to his bunk, that Hibbert is "another little worm trying to wiggle home." If he is he is doomed to disappointment.

Osborne is inclined to think that Stanhope is a little hard on Hibbert, but does not pursue the subject when he notes his captain's excited anger. He turns the subject abruptly to the new arrival.

"Raleigh looks a nice chap."

"Yes," Stanhope agrees, after a pause.

"Good-looking youngster. At school with you, wasn't he," persists Osborne.

"Has he been talking already?" sharply demands Stanhope.

OSBORNE—He just mentioned it. It was a natural thing to tell me when he knew you were in command. (STANHOPE *is lounging at the table with his back to the wall.* OSBORNE, *sitting on the right-hand bed, begins to puff clouds of smoke into the air as he lights his pipe.*) He's awfully pleased to get into your company. (STANHOPE *makes no reply. He picks up a pencil and scribbles on the back of a magazine.*) He seems to think a lot of you.

STANHOPE (*looking up quickly at* OSBORNE *and laughing.*)—Yes, I'm his hero.

OSBORNE—It's quite natural.

STANHOPE—You think so?

OSBORNE—Small boys at school generally have their heroes.

STANHOPE—Yes. Small boys at school do.

OSBORNE—Often it goes on as long as—

STANHOPE—As long as the hero's a hero.

OSBORNE—It often goes on all through life.

STANHOPE—I wonder. How many battalions are there in France?

OSBORNE—Why?

STANHOPE—We'll say fifty divisions. That's a hundred and fifty brigades—four hundred and fifty battalions. That's one thousand eight hundred companies. (*He looks up at* OSBORNE *from his calculations on the magazine cover.*) There are one thousand eight hundred companies in France, Uncle. Raleigh might have been sent to any one of those, and, my God! he comes to mine.

OSBORNE—You ought to be glad. He's a good-looking youngster. I like him.

STANHOPE—I knew you'd like him. Personality, isn't it? (*He takes a worn leather case from his breast pocket and hands a small photograph to* OSBORNE.) I've never shown you that, have I?

OSBORNE (*looking at the photograph.*)—No. (*Pause.*) Raleigh's sister, isn't it?

STANHOPE—How did you know?

OSBORNE—There's a strong likeness.

STANHOPE—I suppose there is.

OSBORNE (*intent on the picture*)—She's an awfully nice-looking girl.

STANHOPE—A photo doesn't show much, really. Just a face.

OSBORNE—She looks awfully nice. (*There is a silence.* STANHOPE *lights a cigarette.* OSBORNE *hands the photo back.*) You're a lucky chap.

STANHOPE (*putting the photo back into his case*)—I don't know why I keep it, really.

OSBORNE—Why? Isn't she—I thought—

STANHOPE—What did you think?

OSBORNE—Well, I thought that perhaps she was waiting for you.

STANHOPE—Yes. She is waiting for me—and she doesn't know. She thinks I'm a wonderful chap—commanding a company. (*He turns to* OSBORNE *and points up the steps into the line.*) She doesn't know that if I went up those steps into the front line—without being doped with whiskey—I'd go mad with fright.

(*There is a pause,* OSBORNE *stirs himself to speak.*)

OSBORNE—Look here, old man. I've meant to say it, for a long time, but it sounds damned impudence. You've been longer out here than any man in the battalion. It's time you went away for a rest. It's due to you.

STANHOPE—You suggest that I go sick, like that little worm in there—neuralgia in the eye? (*He laughs and takes a drink.*)

OSBORNE—No. Not that. The colonel would have sent you down long ago, only—

STANHOPE—Only—what?

OSBORNE—Only he can't spare you.

STANHOPE (*laughing*)—Oh, rot!

OSBORNE—He told me.

STANHOPE—He thinks I'm in such a state I want a rest, is that it?

OSBORNE—No. He thinks it's due to you.

STANHOPE—It's all right, Uncle. I'll stick it out now. It may not be much longer now. I've had my share of luck—more than my share. There's not a man left who was here when I came.

But it's rather damnable for that boy—of all the boys in the world—to have come to me. I might at least have been spared that.

OSBORNE—You're looking at things in rather a black sort of way.

STANHOPE—I've just told you. That boy's a hero-worshipper. I'm three years older than he is. You know what that means at school. I was skipper of Rugger and all that sort of thing. It doesn't sound much to a man out here—but it does at school with a kid of fourteen. Damn it, Uncle, you're a schoolmaster; you know.

OSBORNE—I've just told you what I think of hero-worship.

STANHOPE—Raleigh's father knew mine, and I was told to keep an eye on the kid. I rather liked the idea of looking after him. I made him keen on the right things—and all that. His people asked me to stay with them one summer. I met his sister then—

OSBORNE—Yes?

STANHOPE—At first I thought of her as another kid like Raleigh. It was just before I came out here for the first time that I realised what a topping girl she was. Funny how you realise it suddenly. I just prayed to come through the war—and—and do things—and keep absolutely fit for her.

OSBORNE—You've done pretty well. An M.C. and a company.

STANHOPE (*taking another whiskey*)—It was all right at first. When I went home on leave after six months it was jolly fine to feel I'd done a little to make her pleased. (*He takes a gulp of his drink.*) It was after I came back here—in that awful affair on Vimy Ridge. I knew I'd go mad if I didn't break the strain. I couldn't bear being fully conscious all the time—you've felt that, Uncle, haven't you?

OSBORNE—Yes, often.

STANHOPE—There were only two ways of breaking the strain. One was pretending I was ill—and going home; the other was this. (*He holds up his glass.*) Which would you pick, Uncle?

OSBORNE—I haven't been through as much as you. I don't know yet.

STANHOPE—I thought it all out. It's a slimy thing to go home if you're not really ill, isn't it?

OSBORNE—I think it is.

STANHOPE—Well, then. (*He holds his glass up to* OSBORNE.) Cheero, and long live the men who go home with neuralgia. (*He puts his glass down.*) I didn't go home on my last leave. I couldn't bear to meet her, in case she realised—

OSBORNE—When the war's over—and the strain's gone—you'll soon be as fit as ever, at your age.

STANHOPE—I've hoped that all the time. I'd go away for months and live in the open air—and get fit—and then go back to her.

OSBORNE—And so you can.

STANHOPE—If Raleigh had gone to one of those other one thousand eight hundred companies.

OSBORNE—I don't see why you should think—

STANHOPE—Oh, for Lord's sake don't be a damn fool. You know! You know he'll write and tell her I reek of whiskey all day.

OSBORNE—Why should he? He's not a—

STANHOPE—Exactly. He's not a damned little swine who'd deceive his sister.

OSBORNE—He's very young; he's got hundreds of strange things to learn; he'll realise that men are—different—out here.

STANHOPE—It's no good, Uncle. Didn't you see him sitting there at supper?—staring at me?—and wondering? He's up in those trenches now—still wondering—and beginning to understand. And all these months he's wanted to be with me out here. Poor little devil!

OSBORNE—I believe Raleigh'll go on liking you—and looking up to you—through everything. There's something very deep, and rather fine, about hero-worship.

STANHOPE—Hero-worship be damned! (*He pauses, then goes on, in a strange, high-pitched voice.*) You know, Uncle, I'm an awful fool. I'm captain of this company. What's that bloody little prig of a boy matter? D'you see? He's a little prig. Wants to write home and tell Madge all about me. Well, he won't; d'you see, Uncle? He won't write. Censorship! I censor his letters—cross out all he says about me.

OSBORNE—You can't read his letters.

STANHOPE (*dreamily*)—Cross out all he says about me. Then we all go west in the big attack—and she goes on thinking I'm a fine fellow for ever—and ever—and ever. (*He pours out a drink, murmuring "Ever—and ever—and ever."*)

Osborne takes Stanhope's blanket from his pack and spreads it on the bed by the table. With gentle insistence he gets his now slightly unsteady captain to agree to lie down, though the latter still is of a mind to combat the suggestion and to continue the recital of his determination to be even with Raleigh for having forced his way into "C" company.

Slowly, as the older man makes him comfortable on the bed, Stanhope falls into a deep sleep. . . . Mason comes to report the arrival of the pepper. . . . Osborne shades the lights so they will not waken the sleeper. . . .

The curtain falls.

ACT II

It is early next morning. In the dugout, "a pale shaft of light shines down the steps, but candles still burn in the dark corner where Osborne and Raleigh are at breakfast."

Now Trotter comes in, off duty temporarily and full of thoughts of bacon and breakfast. It would be nice, thinks Trotter as he throws his equipment aside, if he could have a bit of lean with his bacon. And he can have, Mason assures him, if he learns how to look at it. Let him look straight down on bacon from above and he can often see a streak of lean that might quite escape the vision from any other angle. . . .

Trotter is not at all pleased with the look of things, he reports to Raleigh and Osborne. Nor yet with the unnatural quiet. The Boche, he is impelled to repeat, is certainly up to something.

On the other hand it is a gorgeous morning. Quite springlike. Makes Trotter think of gardening, and things like that; a mood that was definitely stimulated earlier in the morning, he reports, when he had distinctly heard a small bird singing above the ruins of an old trench.

Osborne is rather keen on gardening, too. And if Trotter is proud of the grass plot in front of his house, bordered with geraniums, lobelia and calsularia, not to mention his 'olly-'ocks in the back, Osborne is no less proud of the fact that his last time home on leave he had built a rockery and even induced a primrose from the woods to grow in it, once he had thought to press a bit of moss around it. They'll be coming out again soon, too, those primroses, if they are having the sun at home.

Which reminds Trotter of the time last spring when his company was moving out of a salient about dawn one morning when they began to smell something sweet. It was just the time the Bosche was sending over a lot of that phosgene gas—and every man got into his gas mask. Then Trotter discovered that it was nothin' but a blinkin' may-tree all out in bloom and they did feel silly!—puttin' on gas masks because of a damned may-tree! . . .

Raleigh admits getting the feel of the trenches now. He's been there twelve hours and it seems ages. It's hard to get used to; it's hard to think of the German lines being no more than the width of a Rugger field away!

Osborne admits he always thinks of distances at the front in the terms of a Rugger field. Keeps them in proportion. He, too, used to play Rugger once. With the old Harlequins, in fact.

"I played for the English team on one great occasion," Osborne admits, modestly.

"What! For *England!*" Raleigh can hardly trust his ears.

OSBORNE—I was awfully lucky to get the chance. It's a long time ago now.

RALEIGH (*with awe*)—Oh, but, good Lord! that must have been simply topping! Where did you play?

OSBORNE—Wing three.

RALEIGH—I say, I—I never realised—you'd played for England?

OSBORNE—Tuppence to talk to me now! Anyhow, don't breeze it about.

RALEIGH—Don't the others know?

OSBORNE—We never talk about Rugger.

RALEIGH—They ought to know. It'd make them feel jolly bucked.

OSBORNE (*laughing*)—It doesn't make much difference out here!

RALEIGH—It must be awfully thrilling, playing in front of a huge crowd—all shouting and cheering—

OSBORNE—You don't notice it when the game begins.

RALEIGH—You're too taken up with the game?

OSBORNE—Yes.

RALEIGH—I used to get wind up playing at school with only a few kids looking on.

OSBORNE—You feel it more when there are only a few. (*He has picked up a slip of paper from the table; suddenly he laughs.*) Look at this!

RALEIGH (*looking at it curiously*)—What is it?

OSBORNE—Trotter's plan to make the time pass quickly. One hundred and forty-four little circles—one for each hour of six days. He's blacked in six already. He's six hours behind.

RALEIGH—It's rather a good idea. I like Trotter.

OSBORNE—He's a good chap.

RALEIGH—He makes things feel—natural.

OSBORNE—He's genuine sort of chap.

RALEIGH—That's it. He's genuine. (*There is a pause. He has been filling a new pipe.* OSBORNE *is puffing at his old one.*) How topping—to have played for England!

OSBORNE—Well, aren't you, now?

RALEIGH (*laughing*)—It's not quite the same. I wasn't picked specially, like you were. (*There is a pause.*) The Germans are really quite decent, aren't they? I mean, outside the newspapers?

OSBORNE—Yes. (*Pause.*) I remember up at Wipers we had a man shot when he was out on patrol. Just at dawn. We couldn't get him in that night. He lay out there groaning all day. Next night three of our men crawled out to get him in. It was so near the German trenches that they could have shot our fellows one by one. But, when our men began dragging the wounded man back over the rough ground, a big German officer stood up in their trenches and called out: "Carry him!"—and our fellows stood up and carried the man back, and the German officer fired some lights for them to see by.

RALEIGH—How topping!

OSBORNE—Next day we blew each other's trenches to blazes.

RALEIGH—It all seems rather—silly, doesn't it?

OSBORNE—it does rather!

Raleigh has gone into his tunnel to write his first letter home. . . . Now Stanhope is back from the line and a visit to the colonel. . . . The big German attack, it has been confessed by a prisoner, will come the morning of the 21st, two days from then!

Stanhope, of course, will prepare to meet it as best he can, he tells Osborne. He plans to wire his company in their position with lines of wire down both sides of them as well as in front. They can't expect any help from behind, the colonel says, and they will just have to stick it.

The nearness of the attack makes both Stanhope and Osborne thoughtful.

The older man finds a kind of relief in knowing that the thing is really going to happen at last. They have been waiting so long. . . .

Stanhope has grown increasingly introspective. A lot of things have happened recently to sharpen his imagination. Sometimes he has a queer feeling that perhaps he may be "going potty," but Osborne tries to convince him that his trouble is no more serious than nerve strain, and quietly to suggest that whiskey this early in the morning is not particularly helpful.

Then Stanhope hears that Raleigh is writing a letter home and the old misery comes back into his eyes. Has Raleigh been told about the censorship? Does he know that his letters shall be read?

Osborne has not taken that order seriously. Stanhope cannot mean really to read the boy's letters!

"Officially," snaps Stanhope, "I'm supposed to read all your letters. Damn it all, Uncle! Imagine yourself in my place—a letter going away from here—from that boy—"

"He'll say nothing—rotten—about you."

"You think so! . . . I heard you go on duty last night. After you'd gone, I got up. I was feeling bad. I forgot Raleigh was out there with Trotter. I'd forgotten all about him. I was sleepy. I just knew something beastly had happened. Then he came in with Trotter—and looked at me. After coming in out of the night air, this place must have reeked of candle-grease, and rats—and whiskey. One thing a boy like that can't stand is a smell that isn't fresh. He looked at me as if I'd hit him between the eyes—as if I'd spat on him—

"You imagine things!"

Now Raleigh has come from the tunnel. He is on his way to inspect his platoon's rifles. He has the letter he has written in his hand and would put it on the table to be picked up by the quartermaster-sergeant. He is about to seal it when Stanhope calls to him to leave it open. Raleigh is taken quite by surprise. He has been careful, he explains, not to say anything about their location, and—

Stanhope is firm. All letters must be censored. In which case, Raleigh decides, he will just let it go. He is putting the letter back in his tunic when Stanhope jumps from his chair and faces him.

STANHOPE—Give me that letter!
RALEIGH (*astonished*)—But—Dennis—
STANHOPE (*trembling*)—Give me that letter!
RALEIGH—But it's—it's private. I didn't know—
STANHOPE—D'you understand an order? Give me that letter!

RALEIGH—But I tell you—there's nothing—(STANHOPE *clutches* RALEIGH'S *wrist and tears the letter from his hand.*) Dennis—I'm—

STANHOPE—Don't "Dennis" me! Stanhope's my name! You're not at school! Go and inspect your rifles. (RALEIGH *stands in amazement at the foot of the stairs.*)

STANHOPE (*shouting*)—D'you understand an order?

(*For a moment* RALEIGH *stares wide-eyed at* STANHOPE, *who is trembling and breathing heavily, then almost in a whisper he says: "Right," and goes quietly up the narrow steps.* STANHOPE *turns toward the table.*)

OSBORNE—Good heavens, Stanhope!

STANHOPE (*wheeling furiously on* OSBORNE)—Look here, Osborne, I'm commanding this company. I ask for advice when I want it!

OSBORNE—Very well.

(STANHOPE *sinks down at the table with the letter in his hand. There is silence for a moment. Then he throws the letter on the table and rests his head between his hands.*)

STANHOPE—Oh, God! I don't want to read the blasted thing!

OSBORNE—You'll let it go then?

STANHOPE—I don't care. (*There is a pause.*)

OSBORNE—Shall I glance through it—for you?

STANHOPE—If you like.

OSBORNE—I don't want to.

STANHOPE—You better. I can't.

(OSBORNE *crosses and takes the letter from the table. He turns to his bed, sits down, and opens the letter.* STANHOPE *sits with his head in his hand, digging a magazine with a pencil. After a while,* OSBORNE *glances up at* STANHOPE.)

OSBORNE—D'you want to hear?

STANHOPE—I suppose I better know.

OSBORNE—He begins with a description of his getting here—he doesn't mention the names of any places.

STANHOPE—What does he say then?

OSBORNE—The last piece is about you.

STANHOPE—Go on.

OSBORNE (*reading*)—He says: "And now I come to the great news. I reported at Battalion Headquarters, and the colonel looked in a little book, and said, 'You report to "C" Company—Captain Stanhope.' Can't you imagine what I felt? I was taken along trenches and shown a dug-out. There was an awfully nice officer there—quite old—with grey hair"—(OSBORNE *clears his throat*)—"and then later Dennis came in. He looked tired, but that's because he works so frightfully hard, and because of the responsibility. Then I went on duty in the front line, and a sergeant told me all about Dennis. He said that Dennis is the finest officer in the battalion, and the men simply love him. He hardly ever sleeps in the dug-out; he's always up in the front line with the men, cheering them on with jokes, and making them keen about things, like he did the kids at school. I'm awfully proud to think he's my friend." (*There is silence.* STANHOPE *has not moved while* OSBORNE *has read.*) That's all. (*Pause.*) Shall I stick it down?

(STANHOPE *sits with lowered head. He murmurs something that sounds like "Yes, please." He rises heavily and crosses to the shadows by* OSBORNE's *bed. The sun is shining quite brightly in the trench outside.*) . . . The curtain falls.

Later that afternoon Stanhope is giving instructions to his sergeant-major as to what shall be expected of "C" company when the big attack comes. Principally, the captain is particular about the screens of wire that he wants run down both sides of the "C" company position. They will provide a measure of protection should the companies on their right and left flanks give way. Whatever may come, "C" company is to stick where it is.

The sergeant-major is not altogether clear as to the captain's intentions. What, for instance, is likely to happen if the attack should continue for two or three days? What if finally the Bosche does break through? What will "C" company do if it should find itself with the enemy all around and back of it?

"Then we advance and win the war," calmly answers Stanhope. They have been told to stick and stick they will! They may be able to delay the advance a whole day. . . .

The Colonel has called and brings with him serious news. The Brigadier has ordered a raid. The Bosche has been changing his front-line troops and everything points to the fact that the big push will start at dawn on Thursday. Meantime it has become increasingly important that the Brigadier should know who's come into line opposite his regiment. He suggested a raid that night, with the object of snaring a Bosche prisoner or two, but the Colonel has convinced him that a daylight raid the following afternoon would be much more practical and far more promising.

The Colonel is also of the opinion that the raiding party should consist of two officers and ten men. He doesn't want Stanhope to go. Can't risk that. But he does suggest Osborne as the level-headed sort who should lead a venture of that kind. Dismissing Trotter as too fat for an effective dash across No-man's land, and Hibbert as none too promising a substitute, the Colonel has hit upon young Raleigh as the best man for the second job. Raleigh is fresh and eager and has plenty of guts.

Stanhope is reluctant to send Raleigh. "It's rotten to send a fellow who's only just arrived," he protests. But, like the Colonel, he can think of no one else in his company so good. And thus it is arranged, with details as to smoke screens and holes to be blown in enemy wire to be settled later. . . .

Lieutenant Hibbert comes in to report that his neuralgia is getting much worse and to ask that he be permitted to go down the line to a hospital. He can't bear the pain longer.

STANHOPE (*quietly*)—You're going to stay here.

HIBBERT—I'm going down to see the doctor. He'll send me to hospital when he understands.

STANHOPE—I've seen the doctor. I saw him this morning. He won't send you to hospital, Hibbert; he'll send you back here. He promised me he would. (*There is silence.*) So you can save yourself a walk.

HIBBERT (*fiercely*)—What the hell—!

STANHOPE—Stop that!

HIBBERT—I've a perfect right to go sick if I want to. The men can—why can't an officer?

STANHOPE—No man's sent down unless he's very ill. There's nothing wrong with you, Hibbert. The German attack's on Thursday; almost for certain. You're going to stay here and see it through with the rest of us.

HIBBERT (*hysterically*)—I tell you, I can't—the pain's nearly sending me mad. I'm going! I've got all my stuff packed. I'm going now—you can't stop me! (*He goes excitedly into the dug-out.* STANHOPE *walks slowly towards the steps, turns and undoes the flap of his revolver holster. He takes out his revolver, and stands casually examining it.* HIBBERT *returns with his pack slung on his back and a walking-stick in his hand. He pauses at the sight of* STANHOPE *by the steps.*)

HIBBERT—Let's get by, Stanhope.

STANHOPE—You're going to stay here and do your job.

HIBBERT—Haven't I told you? I can't! Don't you understand? Let—let me get by.

STANHOPE—Now look here, Hibbert. I've got a lot of work to do and no time to waste. Once and for all, you're going to stay here and see it through with the rest of us.

HIBBERT—I shall die of this pain if I don't go!

STANHOPE—Better die of pain than be shot for deserting.

HIBBERT (*in a low voice*)—What do you mean?

STANHOPE—You know what I mean—

HIBBERT—I've a right to see the doctor!

STANHOPE—Good God! Don't you understand!—he'll send you back here. Dr. Preston's never let a shirker pass him yet—and he's not going to start now—two days before the attack—

HIBBERT (*pleadingly*)—Stanhope—if you only knew how awful I feel—Please do let me go by—

(*He walks slowly round behind* STANHOPE. STANHOPE *turns and thrusts him roughly back. With a lightning movement* HIBBERT *raises his stick and strikes blindly at* STANHOPE, *who catches the stick, tears it from* HIBBERT'S *hands, smashes it across his knee, and throws it on the ground.*)

STANHOPE—God!—you little swine. You know what that means—don't you? Striking a superior officer! (*There is silence.* STANHOPE *takes hold of his revolver as it swings from its lanyard.* HIBBERT *stands quivering in front of* STANHOPE.) Never mind, though. I won't have you shot for that—

HIBBERT—Let me go—

STANHOPE—If you went, I'd have you shot—for deserting. It's a hell of a disgrace—to die like that. I'd rather spare you the disgrace. I give you half a minute to think. You either stay here and try and be a man—or you try to get out of that door—to desert. If you do that, there's going to be an accident. D'you understand? I'm fiddling with my revolver, d'you see?—cleaning it—and it's going off by accident. It often happens out here. It's going off, and it's going to shoot you between the eyes.

HIBBERT (*in a whisper*)—You daren't—

STANHOPE—You don't deserve to be shot by accident—but I'd save you the disgrace of the other way—I give you half a minute to decide. (*He holds up his wrist to look at his watch.*) Half a minute from now—

(*There is silence; a few seconds go by. Suddenly* HIBBERT *bursts into a high-pitched laugh.*)

HIBBERT—Go on then, shoot! You won't let me go to hospital. I swear I'll never go into those trenches again. Shoot!—and thank God—

STANHOPE (*with his eyes on his watch*)—Fifteen more seconds—

HIBBERT—Go on! I'm ready—

STANHOPE—Ten. (*He looks up at* HIBBERT, *who has closed his eyes.*) Five.

(*Again* STANHOPE *looks up. After a moment he quietly drops his revolver into his holster and steps towards* HIBBERT, *who stands with lowered head and eyes tightly screwed up, his arms stretched stiffly by his sides, his hands tightly clutching the edges of his tunic. Gently* STANHOPE *places his hands on* HIBBERT'S *shoulders.* HIBBERT *starts violently and gives a little cry. He opens his eyes and stares vacantly into* STANHOPE'S *face.* STANHOPE *is smiling.*)

STANHOPE—Good man, Hibbert. I liked the way you stuck that.

HIBBERT (*hoarsely*)—Why didn't you shoot?

STANHOPE—Stay here, old man—and see it through—

(HIBBERT *stands trembling, trying to speak. Suddenly he breaks down and cries.* STANHOPE *takes his hands from his shoulders and turns away.*)

HIBBERT—Stanhope! I've tried like hell—I swear I have. Ever since I came out here I've hated and loathed it. Every sound up there makes me all—cold and sick. I'm different to—to the others—you don't understand? It's got worse and worse, and now I can't bear it any longer. I'll never go up those steps again—into the line—with the men looking at me—and knowing—I'd rather die here. (*He is sitting on* STANHOPE'S *bed, crying without effort to restrain himself.*)

STANHOPE (*pouring out a whiskey*)—Try a drop of this, old chap—

HIBBERT—No, thanks.

STANHOPE—Go on. Drink it. (HIBBERT *takes the mug and drinks.* STANHOPE *sits down beside* HIBBERT *and puts an arm round his shoulder.*) I know what you feel, Hibbert. I've known all along—

HIBBERT—How can you know?

STANHOPE—Because I feel the same—exactly the same! Every little noise up there makes me feel—just as you feel. Why didn't you tell me instead of talking about neuralgia? We all feel like you do sometimes, if you only knew. I hate and loathe it all. Sometimes I feel I could just lie down on this bed and pretend I was paralysed or something—and couldn't move—and just lie there till I died—or was dragged away.

Hibbert is stronger now, though still not resigned. He will stick it, or try to. And whatever comes, whether he is wounded and goes back feeling proud, or is killed and gets away from all the hell of it, or comes through as every one of them has a clean fighting chance of doing, Stanhope is positive he will be grateful that he can look his fellow men straight in the eyes the rest of his life. For the rest, nobody will ever know what has happened in the dugout that afternoon. . . .

Osborne is the first off-duty and the first to hear of the raid. If he is startled by the news of it there is only the pause in his speech to indicate his feelings. He, too, is a little sorry Raleigh should have been chosen. Seems— But it is the Colonel's suggestion. That settles it. When are they to go?

OSBORNE—To-morrow? What time?

STANHOPE—I suggest about five o'clock. A little before dusk—

OSBORNE—I see.

STANHOPE—I'm damn sorry.

OSBORNE—It's all right, old chap.

STANHOPE—I'm dining with the Colonel to arrange everything. Then I'll come back and go through it with you.

OSBORNE—Where do we raid from?

STANHOPE—Out of the sap on our left. Straight across.

OSBORNE—Where's the map?

STANHOPE—Here we are. Look. Straight across to this sentry post of the Boche. Sixty yards. To-night we'll lay out a guiding tape as far as possible. After dark the tochemmas are going to break the Boche wire and we'll cut a passage in ours.

OSBORNE—Will you fix up the men who are to go?

STANHOPE—Are you keen on any special men?

OSBORNE—Can I take a corporal?

STANHOPE—Sure.

OSBORNE—May I have young Crooks?

STANHOPE—Righto.

OSBORNE—You'll ask for volunteers, I suppose?

STANHOPE—Yes. I'll see the sergeant-major and get him to go round for names. (*He crosses to doorway as* MASON *comes in with the tea.*)

MASON—Your tea, Sir!

STANHOPE—Keep it hot, Mason.

MASON—Will you take this cup, Mr. Osborne?

STANHOPE—Take the other in to Mr. Hibbert, in there.

MASON—Very good, sir. (*He goes in to* HIBBERT'S *dug-out.*)

STANHOPE—Shan't be long, Uncle. (*He goes up the steps.*)
OSBORNE—Righto.

Trotter is not so very helpful about the raid. He doesn't like the idea of it. Raids are a damned nuisance. And probably the Boche will be ready and waiting for this one. There was a raid down the line a few nights ago, Trotter reports, in which the men were sent out even after the Boche had discovered the holes in the wire that were to be their path. Nothing short of murder, that raid.

"It's damn ridiculous, making a raid when the Boche are expecting it," Mr. Trotter concludes.

"You might avoid talking to Raleigh about it," Osborne suggests. "There's no use telling him it's murder—"

"Oh, Lord, no!" Trotter agrees. He, too, regrets Raleigh's choice. "I'm sorry 'e's got to go. 'E's a nice young fellow—"

Osborne turns to reading a small well-worn pocket volume. Curious time to read, thinks Trotter. Curious book to read—"Alice's Adventures in Wonderland!" A kid's book—that's what that is! A *kid's* book! Osborne certainly is a funny chap! . . .

Stanhope returns to report that the sergeant-major is collecting volunteers and to round up Hibbert, who is to relieve Raleigh. Stanhope and Hibbert leave the dugout together. Something in their attitude attracts Trotter's attention.

TROTTER—Can't understand that little feller, can you?
OSBORNE—Who?
TROTTER—Why, 'Ibbert. D'you see 'is eyes? All red. 'E told me in there 'e'd got 'ay-fever.
OSBORNE—Rotten thing, hay-fever.
TROTTER—If you ask me, 'e's been crying—(OSBORNE *is writing at the table.*)
OSBORNE—Maybe.
TROTTER—Funny little bloke, isn't 'e?
OSBORNE—Yes. I say—d'you mind? I just want to get a letter off.
TROTTER—Oh, sorry. They 'aven't collected the letters yet, then?
OSBORNE—Not yet.
TROTTER—I'll get one off to my old lady. (*He goes towards his dug-out.*) She's wrote and asked if I've got fleas.
OSBORNE—Have you?

TROTTER (*gently rotating his shoulders*)—I wish it was fleas. (TROTTER *goes into his dug-out;* OSBORNE *continues his letter.* RALEIGH *comes down the steps from the trench.*)

RALEIGH (*excitedly*)—I say, Stanhope told me about the raid!

OSBORNE—Has he?

RALEIGH—Just you and me, isn't it—and ten men?

OSBORNE—Yes, to-morrow. Just before dusk. Under a smoke cloud.

RALEIGH—I say—it's most frightfully exciting.

OSBORNE—We shall know more about it after Stanhope sees the Colonel to-night.

RALEIGH—Were you and I picked—specially?

OSBORNE—Yes.

RALEIGH—How topping!

The curtain falls.

ACT III

It is getting on toward sunset the following day. "The earth wall of the trench outside glows with a light that slowly fades with the sinking sun."

Stanhope has ordered Mason to have a pot of hot coffee ready in five minutes. The Colonel stops by for a final check up on the raid arrangements. The Colonel has done what he could to suggest a postponement of the raid, but the Brigadier is obdurate. His report must be in by seven o'clock.

"They can't have it later because of dinner, I suppose," mutters Stanhope, bitterly. "Meanwhile the Boche are sitting over there with a dozen machine guns trained on that hole—waiting for our fellows to come!"

"Well, I can't disobey orders!" protests the Colonel.

"Why didn't the trench mortars blow a dozen holes in different places—so the Boche wouldn't know which we were going to use?"

"It took three hours to blow that one. How could they blow a dozen in that time? It's no good worrying about that now. It's too late."

By their watches there are nineteen minutes to go. The smoke bombs will be dropped thirty yards to the right. The wind is just right. When the smoke blows across the opening in the wire the men will start. They are to bring their prisoners directly back to Stanhope's dugout. Not so safe to take them to headquarters. The Boche will be shelling headquarters by way of reprisal.

"It's no good getting depressed," the Colonel insists, noting Stanhope's mood. "After all it's only sixty yards. The Boche'll be firing into a blank fog. Osborne's a cool, level-headed chap, and Raleigh's the very man to dash in. You've picked good men to follow them?"

"The best. All youngsters. Strong, keen chaps."

"Good." (*A pause.*) "You know quite well I'd give anything to cancel the beastly affair!"

"I know you would, sir."

Osborne and Raleigh are back from a last-minute inspection of the sap from which they are to make the dash. The Colonel is a trifle husky as he bids them luck. He knows they will put on a good show. And when they get their German, or Germans, they are to bundle them right back to Stanhope's dugout. If they succeed he promises to recommend them both for the M.C. As a final thought, let them not forget to empty their pockets of papers and things!

Raleigh will leave his trinkets with his other things at his bunk. Osborne would like Stanhope to take charge of one or two things: His watch and his ring! Just in case anything should happen, he would like to have them sent on to Mrs. Osborne!

"You're coming back, old man," insisted Stanhope, with a forced optimism. "Damn it, what on earth should I do without you?"

"Goodness knows!"

"Must have somebody to tuck me up in bed. . . . Well, I'll see you up in the sap, before you go. Just have a spot of rum in that coffee."

"Righto!"

Stanhope has disappeared in the trench. Raleigh is in from his dugout. There's just time, Osborne thinks, for a small pipe before they go. And perhaps a cup of coffee. How about a drop of rum in it? Rum might make them a bit muzzy, Raleigh thinks. They'll have the rum afterward, suggests Osborne, to celebrate. . . .

They are both feeling all right. Osborne admits a sort of empty feeling inside, and Raleigh finds himself wanting to yawn. But they'll be fine directly they get started.

RALEIGH (*taking a deep breath*)—I wish we could go now.

OSBORNE (*looking at his watch on the table*)—We've got eight minutes yet.

RALEIGH—Oh, Lord!

OSBORNE—Let's just have a last look at the map. (*He picks up the map and spreads it out.*) Directly the smoke's thick enough, I'll give the word. You run straight for this point here—

RALEIGH—When I get to the Boche wire I lie down and wait for you.

OSBORNE—Don't forget to throw your bombs.

RALEIGH (*patting his pocket*)—No. I've got them here.

OSBORNE—When I shout "Righto!"—in you go with your eight men. I shall lie on the Boche parapet, and blow my whistle now and then to show you where I am. Pounce on the first Boche you see and bundle him out to me.

RALEIGH—Righto.

OSBORNE—Then we come back like blazes.

RALEIGH—The whole thing'll be over quite quickly?

OSBORNE—I reckon with luck we shall be back in three minutes.

RALEIGH—As quick as that?

OSBORNE—I think so. (*He folds up the map.*) And now let's forget all about it for—(*he looks at his watch*)—for six minutes.

RALEIGH—Oh, Lord, I can't!

OSBORNE—You must.

RALEIGH—How topping if we both get the M.C.!

OSBORNE—Yes. (*Pause.*) Your coffee sweet enough?

RALEIGH—Yes, thanks. It's jolly good coffee. (*Pause.*) I wonder what the Boche are doing over there now?

OSBORNE—I don't know. D'you like coffee better than tea?

RALEIGH—I do for breakfast. (*Pause.*) Do these smoke bombs make much row when they burst?

OSBORNE—Not much. (*Pause.*) Personally, I like cocoa for breakfast.

RALEIGH (*laughing*)—I'm sorry!

OSBORNE—Why sorry? Why shouldn't I have cocoa for breakfast?

RALEIGH—I don't mean that. I—mean—I'm sorry to keep talking about the raid. It's so difficult to—to talk about anything else. I was just wondering—will the Boche retaliate in any way after the raid?

OSBORNE—Bound to—a bit.

RALEIGH—Shelling?

OSBORNE—" 'The time has come,' the Walrus said,
'To talk of many things:
Of shoes—and ships—and sealing-wax—
Of cabbages—and kings.' "

RALEIGH—" 'And why the sea is boiling hot—
And whether pigs have wings?' "

OSBORNE—Now we're off! Quick, let's talk about pigs! Black pigs or white pigs?

RALEIGH—Black pigs. In the New Forest you find them, quite wild.

OSBORNE—You know the New Forest?

RALEIGH—Rather! My home's down there. A little place called Allum Green just outside Lyndhurst.

OSBORNE—I know Lyndhurst well.

RALEIGH—It's rather nice down there.

OSBORNE—I like it more than any place I know.

RALEIGH—I think I do, too. Of course, it's different when you've always lived in a place.

. . . .

RALEIGH—I say, here's your ring.

OSBORNE—Yes. I'm—I'm leaving it here. I don't want the risk of losing it.

RALEIGH—Oh! (*There is silence. He puts the ring slowly down.*)

OSBORNE (*rising*)—Well, I think perhaps we ought to get ready.

RALEIGH—Yes. Righto. (*He also rises.*)

OSBORNE—I'm not going to wear a belt—just my revolver, with the lanyard round my neck.

RALEIGH—I see. (*He puts his lanyard round his neck and grips his revolver.*) I feel better with this in my hand, don't you?

OSBORNE—Yes. Something to hold. Loaded all right?

RALEIGH—Yes.

(*They put on their helmets.* OSBORNE *takes his pipe from his mouth and lays it carefully on the table.*)

OSBORNE—I do hate leaving a pipe when it's got a nice glow on the top like that.

RALEIGH (*with a short laugh*)—What a pity! (*There is another pause.* OSBORNE *glances at his watch as it lies on the table.*)

OSBORNE—Three minutes to. I think we'd better go.

RALEIGH—Righto. (*Their eyes meet as* OSBORNE *turns from the table.*)

OSBORNE—I'm glad it's you and I—together, Raleigh.

RALEIGH (*eagerly*)—Are you—really?

OSBORNE—Yes.

RALEIGH—So am I—awfully.

OSBORNE—We must put up a good show.

RALEIGH—Yes. Rather! (*There is a short pause.*)

OSBORNE—Let's go along, shall we?

RALEIGH—Righto. (*They go towards the steps.*) (MASON *comes to the entrance of his dugout as they pass.*)

MASON—Good luck, sir.

OSBORNE—Thanks, Mason.

MASON—It's a lovely chicken for dinner, sir.

OSBORNE (*slowly going up the steps*)—Splendid!

MASON—Good luck, Mr. Raleigh.

RALEIGH—Thanks.

Osborne and Raleigh go up the steps "into the pale evening sun." There is a moment's silence as Mason tidies the table and puts the coffee mugs away. Suddenly there is the "dull crash of bursting smoke bombs," and afterward the screech of bombs, the whine of shells, the rat-tat-tat of machine guns. The noise is somewhat deadened by the earth walls, but through the dugout door the havoc being wrought by the shells that hit is to be seen. . . . Gradually the noise dies away. The machine guns rattle a last time and stop. There is the sound of voices in the trench above. Stanhope is directing the Colonel!

Now the Sergeant-major has brought in a captured German soldier. He is a bare-headed boy, in field gray, and is sobbing bitterly. Nor does the Sergeant-major's assurance that he is not to be hurt calm the prisoner's fears. He falls on his knees and pleads for mercy.

The Colonel's examination is conducted in such German as he commands. Once or twice the prisoner answers in equally uncertain English. Readily he tells the Colonel that his regiment is the 20th Württembergers and that they came into line the night before. But he will not tell from what town he came up to the line, and the Colonel lets it pass. The Sergeant-major searches him, finds his pay book, a pocket knife, an assortment of trinkets and a bar of chocolate. He gets everything back except his knife. Then they march him away to headquarters for further questioning.

The Colonel is vastly pleased with the results of the raid, and is sure the Brigadier will feel the same way about it. The Colonel's satisfaction fails to cheer Stanhope. The thought of the Brigadier's pleasure is also something less than thrilling. Stanhope has had a report from the raiding party. Four men and Raleigh came back safely.

COLONEL—Oh, I say, I'm sorry! That's—er—six men and—er—Osborne?

STANHOPE—Yes, sir.

COLONEL—I'm very sorry. Poor Osborne!

STANHOPE—Still it'll be awfully nice if the Brigadier's pleased.

COLONEL—Don't be silly, Stanhope. Do you know—er—what happened to Osborne?

STANHOPE—A hand grenade—while he was waiting for Raleigh.

COLONEL—I'm very sorry. And the six men?

STANHOPE—Machine-gun bullets, I suppose.

COLONEL—Yes, I was afraid—er—(*His words trail away; he fidgets uneasily as* STANHOPE *looks at him with a pale, expressionless face.* RALEIGH *comes slowly down the steps, walking as though he were asleep; his hands are bleeding. The* COLONEL *turns to the boy with enthusiasm.*) Very well done, Raleigh. Well done, my boy. I'll get you a Military Cross for this! Splendid! (RALEIGH *looks at the* COLONEL *and tries to speak. He raises his hand to his forehead and sways. The* COLONEL *takes him by the arm.*) Sit down here, my boy. (RALEIGH *sits on the edge of* OSBORNE'S *bed.*) Have a good rest. Well, I must be off. (*He moves towards the steps, and turning once more to* RALEIGH *as he leaves.*) Very well done. (*With a quick glance at* STANHOPE, *the* COLONEL *goes away.*)

(*There is a silence now in the trenches outside; the last shell has whistled over and crashed. Dusk is beginning to fall over the German lines. The glow of Very lights begins to rise and fade against the evening sky.* STANHOPE *is staring dumbly at the table—at* OSBORNE'S *watch and ring. Presently he turns his haggard face towards* RALEIGH, *who sits with lowered head, looking at the palms of his hands.* STANHOPE *moves slowly across towards the doorway, and pauses to look down at* RALEIGH. RALEIGH *looks up into* STANHOPE'S *face, and their eyes meet. When* STANHOPE *speaks, his voice is still expressionless and dead.*)

STANHOPE—Must you sit on Osborne's bed?

RALEIGH—I'm sorry. (*He rises.*)

(STANHOPE *turns and goes slowly up the steps.* RALEIGH *stands with lowered head. Heavy guns are booming miles away. The curtain falls.*)

. . . .

Only Stanhope, Trotter and Hibbert attend the "celebration" that night. They have the chicken and the champagne and do their best to be gay about it. Especially the champagne. Talk about their times on leave; of the women they met; of the experiences they had. Hibbert manages to stir up a thrill of sorts getting out his souvenir postcards and passing them around. Pictures of women's legs, mostly. Not so good, either. Too fat, usually, to suit Stanhope. Or too thin. Scraggy, a lot of them, if you'll believe Trotter.

Stanhope would put a load of whiskey on top of the champagne, despite Trotter, who intimates that in his opinion such a combination might easily be attended with grave danger to the experimenter. Stanhope, however, is recklessly inclined to-night and much put out to find that of the six bottles of whiskey with which they arrived in line three days before only one is left. Fortunately that one will be enough to last until dawn. . . .

Raleigh is standing duty. He hasn't been in the dugout much since the raid. Seemed rather to resent the thought of a celebration, Hibbert reports.

"Well, I 'ope 'e gets the M.C., that's all," hopes Trotter. "'E's just the kid I'd like if ever I 'ave a kid—strong and plucky!"

"Oh, for God's sake, forget that bloody raid!" shouts Stanhope, hysterically. "Think I want to talk about it?" . . .

The party's over. Hibbert would like to go on, but Stanhope is through—and a little ugly about it. Trotter has gone to relieve Raleigh, whose dinner has been brought in by Mason and put on the table. . . .

Now Raleigh stands at the bottom of the trench stairs and hesitates about coming forward. Stanhope calls a little sharply to him. Wasn't he told to come down to dinner at eight? He didn't think they would mind? What right had he to assume that, having been invited, no one would mind if he did not come?

However, his dinner has been saved for him. Let him eat it. He doesn't care for it? He has had something with the men? Tea and bread and cheese—with the men? Stanhope's disgust mounts with the thought of such a situation.

"I know you're new to this, but I thought you'd have the common sense to leave the men alone to their meals," he growls. "Do you think they want an officer prowling around eating their rations, and sucking up to them like that? My officers are here to be respected—not laughed at."

Raleigh is apologetic. He had not intended any offense. The men asked him to share with them—

Stanhope's state of temper does not admit of his accepting explanations.

STANHOPE—You insulted Trotter and Hibbert by not coming. You realise that, I suppose?

RALEIGH—I didn't mean to do anything like that.

STANHOPE—Well, you did. You know now—don't you? (RALEIGH *makes no reply. He is trying to understand why* STANHOPE'*s temper has risen to a trembling fury.* STANHOPE *can scarcely control his voice. Loudly.*) I say—you know now, don't you?

RALEIGH—Yes. I'm sorry.

STANHOPE—My officers work together. I'll have no damn prigs.

RALEIGH—I'll speak to Trotter and Hibbert. I didn't realise—

STANHOPE *raises his cigar. His hand trembles so violently that he can scarcely take the cigar between his teeth.* RALEIGH *looks at* STANHOPE, *fascinated and horrified.*)

STANHOPE—What are you looking at?

RALEIGH (*lowering his head*)—Nothing.

STANHOPE—Anything—funny about me?

RALEIGH—No. (*After a moment's silence,* RALEIGH *speaks in a low, halting voice.*) I'm awfully sorry, Dennis, if—if I annoyed you by coming to your company.

STANHOPE—What on earth are you talking about? What do you mean?

RALEIGH—You resent my being here.

STANHOPE—Resent you being here?

RALEIGH—Ever since I came—

STANHOPE—I don't know what you mean. I resent you being a damn fool, that's all. (*There is a pause.*) Better eat your dinner before it's cold.

RALEIGH—I'm not hungry, thanks.

STANHOPE—Oh, for God's sake, sit down and eat it like a man!

RALEIGH—I can't eat it, thanks.

STANHOPE (*shouting*)—Are you going to eat your dinner?

RALEIGH—Oh! Good heavens! Don't you understand? How can I sit down and eat that—when (*his voice nearly breaking*) —when Osborne's—lying—out there—

(STANHOPE *rises slowly. His eyes are wide and staring; he is fighting for breath, and his words come brokenly.*)

STANHOPE—My God! You bloody little swine! You think I don't care—you think you're the only soul that cares!

RALEIGH—And yet you can sit there and drink champagne—and smoke cigars—

STANHOPE—The one man I could trust—my best friend—the one man I could talk to as man to man—who understood everything—and you think I don't care—

RALEIGH—But how can you when—?

STANHOPE—To forget, you little fool—to forget! D'you understand? To forget! You think there's no limit to what a man can bear? (*He turns quickly from* RALEIGH *and goes to the dark corner by* OSBORNE'S *bed. He stands with his face towards the wall, his shoulders heaving as he fights for breath.*)

RALEIGH—I'm awfully sorry, Dennis. I—I didn't understand. (STANHOPE *makes no reply.*) You don't know how—I—

STANHOPE—Go away, please—leave me alone.

RALEIGH—Can't I—

(STANHOPE *turns upon* RALEIGH.)

STANHOPE—Oh, get out! For God's sake, get out!

(RALEIGH *goes away into his dug-out, and Stanhope is alone. The Very lights rise and fall outside, softly breaking the darkness with their glow—sometimes steel-blue, sometimes grey. Through the night there comes the impatient grumble of gunfire that never dies away. The curtain falls.*)

It is near dawn the next day. The dugout is in heavy darkness, save for the faint glow of the Very lights in the sky beyond the doorway. Mason, coming from the men's quarters, lights a candle. It is time to awaken Stanhope, sleeping heavily upon his cot. He is not easy to waken.

Trotter is up and half shaved, a job he soon finishes. Soon Mason has hot tea for them. Now the sergeant-major is in to report the wiring job all set. No signs of activity just opposite, he reports, but the guns are goin' 'ard down south. An 'eavy bombardment, in fact. Looks like it's spreading.

The men, Stanhope orders, are to have a decent drop of rum

with their tea. They will stand-to, ready for an attack, till midday. If it doesn't come by that time, it probably will not come until the next day.

Mason has prepared packets of sandwiches for his officers. " 'Arf bully beef and 'arf sardine. Sardine on top, sir," he explains.

"How delicious," praises Stanhope. "No *pâté de foie gras?*"

"No what, sir?"

"No *pâté de foie gras?*"

"No, sir. The milkman 'asn't been yet."

Trotter is dressed and ready to inspect the line. He calls Hibbert and Raleigh. Stanhope is writing when Raleigh comes. For a moment the boy stands at the foot of the steps. Shyly turns and calls:

"Cheero, Stanhope!"

"Cheero, Raleigh!" Stanhope answers. "I'll be coming up soon."

Raleigh goes up the steps.

It takes some pursuasion to get Hibbert started. Hibbert can't see any necessity for such appalling hurry! His mouth is dry! He wants water! A lot of water! There is a call "floating through the dawn" from down the trench that does not help him. "Stretcher bear-ers!"

Hibbert manages to make the steps finally, with Mason going along as moral support. Stanhope continues his writing. . . .

The Sergeant-major is back to report that the firing is getting 'ot; that Corporal Ross has been 'it; that it will be practically impossible to get the wounded back. It will be better, Stanhope decides, to carry them to the big dugout and let the stretcher-bearers do what they can there until the situation clears. Again Stanhope is alone—

"Flying fragments of shell whistle and hiss and moan overhead. The sharp 'crack' of the rifle grenades, the thud of the shells, and the boom of the Minenwerfer mingle together in a muffled roar."

Stanhope is at the foot of the steps when the Sergeant-major returns excitedly. It is Mr. Raleigh this time—Mr. Raleigh has been 'it. A bit of shell got 'im in the back. Might of broken 'is spine. He can't move his legs. . . .

The Sergeant-major carries Raleigh like a child into the dugout. Stanhope has rolled a trench coat into a pillow, taken the blanket from his own bed and put it on Osborne's. The Sergeant-major lays Raleigh gently down. Slowly he regains consciousness. As he turns his head he sees Stanhope.

"Hullo—Dennis—"

"Well, Jimmy (*he smiles*)—you got one quickly."

For a moment there is no response. Stanhope sits on a box by the side of the bed anxiously watching his second lieutenant. When Raleigh speaks again it is in a wondering voice.

RALEIGH—Why—how did I get down here?

STANHOPE—Sergeant-major brought you down.

(RALEIGH *speaks again, vaguely, trying to recollect.*)

RALEIGH—Something—hit me in the back—knocked me clean over—sort of—winded me—I'm all right now. (*He tries to rise.*)

STANHOPE—Steady, old boy. Just lie there quietly for a bit.

RALEIGH—I'll be better if I get up and walk about. It happened once before—I got kicked in just the same place at Rugger; it—it soon wore off. It—it just numbs you a bit. (*There is a pause.*) What's that rumbling noise?

STANHOPE—The guns are making a bit of a row.

RALEIGH—Our guns?

STANHOPE—No. Mostly theirs.

(*Again there is silence in the dugout. A very faint rose light is beginning to glow in the dawn sky.* RALEIGH *speaks again—uneasily.*)

RALEIGH—I say—Dennis—

STANHOPE—Yes, old boy?

RALEIGH—It—it hasn't gone through, has it? It only just hit me?—and knocked me down?

STANHOPE—It's just gone through a bit, Jimmy.

RALEIGH—I won't have to—go on lying here?

STANHOPE—I'm going to have you taken away.

RALEIGH—Away? Where?

STANHOPE—Down to the dressing-station—then hospital—then home. (*He smiles.*) You've got a Blighty one, Jimmy.

RALEIGH—But I—I can't just for—for a knock in the back. (*He stirs restlessly.*) I'm certain I'll be better if—if I get up. (*He tries to raise himself, and gives a sudden cry.*) Oh—God! It does hurt!

STANHOPE—It's bound to hurt, Jimmy.

RALEIGH—What's—on my legs? Something holding them down—

STANHOPE—It's all right, old chap; it's just the shock—numbed them.

(*Again there is a pause. When* RALEIGH *speaks there is a different note in his voice.*)

RALEIGH—It's awfully decent of you to bother, Dennis. I feel rotten lying here—everybody else—up there.

STANHOPE—It's not your fault, Jimmy.

RALEIGH—So—damn—silly—getting hit. (*Pause.*) Is there —just a drop of water?

STANHOPE (*rising quickly*)—Sure. I've got some here. (*He pours some water into the mug and brings it to* RALEIGH. *Cheerfully.*) Got some tea-leaves in it. D'you mind?

RALEIGH—No. That's all right—thanks—(STANHOPE *holds the mug to* RALEIGH'S *lips, and the boy drinks.*) I say, Dennis, don't you wait—if—if you want to be getting on.

STANHOPE—It's quite all right, Jimmy.

RALEIGH—Can you stay for a bit?

STANHOPE—Of course I can.

RALEIGH (*faintly*)—Thanks awfully. (*There is quiet in the dugout for a long time.* STANHOPE *sits with one hand on* RALEIGH'S *arm, and* RALEIGH *lies very still. Presently he speaks again—hardly above a whisper.*) Dennis—

STANHOPE—Yes, old boy?

RALEIGH—Could we have a light? It's—it's so frightfully dark and cold.

STANHOPE (*rising*)—Sure! I'll bring a candle and get another blanket. (STANHOPE *goes to the left-hand dugout, and* RALEIGH *is alone, very still and quiet, on* OSBORNE'S *bed. The faint rosy glow of the dawn is deepening to an angry red. The grey night sky is dissolving, and the stars begin to go. A tiny sound comes from where* RALEIGH *is lying—something between a sob and a moan.* STANHOPE *comes back with a blanket. He takes a candle from the table and carries it to* RALEIGH'S *bed. He puts it on the box beside* RALEIGH *and speaks cheerfully.*) Is that better, Jimmy? (RALEIGH *makes no sign.*) Jimmy—

(*Still* RALEIGH *is quiet.* STANHOPE *gently takes his hand. There is a long silence.* STANHOPE *lowers* RALEIGH'S *hand to the bed, rises, and takes the candle back to the table. He sits on the bench behind the table with his back to the wall, and stares across at the boy on* OSBORNE'S *bed. The solitary candle-flame throws up the lines on his pale, drawn face, and the dark shadows under his tired eyes. The thudding of the shells rises and falls like an angry sea. A private soldier comes scrambling down the steps, his round, red face wet with perspiration, his chest heaving for breath.*)

SOLDIER—Message from Mr. Trotter, sir—will you come at once. (STANHOPE *gazes round at the soldier—and makes no other sign.)* Mr. Trotter, sir—says will you come at once!

(STANHOPE *rises stiffly and takes his helmet from the table.*)

STANHOPE—All right, Broughton, I'm coming.

(*The soldier turns and goes away.* STANHOPE *pauses for a moment by* OSBORNE'S *bed and lightly runs his fingers over* RALEIGH'S *tousled hair. He goes stiffly up the steps, his tall figure black against the dawn sky. The shelling has risen to a great fury. The solitary candle burns with a steady flame, and* RALEIGH *lies in the shadows. The whine of a shell rises to a shriek and bursts on the dugout roof. The shock stabs out the candle-flame; the timber props of the door cave slowly in, sand-bags fall and block the passage to the open air. There is darkness in the dugout. Here and there the red dawn glows through the jagged holes of the broken doorway. Very faintly there comes the dull rattle of machine-guns and the fevered spatter of rifle fire.*)

The curtain falls.

WINGS OVER EUROPE

Drama in Three Acts

BY ROBERT NICHOLS AND MAURICE BROWNE

HAVING begun its season with a revival of Shaw's "Major Barbara" at the home theatre in November the Theatre Guild took over a lease of the Martin Beck Theatre for its second production, that of "Wings Over Europe," on December 10, 1928.

This extremely serious drama was received with profound salaams by the slightly mystified but deeply impressed reviewers of the press and with mingled cheers and gentle ravings by the subscribers of the Guild. It was played for something more than a hundred performances, however, and should continue in the Theatre Guild repertory for many seasons to come.

The play's authors, the Messrs. Nichols and Browne, are both English, both graduates of Cambridge, both interested in a better drama (Mr. Browne being, in historic fact, the very creator of the name Little Theatre as a classification for the experiments of artistically eager amateurs) and both in their thirties. They thought originally of "Wings Over Europe" as a protest against all war and a vision of the advantages of universal peace.

Their hero is a youthful scientist who, by discovering a formulæ by which he can control the atom, harnessing its boundless energy and releasing man for all time from his slavery to matter, hopes to divert his discovery to the everlasting glory of mankind. Because he is the nephew of the Prime Minister of England he first seeks Britain's aid rather than that of the League of Nations and brings his proposition to the British Cabinet.

"The play does not aim at a realistic presentation of what would occur were a Francis Lightfoot to enter No. 10 Downing street to-morrow morning," writes Mr. Nichols. "It is an extravaganza, a ballet of ideas. It is no more realistic in intention than Mozart's 'Don Juan' (the music of Mozart was constantly in my head as I did my share of the play) which is, as you know, opera bouffe, but which under the Victorians had become a severe tragedy of a declamatory sort. . . . To me the theatre does not exist to discuss problems, or take sides, or ventilate grievances (no, not though it be man's grievance with the order of the universe itself) but to establish as often as possible in a piece the reign of the mysterious influence Beauty. (That is why I admire Tchekov so intensely—in his best plays Beauty is constantly with us; descending upon our hearts like a refreshing dew.")

In the Cabinet Council Room at No. 10 Downing Street, London, "we have our backs to the Horse Guards Parade," advise the authors, "and we are looking toward the Georgian clock on the marble mantelpiece, set precisely in the middle of the farther wall. A cheerful fire is burning in the grate, but we can scarcely see it because the entire middle of the cream-panelled, book-shelved room is occupied by a lengthy table, round the circumference of which are neatly arranged no less than thirteen (ominous number) leather-covered blotting-books, as if to hem in the long array of ink-pots, stationery boxes, etc., which form, as it were, the backbone of the table."

It is a cheerful and comfortable room, lined with bookshelves that are packed with "brown leather-jerkined volumes of law." There are tall double doors letting into an ante-room at the right; the sunlight of a spring morning falls through tall windows at the left, double-paned to keep out the noise.

Two messengers have just finished putting the last chair, the last pen, the last bit of stationery in place; the table clock reads half-past nine. The hour of an appointment has arrived and the Prime Minister, who has been standing quietly warming his hands at the fire, bids the head messenger summon the gentlemen who are waiting outside.

The Prime Minister "is in well-preserved later middle age. He is a country gentleman and a conservative. He wears pince-nez." The gentlemen summoned are "Sir Berkeley Rummel, tall, clean-shaven, gold-spectacled, grizzled; and Sir Henry Hand, stoutish, bearded, philosophically-twinkling."

These two, it transpires, are among the greatest of Britain's nerve-specialists and have been examining with greater care than the subject of their investigation has been aware the mental condition of the Prime Minister's nephew, young Francis Lightfoot, already a physicist of conspicuous achievement though only in his 25th year. Their report now delivered is that Mr. Lightfoot is perfectly normal.

"The young man," admits Sir Henry Hand, "is what is popularly known as highly-strung, but not more so than any sensitive man of his attainments. Extraordinary results only originate in fine organizations. He is the type of artist-scientist, a type not uncommon among great physicists. Pascal belonged to it, and Newton, at least mentally."

"Charles Darwin, one of the sanest men who ever lived," adds Sir Berkeley Rummel, "was of a not dissimilar type. Your nephew, Mr. Grantly, though highly-strung, as Sir Henry says, is altogether normal."

"How did he take the examination? Did he spot what you were after?"

"No, no. Oh, dear no," Sir Berkeley is sure. "No, we told him that—as he's staying with you here—you had asked us to your breakfast table that we might make his acquaintance, because we had a special interest in the neurological make-up of men of remarkable aptitudes; above all, of eminent physicists. He said he was honored. Completely unsuspecting."

They have been mildly surprised to find that young Lightfoot lives a life quite completely retired from the world. His laboratories are in North Wales where he works with his assistants, taking into his confidence no other physicist. Having thirty thousand pounds a year he is independent as to means and, his trust in humanity having been shaken when he was 16, he has definitely refused to take further risks.

The Prime Minister and his visitors are still discussing Francis Lightfoot's peculiarities as well as his promised eminence when that young man sidles youthfully through the tall doors, putting the older men to some slight embarrassment as they try to change their subject gracefully.

"Francis Lightfoot is twenty-five years old but looks much younger," as his authors see him. "He is dressed in a striped gray double-breasted coat and waist-coat, gray 'bags,' soft brown shoes; he wears no tie; all his clothes are well cut, but worn with carelessness. He is slightly below medium height and of graceful build; he has small hands and feet and a shock of brown hair. His face is very beautiful and rather unearthly. To prosaic people there is something rather noxious in this unearthliness, just as to poetic people there is something angelic in it. He has fine eyes which, in repose, alternate between dreaminess and daring; in action they betray, as do his brows, nostrils, and mouth, a fiercely petulant wilfulness and an extreme pride—a pride entirely what the Bible would call 'ghostly.' His manner is nervous and constrained, for he is not at his ease in the world of affairs. . . . At present he is evidently suffering from a profound inward happy excitement, but is endeavoring to appear calm, and this endeavor results in his casting quick and uneasy glances in every direction."

As he bids his investigators good-by Francis is quite frank to ask them their verdict. Is he or is he not sane? And when they assure him that he is quite sane his elation is apparent. Now his eminent uncle must admit that everything is as it should be and there can be no more doubts as to the discovery, the proposed revealing of which has been the cause of these preliminaries. Yet the prime Minister advises caution.

PRIME MINISTER—Don't let yourself get excited, my boy. It's not going to be easy. I fear you may have some disappointments in front of you.

FRANCIS LIGHTFOOT—Disappointments?

PRIME MINISTER (*taking him past precipices at a good round trot*)—Man will be man; but everybody will, I am sure, do their best to help you—

FRANCIS LIGHTFOOT—Help me? I am going to help them.

PRIME MINISTER—To help you help them, I should have said. Well, well, all is ready. You'll seat yourself just behind me and draw up when the battle begins.

FRANCIS LIGHTFOOT—Battle!

PRIME MINISTER (*who has timed his stroke*)—Public affairs are always a battle—I don't know why (*genially*) perhaps it's because, as the Chinese sage used to say, those who speak don't know, and those who know don't speak.

FRANCIS LIGHTFOOT—I am going to make a statement, nothing more. You and the Cabinet Committee will then act on it for the public good.

PRIME MINISTER (*soothingly*)—Of course, of course. (*Returning to his point.*) But has it ever struck you, Francis, that there's nothing on earth—except religion—on which men are so divided as the public good?

FRANCIS LIGHTFOOT—Not when the question is large enough, and the issue simple.

PRIME MINISTER—It takes genius to tell which questions are large, and, except Evelyn Arthur, there is no genius in my Cabinet. The rest of us are just, I hope, sound men doing our best. As to a simple issue, in a public life of over thirty years (*cheerily*), I have never yet met one.

FRANCIS LIGHTFOOT—But, Uncle, if I were to say to you:

"I am a terrible angel and I come to offer you a choice on which you must decide in the next five minutes—and that choice is 'Will you live or die?' "

PRIME MINISTER—I fear that in my public capacity I should certainly have to say, "I choose to live"; in my private capacity . . . I don't know . . . my son killed, my daughters married, my wife dead . . . If I hadn't my grand-daughter—

FRANCIS LIGHTFOOT—But you have. There's Marjorie, and there's your duty. So the issue's simple, and you say, "I choose to live."

PRIME MINISTER (*shrugging*)—Yes, I suppose so.

FRANCIS LIGHTFOOT (*ardently*)—Very well. That is precisely the question I put to you, and not to you only, but to Europe and, for the matter of that, to the entire world. And (*triumphantly*) the answer will be the same—for the world will have life and will have it more abundantly!

PRIME MINISTER—Don't you—er—just a trifle—in the enthusiasm of an adept, you understand—overstate the case?

FRANCIS LIGHTFOOT—Not one jot.

PRIME MINISTER (*leaving it*)—Well, if the issue's as simple as that, let us hope the others will see it. Most men want to live, I believe; certainly most of my Cabinet do, if only for the abundance of—er—life, which will be theirs when they step into my shoes.

There is one man in the cabinet upon whom the Prime Minister advises his nephew to concentrate. He is Evelyn Arthur, the Secretary for Foreign Affairs, an understanding man and also something of a genius. But Francis cannot understand the need of concentrating on any man or any group; his statement of his discovery will be simple; it should appeal to all men of intelligence; if they take it, well and good; if they do not, on their heads be it. . . .

Francis has rushed out to provide himself with a necktie when Evelyn Arthur arrives. The secretary is slightly disturbed by the early hour of this special meeting, but he is genially pleased to meet the Prime Minister and greatly interested in the genius nephew. Evelyn Arthur has talked, he reports, with the great Einstein and been somewhat amazed at that scientist's marked enthusiasm for Francis Lightfoot.

He is also pleased to learn in his first talk with young Lightfoot that they share a love of Shelley, not only as a poet but because Francis believes with others that if he had been born later

Shelley would undoubtedly have been a great chemist. "His poems seem almost like my own voice talking to me," Francis confesses, "for physics are my passion and humanity my religion."

Now the doors are opened and the Cabinet Committee enters, buzzing busily with casual affairs. Soon each is seated before his respective inkwell and blotter.

"You and I may think that the Prime Minister reminds us a little, in some respects, of Sir Arthur Campbell Bannerman, Lord Oxford, and Mr. Baldwin," suggest the authors, "the Secretary for Foreign Affairs, of Lord Salisbury, Lord Balfour, and Sir Austen Chamberlain, and the others of a number of eminent personages, with whose outward aspects the Daily Press has made us not unfamiliar. But we assure you that, till the Censor assures us that we are not mistaken, the less said about these misapprehensions of ours, and the sooner we all get on with the play, the better."

The Prime Minister, rapping for order and making sure that all the doors are shut, now proceeds to acquaint the gentlemen present with the purpose of the meeting. It has been a carefully guarded secret, he explains, because of its unique and very grave nature. He has even dispensed with the services of a secretary, as had been done in war times when matters of grave import were before the committee.

"You know me well enough, gentlemen," the Prime Minister continues, "to be sure that I do not take such steps without due cause, and I should like to make it plain from the start, that, extraordinary as the statements you are shortly to hear must sound to our inexpert ears, they are well-founded, and I take full responsibility for them. I need not enlarge on the capacities of Francis Lightfoot; his name and achievements are familiar to every reader of the daily press, despite the fact that, as perhaps some of you have heard, not only does he not associate with his fellow-physicists, but he also shuns all publicity and is known to the world only by two things: his immense scientific prestige and his reputation as a recluse. I will therefore content myself, in respect to his capabilities, with two facts only: last time Mr. Arthur saw the world-famous Albert Einstein, Professor Einstein spoke of little else but Mr. Lightfoot's work—that is the first fact. This is the second: I have this morning heard, on unimpeachable authority, that Mr. Lightfoot will receive next year, at the unprecedented age of twenty-five, the Nobel Prize."

He tells them of his acquaintance with his nephew all the

latter's life, of his complete trust in him, of the nerve-specialists' report. He warns them that, although all Francis Lightfoot purposes to do is to make a statement in which he will try to accommodate his exposition of his discoveries in the vastly complicated world of physics to their lay intelligences, leaving such action as may suggest itself to their own decision, that the thing they are about to hear is quite unprecedented. He can only hope that, with all their help, the committee will be able to "tackle it in that spirit of hopeful resolution for which this ministry has, we like to believe, made itself famous."

Gracefully the Prime Minister presents his nephew to the Cabinet, and then as gracefully, with a touch of dignified banter, he presents the Cabinet individually to Francis Lightfoot.

Francis, beginning his statement a little haltingly, is at first made more nervous by the interruptions of his hearers. His statement, for example, that he has brought his discovery to them despite the fact that he does not believe in government, seeing that all government is founded on force, distresses Lord Dedham to such an extent that he is constrained to protest.

Evelyn Arthur manages, however, to gain a measure of protection from heckling for the young speaker and shortly Lightfoot, past the preliminaries of explaining his trust in his uncle, the Prime Minister, and in this committee of the British Commonwealth of Nations, is launched upon his main statement.

Francis Lightfoot—In science there are two main modes by which great conclusions, like mine, are arrived at. There's the Commonsense Mode: long and arduous spade-work, by lots of people, followed by a stroke of luck; and there's the Uncommonsense Mode: that depends on a unique combination of gifts in a particular individual—Newton, for instance, or Einstein, or myself. People who don't like or understand the Uncommonsense Mode call it Inspired Guessing. My own genius is for short cuts. And my discovery is a by-product of a five-year-long short cut in an investigation I'm making—

Sir Romilly Blount—Here, Mr. Lightfoot, or abroad?

Evelyn Arthur—I understand Mr. Lightfoot's laboratory is in North Wales.

Francis Lightfoot—This investigation aims at solving the old riddle: "What is energy?" (*Warming up to his subject.*) So far as we know—we really know nothing—all energy resolves itself at the last analysis into what's popularly known as electricity—though what electricity is . . . well, none of us know. However, apparently electricity is the thing-in-itself, just as that mysterious thing we call life, which moves in all of us, in me, and in you, is the thing-in-itself. Now, just as life manifests itself in constantly changing structures known as bodies, which tend to perish and be re-created from hour to hour, so electricity manifests itself in the perpetual dance of entities known as negative electrons round a positively charged nucleus. Such groups are, in fact, infinitesimally small solar systems, and of the different combinations of these systems all matter is, as far as we know, made up. It follows, therefore, that the physicist has two main interests—first, the varieties of combinations of these solar systems which, being combined, make up the ninety odd elements of which, in variegated structure, the substance of the universe is composed. And, second, that force which holds each solar system together; in other words, the thing-in-itself. Now my investigations—

Lord Sunningale interrupts. He would like to have Mr. Lightfoot "cut the cackle and come to the hosses," for the benefit of those old codgers who have not enjoyed the speaker's advantages.

Sir Humphrey Haliburton is also of the opinion that they should not spend a great deal of time with contemplating infinitesimal solar systems. Sir Humphrey has work to do.

Even the Prime Minister and Evelyn Arthur are inclined to think perhaps Francis should come to his point as quickly as possible. Somewhat discouraged, but still willing to do his best, Francis begs a moment to collect his thoughts and the committee generously grants his request by drifting into a casual buzzing about those matters of trivial importance nearest to each of them at the moment.

Suddenly Francis jumps to his feet. "Gentlemen," he cries, "I can control . . . the energy . . . in the atom!"

Evelyn Arthur's monocle drops from his eye. Sir Humphrey Haliburton and Richard Stapp find themselves being stared at intently by an excited young man. Stapp would again change the subject.

FRANCIS LIGHTFOOT (*staring in front of him, hoarsely*)—I said . . . I can control . . . the energy . . . in the atom. (EVELYN ARTHUR *restores his monocle to its place.* H. G. DUNNE *jumps up.*)

H. G. DUNNE (*excitedly*)—What! Man alive! Is that the . . . ? (*To the others*)—Gentlemen! D'you realize what that means?

MATTHEW GRINDLE (*dryly*)—No, Mr. Dunne, we do not; or perhaps I should say, I do not. If you will be so good—we are hoping to hear. (*He pulls out his watch.*) My Budget proposals—

H. G. DUNNE (*losing his head*)—Damn your Budget proposals! Go ahead, Lightfoot, rub it in. Tell 'em what's what! (*The* PRIME MINISTER *frowns and raps.*)

PRIME MINISTER (*magisterially*)—Mr. Dunne, your engineer's training has given you a certain advantage over some of us, but that is no reason I should have to remind you that you are addressing a Cabinet Committee.

H. G. DUNNE—I beg your pardon. I beg your pardon, Grindle. (*He sits down. Weakly, with traces of hysterical laughter*)—But if you knew, if you only knew . . . (*Pause. Silence. The* PRIME MINISTER *turns to* FRANCIS LIGHTFOOT.)

PRIME MINISTER—Go on. (FRANCIS LIGHTFOOT *is silent.*) Tell them what you told me last night. Tell them what it means.

FRANCIS LIGHTFOOT (*patiently, but not without a trace of scorn*)—It all seems so elementary to me. Well . . . it means that the present, all this, all that you're accustomed to call civilization, is—is relegated at last to its proper place as the confused remembrance of an evil dream of no more account than a child's nightmare. Yesterday, Man was a slave; to-day, he's free. Matter obeys him!

(*The Cabinet Committee is divided between those who glance at each other and those who carefully refrain from doing so.*)

LORD DEDHAM (*indulging his truculence*)—Mr. Lightfoot, I'm Lord Chancellor, and I've risen to my present position by my obstinate preference for facts as opposed to verbiage. Rhapsodies, however eloquent, are not evidence. Stick to facts, please. (*He snaps his fingers.*)

FRANCIS LIGHTFOOT—Who the devil d'you think you're talking to?

H. G. DUNNE—Hear, hear!

PRIME MINISTER—Francis—

FRANCIS LIGHTFOOT—I've given you facts. I've tried to tell you of the miniature solar systems of the atom, but you wouldn't listen. Well, perhaps you'll listen to this: so far as matter is concerned, what I will to be, will be, and what I will not to be, will not be. Is that fact enough?

PRIME MINISTER—Francis—

LORD DEDHAM—Mr. Lightfoot, kindly refrain from indulging your predilection to mystify. You are here to explain.

H. G. DUNNE—Order!

EVELYN ARTHUR (*sweetly*)—Lord Dedham, may I remind you that Mr. Lightfoot is here of his own free will?

LORD DEDHAM—This is a Cabinet Committee, and—

EVELYN ARTHUR—Lord Dedham, your position and mine in the world of politics simply do not exist, compared with this young man's in the world of science. We must be patient. Mr. Lightfoot, will you permit me to play the part of magician's assistant for a moment? (*There is something so charming and not without a hint of Puck in* EVELYN ARTHUR'S *glance that* FRANCIS LIGHTFOOT *smiles assent.*) Thank you. Now, gentlemen, here we have a table made of—let me see—oak, isn't it? Yes, oak. Very well. Now, if Mr. Lightfoot were so vulgar as to wish to turn this table into gold, hey, presto, he could do so. And if he happened to dislike it as much as I do, he could, hey, presto, abolish it. Is that clear? (*He smiles, takes out his monocle, puts it back, sits down.*)

LORD DEDHAM—Look here, what are you up to, Arthur, pulling our legs?

EVELYN ARTHUR (*with sweet acerbity*)—Lord Dedham, you reminded Mr. Lightfoot that he was addressing a Cabinet Committee. Are you reminding me?

LORD DEDHAM—But—

PRIME MINISTER—I suggest that we postpone discussion until the end of Mr. Lightfoot's statement. (LORD DEDHAM *retires into the sulks.*)

FRANCIS LIGHTFOOT (*nervously*)—Mr. Arthur has—has put it a little oddly; but—yes, that's what it means. Oh, please, please, don't waste time asking silly questions; consider what you're going to do. (*Very earnestly and as if repeating a peroration.*) You see—the history of Man up to now has been one long horrible narrative of his slavery to matter. To-day I put into your hands power over matter; ultimate power over matter; the power of—of a god, to slay and to make alive. Incidentally it means food, shelter, abundance, for every one. But that's just incidental. Beyond that—a mere matter of organization—rises the New World, the Summer of Mankind, the Golden Age. Don't you see, gentlemen? It's—Man's free! And now, now, he can live as the sages of all countries have always dreamed he might live—not—not a feebly struggling parasite, not a thing oppressed by needs and fears, with no security, no leisure, but Man, a Titan, a Prometheus, a Prometheus Triumphant, all his days and nights one long hymn of praise to Beauty and to Truth, the Beauty and the Truth which from hour to hour Man discovers and Man creates! (*Quietly, exhausted.*) That's what it means, gentlemen; that's what my discovery means. You're the first—except my uncle—to know. Now I'm going to leave you to organize. That's your job; the new organization. I'll come back, a week from to-day, at the same time. Have your plans ready.

Now, as Evelyn Arthur attempts to control the situation by putting through a vote of thanks to Francis Lightfoot the committee works itself into a state of considerable agitation. Several of the gentlemen are crying for more. Lord Dedham is still demanding the facts that he has missed.

Calmly, a little wearily, Lightfoot tries to answer the questions that are more or less indiscriminately flung at him. Under the new conditions, he explains, there will be no law, because law at bottom relies upon force. With all men equally master of a force that shall be completely destructive arbitration must follow.

"By the use of one small piece of mechanism," he explains to Lord Dedham, "constructed according to formulæ of which only I am master, one man, any one man, can defy all the policemen in London. . . . He touches a spring; the atoms about the piece of mechanism begin to redistribute themselves at an undreamt-of speed—at such a speed that not only he, but his house, his street, his borough, London itself, disappears if he so wishes . . . Is blown up . . . Any explosion is only a sudden redistribution of atoms."

Again there is consternation, a consternation that grows with each additional assertion of the young scientist that his discovery shall not be employed to the advantage of any group or any nation, but for all humanity.

He sharply declines an invitation to consult with Richard Stapp at the War Office relative to making England the dominant nation of the world. He tries to convince Lord Cossington that it is quite possible for him, if he wanted to do it, to change the table at which they are sitting into gold; that thereafter all materials shall be raw materials. He explains to St. John Pascoe that all colonies henceforth shall represent humanity and never again be looked upon merely as sources of raw materials. Even the system of credits, he tells Matthew Grindle, being founded on gold, must cease to exist. And as for labor, that too, as they know it, shall cease to be.

LORD SUNNINGDALE—Look here, young man, I like you, but this joke has gone far enough. A farce is—

FRANCIS LIGHTFOOT (*fiery, jumping up*)—Farce! Farce, gentlemen? It's you who are making the farce. Behave like adults; stop babbling like children about your departments. Wake up. All that stuff is totally and for ever scrapped. Put it out of your minds. Concentrate on something serious.

SIR ROMILLY BLOUNT—Serious? Where d'you suppose you an' your crazy experiments 'ud be, if it weren't for the Navy?

ST. JOHN PASCOE—You wouldn't exist—you wouldn't exist!

SIR ROMILLY BLOUNT—I s'pose you'll tell us the Empire—

FRANCIS LIGHTFOOT—Empire? What Empire? I'm talking about Mankind.

LORD DEDHAM—D'you realize what you're saying?

FRANCIS LIGHTFOOT—Of course I do, and it's high time you—

EVELYN ARTHUR (*jumping up*)—It is indeed! (*Tumult in which* LORD DEDHAM *can be heard bawling*)—

LORD DEDHAM—Traitor!

PRIME MINISTER (*rapping with a heavy ruler*)—Quiet! I will have quiet! This is a Cabinet Committee, not Bedlam! Silence, gentlemen! Silence! Silence! (*He is evidently very angry. The tumult dies away.*) Gentlemen, this is a disgraceful scene. Disgraceful. Mr. Arthur and I will thank you gentlemen to listen to him in silence.

EVELYN ARTHUR (*suavely*)—Gentlemen, in the heat of the moment I think we have tended, as Mr. Lightfoot suggests, to overlook the larger issues. Our amazement, concerned, honorably, as we are, with those duties which the State has entrusted to us, is natural; but we have no time for amazement. Has it struck you, gentlemen, that Mr. Lightfoot is in a position to carry this news to other, and perhaps he would consider, more enlightened groups, either at home or abroad? I trust he will not do so; I do not think he will; possibly he already regrets imparting it even to us. But I ask Mr. Lightfoot to remember that these implications, which from long familiarity seem so much a matter of course to him, are an extraordinary, a staggering novelty to us. The illimitable hopes so abruptly revealed are hard to grasp in a moment. But, Francis Lightfoot, those hopes are sublime; and our stupefaction is but the measure of their magnificence.

We have done our duty in the past; we shall rise to it now. Soon the unfamiliar air of this exalted frontier will become native to us; and, inspired by your example, your achievement, your trust, we shall perform our task, the task which you have honored us by setting, and for which we thank you, not only in our names, but in the name of Humanity. (*He holds out his hand.*)

FRANCIS LIGHTFOOT (*moved*)—Thank you, Mr. Arthur. You have understood.

EVELYN ARTHUR—Not only I. Prime Minister, I call on you to ask this Cabinet Committee to rise in Mr. Lightfoot's honor.

FRANCIS LIGHTFOOT (*looking up, covering his eyes with his hands*)—No, no, not in mine (*stretching up his arms*), in honor of the coming glory to Humanity. (EVELYN ARTHUR *on one side the* PRIME MINISTER *on the other, signal with frantic but hidden gestures for the Cabinet Committee to rise. The Committee takes the cue.* FRANCIS LIGHTFOOT, *exulting, with his arms yet raised, looks round on them.*) At this hour, the New World begins. Thank you, gentlemen. This day week, at the same time. Meanwhile, I undertake to say nothing to any one else, and you undertake to draw up your program. (*He pulls out a paper.*) Here are details of time and place for the tests which I have arranged, for you and for any experts you like to bring. My assistants will carry them out; I shan't be there; demonstrations are so futile. However, though they are just simple tests, they will prove without revealing my method, that I can do what I say. Good day, gentlemen. (*Amid complete and astonished silence he makes for the doors. At the door he turns.*) I have called on you to build a House for Man. To-day week will disclose whether you have risen to your opportunity. The responsibility is yours.

Lightfoot's withdrawal leaves the Cabinet Committee rather stunned. Some little attempt is made by Lord Dedham to joke himself and his confreres back to a normal state of mind, but even joking seems suddenly to have also ceased to exist. It is Evelyn Arthur who puts Dedham in his place.

"My friend," says he seriously, tapping Dedham on the chest with his monocle, "this is no time for schoolboy-horseplay. (*The others drift nearer.*) Kindly realize that every word that young man said is—I am convinced—literally true."

"Oh, c-c-come, surely—" begins Lord Cossington.

"Every word! And I solemnly say to you all, it would be

better for that poor young man and for the world had he never been born."

The curtain falls.

ACT II

A week later the Cabinet Committee is again in session. Their slumped attitudes give unmistakable signs of "strain, weariness and jangled nerves."

During the week that has elapsed the two greatest scientists in England, barring Francis Lightfoot, have submitted a report on the Lightfoot tests. The impossible, they are free to admit, has been accomplished. And then these scientists have calmly gone off to Switzerland on a walking tour.

During the tests, it appears, Lightfoot had, by detonating what Sir Romilly Blount describes as a lump of sugar, blown a crater in the earth as big as St. Paul's. And as successfully transformed Lord Sunningdale's latchkey into gold and from gold into India rubber.

The Cabinet has been, as Lord Cossington expresses it, "struck all of a 'eap" and is as near its wit's ends as it is possible for a British cabinet to approach with impunity.

They are agreed, however, on a kind of program. Evelyn Arthur cannot believe that the problem presented by this one boy can really be so tremendously difficult a problem. After all they are twelve. Nor does it appear as difficult to the Prime Minister. "My nephew may be rather a queer fish," agrees he, "but he's a nice boy and a gentleman!"

The agreement then, as Evelyn Arthur understands it, is that they shall first try to pursuade Francis Lightfoot and carefully avoid bullying him. But if persuasion should fail! Shall Mr. Lightfoot be free then to go elsewhere with his discovery?

Richard Stapp, as Secretary for War, is definitely opposed to any such freedom being permitted so dangerous a young person. So is Lord Dedham. So are several of the others. And yet most of them would hesitate to take extreme measures—such as to "deceive and shoot" young Lightfoot, as the War Minister suggests.

"Now, then, yer benevolent, bloodthirsty barbarians," protests the jovial Lord Sunningdale, "we're in London, not Moscow. (*Murmurs of 'Hear. Hear!'*) There's no need ter try an' pull all this Napoleon-Trotsky-Mussolini stuff. Damned unsportsmanlike, I'd call it: lockin' up an' murderin' an' poisonin' a nice young feller whose only fault is he's too full o' faith, hope an' charity. The lad's a good lad: mettlesome but gentlemouthed.

He's lookin' ter us: an', as Arthur says, if twelve of us old stagers can't put an idealistic colt through his paces on the snaffle—well, it's high time we took ter our beds an' hallooed for the parson."

The Committee votes, however, on motion of Sir Humphrey Haliburton, that should Francis Lightfoot refuse to be persuaded to the Committee's way of thinking that he be immediately arrested and placed in strict confinement. The motion is carried over the gentle protests of the Prime Minister.

So the matter stands as Lightfoot is summoned: First, persuasion. If that should fail Lord Dedham, Lord High Chancellor, is to act.

A moment later Francis enters the room. The Committee greets him in silence and then slowly, and with a show of reluctance on the part of some, rises to its feet. The boy begs them to sit down, but prefers to remain standing himself.

They begin by flattering him. They are still all amazed at what he, a great genius, has been able to do. But Francis is of no mind to listen to compliments. He is eager to know their program. They have, they tell him, passed a resolution, with only one dissenting vote. It reads:

"His Majesty's Cabinet Members, in Committee assembled, most earnestly and solemnly request and entreat Francis Lightfoot to communicate his overwhelming discovery to no other human being, and to destroy its secret."

Lightfoot is amazed! For a second he cannot believe his ears! "And to destroy his secret!" It's incredible!

"Never!" he shouts, wildly. "Never, while there are stars in heaven or a man on earth!"

"Has it struck you, Francis," suavely inquires Evelyn Arthur, "that if you don't there may soon be no man on earth, and, quite possibly, one less star in heaven?"

"No," Lightfoot answers. "Humanity's not like that! It can't be: I know it can't; my heart tells me it can't."

Solemnly, but very kindly, Evelyn Arthur would bid Francis good-by. There is no reason why they should part in anger and the older man is hopeful that the younger will find it possible to use his *future* knowledge aright.

Lightfoot senses the determination of the Cabinet. Now he knows they would be rid of him! But he is not to be disposed of so easily! They are jealous of their power! They're afraid he will end it! Very well, he will!

With the aid of the man in the street, asserts Lightfoot—those potential followers of Shelley and Clark Maxwell—he will fight them! And when Evelyn Arthur questions if the man in the street has ever heard of either Shelley or Clark Maxwell, Francis agrees to go out on the street, pick up the first three passers-by and bring them in to prove his point.

With smiling vision of a plausible victory through this simple test the Committee chuckles as Evelyn Arthur and Lightfoot go to bring in their men. Shortly they are back.

EVELYN ARTHUR—We found two, just outside the front door, going in opposite directions. There was no one else in sight, so —er—we agreed that—(*to the* PRIME MINISTER)—you might ask your secretary to procure the third: would you mind?

PRIME MINISTER—Certainly. (*Telephoning.*) Grantly speaking: is that you, Eddie? Would you be so good as to go out on the Downing Street steps and ask the first man you meet to come in here for a moment . . . yes, that's what I said. Wait a moment. (*To* EVELYN ARTHUR.) Where are the two others?

EVELYN ARTHUR—In the front ante-room.

PRIME MINISTER (*telephoning*)—Put him in the front anteroom; you'll find two others there: then show them in here, one at a time. Don't scare him . . . oh, say we've a little bet on.

LORD SUNNINGDALE (*laughing*)—Every Englishman likes a bet. Gives him somethin' ter think about.

FRANCIS LIGHTFOOT (*anxious, to* EVELYN ARTHUR)—I'd say the big chap was a plumber?

EVELYN ARTHUR (*vaguely*)—I haven't the remotest idea: but, then, I never have. All workmen seem the same to me: some smell of onions, some of beer. I prefer onions.

FRANCIS LIGHTFOOT—The other's a clerk, I suppose.

EVELYN ARTHUR (*dreamily*)—A subsidiary ruler, and a subsidiary ruled. Yes, our business is with . . . what is. Once we lose touch with that, we're done for. (*Change of tone.*) Shall we sit down? (*They sit.*) Tell me, Francis, wasn't it held in Newton's day that the planets marched upon their orbits in accordance with the law of an imperious necessity, which imposed upon each its course? (FRANCIS LIGHTFOOT *nods. Dreamily again.*) And to-day it is agreed, I suppose, that the affair is hardly so exalted. The planets move upon their course according to the law of least resistance, casually, as it were; taking the easiest path. The easiest path. Not unlike humanity. (EVELYN ARTHUR *checks* FRANCIS LIGHTFOOT, *who seems about to speak.*) Despite all our talk about progress, the law would seem to be that humanity exerts, not its maximum, but its minimum energy, and progresses only when it is easier to progress than to retrogress or to stand still. (*Change of tone.*) Civilization cannot be imposed, Francis: it can only be induced: the art of government consists in making retrogression difficult, stagnation dull, and progress—apparently—easy. (*The doors open.*) Ah, here's our man. (*Quickly to* FRANCIS LIGHTFOOT.) Shelley or Clark Maxwell?

FRANCIS LIGHTFOOT (*similarly*)—Shelley for a workingman: otherwise Clark Maxwell. Is that fair?

EVELYN ARTHUR—I . . . think so.

The first of the proletarians is Albert Cummins, workman, and he never 'eard of Shelley, unless they might mean a Hadmiral.

The second is Mr. Hart-Plimsoll, a young gentleman in a short morning coat carrying a briefcase. Mr. Hart-Primsoll is a division clerk in the foreign office, and therefore one of Evelyn Arthur's myrmidons. He recalls the name of Clark Maxwell vaguely as that of some sort of scientist who had to do with magnetism or, perhaps, electric light. But science does seem awfully inhuman to Mr. Hart-Plimsoll. More important things, it seems to him, taking life in the large, are love and Anglo-American relations.

The third man from the street is Mr. Taggert, "a red-headed little man of about thirty-five" who wears a check overcoat too big for him, a red necktie and a felt hat. He is a bit determined to set himself right with the committee. First off Mr. Taggert is a socialist and he recognizes the committee as a ring of capitalist bosses. He is, however, ready to answer any fair question. Shelley? Yes. Revolutionary poet, wasn't he? But that's about all Mr. Taggert remembers of him. He is not strong on poetry. Prefers fax—Marx fax. Strong, too, for eddication, more and more eddication. It would take the eddicated socialist really to determine whether bombs would be necessary and proper in a revolution. But he does not think much of the Secretary of Education's Adult Education bill. "Milk fer bibes!" That's what that is, if you ask Mr. Taggert.

Mr. Taggert pauses on his way out long enough to exchange a friendly greeting with Lord Sunningdale—"ole Sunny" he calls him—and to try to extract from the Lord Privy Seal a tip on the next day's races.

Evelyn Arthur turns to Francis. "Well, Francis? They were not intimately acquainted with your two friends. . . . We are representative of millions such; we are no better, no worse; certainly luckier; possibly more knowledgeable; but representative. We—"

FRANCIS LIGHTFOOT—I've got it! Not knowledge! There's something more important. And they all had it. Goodwill!—That's right, smile! I wouldn't have your heart for—you're the mummy whose hand kills!

LORD SUNNINGDALE—Easy, boy, easy.

PRIME MINISTER—Francis! To my oldest friend—

FRANCIS LIGHTFOOT—I don't care: he shall not sit there, gentle, courteous, pitying. I know him—history knows him—Antichrist! What can you know of Humanity, if you don't love?

EVELYN ARTHUR—I beg your pardon for smiling, Francis. But—how can you love humanity, if you don't know it?

FRANCIS LIGHTFOOT—I trust it, and love begins with trust.

EVELYN ARTHUR—Are you quite sure love doesn't begin with . . . forgiveness?

FRANCIS LIGHTFOOT—Never! Despair always says that. There's the body of common goodwill. (*Pause.*)

SIR ROMILLY BLOUNT—Young man: you said you went to a Public School?

FRANCIS LIGHTFOOT—Yes.

SIR ROMILLY BLOUNT—Why? Was it because o' the body o' common goodwill? If it's so general, why am I at this table? Why's Lord Dedham, Sir Humphrey Haliburton, Esme Faulkiner, Richard Stapp?

FRANCIS LIGHTFOOT—Because you don't trust, or hope, or believe.

EVELYN ARTHUR—We trust as we dare, Francis; we hope as we may; we believe as we can.

LORD DEDHAM (*harshly*)—Government's not here to trust or hope or believe. We're here to govern.

FRANCIS LIGHTFOOT (*rising*)—You're here to believe and, by God, I'll make you!

SIR ROMILLY BLOUNT (*half rising*)—You'll make . . . ?

EVELYN ARTHUR (*quietly*)—Francis, do you believe?

FRANCIS LIGHTFOOT (*standing*)—Yes, absolutely.

EVELYN ARTHUR (*very gently*)—Poor boy!

PRIME MINISTER—Francis, you spoke of the body of common goodwill. You were right. It exists, and all government is founded on it. But it takes many forms; and some of them issue an abnegation. In the splendor of youth we sometimes despise abnegation, but old hearts understand it, and prize it more every year. To you, we may seem ignoble in our disillusion; but I know, and all here know, if we know nothing else, that we have to die for Man before we can live for him; so that our death may increase the honor and might of the only god left living, that unknown god whom, as the Scripture says, "we ignorantly worship."

FRANCIS LIGHTFOOT—Whose name is Compromise!

PRIME MINISTER—It is the gods who are most abused who survive. My boy, you are not the first to suffer; the highest heroism begins with just such abnegation; and there is probably not one man in this room who has not laid down some ideal on the altar of the common goodwill.

FRANCIS LIGHTFOOT—What ideal has a fellow like Sir Romilly Blount ever sacrificed?

SIR ROMILLY BLOUNT—You're addressin' me, young man? (*He rises.*) Did you ever hear o' the Minotaur class o' battleship?

FRANCIS LIGHTFOOT—No.

SIR ROMILLY BLOUNT—Then I'll tell you. The keels o' the Minotaur class were on the slips. They'd 'a' been the handsomest, the grandest ships ever known. What your physics is to you, those ships were to me. I foresaw 'em, I planned 'em, I toiled for 'em, I fought for 'em; an', when somebody I loved died, I prayed for 'em, knowin' as they alone could keep my heart from breakin' in my body. An' then, at this table, sittin' where I am now, I had to listen to these new disarmament proposals, an' the general feelin' was—they had to go. You may think it funny, young man, you may sneer at me, but every night for three nights I had to wrestle in prayer to be delivered from the temptation to speak up for my ships; I had to take the part of a Christ I didn't believe in, against the part of a Jehovah, god of battles, in whom I did. An' I came back, an' I sat down here, an' I never said a word; an', when they'd voted 'em away, I fell with my head on this table, as Esme Faulkiner here can tell you, an' your uncle—he was at the Home Office then—came an' patted me on the back an' led me home. An' I never come into this room but I see the ghosts o' those ships before me floatin' above this table. You're young, my boy, an' you think you know a lot, but an old salt like me can tell you there's bitterer waters swallowed in this room than can be found in all the seven seas.

FRANCIS LIGHTFOOT—I beg your pardon, sir. (*Change of voice.*) Just the same, if he can live up to that ideal, surely the world . . .

LORD VIVIAN VERE—Damn it, boy, the mass of mankind is still unimaginably ignorant. One must do what one can.

FRANCIS LIGHTFOOT—Rubbish! One must do what one can't. That's why I tackled the atom.

LORD VIVIAN VERE—We're not all geniuses. And the man of to-day who's not quite ignorant has lost his old beliefs without acquiring new ones. A man without belief won't take responsibility, and it's responsibility you're trying to thrust on him. Besides, in even the best there's the residuum of the savage. Teach it no new ways to evil.

SIR HUMPHREY HALIBURTON (*genially*)—Life's a penny-i'-the-slot machine, my boy. Put in happiness, and you get out happiness; put in discontent, and you get discontent out. Everybody's got his limit and is happy or unhappy up to it. Let folks be comfortable their own way.

FRANCIS LIGHTFOOT—Comfortable!

SIR HUMPHREY HALIBURTON—Yes, my boy, comfortable. Live and let live.

FRANCIS LIGHTFOOT—Such living is death.

SIR HUMPHREY HALIBURTON—Well, Nature's for it—breeds 'em by the million.

LORD SUNNINGDALE (*even more genially*)—Why this itch ter make folks better, sonny? You fellers'll never admit a pippin's juicy, if it ain't off yer own tree. Damme, a blood-horse, all fire an' satin skin, is as satisfyin' as—as any highbrow kafoozelum. You brainy birds are all bilious bodies. Everythin' that's good of its kind is all right, an' failures are only stuff that's tryin' to be itself an' ain't succeedin'.

FRANCIS LIGHTFOOT—It's because I want them to succeed . . .

LORD SUNNINGDALE—An' if they did, my son, they wouldn't have the qualities that's theirs.

One by one the statesmen voice their objections and their distrust of Francis Lightfoot's vision of a perfect humanitarianism and express their own conclusions, each slightly veiling his own philosophy.

"The universe is a phantasmal flux; our task is to redeem it to a temporary concreteness," declares Matthew Grindle, a godly Chancellor of the Exchequer. "Don't make that task easy; in its terror lies the sole dignity of a race of phantoms."

"You have required us to build a house for man; a wrong analogy," corrects the Prime Minister. "We politicians are not architects. Our task is more homely; that of the gardener. We seek only to fertilize, to sow, to prune; the rest depends on . . . the qualities of the plant."

"I object on higher grounds," stammers Lord Cossington. "You're ups-s-setting the balans-s of Nature. There's no progress without a s-struggle, unceas-sing s-struggle."

"Lightfoot, I believe that if in this life we strive hard enough we shall live again," ventures Esme Faulkiner. "You want to make the World safe for Democracy—a cushy place. I want for man the immortality of heroes."

Unexpectedly from Richard Stapp there comes a measure of agreement. "I've fought these chaps for the last two days and nights," he shouts at Lightfoot: "the only one among 'em who cursed their 'Safety First!' Why? Because the battle's to the strong; an' with this weapon the Americans an' ourselves could be cock o' the walk an' teach all other peoples on the globe where they got off."

Cowards, Lightfoot calls them, one and all! Cowards with, it may be, the courage to die but not one of them with the courage to live!

"Francis!" cautions the Prime Minister. "The fact that your ideas and ours do not chime—"

"Ideas!" interrupts Lightfoot; "the very substance of our beings doesn't chime. Yours is the Spirit of Yesterday; mine is the Spirit of To-morrow. (*Murmurs.*) Must I tell you what every board-school urchin knows?—that, among the myriad orbs of the Milky Way there gyrates, in a minor solar system, a negligible planet, and that on this pea of a planet creeps a race of parasites? But parasites who know themselves for what they are! Isolated! Isolated between the abyss of the unimaginably small, the atom, and the abyss of the unimaginably great, the night about us. In that isolation, what refuge have we but one another? what future but the future of all? what ethic but the good—not of one person, or of one nation—but of Mankind? Answer me that; you can't! The day of the Takers is over, I tell you; the day of the Givers dawns. And I inaugurate it—with the greatest of all possible gifts: mastery over matter. At last, Man is free to enlarge the Kingdom of the Spirit; and so, whether the Sum of Things is justified or not, to justify himself. And do you think, because the Spirit of Yesterday in you is afraid, the Spirit of To-morrow in me will run away?"

"Then . . . you refuse to destroy the secret?"

"Utterly!"

Again they are at him, offering, this time, what he classifies as a bribe by agreeing to give him all the help the government can bring to his aid in any scientific research for the ultimate good of humanity that he might care to undertake. But this suggestion of little men trying to bribe the master of the atom fills him with nothing more than laughter. Suddenly he grows serious again:

"To hell with the lot of you!" he shouts, and would leave the room.

Now Lord Dedham would take command. There is a threat of serious consequences in both his voice and actions. Neither of these frightens Francis. As fast as the Cabinet suggest other plans of curbing him he belittles them utterly with ridicule or defiant banter. The repeated threat that a police inspector is to be summoned and Lightfoot given into custody, with no favors extended and an untimely exit threatened, worry him not in the least. So long as they have reduced the whole show to a game he is willing to play.

"When I first took my place among you, by right, as the greatest benefactor Mankind has ever known," he shouts, "the first word my uncle spoke was 'War.' And since then: 'War, Death, Despair'—to me who bring Love, Life, and Hope. Only one man among the lot of you wanted my gift—and what for? Humanity? No, To be 'cock of the walk . . . the game for the game's sake.' You've dragged me down—you've made me fight —very well then, by God, I'll meet you on your own atrocious level. Dedham, you death's head, summon your policemen." (*He shoves his hands into his pockets and sits down.*)

Again they seek to temporize. Again they offer reason and excuse and hint at mysterious plans. To none will he listen seriously. Sir Humphrey Haliburton reaches for the bell to summon the guard when Francis stops them. He still has one thing to say.

"Listen, you," he shouts as he faces the circle of tense faces. "Last week, I came here—a boy, full of hope: to-day I stand here—a man, whose despair almost equals your own. But one learns in this room. Last week, when I left here, my heart knew —though my brain refused to believe—your wickedness. And I made my preparations.

"What's he mean? What's hc talking about?—Preparations?"

FRANCIS LIGHTFOOT—My preparations! Aren't I to be shot at dawn? or buried alive? Understand this: either, by noon tomorrow, you will be prepared to formulate, under my supervision, a constructive program satisfactory to me, or at one o'clock to-morrow England ends! (*Uproar.*) Where this island was, will be a whirlpool of disintegrating atoms! (*He turns to go.*)

VOICES—Stop him! He's mad! Arrest him!

FRANCIS LIGHTFOOT (*dominating them*)—If—if I am interfered with in the slightest degree, or if, in the meantime, (*quietly*) I should come to an unlooked-for—and convenient—end, no power at present known to man can avert that catastrophe. (*Smiling.*) That accident will guarantee the detonation.

PRIME MINISTER—Can you do that?

FRANCIS LIGHTFOOT—I can.

PRIME MINISTER—Will you do that?

FRANCIS LIGHTFOOT—I will. Good morning, gentlemen.

ESME FAULKINER—How?

FRANCIS LIGHTFOOT—That's my affair. But I assure you that, with this brain, these hands, I can destroy England, Europe, the entire planet—to-day, to-morrow, at any moment!

SIR ROMILLY BLOUNT—What d'yer mean? A bomb?

FRANCIS LIGHTFOOT—Nature is not as simple as you, First Lord; nor, I may add, am I.

SIR ROMILLY BLOUNT—Damned puppy!

FRANCIS LIGHTFOOT—Besides, most of all, when they're sentimental, I don't like men with warts on their noses.

SIR ROMILLY BLOUNT (*going for him*)—You'll pay for that, you little . . . (EVELYN ARTHUR, RICHARD STAPP *and others hold him back.*)

FRANCIS LIGHTFOOT (*to* EVELYN ARTHUR)—So the understudy can talk to the Olympians? Clever of you to remember (*blowing across the palm of his hand*), that, if he blows, you—vanish.

ST. JOHN PASCOE—I don't believe you.

FRANCIS LIGHTFOOT—You don't, don't you? Dear, dear. If you don't believe me (*he takes out his watch—a large hunter—opens and looks at it*), by noon to-morrow . . . (*Closes the watch with a click.*) Good day. (*Again he starts to go.*)

EVELYN ARTHUR (*between him and the door*)—In all sincerity, don't be so hard. Forgive Man for being what he is.

FRANCIS LIGHTFOOT—My hardness will make Man what he might be.

EVELYN ARTUR—Have pity.

FRANCIS LIGHTFOOT—Where your pity ends, my love begins.

EVELYN ARTHUR—Your pride!

FRANCIS LIGHTFOOT—My love's pride.

EVELYN ARTHUR—My boy, you don't know what love is. If you did, you would know right and wrong.

FRANCIS LIGHTFOOT (*hesitating*)—Right and wrong? (*Proudly.*) Your right and wrong are Yesterday's; mine are To-morrow's.

EVELYN ARTHUR—Then you will crucify Man on the cross of your impossible hopes?

FRANCIS LIGHTFOOT—I will raise Man, though it be upon a cross, and crown him, though it be with thorns.

(FRANCIS LIGHTFOOT *goes out.*)

RICHARD STAPP—Quick, Hal—your men—after him—watch him, every moment; don't let him know they're following him, and, for God's sake, tell them not to touch him!

The curtain falls.

ACT III

It is just before noon the following day. The Cabinet Committee is again in session, waiting. "Profound depression on every face, save Evelyn Arthur's, which is calm and stern."

A messenger announces the arrival of Francis Lightfoot. A moment later the young scientist enters the room. He, too, appears crushed and hopeless. "His dress is untidy, his hair not brushed, his face haggard; he drags his legs like a man who has tramped far." Under his arm is his volume of Shelley. He leans against the pillar by the door "like a weary Samson."

The Prime Minister quietly tells him that the Cabinet has decided with one dissentient, to capitulate.

The news does not stir Lightfoot. Without raising his head he answers that he is the beaten one. Absently he addresses them.

"Something Evelyn Arthur said has entered my heart and, as far as this world is concerned, has broken it," he says, slowly. "He told me I had no knowledge of right and wrong. (*To the* PRIME MINISTER.) What did you say? 'Destroy the secret?' (*With wearied and subdued scorn.*) How can it be destroyed? Have I the right to wrong the Mind of Man and destroy it? Where action is, Right and Wrong are; and both are implacable. And, if I did destroy it, what use would that be? Hundreds of men are working on this thing. What has been surrendered to genius may be granted to labor. At this very moment, while the world, in you (*his unconscious gesture includes the audience*)

—its representatives—listens, somewhere on the globe a group of men may be bent over a paper which contains the solution. And, when that solution is once more found, the decision between Right and Wrong must be taken. But how can it be taken when I, the furtherest reach of Man's Mind, cannot take it? (*Bitterly.*) I? the furtherest Reach! (*Quietly and sadly, as stating a fact.*) Man has not yet sufficiently evolved to face life, nor I to decide whether I have the right to force Man to face it."

"Then you despair—and out of that despair springs humanity, and out of humanity that modicum of modest hope which is alone useful to man." Evelyn Arthur's voice is soft, even affectionate, but firm. "Faith, dear Francis, is only the shadow, not the substance of things hoped for. The House of Man is not to be built upon the quicksands of hope—they will only engulf him and his. Build, as I do, upon the rock of despair. It is a process, harder, less romantic, so slow that time itself hardly notices the accretions. Thus to build, demands patience and tenacity, and, above all, courage. But on these foundations the House of Man, however humble, can endure."

"You speak of hope and humility, of time and courage," replies Francis. His head is raised, his eyes are radiant; now there is a suggestion of mysterious exaltation in his voice. "I too, have hope, but my hope is wider than yours, for it is not personal; my humility is deeper than yours, for it was born of the contemplation of night and the stars; my trust in time is stronger than yours, my courage stouter, for it is Nature's own. (*Drawing himself up.*) Now I am dangerous, for I am with Her: I am her Sibyl and I speak from the recesses of her heart. (*Ominously.*) Do you not even now feel her gather her forces? Man will be delivered from his burden.

"Francis!"

"Yes, Evelyn Arthur?"

"Yes . . . you are . . . an angel; with an angel's pride."

"Not I, but She. And, as I have some shadow of her capacity, so I have some fragment of her courage. You have guessed; I thought you might. (*To the others, strangely, as if pronouncing an elegy.*) Gentlemen, there was a planet the Earth. After inconceivable millennia, sentience emerged from that planet's slime. Again æons passed, and unimaginable agonies, and at last that sentience, which was now none other than the Mind of Man—of you, gentlemen, and of me—earned the right to such an intensity of apprehension that it seemed on the brink of unriddling the profoundest enigma of the universe; with that unriddling, the universe would have become conscious of itself. Suddenly, every dream was shattered, not by a sidereal accident, but by the very constitution of Man himself. But the genius of Nature is inexhaustible: on another star that consciousness will be accomplished, and, to hasten that process and to assist Nature correct one of her casual blunders I, who gave Man his opportunity, am about to take it away. In a brief moment, this planet and all upon it, with all its history, its hopes, and its disillusions, will be wiped out. (*Sensation.*) You see the clock? When the two arms of that clock coincide on noon, I will return to stand among you, a man among his fellows, and with you pass away, even as all men and this very globe itself will pass away. Our midget has spun long enough. I give it fifteen minutes more—fifteen minutes for you to come to terms with your gods."

Consternation is again upon them. Lightfoot remains outwardly unperturbed, but the strange light in his eyes fascinates them. At the door he turns to announce that he is going "To look at the narcissi in the park." He glances at the clock. "In fourteen minutes I shall return to die among my friends: Man, the enemy!"

The Committee members are variously affected. Evelyn Arthur calmly requests his right to read the moments away quietly. St. John Pascoe is at the verge of hysteria. Sir Humphrey Haliburton excitedly tries to free himself from the confusion that he may devote his time to serious thought.

Lord Cossington, at the window, wonders at the new aspect everything is taking on. He never thought the end of the world would be as it appears to be.

Lord Dedham and Richard Stapp are the ones who seek to do something. Surely something can be, something must be done! But their excitement fails to excite the others. Lord Sunningdale is resigned. He's often wondered whether he would stay the course. He's rather pleased to discover that he probably will.

Out of Stapp's wild reasoning practical conclusions finally take form. It follows that if Lightfoot plans to blow up the world within the next few minutes the controlling mechanism that is to release the atomic energy must be on his person. Sir Humphrey Haliburton's men have not lost sight of the scientist since last he left the committee. The control must be some clockwork thing. Yet the men have seached Lightfoot's clothes while he slept the night before and found nothing "except a notebook of mathematical symbols, a faded snap of his mother and that old turnip of a watch."

SIR ROMILLY BLOUNT—Looks like the end.

LORD DEDHAM—Blast it, such things don't happen!

RICHARD STAPP—Then why's your eye on the clock?

ESME FAULKINER—I do hate this helpless feeling. (*The* PRIME MINISTER *crosses to peer at the clock, and returns to the window.*)

RICHARD STAPP—Dunne! Dunne! Dunne, you're an engineer. What do you make of it?

H. G. DUNNE—Nothing. Flatly, I think he can do it.

RICHARD STAPP—How?

H. G. DUNNE—Damned if I know.

ESME FAULKINER—Perhaps he won't come back. Perhaps he's simply standing out there laughing at us.

SIR ROMILLY BLOUNT—Hell, I do hate his laughter!

SIR HUMPHREY HALIBURTON (*going to the window and beckoning*)—No, he isn't. There—see? Beyond the car—my men are in that—next to the soldier in khaki.

ESME FAULKINER—By the railings?

SIR HUMPHREY HALIBURTON—Feeding the swan . . .

H. G. DUNNE—Look!

SIR ROMILLY BLOUNT—Well, I'll be damned! Emptyin' his pockets . . . buyin' sweets from the ex-service men . . . givin' 'em ter the children!

LORD DEDHAM—Murderer! Blast him!

ESME FAULKINER—Seems to be telling the kids to hurry. (*They glance at each other. The* PRIME MINISTER *crosses to peer at the clock and returns to the window.*)

RICHARD STAPP—An' now he's quite still, lookin' at the narcissi. Phew! (*He wipes his forehead.*)

SIR ROMILLY BLOUNT—Arrest him, Hal!

LORD DEDHAM—Touch him, and the damned thing goes off!

H. G. DUNNE—Dished! Got us cold! (*They turn away.* SIR HUMPHREY HALIBURTON *remains at the window.*)

RICHARD STAPP—But how? How?

H. G. DUNNE—God knows. Can't we all feel it? He's all round us, over us, under us, outside there, and yet—somehow—in this room . . . It's foul, having nothing to pray to.

RICHARD STAPP—HE MUST control it . . . an' our job is to get hold o' the control.

SIR ROMILLY BLOUNT—Catch him lettin' us.

ESME FAULKINER—You bet he's popped it somewhere, and it's ticking away.

SIR HUMPHREY HALIBURTON—He can't have. My men are watching.

H. G. DUNNE—He may have left it in the house, on the way out—

SIR ROMILLY BLOUNT—Or slipped it into the ex-service man's basket—

LORD DEDHAM—Or the children's bags of sweets—

SIR ROMILLY BLOUNT—Or given it to the swan—

RICHARD STAPP (*savagely*)—Or swallowed it!

SIR HUMPHREY HALIBURTON—Even if you got it, you wouldn't know how to use it.

ST. JOHN PASCOE (*with sepulchral mirth*)—The Agenda having been read, and a resolution passed, the committee adjourned. (*Singing.*) "The Committee then adjourned, ha, ha! The Committee then adjourned."

Lord Cossington thinks perhaps they should warn the palace. Richard Stapp decides he will go home to see his wife. Matthew Grindle also thinks suddenly of his "white darling" which throws Dedham into a state of hysterical elation.

"Your white darling?—You fatuous ass—she's mine!" he yells. And proves his assertion by indicating the location of a mole upon the lady's right hip.

Now there is turmoil with Dedham and the crushed Grindle its center. There are other things about the other members that Dedham feels free to say, now that the truth may be told. Vere is a fake! Blount is a cheat! Cossington is an asinine fop! Pascoe is a prig and a fool! Grantly is the feeblest Prime Minister the country has ever known!

Now St. John Pascoe and Dedham are at each other's throats. Pascoe pushes Dedham back into a chair. He may be a prig and a fool, admits Pascoe, but at least he knows how "to die like a simple, honest, upright English gentleman!" a classification that causes Dunne to shake with laughter—or nerves.

As their hysteria mounts some would sing and some would pray. And some would die standing and some would count the seconds as Big Ben is tolling them off. Across the street they still can glimpse Lightfoot still leaning against a tree reading Shelley!

The faint notes of a barrel organ in the distance convicts it of playing "The Minstrel Boy"—"The minstrel boy to the war has gone—" The lilt of the tune throws St. John Pascoe into uncontrollable laughter.

"Gentlemen, for the last time I exert my authority." The Prime Minister interrupts them. "Silence, please. (*He crosses to peer at the clock.*) "We have seven minutes left. If you can pray, pray for the soul of that deluded boy and give thanks for the beauty and bravery that have been on earth; failing that, at least preserve man's dignity by silence. (*He turns to the window again. Pause.*)

The seriousness of their situation brings them to silence again. When they break that silence Matthew Grindle is impressed with the noises the passing buses make. H. G. Dunne has found a sort of peace.

"Now I know I shall find the thing I have always missed," he muses.

"You'll find—ping! Nothing!" insists St. John Pascoe.

Lord Vivian Vere wonders about life—why have any of them lived?

Outside Big Ben continues to tick away the precious seconds. In the distance the barrel organ has changed its tune to "Nearer, My God, to Thee." The notes of the hymn have a profound impression.

"The boy is right," agrees Evelyn Arthur. "Nature, not he, has put Humanity on trial, and because we have failed to evolve a faith adequate to our opportunities she rejects us for new experiments. That is the truth, and I am glad to have come to it."

Richard Stapp is not convinced. Richard Stapp is not a quitter. While they have been mooning he has been thinking. He draws a revolver from his pocket. "Man is and always has been the slave of force," he declaims, excitedly. "Blessed are the strong for they shall inherit the earth!"

It is Stapp's plan to stop Lightfoot. Let none of them bar the way. The moment the would-be destroyer shall appear in the doorway Stapp will shoot and shoot to kill.

"I'm not doin' this for humanity, but for myself," he boastfully admits; "the old original Satan you're all so ashamed of!" . . .

The doors open. The Cabinet members group themselves out of range of Stapp's fire. Lightfoot crosses the threshold. There is a shot. Lightfoot falls. Dedham and Blount catch him and carry his body to the conference table.

"D two chi D T squared minus C delta squared chi equals . . . nought!" the boy murmurs.

"Gibberish, eh!" ventures Stapp.

"No," replies Evelyn Arthur; "Clark Maxwell's formulation of the Theory of Light; pure beauty."

"Pure bunk," answers Stapp.

Lightfoot's lips move. "Farewell, hapless humanity," he mutters. "We go to the eternal mind."

Excitedly they search the dying Lightfoot's clothing. They find his "old turnip of a watch." Gingerly they examine it. It is as Faulkiner, the engineer, discovers, associated with the same wireless mechanism with which the flight of airplanes has been directed from the ground.

"I have it," cries Faulkiner. "There are two controls—one for what he will destroy, the other for when he will destroy it. We know the machine is set for world-destruction; so that's that. Now for the when. There are only three possible positions for a time control; one—instantaneous, but it didn't go off instantaneously—our presence here proves it; two, safety; three, a timed explosion; and this pointer (*to* DUNNE)—see?

They are a little hysterical at the thought that they are safe.

"Everything that has been spoken in this room the last twenty minutes is to be forgotten," commands the Prime Minister.

"The clock, to the great scandal of all hopeful souls, having been set back, the tortoise humanity will now cover its inch during the ensuing century," solemnly declares Evelyn Arthur.

A messenger enters the room. He bears a letter that has been left by a tall, dark gentleman, for the Prime Minister.

PRIME MINISTER—What's this? (*Reading the envelope.*) "Urgent." "From the League of United Scientists of the World." What's that? (*Handing letter to* DUNNE.) Dunne.

DUNNE—Never heard of it. I say! I say!

PRIME MINISTER—Well?

DUNNE—But it's . . .

PRIME MINISTER—Read it.

DUNNE—"To the Prime Minister and Cabinet of Great Britain, from the League of United Scientists of the World, secretly assembled in Geneva. The League informs the Prime Minister that it is aware a scientist outside the League has proved he can control the atom . . ."

DEDHAM—What? How did they know?

HALIBURTON—Geneva!

FAULKINER—Charlton and Eldridge.

DUNNE (*reading*)—"You are hereby given notice that, after

years of coördinated labour, the League, also, has just discovered the secret of the Atom. The League has prepared its programme. And it serves notice that it requires the attendance of the Prime Minister and such of his associates as he shall select, at Geneva immediately. The League, obviously, is in a position to enforce its demands. A similar notice is being served simultaneously on the Chancellories of every civilized country in the world."

STAPP (*peering over* DUNNE'S *shoulder*)—Charlton and Eldridge at the head of the list. Hello, there's a postscript. (*The drone of aeroplanes is faintly heard.*)

DUNNE (*reading*)—"Six aeroplanes are over you as you read this. They contain atomic bombs. Such bombs hang over the capitols of every civilized country."

FAULKINER—What?

STAPP—Ssh! Listen! (*Noise of planes is louder.* STAPP *dashes to the window.*) Green! Enormous! They're right over us. (*All save* ARTHUR *crowd to the windows.*)

HALIBURTON (*at back of crowd*)—Damn them; they're as bad as Lightfoot.

ARTHUR (*softly, to the corpse*)—Five minutes past twelve. The clock cannot be set back. If not you, Francis . . . another.

DEDHAM—Give me room; don't crowd me!

ARTHUR—Nature doesn't often give us a second chance. Perhaps she believes in us, even if we don't believe in ourselves.

STAPP—I can't see; they're in the sun.

ARTHUR (*to the corpse*)—Thank you, Francis. (*He bends down, kisses the face, then he takes the watch from the mantelpiece.*)

PRIME MINISTER (*left of table*)—Gentlemen, those wings even now sound over Europe. Are we with them, or against them? What is our reply?

(*They all talk.* ARTHUR *makes for the door right. As he looks at the unconscious backs of his colleagues, a last flicker of Puck comes over him. He raises his arm as if to throw the watch like a bomb. Pause.* STAPP *turns about, faces right.*)

STAPP (*crosses to right center below table*)—Hello! Where are you off to?

ARTHUR (*fiddling with the lock, tersely*)—Geneva. (*They gape. The door slams behind him.* STAPP, DEDHAM, *and the others come forward to right and left center.* BLOUNT, DUNNE, PRIME MINISTER, FAULKINER, SUNNINGDALE, VERE—LIGHTFOOT *on table*—STAPP, DEDHAM, PASCOE, GRINDLE, COSSINGTON, HALIBURTON.)

DUNNE (*running after* ARTHUR, *right*)—Arthur, wait for me! I, too, have hope. (*He rattles the door. Locked! They all move a step or so to right.*)

FAULKINER—My God, he's taken it!

HALIBURTON—Taken what?

STAPP—It! The thing! The watch! (*Striking his breast.*) Oh, God damn! Why didn't I get it? (*The roar of a car's cut-out.*)

HALIBURTON (*at the window, highly excited*)—There he goes! Out past the Admiralty. Stepping on the gas like a kid!

FAULKINER—Croydon aerodrome at sixty an hour!

HALIBURTON—By God, I love that man!

SUNNINGDALE—Hooray!

DUNNE—Good luck to him! Hooray!

DEDHAM (*savagely*)—Idiot! Geneva! Between them, the end!

PRIME MINISTER (*in a ringing voice*)—No, gentlemen, between them, if Man can find faith, the Beginning! (*The roar of planes fills the entire theatre.*)

The curtain falls.

HOLIDAY

Comedy in Three Acts

BY PHILIP BARRY

FOLLOWING an impulse inspired by the popularity of a character in his previous season's best-selling comedy, "Paris Bound," Philip Barry wrote a companion comedy to that play for the season of 1928-29. He managed this by the simple expedient of writing the second piece not only around the popular character aforementioned, but also around the personality of the actress who played it.

The actress is Hope Williams. Being both a gifted amateur and a social registerite, Miss Williams was selected for the rôle of Fanny Shippan in "Paris Bound." Fanny, it may be recalled, was a friend of the heroine, a wise and witty person considerably fed up with the artificialities of her own social set and more than a little suspicious of all similar social groups. Being a natural comedienne by grace of God and an actress by reason of a partially developed talent for drama Miss Williams proved a happy inspiration for Mr. Barry.

This second play is called "Holiday." It is peopled by a society group considerably richer than was that of "Paris Bound," and its problem is greatly different. It was promptly bought by Arthur Hopkins and produced by him at the Plymouth Theatre, New York, November 26.

The scene is a room on the third floor of Edward Seton's house in Fifth Avenue, New York. "It is a very large, rectangular room of the Stanford White period," explains Mr. Barry. "The panelling is heavy, the mouldings are heavy, the three long windows looking out over the park at back are hung with heavy curtains. . . . It is a handsome room and quite a comfortable room, but rich, very rich."

Julia Seton is writing at a desk. "She is twenty-eight and quite beautiful." It develops that she is just home from the Lake Placid Club and the winter sports.

It also develops that Miss Julia has brought back from Placid more than she took there, since she has annexed a young man named Case—Johnny Case. Mr. Case who, by previous arrangement, has come to call on Miss Julia this bright Sunday morning in December, "is thirty, medium-tall, slight, attractive-looking and luckily not quite handsome."

Johnny and Julia, being finally left to themselves by the house servants, fall promptly and quite enthusiastically into each other's arms. But while the warmth of Julia's greeting is at least reassuring Johnny is still slightly befuddled by his surroundings. The Seton home is much too much for him to take in immediately. It is, it seems to him, something like the Grand Central and must be awful hard to live in.

Julia, amused, is proud and still a little apprehensive as she explains to Johnny that his worst fears are probably about to be realized. The Setons are very rich. They are, in fact, *those* Setons. Johnny had never suspected that.

He thinks Julia should have told him. Still he is not as startled by the news as he might have been. Had he known, he admits, he probably would have asked her to marry him days before he did.

"I went through an awful struggle," confesses Johnny. "You've no idea. I had very definite plans for the next few years, and at first a wife looked like quite a complication."

"What were the plans?" Julia wants to know.

"For one thing, I was worried about having enough for both of us. If I'd known I'd have spared myself. It's simply swell now. Good Julia!"

"Aren't you funny, Johnny?"

"Why?"

"To talk about it."

"It? Money? Why? Is it so sacred?"

"Of course not. But—"

"I'm simply delighted, that's all."

"—That I have—uh—money?"

"Yes. Sure."

"You're amazing!"

"But, why not? If I'd suddenly discovered you could play the piano I'd be delighted, wouldn't I?"

"Is it like knowing how to play the piano?"

"Well, they are both very pleasant accomplishments in a girl."

Julia does not really mind Johnny's attitude. She knows he is going to make millions himself. But Johnny is just as convinced and equally frank in stating that he is going to do nothing of the kind. Before he can fully explain; in fact, before he has more than satisfied himself that Julia's acceptance of him has been honestly due to the fact that she fell in love with him at Placid and is quite convinced that she will never want to let him go, there are interruptions and the subject is changed. . . .

Johnny's presence at the Seton house this Sunday morning, it now transpires, has been planned by Julia for his meeting with her father. Decisions as to a wedding date and so forth she hopes will follow.

Julia has broken the news to father in church, where, she figured, he would have a chance to think before he began to talk. She had left Mr. Seton a little cheered by the fact that he knew a member of Johnny's law firm, but still in rather a seriously prayerful state of mind.

Now she knows that although the meeting will be something of an ordeal, Johnny will face and conquer it, and she has not the slightest sympathy with his suggestion that their engagement would have been a "swell guilty secret" to have kept for awhile.

Father had to be told, and he had to be told at once because it is Julia's hope that she and Johnny can be married in two weeks. Father, of course, will have something to say about that, and also about the kind of wedding it shall be—simple, as Johnny would prefer, or churchly and grand, according to the Seton tradition. The thought is depressing to Johnny.

JOHNNY—I just hate the thought of sitting down with a man and being practical about you—so soon, I mean. (JULIA *softens.*)

JULIA—Angel! (*She kisses him, lightly.*) It's got to be done, though.

JOHNNY—All right. I'll gird up my loins. You know, I bet he'll hate this necktie. It doesn't look substantial.

JULIA—You might sit like this—covering it with your hand.

JOHNNY—I love you, Julia.

JULIA—I love you, Johnny.

JOHNNY—That's the main thing, isn't it?

JULIA—Darling, that's everything—

JOHNNY—Kiss?

JULIA—With pleasure. (*They kiss.*)

JOHNNY—Don't go.

JULIA—I wouldn't think of it.

JOHNNY—It'd be swell to have this whole day free with no ordeals to face.

JULIA—It'll be over soon.—I think we'll have Ned and Linda on our side.

JOHNNY—Lord, do they have to mix in, too?

JULIA—Well, they're my brother and sister.

JOHNNY—Are they good guys?

JULIA—Dears. Ned's a little inclined to drink too much, but I think he'll outgrow it. You ought to be able to help him, I think. Linda's a curious girl, she has developed a curious—I don't know—attitude toward life. I can't make her out. She doesn't think as we do at all, anymore.

JOHNNY—We?

JULIA—The family. Father's worried sick about her. I think we can help her a lot though—I hope we can.

JOHNNY—She might prefer to work it out for herself. So might Ned.

JULIA—You *are* strange this morning, Johnny.

JOHNNY—How?

JULIA—You seem—not to like things quite as much as you might.

JOHNNY—Oh, yes, I do!

JULIA—We can't just wander forever up snowy mountains through pine woods with never a care, you know."

JOHNNY—Come here, darling. (*She rises and goes to him.*) We can do better than that. (JULIA *looks at him.*)

JULIA—Do you suppose?

JOHNNY—I know.

JULIA (JULIA's *head drops*)—Oh, I feel so awfully sad all at once.

JOHNNY—Don't—*don't.* Don't ever— (*His grasp tightens on her shoulders.*) Look up here! (*With an effort,* JULIA *looks up.*) Now please kiss me several times. (JULIA *kisses him, once, twice, lightly.*)

JULIA—Is that all right?

JOHNNY—All right, hell. It's perfect.

Johnny is for continuing the lesson and is bending over to kiss Julia again when Linda Seton enters the room. Linda "is twenty-seven and looks about twenty-two." When she removes the fur coat that covers her she is seen to be a "slim, rather boyish, exceedingly fresh" young woman. "She is smart, she is pretty, but beside Julia's grace, Julia's beauty, she seems a trifle gauche, and almost plain."

She stops short at sight of Julia and Johnny, but she is not greatly perturbed. This may not be exactly the way for sister to be spending Sunday morning, but Linda is willing to leave the question open. Much no doubt depends upon who the young man happens to be. Linda devotes the next few moments to finding out.

From Johnny she gets no more than monosyllabic pleasantries, but from Julia she learns of how one frosty morning at Placid Julia, properly chaperoned, was on her way to the rink when whom should they meet but Johnny carrying ski. It was quite apparent to Julia that there was something wrong with Johnny's nose; that it was in fact frozen. Realizing then that Johnny did not know his nose was frozen Julia stepped up and politely told him.

"I suppose you don't realize it," Julia had said, "but your nose is frozen."

"Thanks, I hadn't realized it," replied Johnny.

"Well, it is," said she.

"I don't suppose there is anything you personally could do about it?" said he.

Which, Linda admits, was a bit fresh, though probably no more fresh, as Johnny insists, than Julia's mentioning it in the first place.

Ned Seton, the girls' brother, comes in and is a trifle annoyed. Some one, and he suspects Julia, has taken his cocktail shaker from his room and he doesn't like it. Ned is twenty-six and as handsome in his way as Julia is in hers. "His features are fine, a little too fine; he displaces very little, but no one minds and most like him."

Now Ned has met Johnny and heard of Julia's intention of marrying him. Ned, too, is mildly surprised but not at all displeased. He knows this Johnny Case. At least he knows of him. Johnny and Ned had been at the same football game in New Haven and Johnny had helped Ned (who needed help) to get somewhere and to bed. Which, in a way, makes for a brotherly respect or something.

It is Linda's opinion, however, that with everything he may have in his favor in the way of friendly interests and a good appearance Johnny still will need more if he is going to impress properly the head of the Seton family. She thinks Johnny will need a bit of coaching. Is he, for one thing, a man of means? Money being the god of the Seton family that is most important.

JOHNNY (*rising*)—I have in my pocket now thirty-four dollars and a package of Lucky Strikes. Have one?

LINDA—Thanks. (*She takes cigarette.*) But no Gilt-Edged Securities? No rolling woodlands?

JOHNNY—I've got a few shares of Common Stock tucked away in a warm place.

LINDA—Common? Don't say the word. (*She accepts a light from* JOHNNY, *and seats herself, sighing.*) I'm afraid it won't do, Julia.—He's a comely boy, but probably just another of the vast army of clock-watchers.

NED (*from behind his newspaper*)—How are you socially?

JOHNNY—Nothing there, either.

LINDA—You mean to say your mother wasn't even a Whoosiz?

JOHNNY—Not even that.

JULIA—Linda, I do wish you'd shut up.

NED—Maybe he's got a judge somewhere in the family.

LINDA—Yes, that might help. Old Judge Case's boy. White pillars. Guitars a-strummin'. Evenin', Massa.

NED—You must know some prominent people. Drop a few names.

LINDA—Just casually, you know: "When I was to Mrs. Onderdonk's cock-fight last Tuesday, whom should I see but Mrs. Marble— Well, sire, I thought we'd die laughing—

JULIA (*to* JOHNNY)—This is a lot of rot, you know.

JOHNNY—I'm having a grand time.

LINDA—"Johnny," she says to me—she calls me "Johnny"—

JULIA—Oh, will you be *quiet!* What on earth has set you off this time?

LINDA—But it's dreadful, sister. (*To* JOHNNY.) Just what do you think you're going to prove with Edward Seton, financier and cotillion-leader?

JOHNNY—Well, I'll tell you: when I find myself in a position like this, I ask myself: What would General Motors do? Then I do the opposite.

Linda likes this Case boy. It will be a pity, she now believes —a great pity—if Julia's wedding doesn't come off. But Julia isn't afraid of that, however difficult her father may be. Julia plans, gaining father's consent, that the wedding shall be announced immediately and held within a few weeks.

Linda, enthused at the prospect, wants to give the announcement party. She is not much for parties as a rule, particularly father's parties. But she would love to give a party of her own, just inviting the right people over the telephone. It would come on New Year's Eve, too. That would be great.

"Oh, Lord, Lord! Let's have some fun in this house before you leave it," thrills Linda. "And just a few people—very few. Not a single bank or pink roses and no string quartet during supper. All I want by way of entertainment is just one good tap dancer!"

Linda's enthusiasm mounts with the thought that for once she, alone, is going to do something for Julia and do it in her own way.

"It won't be a ball, it'll be a simple sit-down supper—and, you know where?—the old playroom!—because the playroom's the one room in this house any one's ever had fun in!"

Now the closing of the front door indicates that the senior Seton is home and probably gone first to his sitting-room. Julia wants to see father before father sees Johnny, and insists on carrying Ned with her. Which leaves Linda and Johnny to continue getting acquainted. They are great kidders, these two.

"However do you do, Mr. Case?" echoes Linda in her best society manner.

"And you, Miss—ah—" replies Johnny in kind.

"Seton is the name."

"Not one of the bank Setons?"

"The same."

"Fancy! I hear November cats are up four points."

"Have you been to the opera lately?"

"Only in fits and starts, I'm afraid."

"But, my dear—we must do something for them! They entertained us in Rome."

"And you really saw Mt. Everest?"

"Chit."

"Chat."

That, Linda thinks, will do for the preliminaries. Now for serious matters. Linda loves her sister Julia more than she loves anything else on earth. Julia's sweet, she's beautiful, she's even exciting, and it is terribly important that she shall marry the right man.

Johnny is a strange bird, so far as the Setons are concerned. Not at all the type they are used to meeting. Linda would like to know something about him; where he's been, what he's been doing.

Johnny is frank to say that he has never done anything much beside work. The vacation trip to Lake Placid happens to have been the first holiday he has ever had, and he has been working since he was 10. The last few years he has been studying law. Ambitious? Yes. Ambitious to live.

"Awhile ago you asked me if I knew any living people," says Johnny. "I know damn few."

"There aren't but damn few."

"Well, I mean to be one of them some day. Johnny's dream."

"So do I. Linda's longing."

It happens that both Linda and Johnny know the Potters—Nick and Susan Potter—and they are agreed that perhaps the Potters get more fun out of nothing than any other two in the world.

"Compared to the time I have," says Linda, "the last man in a chain gang thoroughly enjoys himself."

"What's the matter? Are you fed up?"

"To the neck. Now tell me about *your* operation."

They are of a mind as to the emptiness of everyday existence as most people live it. They are convinced that what they both need is a change, time off, days off, years off from what they are doing. "And of course *that's* so easy," protests Linda.

JOHNNY—It can be done. I intend to do it. I intend to take quite a lot of it—when I'm not so busy just making the wherewithal.

LINDA—Case, you astonish me. I'd have thought you a Willing Worker.

JOHNNY—I am if I can get what I'm working for.

LINDA—And what would that be?

JOHNNY—Mine is a simple story: I just want to save part of my life for myself. There's a catch to it, though. It's got to be part of the young part.

LINDA—You'll never get *on and up* that way.

JOHNNY—All right, but I want my time while I'm young, and let me tell you, the minute I get hold of just about twenty nice round thousands, I'm going to knock off for as long as they last, and—

Linda—Quit?

JOHNNY—Quit. Retire young, and work old. That's what I want to do.

LINDA—Grand. Does Julia know about it?

JOHNNY—No—there's no use getting her hopes up until it happens—don't tell her, will you?

LINDA—She has enough of her own for two right now—or ten,

for that matter. Mother and grandfather did us pretty, pretty. (JOHNNY *shakes his head.*)

JOHNNY—Thanks, but I've got to do myself only just pretty enough.

LINDA—I see. That's foolish—you're all right, though, Case, You haven't been bitten with it yet—you haven't been caught by it.

JOHNNY—By what?

LINDA—The reverence for riches.

JOHNNY (*laughing*)—You are a curious girl.

LINDA—Curious, am I, and what about you, you big stiff?

JOHNNY—Just take Johnny's hand, and come into the Light, Sister. (JULIA *enters.* JOHNNY *turns to her.*) Did you see him?

JULIA—I saw him.

LINDA—Julia. How was he?

JULIA—I don't know yet. Johnny, you go up to Ned's room. You haven't arrived yet. Take the elevator—Father's coming down the stairs. Quick, will you?

JOHNNY—When do I arrive?

JULIA—One o'clock. It's quarter to.

JOHNNY—This is getting a little complicated, if you ask me.

JULIA—Nobody asked you. Go on! Do as you're told!

JOHNNY—See here, you saucy—

LINDA—Go on, Case. Don't expect simplicity here—just think of our Fifth Avenue frontage.

Julia's interview with her father has not been any too promising. It is the same old story, of course—she is being married for her money.

Linda doesn't believe that's true, but even if it were she can't think of any better investment into which to put the family jack than that of acquiring a superior type of husband. And she has an idea that if Johnny Case had known about the Seton money he would have been running yet.

"You do like him, don't you?" pleads Julia.

"She asks me if I like him!" Linda's enthusiasm is perfect. "My dear girl, do you realize that *life* walked into this house this morning? Marry him quick. Don't let him get away. And if father starts the usual—where *is* Big Business, anyway?"

"He said he'd be right down."

"Stand your ground, Julia. If you don't know your own mind

by now you haven't got a mind. Name your date and stick to it. I'm telling you."

"I want father to see that Johnny has the self-same qualities grandfather had—and that there's no reason why he shouldn't arrive just where he did," insists Julia.

"—If he wants to," adds Linda, significantly.

When Edward Seton enters the room he is seen to be a man of 58, "large, nervous, distinguished. He wears a black morning coat, a white carnation in his buttonhole and gray striped trousers. He takes glasses from his nose and folds them away in a silver case."

Mr. Seton is quite patient with Julia's impatience. Naturally there are many things he will want to know about this young Mr. Chase—Case, rather, but of one thing he is quite sure— It will be out of the question for Julia to think of being married by the 10th of January. It isn't an affair that can be rushed into. Even though Linda is also convinced that Johnny is a boy with loads of charm and great possibilities, there is the matter of background to be gone into. Has any one seen the financial section of the *Morning Times?*

The Seton sisters will not be put off, however. They insist upon discussing Johnny Case and forcing an early decision from their father as to the young man's eligibility. Linda, particularly, is frankly irritated at the plans her father makes so casually for the investigation of Johnny.

"I propose not to allow the subject of an engagement to come up in my first talk with him," Mr. Seton insists. "I believe I am competent to direct the conversation. You and Ned, Julia, may excuse yourselves on one pretext or another. I should like you to stay, Linda."

"Couldn't we rig up a dictagraph? My shorthand's weak," Linda suggests.

Now Johnny, formally announced by the butler, is as formally received by Edward Seton and formally introduced to Miss Linda Seton and Mr. Ned Seton.

"I recall your face, but your figure puzzles me," admits Ned.

Now Ned and Julia have been reminded of the telephoning father has asked them to do and the examination of Johnny Case has been formally inaugurated with almost impressive dignity.

Yes, there has been quite a bit of snow. No, Johnny will not smoke before lunch. Yes, he is in business in New York—with Sloan, Hobson. No, he is not a born New Yorker. He was born in Baltimore in 1897 July 6th—and he is thirty years old.

No, Johnny doesn't know the Clarence Whites, of Baltimore. Nor the Archie Fullers. Nor Colonel Evans—old Philip Evans. Johnny doesn't know any of them. Which gives Mr. Seton pause. There is a silence, broken by Johnny.

"I haven't been in Baltimore in some years," reports Johnny, his "confession" gaining a certain defiant speed as he proceeds. "And I shouldn't be likely to know them anyway. My father had a small grocery store in Baltimore—which he was never able to make a go of. He left a number of debts which my mother worked very hard to clear up. I was the only child, and I wasn't in a position to help very much. She died the May before my sixteenth birthday.

EDWARD—But how sad.

JOHNNY—It *was* pretty sad.—I hadn't any—connections except for an uncle who's in the roofing business in Wilmington. He wasn't much good though—he was inclined to get drunk—still is—

LINDA—We have an uncle like that, but he keeps off roofs. (JOHNNY *smiles at her, and continues.*)

JOHNNY—But I was what's called a bright boy, and I managed to wangle a couple of scholarships. They helped a good deal in school and college, and there was always plenty of ways to make up the difference. In term-time I usually ran eating-joints and typed lecture notes. In the summers I sold aluminum pots and pans—

EDWARD—Linda, are you there? Linda! (*Weakly.*)

JOHNNY—Or worked in a factory—or on a newspaper. Once I got myself engaged as a tutor. That was pretty unpleasant. Then there were department stores at Christmas and florists at Easter. During law school I slept all night on a couch in a doctor's office, and got fifteen a week for it. That was soft.

EDWARD (*weakly*)—Admirable.

JOHNNY—No—it simply happened to be the only way to get through. (*A brief pause, then:*) Anything else, sir?

EDWARD—I beg your pardon?

LINDA—I should think you would.

JOHNNY—Is there anything more I can tell you about myself?

EDWARD—Why, uh—that is to say, uh—(*He flounders, and stops.*)

JOHNNY—Well, Mr. Seton, how about it?

EDWARD—About it? About what?

JOHNNY—Julia and me.

EDWARD—You and Julia? I'm afraid I—

JOHNNY—About our getting married. (*There is a silence.*)

EDWARD—This is a complete surprise, Mr. Case. I don't know quite what to say to you.

JOHNNY (*smiling*)—Yes would be pleasant.

EDWARD—I am sure it would. However, we must go into it rather more carefully, I am afraid.

JOHNNY—The only difficulty is the time. Julia's idea is January tenth. It's mine, too.

EDWARD—We shall see about that.

JOHNNY—May I ask *how* we shall see, sir?

EDWARD—Mr. Case, I do not know you at all.

JOHNNY—I'll give you every opportunity to if you'll permit me. How's lunch to-morrow?

EDWARD—To-morrow I have several.

JOHNNY—Tuesday? (EDWARD *hesitates.*)

EDWARD—Will you meet me at the Bankers' Club at one on Friday?

JOHNNY—I'm terribly sorry, but Friday's out. I've got to go to Boston on business. Better make it to-morrow.

(NED *and* JULIA *reënter.* EDWARD *speaks, hastily.*)

EDWARD—Very well, I shall arrange my appointments.—Ah, Ned, Julia,—and what do you suppose can be keeping the Crams?

JOHNNY (*cutting in before they can reply*)—Thank you. In the meantime, I think Mr. Hobson or Mr. Sloan might say a good word for me. I'm nobody at all, as things go. But I'm quite decent and fairly civilized, and I love your daughter very much—which isn't a bit hard. She seems to like me quite a lot too, and that's about all that can be said for me—except that I think we've a simply grand chance to be awfully happy—what do *you* say, Julia?

JULIA—Oh, so do I!

LINDA—Come on, Father, be an angel, ***I*** think he's a very good number.

EDWARD—I am afraid it is too important a matter to be decided off-hand.

JULIA—But I want to be married on the—

EDWARD (*with sudden sharpness*)—You will be married, Julia, when I have reached a favorable decision—and upon a day which I will name.

JULIA—I—our plan was—the tenth, and sail that night on—

EDWARD—The tenth is out of the question.

JULIA—Oh, but, Father,—! I—

EDWARD—And we shall let it rest at that for the moment.

LINDA—But you'll come round, Father! I have a swell hunch you'll come round. Oh, Lordy, what fun! Let's all join hands.

Seton Cram is 36, "somewhat bald, inclined to a waistline, but well turned out in a morning-coat, striped trousers and spats. Laura is thirty-two, a shade taller than Seton, with a rather handsome, rather disagreeable face. She is as smartly dressed as a poor figure will allow." The Crams are duly presented to Johnny, the conversation drifts naturally into the effects of the severe cold on chapped hands and out again to the preparations for lunch.

Ned is inclined to think Johnny will want to brush up a bit and as they are leaving the room Linda suddenly discovers that she, too, is simply covered with dust. She follows rapidly after them. She has heard Ned ask the whereabouts of his cocktail shaker.

The Crams and Edward Seton are a bit bewildered as the curtain falls.

ACT II

The Seton party, by New Year's Eve, has assumed the usual extensive proportions of a society event. The playroom at the top of the Seton house, as Linda had predicted, is the only place not swarming with socially important celebrants.

"The playroom is a long and spacious, high-ceilinged room with white woodwork and pale blue walls as a background for story book designs done in silver, white and green in the Arthur Rackham manner."

There are two trapezes swinging from the ceiling and tied up so as to be out of the way. The furniture is light and plain and mostly low. There is a victrola and an old-fashioned music box and a settee.

For the moment the room is in darkness, but soon Julia and Ned have come from below stairs in search of Linda. They can't find Linda and the playroom, Ned says, is her usual retreat when she is in a jam.

Linda has not had a happy evening. Her party has been taken away from her by Julia and her father. Then Linda has refused to appear at dinner, which has made Edward Seton furious. Julia has told the company that her sister is suffering from a splitting headache and will be down later. Still Linda hasn't appeared, and now they fear she has left the house and run out on what is ostensibly her own party.

young man and pleased to hear him report that he even likes his prospective father-in-law. Johnny, in fact, is quite prepared to discount Nick's warning that the elder Seton expects him to devote his life to a money-making career and would be "down on him like Levine took Richmond" if he tried to quit. And yet to quit and enjoy himself while he is still young is still Johnny's ambition. Julia will understand, he is sure.

Now Susan and Linda have arrived, Susan full of cheers and congratulations. Linda, still determined to have nothing to do with "that low class dancehall downstairs," only hopes the crowd will leave them alone. . . .

Johnny and Linda, at least, are agreed on Johnny's idea of getting something out of life.

"I wish some one would tell what I'm to do in 1928-29 and '30 and all the rest of them," muses Linda.

"What you need is a husband, Linda," ventures Susan.

"Have you any addresses?"

"He'll arrive. I only hope you'll know how to act when he does."

"Well, I won't take no for an answer," promises Linda.

Julia and Johnny's wedding day has been fixed for the 12th. They had decided on the 10th, but Papa Seton has a corporation meeting scheduled for that date.

Johnny thinks perhaps he and Julia will stay on the other side indefinitely. He has accumulated a bunch of common stock at a low price and there is a chance it may shoot up. If it does he will be ready to quit for awhile. Susan and Linda are strong for that resolve, but Nick is still doubtful. Has Johnny told Julia? He hasn't? Well, right there is the beginning of a complication, Linda warns. Julia and her father are pretty much of a mind on some things. . . .

Laura and Seton Cram are in, much to Linda's disappointment. She doesn't like the Crams. Never has. Seton brings good news for Johnny, however. There is a well-founded rumor that the Seaboard stock Johnny holds is in for a sharp rise. It ought to make him thirty or forty thousand. And Johnny, by the same rumor, has had a lot to do with putting Seaboard on the map. More than that, Seton is convinced that his own firm of brokers is going to make Johnny an offer to join the firm, with a chance of being made an executive at a large salary. Johnny is excited by the news about the stock, but he has little interest in the business offer.

It is nearing the midnight hour. Laura is insistent that they all, especially Linda, should go downstairs and join the party. But again Linda flatly refuses. Let the rest of them go. She is staying in the playroom.

"If you ask me, it's one of the worst cases of downright rudeness I've ever seen," explodes Seton Cram.

"And has some one asked you—" counters Linda.

"When a girl invites three hundred people to her house—" adds Laura.

"I invited six people—three of whom you see before you—the others came on some one else's say-so—yours and father's, I believe."

The Crams decide that they had better go. Which relieves the situation greatly.

Now Linda and Johnny, Susan and Nick proceed to enjoy themselves. The witching hour approaches and they are irresponsibly joyous. Johnny is moved to enthuse over the lucky stock break, this night of all nights, and Linda was never as happy for anybody in her life. And then Edward Seton and Julia arrive.

Father is plainly perturbed. He wants everybody downstairs to help usher in the new year. Linda is still obdurate. There are two parties. She is only interested in her own. She had asked and been granted permission to have it and she does not intend to change her plans. She is angry because they have stopped her other guests, Peter Jessup and Mary Hedges, downstairs. She sends Nick and Susan to rescue them.

LINDA—Listen to me, Father: to-night means a good deal to me—I don't know what, precisely—and I don't know how. Something is trying to take it away from me, and I can't let it go. I'll put in an appearance downstairs, if you like. Then I want to bring a few people up here—the few people in the world I can talk to, and feel something for. And I want to sit with them and have supper with them, and we won't disturb any one. That's all right with you, isn't it?

EDWARD—Your place is downstairs.

LINDA—Once more, Father: this is important to me. Don't ask me why, I don't know. It has something to do with—when I was a child here—and this room—and good times in it—and—

EDWARD—What special virtue this room has, I'm sure I don't see.

LINDA—You don't, do you—no—you can't. Well, I'll tell you this room's my home. It's the only home I've got. There's something here that I understand, and that understands me. Maybe it's Mother.

EDWARD—Please do as I have told you, Linda.

LINDA—I suppose you know it's the end of us, then.

EDWARD—Don't talk nonsense. Do as I say.

LINDA—It *is* the end. But all the same, I'm going to have supper here to-night in my home with my friends.

EDWARD—I have told you—

LINDA—You thought I'd come around, didn't you? You always think people will come around. Not me; not to-night. And I shan't be bothered here, either. Because if there's one thing you can't stand, it's a scene. I can promise you one if you interfere. I can promise you a beauty.

Father tries to change the subject, but Linda is insistent. Thoughts of her mother crowd in upon her. Was she a sweet soul? Was she exciting? Edward Seton is short in his answers. Again he would change the subject. He would talk with Johnny now, and asks Linda to go.

Mr. Seton is eager to congratulate Johnny on his prospects. He is proud of Johnny and has already begun to make plans for him. Eventually, of course, he will come into the Seton firm. Let him go with Pritchard-Ames for the present.

But Johnny is not of the same mind. "I don't want to get tied up for life quite so soon," he explains. "You see, I'm a kind of a queer duck, in a way. I'm afraid I'm not as anxious as I might be for the things most people work toward. I don't *want* too much money. . . . You see it's always been my plan to make a few thousands early in the game, if I could, and then quit for as long as they last, and try to find out who I am and what I am and what goes on and what about it—now, while I'm young, and feel good all the time. I'm sure Julia understands what I'm getting at—don't you, Julia?"

Julia is not so sure that she does. Edward Seton can't understand. Perhaps Johnny wants to occupy himself otherwise—with some art or other?

JOHNNY—Oh, no, I've got no abilities that way. I'm not one of the frail ones with a longing to get away from it all and indulge a few tastes, either. I haven't any tastes. Old China and first editions and gate-legged tables don't do a thing to me. I don't want to live any way or in any time but my own—now—in New

York—and Detroit—and Chicago—and Phoenix—any place here, —but I do want to live.

EDWARD—As a gentleman of leisure.

JOHNNY—As a man whose time, for awhile at least, is his own. That's what I've been plugging for ever since I was ten. Please don't make me feel guilty about it, Sir. Whether I'm right or wrong, it's more important to me than anything in the world but Julia. Even if it turns out to be just one of those fool ideas that people dream about and then go flat on—even if I find I've had enough of it in three months, still I want it. I've got a feeling that if I let this chance go by, there'll never be another for me. So I don't think any one will mind if I—just have a go at it—will they, Julia? (JULIA *is silent.*)—Will they, dear?"

JULIA—Father—will you let Johnny and me talk a while?

EDWARD—Just a moment—(*to* JOHNNY) As I understand it, you have some objection, perhaps, to our manner of living.

JOHNNY—Not for you, sir. I haven't the slightest doubt it's all right for you—or that it's the answer for a lot of people. But for me—well, you see I don't *want* to live in what they call "a certain way." In the first place I'd be no good at it, and besides that I don't want to be identified with any one class of people. I want to live every which way, among all kinds—and know them—and understand them—and love them—that's what I want, don't *you,* Julia?

JULIA—Why, I— It sounds—

EDWARD—In all my experience, I have never heard such a—

JOHNNY—I want those years now, Sir.

JULIA—Father—please— (*He turns to her. Their eyes meet.*) It will be all right, I promise you.

EDWARD (*turning at the door*)—Case, it strikes me that you chose a strange time to tell us this, a very strange time.

JOHNNY (*puzzled*)—I don't quite—

EDWARD—In fact, if I had not already sent the announcement to the newspapers—asked a number of our friends here to-night to—

JULIA—Father!

JOHNNY (*very quietly*)—Oh, I see.

JULIA—Father—please go down. We'll come in a minute.

After Edward Seton has gone Johnny tries to explain to Julia, but she is furious with him. The idea of his choosing this night to make such a foolish declaration and to antagonize her father!

The idea of his thinking that a young man of his energy and his ability could quit at thirty! Ridiculous! She is willing, if he is tired, that he should take a holiday, but to give up his career—Why does he take delight in torturing her as he does?

It is hard for Johnny to understand Julia in this mood. There is an expression in her eyes now that he has never seen before. Of course, he explains, he would not expect her to live on his income. She has plenty and to spare. The "looks of the thing" don't mean a thing to him.

"I shouldn't mind it," he explains, "and I think that lookout's mine. Oh, darling, you don't see what I'm after, either—but try a little blind faith for awhile, won't you? Come along with me—the whole way, dear."

"Wait till next year—or two years, and we'll think about it again," pleads Julia. "If it's right it can be done then as well as now. You can do that for me—for us—can't you?"

He is looking her squarely in the eyes now. "You think by then I'd have come 'round," he says, "that's what you think, isn't it? I'd have come 'round—"

Linda is back before Julia can answer. She couldn't find Peter and Mary. They had missed her and gone on. Nick and Susan have followed. Linda is expected to join them later, but she doesn't think she will. She thinks she will stay in the playroom by herself. She can be quite amusing by herself at times. Johnny thinks he will stay, too. And Julia, angry with them both, flounces out. . . . Linda starts the music box. . . . It's a waltz.

"You wouldn't care to step into a waltz, Mr. Case?" she says.

"I'd love it."

She extends her arms, he takes her in his, they begin to waltz slowly.

JOHNNY—There's a conspiracy against you and me, child.

LINDA—What's that?

JOHNNY—The Vested Interests—

LINDA—I know.

JOHNNY—They won't let us have any fun, and they won't give me time to think.

LINDA—I suppose, like the great fathead you are, you told them all your little hopes and dreams.

JOHNNY—Um.

LINDA—Pretty disappointing?

JOHNNY—Bad enough.

LINDA—Poor boy.

JOHNNY—How about your own evening?

LINDA—Not so good, either.

JOHNNY—Poor girl.

LINDA—But we won't mind, will we?

JOHNNY—Hell, no, we won't mind.

LINDA—We'll get there—

JOHNNY—We'll get there! (*She stops in the dance and looks up at him for a moment, curiously. Then he smiles at her and she smiles back.*) Place head, A, against cheek, B, and proceed as before—(*they begin to dance again.*) Of course they may be right.

LINDA—Don't you believe it!

JOHNNY—They seem—awfully sure.

LINDA—It's your ride still, isn't it? You know where you want to go, don't you?

JOHNNY—Well, I thought I did.

LINDA—So did I. Pathetic, wasn't it—all my fuss and fury over anything so unimportant as this party.

JOHNNY—Maybe it was important.

LINDA—Well, if it was, I'm not. And I guess that's the answer.

JOHNNY—Not quite.

LINDA—Me and my little what-d'you-call-it—defense mechanism—so pathetic. Yes, I'm just chock-full of pathos, I am.

JOHNNY—You're a brick, Linda.

LINDA—Oh, shut your silly face. . . . You're right, you know—there *is* nothing up the fun-alley.

JOHNNY—Fun-alley?

LINDA—I had a nice little seven-word motto for my life, but I guess she don't work.

JOHNNY—What was it?

LINDA—"Not very important—but pretty good entertainment."

JOHNNY—Hum.

LINDA—For "pretty good" read "rotten." (*She stops dancing.*) There. That's enough. I'm getting excited.

JOHNNY—What?

LINDA—It was grand. Thanks. You can go now. (*She has not yet left his arms. Suddenly from outside comes the noise of bells tolling. Her grasp tightens upon his arm.*) Listen! (*She looks over her shoulder toward the window. Horns begin to sound, sirens, shots.*)

JOHNNY—It's it, all right. (*Again she turns her face to his.*)

LINDA—Happy New Year, dear.

JOHNNY—Happy New Year, dear. (*He bends and kisses her. For an instant she clings to him, and then averts her face.*)

LINDA (*in a breath*)—Oh, Johnny, you're so attractive—

JOHNNY (*with difficulty*)—You're—you're all right yourself— (*There is a dead silence. Then she leaves his arms, turns and smiles to him.*)

LINDA—You can count on Sister Linda—Run on down now—quick? They'll be waiting.

JOHNNY (*hesitating*)—Linda—

LINDA—What?

JOHNNY—They've—your father—I've been put in a position that—

LINDA—Do you love Julia, Johnny? (JOHNNY *turns away.*)

JOHNNY—Of course I do.

LINDA—Well, if ever she needed you, she needs you now. Once it's announced she'll go through with it. Then you can help her. I can't do anything any more. I've tried for twenty years. You're all that's left— Go on, Johnny—(*He goes to the door and opens it. From downstairs comes a swelling chorus of male voices singing "Auld Lang Syne"*)—and tell those choir-boys for me, that I'll be in Scotland before them.

Johnny leaves the door open as he goes. From below stairs there is a roll of drums. The music and voices stop. Linda has shut off the music-box and is standing by the window. Through the door the voice of Edward Seton is heard.

"Ladies and Gentlemen," he is saying, "my very good friends, I have the honor to announce to you the engagement of my daughter, Julia, to Mr. John Case—an event which doubles the pleasure I take in wishing you—*and* them—a most happy and prosperous, New Year." (*There is loud applause, congratulations.*)

Ned wanders in. He is plainly intoxicated. Linda wonders what it would be like to get drunk. It's great, Ned assures her. It brings you to life. You feel important. It's a swell game, too, as it goes on, every move, every sentence, is a problem that gets pretty interesting. And when finally you're beaten you don't mind. You sleep.

LINDA—Oh, Ned—that's awful!

NED—Think so? Other things are worse.

LINDA—But—but where do you end up?

NED—Where does everybody end up? You die.—And that's all right, too.

LINDA—Ned, can you do it on champagne?

NED—What's the matter, Linda? (*She drinks her glass and sets it down.*)

LINDA—Nothing.

NED—I know.

LINDA—Yes?

NED—Johnny.

LINDA—Give me some more, Ned.

NED—He's a funny boy, isn't he?

LINDA—Give me some, Ned—(NED *fills her glass.*)

NED—You can tell me about it.

LINDA—I love the boy, Neddy.

NED—I thought so. Hell, isn't it?

LINDA—I guess it will be.

NED (*raising his glass*)—Here's luck to you—(*He drains his glass.* LINDA *stares at hers.*)

LINDA—I don't want any luck. (NED *falls over on his side, asleep.*) Ned— (*He does not answer.* LINDA *slowly walks up to the door.*) Ned—Maybe I ought—I'm not sure I *will* stay up here. Do you mind? (*No answer. She turns and sees him.*) *Ned!* (*No answer. She goes to him swiftly and bends above him.*) Poor lamb. (*She kisses his cheek. Walks up to the door, turns off the lights, the door opens and the voices are heard from downstairs laughing and talking. She raises her head and goes out calling.*) Hello—Hello, every one!

The playroom is dark, except for the light from the windows. The curtain falls.

ACT III

It is the evening of the day that was to have been Julia and Johnny's wedding day. In the Seton living room Nick and Susan Potter and Linda are taking coffee. Their conversation concerns the present whereabouts of young Mr. Case.

That Johnny and Julia should have disagreed and decided to postpone the wedding for the present is plain enough, and that Johnny should want to go away by himself to think things out is reasonable. But where he could have gone, and where he is at the moment, is puzzling.

Linda seems to be the only one who really is interested. Julia is taking the matter quite calmly and with complete confidence.

She has her father on her side, and he, too, is unperturbed and confident. Nick and Susan, as outsiders, are no more than mildly interested. They, as a matter of fact, don't blame Johnny a bit for having taken to the woods—

The woods! That's a suggestion. Now Linda thinks she has it. Johnny Case is at Lake Placid. Most natural place in the world for him to go. A minute more and she has set long distance tracing him. . . .

Nick and Susan are sailing at midnight. Before they go they are rather plainly anxious to get the thought across to Linda that there are other girls, and one girl in particular, who might be a lot better for Johnny Case than Julia Seton could ever be, seeing how divergent are their views of life. Susan is certain Linda is in love with Johnny—

The answer from the Placid Club is in. . . . Mr. Case had been there but had left on the noon train for New York.

Now Nick has confessed. Johnny is not only in New York right then, but he has engaged a single stateroom on the steamer on which the Potters are sailing. Nick had bought it for him. Johnny is going to Europe alone.

Linda is surprised, but also confident that if Johnny is in town he will be at the house before he sails. She is also confident that Johnny and Julia are still deeply in love with each other, and that once they are married Johnny will be able to adjust all their differences, even including the management of father. What she can't understand is Julia's stubbornness and her arrant shortsightedness. Some way Linda feels that she must make Julia listen to her; that Julia must be made to realize that men like Johnny Case do not grow on every bush.

"But you see," Susan explains, "the things you like in him are just what she can't stand, Linda. And the fate you say he'll save her from is the one fate in this whole world she wants."

"I don't believe it. Even so, she loves him—and there's been a break. Wouldn't you think she'd be woman enough to hang on—*hang on!*"

"I don't know," Susan answers, significantly. "There's another who isn't woman enough to grab."

"I don't quite get you, Susan."

"Well, to make it plain, no man's lost this side of the altar."

Slowly Linda answers her. "Julia has never loved anybody in her life but Johnny—and me," she says. It is rotten of them to suspect—

Nick and Susan are duly sorry. Linda is on the verge of tears. Then Julia comes. She is apparently quite unconscious of any worry. She is glad to see the Potters, sorry they won't be home for the wedding, which she expects will take place in the spring, or earlier, and hopes they will have a lovely trip.

She is, however, visibly startled by their report of Johnny Case's sailing. She doesn't believe that. Certainly if he had planned any such trip he would have let her know.

The Potters gone, Linda tries to arouse Julia's interest in the possibility of Johnny's going. If she doesn't want him to sail and make hash of both their lives she had better send some word to the boat. Julia doesn't purpose doing anything of the kind. Furthermore she is not greatly interested. When Linda accuses her of deliberately shutting her out of her confidences of late Julia is also at pains to deny that accusation.

JULIA—If there's been any shutting out done, it's you who've done it, Linda.

LINDA—Me?

JULIA—Johnny and I have had a difference of opinion, and you're siding with him, aren't you?

LINDA—But he's right! He's right for you as well as for himself—

JULIA—I think that's for me to decide.

LINDA—Not father?

JULIA—Father has nothing to do with it—

LINDA—Oh, no!

JULIA—He happens to agree with me where you don't, that's all.

LINDA—We've always agreed before—always.

JULIA—No—I think quite often I've given in, in order to avoid scenes and upsets and—oh, well—

LINDA—Is that true, Julia?

JULIA—You've always been the "stronger character," haven't you? At least people have always thought so. You've made all the decisions—you've always had the ideas—

LINDA—And you've been resenting me right from the very—(*She turns away*)—Oh—I can't believe it.

JULIA—It's nothing to get in a state about, and I didn't say I resented you. You've been an immense help, often. But when it comes to determining my future, and the future of the man I'm going to marry—

LINDA (*turning on her sharply*)—Your future! What do you want, Julia—just security? Sit back in your feather-boa among the Worthies of the World?

JULIA—Well, I'm certain that one thing I *don't* want is to start this endless, aimless discussion all over again.

LINDA—But I tell you, you can't stand this sort of life forever, not if you're the person I think you are, and when it starts going thin on you, what'll you have to hold on to? Lois Evans shot herself, why? Fanny Grant's up the Hudson in a Sanatorium—why?

JULIA—I'm sure I don't know.

LINDA—Nothing left to do or have or want—that's why—and no insides! There's not a poor girl in town who isn't happier than we are—at least they still want what we've got—*they* think it's good. (*She turns away.*)—If they knew!

JULIA—And I think it's good.

LINDA—Lord, Julia, don't tell me that you *want* it!

JULIA—I want it, and it's all I want.

LINDA—Then it's good-bye, Julia.

JULIA—Oh, Linda, for heaven's sake don't be so ridiculous. If you're so damn set on being violent, get a few Russians in and talk Life with a great big L to them.

Edward Seton enters the room in time to hear the last of the quarrel and is gently chiding. Quite as calm in his confidence, too, as Julia. He does not, he assures Linda, think that Johnny is a fortune-hunter. Merely a strong-willed young man who has become momentarily confused in his outlook—particularly his outlook toward work—an attitude in general that appeals to Mr. Seton as being quite un-American.

LINDA—Then he's a bad one and will go to hell when he dies. Because apparently he can't quite believe that a life devoted to piling up money is all it's cracked up to be. That's strange, isn't it—when he has us, right before his eyes, for such a shining example.

JULIA—I thought you were the one who found leisure so empty.

LINDA—And so it may be for him—yes—maybe it will! But he's got a right to discover that for himself. Can't you see that?

JULIA—I can see the discovery would come, quick enough.

LINDA—And you don't want to be with him to lend a hand, if it should? (JULIA *is silent.*)

EDWARD—Linda, I listened most attentively to our young dreamer the other day. I have listened quite as attentively to you this evening. I am not entirely without intelligence, but I must still confess that most of your talk seems to me to be of the seventeen-year-old variety.

LINDA—I'm glad if it is! We are all grand at seventeen. It's after that that the—sickness sets in.

EDWARD (*chuckling*)—I feel very well, myself—and you look in perfect health, my dear.

LINDA—You both think he'll come around, Father. Compromise, anyway. You'll get fooled. He won't give way one little inch.

EDWARD (*at the door*)—Stubborn—?

LINDA—Right! And sure he's right!

EDWARD—We shall see—(*He goes out, victor.*)

JULIA—Is that all, Linda?

LINDA—Where are you going?

JULIA—To bed.

LINDA—Now?

JULIA—Yes. Have you any objections?

LINDA—You actually won't lift a finger to keep him off that boat to-night?

JULIA—He has no idea of taking it.

LINDA—You don't know him!

JULIA—Well, I think I know him a little better than you. I happen to be engaged to him.

Ned is home early from the theatre. He didn't like it and he left. He likes his drinks better. Ned would comfort Linda if he could. He doesn't see any reason she shouldn't love Johnny Case if she wants to.

Both she and Ned are in a jam as Linda sees it, and they've both got to work out. Ned can't go on drinking his life away just because he is disgusted. After the wedding they'll go out to Colorado and live naturally for awhile. That will bring them back to normal and clear their minds.

Ned is not so sure that he wants to go anywhere. He is pretty well through and doesn't care. But he is keen that Linda should go on. Eager that she should not try to forget Johnny Case if she doesn't want to forget him.

"Are you so sure you *want* to get over him?" he demands.

"No, I'm not," confesses Linda. "And that's what scares me most. I feel alive, and I love it. I feel at last something's happening to me. But it can't get anywhere so it's like living on—*your* stuff. I've *got* to get over it."

"Because it seems so hopeless, is that it?"

"Seems! What do you mean?"

"Don't you know? Then let me tell you something: you're twice as attractive as Julia ever thought of being. You've got twice the looks, and twice the mind and ten times the guts. You've lived in her shade for years, now, and there's nothing to it. You could charm a bird off a tree, if you would. And why not? If you were in her way, she'd ride you down like a rabbit."

Linda is furious, or tries to be, that Ned should think such things knowing, as he must, how much Julia loves Johnny. And then the butler announces Mr. Case.

Johnny has come prepared to make a compromise. He still loves Julia. Nothing else seems important. Linda can understand that. Someway the fun seems to have gone out of him, out of his voice, but she understands.

JOHNNY—Linda—*you* agree that there's only the one thing for me to do now?

LINDA (*smiling*)—Compromise—

JOHNNY—Yes, damn it! But *you* think that's right, don't you?

LINDA—I don't think it matters a bit what I think—(JOHNNY *goes to her suddenly and seizes her wrists.*)

JOHNNY—It does, though! You think it's right, don't you? Say you think it's right!

LINDA—Shall I send for Julia?

JOHNNY—Say it first!

LINDA—Johnny—when two people love each other as much as you say, anything that keeps them apart must be wrong. Will that do? (JOHNNY *throws her hands down and moves away from her.*) And shall I send for her now?

JOHNNY (*almost inaudibly*)—Go ahead. (LINDA *presses a button in the box behind the telephone.*)

LINDA—With luck, we'll manage not to include Father this time.

JOHNNY—Oh, God, yes! (LINDA *again presses the button, and again several times.*) Asleep, probably.

LINDA—Of course not. (*She presses it again. Then:*) Julia—yes—would you come down a minute? No—but there's no telegram to send up! Will you come, Julia? (*Her voice changes.*) Julia, it's terribly important that you come down here at once. (*She replaces the telephone and turns to* JOHNNY.) She'll be right down.

JOHNNY—If she doesn't fall asleep again.

LINDA—Johnny—don't talk like that. I can't stand to hear your voice do that.

JOHNNY—You care more what happens to me than she does.

LINDA (*startled*)—What? Don't be silly. (*Then with difficulty.*) Maybe I feel things about you that she doesn't because —well, maybe just because I'm not in love with you.

JOHNNY—You know what I think of you, don't you?

LINDA (*smiling*)—I'd be glad to hear.

JOHNNY—I like you better than any one else in the world.

LINDA—That's very nice, Johnny—because I like you a good deal, too.

Edward Seton is home. Beams as he meets Johnny. Confident that all will be well. It is Linda's idea that they should all clear out when Julia comes, or before. It is Johnny's idea that Julia, who is there now, should get on her wraps and that they should go out. But it is Edward Seton's idea that they should stay and hear what he has to say to them. He has no idea of coming between two young people in love. Certainly true love is a very rare and beautiful thing. But—

Johnny is prepared to agree to almost anything. He will, if they like, take the position with Pritchard-Ames. For a year or so at least. He still is convinced it is not the thing for him to do, but if Julia wants it—he'll try it for, say, three years.

Now it is arranged that the wedding shall be immediately announced. It can take place any time Mr. Seton agrees, after the invitations have been out ten days, and the newlyweds can sail the end of the same week.

It will be well, Mr. Seton also thinks, to arrange the honeymoon a bit in advance. He will help them plan it. He knows some very good and influential people both in London and Paris he shall want them to visit. And there is no reason, of course, why they should not combine a little business with pleasure, even if Johnny was of the opinion his wedding trip was going to be more of a lark than a business trip.

When they get back father will see that their home is ready for them in Sixty-fourth street—a sweet place he is prepared to lend them. He has also decided to turn the Poplars over to them for the summer. A cute little place, the Poplars, Ned agrees. Hasn't even got a ballroom.

"This is not a deed of gift, you know," Edward warns them. "Not yet. Perhaps when you have occupied them—er—five years or so, my hard old heart may soften."

"Listen to him—*his* hard old heart," laughs Julia, turning happily to Johnny. "Have you ever known any one so sweet?"

JOHNNY (*after a moment*)—Julia—I'm sorry—but I can't stand it.

JULIA (*after a pause*)—Would you—mind telling me what you mean?

JOHNNY—If we begin loaded down with possessions, obligations, responsibilities, how do we ever get out from under them? We never would.

EDWARD—Ah?

JOHNNY—No. You're extremely generous—and kind—but it's not for me.

EDWARD—And may I ask what *is* for you?

JOHNNY—I don't know yet, but I do know it's not this.

EDWARD (*very quietly*)—We are to understand, then, you are *not* returning to work?

JOHNNY—That work? For this?—No.

JULIA—But you said!—

JOHNNY—I'm back where I was, now. I can see now that it's got to be a clean break, it's simply got to be.

EDWARD (*softly*)—But the other day, if I remember correctly, you intimated that you might follow some occupation—

JOHNNY—Eventually, yes. I think I may still be fairly active at thirty-five or forty.

EDWARD—And in the meantime you expect just to lie fallow, is that it?

JOHNNY—Not lie—be! I expect to dig and plow and water for all I'm worth.

EDWARD—Toward the—er—eventual occupation which is to overtake you—

JOHNNY—Exactly.

EDWARD—I see.—Julia, if you marry this young man now, I doubt if he will ever again earn a penny.

JOHNNY—Julia, if it's important to you, I'll promise you I shall earn my own living. And what's more, if there's need of it, I'll always earn yours.

JULIA—Thanks.

JOHNNY—Oh, my dear, we've got to make our own life—there's nothing to it, if we don't—there's no other way to live it. Let's forget wedding invitations and two weeks from Wednesday. Let's go now. The Captain will marry us.

JULIA—I must decide now, must I?

JOHNNY—Please—

JULIA—And if I say No—not unless you—?

JOHNNY—Then I'm going to-night, by myself.

JULIA—Very well—you can go. Because I don't quite see myself with an idler for a husband.

JOHNNY (*after a pause*)—I suppose the fact is, I love feeling free inside even better than I love you, Julia.

JULIA—Apparently—or what you call feeling free.

JOHNNY (*turns to* EDWARD)—Good-bye, sir, I'm sorry we couldn't make a go of it. Thanks for trying anyhow. (*Goes to* LINDA *and takes both her hands. Behind table left.*) Good-bye to you, Linda. You've been sweet.

LINDA—Good-bye, Johnny. So have you.—I hope you find what you're looking for.

JOHNNY—I hope *you* do.

LINDA—You did want some one along with you on the big search, didn't you?

JOHNNY—I did, you know.

LINDA—Poor boy.

JOHNNY—But we won't mind, will we?

LINDA—Hell, no—*we* won't mind.

JOHNNY—We'll get there—

LINDA—Sure. *We'll* get there! (JOHNNY *tightens his grasp on her hands.*)

JOHNNY—Linda—(*She leans toward him.*)

LINDA—Oh, please do—(JOHNNY *bends, kisses her briefly.*)

JOHNNY—Good-bye, Ned (*He goes out.*)

LINDA (*a murmur*)—I'll miss that man.

Johnny's departure leaves Julia and her father a little stunned, but they quickly recover. Edward Seton is more pleased than otherwise and even Julia admits a sense of relief. She has no time to waste persuading "a lightweight like him that there's something more to life than having fun and more fun."

Suddenly Linda is by her sister's side, grasping her by the arm, and shouting a little excitedly:

JULIA—What's the matter with you?

LINDA—You don't love him.

JULIA—Will you kindly let go my arm?

LINDA—You don't love him!

JULIA—Will you please—

LINDA—Answer me! Do you or do you not?

JULIA—And what's that to you, may I ask?

EDWARD—Now, children—

LINDA—What's it to me! Oh, what's it to me! (*Her grasp tightens on* JULIA's *arm.*) Answer me!

JULIA—Father—what's the matter with her?

LINDA—You don't, do you? I can *see* you don't. It's written all over you. You're *relieved* he's gone—relieved.

JULIA—And suppose I am?

LINDA (*to* NED)—She asks me to suppose she is! *She confronts* JULIA.) Are you? Say it!

JULIA—I'm so relieved, I could sing with it. Is that what you want?

LINDA—Yes! Thanks—(*She throws back her head and laughs with joy*)—Oh, Lordy, Lordy—have I got a job now!

From her handbag Linda fishes two brown envelopes and passes one to Ned. They are passports. Is he ready to go with her—now—to-night! Ned's afraid he couldn't. Linda doesn't hear her father, doesn't mind Julia. She sees only Ned. Will he go with her? Ned wavers but hasn't the courage. He's caught! He will have to stick. Then, promises Linda, she will be back for him.

Now the maid is in to tell her that the Potters are waiting below. Her week-end bag is in their car. She will take her fur coat and throw a couple of hats in a box and be ready. Then she turns to Julia.

LINDA—You've got no faith in Johnny, have you, Julia? His little dream may fall flat, you think—yes! So it may! What about it? What if it should? There'll be another—the point is, he *does* dream! Oh, I've got all the faith in the world in Johnny! Whatever he does is all right with me. If he wants to sit on his tail, he can sit on his tail. If he wants to come back and sell peanuts, Lord, how I'll believe in those peanuts! (*She kisses her briefly.*) Good-bye, Julia. (*Turns to her father.*) Good-bye, Father. (*And goes to* NED.) Good-bye, Neddy—

NED—Good-bye, kid—good-luck—(*For a moment they cling together.*)

LINDA—Oh, never you fear, I'll be back for you, you fine bucko!

NED—All right, kid. (*She moves toward the door.* NED *is drawn after her.*)

EDWARD—As yet you have not said where it is you are—

JULIA—I know.

LINDA—And try to stop me, some one! Oh, please—some one try to stop me! (*She goes out.*) (NED *closes the door after her and stands against it, head down, murmuring:*)

NED—Oh, God—oh, God—

EDWARD—I shall not permit it. I shall—

NED—Permit it, permit Linda? Don't make me laugh, Father.

JULIA—She's going *with* them, isn't she? *Isn't* she?

NED (smiling)—Going to get her Johnny.

JULIA (*laughing*)—A fine chance she's got!

NED—Any bets? (*Then savagely.*) Any bets, Julia? (*He raises glass for a toast.*) To Linda! (*Sees the picture of Grandfather.*) And while we're at it, Grandfather—

The curtain falls.

THE FRONT PAGE

A Drama in Three Acts

By Ben Hecht and Charles MacArthur

THE first hit of this particular theatre season, scored in mid-August, was that of a newspaper melodrama called "The Front Page." The hit came as something of a surprise—especially to newspaper men.

There have been from time to time other newspaper plays produced, but few of them have ever attained anything like a paying popularity. Usually objection revolves about their being too freely technical to achieve a convincing actuality. The newspaper men who write them live their stories over with a vivid personal interest, yet seem unable to inspire an understanding interest on the part of their audiences. Their romances and their plots, insists John Average Citizen, are purely artificial and their conclusions highly implausible.

It may be the Messrs. Ben Hecht and Charles MacArthur carried these objections in mind when they wrote "The Front Page" and were determined to produce at least one newspaper drama that should be real.

They would have no traffic with the "What the heck!" school of lip-pursed profaners, nor even with the "Jeez" or impersonal "goddam" boys. They would speak the language as it was spoken to them when they were newspaper men. Let press, public and producer decide whether or not they were justified.

A majority of the play's reviewers were enthusiastic. Here, they severally shouted the morning and afternoon following the play's production on August 14,—here was the first real newspaper drama they had ever seen!

The public, too, for several months thereafter endorsed this enthusiasm. Playgoers to whom the coarser profanities were still something of a shock when spoken in a playhouse took "The Front Page" blows with a smile. Even those newspaper men who insisted that in so and so many years of service they never had met so rough and tough a crew of reporters were willing to admit the Hecht-MacArthur drama was atmospherically veracious and emotionally exciting. Thus the verdict was permitted to stand. Acceptance or rejection of the drama thereafter became largely a matter of individual taste and cultural standards.

Being one of the audience at a performance of "The Front Page" you find yourself looking into the press room of the Criminal Courts building in Chicago, "a chamber set aside by the City Fathers for the use of journalists and their friends."

"It is," state the authors, "a bare, disordered room peopled by newspaper men in need of shaves, pants pressing and small change. Hither reporters are drawn by an irresistible lure—the privilege of telephoning free."

Seven telephones connect the press room with the seven newspapers of Chicago. The place is sparsely furnished with a couple of tables and an assortment of chairs.

"There is one elegant item, however," reads the description; "A huge, ornate, black walnut desk, the former property of Mayor Fred. A. Busse, deceased about 1904." . . . "The walls, unpainted since the building was erected in 1885, sport a frieze of lithographs, hand painted studies, rotogravure cuttings and heroic pencil sketches, all on the same theme: Woman."

There is a door letting into a room labelled "Gents," and double doors at back opening into the main corridor. There are tall windows at the side of the room looking down upon the Cook County jail.

"It is 8.30 in the evening. Four men are playing poker at the main table in the center of the room. They are Murphy of the *Journal,* Endicott of the *Post,* Schwartz of the *News* and Wilson of the *American;* four braves known to their kind as police reporters. Katatonic, seedy Paul Reveres, full of strange oaths and a touch of childhood."

Ernie Kruger of the *Journal of Commerce,* being gifted beyond his comrades, sits detached from the group playing a banjo and singing, more or less dreamily, "By the Light of the Silvery Moon."

At the ornate desk, previously mentioned, now the property of Roy Benzinger, chief feature writer of the *Tribune,* McCue of the *City News* is telephoning all the police stations, hospitals, etc., on behalf of his companions in a never-ending quest for news. "His reiterations, whined in a manner intended to be ingratiating, have in them the monotonous bally-hoo wail of the press."

The card players talk through the whining of McCue and the one-man concert of Kruger, pausing occasionally to voice in picturesque profanity their irritation at being disturbed. Now and again, with their news ears cocked, they pause long enough to catch the drift of what McCue is getting over the phone, as, they do, for instance, when he succeeds in raising Mrs. Margolies.

McCue (*into phone*)—Is this the home of Mrs. F. D. Margolies?

Murphy—I'd like a deck with some aces in it.

McCue (*cordially, into phone*)—This is Mr. McCue of the *City News* Bureau. . . . Is it true, Madame, that you were the victim of a Peeping Tom?

Kruger—Ask her if she's worth peeping at.

Wilson—Has she got a friend?

McCue (*into phone*)—Now, that ain't the right attitude to take, Madame. All we want is the facts. . . . Well, what did this Peeping Tom look like? I mean, for instance, would you say he looked like a college professor?

Endicott—Tell her I can run up for an hour.

Kruger—I'll accommodate her if she'll come down here.

Schwartz—By me.

McCue (*into phone*)—Just a minute, Madame. Is it true, Mrs. Margolies, that you took the part of Pocahontas in the Elks' Pageant seven years ago? . . . Hello. (*To the others.*) She hung up.

Murphy—The hell with her! A dime. (*The fire-alarm box, over the door, begins to ring.*)

Endicott—Where's the fire?

Wilson—Three-two-one!

Schwartz—Clark and Erie.

Kruger (*wearily as he strums*)—Too far.

McCue (*into phone*)—Harrison four thousand.

Schwartz (*rises; stretching; ambles over and looks out the window*)—Oh, Christ!—what time is it, anyway?

Wilson—Half past eight. (*Rises; goes to the water cooler.*)

Murphy (*drawing cards*)—One off the top.

Wilson—How's the wife, Ed? Any better?

Schwartz—Worse.

Wilson—That's tough.

Schwartz—Sitting here all night, waiting for 'em to hang this bastard! (*A gesture toward the jail.*)

Kruger—It's hard work, all right.

McCue (*into phone*)—Hello, Sarge? McCue. Anything doing? . . . Yeah? That's swell. . . . (*The players pause.*) A love triangle, huh? . . . Did he kill her? . . . Killed 'em both!

Ah! . . . Was she good looking? . . . (*A pause. With vast disgust.*) What? Oh, niggers! (*The players relax.*)

KRUGER—That's a break.

MCCUE (*in phone*)—No, never mind—thank you, Sarge.

There is some mystery, it appears, surrounding the failure of Hildy Johnson of the *Examiner* to show up for this particular vigil. Frequently the phone rings and the call is from Walter Burns, Johnson's managing editor. Burns is evidently keenly restive about getting in touch with his reporter.

Schwartz of the *News* has the dope, if any care to know what has happened to Johnson. Hildy's quit! More than that, believe it or not, he's quit to get married, Burns or no Burns. . . .

The poker game goes on; the telephoning goes on; the harmonizing of Kruger continues spasmodically. . . . Bensinger of the *Tribune* arrives—"a studious and slightly neurotic fellow who stands out like a sore thumb owing to his tidy appearance." Bensinger also tries to recover his desk, but his success is in no way satisfying. His conferees are inclined to hoot and make other noises at him when he protests that he has tried to keep his desk and his telephone clean and shall demand that they respect his property. He is tired of finding their dirty underclothing and parts of their discarded lunches parked in the lower drawers of his property.

Bensinger has been trying to see the sheriff, he admits, but he is not inclined to give up the news he got, if any. Let these others get their own news.

Mrs. Herman Schlosser is in looking for Herman. She can't find him. Nor does she get much help from any of "these bravos of the press." Herman may be here, he may be there. He may still be drinking. He may be broke or he may be in funds. Nobody knows.

"He can't come home," bitterly announces Mrs. Schlosser. "I kept dinner waiting till 11 o'clock last night and he never even called up. . . . You know where he is! You're covering up for him!"

MCCUE—Honest to God, Mrs. Schlosser—

ENDICOTT (*into phone*)—No. Mr. Burns, Hildy ain't showed up yet.

MRS. SCHLOSSER—Is that Walter Burns? Let me talk to him!

ENDICOTT (*into phone*)—Just a minute, Mr. Burns. Herman Schlosser's wife wants to talk to you.

MRS. SCHLOSSER (*taking the phone; honeyed and polite*)—Hello, Mr. Burns.

MURPHY—Come on—who opened?

ENDICOTT—Check it.

MURPHY—A dime.

MRS. SCHLOSSER—This is Mrs. Schlosser. . . . Oh, I'm very well, thank you . . . Mr. Burns, I was just wondering if you knew where Herman was. He didn't come home last night, and you know it was pay day . . . (*tearfully*). But it won't be all right. I'm just going crazy. . . . I've done that, but the cashier won't give it to me . . . So I thought maybe if you gave me some sort of order—oh, will you, Mr. Burns? That's awfully nice of you . . . I'm sorry to have to do a thing like that, but you know how Herman is about money. Thank you ever so much. (*Hangs up; turns to the reporters viciously.*) You're all alike, every one of you! You ought to be ashamed of yourselves!

MURPHY—All right, we're ashamed. (*To* WILSON)—A dime's bet.

MRS. SCHLOSSER—Sitting around like a lot of dirty, drunken tramps! Poker! (*She grabs* MURPHY's *cards.*)

MURPHY (*leaping up in fury*)—Here! Gimme those! What the hell!

MRS. SCHLOSSER—You know where he is, and I'm going to stay right here till I find out!

MURPHY—He's at Hockstetter's, that's where he is! Now give me those cards!

MRS. SCHLOSSER—Where?

WILSON—The Turkish Bath on Madison Street.

ENDICOTT—In the basement!

MURPHY—Give me those!

MRS. SCHLOSSER—So! You did know. (MURPHY *nervously awaits his cards.*) Liars! (*She throws the cards face up on the table.*)

MURPHY (*as she throws them*)—Hey! (*They spread out on the table.*)

MRS. SCHLOSSER—You're a bunch of gentlemen, I must say! Newspaper men! Bums! (*Exits.*)

MURPHY (*almost in tears*)—Look! The second straight flush I ever held.

ENDICOTT—Jesus.

MURPHY—Eight, nine, ten, jack, and queen of spades. If I was married to that dame I'd kick her humpbacked.

"I don't know what gets into women," ruminates Endicott, as Mrs. Schlosser disappears. "I took Bob Brody home the other night and his wife broke his arm with a broom." . . .

Bensinger has cleaned his desk with a rag and a bottle of antiseptic and phoned in a new lead for his story. He has seen the sheriff, he reports to his office, and that official refuses to move the hanging up a minute. The execution is set for 7 and the sheriff will hold to that hour, no matter if it does mean the morning papers can't make their city editions.

"He gives a damn if we stay up all night!" sneers Kruger.

"You've got no kick coming," protests Endicott. "I've had two dinners home in the last month."

BENSINGER (*into phone*)—Hello, Jake? . . . New lead on the Williams' hanging. And listen—don't put Hartman's name in it. Just say "The Sheriff." (*The reporters listen.*) Ready? . . . The condemned man ate a hearty dinner . . . Yeah, mock turtle soup, chicken pot pie, hashed brown potatoes, combination salad, and pie à la mode.

KRUGER—Make mine the same.

BENSINGER (*into phone*)—No—I don't know what kind of pie.

MURPHY—Eskimo!

McCUE (*wistfully*)—I wish I had a hamburger sandwich.

BENSINGER (*into phone*)—And, Jake, get this in as a big favor. The whole dinner was furnished by Charlie Apfel. . . . Yeah—Apfel. A for adenoids, P for psychology, F for Frank, E for Eddie, and L for—ah—

MURPHY—Lay an egg.

BENSINGER—Proprietor of the Apfel—wants—to—see—you—restaurant.

WILSON—That means a new hat for somebody. (*A soft cadenza from the banjo.*)

MURPHY—I better catch the fudge, fellas. (*Without dropping his cards,* MURPHY *picks up a telephone. He pantomimes for three cards.*)

BENSINGER (*into phone*)—Now here's the situation on the eve of the hanging. The officials are prepared for a general uprising of radicals at the hour of execution, but the Sheriff still refuses to be intimidated by the Red menace.

MURPHY (*into his phone, while accepting three cards*)—Give me a rewrite man, will you? . . . Yeah. Some more crap on the Earl Williams hanging.

BENSINGER (*into phone, as the reporters listen*)—A double guard has just been thrown around the jail, the municipal buildings, railroad terminals, and elevated stations. Also, the Sheriff has just received four more letters threatening his life. He is going to answer these threats by a series of raids against the Friends of American Liberty and other Bolshevik organizations. Call you later. (*Hangs up.*)

SCHWARTZ—Bet a dime.

MURPHY (*into phone*)—Ready? . . . Sheriff Hartman has just put two hundred more relatives on the payroll to protect the city against the Red army, which is leaving Moscow in a couple of minutes. (*Consults his hand.*) Up a dime. (*Back to phone.*) And to prove to the voters that the Red menace is on the square, he has just wrote himself four more letters threatening his life. I know he wrote them on account of the misspelling.

ENDICOTT—Drop.

MURPHY (*into phone*)—That's all, except the doomed man ate a hearty dinner. As follows: Noodle soup, rustabiff, sweet a-potat', cranberry sauce, and pie-à-la-Mud.

SCHWARTZ—I raise another dime.

MURPHY (*consults his cards*)—Wait a minute. Up again. (*Back to phone.*) Statement from who? The Sheriff? . . . Quote him for anything you want—he can't read. (*Hangs up.* BENSINGER'S *phone rings.*)

THE CARD PLAYERS—Call. . . . Three bullets. . . . Pay at this window . . . Shuffle that deck. . . . I get the same hand every time.

BENSINGER (*answering his phone*)—What? (*To* MCCUE, *as* SCHWARTZ *starts to shuffle.*) Didn't you send that in about the new alienist?

MCCUE (*flat on his back on the smaller table*)—I got my hands full with the stations.

BENSINGER (*into phone*)—All right, I'll give you what I got. Dr. Max J. Eglehofer. From Vienna. There's a dozen envelopes on him in the morgue. . . . Well, he's going to examine Williams at the request of—ah—wait a minute—(*shuffles through his notes*)—the United Federation for World Betterment.

KRUGER—I'm for that.

BENSINGER—Sure. He's one of the biggest alienists in the world. He's the author of that book, "The Personality Gland."

MCCUE—And where to put it.

BENSINGER (*modestly into phone*)—He just autographed it for me.

MURPHY—Did he bite his initials in your pants, too? . . . Nickel.

KRUGER (*into phone lazily*)—Give me the City Desk!

BENSINGER (*into phone*)—All right. He's going to examine him in about fifteen minutes. I'll let you know. (*He hangs up and resumes his study of "The Personality Gland."*)

Outside, from the direction of the jail, there is a whirr and a crash. The jailers are testing the gallows with sandbags. . . .

A call from Hildy Johnson in the Mayor's office locates that missing scribe. Hildy is, he reports, kissing the Mayor good-by and also (MCCUE *adds as he takes the message*) Hildy "is stinko!" He's coming over to the press room presently. Perhaps he'll kiss them good-by, too. . . .

Woodenshoes Eichorn, "a big, moon-faced, childish and incompetent German policeman," has brought the boys his theory that the man who is about to be hung is a dual personality on account of the shape of his head, but no one seems to care.

"I thought you fellas might be interested in the psychological end of it," persists the disappointed Woodenshoes. "None of the papers have touched that aspect."

"Listen, Woodenshoes," answers Murphy, "this guy Williams is just a bird that had the tough luck to kill a nigger policeman in a town where the nigger vote is important."

"Sure! If he'd bumped him off down south they'd have given him a banquet and a trip to Europe."

"Oh, the South ain't so bad," protested McCue. "How about Russia, where they kill all the Jews and nobody says anything?"

"Williams was a bonanza for the City Hall," continues Murphy. "He gets hung—everybody gets elected on a law and order ticket."

"Reform the Reds with a Rope."

"When that baby drops through the trap to-morrow it's a million votes." . . .

When Hildy Johnson breezes in he is discovered to be "a happy-go-lucky Swede with a pants-kicking sense of humor. He is barbered and tailored like a normal citizen—a fact which at once excites the wonder and mirth of his colleagues. Hildy is of a vanishing type—the lusty, hoodlumesque, half drunken caballero that was the newspaper man of our youth. Schools of journalism and the advertising business have nearly extirpated the species. Now and then one of these boys still pops up in the profession and is hailed by his editor as a survival of a golden age. The newspaper men who have already appeared in this press room are in reality similar survivals. Their presence under one roof is due to the fact that Chicago is a sort of journalistic Yellowstone Park offering haven to a last herd of fantastic bravos that once roamed the newspaper offices of the country. Mr. Johnson carries a new suitcase, two paper parcels and—a cane!"

It is a rowdy reception the reporters give Hildy. He has never, in all history, appeared before them before with a shave, a crease in his pants—and a cane! It is almost too much!

Hildy is happy and free. He would sing, if they would give him a chance, that stirring melody, "Good-bye, forever—" but they are not interested in his song. They would have him talk to Walter Burns on the phone instead. Walter has just called for the nine millionth time. They're tired of answering the phone and stalling for Hildy. Is he scared or something? Hildy Johnson scared? He takes the phone from McCue.

HILDY—I'll talk to that maniac—with pleasure. (*Into phone, with mock formality*): Hello, Mr. Burns. . . . What's that, Mr. Burns? . . . Why your language is shocking, Mr. Burns. . . . Now, listen, you lousy baboon. Get a pencil and paper and take this down: Get this straight because this is important. It's the Hildy Johnson curse. The next time I see you—no matter where I am or what I'm doing—I'm going to walk right up to you and hammer on that monkey skull of yours until it rings like a Chinese gong. . . .

McCUE—Oh, boy!

ENDICOTT—That's telling him!

HILDY (*holding sizzling receiver to the nearest reporter*)—Listen to him! (*Into phone.*) No, I ain't going to cover the hanging! I wouldn't cover the last supper for you! Not if they held it all over again in the middle of Clark street. . . . Never mind the vaseline, Jocko! It won't do you any good this time! Because I'm going to New York like I told you, and if you know what's good for you you'll stay West of Gary, Indiana! A Johnson never forgets! (*He hangs up.*) And that, boys, is what is known as telling the managing editor. (*The reporters agree loudly.*)

BENSINGER—Can't you guys talk without yelling?

HILDY (*his song rising again*)—"Good-bye, Forever!"

VOICE (*from jail yard*)—Hey, cut the yodeling! Where do you think you are!

HILDY (*moving toward window, takes out his pocket flask*)—Jacobi! Pickle-nose! (*He takes a final drink from the flask, then aims and throws it out the window.. A scream of rage rises from the jail yard.* HILDY *smiles and salutes his victim.*) On the button! (*Turns to* ERNIE, *resumes his song.*)

BENSINGER (*pleading*)—Oh! shut up.

WILSON—What did you quit for, Hildy?

SCHWARTZ—We hear you are going to get married?

HILDY—I'm getting married, all right. (*Shows tickets.*) See that? Three tickets to New York! Eleven-eighteen to-night!

WILSON—To-night!

MCCUE—Jesus, that's quick!

MURPHY—What do you mean three?

HILDY—Me and my girl and her goddam ma!

ENDICOTT—Kinda sudden, ain't it?

SCHWARTZ—What the hell do you want to get married for?

HILDY—None of your business!

MURPHY—Ooooh! He's in love! Tootsie-wootsie!

MCCUE—Is she a white girl?

ENDICOTT—Has she got a good shape?

WILSON—Does Walter know you're getting married?

HILDY—Does he know I'm getting married? He congratulated me! Shook hands like a pal! Offered to throw me a farewell dinner even.

ENDICOTT—That's his favorite joke—farewell dinners.

MURPHY—He poisons people at them.

HILDY—He gets me up to Polack Mike's—fills me full of rotgut— I'd have been there yet if it hadn't been for the fire escape!

SCHWARTZ—That's what he done to the Chief of Police!

HILDY—Can you imagine? Trying to bust up my marriage! After shaking hands! . . . (*Anxiously.*) Say, my girl didn't call up, did she, or come in looking for me? What time is it, anyway?

SCHWARTZ—Quarter past nine.

MCCUE—Eighteen minutes after.

HILDY (*starting to take off his coat*)—I got to be at this house at seven.

ENDICOTT—What house?

HILDY—Somebody giving a farewell party to my girl.

WILSON—At seven to-night?

HILDY—Yeah.

MURPHY—You got to run like hell.

HILDY—Oh, that's all right. Fellow doesn't quit a job every day. Especially when it's Walter Burns. The lousy baboon.

ENDICOTT—When's the wedding, Hildy?

HILDY—It's in New York, so you guys ain't going to have any fun with it. None of them fake warrants or kidnapping the bride, with me! (HILDY *folds his old shirt and puts it in* BENSINGER'S *drawer.*)

BENSINGER—Aw, for God's sake! Cut that out! (*Throws the shirt on the floor.*)

WILSON—Everybody's getting this New York bug. It's just a rube town for mine.

SCHWARTZ—I was on a New York paper once—the *Times.* You might as well work in a bank.

MURPHY—I hear all the reporters in New York are lizzies.

MCCUE—Remember that fellow from the New York *World?*

ENDICOTT—With the derby?

MURPHY (*presumably mimicking a New York journalist*)—Could you please instruct me where the telegraph office is? (*Makes a rude noise.*) You'll be talking like that, Hildy.

HILDY—Yeah?

ENDICOTT—Which one of them sissy journals are you going to work for?

HILDY—None of them! Who the hell wants to work on a newspaper? A lot of crumby hoboes, full of dandruff and bum gin they wheedle out of a nigger Alderman.

MURPHY—That's what comes of stealing a cane.

ENDICOTT—What are you going in for—the movies?

HILDY—I am not. Advertising business. One hundred and fifty smackers a week.

MCCUE—Yeah?

ENDICOTT—One hundred and fifty what?

SCHWARTZ (*a sneer*)—A hundred and fifty?

HILDY—Here's the contract. (*Hands it to* MCCUE, *who starts to look through it. They crowd around this remarkable document.*) I was just waiting to get it down in black and white before I walked in and told Walter I was through.

MCCUE (*with contract*)—Jesus, it is a hundred and fifty!

Walter Burns is not only sore but positively ungrateful. That's what Hildy calls it. After he (Hildy) had been "sweating his pants off for practically nothing" for ten years to be balled out like a servant girl when he quit! It was enough to make a fellow heat up. But he's quit just the same and he's going to stay quit.

They can laugh at Hildy, but they can't discourage him. He knows what he's getting out of and he knows what he's getting into, and believe him, he's set. Why? Because his girl's uncle owns the business for one thing. And uncle's got so much jack it's choking him. Look what he sent them for a wedding present—five hundred in cash! And there it is, right there in Hildy's pocket—or most of it. It's all there except what the three railroad tickets cost! And he ain't loaning any guy a cent of it, either. Which reminds him that perhaps, now he's going away, he can collect a little? . . . Fat chance! . . .

Jennie, the "slightly idiotic scrubwoman," ready to clean up, receives an ovation. Jennie would get busy with her pail of water and her mop and everybody knows the place smells like a monkeyhouse, but this is a sort of holiday for Hildy Johnson so he won't let Jennie work. To the contrary she is to go with him, all over the building, bidding everybody good-by!

Jennie's protests are giggly and ineffective. Dumping her pail of water out the window onto the gallows workmen below, Hildy grabs the coy matron of the mop and waltzes her grandly out the door, kicking the bucket before them as they go. . . .

Hildy's girl calls up. She's pretty sore. But there is nothing to tell her except that Hildy is on his way! . . .

Mollie Malloy is in. Molly belongs to North Clark street—"cheap black sateen dress, red hat and red slippers run over at the heels. She is a soiled and gaudy houri of the pavement." The boys are rough with Mollie and she as rough with them. She has come to express a grievance. They've been using Mollie in their stories and she's sore. Trying to make out she's the condemned man's affinity!

MOLLIE (*blowing up*)—That's a lie! I met Mr. Williams just once in my life, when he was wandering around in the rain without his hat and coat on like a sick dog. The day before the shooting. And I went up to him like any human being would and I asked what was the matter, and he told me about bein' fired after working at the same place twenty-two years and I brought him up to my room because it was warm there.

ENDICOTT—Did he have the two dollars?

MURPHY—Aw, put it on a Victrola.

MOLLIE—Just because you want to fill your lying papers with

a lot of dirty scandal, you got to crucify him and make a bum out of me!

ENDICOTT—Got a match, Mollie?

MOLLIE (*heedless*)—I tell you he just sat there talkin' to me . . . all night . . . just sat there talkin' to me . . . and never once laid a hand on me! In the morning he went away and I never saw him again till the day at the trial!

ENDICOTT—Tell us what you told the jury! (*They laugh reminiscently.*)

MOLLIE—Go on, laugh! God damn your greasy souls! Sure I was his witness—the only one he had. Yes, me! Mollie Malloy! A Clark street tart! I was the only one with guts enough to stand up for him! And that's why you're persecuting me! Because he treated me decent, and not like an animal, and I said so!

ENDICOTT—Why didn't you adopt him instead of letting him run around shooting policemen?

SCHWARTZ—Suppose that cop had been your own brother?

MOLLIE—I wish to God it had been one of you!

MURPHY (*finally irritated*)—Say, what's the idea of this song and dance, anyhow? This is the press room. We're busy.

SCHWARTZ—Go on home!

MURPHY—Go and see your boy friend, why don't you?

McCUE—Yeah—he's got a nice room.

ENDICOTT (*with a wink at the rest*)—He won't have it long. He's left a call for seven A.M.

MOLLIE (*through her teeth*)—It's a wonder a bolt of lightning don't come through the ceiling and strike you all dead! (*Again the sound of the gallows.*) What's that? Oh, my God! (*She begins to cry.*)

BENSINGER (*rising*)—Say, what's the idea?

MOLLIE—Talking that way about a fellow that's going to die.

ENDICOTT (*uncomfortable at this show of grief*)—Don't get hysterical.

MOLLIE (*sobbing*)—Shame on you! Shame on you!

McCUE (*to the rest*)—It wasn't my fault. I didn't say anything.

MOLLIE (*hysterically*)—A poor little crazy fellow that never did any harm. Sitting there alone this minute, with the Angel of Death beside him, and you cracking jokes.

MURPHY (*getting up meaningly*)—Listen, if you don't shut up, I'll give you something good to cry about!

MOLLIE (*savagely*)—Keep your dirty hands off me!

MURPHY (*in a short and bitter struggle with her*)—Outside, bum!

The entrance of Sheriff Hartman is the signal for another reception, somewhat milder than that accorded Mollie Malloy. The sheriff "is a diabetic and overwrought little fellow, an incompetent fussbudget. He has come to raise hell, but the ovation checks him."

The sheriff wants to know who threw the bucket of water out the window. That's what he wants to know! Who threw out the water and who threw out the bottle? He thinks he knows. He thinks it was Hildy Johnson. Personally he don't give a dam, the sheriff is free to admit, but it don't look right things being thrown out windows thataway. And how must the man in the death house feel about it?

Another thing, there's that name of "Pinky" they been fastening on him. That's got to stop, too. That ain't no name to hang on a man who has the perfectly good name of Peter B. Hartman. "Pinky Hartman! How's that look to the voters? Like I had sore eyes or something," protests the sheriff.

Bensinger repeats his request. It's the last favor he'll ask of Pete Hartman: Will he or will he not hang that guy at 5 o'clock instead of 7 and let them catch their city editions?

"Aw, now, Roy," sincerely protests the Sheriff, "that's kind of raw. You can't hang a fella in his sleep, just to please a newspaper."

"No, but you can reprieve him twice so the hanging'll come three days before election!" charges Murphy. "So you can run on a law and order ticket! You can do that all right!"

The Sheriff disclaims any responsibility for what the Governor may have done in the way of reprieving the prisoner. Neither does he think there will be another reprieve. True, there is to be another examination of Williams by an alienist, but it won't mean anything. The alienist was sent by the Personal Liberty people, a bunch of Bolsheviks, but there isn't anything he will be able to find out that everybody doesn't know. The hanging will come off at 7 per schedule. The Sheriff does not want to be unfriendly with the newspapers, but he does want some co-operation in helping him to crush this Red Menace. . . .

Hildy Johnson is back. He still has Jennie's mop, but he has mislaid Jennie. The Sheriff is moved again to protest. He is tired of the liberties Johnson has taken around there; tired of his thinking that he and Walter Burns are running the town. The

Examiner is going to get a bill for all the damage that has been done in the building in the last year. See how they like that. Furthermore, he (Hildy) can pass the word on to Walter Burns that there will be no tickets for the *Examiner* at the hanging; they can make up their story out of whole cloth, as they do everything else. Hildy is not impressed.

HILDY—Listen, you big pail of lard! If I wanted to go to your God dam' hanging I'd go! See? And sit in a box!

SHERIFF—The hell you would!

HILDY—And I'd only have to tell half of what I know, at that!

SHERIFF—You don't know anything.

HILDY—No? Tell me, Mr. Hartman, where'd you spend the night before that last hanging! At the Planter's Hotel with that librarian. Room Six Hundred and Two. And I got two bell boys and a night manager to prove it!

SHERIFF—If I didn't have to go and see that alienist I'd tell you a few things. (*Exit.*)

HILDY (*calling after him*)—And if I were you I'd get two tickets for the hanging over to Walter Burns pretty fast, or he's liable to come over here and stick a firecracker in your pants!

The Sheriff has gone and Hildy is trying to pack his things in his suitcase. He is beginning to worry now about his girl and his 7 o'clock party date. Getting Peggy on the phone he tries, above the ribald comments of the listening reporters, to tell his love and make his explanations; to win forgiveness and explain about the railroad tickets in his pocket and his waiting taxi, but he has a hard time of it, what with incidental music by Kruger and his banjo and interruptions by everybody. Finally all is well in that quarter—and then Walter Burns calls again! Hildy settles the Burns matter quickly. "You're just making a dam' nuisance of yourself," he tells his managing editor. "What's the idea of calling me up all the time? *No!* I'm through with newspapers. I don't give a damn what you think of me! I'm leaving for New York to-night! Right now! This minute!"

With which information Hildy hangs up the receiver. When the phone rings again, he yanks it from its fastenings and, despite the protests of the other reporters, hurls it through the window into the jail yard.

HILDY (*yelling out the window*)—Tell Pinky to stick that among his souvenirs! (*To the rest.*) If that lunatic calls up again tell him to put it in writing and mail it to Hildebrand Johnson, care of the Waterbury-Adams Corporation, Seven Thirty-five Fifth Avenue, New York City. . . .

MURPHY—Put it on the wall, Mike.

ENDICOTT (*going to the rear wall*)—Waterbury what?

McCUE—Adams.

HILDY (*opening a parcel and showing a pale pair of gloves*)—How do you like those onions? Marshall Field!

McCUE—Very individual.

HILDY—Where's my cane?

ENDICOTT—What cane?

HILDY (*suddenly desperate*)—Come now, fellas. That ain't funny, who's got my cane?

MURPHY (*in a Central Office manner*)—Can you describe this cane?

HILDY (*frantic*)—Aw, for God's sake! Now listen, fellas—

KRUGER (*solicitous*)—Are you sure you had it with you when you came into the room?

WILSON—Was there any writing on it?

HILDY (*diving into* BENSINGER'S *desk*)—Come on! Cut the clowning! Where is it?

BENSINGER—Keep out of my desk! Of all the God-damn kindergartens!

HILDY—Jesus! I only got fifteen minutes. Now, cut the kidding! My God, you fellows have got a sense of humor!

MURPHY—Aw, give him his fairy wand!

ENDICOTT (*a Uranian for the moment, he produces cane from trouser leg*)—Here it is, Gladys.

HILDY—God! You had me worried. (*He picks up his suit-case. Bravura.*) Well; good-bye, you lousy wage slaves! When you're crawling up fire escapes, and getting kicked out of front doors, and eating Christmas dinner in a one-armed joint, don't forget your old pal, Hildy Johnson!

ENDICOTT—Good-bye, Yonson.

McCUE—So long, Hildy.

MURPHY—Send us a postcard, you big stewbum.

KRUGER—When'll we see you again, Hildy?

HILDY—The next time you see me I'll be riding in a Rolls-Royce, giving out interviews on success-y.

BENSINGER—Good-bye, Hildy.

WILSON—Good-bye.

SCHWARTZ—Take care of yourself.

HILDY—So long, fellows! (*He strikes a Sidney Carton pose*

in the doorway; starts on a bit of verse.) "And as the road beyond unfolds"— (*He is interrupted by a terrific fusillade of shots from the courtyard. A roar of voices comes up from the jail yard. For a tense second every one is motionless.*)

VOICES (*in the courtyard*)—Get the riot guns! Spread out, you guys! (*Another volley.*)

WILSON—There's a jail break!

MURPHY (*at window, simultaneously*)—Jacobi! What's the matter? What's happened?

VOICES (*in the jail yard*)—Watch the gate! He's probably trying the gates! (*A huge siren begins to wail.*)

SCHWARTZ (*out the window*)—Who got away? What was it?

VOICE (*outside*)—Earl . . . Williams!!!

THE REPORTERS—Who? Who'd he say? Earl Williams! It was Earl Williams! He got away!

MCCUE—Holy God! Gimme that telephone! (*He works hook frantically.*) Hurry! Hurry up! Will you! This is important. (*Others are springing for the telephones as searchlights sweep the windows from the direction of the jail.*)

SCHWARTZ—Jeez, this is gonna make a bum out of the Sheriff! (HILDY *stands paralyzed, his suitcase in his hand. There is a second rifle volley. Two window panes crash within the room. Some plaster falls. Gongs sound above the siren.*)

MCCUE (*screaming*)—Look out!

MURPHY (*out of the window*)—Where you shooting, you God-damn fools! For Christ's sake! (*Another pane goes.*) Look out where you're aiming, will you!

SCHWARTZ—There's some phones in the state's attorney's office!

KRUGER—Yeah! (*There is a general panic at the door. The* REPORTERS *leave as if a bomb had broken in a trench.* HILDY *is left alone, still holding his suitcase. It falls. He moves back into the room, absently trailing a chair. Another shot.*)

HILDY—Ah-h, Jesus Christ! (*He lets go of the chair and takes one of the telephones.*) *Examiner?* Gimme Walter Burns! Quick! (*Very calmly he sits on one of the long tables, his back against the wall. Then, quietly.*) Hello, Walter! Hildy Johnson! Forget that! Earl Williams just lammed out of the County Jail! Yep . . . yep . . . yep . . . don't worry! I'm on the job! (*There is a third volley.* HILDY *sails his hat and coat into a corner and is removing his overcoat as*—)

The curtain falls.

ACT II

It is twenty minutes later. Searchlights are being played into all angles of the building outside the window. Jennie, the scrub-woman, is sweeping up the broken glass. Woodenshoes, the policeman, is searching for the reporters. He would like at least one of them to print something about his theory of crime prevention.

Endicott of the *Post* is the first to get to his wire. He has practically to wade through Woodenshoes to make it, but he finally manages that stunt.

ENDICOTT (*into phone*)—Ready, Gill. . . . Now, here's the situation so far. . . . Right! . . . At ten minutes after nine Williams was taken to the Sheriff's private office to be examined by this Professor Eglehofer, and a few minutes later he shot his way out. . . . No—nobody knows where he got the gun. Or if they do they won't tell. . . . Yeah. . . . Yeah. . . . He run up eight flights of stairs to the infirmary, and got out through the sky-light. He must have slid down the rainpipe to the street. . . . Yeah. . . . No, I tell you nobody knows where he got it. I got hold of Jacobi, but he won't talk. (MURPHY *enters.*) They're throwing a dragnet around the whole North Side. Watching the railroads and Red headquarters. The Chief of Police has ordered out every copper on the force and says they'll get Williams before morning. . . . The Crime Commission has offered a reward of ten thousand dollars for his capture. . . . Yeah. I'm going to try to get hold of Eglehofer. He knows what's happened, if I can find him. Call you back. (*Hangs up and exits swiftly.*)

Murphy of the *Journal* also reaches his telephone, after hurdling the scrubbing Jennie. So much as we hear of Murphy's story is concerned with facts and details. There is the item of a tear bomb that went off in the hands of one of the Sheriff's bombing squads and Murphy thinks this should be mentioned, much to the disgust of that official, who, palpitant and perspiring with excitement, has dropped in.

Kruger of the *Journal of Commerce* enters the competition with the report that Motorman Julius L. Roosevelt, of the Cottage Grove avenue line, reports having seen a man answering Earl Williams' description boarding a car at Austen avenue—

McCue of the *City News* adds a human note with a story that Mrs. Irma Schlogel, 55, scrublady, "was shot in the left leg while at work scrubbing the eighth floor of the Wrigley building by one of Sheriff Hartman's special deputies."

They have all gone back to the chase when Hildy Johnson makes a dash for the *Examiner* phone. He, too, is vibrant with suppressed excitement but he manages to appear reasonably calm until he has the room to himself.

HILDY (*quickly picking up receiver*)—Gimme Walter Burns! (*He gets up and closes the door carefully; comes back to his phone.*) Walter? Say, listen. I got the whole story from Jacobi and I got it exclusive. . . . That's right, and it's a pip. Only listen. It cost me two hundred and sixty bucks, see? . . . Just a minute—I'll give you the story. I'm telling you first I had to give him all the money I had on me and it wasn't exactly mine. Two hundred and sixty bucks, and I want it back. (*Yells.*) Well, did you hear what I said about the money? . . . All right, then here's your story. It's the jail break of your dreams. . . . Dr. Max J. Eglehofer, a profound thinker from Vienna, was giving Williams a final sanity test in the Sheriff's office—you know, sticking a lot of pins in him to get his reflexes. Then he decided to reënact the crime exactly as it had taken place, so as to study Williams' powers of coördination. . . . Well, I'm coming to it, God damn it. Will you shut up? . . . Of course he had to have a gun to reënact with. And who do you suppose supplied it? . . . Peter B. Hartman! . . . "B" for brains. . . . I tell you, I'm not kidding. Hartman gave his gun to the Professor, the Professor gave it to Earl, and Earl shot the professor right in the belly. . . . Ain't it perfect? If the Sheriff had unrolled a red carpet like at a Polish wedding and loaned Williams an umbrella, it couldn't have been more ideal. . . . Eglehofer? No, not bad. They spirited him away to Passavant Hospital. . . . No, we got it exclusive. Now listen, Walter. It cost me two hundred and sixty bucks for this story, and I want it back. . . . I had to give it to Jacobi before he'd cough up his guts. Two hundred and sixty dollars—the money I'm going to get married on. . . . Never mind about fine work—I want the money. . . . No, I tell you, I'm not going to cover anything else.—I'm going away. (PEGGY *appears in the doorway. She is a pretty girl of twenty.* HILDY *has his back to the door.*) Listen, you lousy stiff. I just did this as a personal favor. Now I'm leaving town and I gave Jacobi every cent I got, and I want it back right away! . . . When will you send it over? . . . Well, see that you do or I can't get married! . . . All right, and tell him to run. I'll be waiting right here in the Press— (*He hangs up and sees* PEGGY. *With a guilty start.*) Hello, Peggy.

PEGGY—What was that, over the telephone?

HILDY—Nothing. I was just telling Walter Burns I was all through that's all. Hello, darling.

(PEGGY, *despite her youth and simplicity, seems overwhelmingly mature in comparison to* HILDY. *As a matter of fact,* PEGGY *belongs to that division of womanhood which dedicates itself to suppressing in its lovers or husbands the spirit of D'Artagnan, Roland, Captain Kidd, Cyrano, Don Quixote, King Arthur or any other type of the male innocent and rampant. In her unconscious and highly noble efforts to make what the female world calls "a man" out of* HILDY, PEGGY *has neither the sympathy nor acclaim of the authors yet—regarded superficially, she is a very sweet and satisfying heroine.*)

PEGGY—You haven't done something foolish with that money? Our money!

HILDY—No. No!

PEGGY—You still have got the rest of it?

HILDY—Of course. Gee, darling, you don't think for a minute—

PEGGY—I think I'd better take care of it from now on!

HILDY—Now listen, honey, I can look after a couple of hundred dollars all right . . .

PEGGY—Hildy, if you've still got that money I want you to give it to me.

HILDY—Now, sweetheart, it's going to be perfectly all right. . . .

PEGGY (*she divines, alas her lover's failing*)—Then you haven't got it.

HILDY—Not—this minute, but I—

PEGGY—You did do something with it!

HILDY—No, no. He's sending it right over—Walter, I mean. It'll be here any minute.

PEGGY (*her vocabulary is reduced to a coal of fire*)—Oh, Hildy!

HILDY (*a preposterous fellow*)—Listen, darling, I wouldn't have had this happen for the world. But it's going to be all right. Now here's what happened: I was just starting out to the house to get you when this guy Williams broke out of jail.

You know, the fellow they were going to hang in the morning.

PEGGY (*intolerant of the antics of the Cyrano sex*)—Yes, I know.

HILDY—Ah, now, listen, sweetheart, I had to do what I did. And—and the same thing when it came to the money. (*She turns away.*) Peggy! Now listen. I shouldn't tell you this, but I haven't got any secrets from you. Do you know how this guy escaped? He was down in the Sheriff's office when Hartman—that's the Sheriff—and Eglehofer—that's this fellow from Vienna—

PEGGY—Hildy!

HILDY—Aw, now I can't tell you if you won't listen. I had to give him the money so he wouldn't give the story to anybody else. Jacobi, I mean. That's the assistant warden. I got the story exclusive—the biggest scoop in years, I'll bet.

PEGGY—Do you know how long mother and I waited, out at that house?

HILDY—Aw, Peggy, listen. You ain't going to be mad at me for this. I couldn't help it. You'd have done the same thing yourself. I mean, the biggest story in the world busting, and nobody on the job.

PEGGY—I might have known it would happen again.

HILDY—Aw, listen—

PEGGY—Every time I've ever wanted you for something—on my birthday, and New Year's Eve, when I waited till five in the morning—

HILDY—But a big story broke; don't you remember.

PEGGY—It's always a big story—the biggest story in the world, and the next day everybody's forgotten it, even you!

HILDY—What do you mean forgotten? That was the Clara Hamon murder—on your birthday. Now, for God's sake, Peggy, it won't hurt to wait five more minutes. The boy's on his way with the money now.

PEGGY—Mother's sitting downstairs waiting in a taxicab. I'm just ashamed to face her, the way you've been acting. If she knew about that money—it's all we've got in the world, Hildy. We haven't even got a place to sleep in, except the train, and—

HILDY—Aw, gee. I wouldn't do anything in the world to hurt you, Peggy. You make me feel like a criminal.

It is all that Walter Burns' fault, Peggy is convinced of that. She will never be happy until she gets Hildy away from that man's influence.

Now Peggy's mother, tired of waiting in the taxi and a little frightened to see the meter click past the $2 charge, has also come in search of Hildy. "She (Mrs. Grant) is a confused little widow who has tried her best to adjust her mind to Hildy as a son-in-law." She listens now patiently to his explanations of the delay and is finally shooed back to the taxi to wait a little longer. . . .

The Mayor is in search of the Sheriff. So far as the newspaper men are concerned the Mayor has no statement to make, nor can they shame one out of him. He refuses to be quoted on the escape, on the political situation, or on the Red Menace. . . .

The Sheriff also refuses to talk, but he has brought the exciting news that Williams has been surrounded in the house he used to live in on Clark street. The Rifle Squad is just going out. Excitedly reporters rush after the Rifle Squad. . . .

The Mayor is extremely peevish with the Sheriff. This is the second or third time that he has balled things up for his party and something, the Mayor is convinced, will have to be done about it.

The Sheriff is contrite but convinced that given half a chance he can yet save the day. With Williams surrounded and his hanging sure there need be no worry about the colored vote.

At which moment a small man named Pincus arrives with a message for the Sheriff from the Governor. It is a third reprieve for Earl Williams, and it isn't any joke. There is reasonable doubt as to the prisoner's sanity, reads the reprieve. And after the Governor giving his word of honor, too, that he wouldn't interfere!

There is only one way to meet this new crisis, as the Mayor sees it. They must bribe Pincus to report that he never has delivered the reprieve. Let him say he couldn't find the Sheriff. And for this helpful job of forgetting Mr. Pincus will be brought from Springfield to Chicago and given a fat job in the City Sealer's office. Pincus, reluctant to agree to the plan, is momentarily convinced that it may be right at that.

The Mayor and the Sheriff are still busily conspiring—this time to have the prisoner Williams shot by the Rifle Squad and thus avoid all possibility of his being reprieved before election day,—when Hildy Johnson again bursts in upon them. They are glad to escape his withering sarcasm by remembering suddenly that their investigations call them elsewhere.

Hildy is in a state of nerves. The boy hasn't come from the office with the money Walter Burns has promised him, and he can't get Walter on the phone. He tries to borrow the money from Woodenshoes, the psychologist; he even turns to Diamond Louie, a racketeer, and finally, in desperation, accepts one hundred and fifty dollars and gives Louie an order on Walter Burns for the two hundred and sixty.

Louie has gone and Hildy is nervously trying to get his packages together and get out of the "lousy place" when his attention is suddenly directed to a noise at the window.

"The sound is caused by Earl Williams falling through the window into the room. Mr. Williams is a little harmless-looking man with a moustache. He is coatless and is shod with death-house sneakers. He carries a large gun. He is on the verge of collapse and holds on to a chair for support. He talks in an exhausted voice. Hildy at the right of him, drops his packages and stands riveted."

EARL—They're after me with searchlights. . . .

HILDY—Put—put down that gun!

EARL (*supporting himself*)—It ain't loaded. I fired all the bullets already.

HILDY—Holy God Almighty! . . .

EARL (*weakly—handing* HILDY *the gun*)—I surrender . . . I couldn't hang off that roof any longer.

HILDY—Holy God!—Get away from that window. (EARL *obeys.* HILDY *strides to the door and locks it. He comes back and stands staring at* EARL *and scratches his head.*) Well, for God's sake. . . .

EARL—I'm not afraid to die. I was tellin' the fella that when he handed me the gun.

HILDY—Shut up a second! (*He locks the door.*)

EARL (*babbling on*)—Wakin' me up in the middle of the night . . . talking to me about things they don't understand. Callin' me a Bolshevik. I ain't a Bolshevik. I'm an anarchist. (HILDY *is pulling down the blinds and putting out the lights.*) It's got nothin' to do with bombs. It's the one philosophy that guarantees every man freedom. (*Weakly.*) All those poor people being crushed by the System. And the boys that were killed in the war. And in the slums—all those slaves to a crust of bread—I can hear 'em cryin'—

HILDY—Be quiet! The hell with that. Shut up! . . . will you? (*He is hunting for a hiding place.*)

EARL—Go on . . . take me back and hang me. . . . I done

my best . . . (*He crumples and falls to the floor.* HILDY *stands for a second, desperate. His eye falls on the toilet door. He considers, picks up Williams and hurriedly dumps him inside the toilet. He closes the door and springs for the telephone.*)

HILDY (*into phone*)—Hello . . . Gimme Walter Burns, quick! (*Second phone rings.* HILDY *hesitates, then answers it, propping first receiver between ear and shoulder.*) Hello! . . . Hello! . . . Oh, hello, Peggy. . . . Listen, for God's sake have a heart, will you? Something terrific has happened! (*Into first phone.*) Walter? Hildy. . . . No, the hell with that. Listen—come right over here. . . . Come over here right away. . . . Wait a minute. (*Into second phone.*) For God's sake, Peggy, quit bawling me out, will you? I'm in a hell of a jam! (*Back to* WALTER.) Walter! Get this—I only want to say it once. . . . I got Earl Williams. . . . Yes! . . . Here in the press room! . . . Honest to God! . . . For God's sake, hurry! I need you. . . . I will. (*Hangs up. Into* PEGGY'S *phone again.*) Listen, darling, this is the biggest thing that ever happened. . . . Now, wait. Don't cry. Wait till I tell you. (*Lowers his voice.*) I just captured Earl Williams! (*In an intense whisper.*) Earl Williams . . . the murderer! I got him. . . . For God's sake, don't tell anybody. . . . Aw, Peggy. . . . Peggy. . . . I can't. . . . I can't. . . . now! . . . Good Lord! Don't you realize. . . . I know, but Peggy . . . (*She has hung up.*) Hello, Peggy. . . . Peggy! (HILDY *hangs up the phone dejectedly. During the last few speeches, there has been a knocking on the door.* HILDY *glares apprehensively and holds himself ready for fight. He moves to the door, and as he approaches it, cries:*) Who is it? (*There is no answer.* HILDY *opens the door cautiously.* MOLLIE *bounds in like a wildcat. He seizes her and wrestles with her.*) Wait a minute! What the hell do you want?

MOLLIE (*wildly*)—Where they gone? You know where they are.

HILDY—Get outa here, Mollie!

MOLLIE—They got him surrounded. They're gonna shoot him—like a dog.

HILDY—Listen! They're lookin' for you, too! If you're smart, you'll get outa here.

MOLLIE—For God's sake, tell me where they've gone. I ain't afraid of them, the yella murderers. . . .

HILDY—I'll tell you where they are. They're out at Clark Street! That's where they are! Clark and Fullerton!

MOLLIE—Where? Where? . . . (*The toilet door opens and* EARL WILLIAMS *appears, dazed and blinking.* MOLLIE *sees him.*) Oh! (*A knock on the outer door is heard.*)

HILDY (*with a desperate look at the door*)—Oh, for Christ's—! . . . Sh—! (*With a desperate gesture for silence, and tiptoeing towards the door.*) Who is it?

WOODENSHOES (*outside*)—It's me.

HILDY—What do you want, Woodenshoes?

WOODENSHOES (*outside*)—I got some important information for you . . . a clue. . . .

HILDY—I'll be right with you. I'm making a personal call. . . . (*Turning to the two, tensely.*) Get back in there! (*Indicating toilet.*)

MOLLIE—What's this . . . a double cross?

HILDY—Damn it! I'm trying to save him. . . .

WOODENSHOES (*outside*)—This is very important.

MOLLIE (*to* EARL)—What are you doing here?

HILDY (*to* MOLLIE)—Keep him quiet! It's a cop! (*On his way to the door.*) I'll get rid of him. . . . (*He opens the door cautiously and steps quickly into the hall, leaving his arm behind him, his hand on the inside knob of the door. Loud and friendly.*) Hello, Woodenshoes! What's on your mind? (*During the ensuing scene a hardly audible conversation takes place between* HILDY *and* WOODENSHOES. HILDY'S *shoulder is visible in the door.*)

EARL—Thank you for those roses. . . .

MOLLIE—How did you get here? Does anybody know?

EARL—I came down the rainpipe. I didn't mean to shoot him. I don't know what happened.

MOLLIE—But what are you going to do? You can't stay here! They'll get you!

EARL—I don't care any more.

MOLLIE—You've got to hide! You've got to hide somewhere! the rats!

EARL—No. Don't do anything. I'm ready to go. I don't care. It's better to die for a cause than the way most people die —for no reason.

MOLLIE—You won't die. They'll never get you.

EARL—I ain't important. It's humanity that's important, like I told you. Humanity is a wonderful thing, Mollie.

MOLLIE—No, it ain't. They're just dirty murderers. Look what they done to you . . . and to me. . . .

EARL—That's because they don't know any better.

MOLLIE—You're too good for 'em . . . that's why.

EARL—You're good, too.

MOLLIE (*with wonder*)—Me?

EARL—Yeah, I think you're wonderful. . . . I wrote out a statement to-day and left it with Mr. Jacobi, so that when I was dead people would understand what I meant. There was a lot about you in it. I said you were the most beautiful character I ever met.

MOLLIE (*blinking and dazed*)—Yeah?

HILDY (*entering, indicating toilet*)—Get back in there! The fellows are coming down the hall now! (*He locks the door.*)

MOLLIE—They'll find him there!

HILDY—Well, there isn't any place else. (*He looks helplessly around the room; at that moment some one tries the door knob.*)

MOLLIE—There's somebody!

HILDY—Sssh!

ENDICOTT (*outside*)—Who locked the door?

HILDY—Coming right away, Mike. (*Whispers to* MOLLIE)—He's got to go in there!

ENDICOTT (*outside*)—Well, for God's sake, hurry.

MOLLIE—Oh, my God!

HILDY—Wait a minute! I got an ide! (*Springs and opens the desk.*) Can you get in this desk?

WILSON (*outside*)—What the hell's going on in there? (*Starts to pound on door.*)

EARL—What good'll it do?

HILDY—We'll get you out in ten minutes.

WILSON (*outside*)—Open up there, will you?

HILDY—All right, all right. God damn it!

EARL—Please, don't talk like that in front of her.

MOLLIE (*to* EARL)—Go on! Please! Please!

EARL—They'll find me, anyhow. (*More pounding.*)

HILDY—All right, I'm coming! (*To* EARL)—Keep dead quiet. Don't even breathe.

MOLLIE—I'll be right here. I won't leave you.

ENDICOTT (*outside, shouting*)—Hey, what the God damn Hell.

HILDY—Keep your shirt on! (*He opens the door.*) What are you trying to do! Kick down the building?

Endicott and Wilson, followed by Murphy, rush for their phones to make their latest reports. The Rifle Squad had surrounded the Williams house all right, only Williams wasn't there. They had, however, succeeded in shooting some one. The Sheriff's brother-in-law, according to Murphy, was looking for Williams under a bed when Deputy Watson, mistaking him for the murderer, shot him right in the pants. . . .

Now they turn to Mollie Malloy, sitting nervously in Bensinger's chair in front of his desk. The nerve of her, parking herself around there all the time. Let her get out, and if she won't get out Murphy will put her out! When Hildy speaks a word for Molly they begin to grow suspicious. Why were the two of them there together—with the door locked, too? What's Hildy waiting around for, anyway? Why ain't he on the way to his train?

Suddenly they notice the twitching of the muscles in Mollie's face. She has the shakes, too! Now their suspicions grow! Looks like Hildy's trying to hang something on 'em, if you ask Endicott. And Schwartz has an idea that Williams is most likely to be some place nobody's thought of looking for him. The roof—for instance—

That's an idea. McCue, at the window, can see how he might have made the jail roof and jumped four feet to this other roof—

And come down the rainpipe, adds Schwartz. And crawl right into any one of the press room windows—

Bensinger's arrival arrests their detective work, because Bensinger is anxious to get into his desk and get some aspirin. He feels something coming on, and anything that is wrong with Bensinger is always good for at least one laugh. Now Bensinger is also upset at sight of Mollie Malloy sitting in his chair, and probably breathing germs all over the phone and everything!

Suddenly Hildy develops a terrible cough and, try as he may he can't seem to avoid coughing in Bensinger's face. Hildy feels that he is catching something, too! Diphtheria, maybe! Bensinger decides the quicker he gets Doc Springer to fumigate the place the safer it will be for all of them. . . .

The desk is saved for the moment, but now Schwartz is back on the trail again, and McCue with him. What if Williams SHOULD be right there in the building? What if they COULD cop that reward! Why not call the cops and make a search—

Yeah, and if they do call the cops who'll get the reward? The cops, of course, points out Hildy. If they're going to search the building why not let each of them take a floor and whoever finds him everybody is in on the split! That's a good idea, but—

Just then Mrs. Grant comes back for Hildy. She isn't going to be put off this time. She's going to wait until she gets him.

And she doesn't believe any of that gibberish he told Peggy over the phone, either—all that stuff about catchin' a murderer!

Now hell and a lot of reporters are loose! Hildy tries to explain that he only said he was trying to catch a murderer, not that he *had* caught one, but they refuse to listen.

And Mollie! What does she know about it? Perhaps a few good stiff socks in the jaw will make her tell a few things! Or Hildy, the dirty double-crosser! Either he'll come clean or they'll beat it out of him!

For the moment Mollie saves Hildy. She's the only one who knows where Williams is, she cries, shrilly, and she won't tell! Let 'em find out, the lousy heels! Do they think she's gonna tell?

She'll either tell or they'll make her tell, announces Murphy. She'll either tell or they'll kick her teeth out!

Now they're closing in on Mollie, and have barred the door! Now she circles the room, picks up a chair to defend herself with and tries to swing it. Now she is over by the windows, and they are closing in on her.

"You'll never get it out of me! Never!" she cries, as she jumps for the open window and disappears.

"Her scream of terror and exultation is heard as she drops through the darkness to the ground. The reporters stand riveted for an instant, powerless before the tragedy. Then they rush forward. An assortment of awed and astonished oaths rise from them. They lean out of the window. Woodenshoes the Theorist, stands sick at heart. His body is doubled up with pain for a moment. Through the babble of cries his voice comes thickly."

"Oh, I never thought she'd do that! That's terrible. . . ."

"Take me out of here!" wails Mrs. Grant, coming out of a trance. "Take me out of here! Oh, my God!"

"She ain't killed! . . . No. . . . She's moving. . . . Get the cops, Woodenshoes. . . . Come on, fellas. . . ."

"Holy God! The poor kid!" mutters Hildy.

Now the reporters have rushed down to the courtyard, from which the calls are for a doctor and for help.

"Hildy stands dazed, looking out of the window. Mrs. Grant moans through her hands. As the vibrations subside a newcomer is standing in the door. This is Mr. Walter Burns, the Managing Editor. Beneath a dapper and very citizen-like exterior lurks a hobgoblin, perhaps the Devil himself. But if Mr. Burns is the Devil he is a very naïf one. He is a Devil with neither point nor purpose to him—an undignified Devil hatched for a bourgeoise Hallowe'en. In less hyperbolic language Mr. Burns is that product of thoughtless, pointless, nerve-drumming unmorality that is the Boss Journalist—licensed eavesdropper, trouble maker, bombinator and Town Snitch, misnamed The Press. At this moment Mr. Burns, in the discharge of his high calling, stands in the door, nerveless and meditative as a child, his mind open to such trouble as he can find or create."

Walter Burns isn't interested in the tragedy of Mollie Malloy, or in Hildy's reaction to it. Walter has come to get the murderer Williams, or to learn where Hildy has hidden him. When he learns Williams is in the desk, and discovers at the same moment that Mrs. Grant is in the room, his chief concern is one of fear that she will spill the story. When Mrs. Grant gains strength she protests shrilly that she knows they are doing something wrong. Then Walter Burns calls his friend, Diamond Louie, and orders that Mrs. Grant be taken to Polack Mike's and kept there where she can't talk to anybody. "Tell 'em it's a case of delirium tremens," instructs the Managing Editor, as the kidnapping is completed.

HILDY (*helplessly*)—Listen, Walter, this'll get me in a hell of a jam. . . . (*To* MRS. GRANT, *who, a hand over her mouth, is being dragged off, her heels trailing*)—Now don't worry, mother, this is only temporary. . . . Honest to God, Walter. . . .

MRS. GRANT (*vaguely heard*)—Peggy, Peggy! Oh, my God! (*Exit* TONY, LOUIE *and* MRS. GRANT. HILDY *starts out.*)

WALTER (*grabs his arm*)—Where the hell do you think you're going?

HILDY—Let go of me! I gotta get my girl! She's downstairs in a cab all alone.

WALTER—Your girl! Good God, what are you? Some puking college boy! Why, in time of war you could be shot for what you're doing—for less than you're doing!

HILDY—To hell with you—there's your story—locked up in that desk! Smear it all over the front page--Earl Williams caught by the *Examiner*—and take all the credit. . . . I covered your story and I covered it God damn right. . . . Now I'm gettin' out. . . .

WALTER—You drooling saphead. . . . What do you mean—a story? You've got the whole city by the seat of the pants!

HILDY—I know all about that, but . . .

WALTER—You know hell— You got the brains of a pancake. . . . Listen Hildy, if I didn't have your interests at heart would

I be wastin' time now arguin' with you! You've done somethin' big—you've stepped into a new class. . . .

HILDY (D'ARTAGNAN *never gave* RICHELIEU *an ear more startled or more innocent*)—Huh?

WALTER—Listen, we'll make such monkeys out of these ward heelers that nobody will vote for them—not even their wives.

HILDY—Expose 'em, huh. . . .

WALTER—Expose 'em! Crucify 'em! We're gonna keep Williams under cover till morning so's the *Examiner* can break the story exclusive . . . Then we'll let the Senator in on the capture —share the glory with him.

HILDY—I see—I see! (*Blinking and warming up.*)

WALTER—You've kicked over the whole City Hall like an applecart. You've got the Mayor and Hartman backed against a wall. You've put one administration out and another in. . . . This ain't a newspaper story—it's a career. And you standin' there bellyachin' about some girl. . . .

HILDY—Jesus, I—I wasn't figuring it that way, I guess. We'll be the white-haired boys, won't we?

WALTER—Why, they'll be naming streets after you. Johnson Street! You and I and the Senator are going to run this town. . . . Do you understand that?

HILDY—Yeah. . . . Yeah! But—wait a minute—we can't leave Williams here. . . . One of those reporters'll . . .

WALTER—We're going to take him over to my private office right away. . . . Where's the *Examiner* phone?

HILDY—That one. The red one. How the hell you gonna do it? They'll see him!

WALTER—Not if he's inside the desk. . . . We'll carry the desk over. (*Into phone*)—Hello! *Examiner.* Give me Duffy. . . . I'd have had him there now if you hadn't give me such an argument.

HILDY—You can't take that out. It's crawling with cops outside.

WALTER—We'll lower it out of the window with pulleys. Quit stallin'. . . . (*To* HILDY)—Hildy! Get that machine and start pounding out a lead, will you. . . . Come on—snap into it. . . .

HILDY—How much you want on it? . . .

WALTER—All the words you got. . . .

HILDY—Where the hell is there some paper?

WALTER (*into phone*)—Hello. . . . Hello!

HILDY (*moving for* BENSINGER'S *desk*)—Can I call the Mayor an animal at bay?

WALTER—Call him a nigger if you want to! Come on! Come on!

HILDY—How about that time he had his house painted by the fire department.

WALTER—Give him the works. . . . (*Into phone*)—Hello Duffy. Get set! We got the biggest story in the world. Earl Williams caught by the *Examiner* . . . exclusive. . . . (HILDY *has opened the drawers of* BENSINGER'S *desk and in a frantic search for paper is tossing play manuscripts, syringes, patent medicines and old socks in the air.*)

WALTER (*continuing into phone*)—Duffy! Send down word to Butch McGuirk I want ten huskies from the circulation department to lam right over here—press room, criminal courts building. That's what I said—Butch McGuirk. (*To* HILDY)—He'll get that desk out—nothin' ever stopped those boys yet. (HILDY *has unearthed a full package of* BENSINGER'S *personal stationery. He now picks up the typewriter.*) What if they start shootin'?

WALTER—Fine! (*Into phone*)—Now listen, Duffy. I want you to tear out the whole front page. . . . That's what I said—the whole front page . . . out . . . (*into phone*)—Johnson's writing the lead . . . (PEGGY *enters—a desperate and strident antagonist.*)

PEGGY—Hildy!

WALTER—What the hell do you want!

PEGGY—Hildy!

HILDY (*holding the typewriter in his arms. Dazed*)—What?

WALTER—Listen, Miss, you can't come in here! (*Into phone*)—To hell with the Chinese earthquake! . . . What's that?

HILDY—Listen, darling—

PEGGY—Where's mother?

WALTER (*into phone*)—I don't care if there's a million dead.

HILDY—Peggy, I got to ask you to do something! A big favor!

PEGGY—You're not coming.

WALTER (*into phone*)—What? I don't hear you.

HILDY—Now don't get sore and fly off the handle, darling. What happened was—

PEGGY—You're not! Are you? Tell me, Hildy! Tell me the truth!

WALTER (*into phone*)—Take all those Miss America pictures off Page 6. Wait a minute, Duffy. (*Turns.*) Now look here, little girl—

PEGGY (*wheels on* WALTER)—You're doing this to him! He was going and you stopped him!

HILDY—Something terrific's happened, Peggy! Wait till I tell you! I couldn't—

WALTER—You'll tell her nothing! She's a woman, you damn fool!

PEGGY—Well, I'm not going to let you do it! You're coming right now! With me!

WALTER—Holy God!

HILDY—But it's the biggest chance of my life. Now listen, darling—

WALTER (*frenzied*)—Shut up, will you?

PEGGY—You don't want to marry me! That's all!

HILDY (*putting down the typewriter*)—That ain't true! Just because you won't listen you're saying I don't love you when you know I'd cut off my hands for you! I'd do anything in the world for you! Anything!

WALTER (*into phone*)—Hello, Duffy! What? . . . What's that? . . . To hell with the League of Nations! Spike it!

PEGGY—You never intended to be decent and live like a human being! You were lying all the time!

HILDY—Peggy, don't keep saying that!

WALTER (*into phone*)—What's that? What?

PEGGY—Lying! That's what you were! Just lying!

HILDY (*his tortured male spirit takes refuge in hysteria*)—All right! If that's what you think!

WALTER (*shouting at the lovers*)—H. Sebastian God! I'm trying to concentrate!

PEGGY—I see what you are now! You're just a bum! Like him—(*indicates* WALTER)—and all the rest!

HILDY—Sure! That's what I am!

WALTER (*into phone*)—No. Leave the rooster story alone—that's human interest!

PEGGY—You're just a heartless selfish animal without any feelings! (*To* WALTER)—And you're worse! It's all your fault and if you think I'm going to put up with it—

WALTER—Shut up, will you? . . . (*Into phone*)—Duffy, let me talk to Butch—

HILDY—Shut up, will you? Yeah! That's what I am! A bum! Without any feelings! And that's all I want to be!

WALTER (*into phone*)—Get a hold o' Butch as fast as you can.

PEGGY—You never did love me or you couldn't talk to me like that (*The desk top opens slowly and* EARL WILLIAMS *sticks his head out.*)

WALTER (*screaming across the room*)—Get back in there-you God damn turtle. . . . (*The desk top falls, the fugitive disappears within and* PEGGY, *her heart break audible in her sobs, moves blindly toward the door.*)

HILDY (*sitting before his typewriter calls after her, his voice tormented but his egoism intact*)—If you want me you'll have to take me as I am instead of trying to turn me into some lah de dah with a cane! I'm no stuffed shirt writing peanut ads. . . . God damn it—I'm a newspaper man. . . . (PEGGY *exits, her sobs filling the room and corridor.*)

WALTER—Shut up! (*Into phone as the curtain is falling*)—Hello Duffy! The edition gone in yet? . . . Well, don't. . . . Never mind the mail trains. . . . You ain't working for the advertising department. . . . The hell with Marshall Field's!! Stick on this wire!

HILDY (*has started typing. The click of the keys stops suddenly and he rips the piece of copy paper from the machine. He is not quite himself—he has made an error in his lead*) . . . God damn it—

The curtain falls.

ACT III

Five minutes later Hildy Johnson has made some little progress with his story, beating it furiously out of a typewriter that sounds quite as though it had been beaten before.

Walter Burns is pacing the room, threatening to explode at any moment. Butch and the circulation huskies who are coming to move the desk have failed to put in an appearance; Duffy, Walter's city editor, has failed to stay on the phone, as instructed, and Hildy isn't doing any too well with the story. It is a tough moment for a managing editor.

"What's your lead?" demands Burns of Hildy.

" 'While hundreds of Sheriff Hartman's paid gunmen stalked through Chicago shooting innocent bystanders, spreading their reign of terror,' proudly reads Hildy, 'Earl Williams was lurking less than twenty yards from the Sheriff's office where . . .' "

"That's lousy," interrupts Burns. "Aren't you going to mention the *Examiner?* Don't we take *any* credit?"

"I'm putting that in the second paragraph. . . ."

"Who the hell's going to read the second paragraph? Ten years I've been telling you how to write a newspaper story—My God, have I got to do everything?" . . .

Roundly they curse each other out and then the Managing Editor returns to the attack.

"Here's your lead: 'The *Chicago Examiner* again rode to the rescue of the city last night in the darkest hour of her history! (*Lowering his voice.*) Earl Williams—Earl Williams, the Bolshevik Tiger, who leaped snarling from the gallows upon the flanks of the city, was captured . . ."

"I got you! I got you!" shouts the newly inspired Hildy. "Go on from there. . . ."

There is a knock at the locked door. Bensinger of the *Tribune* is back again and naturally will want his desk. But the Managing Editor of the *Examiner* is equal to that crisis. He doesn't know Bensinger, but he knows the type.

He opens the door, lets Bensinger in and is fearfully glad to meet him. Meeting the *Tribune* man is certainly quite a coincidence, in fact, seeing that he had just been asking Hildy Johnson about him. Wanted to congratulate him on the story he had in the *Tribune*. Wanted to congratulate him especially on the Bensinger poetry that gave it just the right touch. That's what the *Examiner* needs; somebody who can do a story with a poetic touch like that. What's Bensinger getting on the *Tribune?* Seventy-five? Would he be willing to come to the *Examiner* for $100 and a by-line? And start right in—with a good, big smashing human interest story of the man hunt?

Bensinger is slightly flabbergasted and momentarily puzzled as to the ethics involved. Would it be right for him to quit the *Tribune* that way? Still, as Mr. Burns says, what had the *Tribune* ever done for him? Nothing but butcher his copy and cut his stories. On the *Examiner* he'll have the Managing Editor's personal guarantee of freedom to write what he wants to. So—

Bensinger is barely out the door on his way to the *Examiner* when Burns picks up the office phone. "Duffy! Listen!" he shouts. "Now get this! A God damn *Tribune* sneak is coming over to get a job. Yeah, Bensinger, the fellow I told you about. Now listen, handle him with kid gloves and tell him to get busy writing poetry. No . . . no! We don't want him. But wait till he gets through. Then tell him his poetry stinks and kick him down the stairs." . . .

Now Hildy is beginning to worry about his girl again. What a bum he has turned out to be to treat her that way. . . . This, suggests Walter Burns, is no time to begin snivelling about a girl. What's being in love get you, anyway. The Managing Editor was in love with his third wife—and treated her fine. What did that get him? A week after she met a certain *Tribune* party Walter sneaked home, crawled through the bathroom window and found them in bed. And the next morning, all over the *Tribune's* front page, was the traction story he had been saving for two months! That's what a woman can do to you!

Another knock at the door. This time its Diamond Louie. The kidnapping of Mrs. Grant, Louie reports, has gone a little wrong. They were taking the old lady down Wentworth Avenue, going sixty-five miles an hour, when what should they smash into but a police patrol! The next thing Louie knew he was running down Thirty-fifth Street. What became of Mrs. Grant he doesn't know, but he has an idea.

Hildy is hysterical with anxiety! He is responsible for this! Peggy's mother is dead and he killed her! He tries to rush out in search of her, but Walter Burns stops him. Let them telephone first. They can get all the particulars over the phone.

More trouble. While Hildy is calling up the hospitals trying to locate Mrs. Grant, Walter Burns is hearing over another phone from Butch, and Butch is not only not on his way with the circulation boys to remove the desk, but he isn't coming. Butch is with a dame and he isn't passing up no dame for Walter Burns or anybody else.

Now what to do with the desk? Diamond Louie will have to hustle a gang of men from the building, from the street, from anywhere . . . and if Louie fails him Walter has other ideas.

"Listen, Hildy," he says, "if Louie don't come back in five minutes we'll get it out alone! There's millions of ways! We can start a fire and get the firemen to carry it out in the confusion! . . ."

Hildy isn't interested. He's too busy trying to get in touch with the hospitals to locate Mrs. Grant. It's a terrible position for an unmarried bridegroom to be in. Nor can all Walter Burns' sarcasm move him. Hildy is starting for the morgue to continue his frenzied search when Sheriff Hartman, a couple of deputies and several suspicious and disgusted reporters swarm into the room.

The Sheriff means business this time. He has the backing of the other reporters, too. They are all convinced now that Hildy knows where Williams is; that he and Mollie were trying to hide him. If Hildy won't talk, the Sheriff is prepared to take measures. In fact he starts now with orders to the deputies to grab, hold and search Hildy. Nor can the protests of Walter Burns stop him. In the search the deputies uncover the gun

Hildy has taken away from Williams. Hartman recognizes the gun as his own!

Now the reporters are swarming forward again, demanding their rights to the story they believe Hildy and his Managing Editor are holding out. Now Sheriff Hartman, egged on by the reporters and with a brave attempt at authority, has placed both Hildy and Burns under arrest. And now the whole lot of them have been thrown into a further state of confusion by the sudden appearance of a patrolman leading in Mrs. Grant, her hat over one ear, her eyes flashing an anger so hot it is difficult for her to express it. Hildy would hug Peggy's mother for sheer joy at seeing her alive, but she shakes him off. For the moment Walter Burns is the target of her wrath. It was he who organized her kidnapping! It was he who told the brutes to take her, the brutes who dragged her all the way down stairs, pinched her until she was black and blue all over when she tried to scream for help, and finally ran her into another automobile and nearly killed her! Walter is round-eyed at the accusation.

"Now, Madame, be honest," he warns Mrs. Grant. "If you were out joy-riding,—drunk! . . . And got in some scrape . . . why don't you admit it instead of accusing innocent people!"

And then, to make her charges good, Mrs. Grant makes further revelations. The reason they had her kidnapped was because they were hiding some kind of murderer!

With righteous indignation Walter Burns pounds the Bensinger desk to emphasize his declaration that Mrs. Grant is a liar. And from inside the desk come three answering knocks from the misunderstanding Williams.

SHERIFF (*leaping as if the desk had bitten him*)—What was that?

REPORTERS—My God, he's in the desk! For the love of Christ! Holy God, he's in there! etc.

SHERIFF—Aha! I thought so! Stand back, everybody!

DEPUTY—Look out, Sheriff! He may shoot!

SHERIFF—Get your guns out! (*The police all take out guns.*)

HILDY—He's harmless, for God's sake!

SHERIFF—Don't take any chances! Shoot through the desk!

HILDY—He can't hurt anybody! You got his gun!

MRS. GRANT (*panic-stricken*)—Oh, dear! Oh, dear!

WALTER (*to* MRS. GRANT)—You gray-haired old Judas!

MRS. GRANT—Let me out! Let me out of here! (*Streaks for*

the door; exits. The reporters are going for the telephones.)

MURPHY (*into phone*)—City desk! Quick!

MURPHY (*to policeman*)—Close the door. You stand there. You cover the windows! (*Indicates with his gun.*)

MURPHY—Look out where you're pointing that gun, Pinky!

MCCUE (*into phone*)—Gimme Emil.

MURPHY—Hold the wire! I've got a flash for you.

WALTER (*to* HILDY)—Call Duffy.

SHERIFF—No, you don't!

WALTER—Do you want us to get scooped?

MCCUE (*into phone*)—Emil? Hang on for a second.

SHERIFF—Now then! Everybody aim right at the centre. And when I say three—

HILDY—God damn it! That's murder!

SHERIFF—Carl! Frank! One of you get on each side of the desk. Take hold of the cover. Now then! We got you covered, Williams—don't try to move! Now! Everybody quiet and ready for any emergency. I'm going to count three!

MURPHY (*phoning in the silence*)—I'll have it in a minute. . . .

SHERIFF—One! . . .

KRUGER—Right away now!

SHERIFF—Two! . . . (DIAMOND LOUIE *enters, accompanied by three people he has picked up in the street. One is a boy in short pants, the second is a sailor, the third is a seedy old man of the Trader Horn type.*)

POLICEMAN (*at the door, opposing them*)—What do you want? (WALTER *waves violently,* LOUIE *and his assistants disappear.*)

SHERIFF (*wheeling*)—Who was that?

WALTER (*white with rage*)—Double-crossing Sicilian!

SHERIFF—Shut up!

KRUGER (*into phone*)—Keep holding it!

SHERIFF—Now then! Keep everybody out of here! I want quiet! . . . There's a dozen guns on you, Williams! You can't escape! Do you surrender or not?

WALTER (*into phone*)—Duffy!

SHERIFF—Are you ready, boys?

CARL—Yah. . . .

SHERIFF—All right. Now everybody aim right at the center. (*Looking around*)—Are you all ready? (*To the men at the desk.*) You boys? (*From the deputies comes a whispered "Yes."*) Ready back there? (*This to the men at the door and windows; they give quick nods in reply.*) All right. Now then

—up with it. (CARL *and* FRANK *raise the cover. The* SHERIFF *waits a discreet distance until he sees there is no danger.* WILLIAMS *is cowering in the desk, his hands over his face. The* SHERIFF *rushes on him, jabbing his gun into him.*)

WILLIAMS (*a wail*)—Go on—shoot me!

SHERIFF—Got you, Williams!

THE POLICE AND DEPUTIES—Grab him, there! That's him! That's him. Don't let him shoot! Stick 'em up, you! Clout him! Give him the boots! Hold his arms! (*Through this the reporters are telephoning in. As they talk, the police drag the screaming little anarchist out.*) (*The* SHERIFF *follows them.*)

MURPHY (*into the phone*)—Earl Williams was just captured in the press room o' the Criminal Court building hiding in a desk.

MCCUE (*into phone*)—The Sheriff just caught Williams in a roll top right here in the room.

KRUGER (*into phone*)—Just nabbed Williams hiding in a desk, Criminal Court press room.

MCCUE (*into phone*)—Williams put up a desperate struggle but the police overpowered him.

MURPHY (*into phone*)—Williams tried to shoot it out with the cops but his gun wouldn't work.

KRUGER (*into phone*)—Williams was unconscious when they opened the desk. . . .

WALTER (*into phone*)—Duffy! The *Examiner* just turned Earl Williams over to the Sheriff. . . . (*The* SHERIFF *rushes back.*)

SHERIFF (*indicating* WALTER *and* HILDY)—Just a minute! Put the cuffs on those two! (*The police obey.*) Harboring a fugitive from justice!

MURPHY (*into phone*)—A well-dressed society woman tipped off the cops. Call you back in a minute. . . .

KRUGER (*into phone*)—An old sweetheart of Williams' double crossed him. . . . Call you back. . . .

MCCUE (*into phone*)—More in a minute.

REPORTERS—Where's that old lady? Hey, madam. . . . Wait a minute! . . . Where's the old dame? (*They exit in a hurry.*)

SHERIFF (*into phone*)—Hello, girlie! Gimme Jacobi! Quick! . . .

WALTER—Hartman. . . you're going to wish for the rest of your life you'd never been born! (*The* MAYOR *enters.*)

MAYOR—Fine work, Pete! You certainly delivered the goods! I'm proud of you!

SHERIFF (*over his shoulder as he phones*)—Look kind of natural, don't they, Fred? (*Referring to the handcuffs.*)

MAYOR (*happily*)—A sight for sore eyes! Well, it looks like you boys stepped in something up to your neck!

HILDY (*to* HIS HONOR)—Go on! Laugh! You big tub of guts!

MAYOR—That's pretty, isn't it? Aiding an escaped criminal, huh?

SHERIFF (*rolling in catnip*)—And a little charge of kidnapping I'm looking into!

There is much gloating now. The Sheriff and the Mayor see two of their enemies of the press started for state's prison with about ten years chalked up against each of them.

Neither Hildy nor Walter Burns is impressed, however. Hildy is flippant, Walter menacing as he recalls to their memory things that have happened to certain others who tried to get the *Examiner*. Frequently they had taken their own lives. Occasionally they had met with fatal and mysterious accidents. It seems there is a special Providence that watches over certain newspapers.

The exchange of compliments, of dares and double dares, gathers momentum as the Sheriff calls for the District Attorney to come over and take the confessions of his important prisoners and Walter Burns manages to shout into the phone for Duffy to get Clarence Darrow!

And then Mr. Pincus, the Governor's messenger, reels into the room!

Mr. Pincus is drunk. He has decided that he does not want to come to the city and be a City Sealer. He would like, on the other hand, to have the world know that he brought a reprieve for Earl Williams from the Governor and tried to deliver it to this Sheriff and this Mayor and that neither would take it. Furthermore he would like to testify that they had started right in trying to bribe him and he did not want to be bribed!

Now the celebrating is being done by Hildy and his Managing Editor. And the apologizing by the Mayor and the Sheriff. After all, newspaper men should be intelligent, and intelligent newspaper men should understand.

"I can't tell you how badly I feel about this, Walter," ventures the Mayor, as he orders the Sheriff to release the prisoners. "There was no excuse for Hartman flying off the handle."

"I was only doing my duty," protests the Sheriff, weakly. "There wasn't anything personal intended."

"You guys had better quit politics and take in washing," advises Hildy.

The Mayor and the Sheriff, with Messenger Pincus, are starting for the warden's office to deliver the reprieve when Peggy dashes in. Her mother had reported that Hildy was being arrested and she was worried. Now she is relieved.

The Sheriff is reminded that there was to have been a little feed after the hanging and he can see no reason why they shouldn't have it anyway. He thinks perhaps Walter Burns would enjoy coming. But Walter is cold to the suggestion.

"Wait until those two Greeks read the *Examiner* to-morrow!" he mutters, as the Sheriff disappears. And then he snaps back to life. "Hildy, I'll tell you what I want you to do."

"What?"

WALTER—I want you to get this guy Pincus over to the office to-morrow—

HILDY—Nothing doing, Walter. I'm all washed up. I mean it this time, Walter.

PEGGY—Oh, Hildy, if I only thought you did.

HILDY—Listen, Peggy—if I'm not telling you the absolute truth may God strike me dead right now. I'm going to New York with you to-night—if you give me this one last chance! I'll cut out drinking and swearing and everything connected with the God damn newspaper business. I won't even read a newspaper.

WALTER—Listen, Hildy, I got an idea—

HILDY (*to* WALTER)—There's nothing you can say can make me change my mind. This time I'm through, and I mean it. I know I don't deserve you, Peggy. I've done everything in the world to prove that, I guess.

PEGGY—Hildy, please! Don't say things like that.

HILDY—I've gotta hell of a nerve to ask you to marry me. I'm a prize package, all right. But if you'll take me, here I am.

PEGGY—Darling, don't talk that way. I want you just the way you are. (*Anyway* PEGGY *will always remember that she said this and always forget that she didn't mean it.*)

WALTER—God, Hildy, I didn't know it was anything like this. Why didn't you say something? I'd be the last person in the world to want to come between you and your happiness.

HILDY (*staggered*)—What?

WALTER—You ought to know that. . . . (*As* HILDY *continues to blink*)—I love you, you crazy Swede! (*To* PEGGY)—You're getting a great guy, Peggy.

HILDY—Never mind the Valentines. Good-bye, you lousy bohunk. (*They shake hands.*)

WALTER—You're a great newspaper man, Hildy. I'm sorry to see you go. Damn sorry.

HILDY—Well, if I ever come back to the business—(*To* PEGGY) which I won't. . . . (*To* WALTER, *his arm around* PEGGY)—There's only one man I'd work for. You know that, don't you?

WALTER—I'd kill you if you ever worked for anybody else.

HILDY—Hear that, Peggy? That's my diploma. (*He hesitates*)—Well, Walter . . . I don't know what to say . . . except I'm going to miss you like hell.

WALTER—Same here, son.

HILDY (*to* PEGGY)—Twelve years we've been knocking around together . . . before you were born. . . . (*To* WALTER *his face lighting up*)—Remember the time we hid the missing heiress in the sauerkraut factory?

WALTER—Do I (*To* PEGGY)—Get him to tell you some time about how we stole Old Lady Haggerty's stomach . . . off the coroner's physician. We proved she was poisoned. . . .

HILDY (*laughing*)—We had to hide for a week!

PEGGY—Darling . . .

HILDY (*back to life*)—What?

PEGGY—You don't want to go to New York . . . down deep.

HILDY—Aw . . . what do you mean? I was just talking. (*With a nervous laugh*)—I'd feel worse if I stayed, I guess. . . .

PEGGY—Hildy, if I thought you were going to be unhappy—I mean, if you really wanted to—(*firmly*)—No. No. It's your chance to have a home and be a human being—and I'm going to make you take it.

WALTER (*to* PEGGY)—Why, I wouldn't let him stay. . . . Go on, Hildy, before I make you city editor.

HILDY (*starting*)—Hurry up, Peggy. He means it.

WALTER (*as* PEGGY *follows*)—Any objection to my kissing the bride?

HILDY (*stopping*)—It's O.K. with me. (*He looks at* PEGGY. *She smiles.*) Go ahead, Mrs. Johnson.

WALTER (*removing his hat and kissing her chastely*)—Thank you. . . . What time does your train go?

PEGGY—There's another one at twelve-forty. (*To* HILDY)—We came awfully near going without you.

WALTER—New York Central, eh? (*To* HILDY)—I wish there was time to get you a little wedding present . . . but it's awful short notice.

PEGGY (*straining to be gone*)—Thank you, Mr. Burns, but Hildy's all the wedding present I want. . . . (*Laughing a little*) —If I've really got him.

HILDY—Ah, forget it, Walter. (*He, too, is leaving.*)

WALTER—Hold on! I want you to have something to remember me by. You can't leave like this. . . . (*Thoughtfully reaching for his watch*)—And I know what it's going to be. . . . (*Produces the watch.*)

HILDY (*embarrassed*)—Aw, Jesus, no, Walter! You make me feel like a fairy or something!

WALTER (*with affected brusqueness*)—Shut up! You're going to take it, I tell you! It was a present from the Big Chief himself! And if you'll look inside. . . . (*Opening the watch*)—You'll find a little inscription—"To the Best Newspaper man I know." . . . When you get to New York, you can scratch out my name and put yours in its place, if you want to. . . .

HILDY—You know I wouldn't do that . . .

WALTER—Here. . . . (*giving him the watch.*)

HILDY—Aw, Walter! It's too good for me! I can't take it!

WALTER—You got to! (*To* PEGGY)—Make him!

PEGGY—Go on, Hildy—if Mr. Burns wants you to. You don't want to hurt his feelings. . . . (HILDY *takes it.* WALTER *pats him on the shoulder, his face averted.*)

HILDY (*a lump in his throat*)—Well, this is the first and last thing I ever got from a newspaper. . . .

PEGGY—Good-bye, Mr. Burns. . . . I always had a queer opinion of you, Mr. Burns. I still think you're a little peculiar, but you're all right . . . underneath. I mean I think you're a peach.

WALTER (*winningly*)—So are you! You look just like a little flower.

HILDY (*ushering* PEGGY *out*)—Good-bye, you big baboon. . . .

PEGGY—Good-bye. . . . (*they exit.*)

WALTER (*calling after, leaning against the door*)—Good-bye, Johnson! Be good to yourself . . . and the little girl. . . .

HILDY'S VOICE—The same to you and many of them!

(WALTER *waits till* HILDY *and* PEGGY *are out of sight and earshot, then closes the door. He walks slowly to the telephone. The receiver is still off the hook, the obedient* DUFFY *still on the other end.* WALTER *hesitates sentimentally, the receiver in his hand. Then he heaves a huge sigh and speaks*)

WALTER—Duffy! . . . (*He sounds a bit tired*)—Listen! I want you to send a wire to the Chief of Police of La Porte, Indiana. . . . That's right. . . . Tell him to meet the twelve-forty out of Chicago. . . . New York Central . . . and arrest Hildy Johnson and bring him back here. . . . Wire him full description. . . . The son of a bitch stole my watch!

The curtain falls.

LET US BE GAY

A Comedy in Prologue and Three Acts

By Rachel Crothers

EARLY in the new year Rachel Crothers brought a comedy in from her Connecticut studio and offered it to John Golden. "Let Us Be Gay" she had called it.

Mr. Golden, being a producer of quick decisions, liked the play, approved its production, made certain suggestions as to the cast, remodeled the scenery and bowed gracefully out of the picture. It was Mr. Golden's time for going south to take up the more serious work of trap shooting over the Florida golf courses and he could not be delayed.

Miss Crothers thereupon took charge of the play's staging and rehearsals and on February 21 produced "Let Us Be Gay" at the Little Theatre. Night letters sent to Mr. Golden on that occasion ventured the prediction that the play was a hit. The support of the reviewers was enthusiastic and that of the public consistently steady. As the season wore on the popularity of the Crothers comedy grew, and in late June it still was prospering enormously.

This is a pleasant social comedy in which the characters gathered at a curiously assorted house party are faithfully and revealingly dissected. There is back of the play that touch of strengthening purpose characteristic of Miss Crothers' work. She is prepared to permit her characters to be as gay as they please but she reserves her right to point a subtle moral or two in their revealment.

There is domestic tragedy at the beginning of "Let Us Be Gay." It is 12 o'clock midnight. The scene is a corner of Kitty Brown's bedroom in the California home of the Browns. "The appointments are feminine and charming," a fact to be easily discerned even though the room lies mostly in shadow, a reading lamp throwing a single band of light across the bed.

The room is empty until Kitty Brown lets herself in the door and turns the key after her. "Kitty is twenty-five, small, delicate, vivid. She wears a soft dressing robe over her nightgown." Kitty is smothering her sobs as she tries to clear the dressing table of toilet articles and get them into a small travelling bag.

There is a knocking at the door which Kitty at first pretends she does not hear. Outside the voice of a man is heard declaring that he has read the damned thing she has written for him and that he is convinced she does not mean a word of it. Let her open the door and face him. If she doesn't he will break the door down. And to indicate that the breaking is possible he attacks the door violently.

A little frightened Kitty bids him begone. She never wants to see him again so long as she lives. Besides, everybody in the house will hear him.

He refuses to begone. He refuses to stir until she faces him and talks things out. She will have to talk things out sooner or later, why not now? There are things he must tell her; there are things she must know.

Finally he (Bob Brown) makes so great a racket that Kitty unlocks the door and lets him in, backing away until she stands against the bed "staring with dread in her eyes."

Bob holds an open letter in his hand and as he waves it he repeats that she could not have meant what she has written. He isn't in love with any other woman. He is in love with her. For anything, for everything, he has done he is sorry. The bare facts of the sin she alleges he has committed may be true—but not in the sense she has taken them. He wishes he had told her himself. He is amazed to learn that she had the facts from the other woman—from Alice herself. But that's all over now—

Bob—It's all over and I—I'm sorry. You—good God—don't take it like this!—It has nothing to do with you—nor the way I feel towards you—nor what I am to you! That's what you've got to see. That's what—

Kitty—Go away—out of the house—till I get my things together. I'm going to take the children to mother, and I'm going to get my divorce as quickly as I possibly can.

Bob—You're shaking and cold. I'm going to give you some whiskey.

Kitty—Go out of this room and don't come back.

Bob (*turning back at the door*)—I'll be damned if I will! You've got to hear my side of it. We've got to talk it out.

Kitty—I'm going to take the children to mother.

Bob—No, you're not. Not unless I say you can.

Kitty—They're not yours. They're all mine. They're mine.

Bob—Don't be a fool, Kitty. The whole business doesn't mean anything more to me than getting drunk. In fact, that's just about what it is. It's over. I'm sorry. I wouldn't hurt you for anything in the world.

KITTY—You don't even know what you've done to me.

BOB—The whole bloomin' trouble is, Kitty, you don't understand. You still think and feel and expect just what you did when you were a girl. She's not in love with me. She's all right. She knows her way about.

KITTY—Oh—

BOB—You still don't know the actual honest to God truth about the man and woman business. If you did understand you'd forgive me. You'd say forget it, old man, and let's go on.

KITTY—I've made up something that never was at all. I believed you were just exactly to me—what I was to you. I thought that being that way made—the children—more wonderful—made—made everything more— (*Her voice breaks.*) I know I was a fool. I thought it was the most beautiful thing in the world and it never was there at all.

Again Bob pleads with Kitty, insisting over and over that their sacred love has not been, could not be, affected by anything that has happened. How can she be jealous of some one he does not love?

It isn't jealousy, Kitty insists. It is the hurt, the lie he has told her, the lie he has lived. Nothing's been true.

"If you're like this," sobs Kitty, "nothing in the world is what I thought it was. I can't ever believe in anything or anybody—ever—*again!*"

"It's horrible what you're doing," answers Bob. "Killing everything, busting it all up. You're doing a great deal worse thing now than I ever did in my life. I never meant to hurt you —never—and you're hurting me as much as you can. You're smashing up the only thing in the world I care a hang about and the only thing that means a damned thing anyway."

Again she dismisses him. In spite of his threat that if she lets him go out the door of that room he will never come back, she lets him go. He slams the door after him. Kitty falls sobbing across the bed as the prologue curtain falls.

ACT I

On an afternoon in August three years later, at the country house of Mrs. Boucicault "somewhere in Westchester," Perkins, a maid, is busily arranging a chair and cushions for the impending approach of, her attitude indicates, a somewhat exasperating person who is to rest there. Perkins is followed by Whitman, an English major-domo, gray, venerable, observant and intolerant, after the fashion of English butlers, come to inspect the arrangements and suggest such changes as forty years of service in Mrs. Boucicault's employ has taught him his mistress will expect.

Mrs. Boucicault, whose arrival is shortly negotiated with no more servant confusion than customarily attends such an event, "is seventy-six—half Victorian, half ultra-modern—an enormous amount of dominating personality radiating from her hardness and her insatiable thirst for life. Her clothes have rather a grand manner of having been well made but not modish—and a good deal of jewelry is mixed up with chains and three kinds of glasses hung about her neck. Her hair—iron gray—is worn rather high in puffs—her voice is warm and deep and her sense of humor dry and sharp. She has one slightly stiff knee and walks with a stout stick with a curved handle."

Seated finally, and a little heavily, among her cushions Mrs. Boucicault concludes the instructions she has been issuing from time to time regarding the expected arrival of a Mrs. Brown—Mrs. Courtland Brown—who is to be met on the five-fifteen or such later train as she may have taken and properly assigned a room in the north wing—the *north* wing, despite Whitman's protest that the lady would be much more comfortable in the south wing.

The weather is hot and Mrs. Boucicault is bored by the heat. She is also bored by the fact that she has been obliged to dress and she is none too happy in the knowledge that she is growing older and older, and that "the longer you live the more you have to regret."

She is cheered for the moment by the appearance of her granddaughter, Dierdre Lessing, "a tall, dark, exotic creature of 20—just now very startlingly beautiful in a one-piece bathing suit of orange and black and a black coat."

Dierdre is on her way to the pool, and is taking the living room way as a short cut. A moment later she is followed by Bob Brown and the coincidence explains much.

Mrs. Boucicault was sure both Dierdre and Bob were playing golf, but it appears that they had done their 18 holes in the morning and are just now bored by the heat. Mrs. Boucicault holds them long enough to warn Bob that another very attractive woman is about to join the house party, but the promise fails to excite him. Just now he is finding Dierdre a fairly consuming study.

Kitty Brown's arrival in a ravishing summer outfit finds Mrs. Boucicault eagerly awaiting her and grateful for her coming. The summons, they are agreed, was unexpected and a bit sudden, to say the least of it. The reason for it is still a bit obscure to Kitty. She was packing for a trip to California with her children when the Boucicault call for help was received. Now Kitty would like to know why all the hurry.

Soon she is in possession of the essential facts. First, there is a man. "He's one of those stray dogs I get interested in. I don't know much about him—except that he's been divorced—at least once, and seems to be rather humble as men go—and to have a fair amount of money. With your alimony it wouldn't be bad at all."

Secondly there is a girl, Dierdre, the granddaughter. "She's one of those gorgeous young things that are running around loose now. Lives alone—is alone—father one place—mother another—knows everything—everybody—done everything—and only twenty years old."

"I know," murmurs Kitty. "I know. Wonderful—isn't it. They get such a good start now. I've been *made*. They just *are*."

But Kitty has no intention of ever marrying again. Nor does she plan, as Mrs. Boucicault slyly intimates, to meet the economical pressure by living in sin, as old-fashioned folk used to say. Her talent for clothes is beginning to pay dividends, she reports, and with an income assured men may come and men may go so far as she is concerned. But, as to this commission that Mrs. Boucicault would assign her—

"Kitty," the older woman frankly asks, "will you do this for me? Take him away from the girl?"

"I thought your religion was hands off?"

"It is. But it doesn't work when it comes home. She's *my own grandchild*."

MRS. BOUCICAULT—I've got to keep her from going to the dogs before the first of October.

KITTY—Why the first of October?

MRS. BOUCICAULT—She's going to marry a nice boy the first of October—an awfully nice boy. He's here too. They've got everything in common to make a go of it—when—bing—out of the blue she takes this shameless damnable passion for this man.

KITTY—You don't think you can do anything about that—do you?

MRS. BOUCICAULT—That's why I sent for you.

KITTY—You never seemed like an old woman to me before, Bouci—not a bit. Always as fresh and open minded about life as—

MRS. BOUCICAULT—Shut up. I'm not talking about life, I'm talking about my own granddaughter.

KITTY—Oh, well then, of course you can't be expected to use your common sense at all.

MRS. BOUCICAULT—She's in a kind of danger I don't want to recognize—but I'm frightened, Kitty. I want to beat her over the head and make her behave, but I'm pretending I don't see anything. Now the best thing that could possibly happen is for you to take the man.

KITTY—I'm tremendously flattered that you think I could get a man away from a stunning young thing like that—but even if I could, don't you know the sooner she finds out everything for herself—the sooner she loses her romantic illusions—the happier and safer she's going to be?

MRS. BOUCICAULT—I'm not so sure. Women are getting everything they think they want now, but are they any happier than when they used to stay at home—with their romantic illusions—and let men fool them?

KITTY—At least they're more intelligent. That's one thing I refuse to be—a happy fool.

MRS. BOUCICAULT—Un! I'd like to live another fifty years—without the bother of living—to see this thing through. I've watched a long procession of men, women and morals through three generations. I'm seventy-six, and I don't know anything.

KITTY—That's why you're so wise, dearest.

MRS. BOUCICAULT—I always knew my husband wasn't faithful to me, but I lived in hell with him for fifty years because divorce wasn't respectable. My only daughter had three divorces—which I was tickled to death to see her get—and there's my grandchild in the middle of this modern moral revolution and I'm helpless—can't do a thing for her. She's grown up before I knew it—dumped herself in my lap and this thing has happened right under my nose.

KITTY—Then for Heaven's sake, let it happen. Let it alone.

MRS. BOUCICAULT—No—by God—I won't. She's got to walk up that aisle a perfectly decent girl if I have to lock her up till—

KITTY—Now see here, Bouci. I don't think I'm clever enough for this job if it's as important as all that.

Mrs. Boucicault—You can do it if you want to. Didn't I see you take the Russian away from the Italian princess before she even knew it?

Kitty—I didn't take him away. I just borrowed him for the week-end. Who else is here besides your pièce de résistance?

Mrs. Boucicault—I can't remember. I never see any one till tea. From then on to midnight is as much as I can stand of any guests.

Kitty—You don't care what they do after midnight—just so they let you alone.

Mrs. Boucicault—Not a bit!

As the house party assembles Kitty is introduced. First to Townley Town who is "forty, tall, plain and charming; not very vivid, not very weak; indestructible in his inscrutable agreeableness."

"How do you do," smiles Kitty. "Oh, you magnificent, long-legged Britishers. I've been avoiding you in Paris—but you are wonderful—aren't you?"

"Yes, we are—aren't we?"

A wasted approach on Kitty's part, as it turns out. Townley isn't the man. Townley is only a sort of professional guest, subject to "Bouci's" call that she is a man shy.

Next comes Bruce Keen—"young, tall and good looking in a fresh, straightforward way"—looking for Dierdre.

"This is Bruce Keen," admits Townley, when the introduction is forced upon him; "young, handsome and very much in demand both with the upper bums and the best people. But by Monday morning you'll find me very much more satisfactory."

"Do you think that's clever?" scowls Bruce.

"I didn't hear him," coos Kitty. "I was looking at you. How magnificent you long-legged Americans are! I've been avoiding you in Paris—but you—"

Only Bruce is mystified by the laugh that follows.

Now there is a flurry of tea, highballs and epigrams. Kitty has moved out to the porch and is more or less surrounded by the men. Madge Livingstone drifts in. She is "possibly thirty-eight—looking younger—tall and frail and beautiful in a pale patrician way. She is now wearing something diaphanous and trailing, which adds to her illusiveness. She moves with a slow grace and slight hauteur."

Mrs. Livingstone has been spending a languid day, listening a good part of the time to Wallace Grainger read aloud. Wallace has such a good mind and writes such clever books Mrs. Livingstone is quite proud of having been his inspiration these last ten years.

Now Mr. Grainger joins the group. "He is about forty. A man with a great deal of manner—the perfection of which seems trying to make up for lost enthusiasms. He is wearing flannels and is in most perfect style. He carries a paper novel and paper knife."

Kitty is still on the terrace chatting and laughing with the men. Mrs. Livingstone, having been told that Kitty is a Mrs. Courtland Brown from California, has been struck with the fact that not only does Boucicault appear to be "going in for Browns" this season, but that Dierdre also appears to have taken a sudden fancy to a charming gentleman of the same name.

And then Bob Brown appears. He has a sofa pillow poised, ready to add his bit to the present comfort of Mrs. Livingstone, when he hears Kitty laugh. He is for the moment visibly paralyzed with wonder.

A moment later Kitty and the others have come in from the terrace, and Mrs. Boucicault is presenting her newest guest.

"You two Browns must know each other," she is saying. "Mr. Bob Brown this is Mrs. Courtland Brown."

There is a sufficient pause to attract Mrs. Boucicault's attention as Bob and Kitty quite frankly stare at each other. Then Kitty catches her breath and the situation is saved.

"How wonderful you long-legged Americans are!" she says. "I've been avoiding you in Paris, but it *is* wonderful to see you again."

"Do you mean that?"

"Don't flatter yourself too much," laughs Townley Town. "She thinks we *all* have long legs."

KITTY—Has anybody got a cigarette? (*The three men near her offer her one.*) Oh, not three. That's my unlucky number. The third of June was my wedding day, to-day is the third of August, and three years ago—thanks. (*Taking a cigarette from one, and a light from another.*)

BOB (*not taking his eyes away from* KITTY)—What were you going to say—Mrs. Brown? Did anything unlucky happen to you three years ago?

KITTY (*as* WALLACE *lights her cigarette*)—I thought so then. I've grown wiser since. Have you ever been in California, Mr.

Brown? I keep thinking I've seen you some place. (*Moving a little towards* BOB.)

BOB—Yes—I have—but I don't seem to remember the Courtland Browns.

KITTY—Courtland was my maiden name. I took it back after my divorce, of course, and I'm crazy about it. Mrs. Courtland Brown. Not bad, eh?

TOWNLEY—No—if one must be a Brown—Courtland certainly helps.

KITTY—That's the way I feel about it. Perhaps you don't mind being Brown. I did, horribly.

BOB—You seem to have got rid of it pretty successfully.

KITTY—Where's that nice girl you were telling me about, Boucicault?

MRS. BOUCICAULT—Where is she, Bob?

BOB—I left her in the pool. She wouldn't come out.

MADGE (*still on the sofa*)—I'm Madge Livingstone, Mrs. Brown. Nobody seems to be introducing us.

KITTY (*going to* MADGE *with gracious charm and putting out her hand*)—Oh, how do you do.

MADGE—I've been admiring you.

KITTY—How nice! I'm grateful!

MRS. BOUCICAULT—Go get your tea, Bob. (BOB, *staring at* KITTY, *doesn't hear.*) Don't stand around looking indefinite, Bob! Tea!

BOB—What? Oh—yes—thanks. I'll have about the longest drink of Scotch I've ever had in my life—I think. (*He goes to the tea table.*)

KITTY (*watching him as he goes*)—There's something strangely familiar about that man.

TOWNLEY—I dare say all Browns have something in common.

Dierdre is the last to be introduced to Kitty, and their mutual admiration is immediately spoken. Kitty, particularly interested in the plans for Dierdre's wedding, recalls that she, too, was married in a little church, in the spring, when everything was just beginning instead of dying, and it was the most perfect of Junes.

She must have been a perfect bride, Bob Brown suggests, and Kitty is ready to agree with him. She believed it all then, the holy sacrament and everything.

"There never was such sunshine as it fell across the altar.

There never were such flowers—and such bridesmaids. They wore large soft hats and green tulle frocks. Darlings—every one of them. They all have their divorces now." They all laugh a little, with the exception of Bob and Madge.

Bob is curious about the bridegroom, too. Was he also satisfactory—at the time?

"He was the most perfect part of it," promptly admits Kitty. "And I was more in love than any girl—any place—ever was."

Kitty is inclined to believe, however, that it is time for a change in the old-fashioned marriage customs. Dierdre and Bruce should be smart enough to evolve something new—"some graceful arrangement with all the little annoying things like love and fidelity entirely left out. It's absolutely fatal to marry the ones we are in love with."

Now Kitty thinks she would like to take a walk and see the grounds. She doesn't mind much whether she walks with Mr. Town or Mr. Grainger. She would, of course, like to accept Mr. Brown's invitation, but unfortunately the others had spoken first. Kitty is really having a gorgeous time, she admits to Bob. The unexpectedness of everything is so thrilling. . . .

Kitty and Wallace Grainger are seeing the grounds. . . . Mrs. Boucicault and Townley Town have followed after. . . . Dierdre and Bruce Keen can't hit upon anything to do except quarrel.

It seems to Bruce that Dierdre is especially hard to please of late, and not at all keen about being with him or talking with him. And yet he is just as keen about her as ever. As a matter of fact Bruce is as jealous as a pup of this Brown guy and about convinced that Dierdre is making a congenital idiot of herself. They are still arguing the question when Kitty comes back to change her shoes for a longer walk, and Bob Brown follows her in from the terrace.

BOB—Mrs. Brown—I'm awfully anxious to ask you something about California—if you'll be good enough to give me just a minute.

WALLACE (*who has followed* KITTY *in*)—I'll come right back and wait for you here.

DIERDRE (*rising*)—Is this going to be a secret conference? Do you want us to go?

BRUCE—Yes, he does. Come on with me—if you can bear it. (*Giving* DIERDRE *a push as they go off across the terrace to the right.*)

BOB (*after a pause*)—Why did you do this absurd thing? Why didn't you say who we are—at once?

KITTY—Why didn't you?

BOB—I couldn't speak. It was—

KITTY—Neither could I. It was all so quick. If we'd blurted it out at once—but we didn't—and it's infinitely better this way. Much more graceful.

BOB—It's ridiculous. I'm going to tell them now.

KITTY—Oh, no, you're not. I refuse to be made a—conspicuous. It's done now—and much more comfortable this way —for everybody. Why spoil everybody's week-end about a thing that is of no importance really? We were bound to run into each other, some time, some place.

BOB—I don't like it. There's no reason in the world why we shouldn't tell them.

KITTY—There's no reason in the world why we should. What possible difference can it make to anybody in any way? It will only be for such a little while. Any hostess would be grateful to us for keeping still—especially this one.

BOB—Do you want me to go in town?

KITTY (*turning back to look at* BOB)—And leave this nice girl? How absurd!

BOB—She's going to marry the boy.

KITTY—Oh, surely not.

BOB—What?

KITTY—That half baked boy? He isn't up to her. She's ready for life. She's gorgeous. I must tell you something. Bouci sent for me to take you away from her. Now you know that's rather good. (*She laughs.*)

BOB—You can't be as hard as you seem.

KITTY—You didn't expect me to be soft—did you?

BOB—You're making them misunderstand you. They think you're a hard boiled woman of the world—to put it mildly. Is that what you want them to think?

KITTY—I think it's all a very amusing situation myself. For goodness' sake, let's be gay about it.

BOB—I refuse to accept the situation. It's uncomfortable and absurd.

KITTY—If this is uncomfortable what would it be if you told? Curiosity—watching. Why did it happen?—Who began it? What was it?—Feeling so sorry for me because I lost you.

BOB—Oh—

KITTY—Spoiling the girl's fun.

BOB—Absurd.

KITTY (*with sudden fire*)—I won't have it all brought back. It's a very trivial thing to ask—it seems to me. I do ask it. I—I shall leave at once if you're going to do it.

BOB—If you put it that way—I won't.

KITTY—Thanks.

WALLACE (*coming back from the hall*)—I hope I haven't kept you waiting?

KITTY (*after a slight pause—remembering*)—Oh—my shoes. I won't be a minute. (*She gets her coat from the piano quickly and crosses to the hall entrance.*) Mr. Brown and I have found a distant relation—by marriage—but very distant. (*She goes off quickly as the curtain falls.*)

ACT II

Dinner is about over the Sunday evening following when Madge Livingstone, having abruptly left the table, followed by Wallace Grainger, storms out into Mrs. Boucicault's living room.

Mrs. Livingstone, judging from her remarks, has stood about all she can stand. She doesn't mind the other men acting as though they had never seen anything like Kitty Brown before, but she does most seriously object to Wallace acting that way. If she is no longer his inspiration, Mrs. Livingstone points out, then no part of their beautiful friendship is justified.

Mrs. Boucicault and Dierdre follow Mrs. Livingstone and Mr. Grainger. Mrs. Boucicault comes to hurry the arrangement of the bridge tables on the terrace. If they are to play at all they had better get started. Dierdre's interest at the moment is divived. She is lost in admiration of the executive ability of her grandmother and she finds the liqueurs and highballs on a side-table appealing to her mood. It is the highball that adds a touch to her loquaciousness as well as her frankness. She lets Mrs. Boucicault know that she (Dierdre) is fully aware of the conspiracy to bring Kitty Brown to the house party to turn Bob Brown's attention from other interests. She not only knows all about it, but she is greatly amused that it is not working.

"You're forgetting who you are," sharply suggests Mrs. Boucicault.

"I know damn well who I am," answers Dierdre. "That's why I'm going to manage my own business." And she storms out on to the terrace.

Mrs. Boucicault is slightly upset by her granddaughter's attitude, but not enough to accept Mrs. Livingstone's sympathy. Neither her sympathy nor her advice. And as for Mrs. Livingstone being shocked—that's all poppycock!

"Don't pose with me, Madge," snaps Mrs. Boucicault. "She's the only one of the whole pack I care a thing about. I love her. I've actually been fool enough to let myself love her. I'd begun to have some pride in her. I'd begun to think the good old stock was coming out. Why did this thing have to hit her? Why? And no matter what happens I can't blame her. I blame myself and my respectable friends and the disrespectable things they are doing."

With this relief Mrs. Boucicault takes a tiny cigar from her case, borrows a light from Bob Brown, and recovers at least a moderate degree of amiability.

Now they are all in from the dining-room. Dierdre carries a cup of coffee in one hand and a highball in the other. The coffee is for her grandmother and the highball for herself. Nor will she let Bob take it away from her.

Kitty is surrounded by the men, as usual. Townley Town, Bruce Keen and Wallace Grainger hang upon her recollections of certain Paris music hall singers. This takes them to the piano where they get more fun than harmony out of their effort to duplicate the more popular songs.

Dierdre is still defiant. She has no interest in a swim in the pool, now or later, with Bruce. Nor will she "talk things out" with him about Bob Brown. If they were to try to talk now they would only ball things up. For the present she wants to be let alone.

And Kitty Brown refuses to talk things out with Bob. There may be many things he wants to ask her, as he insists, but she can't imagine herself answering any of them. She quite deliberately discourages every effort Bob makes toward a better understanding.

There is no lessening of Dierdre's interest in Bob, however. She has managed now to get him to herself, as Kitty leaves him.

DIERDRE—Let's hop in the pool after awhile. It's so beastly hot.

BOB—Is it? I don't think so.

DIERDRE—Oh—you don't need the pool to cool off. Why the sudden drop in temperature?

BOB—All your imagination.

DIERDRE—Am I as dark and glowing and mysterious as ever?

BOB—You're marvellous.

DIERDRE—What are you looking at? (*As he glances at* KITTY.)

BOB—I'm looking at you.

DIERDRE (*lifting her face close to his*)—And I'm looking at you, darling—and seeing the most wonderful things in the world.

BOB (*touching her highball glass*)—Isn't that enough?

DIERDRE—Don't be so paternal. Come on. You need one yourself. (DIERDRE *goes out*—BOB *follows her.*)

KITTY—Townie, are you trying to persuade me you've fallen in love with me or is this just your week-end charm?

MRS. BOUCICAULT (*coming down to* KITTY)—Go on, Townley.

TOWNLEY (*rising*)—Where shall I go?

MRS. BOUCICAULT—Go to hell.

KITTY (*calling to* TOWNLEY *as he goes*)—And if you return —bring me some very hot coffee. (TOWNLEY *goes onto the terrace to the table to get the coffee.*)

MRS. BOUCICAULT (*suddenly flaring at* KITTY)—Why don't you do what I want you to do? Get Bob Brown away from Dierdre?

KITTY (*rising quickly*)—Really, Bouci, this is rather disgusting. You're putting a ridiculous thing up to me—an impossible thing.

MRS. BOUCICAULT—You're efficient enough with the others. Why are you so mulish about it? This is the first time I've seen you even speak to Bob. I've been watching Dierdre. I heard something she said to him just now. Help me, Kitty.

KITTY—I've been watching her too. She is in love with him. Why on earth don't you let them alone? Isn't your Bob Brown as good as the other one for her to marry—better—since he's the one she really wants?

MRS. BOUCICAULT—He hasn't the slightest intention of marrying her—and she's throwing herself at him. Hot headed young daredevil! Anything could happen. I'm frightened, Kitty. (TOWNLEY *comes back with a cup of coffee.*) What is it, Townley? Go away. Go away and mind your own business.

TOWNLEY—This is my business. Don't snort at me, angel. I was sent for this.

Mrs. Boucicault is still having considerable trouble getting her bridge started. She manages to herd some of her prospective partners toward the terrace, but loses others in the process. Now she finds Wallace Grainger trying desperately to recite a bit of poetry to Kitty Brown. And with Wallace started for the game Townley Town holds Kitty back while he tries as desperately to get her to promise to go to dinner with him in town as soon as they shall both get back. Now Townley has heard his hostess's call and only Bob is left with Kitty.

"The situation is getting more amusing every minute," observes Kitty. "Isn't it?"

BOB—No. I don't think it is. It's getting more ridiculous every minute. We ought to have told them in the first place. Let's tell them now. It would clear the whole atmosphere.

KITTY—The atmosphere doesn't need clearing. Surely you aren't embarrassed—are you? Don't let my being here make the slightest difference to you in any way.

BOB—About Dierdre—you mean?

KITTY—About anything.

BOB—You don't think I'm in love with her?

KITTY—Aren't you? I'm no judge—of that.

BOB—And you don't think for a minute she's—it's anything serious with her?

KITTY—Oh—isn't it? I should have said it was something very serious. But perhaps I'm no judge of that either.

BOB—You're implying a lot—but you surely don't think I was skunk enough to go after her.

KITTY (*moving away*)—And you surely don't think you have to explain anything to me.

BOB—I want you to know how it is. I was flirting with her—a little—a little too much—perhaps—before you came—but seeing you has made me stop.

KITTY—Oh—sorry. (*Half turning back to him.*) But I'll be gone in the morning—and it will be just as though I'd never been here at all. (*Starting again to go.*)

BOB—Wait—please.

KITTY—Yes?

BOB—I'm not going to ask to see the children—though I want to—horribly.

KITTY (*having looked at him quickly with startled wistful eyes—and speaking with difficulty*)—Bob—it is better for them to know only one side—even if that side is—me.

BOB—Are they well?

KITTY—Very. Robert is getting to be more like you every minute. And Katherine is marvellous.

BOB (*looking at her eagerly and moving a little towards her*) —Like you?

KITTY—Yes, only more so.

BOB—I hope she'll be just exactly like you—just exactly—as you were, I mean.

KITTY—She won't, I assure you. She'll be much more intelligent—and much more prepared. I believe in preparedness.

BOB—You're changed, Kitty.

KITTY—I hope so. Three years of Paris ought to improve any woman.

BOB—You seem to have had a pretty good time.

KITTY—I've been awfully lucky in the people I've known. Gay, delightful people.

BOB—Like these, you mean?

KITTY—Um—all sorts.

BOB—Tell me some more. You might sit down a minute at least. What have you actually been doing—all this time? (*She hesitates in a long pause and then sits on the sofa back of her.* BOB *brings the arm chair and sits before* KITTY.)

KITTY—I've been working hard, too.

BOB—At what?

KITTY—Clothes. I've made a good connection with a firm in Paris, and I'm going to have a shop out home.

BOB—What?

KITTY—Yes. It will keep me going back and forth, which I shall adore. I can stand one place because I'll always know I'm going to the other.

BOB—Um. There's something in that—possibly. Though the further I go the more I see I'd like to stay put—once I get in the right place.

KITTY—Are there any right places?

BOB—There's just one—for me. But I'm not in it. (KITTY *is about to rise. He goes on quickly.*) Well—and—

KITTY—I think that's about all—except that in a little while I shan't have to have any more alimony—I can take care of the children myself.

BOB—You'll do nothing of the kind.

KITTY—Certainly I will.

BOB—We'll see about that.

KITTY—There's something about one's own money—making

it and spending it—that has—I know now how a man feels—only—he takes it for granted—and it's a new thrill to me.

BOB—And when you're not working?

KITTY—Like you I've been amusing myself with anything and everything that came my way. I know how a man feels about that too.

BOB—You're very glib but I don't know just what you mean. What—do you—exactly?

Dierdre's return interrupts them. Being a little more suspicious than usual Dierdre is beginning to think that perhaps Kitty is trying to vamp Bob, though she hesitates to believe she would even if she could.

The wind on the terrace has driven the bridge players inside, and now again there is considerable confusion and not a little sarcasm spent upon the reorganization of the tables. The play is no sooner started than one table, at least, is decidedly upset by the talkative Dierdre. Her association with the liquor wagon becomes more noticeable by the minute, and when she has some little difficulty separating the hearts from the jumping spades it is, Madge Livingstone insists, time to find out whether they are playing bridge or what.

Even being dummy does not help Dierdre. It gives her an opportunity, rather, to pick up her conversation with Kitty. She wants to tell Kitty just why she was sent for—to take Bob away from her. But it can't be done. That much she wants to say and does say, and neither Bob nor Bruce nor her grandmother can keep her quiet.

"Bruce," demands Mrs. Boucicault, sharply, "take her out of the room."

"Why should I leave the room?" indignantly demands Dierdre. "I'm a great deal more decent than anybody in it."

KITTY (*lifting her head quickly and throwing her cards on the table*)—I don't think there's any doubt about that. Why don't we all leave the room—in the order of our sins?

TOWNLEY—That's a good idea. I'll start the procession. (*He goes up towards the terrace—stopping as* KITTY *speaks.*)

KITTY—I'll come next. (*She goes up—stopping as* DIERDRE *calls out.*)

DIERDRE—But, Kitty—I want you to know.

BRUCE (*in low tone to* DIERDRE*—standing above her*)—Dierdre—please.

DIERDRE—I can't help it, Bruce. (BRUCE *turns away quickly and goes onto the terrace.*)

MRS. BOUCICAULT—You've disgraced yourself, Dierdre.

KITTY—Why do you say that, Bouci? She's only telling the truth. I think it's delightful.

DIERDRE—Gran thinks I'm tight. (*Her head drops a little over the back of the chair.*)

KITTY (*going to* DIERDRE)—Just chatty—aren't you? I am too—when I've had a drink or two. If this had been me—instead of you—my word—the things I could have told about the first time I fell in love. Couldn't you, Mr. Brown?

BOB (*standing at the left of the table*)—I don't think anybody would be interested.

KITTY—Oh, it's always amusing. Why don't we make it an "I confess" game—and cross our hearts to be as honest as Dierdre? How many times has it been the first time with you, Townie?

TOWNLEY—Well—a— You'll have to give me a few minutes to think.

KITTY—While he's thinking—will you, Madge? May I call you Madge? We're all getting so cosy and real now.

MADGE—I find this excessively disagreeable, Mrs. Brown.

DIERDRE—Bob, you tell Kitty how it is with us.

BOB—Don't, Dierdre!

DIERDRE—You wouldn't take him away from me, would you, Kitty? You mustn't now.

KITTY—No danger of that—is there, Mr. Brown?

MRS. BOUCICAULT—Dierdre, leave this room!

DIERDRE—No! I want to tell—

KITTY—Come on, dear. Come outside and tell me. I know just how you feel. How could you resist Bob.

MRS. BOUCICAULT—Katherine! Are you upholding Dierdre?

KITTY—I'll do my best. She's a little tall for me.

BOUCICAULT—Katherine, I'm ashamed of you.

KITTY—That's good, Bouci. I'm ashamed of you, too. You've been very naughty with your heavy intrigue. I told you I wasn't clever enough for this job.

BOB—What job?

KITTY—Oh, to get you, and have you and hold you, forever.

MADGE—Boucicault, I can't stand this brazenness!

KITTY—Now if it were Wallie you wanted me to take away from somebody—there's no telling what might have happened.

(*She smiles at* WALLACE—*much to his excited embarrassment—and turns toward the terrace as the curtain falls.*)

An hour later Kitty Brown walks out from her bedroom onto a balcony flooded with moonlight. She is wearing a charming dressing robe into which Perkins has helped her and she is ready for the night. In the morning she will have her coffee at 8, she warns Perkins, and thus be ready for an early train into town.

In the shadows below the balcony the glow of a cigarette is seen. Behind the cigarette is Townley Town. Before Kitty can stop him he is on the stairs at the end of the balcony and is coming up. They are creaky stairs and apparently none too safe, but Townley manages them. At the top he quiets Kitty's further protests by pulling her down on the top step beside him.

Townley's intentions are apparent but his manners are restrained. He has, he admits, fallen quite in love with Kitty and he is greatly cheered as to the possibilities by her frank admission that she finds him a most agreeable person. Kitty is different, Townley admits. He feels fearfully sorry for Bob Brown, being pursued as he undoubtedly is by Dierdre. It isn't the women who pursue men that are the most attractive. It is the women who keep them wondering, as Kitty has kept Townley wondering.

Now he is of a mind to find out exactly where he stands. Nor will he take gracefully the suggestion that he had better be going. He has followed Kitty to the door of her room and is eagerly bent upon having a good-night kiss. Kitty refuses him when suddenly the shutters of the French windows in an adjoining room are thrown open and Bob Brown walks out upon the balcony.

Kitty is as quick as the shutters, however, and with a push she shoves Townley into her room and closes the door.

BOB—Kitty!

KITTY—Oh—it's your room! Fancy that!

BOB—Kitty, you don't believe anything that girl said—(KITTY *shakes her head at* BOB.) What's the matter? No one can hear us. There's no one about. I don't know what she told you, but you've got to know I haven't done anything you could object to.

KITTY (*calling*)—Townley—did you find the cigarettes? Come out. (*A pause.* TOWNLEY *comes out.*) That's Mr. Brown's room. Isn't it amusing? (*To* Bob.) We were wondering. We've been sitting on the steps—smoking—to keep the mosquitoes away. They're awfully bad to-night—aren't they? The vines, I s'pose. Mr. Townley was just going. Perhaps you'll stay now. Perhaps you'll bring out some chairs, Mr. Brown? (*The men stare at each other amazed—embarrassed.*) No? Oh—well—I'll see you to-morrow night, Townie. Better ring me up in the afternoon at three—sharp. I'll be awfully busy all day. What?

Townley (*after a slight pause*)—I'm afraid I don't understand quite.

Kitty—You will. I shall have something frightfully amusing to tell you at dinner. Good night.

Townley—It seems Boucicault's scheme did work then.

Kitty—Not at all. At least not her way. That's what I'll tell you about. It's unbelievably funny.

Townley (*coldly*)—I see.

Kitty—Oh, do you! You don't in the least. This seems to be rather too staggering for you. Don't be melodramatic I beg. If you want me to dine with you ring me up. If you don't—don't. Good night.

Townley—At three—sharp. Good night. Good night, Brown. (Bob *doesn't speak.*)

Kitty (*putting her hand out impulsively to* Townley)—You're a darling. (Townley *takes* Kitty's *hand for an instant—and goes down the steps.*)

Bob—What does it all mean?

Kitty—All what? Townley on my balcony? That ought not to need an interpretation—for you.

Bob—What?

Kitty—Yes. Good night. (*She starts to go.*)

Bob—Is it—what it looks like?

Kitty—Nothing very novel about it—is there?

Bob—What was he doing in your room?

Kitty—That's a very naïve question—for you. How silly it all is. I'm going to bed. Good night.

Bob—Kitty!

Kitty—Yes?

Bob—It's horrible! I can't believe it. It isn't you

Kitty—I don't think you know much about what is—or isn't—me.

Bob—I do. You can't have changed like this. It simply is not possible.

KITTY—Why not?

BOB—Are you doing this sort of thing all the time? God—what are you laughing at?

KITTY—It's so funny!

BOB—No it isn't! I want you to know I've absolutely done nothing wrong towards Dierdre Lessing. I'm horribly sorry and ashamed about the whole thing downstairs—and you've got to tell me exactly what you mean by this. In the name of heaven, why did you let that man come up here! Is he—

At which moment Dierdre Lessing walks out of Bob Brown's room and joins Bob and Kitty on the balcony. She, too, is plainly suspicious. She is, however, willing to stand by what she has done. She has meant everything she has said and she has come to talk things over with Bob. Bob's idea that Kitty should chaperone Dierdre back to her room, in case some one else might be moving about, strikes her as being decidedly amusing.

Now that she is there Dierdre wants to put her problem up to Kitty. She is engaged to Bruce, but she is crazy about Bob. What would Kitty do if she were in her place?

"If I were in your place," Kitty answers, quite seriously, "I'm sure I would marry Bob. (BOB *turns to watch* KITTY.) I'd believe that he was the one man for me—and that I'd be the one woman for him—always. I'd believe that nothing could ever change him. That's the way I know I'd feel about Bob—but I suppose you're much too intelligent for that."

But that isn't at all what Bob wants. He never has thought of Dierdre in that way, he insists, even in the face of her denials that he was confessedly crazy about her before Kitty arrived. That's it! Dierdre decides. It is Kitty who has worked this change in Bob. She has taken him. That's what their being there together and alone means!

Bob would tell Dierdre of his relation to Kitty, but Kitty will not have that. It is better that Dierdre should believe what she wants to. It is better, anyway, if she is in love with Bob that she find out his unworthiness before rather than after she marries him. And Dierdre, believing the worst, leaves them.

Bob is furious at the thought that Dierdre will think what she does of Kitty. He will not have that. He will clear the whole thing up the first thing in the morning.

If he does he will spoil everything, insists Kitty. As it is the plan has worked just as Mrs. Boucicault wanted it to and no one is hurt. It is an easy way out for Bob. Kitty is not sure that she has not had quite a kick out of it herself. So why not let matters stand.

BOB—Kitty, I'm more in love with you than I ever was in my life.

KITTY—Oh—Mr. Brown, this is so sudden.

BOB—I adore you.

KITTY—It's the moon.

BOB (*taking her by the shoulders and turning her towards him*)—Stop this. Look at me. Talk to me like—like—

KITTY—Like what?

BOB—Like your own honest-to-God self. You haven't said a real thing to me since you came.

KITTY (*getting away from him*)—I don't know any real things —do you?

BOB—Stop bluffing and hedging. I love you! Doesn't that mean anything to you at all?

KITTY—Yes, that I'm something new to you.

BOB—How much does this Townley thing mean?

KITTY—Nothing in particular. Only that you're not used to seeing other men aware of me.

BOB—I'm not used to seeing other men treating you as though they had a right to—to—

KITTY—To what?

BOB—To come up here.

KITTY—Townley had a perfect right to come up here. I invited him.

BOB—God, Kitty, I can't stand this. What does it mean?

KITTY—It means I like him.

BOB—And what else?

KITTY—I don't know what else—yet.

BOB—How far has it gone?

KITTY—Just as far as—as—

BOB—As—what?

KITTY—As the door.

BOB—Are you in love with him?

KITTY—I always like to think I'm in love with somebody.

BOB—Is there nothing left of what you used to feel for me? Is every bit of it gone?

KITTY—Every little bit.

BOB—Is it?

KITTY—Do you think I'm a fool? I've filled my life with other things.

BOB—What things?

KITTY—Things—things—to take the place of the ones I used to think were everything and found were nothing.

BOB—What about you—yourself? What's become of that?

KITTY—I find myself a much easier person to live with than I used to be. I don't take myself as seriously as I used to.

BOB—Oh, Kitty, you were the sweetest thing in the world, and you still are.

KITTY—Was I? I don't remember.

BOB—I don't believe you've changed. You're the same adorable thing I loved, and you're even more so now. Kitty, I—I—

KITTY—No—no—Bob.

BOB (*drawing her close in his arms*)—Please—please—darling.

KITTY—Oh, no—Bob, not that.

BOB—I can't help it, Kitty. Why can't I have you again? (*He kisses her.*)

KITTY—It's over—it's finished. (*Getting away from him.*)

BOB (*after a pause in a low, hard tone*)—Is there anybody else?

KITTY—Yes. Why not?

BOB—Is this the way you've been living? Have there been other men? Have you—have you—

KITTY—And if I have, what of it? (*She stops as a soft whistle is heard from below.*)

WALLACE (*not seen in the darkness*)—Kitty, are you there?

KITTY (*to* BOB)—Well—we're both having a busy evening—aren't we? It's Wallie. Hello, lovely night, isn't it? (*Looking over the railing.*)

WALLACE—I want to say a poem to you.

KITTY—I'm dying to hear it—but you can't now. Somebody else is here.

WALLACE—Oh.

KITTY—Sorry. Ring me up at three o'clock to-morrow—sharp.

WALLACE—At three sharp.

KITTY—Perhaps I'll have dinner with you to-morrow night.

WALLACE—Thanks.

KITTY—Good night.

WALLACE (*softly*)—Good night.

KITTY (*after a slight pause*)—Well—I don't expect anybody else—but perhaps you do—Mr. Brown. Good night. (*She goes in as the curtain falls.*)

ACT III

At 9 o'clock next morning Mrs. Boucicault's week-end guests are variously preparing to depart. Dierdre, the shock of the previous evening's experience still upon her, is trying to avoid Bruce Keen, who insists upon following her wherever it may be she intends going. Dierdre, on the other hand, is equally determined to be by herself. Her impulse is to jump in a car and ride and ride until she is far away from everybody and where she can *think.*

As for her feelings toward Bob Brown, she is not sure what they are, either. Of course Kitty Brown had won him away from her. Dierdre couldn't hope to compete with that type of woman. But what did that matter? What if she had found them alone on Kitty's balcony? She is still desperately interested in Bob.

DIERDRE—If he came down here right now and asked me to go away with him—I'd go.

BRUCE—You wouldn't.

DIERDRE—I would.

BRUCE—You're not in love with him. It's just a—an—infatuation.

DIERDRE—Whatever it is I've got it.

BRUCE (*touching* DIERDRE'S *shoulder and sitting on the seat at left of the sofa*)—You'll get over it. I've been that way—lots of times.

DIERDRE—Of course you have. But I haven't. It means something to me.

BRUCE—Not a thing. Not a damn thing. If you threw yourself away on that man you'd want to kill yourself afterwards.

DIERDRE—Applesauce!

BRUCE (*leaning towards her over the back of the sofa*)—Dierdre—dearest—I want to see you through this. Believe me there's nothing in it but what you'll be terribly sorry for—and ashamed of afterwards.

DIERDRE—Awfully wise—aren't you?

BRUCE—You bet I'm wise. I want to marry you. I love you. I want to make it the—the greatest ever—and we could, too—if you'd—

DIERDRE—Yes—why do you want to marry me? Why do you love me? (*Breaking a little.*) I think it's perfectly marvellous that you do, Bruce—but why?—It's because you've lived enough to be sure. Well, I haven't.

BRUCE—You don't have to go through that.

DIERDRE (*softening and putting a hand over his*)—Listen, Bruce—I like you better than anybody in the world. Maybe we are the best bet for each other. But I'm not crazy about you the way I am about Bob.

BRUCE—Take it from me—liking is a better bet than craziness.

DIERDRE (*drawing her hand away*)—Now, don't talk to me like Santa Claus. I want to know what I'm doing because I know—myself. Not because somebody's telling me what I ought to do.

BRUCE—If you'd use your bean and tell yourself the truth you'd know what to do.

DIERDRE—I am using my bean. That's just it. I'm not swallowing any old stuff.

BRUCE—Now get this. There's no new slant on this old stuff at all. Either a girl's decent or she isn't. There's no half way business about it—and when a fellow gets down to brass tacks, he wants the girl he's going to marry—the one who is going to be the mother of his kids—to be the straightest, finest, cleanest thing in the world.

DIERDRE—Pearls you learned at mother's knee. And if a girl wants the darling boy she marries to be the same thing—where the hell is she going to find him?

That, insists Bruce, man-like, is not the same thing at all. But it is to Dierdre. She can't see, for that matter, why she shouldn't have Bob for a time and marry Bruce, too.

The arrival of Mrs. Boucicault interrupts the discussion. Bouci has come to speed her parting guests and she loathes the job. And yet there is an intense sort of pleasure to her in seeing them go.

Now Bruce has gone and Dierdre has turned on her grandmother. It's a rotten low down thing grandmother has done—sending for Kitty and setting her deliberately on the trail of Bob Brown. It may be some satisfaction to her to know *all* that has happened—that she (Dierdre) had gone to Bob Brown's room the night before and that she found Bob and Kitty together, which is evidence that Mrs. Boucicault's conspiracy had been quite successful. But it hasn't made any difference in Dierdre's feelings toward Bob.

"Just because you cooked up a nasty thing with that kind of

woman—" Dierdre is saying when Kitty Brown comes through the door.

"I suppose I'm the woman," ventures Kitty.

"I know that this is all ridiculous nonsense," explodes Mrs. Boucicault. "Kitty, I don't believe a word of it!"

"Why don't you? You wanted it to happen, didn't you? That's why you offered me your hospitality, isn't it?"

Mrs. Boucicault still refuses to believe what she has heard. Again she demands that Kitty deny Dierdre's charge, and again Kitty refuses to clear herself. But there are angry flashes in her voice when Dierdre repeats her own conviction of Kitty's sin.

"Don't take me for a blithering idiot, Gran," sneers Dierdre. "I *know.*"

"And *what* do you know?" snaps Kitty. "There was just a minute last night when I wanted you to believe I'd done that rotten thing—because I thought it would save you a bigger headache—later on. More or less the same thing happened to me—once—and I was sorry for you—with all my heart. I intended to hold my tongue—and go through with it. But since you've talked—in not quite a good sportsman way—we'll talk a little more. You came to the gentleman's—balcony—and found me there first. Surely you can allow me the same comfortable freedom—without question—which I grant you. Besides—I wasn't alone with him—remember. Mr. Townley was there too."

Townley, a little flustered, is forced to admit that he was there. And Wallace Grainger, following him into the room, also confesses that he, too, played a small though obscure part in the famous balcony scene.

These revelations are almost too much for Mrs. Boucicault. And when the situation is further complicated by the arrival of Bob Brown, followed by Dierdre's insistence that, so long as Kitty is revealing so much she tell about Bob's part in the adventure, too, the air is at least vibrant with expectancy.

Bob refuses to permit Kitty to stand as charged before this house party, even if she doesn't, as she says, care a hang what any of them may choose to think of her. But Kitty holds him to his promise not to mention the true state of affairs. She will not, however, let Dierdre's charge that she is trying to "make a joke of the whole rotten affair" pass unanswered.

"And what are you trying to make out of it?" she demands, spiritedly. "I know I asked you to believe that inconceivably vile thing—and now I ask you not to. That's where the joke comes in. I'm afraid I've tried to be a little too clever, Bouci.

I'm afraid I've got myself in too deep. There doesn't seem to be anything about me to tell—what I am—(*her voice breaks*)—or how things are. That's rather a joke, too. I know exactly what each and every one of you is thinking about me—each in his own way. (*To* DIERDRE.) If you think I took your Mr. Brown away from you last night—allow me to give him back to you this morning."

Kitty starts to go, but Bob stops her.

"Dierdre—listen! Kitty is my wife—or was!" he says, as a murmur of amazement sweeps the group. "She divorced me three years ago. But she still is my wife—to me. There never has been and there never will be any one to take her place. The greatest thing that could happen to me would be for her to take me back—but that—I know—is a lost hope."

"You always have had good manners, Bob," admits Kitty. And then to the others: "He's only being magnificent, Bouci. This accidental meeting doesn't change anything for us. That was settled three years ago. Don't let it change anything for anybody else."

They have nearly all left now, both Townley and Wallace thrilled with the expectation of calling Kitty at 3 in town. Mrs. Boucicault, though reluctant to have Bob and Kitty speak their farewells alone, has returned to the routine of her household. She would love above all other things to hear what they have to say to each other but she leaves them.

What Kitty has to say is, she thinks, good-by and no more. What Bob has to say is that he will not accept this good-by. He has not slept a wink all night and he must know the truth. The truth about the men he had found on Kitty's balcony, the truth about her life since she has been a divorcee. If what she would let him believe is true, then obviously she cannot keep the children, a statement that fills her with a momentary fear.

There is something to confess between them, and much to reiterate. It has been a miserable three years of separation for Bob, and, despite a courageous determination to be gay about it, it has not been a happy time for Kitty.

But it probably has been better for them—better than for her to have forgiven him that first time and then gone on forgiving and forgiving other lapses. Better for her that she, too, should have had her experiences and come to know how shallow such adventures can be. The confession is a blow to Bob.

"How could you! How could you!" he cries in the bitterness of his disappointment.

"Because I loved you so!" Kitty answers, with sudden full abandon.

KITTY (*letting her feeling carry her away at last*)—Heaven and earth and God were all mixed up in you. When that was gone nothing was left. Can't you understand that? I suppose you think I ought to have stayed at home with a broken heart, for the rest of my life—hugging my ideals. But I didn't seem to be able to do that. I had to get out and find out what it was all about—to see why you did it.

BOB—Well, then if you've found out so much—if you've got so wise and experienced—you know now how little that affair meant to me.

KITTY—Yes, I know now. I know both sides. I wanted to find out whether I'd been a fool or not—whether I had exaggerated what you did. Well, I hadn't. It was just as horrible as I thought it was. Bob, marriage means just one thing—complete and absolute fidelity—or it's the biggest farce on earth.

BOB—I could make our marriage now what you thought it ought to be then.

KITTY (*sitting on the sofa*)—That I should live to hear you say that, Mr. Brown!

BOB (*standing in front of her*)—How can you be so hard?

KITTY—Because I refuse to be made unhappy again.

BOB (*sitting above her on the sofa*)—Kitty, darling, if you'd let me begin again! God—what we've lost! Two people who loved each other as we did!

KITTY—Don't harp on that.

BOB—We had the great chance and muffed it.

KITTY—The chance is gone now, Bob. Let's be sane and look this in the face. What if we did go back—what of it? What is there in it?

BOB—Well, not so much if we're only thinking of ourselves. The thing that's been hitting me in the eye in the last three days is that there is something a damned sight bigger in it than ourselves—and that's what we ought to grab now—and hang on to.

KITTY—The *real* thing, yes. But as it *is*—as we've all *made* it.

BOB—Well, it is the real thing—to plenty of people.

KITTY—To whom, for instance? Anybody you know?

BOB—Yes, of course.

Kitty—Who are they?

Bob—Well—a—a—

Kitty—Exactly. Now let's get over this and not be sorry it happened. And the next time we see each other we'll be more game about it.

Bob—All right. Then we're going to be friends. Have dinner with me to-night in town.

Kitty—I have to eat *two* dinners *now.*

Bob—Eat three. I'll make it any time you say.

Kitty—Why not all dine together?

Bob—Cut out Townley.

Kitty—But not Wallie. You don't mind Wallie. He's having the time of his life. (*They laugh together,* Bob *bends over her and kisses her hair.*)

Bob—Give me a chance to make you love me again. That's fair, isn't it?

Kitty—Love isn't enough, Bob.

Bob—The children.

Kitty—We had the children. We had love—but that didn't keep us together. No, Bob, I'm not going to give you a chance to hurt me again. It's the awfulest hurt in the world and it would still be there, if I'd let it. (*She rises and moves away from him.*)

Bob (*following her a little*)—But I wouldn't hurt you again.

Kitty—No, Bob—I'm not going back. I'm going on. I don't know to just what—but on. For heaven's sake let's be gay about it.

Bob—To see you like this is a worse tragedy than losing you. Aren't you sick of this damned batting around—trying to fool yourself into thinking you're having a good time?

Kitty—Maybe you've had enough—you've been at it longer than I have—maybe you're ready for your slippers at the fire—I'm not. (*Putting on her coat.*)

Bob—Oh, Kitty, marry me again.

Kitty—You're out of your senses.

Bob—It's what I want. It's the only thing I do want—you and the children. Can't we make a fresh start?

Kitty—It's too late.

Bob—Do you hate me?

Kitty (*putting on her gloves*)—No.

Bob—Then why—

Kitty—Oh, it isn't you.

BOB—What is it then?

KITTY—It's myself. I couldn't. Neither could you, Bob. You're just making a gallant gesture.

BOB—No. From the minute I saw you, something pounded in me so hard—an idiotic hope—a something bigger than I ever had—or ever knew there could be. This is tougher than the first time I lost you. Good-by, Kitty. (*Putting out his hand.*)

KITTY (*taking his hand after an instant's hesitation*)—Good-by—and good luck. You'll get over this, Bob, in no time at all.

BOB—Oh—

KITTY—Yes, you will, I know. It doesn't take long.

BOB—Well, how is it going to end? What will you do? Where are you going?

KITTY—I don't know, I am sure. Life's a very complicated business, isn't it?

BOB—Do you think I could make you love me again? That's the point.

KITTY—That's what I'm afraid of. That's why I'm running now.

BOB (*going to her*)—Kitty—

KITTY—If I let myself go, I could be fascinated by you again in no time at all.

BOB—You're adorable!

KITTY (*holding him off*)—No, Bob, let's not make fools of ourselves. It would be no joke for either one of us to try to settle down again.

BOB—But we—

KITTY—No, I'm afraid, Bob. I'm honestly afraid. (*Sitting in the large chair.*)

BOB—Why? Why, dearest?

KITTY—I don't know. I've been so gay—so—so full of—so empty.

BOB (*dropping on his knees in front of her*)—Kitty!

KITTY—So lonely—

BOB—Darling!

KITTY—Oh, Bob, I love you so. (*Putting her arms about his neck.*) Take me back.

The curtain falls.

MACHINAL

A Tragedy in Ten Episodes

By Sophie Treadwell

THE gossiping heralds declared that Sophie Treadwell's drama, "Machinal," scheduled by Arthur Hopkins for September production, was frankly a dramatization of the then barely cold sensation, the Ruth Snyder-Judd Gray murder trial.

Miss Treadwell arose in her place periodically to deny these rumors. She had, she was willing to admit, been influenced to some extent by the grinding forces of a mechanistic world that had played a part in the lowering of Ruth Synder's standards and loyalties, her morals and ambitions, her pathetic and utterly frustrated pursuit of happiness. But "Machinal" was in no sense a dramatization of the Snyder-Gray case nor of any other.

When the play was produced September 7, 1928, the drama reviewers were quick to repeat the charge that here, if not a dramatization of the Snyder woman's life, crime and death, was at least a sort of idealized reflection of it.

It was, in many respects, a perfect presentment of melodrama. Mr. Hopkins and Robert Edmund Jones, his scenic designer, had caught the spirit of Miss Treadwell's deeper message and had illustrated it with impressive effect.

The settings were largely imaginative and partially impressionistic. The episodes were brief and frequently melted one into the other by the blacking out of the conclusion of one scene, the changing of the meagre settings and the raising of the lights on the episode following.

The play was the talk of the early season. Its popularity waned, however, and after ninety odd performances it was withdrawn. The American playgoer never has been one to endorse the tragic drama enthusiastically.

In Miss Treadwell's play the grinding of the machine begins with the introduction of the Young Woman in the office in which she works. "She is any Young Woman, going any day to any business. Ordinary. The confusion of her own inner thoughts, emotions, dreams, cuts her off from any actual adjustment to the routine of work. She gets through this routine with a very small surface of her consciousness. She is not homely and she is not pretty. She is preoccupied with herself—with her person. She has well-kept hands, and a trick of constantly arranging her hair over her ears."

The scene of her employment is the office of the George H. Jones Company; a hive of a place in which telephone girls, stenographers, filing clerks and adding clerks are jumbled together in a kind of orderliness that may promote efficiency but does not make for either comfort or concentration.

Over this office there is the steady drone of business: The whine of the phone girl, with her lifeless repetitions of "George H. Jones Company; good morning; hello; he's in conference; Mr. K. wants you; Spring 1726; hello; George H. Jones Company," etc. The adding clerk's incessant buzz of figures mingles with the filing clerk's mutterings of reports and market matters and the stenographer's strained efforts to read her notes.

Intermingled with these the gossip of the office; the sly references to parties held and parties planned; to personalities with "it" and personalities with none; to the fact that She is late; that She has the boss going and coming; that She lives with her mother—

Jones, the boss, is in. A flabby, smiling, slogan-shouting Jones, given to speeding things up, to hewing to the line, to first being sure he is right and then going ahead. He comes now looking for Miss A; he would see Miss A as soon as she comes in; he would not be disturbed while he is in conference—with Miss A.

The Young Woman arrives, fussed and conscious. The force greets her characteristically.

STENOGRAPHER—You're late!

FILING CLERK—You're late!

ADDING CLERK—You're late!

STENOGRAPHER—And yesterday!

FILING CLERK—The day before.

ADDING CLERK—And the day before.

STENOGRAPHER—You'll lose your job.

YOUNG WOMAN—No!

STENOGRAPHER—No! (*Workers exchange glances.*)

STENOGRAPHER—Can't?

FILING CLERK—Rent—bills—installments—miscellaneous.

ADDING CLERK—One ten—ninety-five—$3.40—35—12.60.

STENOGRAPHER—Then why are you late?

Young Woman—Why?
Stenographer—Excuse!
Adding Clerk—Excuse!
Filing Clerk—Excuse!
Telephone—Excuse it, please.
Stenographer—Why?
Young Woman—The subway!
Telephone—Long distance?
Filing Clerk—Old stuff!
Adding Clerk—That stall!
Stenographer—Stalled?
Young Woman—No—
Stenographer—What?
Young Woman—I had to get out.
Adding Clerk—Out?
Filing Clerk—Out?
Stenographer—Out where?
Young Woman—In the air. I thought I would faint! I had to get out in the air.
Filing Clerk—Give her the air.
Adding Clerk—Free air.
Stenographer—Hot air.
Young Woman—Like I'm dying.
Stenographer—Same thing yesterday. And the day before.
Young Woman—Yes. What am I going to do?
Adding Clerk—Take a taxi! (*They laugh.*)
Filing Clerk—Call a cop!
Telephone—Mr. J. wants you.
Young Woman—Me?
Telephone—You!
Young Woman—Mr. J.?
Stenographer—Mr. J.
Telephone—He's bellowing for you!

The Young Woman, with a final pat to her hair, disappears behind the office door. The buzz of the office is resumed. Now the gossip draws to Him and Her. Will she get Him, the stenographer wonders. She'd hate to get in bed with him, insists the Telephone Girl. . . .

It's a short conference. The Young Woman is back. She can't work. Her typewriter's broken. She is listless and unhappy. She tries sorting the mail to fill in time. The clerks joke her slyly as to her standing with the boss.

Soon Jones has followed her into the office, to her desk. He puts his hand familiarly on her shoulder. The others stop work to stare:

"That letter done?" he asks.

"No," she answers, pulling away from him.

JONES—What's the matter?

STENOGRAPHER—She hasn't started.

JONES—O.K.—want to make some changes?

YOUNG WOMAN—My machine's out of order.

JONES—O.K. Use the one in my room.

YOUNG WOMAN—I'm sorting the mail.

STENOGRAPHER (*sarcastic*)—One thing at a time!

JONES (*retreating*)—O.K. (*To* YOUNG WOMAN.). When you've finished.

STENOGRAPHER—Haste makes waste.

JONES—O.K.—don't hurry. (*Exits.*)

STENOGRAPHER—Hew to the line.

TELEPHONE—He's hewing.

FILING CLERK—Hot dog.

YOUNG WOMAN—(*She gets to her feet—then stops.*)

ADDING CLERK—5,000—10,000—15,000.

FILING CLERK—Profits, plans, purchases.

TELEPHONE—Hello—hello—George H. Jones Company—hello— (YOUNG WOMAN *remains seated and goes into her soliloquy.*)

YOUNG WOMAN—George H. Jones—he likes me—loves me—loves me not—loves me. (*Voices repeat quietly, as in the beginning.*) You are late, my dear—ah, yes—the subway—could fire me. He's an old woman—George H. Jones—Mrs. George H. Jones—Dear Madame—in reply to your—why does he want me? He says he loves my hands—his are fat hands—fat hands that never grow weary—well, my fine lady, how do you think we're going to live if you're too proud to work—is that the way to talk to your mother, your poor old mother that's—Ninety-sixth street—change for express—don't crowd—don't push—I must get out or I'll scream—all those bodies—pressing—I must have air. I don't care if I'm late. I must get out. He's a fine man. He could give me everything. I could rest. I could sleep mornings— Did Madame ring? I will bring your coffee at once, Madame. But he would come home nights. I should be ashamed. When he touches me my blood runs cold—oh, don't! Please don't! He's a good man. He loves me. Anything to get away from Ma—Ma and subways and offices and cheap places! If only he wouldn't put his hands on me. He makes my flesh curl. I'd get used to it—maybe lots of wives' skins curl and they get used to it. I wonder if you do—I'll ask Ma—I'll ask Ma if it makes much difference if your skin curls. Ma must know. She married my father—she had me—she never lets on—she never lets on anything—but she must have been young once—I got to ask somebody—she's the only person I could ask that—anybody else would think I was crazy—George H. Jones—Mrs. George H. Jones. Dear Madame— . . .

STENOGRAPHER—Quit your dreaming, kid—get a move on. (*The others start to speak out loud again—blend speeches.*)

The scene blacks out.

EPISODE II—AT HOME

In a kitchen of one of the cheaper apartment houses the Young Woman and her mother are sitting at table eating. At least the mother is eating. The Young Woman is without appetite for food but keenly eager to know about life. She is restless and jumpy. The call of the janitor for the garbage can startles her. Her mother is a little disgusted with her. What's the matter, anyway? She ought to be grateful for everything she's got.

YOUNG WOMAN—Oh, Ma, don't talk!

MOTHER—You just said you wanted to talk.

YOUNG WOMAN—Well, now—I want to think. I got to think.

MOTHER—Aren't you going to finish your potato?

YOUNG WOMAN—Oh, Ma!

MOTHER—Is anything the matter with it?

YOUNG WOMAN—No—

MOTHER—Then why don't you finish it?

YOUNG WOMAN—Because I don't want it.

MOTHER—Why don't you?

YOUNG WOMAN—Oh, Ma! Let me alone!

MOTHER—Well, you've got to eat! If you don't eat . . .

YOUNG WOMAN—Ma, don't nag.

MOTHER—Nag! Just because I try to look out for you—nag! Just because I try to care for you—nag! Why, you haven't sense enough to eat! What would become of you I'd like to know if I didn't nag!

YOUNG WOMAN—I'm grown up, Ma.

MOTHER—Grown up! What do you mean by that?

YOUNG WOMAN—Nothing much—I guess.

MOTHER—(*Rises—clatters dishes.*)

YOUNG WOMAN—Let's not do the dishes right away, Ma. Let's talk—I gotta!

MOTHER—Well, I can't talk with dirty dishes around—you may be able to but— (*Clattering—clattering.*)

YOUNG WOMAN—Ma! Listen! Listen!—There's a man who wants to marry me!

MOTHER (*sits—stops clattering*)—What man?

YOUNG WOMAN—He says he fell in love with my hands.

The mother isn't particularly interested. Not until she hears the man in love is Vice President of the company. Then she favors marriage and the quicker the better. But the Young Woman doesn't love the Vice President. She doesn't love him, and it's about love that she wants to talk.

"Tell me," she cries, eagerly, "love is real, ain't it? It isn't all just—you fall in love, don't you—and then—your skin oughtn't to curl—ought it—when he just comes near you—ought it? That's wrong, ain't it? You don't get over that, do you—ever, do you or don't you? How is it, Ma—do you?

"Do you what?"

YOUNG WOMAN—Do you get used to it—so that after a while it doesn't matter Or don't you? Does it always matter? You ought to be in love, oughtn't you, Ma? You must be in love, mustn't you? That changes everything—doesn't it—or does it? Maybe if you just like a person it's all right—is it? When he puts a hand on me, Ma, he makes my blood run cold—his hands—his hands are—fat, Ma—don't you see—his hands are fat—and they sort of press—and they're fat—don't you see—don't you see?

MOTHER—(*Stares at her, bewildered.*)

YOUNG WOMAN (*rushing on*)—I've always thought I'd find somebody—somebody young—and—and—attractive—with wavy hair—wavy hair—I always think of children with curls—little curls all over their head—somebody young—and attractive—that I'd like—that I'd love— But I haven't found anybody like that yet—I haven't found anybody—I've hardly known anybody—you'd never let me go out with anybody and . . .

MOTHER—Are you throwing it up to me that . . .

YOUNG WOMAN—No—no—let me finish, Ma. Let me finish! I just mean I've never found anybody—anybody—nobody's ever asked me—till now—he's the only man's ever asked me—and I suppose I got to marry somebody—all girls do—

MOTHER—Nonsense.

YOUNG WOMAN—But I can't go on like this, Ma—I don't know why—but I can't—it's like I'm all tight inside— Sometimes I feel like I'm stifling!—You don't know—stifling— (*She walks.*) I can't go on like this much longer—going to work—coming home—going to work—coming home—I can't— Sometimes in the subway I think I'm going to die—sometimes even in the office if something don't happen—I got to do something—I don't know—it's like I'm all tight inside.

MOTHER—You're crazy.

YOUNG WOMAN—Oh, Ma!

MOTHER—You're crazy!

YOUNG WOMAN—Ma— If you tell me that again I'll kill you! I'll kill you!

MOTHER—If that isn't crazy!

YOUNG WOMAN—I'll kill you— Maybe I am crazy—I don't know. Sometimes I think I am—the thoughts that go on in my mind—sometimes I think I am—I can't help it if I am—I do the best I can—I do the best I can and I'm nearly crazy! (MOTHER *rises, and sits.*) Go away! Go away! You don't know anything about anything! And you haven't any pity—no pity—You just take it for granted that I go to work every day—and come home every night and bring my money every week— You just take it for granted— You'd let me go on forever—and never feel any pity—no pity—you're like a leech—you just suck my life—all my youth—I never had any youth— (MOTHER *rises.*) Go away—go away—or I'll kill you!

From somewhere down in the well-like court of the building the rasping voice of a radio vocalist breaks into a sentimental mother song. The mother begins to cry, the Young Woman to comfort her. These are maudlin tears mixed with a kind of pleading and thick with self-pity.

Now the Young Woman is saving the mother further by doing the dishes. Doing them, however, in rubber gloves to save her hands—the hands, she says, that got her a husband.

"A husband? So you're going to marry him, now?"

"I suppose so."

"If you ain't the craziest!"

Downstairs the mother song has gone faintly jazz. The lights fade slowly. The curtain falls.

EPISODE III—THE HONEYMOON

The Young Woman and her Husband follow the Bellboy into a hotel room. There is a door into a bathroom at back, and the window opens on a dancing Casino across the way. There is a small jazz band playing for dancing in the Casino.

The Bellboy has raised the window, received his tip and is gone. The Husband, smiling a little vacuously as he throws his hat on the bed and calls attention to the fact that they have arrived, is slightly disturbed at the Young Woman's apparent lack of interest in any part of her surroundings save the evident scarcity of exits. It's a good room, he reminds her, a room costing twelve bucks a day. And they're going to get their money's worth out of it.

The Young Woman is standing at the window watching the dancers when her Husband comes out of the bathroom. She had hoped there was to be a view of the ocean from the window, but, as he points out, she can see the ocean from the boardwalk tomorrow. She ought to wash up now. And pull down the blind, if she doesn't want people looking in. What's the matter with her? She looks a little scared. She looks a little white around the gills.

HUSBAND—Nothing to be scared of. You're with your husband.

YOUNG WOMAN—I know.

HUSBAND—Happy?

YOUNG WOMAN—Yes.

HUSBAND (*sitting*)—Then come here and give us a kiss. (*She goes to him. He puts her on his knee.*) That's the girlie. (*He bends her head down—and kisses her along the back of her neck.*) Like that? (*She tries to get to her feet.*) Say—stay there! What you moving for?—You know—you got to learn to relax, little girl— (*Pinching her above the knee.*) Say—what you got under there?

YOUNG WOMAN—Nothing.

HUSBAND—Nothing! (*Laughs.*) That's a good one! Nothing, huh? huh? That reminds me of the story of the Pullman porter and the—what's the matter, did I tell you that one?

YOUNG WOMAN—I don't know.

HUSBAND—The Pullman porter and the tart?

YOUNG WOMAN—No.

HUSBAND—It's a good one—well—the train was just pulling out and the tart . . .

YOUNG WOMAN—You did tell me that one!

HUSBAND—About the . . .

YOUNG WOMAN—Yes! Yes! I remember now!

HUSBAND—About the . . .

YOUNG WOMAN—Yes!

HUSBAND—All right—if I did. You're sure it was the one about the . . .

YOUNG WOMAN—I'm sure.

HUSBAND—Where he asked her what she had underneath her seat and she said . . .

YOUNG WOMAN—Yes! Yes! That one!

HUSBAND—All right—but I don't believe I did.

Her reassurance is positive. He has told her *all* his stories. Still he doubts. She escapes to the bathroom over his protests. Now that she's married there's no need of her being modest. She ought to know she can undress before her Husband. Well, anyway, she can leave the door open—so's they can talk. He wants to tell her all about himself. . . . He's going to enjoy life from now on. Hasn't been so easy for him to get where he is. Perhaps next year they will go to Paris, so's she can buy a lot of that French underwear. So's he can buy a Swiss watch right there in Switzerland.

HUSBAND—All my life I've wanted a Swiss watch that I bought right there. All my life I've counted on having that some day—more than anything—except one thing—you know what?

YOUNG WOMAN—No.

HUSBAND—Guess.

YOUNG WOMAN—I can't.

HUSBAND—Then I'm coming in and tell you.

YOUNG WOMAN—No! Don't! Please don't.

HUSBAND—Well, hurry up, then! I thought you women didn't wear much of anything these days—huh?—huh?—I'm coming in.

YOUNG WOMAN—No—No! Just a minute!

HUSBAND—All right! Just a minute! (*Laughs—takes out watch.*) 13—14—I'm counting the seconds on you—that's what you said, didn't you?—just a minute! 49—50—51—53—54. (YOUNG WOMAN *enters.*)

YOUNG WOMAN (*at the door*)—Here I am. (*She wears a little white gown that hangs very straight. She is very still, but her eyes are wide with a curious, helpless, animal terror.*)

HUSBAND—(*starts towards her—stops. The room is in shadow except for one dim light by the bed. Sound of girl weeping in the dark*)—You crying? What you crying for?

YOUNG WOMAN—Ma! Ma! I want my mother.

HUSBAND—I thought you were glad to get away from her.

YOUNG WOMAN—I want her now—I want somebody.

HUSBAND—You've got me, haven't you?

YOUNG WOMAN—Somebody—somebody—

HUSBAND—There's nothing to cry about—there's nothing to cry about.

The dance music continues. There are shadows of the dancers flickering on the wall and ceiling. The lights gradually fade. In the blackness the curtain is lowered.

EPISODE IV—MATERNAL

In a hospital room the door at back opens into a corridor, the window at the side discloses the steel frame of a building going up. There is the practically incessant tattoo of steel riveting. Outside in the hall a stretcher-wagon passes the door.

On a bed in the center of the room the Young Woman lies very still. A Nurse in white circles professionally about the bed, putting the patient through the periodical third degree: "How you feeling to-day?" "Better?" "No pain?" "You're getting along fine."

She takes the patient's pulse. She writes up the patient's record hanging at the foot of the bed. She assures the patient she has a fine baby; a girl. All men want boys, so all women should want girls. She didn't want either? Oh, but she will when baby begins to nurse.

The noise? Nothing can be done about the noise. It's a new wing. It's being added to this, the biggest maternity hospital in the world.

Her Husband arrives with a large bouquet. He, too, is solicitous. But, of course, she must brace up! And face things!

"Everybody's got to brace up—and face things. That's what makes the world go around. I know all you've been through but— (YOUNG WOMAN *signs "No."*) Oh, yes, I do! I know all about it. I was right outside all the time. (YOUNG WOMAN *gestures "No" again, violently.*) Oh, yes! But you've got to brace up now! Make an effort! Pull yourself together! Start the uphill climb. Oh, I've been down, but I haven't stayed down! I've been licked, but I haven't stayed licked! I've pulled myself up by my own boot straps—and that's what you've got to do! Will power! That's what conquers! Look at me! Now you got to brace up. Face the music! Stand the gaff! Take life by the horns! Look it in the face! Having a baby's natural! Perfectly natural thing—why should—"

The Young Woman is gagging. Choking. The Nurse thinks perhaps the Husband better go. She's been that way before.

Then the Doctor comes. A young, fussy doctor. Full of orders. Full of a sense of responsibility. Full of phrases about these modern neurotic women. Whatever can be done about them.

The patient has no milk? Then bring her baby. Put the baby to the breast. The patient doesn't want to nurse her baby? No?

DOCTOR—What do you want?

YOUNG WOMAN—Let me alone—let me alone.

DOCTOR—Bring the baby.

NURSE—Yes, Doctor—she's behaved very badly every time, Doctor, very upset—maybe we better not.

DOCTOR—I decide what we better and better not here, Nurse!

NURSE—Yes, Doctor.

DOCTOR (*with chart*)—Gagging—you mean nausea?

NURSE—Yes, Doctor, but—

DOCTOR—No buts, Nurse.

NURSE—Yes, Doctor.

DOCTOR—Nausea!—Change her diet.—What is her diet?

NURSE—Liquids.

DOCTOR—Give her solids.

NURSE—Yes, Doctor. (*Starts to go.*)

DOCTOR—Wait. I'll change the medicine. (*Takes a pad and writes a prescription in Latin, hands it to* NURSE.) After meals. Bring her baby— (*He exits.*)

NURSE—Yes, Doctor. (*Exit.*)

YOUNG WOMAN—Oh, let me alone! Let me alone! I've submitted to enough. I won't submit any more. I'm empty . . . Maybe if you love they don't weigh so heavy. . . . Love makes them light. I was dead. . . . I was climbing the golden stairs. . . . I met my baby coming down. . . . All the dead going up to Heaven to rest. . . . All the babies coming down to earth to be born. Dead going up . . . babies coming down. I can't go on. No matter. . . . I'll rest. . . . I'll lie down. Now I lay me down. . . . God's hands are fat . . . no . . . they make you well. He lays on His hands. . . . God never had one. . . . Mary had one. . . . The Virgin Mary. . . . The Holy Ghost . . . dead going up . . . babies coming down. Oh, let me alone . . . let me alone!

The rivet machine is still going on. The lights fade. The curtain is lowered.

EPISODE V—THE SPEAKEASY

There are three tables and an electric piano in this speakeasy. At one table a Man and a Woman are seated. Just an ordinary Man and Woman. At another a Man and Boy. The Man is effeminate. At the third table two men are waiting for two girls. The first of the men "is pleasing, common, vigorous. He has coarse, wavy hair." The second is an ordinary, salesman type.

The First Man is growing impatient. He doesn't think the Girls are coming. But he is induced to wait. . . . The Man and Boy are discussing the virtues of sherry, a real amontillado—and love . . . the Man and Woman are quarreling because the Man wants the Woman to go to a certain doctor and the Woman doesn't want to go to any doctor.

The First Man is about to beat it—when the Girls arrive. One is the Telephone Girl who works for the George H. Jones Company. The other is the Young Woman who married Jones.

The four of them fall into conversation. The Second Man is sore because the Girls are late; the First Man is eager to discover how he stands with the Young Woman. There are drinks. The Second Man remembers that he has a lot of business to get done that afternoon and needs the Telephone Girl to help him. Besides, he's promised to get home to the Wife and Kid before 6. Still, they don't like to leave the others without—

SECOND MAN—All right with you?

YOUNG WOMAN—All right with me.

SECOND MAN—Come on, kid.

GIRL—You be nice to her, now. She's very fastidious. Good-by.

YOUNG WOMAN—I know what business is like.

FIRST MAN—You do—do yuh?

YOUNG WOMAN—I used to be a business girl myself before—

FIRST MAN—Before what?

YOUNG WOMAN—Before I quit.

FIRST MAN—What did you quit for?

YOUNG WOMAN—I just quit.

FIRST MAN—You're married—huh?

YOUNG WOMAN—Yes—I am.

FIRST MAN—All right with me.

YOUNG WOMAN—Some men don't seem to like a woman after she's married. (WAITER *enters.*)

FIRST MAN—What's the difference?

YOUNG WOMAN—Depends on the man, I guess.

FIRST MAN—Depends on the girl, I guess. (*To* WAITER.) The same.

Between interruptions their talk turns to certain exploits of the First Man, who is just back from Mexico. He tells, without great urging the story of how he had killed a couple of "spigs" down there. He had to kill them to get free.

FIRST MAN—There were a bunch of bandidos—bandits, you know, took me into the hills—holding me there—what was I to do? I got the two birds that guarded me drunk one night, and then I filled the empty bottle with small stones—and let 'em have it. I had to get free, didn't I? I let 'em have it—you don't have to have a gun to kill a man—just a bottle and some stones.

YOUNG WOMAN—Oh—then what did you do?

FIRST MAN—Then I beat it.

YOUNG WOMAN—Where to—

FIRST MAN—Right here. (*Pause.*) Glad?

YOUNG WOMAN (*nods*)—Yes.

The Man is telling the Boy more of the glories that are to be his with his first amontillado experience. Poe loved amontillado. . . .

The Man and the Woman have advanced their quarrel to her confession that she does not want to be rid of her baby, no matter what her folks would say, no matter what any one would say. But she's got to keep her job— There's that to consider. Oh, well, what's the doctor's address? . . .

The First Man reaches the end of his story. The bottle was only an ordinary bottle, like that one on the table. Just filled with pebbles—any kind of pebbles; just pebbles off the ground. And it ain't a bad weapon. The Young Woman is kinda fascinated. In weapons she shivers at the thought of a knife, but a hammer's different.

"I didn't like it so much myself—any of it," confesses the First Man; "but I had to get free, didn't I? Now I'm damned glad I did."

"Why?"

"You know why!"

The quarreling Man and Woman have gone. The Man and the Boy have followed. The First Man and the Young Woman are holding hands across the table. He is explaining his surprise that she should be running around with a girl like the Telephone Girl. She isn't that kind.

She did it, the Young Woman confesses, because the Telephone Girl always seems to have a good time and she wanted to have a good time, too. She never has had a good time. Never. That's because she has never met the right guy, he explains. That's all.

"You didn't fall for that business gag—did you—when they went off?" he demands.

"Well, I thought they wanted to be alone, probably, but—"

"And how—"

YOUNG WOMAN—Oh—so that's it?

FIRST MAN—That's it. Come along—let's go—

YOUNG WOMAN—Oh, I couldn't.

FIRST MAN—Don't you like me?

YOUNG MAN—Yes.

FIRST MAN—Then what's the matter?

YOUNG WOMAN—Do you—like me?

FIRST MAN—Like yuh! You don't know the half of it. . . . Listen . . . you know what you seem like to me?

YOUNG WOMAN—What?

FIRST MAN—An angel. Just like an angel.

YOUNG WOMAN—I do?

FIRST MAN—That's what I said! Let's go!

YOUNG WOMAN—Where?

FIRST MAN—Where do you live?

YOUNG WOMAN—Oh, we can't go to my place.

FIRST MAN—Then come to my place.

YOUNG WOMAN—Oh, I couldn't—is it far?

FIRST MAN—Just a step— Come on—

YOUNG WOMAN—Oh, I couldn't—what is it—a room?

FIRST MAN—No—an apartment—a one-room apartment.

YOUNG WOMAN—That's different.

FIRST MAN—On the ground floor—no one will see you—coming or going.

YOUNG WOMAN (*getting up*)—I couldn't.

FIRST MAN (*rises*)—Wait a minute—I got to pay the damage . . . (*She sits and he starts away.*) and I'll get us a bottle of something to take along.

YOUNG WOMAN—No—don't.

FIRST MAN—Why not?

YOUNG WOMAN—Well—don't bring any pebbles.

FIRST MAN—Say, forget that! Will you?

YOUNG WOMAN—I just meant I don't think I'll need anything to drink.

FIRST MAN—You like me—don't you, kid?

YOUNG WOMAN—Do you me?

FIRST MAN—Wait—

He goes into the next room and when he comes back he carries a bottle. A Boy and a Girl pass them at the door. The Boy drops a nickel in the electric piano. The music is just starting as the lights fade. The curtain falls.

EPISODE VI—A DARK ROOM

It is an ordinary room. There are a bed and dresser in it, and on a window sill is a Chinese lily growing in a bowl filled with pebbles. The Man is at the dresser, partly dressed. The Young Woman is sitting up in the middle of the bed, in her silk slip and stockings.

After a long pause the Man draws the Young Woman out of her silence to learn her thoughts. She has been thinking of the sea and of the seashell that stood on the mantel in her grandmother's house, she tells him—a big pink shell that, when you held it to your ear, you heard the sound of the sea. Her voice is soft and beautiful as she tells of the shell.

He is impressed now with the beauty of her, and crosses to the bed to tell her so. He notices her hands particularly. She certainly has pretty hands. Yes, she agrees, she used to have pretty hands, but she hasn't taken much care of them lately. She's going to after this.

Outside a hurdy-gurdy is playing "Cielito Lindo." It means "Little Heaven" he tells her. He tries to sing a bit of the song for her. That's what lovers call each other in Spain—Little Heaven. And Spain's where all the castles are. She remembers that.

She tries to sing, too, when he asks her to. But all she can remember are those foolish little nursery songs kids learn. "Hey diddle, diddle, the cat and the fiddle," and songs like that. . . .

She is thinking now that there must be something in guardian angels. "There must be something that looks out for you and brings you happiness at last—look at us! How did we both happen to go to that place to-day if there wasn't something?"

He agrees she may be right. But he is a little amused at her persistent references to them as one and to their future.

"We belong together!" she almost sings. "We belong together! And we're going to stick together, ain't we?"

"Sing something else," he answers, unconsciously a little bored.

It is while she is singing another kid song about angels that she remembers why she came with him. It was because he had told her that she looked like an angel.

And she did, and does, he admits. But then, all white women look like angels to a man who ain't seen nothing but Indians for a couple of years. "Gee, when I got off the boat here the other day," he confesses fervently, "and saw all the women—gee, I pretty near went crazy—talk about looking like angels—why—"

"You've had a lot of women, haven't you?"

"Not so many—real ones."

"Did you—like one of 'em—better than me?"

"Nope—there wasn't any of 'em any sweeter than you, honey, not as sweet—no—not as sweet—"

She likes to hear that. She is happy when he kisses her. But there is apprehension in her voice when he admits that he's not so sure about their sticking together forever. Of course, he will have to be moving on some day. When? Quien sabe? Who knows?

She'll be learning a lot about "Quien sabe?" if she rides across the Rio Grande with him. But she's afraid that can never be; afraid that she will never get away from where she is; never know that wonderful country where he is so happy because down there he feels free.

Now the street lights are on and suddenly she realizes that it has been dark quite a long time and she must be hurrying. It is while she sits facing the window pulling on her shoes that she notices the lily and is curious about it.

He bought it, he tells her, because it reminded him of the Frisco where he was born. "The bay and the hills," he thrills. "Jeez—that's the life! Every Saturday we used to cross the bay—get a couple nags and just ride—over the hills. One would have a blanket on the saddle, and the other—the grub. At night, we'd make a little fire and eat—and then roll up in the old blanket and—"

"Who? Who was with you?"

"Anybody—" he answers, indifferently. And then his enthusiasm returns. "Jeez, that old dry grass out there smells good at night—full o' tar weed, you know."

She has slipped into her one-piece, one-fastening dress now and stands before him. He is appreciative of her appearance, but there is still a note of indifference in his voice.

MAN—You look in good shape, kid. A couple of months' riding over the mountains with me you'd be great!

WOMAN—Can I?

MAN—What?

WOMAN—Some day—ride mountains with you?

MAN—Ride mountains? Ride donkeys!

WOMAN—It's the same thing!—With you!—Can I, some day—the high dark mountain?

MAN—Who knows?

WOMAN—It must be—great!

MAN—You ever been off like that, kid—high up? On top of the world?

WOMAN—Yes.

MAN—When?

WOMAN—To-day.

MAN—You're pretty sweet.

WOMAN—I never knew anything like this was! I never knew that I could feel like this! So—so—purified!—Don't laugh at me.

MAN—I ain't laughing, honey.

WOMAN—Purified.

MAN—It's a hell of a word—but I know what you mean—That's the way it is—sometimes.

WOMAN (*she puts on a little hat—then turns to him*)—Well—good-by.

MAN—Aren't you forgetting something? (*Rises.*)

WOMAN (*she looks toward him, then throws her head slowly back, lifts her right arm—this gesture that is in so many statues of women—VOLUPTE— He puts his arm around her, kisses her. Her head and her arm go further back—then she brings her arm around with a wide encircling gesture, her hand closes over his head, her fingers spread. Her fingers are protective, clutching. When he releases her, her eyes are shining with tears. She turns away. Stops—looks back at him—and the room—her eyes fasten on the lily*)—Can I have that?

MAN—Sure—why not?

WOMAN—Good-by! (*She takes the flower and goes out. The light fades.*)

The curtain falls.

EPISODE VII—A SITTING ROOM

It is a plain sitting room with a sofa in the center and a table with a telephone on it. The Woman is looking out of the window catching the tail end of the conversation her husband is having with an associate over the telephone.

Now in great jubilation he hangs up the receiver. He is exultant as he tells her the success of the deal and she a little contemptuous as she echoes his set phrases.

"Did you put it over?"

"Sure I put it over."

"Did you swing it?"

"Sure I swung it."

"Did they come through?"

"Sure they came through," and so on until the list is exhausted. The deal's closed; the property's his; they signed on the dotted line! Now watch him!

Again the telephone, and again the repetition of the familiar formula. This call is from Phillips and that reminds the husband that he is not so sure of Mrs. Phillips. He had lunch with them recently and Mrs. Phillips "gave him the knee."

Husband is prepared to be thankful that he married a Pure Woman. No need of her to insist that she is just like everybody else. He knows she's the purest woman that ever lived. Why she was so pure as a girl that she used to flinch whenever he touched her. Can't she remember that? She can!

Evans is phoning now. And Husband is duplicating his exultation. Sure he put it over! Sure they came through! Yes, sir, their little old John Hancocks right on the dotted line!

Strange, he thinks, that she should be so nervous to-night! Must be she inherits her nervousness from her mother. Which reminds the Husband that her mother had been in the office for her first-of-the-month allowance that morning. And she's coming over to see the baby to-morrow. She gets a lot of comfort out of the kid. A mother's a very precious thing— A good mother!

Is she a good mother? Of course she is. Why shouldn't she be: A good home, a husband who does everything for her, a fine child—

"Yes," she agrees, "I have everything. . . . I should be thankful."

"We should both be thankful . . . and now this big deal going through. Well, I guess we're what you call sitting pretty."

Still, she would like to get away for a little while. If he can't go, perhaps she and her mother and the baby could go. "I've been feeling terribly nervous lately. . . . Sometimes I get scared. . . ."

But there is nothing to be scared of. And what fun could she have without him? Wait until they can take a real trip. Wait'll they can go to Europe and see the whole show. And Switzerland. He has always wanted to buy a Swiss watch in Switzerland.

HUSBAND—You don't want to go away now. . . . Wait for me . . . and we'll do it right. Anything in the paper? . . . (*Sits—reads paper.*) Another revolution in Mexico.

WOMAN (*quickly*)—Anybody hurt . . . any Americans?

HUSBAND—No, siree. I guess those greasers know that your Uncle Sam is keeping an eye on things. Some day we'll go in and straighten out that country for good. No business sense . . . no efficiency.

WOMAN—I think I'll go to bed.

HUSBAND—Oh, it's early. It's only 10:46. I don't go to bed yet. Maybe some one else will call me up about that deal.

WOMAN—You can stay up.

HUSBAND—Yes, and if you fall asleep, I won't be able to wake you up. I know you. Come on, sit down. We'll both go to bed before long.

WOMAN—I'm tired.

HUSBAND—Come on, sit down and rest. (*She is seated.*) Do you want anything to read?

WOMAN—No.

HUSBAND (*resuming the paper*)—Before this country gets through, there'll be peace all over the world. . . . The world's spiritual leader, that's what we'll be. (*Hurdy-gurdy is heard playing chorus, then a verse of "Cielito Lindo."*)

VOICES (*off stage, left, singing*)—Ay, ay, ay, ay— (MAN *and* GIRL *enter from right by footlights and cross slowly to left.*)

MAN—They were a bunch of bandidos—bandits, you know, took me into the hills. Holding me there. What was I to do? I got the two birds that were guarding me drunk one night, and then I filled the empty bottle with small stones and let them have it. I had to get free, didn't I? I let them have it. You don't have to have a gun to kill a man, just a bottle and some stones. (*They exit.*)

VOICES—Just a bottle and some stones—just a bottle and some stones. Just a bottle and some stones.

MUSIC—Ay, ay, ay, ay.

OLD MAN (*crosses from right to left*)—Old bottles, new stones, —old bottles, new stones—head stones—old bottles, new stones, stepping stones—old bottles, new stones, tomb stones—old bottles, new stones—

VOICES *and* HURDY-GURDY—Old bottles, new stones—old bottles, new stones, head stones, etc.— Ay, ay, ay, ay. (WOMAN *rises quickly—screams.*)

WOMAN—You must let me get away.

HUSBAND (*rises, crosses to her*)—What's the matter?

WOMAN—You must let me get away.

HUSBAND (*taking her to door*)—You'll be all right.

He is still talking as the door closes. The lights fade. The curtain falls.

EPISODE VIII—THE LAW

The courtroom is crowded and a-buzz. Judge, Jury, Lawyers, Reporters, Law Clerks, a Bailiff, the Young Woman— All are assembled and intent on the proceedings. The Prosecution has closed. The Defense is ready to proceed.

The Lawyer for the Defense begins his statement to the Jury. He has proceeded past one or two exceptions and through his preliminary denial of the guilt of his client—"this little woman —this young mother—this devoted wife"—when suddenly he calls Helen Jones to the stand.

The Young Woman takes the stand amid the excited murmur of the surprised attendants and spectators.

"The defense sprang a surprise at the opening of court this morning by putting the accused woman on the stand," mumbles the First Reporter as he writes—

"Helen Jones, accused of the murder of her husband, George H. Jones, walked calmly to the witness stand at 10.02 this morning to face the battery of prosecution cross questioning," mumbles the Second Reporter—

"Trembling and hardly able to stand, Helen Jones, accused murderess, had to be almost carried to the witness stand this morning when the lawyer—" writes the Third Reporter.

The Young Woman is sworn and her examination, freed finally from the continued objections of the Prosecuting Attorney, proceeds. She is the widow of the late George H. Jones. She was married to him for six years. She had never quarreled with him. In six years they had never had a quarrel. (That in itself is a triumph to the Attorney for the Defense.)

She is the mother of a child—a daughter of 5—of whom she has taken devoted care all its life. The child is now with the defendant's mother—the mother whom she, the defendant, had worked to support as a girl, while she was a stenographer in the offices of the late Mr. Jones, and whose support had been continued since her marriage by Mr. Jones. (Showing her to be a devoted daughter as well as a devoted wife and mother.)

And did she, Helen Jones, on the night of June 2, or the morning of June 3, kill her Husband, the late George H. Jones? She did not!

And will she tell the Jury, in her own words, exactly what happened on the night of June 2 or the morning of June 3?

She was awakened by somebody or something, the Young Woman replies, and saw two men standing by her husband's bed—and her bed, seeing they had always slept in the same bed. They were big, dark men. And before she could do anything, scream for help or do anything, one of the big, dark men raised something in his hand and struck Mr. Jones over the head with it. Mr. Jones gave a sort of groan and tried to raise up. The man struck him again. Then the men turned and ran out of the room.

Mrs. Jones, seeing that Mr. Jones was bleeding from the temple, got towels to stop the flow of blood and then, seeing that he had passed away, decided to call the police. Which she did. And that is all she knows concerning the death of her husband in the late hours of June 2d or the early hours of June 3d last.

"The accused woman told a straightforward story—" mumbles the First Reporter.

"The accused woman told a rambling, disconnected story—" writes the Second Reporter.

The Prosecution takes the witness.

The first inquiry is one concerning the light. Mrs. Jones can't remember much about the light. She couldn't see the big, dark men well enough to describe them very accurately. She thinks they were dark men, but not colored men. Just a little dark. She made no attempt to cry out or follow them from the room because she saw Mr. Jones was hurt.

She saw Mr. Jones was hurt because there was a kind of light in the room that came, she thinks, under the blind. Mr. Jones always wanted the blinds drawn. Probably it was the moonlight.

She had been asleep about an hour, she thinks. She remembered it was exactly 11.12 when they had gone to bed because Mr. Jones said it was 11.12. He always mentioned the time when he went to bed—always looked at his watch to see if it was time to go to bed and always mentioned the time—every night.

She had not called a doctor when she saw Mr. Jones was hurt because she also saw it was useless. The police called the doctor. Yes, she recognizes pieces of a bottle that were found, together with several pebbles, scattered over the bed. It doesn't seem strange to her that there were no finger prints on the bottle. Yes, she was in the habit of wearing rubber gloves to soften her hands when she was first married, but Mr. Jones didn't like the feel of them. No, it isn't true that about a year ago she had taken to being careful of her hands again and wearing the gloves again despite Mr. Jones' wish.

Yes, she had tried to wash bloodstains out of the nightgown she was wearing the night of the murder, and she had put it in the clothes hamper while it was still wet. Any one would have tried to wash the bloodstains away.

No, she had never seen the bottle or the pebbles before the night her husband was done away with. She has no recollection of bringing home a Chinese lily in a bowl filled with pebbles a year before her husband was murdered. She recognizes the bowl, but she doesn't remember the lily. She has no recollection of bringing it into her bedroom about a year ago and thereafter tending it very carefully until it died and then hiding the bowl filled with little stones away on the top shelf of her closet—

"Under the heavy artillery fire of the State's attorney's brilliant cross questioning, the accused woman's defense was badly riddled. Pale and trembling she—" writes the First Reporter.

"Undaunted by the Prosecutor's machine gun attack, the defendant was able to maintain her position of innocence in the face of rapid fire questioning that threatened, but never seriously menaced, her defense. Flushed, but calm she—" writes the Second Reporter.

LAWYER FOR PROSECUTION (*producing paper*)—Your Honor, I'd like to introduce this paper in evidence at this time.

JUDGE—What is it?

PROSECUTION—It is an affidavit taken in the State of Guanajato, Mexico.

DEFENSE—Mexico? Your Honor, I protest. A Mexican affidavit! Is this the United States of America or isn't it?

PROSECUTION—It's properly executed—sworn to before a notary—and certified to by an American Consul.

DEFENSE—Your Honor! I protest! In the name of this great United States of America—I protest—are we to permit our sacred institutions to be thus—

JUDGE—What is the purpose of this document—who signed it?

PROSECUTION—It is signed by one Richard Roe, and its purpose is to refresh the memory of the witness on the point at issue—and incidentally supply a motive for this murder—this brutal and cold-blooded murder of a sleeping man by—

DEFENSE—I protest, Your Honor! I object!

JUDGE—Let me see the document. (*Takes paper, which is handed up to him, looks at it.*) Perfectly regular. Do you offer this affidavit in evidence at this time for the purpose of refreshing the memory of the witness at this time?

PROSECUTION—Yes, Your Honor.

JUDGE—You may introduce the evidence.

DEFENSE—I object! I object to the introduction of this evidence at this time as irrelevant, immaterial, illegal, biased, prejudicial, and—

JUDGE—Objection overruled.

DEFENSE—Exception.

JUDGE—Exception noted—proceed.

PROSECUTION—I wish to read the evidence to the jury at this time.

JUDGE—Proceed.

DEFENSE—I object.

JUDGE—Objection overruled.

DEFENSE—Exception.

JUDGE—Noted.

DEFENSE—Why is this witness himself not brought into court—so he can be cross-questioned?

PROSECUTION—The witness is a resident of the Republic of

Mexico and as such is not subject to subpœna as a witness to this court.

DEFENSE—If he was out of the jurisdiction of the court how did you get this affidavit out of him?

PROSECUTION—This affidavit was made voluntarily by the deponent in the furtherance of justice.

DEFENSE—I suppose you didn't threaten him with extradition on some other trumped up charge so that—

JUDGE—Order—

BAILIFF—Order!

JUDGE—Proceed with the evidence. (DEFENSE *rises.*)

PROSECUTION (*reading*)—In the matter of the State—vs. Helen Jones, I, Richard Roe, being of sound mind, so herein depose and state that I know the accused, Helen Jones, and have known her for a period of over one year immediately preceding the date of the signature of this affidavit. That I first met the said Helen Jones in a so-called speakeasy somewhere in the West 40s in New York City. That on the day I met her, she went with me to my room, also somewhere in the West 40s in New York City, where we had intimate relations—

YOUNG WOMAN—Oh! (*Moans.*)

PROSECUTION (*continues*)—and where I gave her a blue bowl filled with pebbles, also containing a flowering lily. That from the first day we met until I departed for Mexico in the fall, the said Helen Jones was an almost daily visitor to my room where we continued to—

WOMAN—No! No! (*Moans.*)

PROSECUTION—What is it, Mrs. Jones—what is it?

YOUNG WOMAN—Don't read any more! No more!

PROSECUTION—Why not?

YOUNG WOMAN—I did it! I did it! I did it!

PROSECUTION—You confess?

YOUNG WOMAN—Yes, I did it!

DEFENSE (*rises*)—I object, Your Honor.

JUDGE—You confess you killed your husband?

YOUNG WOMAN—I put him out of the way—yes.

JUDGE—Why?

YOUNG WOMAN—To be free.

JUDGE—To be free? Is that the only reason?

YOUNG WOMAN—Yes.

JUDGE—If you just wanted to be free—why didn't you divorce him?

YOUNG WOMAN—Oh, I couldn't do that! I couldn't hurt him

like that! (*Bursts of laughter from all in the court. The* YOUNG WOMAN *stares out at them, and then seems to go rigid.*)

JUDGE—Silence!

BAILIFF—Silence! (*There is gradual silence.*)

JUDGE—Mrs. Jones, why—

YOUNG WOMAN—(*Begins to moan—suddenly—as though the realization of her enormity and her isolation had just come upon her. It is a sound of desolation, of agony, of human woe. It continues until the end of the scene.*)

JUDGE—Why?

YOUNG WOMAN—(*She cannot speak.*)

DEFENSE—Your Honor, I ask a recess to—

JUDGE—Court's adjourned.

FIRST REPORTER—"Murderess confesses—"

SECOND REPORTER—"Paramour brings confession—"

THIRD REPORTER—"'Did it,' woman cries."

There is a great burst of speed from the telegraph instruments. They keep up a constant accompaniment to the woman's moans.

Two policemen are standing by the Young Woman as the lights fade. The curtain falls.

EPISODE IX—IN A PRISON

The bars of the prison room are set back. In front of them the Jailer and a Matron sit. Inside the bars the Young Woman is listening quietly to the prayers of a Priest. Frequently as the Priest intones his plea a Negro prisoner breaks into a spiritual.

"Hear, O Lord, my prayer, and let my cry come to Thee. Turn not away Thy face from me; in the day when I am in trouble, incline Thy ear to me. In what day soever I shall call upon Thee, hear me speedily. For my days are vanished like smoke; and my bones are grown dry, like fuel for the fire—" . . . "The Lord hath looked upon the earth that He might hear the groans of them that are in the fetters, that He might release the children of—"

The song of the Negro breaks again upon the prayer, but the Woman would let him sing. She understands.

WOMAN (*her calm shattered*)—Father, Father! Why was I born?

PRIEST—I came forth from the Father and have come into the world. I leave the world and go unto the Father.

WOMAN—When I'm dead won't I have peace?

PRIEST—Ye shall indeed drink of my cup.

WOMAN—Will I have peace to-morrow?

PRIEST—I will raise Him up at the last day.

WOMAN—To-morrow! Father! Where will I be to-morrow?

PRIEST—Behold the Son cometh, yea is now come, ye shall be scattered every man to his own.

WOMAN—In hell! Father! Will I be in hell?

PRIEST—I am the resurrection and the life.

WOMAN—Life has been Hell to me, Father!

PRIEST—Life has been Hell to you, daughter, because you never knew God!

WOMAN—How could I know Him, Father? He never was around me.

PRIEST—You didn't seek him, daughter. Seek and ye shall find.

WOMAN—I sought something.—I was always seeking something. (*Crosses to bars.*)

PRIEST—What? What were you seeking?

WOMAN—Peace. Rest and peace. (*Sound of aeroplane is heard off.*) Will I find it to-night, Father? Will I find it?

PRIEST—Trust in God.

The roar of an aeroplane is heard over the prison. "He has wings but he isn't free," she says. And still the Woman wonders. Why should she have felt free for the one time on earth when she had committed the mortal sin for which she now must die! And that other sin—that sin of love.

"That's all I ever knew of heaven," she wails. "Heaven on earth. How is that, Father? How can that be? A sin—a mortal sin—all I know of heaven."

Now her mother has come to see the Woman. But she is a stranger. This Woman never knew this mother. Yet now they embrace through the bars and the Woman cries out to her Mother to take care of that strange child she is leaving, the child that will never know her.

And now it is time. The Jailer takes the Mother away. The Matron and a Guard take the Woman by the arms and start through the door. The Priest follows, praying:

"Lord have mercy! Christ have mercy! Lord have mercy—Christ hear us—"

The lights fade. The voice of the Priest dies away. There is darkness.

EPISODE X—IN THE DARK

Out of the darkness come the voices of the Reporters. They are wondering at the delay. They ask each other the time. They shush each other into silence.

The voice of the Priest is heard, dimly, then louder. "St. Peter pray for us—St. Paul pray for us—St. James pray for us—"

"Here they are," reports the First Reporter.

"How little she looks! She's got smaller."

"Hush!" warns the Third Reporter.

"St. Philip pray for us— All ye Holy Patriarchs and Prophets —St. Philip—St. Matthew—St. Simon . . . all ye Holy Innocents pray for us—"

"Suppose the machine shouldn't work!" suggests the First Reporter.

"It'll work. It always works."

"Hush!"

PRIEST—Saints of God make intercession for us—be merciful— Spare us, O Lord—be merciful—

FIRST REPORTER—Her lips are moving— What is she saying?

SECOND REPORTER—Nothing.

THIRD REPORTER—Hush!

PRIEST—O Lord, deliver us from all evil—from all sin—from thy wrath—from the snares of the devil—from anger and hatred and every evil will—from—

FIRST REPORTER—Did you see that? She fixed her hair under the cap—pulled her hair out under the cap.

THIRD REPORTER—Sssshhh!

PRIEST—Beseech Thee—hear us—that Thou wouldst spare us— That Thou would'st pardon us—Holy Mary—pray for us—

SECOND REPORTER—There—

WOMAN (*calling out*)—Somebody! Somebod— (*Her voice is cut off.*)

PRIEST—Christ have mercy—Lord have mercy—Christ have mercy—

Gradually the light increases—first, a faint blue, then red, then pink, then amber. Now all are thrown on full. An indescribable glow suffuses the scene.

The curtain falls.

LITTLE ACCIDENT

A Comedy in Three Acts

BY FLOYD DELL AND THOMAS MITCHELL

THE season had started slowly. There had been considerable melodrama, topped by "The Front Page" and "Machinal," and one high comedy, Lonsdale's "The High Road," that was pleasing the society crowd. But that was all. Early October was a good time for the entrance of a light comedy.

On the 9th "Little Accident" was produced by Crosby Gaige at the Morosco Theatre. Written by Floyd Dell, novelist, and having served its time and purpose as a story called "The Unmarried Father," Thomas Mitchell, actor, and Mr. Dell had made the yarn over into a play the leading male part of which should be suited to the actor-collaborator.

There were many other plays that week and "Little Accident" did not receive the personal attention of the higher-ups of dramatic criticism. The reports of their chief assistants, however, were most favorable. Laughter was said to roar gustily through the Morosco Theatre and many people were made glad by the coming of a play concerned with a new employment of that paternal instinct which is usually accepted as being more comic than important in the drama.

The opening scene of "Little Accident" is the dining room of the Overbeck home in Vickley, Illinois. The time is early morning of a late April day and the Overbeck family is assembling somewhat tardily for breakfast.

So far only Mrs. Overbeck and her youngest daughter, Doris, are down, though a grumbling from the yard would indicate that J. J. Overbeck, the father, is also stirring.

From the conversation of the Overbeck women it appears that the night before this particular morning had not been entirely free from disturbance. Young Norman Overbeck had arrived home quite late, accompanied by his best friend, Gilbert Rand, and the two of them had stood on the porch and serenaded the coming dawn with excerpts from a song called "Maid of Athens." They had also managed, while serenading, to step, or fall, off the porch into Mr. Overbeck's bed of hyacinths.

The whole situation is highly amusing to Doris, but Mrs. Overbeck can see nothing funny in it. As for Mr. Overbeck, when settled at table, he is prepared to express his mind quite freely. Early morning serenades to the Maid of Athens, ventures "J. J." are certainly not his idea of a perfect preparation for a wedding rehearsal, and this is the morning, whether Norman remembers it or not, that he is to rehearse the ceremony that will make him the husband of Madge Ferris.

Mrs. Overbeck is sure everything will be all right and goes on finishing a written account of the approaching wedding which she is to send to such out-of-town papers (including those in Chicago) as should be interested in weddings, whether their editors know the Overbecks and the Ferrises or not.

When Norman Overbeck, a good-looking young man in his twenties, arrives at table he is not particularly interested in breakfast. He can do with a bit of orange juice and a cup of coffee, but more than that would be superfluous. Nor does he react enthusiastically to his father's suggestion that he try "a bowl of gin and some toast."

There is every reason to suspect that father is quite out of patience with Norman. In fact father has a good mind, as he says, to suggest to his prospective daughter-in-law that she make her husband sign the pledge. As he feels this morning, Norman admits he would be glad to sign any number of pledges.

Norman also feels the same way about his mail that he does about breakfast. He is not interested in it. It is mostly ads, anyway. There is, however, one special delivery letter that may mean something. He suggests that Doris read that one to him, and Doris does.

It comes from the Ellen Harris Maternity Hospital in Chicago. As advance advertising that, it seems to Doris, is going pretty far.

> "Mr. Norman Overbeck. Dear Sir: A matter of personal importance to you, and one which I would rather not be obliged to take up in correspondence, unless you prefer it—"

Doris gets no farther. "Well, tie that if you can," she ejaculates with fervor. "Making a bid to bring little Norman, Jr., into the world before you're married even!"

"Damn fools," agrees Norman. "A thing like that shouldn't be allowed."

There is a postscript:

"Perhaps if I recall the Springer exhibit at the Steinbeck Art galleries it will refresh your memory."

The Steinbeck galleries are in Boston. And Norman had been in Boston, too, but—

Suddenly Norman's brain begins to work. He remembers something. He is at some pains, however, to conceal the thought from Doris. Surreptitiously he recovers the hospital letter, reads it thoughtfully and begins quickly and with considerable agitation to count on his fingers.

"Oh, my God!" explodes Norman, just as Doris lets Gilbert Rand in the front door.

Gilbert is another attractive young man of about Norman's age neatly arrayed in a brown and tan combination of suit, tie, socks and shoes. Gilbert is also full of spirits and inclined to joke with the prospective groom. Particularly after Doris calls his attention to the letter from the Maternity Hospital. That's a good one! A bit previous, but good!

Norman sees the joke, but can't exactly laugh at it. As a matter of fact he is much inclined to take it seriously.

NORMAN—Of course this refers to a potential baby—but, suppose they didn't.

GILBERT—I don't get you.

NORMAN—Suppose these people were up to something.

GILBERT—What?

NORMAN—I'm only supposing.

GILBERT—Supposing what?

NORMAN—Well—take a hypothetical case—take me.

GILBERT—All right. Then what?

NORMAN—I'm about to be married.

GILBERT—Yes?

NORMAN (*nervously clasping and unclasping his hands*)—Suppose those people should accuse me.

GILBERT—Of what? Having a baby?

NORMAN (*laughing*)—Yes. Funny, isn't it?

GILBERT—Well, I'll say they'd be picking a pretty time for it. A day before your wedding—all arrangements made. Picture it.

NORMAN (*taking the letter from his pocket and smoothing it out*)—I am picturing it.

GILBERT—What a jam.

NORMAN—Still such things happen.

GILBERT—You bet they do. They happen every day.

NORMAN—That's what I mean.

GILBERT—Why, I've had cases, I've known men, Norman, even during my short practice, to go all through life paying hush money.

NORMAN (*crumpling letter in his fist*)—Gosh!

GILBERT—And yet you know there's a humorous side to it.

NORMAN—Humorous?

GILBERT—Yes, because you see, that sort of thing *could* happen to any of us, but people don't figure that way. If your neighbor happens to escape, he seems all the more ready to condemn you.

NORMAN—Me?

GILBERT—I mean the fellow that's caught. Funny, isn't it?

NORMAN—Certainly is.

GILBERT—Well, I hope this minister won't take all morning.

NORMAN—Gilbert, tell me. This interests me. What happens when a man denies everything?

GILBERT—Doesn't help at all.

NORMAN—No?

GILBERT—No. He may clear himself legally, but that's not the point. He'll always be suspected. . . . You see the sympathy is always with the woman. I don't know why, but it is. You know, poor unfortunate woman—all that bunk. The man seduced her—that's what they say. He's the villain. No sympathy for him. They only see a poor, helpless woman with a fatherless baby. See the point?

NORMAN—Yeh, I see it.

The wedding rehearsal party continues to gather, and Norman's agitation continues to increase. He is constantly going back to the hospital letter until finally Gilbert's suspicions are aroused. He demands a sight of the worrisome document. One glance at it convinces him that it is genuine and that nothing like blackmail inspired its writing. Furthermore he gradually becomes convinced that Norman is not only greatly upset by the letter but that he stands badly in need of advice and help.

Norman, on the other hand, protests complete ignorance of the whole matter. He does not know the writer of the letter, he knows nothing about any maternity hospital and the fact that there is a Steinbeck gallery in Boston and that he has been there means nothing.

GILBERT—Why does she—this Doctor—refer to the Springer Art Exhibit to refresh your memory?

NORMAN—How should I know?

GILBERT—Was this Springer Exhibit in Boston?

NORMAN—Might have been . . . Springer is a well-known painter—nothing unusual about his having a show in Boston.

GILBERT—Do you remember it?

NORMAN—What?

GILBERT—The show in Boston.

NORMAN—I don't know.

GILBERT—Well, try to recall it.

NORMAN—All right, I will. Yes—now that you mention it.

GILBERT—Good, now we're getting somewhere.

NORMAN—Oh, are we? Just where do you think we're getting? What are you driving at, Gilbert? What are you trying to insinuate?

GILBERT—That's easy.

NORMAN—Well, what?

GILBERT—There's a girl in this case.

NORMAN—There is, eh?

GILBERT—That much, I'm sure of.

NORMAN—And what has that got to do with me?

GILBERT—That's what I'm trying to find out.

NORMAN—Well, I won't tell you. I mean I can't tell you. I mean I don't know any girls in Chicago.

GILBERT—Do you know any in Boston?

NORMAN—Yes, but this letter is from Chicago.

GILBERT—A girl from Boston could have a baby in Chicago.

NORMAN—Of course she could. I'm not denying that. She could have twins for all I care. What's a Boston girl having a baby in Chicago got to do with me?

GILBERT—Nothing, unless you happen to know her.

NORMAN—Well, I don't.

GILBERT—You can't be sure of that. You spent three years in Cambridge. Must have a pretty wide acquaintance there.

NORMAN—Not that kind.

GILBERT—What kind?

NORMAN—Boston girls—who have babies in Chicago.

GILBERT—Oh, come now, Norman.

NORMAN—I tell you I haven't looked at another girl since I fell in love with Madge.

GILBERT—When was that?

NORMAN—Oh, ages ago.

GILBERT—Before you left Cambridge?

NORMAN—Of course not. How could I? I hardly knew Madge until after I left Cambridge.

GILBERT—I see. Just when did you leave Cambridge, Norman.

NORMAN—Oh, a long time ago.

GILBERT—I see, now tell me, Norman, did you have any acquaintance, girl acquaintances, about the time you left Cambridge?

NORMAN—Why do you ask that?

GILBERT—Well, answer me, did you?

NORMAN—I suppose I did.

GILBERT—Any intimate—

NORMAN—What do you mean—intimate?

GILBERT—Just that. Any one girl you knew or cared for more than the other?

NORMAN—Now, don't go too far, Gilbert.

GILBERT—My dear boy, I'm trying to get to the bottom of this. We gain nothing by denying it.

NORMAN—But, I'm not—I'm not denying anything.

GILBERT—Then tell me. Did you have a love affair last year in Cambridge?

NORMAN—Yes. If you call it a love affair—it was a girl, that's all.

GILBERT—And you made love to her.

NORMAN (*looking up quickly*)—Sh! Yes! Now, you know.

Little by little Gilbert manages to extract the whole story from Norman. He had, one day when he had missed his train and had an hour to wait, wandered into the gallery. And there, copying a lilypad of Monet's, sat a girl. A fascinating girl. Norman spoke to her. Quite casually at first. Merely to admire her work—and the picture she herself made as she worked.

She was not, as it turned out, a complete stranger. At least Norman had seen her often on the street in Cambridge. They both lived in Cambridge. And, in fact, he had seen her that morning as she was entering the Art Gallery, which may have had something to do with his missing the train.

Anyway, they were soon deeply discussing art and life and things like that and, seeing they both lived in Cambridge, Norman took her home. Isabel Drury was her name.

After that they met at many parties and became awfully well

acquainted. But Isabel was a very serious girl. Completely wrapped up in her art. Ready, she insisted, to give up everything for a career—love, home, everything. And so—

GILBERT (*impatiently*)—Well, go on.
NORMAN—Where was I?
GILBERT—Just leaving Cambridge.
NORMAN—That was in June. You see she didn't know—she didn't realize I was going home—she was that kind—impractical.
GILBERT—Well!
NORMAN—It was the day before I left, last June—
GILBERT—Wait now. Late June, early April, count it up.
NORMAN—I did. First thing I did, was count it up.
GILBERT—Well.
NORMAN—It comes out even. We spent that day, the day before I left, at the Springer show. It was late when we started back to Cambridge. We took a cab and we talked—at least, I talked.
GILBERT—About art?
NORMAN—No—not now. Isabel was silent for a long time, but when the cab drew up at her house she said: "Let's go on." It was a beautiful night, June, you know.
GILBERT—Yes, I know.
NORMAN—We rode—oh, miles out of town,—then some one suggested that we walk.
GILBERT—Who?
NORMAN—Maybe I did. We dismissed the cab and strolled through the woods.
GILBERT—Yes?
NORMAN—We lost ourselves in the woods.
GILBERT—Lost yourselves?
NORMAN—Pretended. It was all pretence, Gilbert. All make-believe.
GILBERT—Well, I hope so.
NORMAN—I'll never forget that night. It wasn't real, I tell you. There seemed to be some sort of summer madness in the air. Why, even now—

Then Madge Ferris comes. From the yard her cheery "Yoo-hoo!" can be heard, and from the room Norman answers with another "Yoo-hoo!" not so cheery and decidedly more throaty.

Madge is a pretty girl and full of life. In her tan knitted jersey and tan pleated skirt she suggests a wholesomely athletic type. She is terribly excited about the rehearsal and thrilled at the thought of her wedding. She can't quite understand why neither of these adventures seems to mean more to Norman than it does. She can't get a rise from him even with a report that Aunt Laura has given them furniture. Madge is still puzzled as she goes to join the girls, but too happy to let anything worry her long. Norman looks after her wonderingly and turns helplessly to Gilbert.

GILBERT—Norman, you've only got a minute, and we must talk fast. This may mean nothing—a false alarm.

NORMAN—Do you think so?

GILBERT—No, I don't.

NORMAN—Neither do I.

GILBERT—Norman, all right. We must assume that it's just as bad as we suspect. I mean that this girl Isabel is in Chicago. She has a baby, and she's blaming it on you.

NORMAN—No, no. You're wrong. Understand me, Gilbert. Isabel wouldn't blame me unless—

GILBERT—Unless you're the father. All right. Now then. Tell me this. Was anything ever said about marriage?

NORMAN (*looking into the hall*)—Sh! Not till afterwards.

GILBERT—After the night in the woods.

NORMAN—Yes. I was rather frightened and I said we must get married.

GILBERT—What did she say?

NORMAN—She laughed.

GILBERT—She laughed?

NORMAN—Yes, she laughed at me. Said I was provincial.

GILBERT—Provincial?

NORMAN—You see, that's Isabel. Well, what could I do? There was nothing I could do or say to persuade her.

GILBERT—Well?

NORMAN—Well, I got mad, she got mad, hell of a row, and that day I left Cambridge.

GILBERT—And that was the last time you saw her?

NORMAN—Yes. I came home here to Vickley.

GILBERT—Ever write to her?

NORMAN—Every day, for weeks.

GILBERT—Any answer.

NORMAN—None. Then I tried to forget her. I did forget her. In the fall I fell in love with Madge.

GILBERT—I see. Now tell me—about this Isabel. Were you her first lover?

NORMAN—Sh! Good God, man, of course.

GILBERT—She told you so?

NORMAN—We didn't talk about it.

GILBERT—No, but she laughed at the idea of marriage. Obviously, not her first experience.

NORMAN—Now, Gilbert—

GILBERT—Now, Norman, she sounds to me like a very sophisticated woman.

NORMAN—You don't know Isabel.

GILBERT—Well, that's not the point.

NORMAN—No; the point is this. I'm in a jam.

GILBERT—Maybe. And if you are, I can get you out of it.

NORMAN—How?

GILBERT—Never mind. You leave it to me. You just forget it.

NORMAN—Forget it? Huh!

GILBERT—Go right ahead with your wedding plans, just as if nothing had happened.

NORMAN—But I can't—not now—I can't when she needs me.

GILBERT—Who?

NORMAN—Isabel—I can't leave her alone with that baby.

GILBERT—Great Scott—Don't get so upset. You don't know—yet.

NORMAN—What? . . . Don't know what?

GILBERT—All this may be your imagination.

NORMAN—Yes, that's right.

GILBERT—Don't you see? Now you keep calm. I'll run up to Chicago. I'll go this morning. (*Looks at watch.*) Just time to catch the morning train.

NORMAN—Good. I'll go with you.

Gilbert is convinced that that would never do. Norman can't leave. Neither of them can leave until after the rehearsal. Then Gilbert will take the afternoon train and Norman will stay on in Vickley as though everything was all right. If there is anything crooked about the affair in Chicago Gilbert will soon find it out.

The girls press Gilbert into dancing while the party is waiting for the minister and Madge manages to have a few minutes with Norman. She can see something is disturbing him. She wishes he would tell her what it is. She doesn't believe in secrets between husband and wife. Doesn't believe they are possible, as a matter of truth. When two people truly love each other it is impossible for one to have a secret from the other. And if Norman should ever have a secret from Madge she would know at once that he did not love her any more.

A ring at the door announces the arrival of Dr. Gifford, who is to conduct the rehearsal, and the party flocks to welcome him. Norman pulls Gilbert back to whisper excitedly to him that he (Norman) cannot go through with their plan. He must tell Madge everything. She doesn't believe in secrets. She couldn't love him if he had a secret from her.

Gilbert is not impressed. Norman already has a secret from Madge and it hasn't affected her love up till now, has it? Well, then—

But Norman has made up his mind. When Madge comes to call him for the rehearsal he blurts out his determination. He can't go on with the reheasal! He is going, he has to go, to Chicago. There is something he wants to tell, something he must tell, them all! He—

Gilbert manages to interrupt enough to keep the dread secret untold until Dr. Gifford providentially opens the door and discovers the missing groom for whom he has been searching.

DR. GIFFORD—Well, well! Here he is! Looking just like any bridegroom ought to look. (*As he offers* NORMAN *his hand.*) Good morning, Norman.

NORMAN (*as he shakes hands*)—How do you do, Dr. Gifford?

GILBERT—We're ready, Doctor, if you are.

DR. GIFFORD—Good! First of all we must decide—some prefer the procession up the aisle.

DORIS—Lois Henderson didn't.

LUCINDA—No, they came from the sacristy.

MRS. OVERBECK—Hush, Lucinda!

GILBERT (*to* NORMAN)—Don't make an ass of yourself. (*To* DR. GIFFORD.) Up the aisle, I say. (*To* NORMAN.) Eh, Norman? (*To* DR. GIFFORD.) Yes, sir, up the aisle, all sails flying.

DR. GIFFORD—Good! You know the order?

MADGE—Yes, Doctor. I have it all written out.

DR. GIFFORD—That's fine. Bride and family—

MADGE—Yes, I know.

DR. GIFFORD—And our friend Gilbert—will look after the groom.

GILBERT—I'll try to, Doctor.

DR. GIFFORD—Then—when we reach the altar, the music stops and the happy pair are left alone.

NORMAN—No!

MRS. OVERBECK—What's the matter with you?

LUCINDA—Pay no attention—he's upset.

MADGE—Norman, dear, what is it?

NORMAN (*going to* MADGE)—I won't—I can't go on with this—

GILBERT—Wait, Norman. Doctor! Norman's upset. I'll explain. (*Turning to* NORMAN *and* MRS. OVERBECK.) An important matter—a very serious matter—came up this morning. A matter which Norman was fully qualified to handle by himself—but—his father interfered.

NORMAN—What?

GILBERT—Now, Norman! I'll do this!

MADGE—Said he didn't have enough experience, I suppose.

GILBERT—Exactly. Now it's business that must be done in Chicago.

MRS. OVERBECK—Chicago?

GILBERT—Yes, that's why Norman insists on going. Am I right, Norman?

NORMAN—Yes! (NORMAN *turns to* MADGE, *taking her by both hands.*) And I've just got time to catch the morning train.

GILBERT—Wait! Norman; no not that.

MADGE—But, Norman, dear, the rehearsal!

DR. GIFFORD—Can't you go after?

NORMAN—No! Sorry, Doctor. It must be done to-day. Am I right, Gilbert?

GILBERT—Yes! No! Wait!

NORMAN—I can't. I haven't got time. (*He rushes out.*)

MADGE (*after the door closes*)—Oh, dear! And I let him go without kissing him. (*Looking out the window after* NORMAN.) Norman! Yoo-Hoo!

NORMAN (*in distance*)—Yoo-Hoo!

The curtain falls.

ACT II

The reception room of the Ellen Harris Hospital in Chicago is immaculate and modern. Everything, including nurses and employés, wears a sterilized look.

The office fixtures are marbelized and glassed in. There is an enamel table and chair at one side of the room. No germ, you feel, has ever settled on the glass knob of the Doctor's Office and lived to boast of its adventure to other germs. There is a measure of comfort suggested by a long reading table and chairs placed stiffly at either end.

The afternoon of the day Norman Overbeck ran out on the wedding rehearsal party in Vickley the reception room of the hospital is occupied by Miss Clark, hospital secretary, and two men.

One man is a nervous fellow named Hicks. The other a complacent Italian. Mr. Hicks is pacing the floor. Miss Clark is keeping track of the incoming phone calls. The Italian is watching Hicks and wondering about Miss Clark.

Hicks, it transpires, has been waiting since dawn for news from his wife. She has been confidently expecting for many hours to present him with an heir, and while the delay is quite understandable and not at all disturbing to the hospital attachés, or even to the Italian, it is entirely beyond the understanding of Mr. Hicks and excessively aggravating as well. Yet nothing that he can do will help matters. Vaguely he senses that. And whenever he fails to remember it some one is quite sure to remind him.

The Italian, on the other hand, is an habituated person so far as hospitals and babies are concerned. He merely is waiting for Mrs. Amendelaro to help her take home a sixth little Amendelaro. The fact that the sixth happens to be a little Rudolpho, after Mr. Amendelaro had been somewhat discouraged by the previous arrival of five daughters, adds to his enthusiasm and likewise contributes to his patience. . . .

When Norman Overbeck arrives he discovers that, so far as Miss Clark knows, there have been no preparations made for his reception. Dr. Zernecke has not mentioned him and nothing has been said about any letter of invitation. As he has no appointment it will be necessary for him to wait until the doctor is disengaged.

Mr. Hicks is consoling. Waiting, he assures Norman, is one of the best things they do around that hospital. Being married and raising a family is all right in a way, Mr. Hicks volunteers further, as soon as he discovers that Norman is still single, but the man free of such responsibilities has something to be thankful for. Yes, sir!

"My wife's as fine a girl as is," ventures Mr. Hicks. "But they're all alike. They marry you thinkin' you're something you ain't. And when they find out you ain't, they get sore . . . —start naggin'—you know, fights and arguments, and a'course you fight back. Why not? A man's got his self-respect, ain't he? But what does it get him? You can't win. About the time you're ready to say so, you know, quit, throw up the sponge and hop back to single bliss, this happens.

"What?"

"They pull this baby gag on you, and there you are. They got you comin' and goin'."

Miss Clark has finally succeeded in making Dr. Zernecke understand that Norman is the young man from Vickley, the one who had a letter referring to an art exhibit, and the doctor has sent word that he is to wait; also that Miss Hemmingway, a nurse, is to get a St. Theckla record from him.

Norman, never having heard of St. Theckla, is something more than merely nonplussed. And by the time Miss Hemmingway has him seated in the enamel chair at the end of the enamel table and has begun to fire questions at him he is unquestionably perturbed.

Has he had a medical examination recently? For insurance? That's good. How old is he? Twenty-five?

MISS HEMMINGWAY—Both parents living?

NORMAN (*as he slowly backs away to the chair*)—Yes—but what—

MISS HEMMINGWAY—Any tuberculosis in your family?

NORMAN—No—

MISS HEMMINGWAY—Epilepsy?

NORMAN—No—

MISS HEMMINGWAY—Insanity?

NORMAN—No—not yet.

MISS HEMMINGWAY—Sit here. Now take off your coat.

NORMAN—What for?

MISS HEMMINGWAY (*assisting him off with his coat*)—This will only take a minute. . . . Now your vest. (MISS HEMMINGWAY *takes out of the top drawer and lays in orderly fashion on the top of the white enameled table a Kiedel Tube—a Stethescope—and a rubber arm Tourniquet. She then removes the corks from a large bottle of alcohol and a bottle of collodium which have been standing on the table. Then removes the protecting cover from the end of the Kiedel Tube and places it ready for use.*)

MISS HEMMINGWAY (*to* NORMAN)—Now, your shirt. . . . Oh! Just unbutton it.

NORMAN (*showing signs of relief*)—Say, this is a Maternity Hospital, isn't it?

MISS HEMMINGWAY—Oh, yes. (*She unbuttons the cuff of his right sleeve and rolls it up, well beyond his elbow.*) Exclusively.

NORMAN—Say, what is this?

MISS HEMMINGWAY (*as she glances at Kiedel Tube*)—This—? A Kiedel Tube. It won't hurt.

NORMAN—But I mean—what is it for?

MISS HEMMINGWAY—A test. The Kahn Blood Test you know. This way you only have to do it once. (*She slips the arm band over Norman's arm and runs it up beyond his elbow and half tightens it.*)

NORMAN—Well, I'm glad of that.

. . . .

NORMAN—Do you always do this?

MISS HEMMINGWAY—Oh, yes—we always keep a complete medical record. (DR. ZERNECKE *enters. She has a chart board with charts on it in her hand.*)

NORMAN—But I mean— Why a medical record?

MISS HEMMINGWAY—Just for future reference.

NORMAN—Oh, future reference.

MISS HEMMINGWAY—Yes. We put them on file—so as to— (*She turns and sees* DR. ZERNECKE.) Oh, Dr. Zernecke— This is Mr. Overbeck.

DR. ZERNECKE (*as she removes her monocle and sees* NORMAN.)—Oh, yes—of course.

NORMAN—How do you do.

MISS HEMMINGWAY—I finished the examination, Doctor.

DR. ZERNECKE—Oh, good. (*Looks up.*) And everything's settled?

MISS HEMMINGWAY—Yes.

DR. ZERNECKE (*to* NORMAN)—Then we won't keep you any longer, Mr. Overbeck.

NORMAN—You mean that's all?

DR. ZERNECKE—Yes, that's all.

NORMAN—That's all you want!

DR. ZERNECKE—Yes. Just to be sure everything is all right, you know.

NORMAN—And I can go back to Vickley?

DR. ZERNECKE—Certainly.

NORMAN—Gosh!

DR. ZERNECKE—You're to be married soon, aren't you?

NORMAN—Yes, to-morrow.

DR. ZERNECKE—So I heard. Well, you may rest assured we'll be very discreet.

NORMAN—Oh, wait! (DR. ZERNECKE *stops.*) You knew about my marriage?

DR. ZERNECKE—Of course!

NORMAN (*hopefully*)—So that's why you—in case I should have—for *future* reference.

DR. ZERNECKE—Yes, we just keep it on file.

NORMAN—Oh! I see.

DR. ZERNECKE—I'm sorry if we disturbed you—

NORMAN—Oh, not at all.

DR. ZERNECKE—But you see a medical record—

NORMAN (*he is quite excited*)—I know. They're the only things to have. Especially when you are getting married. Modern, scientific, up-to-date. I approve thoroughly. (*He shakes hands with* DR. ZERNECKE *again.*) And now, if there's anything else I can do for you—

DR. ZERNECKE—You won't be troubled any further.

NORMAN—Nice place you have here. (*Turns to* MISS HEMMINGWAY, *and shakes her hand.*) Thank you very much.

DR. ZERNECKE—Perhaps before Mr. Overbeck goes he'd like to see the baby.

NORMAN (*looking dazedly after* DR. ZERNECKE)—Huh!

MISS HEMMINGWAY—You really ought to see him.

NORMAN—Him?

MISS HEMMINGWAY—X-21-A-4 is a cute little trick.

NORMAN—X what?

MISS HEMMINGWAY (*laughing*)—That's your baby's name . . . on the file.

NORMAN (*leaning against table weakly*)—Baby?

MISS HEMMINGWAY (*looking at* NORMAN)—Didn't you understand about this, Mr. Overbeck? I thought, of course, you—

NORMAN—But you said—she said—good God!

MISS HEMMINGWAY—The medical record is for purposes of adoption. You knew there was a baby, didn't you?

NORMAN—No—I mean—yes. I mean—of course.

MISS HEMMINGWAY—We're not supposed to bring them downstairs, but if you'll wait, I'll see what I can do. It may be your only chance to see him.

By pursuing her as far as the doorway Norman is able to extract the additional information that the baby is nearly three weeks old, and that Miss Drury is still with her son, although she had made her plans to leave that day. Can he see Miss Drury? Miss Hemmingway will see about that, too.

Now Gilbert Rand arrives. He has been chasing Norman all over town. He finds him as near hysteria as a sane man can be. They are there, Norman explodes—both of them are there—the baby and his mother! They've been there three weeks! What is he going to do? He can't think of going through life with a baby somewhere—nobody knows where—and looking at Madge Ferris every day! Every day—morning, noon and night—and never tell—

Now Isabel Drury is on the phone. Gilbert thinks he had better talk with her, but Norman had rather do it. Gilbert, however, stands by to prompt him should he seem likely to incriminate himself.

Isabel has no intention of making any trouble, she says, over the phone. She does not even want to see Norman. She wants him to go home and get married, as he planned. She is going to Paris to study art, and she doesn't want to go all through a discussion of that again.

The idea of Isabel's going to Paris at a time like this! To Norman it's simply inhuman!

"She obviously wants to end this whole business," deduces Gilbert. "Well, let her."

"How?"

"You go back to Vickley, marry Madge and the incident is over."

"But the baby?"

"He'll be adopted."

"Where? When? How? By whom?—"

Norman does not care for the idea. Even Gilbert agrees that perhaps they had better talk the matter over with Dr. Zernecke. . . .

The doctor is reassuring. The St. Theckla Child Adoption Society is very discreet; there is no possibility of either parent ever being embarrassed. The baby will be placed in a suitable family—there are many nice people on the waiting list—and no one will ever know—

Norman is amazed that such things can be. Not know where his son has been taken or to whom he has been given? *His* son!

To tell him, Dr. Zernecke explains, would never do. Often parents change their minds after giving a baby for adoption, and that causes a lot of trouble. Miss Drury has signed the baby over to the society, it's her baby, and Norman has nothing to say about it.

Miss Drury, Miss Hemmingway reports, is coming. Perhaps it would be well, the doctor suggests, if Norman and the baby's mother were to settle the question of the child's adoption between them.

Gilbert thinks he had better stay, too, but Norman will not have that. He would only make matters worse. . . .

Isabel Drury looks none too strong. She is of medium height and there is an independent swing to her shoulders as she walks across the room. She is wearing an English tweed sport suit, orange jersey, a brown felt sport hat and brown shoes and stockings. She is a bit startled as she looks up and sees Norman.

NORMAN—Thought I'd go, didn't you?

ISABEL—No, Norman, dear, I didn't. I only hoped you would.

NORMAN—But why?

ISABEL—Because you'd talk—you'd argue, and besides I didn't want to upset you now—just before your wedding.

NORMAN—Oh, of course you haven't! Oh, no!

ISABEL—I'm sorry. (*As she puts bag and gloves on white table.*) I'm dreadfully sorry, and if it hadn't been for Doctor Zernecke with that fool medical record you never would have known about it.

NORMAN—Well, I do know about it—and I want to tell you this—I think it was a hell of a thing to do.

ISABEL—What? Have a baby? Well, Norman, dear, you're hardly in a position to criticize me—

NORMAN—I'm not talking about having the baby—that's different—that's another matter.

ISABEL (*casually*)—It was just an accident.

NORMAN (*amazed*)—A what?

ISABEL—An accident—a—a—biological accident—that's all. I didn't know. *I* never dreamed it was going to happen.

NORMAN—Well, I don't know why you should be so damn sure of that. Anyway it has happened, and I want to know what you mean by giving him away?

ISABEL—Oh— That—

NORMAN—Yes, that! I never heard of such a thing. It's inhuman.

ISABEL—Now, Norman, if you raise your voice I'll leave.

NORMAN—But will you please explain—

ISABEL (*sitting at table*)—If you'll be calm—if you'll listen for a moment.

NORMAN—All right. I'll be calm. I'll listen, I'm all ears. But I'll tell you this. I won't agree with you. (ISABEL *removes her hat and puts it on the table.*)

ISABEL—Of course not—having heard of this only ten minutes ago—you naturally know more about it than I do. I'm only the baby's mother.

NORMAN—And I'm the baby's father.

ISABEL—You are—if I say so.

NORMAN—W-H-A-T?

ISABEL (*languidly*)—Oh, I'm not going to deny that you are his father.

NORMAN—Thanks.

ISABEL—Just the same you have nothing to say about it.

NORMAN—Is that so?

ISABEL—Exactly so.

NORMAN—Now look here, Isabel—

ISABEL—Now, Norman, please. I've had a dreadful time these last three weeks and all the months before and if you're going to nag—

NORMAN—I'm not nagging. I'm simply asking you in the nicest way I know.

ISABEL—Well, it isn't very nice.

NORMAN—All right—all right. I'm sorry. Go on.

ISABEL—Why, Norman—you're not even being civil to me.

NORMAN—Civil?

ISABEL—We meet after nearly a year and all you do is bark at me.

NORMAN—I didn't bark.

ISABEL—Yes, you did, Norman. You barked. And I'm in no condition to be barked at— You sit there and tell me you're the baby's father.

NORMAN—Well, I am.

ISABEL—All right, but don't expect me to be impressed. Try being a baby's mother once—and see how you like that. Just why women should have the exclusive rights to motherhood—I don't know!

NORMAN (*quickly*)—Neither do I! Especially when they give their babies away.

ISABEL—I'll explain that. If you can be sensible long enough—

NORMAN—I'm waiting.

Isabel explains that she had many problems to solve. First, there was her family. She had disgraced them and been promptly disowned. She didn't care about that, but there it was.

Then there was the problem of the baby. Giving him for adoption is unquestionably the best thing for him. He'll be happier in a home. Norman can't see that. His baby—happier with strangers? But they won't be strangers to the baby, Isabel points out.

ISABEL—He'll have a home—a real home— That's more than I could give him.

NORMAN—Then why didn't you tell me, Isabel?

ISABEL—I didn't know, dear, till after I heard you were engaged to be married.

NORMAN—Even so—

ISABEL—Yes and ruin your whole career. That's just what it would do, Norman. Break off your engagement—and what chance would you have as a lawyer—with an illegitimate son.

NORMAN—Well, that *is* a nice thing to say.

ISABEL—What?

NORMAN—*Illegitimate son.*

ISABEL—Well, he is.

NORMAN—He's ours, isn't he?

ISABEL—Just the same that's what they'd call him in Vickley. Of course—I get no credit for avoiding that—and I certainly get no thanks for protecting you.

NORMAN—Protecting me?

ISABEL—Yes—shouldering the whole thing. I knew very well, Norman, if I told you—

NORMAN—You might have to marry me.

ISABEL—What?

NORMAN—Hah! You can't fool me, Isabel—I know.

ISABEL—What? You know what?

NORMAN—The trouble with you— The whole trouble with you—in a nut shell.

ISABEL—What?

NORMAN—You don't love me. That's why we're here—that's why this has happened.

ISABEL—That baby happened—because I don't love! I certainly don't see that!

NORMAN—Oh, yes, you do—but never mind, let it go— That's all over now. Go on!

ISABEL—Anyhow, I never said I didn't love you.

NORMAN—No! You just wouldn't marry me, is that it?

ISABEL—Exactly—you or anybody else.

NORMAN—No, you want to paint.

ISABEL—Norman, I won't discuss that.

NORMAN—No?

ISABEL—No! I refuse to talk about it. I'll leave.

NORMAN (*stopping her*)—I'm sorry—I'm sorry— All right, all right!

ISABEL—Just why every one should sneer when I say I want to paint—

NORMAN—I didn't sneer.

ISABEL—Norman, my life is my own—and I'm going to do just exactly as I please with it. If I make a mess of it, all right. It belongs to me. If you think I'm going to settle down in Vickley and raise a dozen babies,—well, I just won't do it! I won't! I won't!

NORMAN—I thought we weren't going to discuss that.

ISABEL—We're not— If you think I'm just going to do nothing but be your wife—

NORMAN—Have I asked you to?

ISABEL—No,—especially since you're going to marry some one else.

NORMAN—To-morrow. I'm going to be married to-morrow.

ISABEL—That suits me.

NORMAN—Fine, then we're both satisfied. Now—go on—about the baby.

ISABEL—Norman—there's nothing else— He's going to be adopted.

NORMAN—Yes—by whom?

ISABEL—Why, the people—

They are both talking at once, now, and neither agreeing with anything the other says. Isabel is satisfied the St. Theckla Society is wonderful and that the baby will be properly looked after by that society and Norman is equally convinced that neither the Theckla's nor any one else is going to take his son and refuse to let him know what they do with him. He doesn't know exactly what he'll do about it, but he'll do something—

If he does anything that embarrasses her, Isabel warns him, she will swear he is not the baby's father. If she does that, Norman counters, he will demand to know who is. Let her produce him?

Isabel repeats that she has made every possible investigation of the St. Theckla's and she is sure she is doing what is right. So she's through.

She's running away, that's what she's doing, shouts Norman. Well, let her! She says there is nothing else for her to do. Why isn't there? She can marry him, can't she?

No, she can't! He's going to marry some one else! He's in love with some one else!

"I'm not," shouts Norman. "You know damned well I'm not. Oh, I'm engaged—yes—I'm going to be married. But why? In self-defense. I pretended even to myself that I was in love with her and all the time I knew—and you know, Isabel—I've never had a thought for any one but you. I forgot, you say . . . when all summer long—I went through hell—I couldn't talk—I couldn't think—I couldn't eat—I couldn't sleep—all night long I'd walk the streets. I did, Isabel, no fooling. The people home—I don't know what they thought. I pretended to be sick— Once I said I had a toothache for fear they'd think I'd gone insane. But I didn't have a toothache—it was you—just you, Isabel. In self-defense and more to please my family I got myself engaged. I know that's a caddish thing to say—she's worth ten of me—and you.

"Thank you. Then why do you prefer me?"

"I don't know—damn it, I don't know!"

Norman is only convinced of one thing: Isabel has no right to walk out on that baby. And Isabel is just as strongly convinced that the only person in the world she owes anything to is herself. He has his ambitions, and she has her ambitions, and her ambition is not to be just a wife and mother. She has other things to do and she purposes to do them. With which statement Isabel walks out and leaves Norman standing somewhat bewildered in the middle of the reception room floor. . . .

Miss Clark is answering the telephone. . . . Hicks is back, his face wreathed in smiles. Hicks is the father of a fine girl and everything's lovely. Anything he's said before about wives and families and responsibilities— That stuff doesn't go.

Now Miss Hemmingway arrives with Miss Drury's baby. Norman is fascinated by the sight of his offspring.

MISS HEMMINGWAY—Isn't he darling? (HICKS *is staring at the group, puzzled.*) He looks like you, Mr. Overbeck.

NORMAN (*looking up and smiling at* MISS HEMMINGWAY)—Do you think so?

MISS CLARK—Miss Hemmingway—there's a call for you.

MISS HEMMINGWAY—Oh, all right—I'll take it here.

MISS CLARK (*in phone*)—Just a moment, please.

MISS HEMMINGWAY (*turning to* NORMAN)—Would you care to hold him?

NORMAN (*anxiously*)—May I?

MISS HEMMINGWAY (*as she offers him the baby*)—Of course. (NORMAN *attempts to take the baby, but shows by his manner that he is unaccustomed to handling babies.* HICKS *has been watching him.*)

HICKS (*in a very superior manner*)—Put one arm under him. (NORMAN *takes the baby and backing up against the center table, half sits on it, looking down into the baby's face as* MISS HEMMINGWAY *gives* HICKS *one look and crosses quickly to the phone.*)

MISS HEMMINGWAY (*into the phone*)—Hello!—Oh, Dr. Allenby—this is Miss Hemmingway— (MISS HEMMINGWAY *continues to carry on a conversation with* DR. ALLENBY.)

HICKS (*to* NORMAN)—Say, buddy, is it yours?

NORMAN (*looking* HICKS *in the face*)—Yes.

MISS HEMMINGWAY (*into phone*)—Hello!—what?— Well, I couldn't till now.

HICKS (*to* NORMAN, *trying to understand the situation*)—But I thought you said you wasn't married.

NORMAN (*looking at* HICKS *defiantly*)—I'm not.

HICKS (*looking away very wisely*)—Oh—! Non-Union, eh?

NORMAN—Yes!

HICKS—Well, what the hell! If he's yours, what's the odds how he got here. The old feeling's there just the same, ain't it?

NORMAN—Yes!

HICKS—Well, that's what counts— Anyhow, that's what I think!

MISS HEMMINGWAY (*into phone*)—What?— But Miss Drury's gone, Doctor—(NORMAN *looks up quickly*) a few minutes ago—yes— Well, we have the father's record. Yes—will they call here— The St. Theckla people?— (NORMAN *straightens up on his feet.*) Oh, very well, Doctor— We'll send the baby right away.

(NORMAN *defiantly looks around the room, first to the left then to the right, and as he watches* MISS HEMMINGWAY, *reaches back on the table and gets his hat, starts for arch. He quickly exits through the arch to the door.*)

MISS HEMMINGWAY (*into phone*)—What?— Yes, I did—they're lovely flowers—I couldn't imagine who sent them—thanks so much.

Miss Hemmingway continues on the phone as the curtain falls.

ACT III

Eight days later Monica Case, whose mother runs a boarding house in Chicago, is trying to tidy up a cheaply furnished room without awaking a sleeping infant comfortably disposed in a Kiddie Koop in an alcove at back.

Monica is evidently more interested in the baby than she is in the sweeping, a fact that irritates her mother excessively. Also it is Mrs. Case's belief that Monica has been devoting considerable attention to making eyes at Mr. Overbeck and has been known to moon about the last few days much more than circumstances call for.

Mrs. Case takes little stock in the excitement Mr. Overbeck and the infant Overbeck have caused and are still causing in her boarding house. The idea of a man's being so crazy over a baby that he must go have the scales tested to discover what's wrong just because the infant's gain is only an ounce a week, and not in accordance with the table in the book. Mrs. Case believes an ounce a week is quite enough. She's had babies and the book hasn't. Mr. Overbeck, if any one should ask Mrs. Case, is a damned fool.

Norman is back from a drug store lugging his baby scales with him. The scales are right—so there must be something wrong with the baby. He isn't gaining, evidently, because he isn't getting the right things to eat. And he isn't getting the right things to eat because Norman doesn't know the formula and is afraid to ask the hospital for it for fear of his own and the baby's whereabouts being discovered. He had trouble with the hospital authorities after his wife died, he explains to Mrs. Case, and he doesn't want to renew the quarrel. Still, he must get hold of the formula some way. Baby can't go on gaining only an ounce a week—52 ounces a year! It would take him twenty years to become a midget! Perhaps if he could get hold of some goat's milk— Perhaps a little tomato juice—

Another thing—the baby must have a lot of fresh air, even though his crib must be kept covered so he will not inhale any of Chicago's soft coal dust. Is it any wonder Chicago has so many gunmen, considering the fact that its babies are raised on soft coal dust?

Norman admits to Monica that he has not yet found a job, but he has had his life insurance transferred to the baby. The thought of what might happen to baby if anything should happen to him is maddening to Norman.

Monica is greatly interested in the baby, too—and in Norman. She is quite frank in saying that she thinks Norman should get married again. Of course he couldn't expect to get another girl just as wonderful as the wife who died, but he should marry some one—some one young who likes children and would love to live in the country. . . .

Mrs. Case has been telephoning the hospital. She told them she wanted the baby's formula. Told them, too, that the father's name was Overbeck.

"She knew you right away," Mrs. Case reports, gleefully. "Stop worrying—she'll give the formula, you'll feed the baby—and we'll all have a little peace around here."

"Oh, my God!" ejaculates Norman, as he realizes what has happened.

MONICA—What's the matter?

NORMAN—They'll take him, Monica—they'll take him back.

MONICA—Who?

NORMAN—Those people from the Hospital.

MONICA—How can they? Aren't you his father?

NORMAN—Yes, I am.

MONICA—Well, then—

NORMAN—Why the hell did I ever let her phone that hospital?

MONICA—Well, if you're the father—

NORMAN—But that isn't enough; you've got to be a mother.

MONICA—But if the mother's dead?

NORMAN—Well, her people.

MONICA—Your wife's?

NORMAN—Yes. That's it. My wife's family. They want him, you see.

MONICA—Yes—but they can't—

NORMAN—Yes, they can— You don't know them—

MONICA—How?

NORMAN—Well, you see, they have legal rights.

MONICA—Why?

NORMAN—Because I'm a bachelor—

MONICA—What?

NORMAN—I mean I'm alone.

MONICA—Oh—and if you were married could you keep the baby?

NORMAN—Yes, I could. I could adopt him.

MONICA—Well—when are they coming?

NORMAN—Any minute.

MONICA—I wish you'd told me sooner—Norman.

NORMAN—I couldn't—Monica!

MONICA—Not at first maybe, but after we became so well acquainted.

NORMAN—I didn't know we were going to be so well acquainted.

MONICA—Well, it doesn't matter now—if they are really coming—

NORMAN—I won't give him back, Monica—I couldn't do it. Not now. A week ago maybe. I know him now, and I think he knows me . . . and—and oh, God! He's so little, that's why!

MONICA (*anxiously*)—Listen, Norman, there is a way.

NORMAN (*turning to* MONICA)—What?

MONICA—Leave, before they come.

NORMAN—What?

MONICA—Yes! Pack up now quick.

NORMAN—I couldn't. I'm nearly broke. I haven't any job. And even if I had one I couldn't take him. What could I do with him?

MONICA—Well—I—*I'll* go with you if you want.

NORMAN—You?

MONICA—Yes.

NORMAN—Oh, but I couldn't—I couldn't let you do that!

MONICA—Why not? *I'll*—just—just be his *nurse*.

NORMAN—I know but—it—it might look funny.

MONICA (*turns and looks towards door then back to* NORMAN) —What do you say, Norman—will you?

NORMAN—Doesn't matter now—it's too late.

MONICA—It isn't too late. You get rid of them—and after they leave we'll go.

NORMAN—I don't know what to say. I can't give him up, I know that.

MONICA—You don't have to, Norman. Look—if you were married.

NORMAN—Yes.

MONICA—Then you could keep him, for sure!

NORMAN—Yes—I know—

MONICA—Well, all right then—I'll get married even—what do you say?

NORMAN—Why—

MONICA—Oh, I love—the baby, Norman.

NORMAN—All right—I'll do it!

MONICA—You will?

NORMAN—Yes, I'll do it now—right away.

MONICA—Oh, Norman! (*She throws her arms around him.*)

Gilbert Rand is startled a trifle when he opens the door and sees Norman being thus embraced, but Gilbert has become a successful shock-absorber. When Norman explains that Monica is helping him with the baby, Gilbert quite understands. He can see, too, that Monica is very good at helping. But at the moment Gilbert has more important things to speak of. Madge Ferris is downstairs—and knows everything: All about Norman and Isabel and the baby.

"At first she was terribly hurt," Gilbert admits; "but I finally convinced her that you're still madly in love with her!"

"What?"

"Now then—all Vickley thinks your marriage was postponed because of illness—and you can thank me, Norman, for all of it." Still there is one little thing that Gilbert has overlooked. What about the baby? Oh, Gilbert has fixed that, too. A certain family of splendid people will take the baby off Norman's hands and let him see his son whenever he wants to! All Norman will have to do now is to go back to Vickley, and forget everything.

Forgetting "the only decent thing that ever happened in his life" does not appeal to Norman. No, he'll not do that. If Madge won't marry him and take the baby he won't marry her —not even to save Gilbert from becoming the greatest liar in Vickley!

Madge is agreeable, Gilbert reports. So long as there is no one else; so long as Norman thinks he has forgotten the baby's mother, Madge is willing to accept the situation and the child with it.

Norman is just trying to explain about Monica and certain newer plans when Mrs. Case arrives to announce that there is still another lady downstairs who would like to see Norman. She is, so far as Mrs. Case can figure it, Norman's dead wife. They must have dug her up!

But Isabel has not come for Norman. All she wants is her baby. And she doesn't plan giving him away again, either. The adoption people wouldn't take him now, anyway.

NORMAN—Won't take him? What do you mean? What's the matter with him?

ISABEL—Nothing's the matter with him. It's you. They say it isn't safe with you around. (NORMAN *turns away.*) But that doesn't matter now, because I want him.

NORMAN (*turning to* ISABEL)—Oh, changed your mind, have you?—And what about me?

ISABEL—I haven't changed my mind about you.

NORMAN—I didn't ask you that—what about me? I want the baby.

ISABEL—You're going to be married.

NORMAN—To-morrow.

ISABEL—Funny—I always seem to meet you the day before your wedding— Well, you can't be married and have the baby too—

NORMAN—Can't I? Shows how little you know.

ISABEL—But your wife won't want another woman's baby.

NORMAN—Won't she? She's not like you.

ISABEL—No, she's worth ten of— I'm sure she's very sweet.

NORMAN—She is—I'm crazy about her.

ISABEL—All right, then marry her and—

NORMAN—And what?

ISABEL—Have babies of your own; that's what.

NORMAN—You needn't tell me what to do.

ISABEL—I'm not.

NORMAN—Anyhow, they won't be like him.

ISABEL—I didn't say they would.

NORMAN—No other baby'll ever be like him. And that's why I won't give him up.

ISABEL—Won't you? We'll see about that.

Now it appears that neither Isabel nor Norman will give up their child. And neither will listen to any suggestion that the baby might be kept jointly. Norman has his marriages to think of and Isabel has her pride. She has been pretty unhappy since the baby disappeared. She has suffered more than she thought it possible to suffer—and then to sit in the doctor's office when Norman telephoned for the formula and have herself pronounced dead!

Then to rush out there and find her baby being fed, of all things, goat's milk and tomato juice out of a can! It's a wonder he's alive at all.

Now Isabel is holding her baby in her arms and smiling down at him. He is beautiful, she thinks, even though he has Norman's nose. Of course they couldn't expect everything. . . .

Madge Ferris takes her introduction to Isabel and Norman's baby very well. She is entirely sympathetic and understanding and, so far as she is concerned, everything will be lovely when she and Norman are married and Isabel has gone on to Paris with the baby.

To Paris? Take Norman's baby to Paris? Not if Norman can stop them! Any of them! All of them! Can't they understand that he doesn't intend to give that baby up? Won't some of them try to realize that he is the baby's father?

MADGE—I think perhaps you and Miss Drury would rather talk alone. (*She starts up toward folding doors.*)

NORMAN (*as he goes to* MADGE)—No—don't go.

ISABEL (*as she goes to* MADGE)—Please don't go, Miss Ferris. He'll calm down.

NORMAN—Here—I'll end this right now— (*To* ISABEL.) Isabel, you're the cause of this.

ISABEL—Of what?

NORMAN—This mess I'm in—I tie myself in a knot trying to hold on to the baby and you come along and calmly announce you'll take him off my hands—well, you won't do it!

ISABEL—Won't I? Now, Norman, please have sense—what can you do?

NORMAN—I can ask you to leave right now.

MADGE—Norman!

NORMAN—Well, I can't help it— (*To* MADGE.) She makes me so damn mad—I can't think straight while she's here.

ISABEL—Very well—I'll go —(*stops and turns to* NORMAN) at least till you come to your senses. Will you show me to the door?

NORMAN—No—I won't—Monica will— (*He calls.*) Monica!

MONICA (*from in the alcove*)—Yes, Norman, dear.

MADGE—Norman dear!

ISABEL—Well—that's a little unexpected.

MADGE—Excuse me—I will wait in here. (*She goes up to the folding doors, opens them, enters the alcove and closes the door after her.*)

ISABEL—Are you engaged to her too, Norman?

NORMAN—Yes, I am.

ISABEL—But why?

NORMAN—To keep the baby.

ISABEL—Two—you need two wives?

NORMAN—I don't know what happened?—they were coming to take him—I could see them carrying him out that door—I was damn near crazy.

ISABEL—Norman!

NORMAN—Leave me alone.

ISABEL—If—it's just so you can have some claim on him, Norman—I—I'll marry you.

NORMAN (*as he turns to* ISABEL)—What?

ISABEL—Just a formal—you know—business-like.

NORMAN—You'll marry me—not because of me?

ISABEL—Oh, no—quite impersonally.

NORMAN—Not if you were the last woman on earth.

ISABEL—But why—

NORMAN—I don't love you—that's why.

ISABEL—Do you love them?

NORMAN—Yes!

ISABEL—Both of them?

NORMAN—Yes—that's different. I don't hate them. I could have peace with them—all I'd ever have with you is misery.

ISABEL—But if you don't love me—

NORMAN—Love you? Huh? I wonder now that I ever did.

ISABEL—But you did, Norman. You did love me once. I remember—the first time you told me. We were leaning against a picket fence and you talked about platonic friendship and you said the reason we would always get along together was because there was nothing physical in our affection. You did, Norman—really—it does seem funny now. Doesn't it?

NORMAN—You think it's funny do you? All right, go on laugh. After a while I'll laugh too.

ISABEL—I'm not laughing, Norman.

NORMAN—You know what's the matter with you, Isabel—you're too damn fresh. You're not attractive, you know.

ISABEL—You used to think I was attractive.

NORMAN (*as he goes to* ISABEL)—Pretended. I didn't want to hurt your feelings. I could see—I could always see . . . petty little traits in you. So sure of yourself. So damn sure of yourself. The way you held your head—your walk.

ISABEL—You used to like my walk.

NORMAN—Pretended. That's all over now, thank God! Now I can say what I think. This is the end.

ISABEL—But, Norman—

NORMAN—I'll tell you this—you'll never torture me—I'm hardened, Isabel. I'm calloused, that's what I am.

ISABEL—Norman, please. I didn't mean—

NORMAN—I don't give a damn what you meant—I'm through.

Norman's father is at the door. He, too, has come to see what can be done about straightening out the affairs of his son and his son's family—or families. He has not, however, come to interfere.

"We all reach corners in our lives that we have to turn alone," admits J. J. "You are standing at one of those corners now. In fact I might say that you are standing at a crossroad—I'd be right sorry, son, to see you lose your way." . . .

Monica has unpacked all the things she previously had packed. Monica is wise enough to know when things are too crowded.

Madge, too, is prepared to back out. She knows Norman would have married her. And she won't pretend that she isn't hurt because he didn't. But she thinks it will be better for a lot of people if she goes back alone to Vickley. J. J. will take Madge to her hotel, and then he will come back to have a peek at his grandson.

Norman throws back the sliding doors in front of the alcove. "Isabel is seated at the center of the archway, holding the baby in her arms with his head on her left arm."

ISABEL—Do we make a pretty picture, Norman?

NORMAN—What the hell did you say to them?

ISABEL—I didn't. They said it to me.

NORMAN—What?

ISABEL—That we loved each other. They heard us talking, you know.

NORMAN—Why—you—

ISABEL—Sh! Don't you wake this baby.

NORMAN—Then stop rocking him. Don't you know he should never be rocked?

ISABEL—No—I didn't.

NORMAN (*takes the baby from her, with its head on his right arm*)—And don't pick him up—ever.

ISABEL—Never?

NORMAN—Except when you feed him and he has to be changed.

ISABEL—Oh, I have so much to learn, Norman.

NORMAN—Well, it's all very simple if you just follow this book— (NORMAN *reaches over to the table and picks up the formula book, and hands it to* ISABEL.) Here, I'll teach you.

ISABEL (*as she wipes her eyes*)—It's no use, Norman. I can't see a line.

NORMAN (*looks at* ISABEL)—What? (*He shows by motions that the baby needs to be changed.*) Well, there's one important lesson you can learn without the book— (*He turns to his left, reaches up on the chest of drawers and picks up the diaper that* MONICA *has left lying on the top and, returning to* ISABEL, *hands it to her.*) Here—fold this in a triangle. (ISABEL *leading, they both start up right toward the bed as the curtain falls.*)

GYPSY

A Drama in Three Acts

By Maxwell Anderson

TO this season's list of plays Maxwell Anderson, author of the highly successful "Saturday's Children" of two years ago, contributed "Gypsy," a fairly ruthless study of a heroine handicapped by ancestry who tries desperately to live a free life and goes down to defeat in the attempt.

She isn't a sympathetic heroine and those aspects of the newer feminine psychology for which she and her mother stand as the exposing medium are none too flattering to their sex. The general public, therefore, notoriously shy of unconventional heroines, particularly when they are unsympathetic, stayed rather persistently away from "Gypsy."

To this editor "Gypsy" represents an honestly written drama inspired by changing social standards and values, a play of purpose, the artistic integrity of which cannot be questioned whatever the reaction may be to its characters and its story. It was one of the distressingly few dramas of native authorship shown during the season to reflect credit upon its author and to provoke debate.

It is a late spring day in New York. In David and Ellen Hastings' apartment on West 18th street, "plainly but happily furnished, somewhat in the village manner, by people who have taste but not too much money," Ellen Hastings and Cleve Christen stand facing each other, "looking at each other as though something disquieting had occured." Ellen is an attractive young woman in her early twenties, Cleve a good-looking, substantial type of young man probably two or three years her senior.

The thing that has happened to disturb them, it transpires, is that in the midst of Ellen's reading aloud Cleve has kissed her. Kissed her because he is in love with her and powerless, he argues, to withstand the temptation.

Ellen has protested, not her dislike of being loved, nor yet of the kiss; but rather her regret that the confession of love had to be made in just that way at just this time. It would have been better for both of them to have kept their feelings under control.

Particularly would it have been better for Cleve. Ellen is, she warns him, a kind of buzzsaw.

"David thinks I'm a terrible flirt," says she, "and the only answer I can make to that is I don't mean anything by it. I guess I flirt with people because—it's amusing—and it doesn't affect me much—so, why not? But don't be serious."

As answer to which Cleve kisses Ellen again, and again she protests, though still feebly. When he would go she begs him to stay. Soon David will be home, she says, and they always have coffee at midnight. It's all right about David. He knew Cleve was to be there.

But about an engagement she and Cleve had for the theatre the next night—Ellen is not sure they had better keep that engagement. In fact she feels strongly that it would be better for her if she never saw Cleve again. That, to Cleve, is quite impossible.

"I don't quite take that in. I tell you I've been walking around in a daze—ever since—well—ever since you came down those stairs—at Peter's party. I didn't know how you felt about it—but— Why have we seen each other every night since we met? Didn't the same thing happen to you?"

"In a way," she admits.

"So—I won't submit to not seeing you again."

"I'm—in love with David, you know," she warns. "I'll have to tell him, sometime."

Later as Cleve becomes more insistent, Ellen tries further to make her attitude clear to him. She hopes there may be no misunderstanding between them.

"I'll have to tell you something, Cleve," she says. "I've had more experience with myself than you have. I am in love with David, and I think I'd always have been faithful to him if I hadn't been married to him. I didn't really want to be married—and I got tired of it and wanted to be free—and—I had a lover. You see, love and faith and trust can be a sort of tryanny. Any way I thought so."

"When was this?"

"About a year ago. But it was terrible for David when I told him, because I was pretty mad about Jerry. That's all, I guess, only I came back to David—and fell in love with him all over again—"

"I see."

"And now I suppose I'm tired of being good again—but I've got to be—the other isn't worth the misery."

"So you just want to flirt with me a little?"

"If you don't mind."

"I mind—but what's that to you?"

"Don't mind, please. Don't be serious."

"All right," Cleve agrees. This time he kisses her lightly upon the forehead.

Now David, a suggestively esthetic young man of open countenance and trusting eyes, is home and has met Cleve for the first time. David brings news, too. He has been made the director of an orchestra in a moving picture house. It's good to have the new job, because of the extra money, but otherwise there is no great thrill in the prospect for David.

"You see, I set out to be a great violinist," he explains to Cleve, "and I'm still a violinist, but not so great."

"I set out to be a second Conrad," confesses Cleve, "and what do I get? I'm the editor of a so-called magazine of so-called Sailor Stories."

There is some satisfaction for all three in their attempted self-justification, however. Cleve has written a novel, David has become a director and Ellen is a pretty fair sort of housewife for a lady who also works in an office.

"At any rate I get breakfast, and I get dinner, except when I'm too late at the office," reports Ellen, "and I wash the dishes and clean house. Oh, I've been so good this winter my own mother wouldn't know me. She doesn't, either. She finds it all quite incredible. Heaven knows I never allowed her to inveigle me into a kitchen. Oh, yes,—and in the long, lonely evenings, while David's at the theatre, I improve my mind by reading a good book."

Whether the mind has been improved or not David admits that Ellen has read a lot of books, even including "The Decline and Fall of the Roman Empire" in ever so many volumes.

It is while Ellen is getting the coffee and sandwiches on the table that Mac and Sylvia arrive. Mac is by way of being an actor, a bum actor some say, but Mac is not sensitive. Sylvia is Mac's most understanding sweetheart and about to take the plunge and become his wife. For years, as Mac explains, they have been ringside spectators; now, with the example of conjugal felicity presented by David and Ellen to inspire them, they are all set for matrimony.

"You see," explains Sylvia, "we're marrying to save each other from the gutter."

MAC—I didn't say the gutter. I said the drain.

SYLVIA—Well, I like the gutter better.

ELLEN (*on the way to the kitchen*)—I wonder where the gutter got its bad reputation.

CLEVE—From the people who lie in it.

MAC—Funny thing, you never find the upper classes in the gutter—always lower classes—well, naturally, the gutter gets a bad name.

SYLVIA—Just like marriage.

MAC—Oh, no, marriage is respectable. The upper classes are always doing it. They do it to set an example.

CLEVE—And just to emphasize it, they do it over and over again.

MAC—Ours is to be a peasant or bourgois marriage. Lifetime lovers—faithful till death.

CLEVE—Faithful?

MAC—That's what marriage is all about.

DAVID—Hold that thought.

MAC—Well, maybe not absolutely.

SYLVIA—Well, if faithful doesn't mean absolutely, what does it mean? Don't you think I'm right, Ellen?

ELLEN (*looking out*)—Just another example of how the ideals of feudalism still permeate modern society.

SYLVIA—Yes?

DAVID—Ellen's quoting Roman history again.

MAC (*as* ELLEN *carries the coffee out of the kitchen*)—Speak, oh, Sibyl, do you or do you not believe husbands and wives ought to be faithful?

ELLEN—Why be so personal?

DAVID—Well, Gypsy, I never noticed you side-stepping before.

ELLEN—I suppose when things happen, one might as well admit them. I never had much use for faithfulness anyway, and less use for telling lies about it.

SYLVIA—But there's something in it, my dear, there's really something in it—two people sort of banding together against the world. It's pretty lonely unless you can trust some one.

ELLEN—But is that the only thing worth trusting people about? I'd much rather be trusted to tell the truth. That, at least, doesn't rob you of your independence.

CLEVE—Oh, doesn't it? You try telling it for a while.

ELLEN—I have! I always have!

CLEVE—Not to everybody?

ELLEN—Pretty close to it.

DAVID—I'll say you have.

MAC—You can always trust Ellen to lay all the cards on the table.

CLEVE—They say one tells the truth to save his own soul—and he may save his own soul—but God, what death and destruction it spreads! So he takes to lying to save other people.

ELLEN—It doesn't save other people much. I never knew a lie to be worth its own agony.

DAVID—They say the truth's more dangerous than firearms, and most people know less about handling it, but for myself I'd rather be shot than lied to.

MAC—If there's anything you can't tell the truth about, why do it at all?

SYLVIA—I guess a person can't be good all the time.

MAC—Is that a threat?

CLEVE—The trouble with telling the truth is that one uses it like the confessional. You think because you're going to confess you're excused for anything—in advance.

ELLEN—That sounds like pure theory. Am I the only person present who has ever had to save his soul by confessing? Are you all pure as the driven snow?

CLEVE—Not me.

MAC—Not me, thank God.

ELLEN—As for David, he never really wanted to be bad. I don't think it's any special virtue in him. He just isn't tempted.

DAVID—I know it's not modern, but personally, I can do without the gutter, and I'd a little rather.

ELLEN—So can I, and I've never been in the drain, either, although you'd never know it from what's said about me. Shall we have our coffee now?

After they have gathered around the table Ellen undertakes to set Cleve right as to what has inspired this discussion of personal morals and specific reactions. It doesn't spring from dozens of love affairs, but from one, and that one her affair with Jerry, which was really quite unimportant—to every one except David. It was pretty sad for him, David admits, the week Ellen was planning to go into vaudeville with Jerry. And it did not help matters that the affair, while aging to him, seemed to make Ellen look younger.

"Is it faithfulness in general that husbands want, or faithfulness from their own wives?" Sylvia would like to know.

"Other men can look after their own wives as far as I'm concerned," announces Mac.

"I wonder sometimes if that is not a good idea," admits David. "I'm going to like Mac a lot better when he's married."

Casually, while the subject is in mind, Ellen mentions that a letter has come from Jerry that day. However, she adds, David need have no cause for alarm in that direction. Jerry is to be in South Bend for three days and, being "a poor, lonely, handsome, benighted soul," he is expecting her there hourly.

The idea may be amusing to Ellen, but it isn't amusing to David. There is nothing very satisfying in the experience of having a wife you're mad about "come running to you in the first blush of spring, snuggle her head on your shoulder and confess how madly she loves somebody else."

"Carramba! I need air!" explodes Ellen, as she starts for the kitchen. "Who wants strawberry jam?"

"Me! That's all I get," protests David.

"You can start in on somebody else's reputation," admits Ellen. "Mine's shot."

The telephone rings. It is Ellen's mother, Marilyn Russell, whose arrival would not be the surprise it is to her daughter, Mrs. Russell explains over the phone, if Ellen had been home any evening during the last week to answer her phone. Marilyn had called Ellen every evening all the way from Boston.

"I wonder she can't stay at home and look after poor Dad instead of blowing in and out of town all the time," suggests Ellen. "I never knew anybody to get such a kick out of riding on trains."

Marilyn wants to come over and have coffee with them, if there is still any left. Mac agrees to fetch her in his car, and Sylvia decides to go with him. She doesn't altogether trust that Russell woman. Cleve goes along, too. Tries to make it a final good-night, but Ellen insists that he should come back with the others.

Now Ellen and David are alone and a little relieved. "Too much company," sententiously comments David. "We never get a chance to get lonesome around here. Do you like Cleve?"

ELLEN—Oh, yes, I like him a lot. Don't you?

DAVID—I think he's a grand guy. I wish I could take you to a show sometime. Is he in love with you?

ELLEN—Maybe he is—a little.

DAVID—Well, they all are, mostly.

ELLEN—Oh, no. They just think I'm pretty, mostly. But Cleve's rather extraordinary.

DAVID—You know, I get to feeling sort of far away from you sometimes, and sometimes it seems to me as if you wanted it that way. I can't help remembering that's the way it all started with Jerry. I couldn't bear that. I don't think I could go through that again.

ELLEN—I couldn't bear it either.

DAVID—Jerry calls you up every once in a while, doesn't he?

ELLEN—Don't talk about Jerry, please.

DAVID—You aren't quite over it, are you—not quite?

ELLEN—Yes, I am. I wish I knew some way to prove it to you.

DAVID—Don't prove it by falling in love with somebody else.

ELLEN—It's the last thing I'd want.

DAVID—Tell me how you feel about Cleve, will you, dear? (ELLEN *pauses, and he goes on.*) Oh, Gypsy, I wonder if you know how much I'm in love with you. I'm so terribly in love with you and I'm tortured sometimes because I look at you and it seems to me that you don't quite belong to me, or anybody—and you never will. It's as if you belonged to me for a little while—and I'm always afraid the time will come when I'll have to give you back.

ELLEN—To whom?

DAVID—To you, I guess.

ELLEN—Darling—I want to belong—I want to be so madly in love there's nothing else in the world. The way it was when we first knew each other.

DAVID—Isn't it that way now?

ELLEN—It is—now. (*She kisses him.*) Oh, David, darling, don't let me get away! Don't let me get away! All my world would collapse away from you.

DAVID—Gypsy, dear, if loving you will keep you—I'll keep you forever.

The doorbell rings. It is Cleve come back upstairs to report the discovery of a messenger boy at the downstairs door with telegrams for Ellen Hastings and Marilyn Russell. He wasn't sure of the Marilyn Russell, so David goes down to sign for that one, which gives Ellen a chance to repeat hurriedly her conclusion that it will be better if she and Cleve do not see each other again. Cleve admits that he feels that way, too, since he has met David.

"I rather pride myself on being a good sport," says Cleve. "I'll take my medicine and like it."

That makes it a lot easier for Ellen. "The best way to quit is just to quit," she says.

"I can call you up sometimes—at the office?"

"I'll want you to, of course. But—"

"Well, I probably will, if I can find an excuse."

David is back. Ellen's telegram is from Jerry. He is coming to town—as if that mattered. And probably Marilyn Russell's telegram is a recall from home. Usually she is sent for before she really arrives.

"My poor mother is still trying to lead her own life," explains Ellen, "but she doesn't get much sympathy from this branch of the family."

And yet David is not entirely in sympathy with Ellen's contention that she is her father's child and not at all like her mother.

"I'll tell you a secret, Ellen," he says. "The things you dislike about your mother are the things you resent in yourself."

"Well, then, I'll never be without a horrible example," says Ellen.

They drift into a discussion of Ellen and Ellen's mother, and the excuse there may be for their feeling as they do toward each other. There was never much home life for Ellen. She frankly has never felt that she knew her mother, and never really liked her.

"I was at boarding school and then I went to work right away and, somehow, I never went back. And then I looked into a university—and then—I just drifted. And I played in stock. Oh, yes—I was an actress."

Marriage also works its way into the discussion, though Ellen is fearfully suspicious of that subject. "Don't bring up marriage," she protests, "it wrecks a home every time it's mentioned."

True, they did get married, she and David. It isn't easy to explain why.

"She pretends to hate being married," says David, "but she doesn't really mind, do you, Gypsy?"

"I mind it about three days out of the week, but the rest of the time I think it's all right."

David—I'll admit marriage does have its drawbacks. It makes people take each other for granted. And it makes other people take them for granted. Just for example, Cleve, you come here to see us, and you know we're married, and so we're just ordinary married people to you. It wouldn't occur to you to think of what's back of it. Now, would it?

CLEVE—Well, no.

DAVID—But a marriage can be the most romantic and thrilling thing in the world. The way Ellen and I found each other and turned everything upside down so we could be together—

ELLEN—Cleve seems fated to learn my whole history this evening.

DAVID—Wasn't it fun, though, Gypsy? I didn't know what to make of her at first. I was playing in an orchestra out West and we happened to hook up with a travelling stock company with this one playing leads in it. She called herself eighteen and looked fifteen and talked philosophy and drove all the men in the company to drink. One of those God-awful companies it was that grow up on the prairies, doing "The Cat and the Canary" for the Missouri farmers. We got acquainted over near-beer and Nietzsche one night and I thought she was flirting with me, too—but, no—she discovered I knew more Karl Marx than she did and it was too much for her and she fell for me.

ELLEN—It was Marx that did it.

DAVID—And then things began to happen. Ellen got a chance to go to Spokane and play in a real troupe and she told me she'd write to me and disappeared. I guess she didn't know she was going to miss me, did you, girl? It hit me pretty hard—but I got a chance to go to New York—and the first mail I received when I got here was a letter from Spokane, just about the loneliest letter ever written, and I couldn't stand it, and telegraphed I'd meet her in St. Louis, just about the time she was wiring me she was on her way to New York. We passed somewhere on the road and then we were both broke and I had to wait for her while she bummed rides out to Missouri with three dollars in her pocket.

ELLEN—I didn't have any trouble getting rides.

DAVID—No, you wouldn't. I was living in a cheap rooming house and this baggage arrived unexpectedly on my door-step without so much as a nightgown at one o'clock in the morning, and you can imagine the hell there was to pay. I swear she was the craziest, most beautiful child that ever walked the earth. I'd never been in love before, and when she came to me it was like—it was like fate—it was like death—it was inevitable—it was beautiful and terrible—for me. I guess I don't know why I'm telling you all this.

CLEVE—But where did you stay that night?

DAVID—Oh, we managed to stay there, and I smuggled her out

before sunrise and found a room for her and we both went looking for jobs. She got one first, of course, and shared her money with me—and all the time we were mad, perfectly mad, and Ellen was the maddest thing that ever ran up against conventions. I had to take a job in Des Moines—because nothing else offered, and we needed money—and I told her she'd have to stay in St. Louis and work hard and be good, but every few days she'd turn up at my place, looking rather shame-faced but very happy, having got to Des Moines, God knows how, across country.

ELLEN—And he was always very good and took me in, little bedraggled wretch that I was.

DAVID—God knows I was glad enough to see you.

CLEVE—And then you were married.

DAVID—Well, we didn't mean to. Ellen had sworn she never would, but when I came back to St. Louis we went to a hotel and told the clerk we were married, but he didn't believe us and they wouldn't let us in anywhere—so we went and got married and showed the clerk the certificate.

ELLEN—Damn his eyes.

DAVID—And the little bride cried all night because she'd gone back on her principles and disgraced herself by swearing away her freedom—and as a matter of fact she's been kicking about it more or less ever since.

CLEVE (*after a moment*)—It's a marvellous story.

DAVID—It was a marvellous story, wasn't it, Gypsy? And it is.

ELLEN—Only it's rather— Well, I may have been crazy but I guess I wasn't very beautiful.

DAVID—I'll decide that.

ELLEN—I'd better put on some coffee and spare my blushes. (*She goes to the kitchen.*)

CLEVE—I wish I'd known her when she was like that.

DAVID—She hasn't changed much. She's just as mad as ever. It doesn't do her any harm. I like her that way.

ELLEN (*pausing in the doorway as she enters the kitchen*)—And even when you aren't mad,—life seems to do such weird things to people.

Now there is another ring at the doorbell and David lets in Mac, Sylvia and Marilyn, Sylvia leading, Mac with his arm about Marilyn's shoulders, giving an imitation of "the young lovers."

Marilyn's greetings are warm and slightly explosive. She would be effusive with her daughter if Ellen would play up to the maternal passion, but Ellen's rather an icicle, according to Marilyn and always has been. . . .

Marilyn's telegram, as expected, is from her husband. He wants her to come home when she has just left home. But, then, she's his first wife and he's her third husband.

"They say husbands are deteriorating," suggests Mac.

"Well, they used to be better before the war," admits Marilyn. "And (*to* ELLEN) before you tell me I can't sleep here to-night because there's only one bed in the house, let me inform you that with unusual forethought, I engaged a room at the Biltmore."

Still Ellen is not at all cheered. She knows her mother will stay there and talk all night as usual, and no one will get to work on time in the morning.

Marilyn, however, is determined on this occasion to go back to her hotel, as planned, if Mac will drive her over. She'll have lunch with Ellen next day, and that also will be in keeping with the customary routine.

After they have gone the echo of Cleve's good-by sticks in David's mind.

"Then if I don't see you, good luck!" Cleve has said to Ellen.

"What does that mean? 'If I don't see you?' " queries David, as he closes the door on Cleve. "Aren't you and Cleve going out together to-morrow?"

ELLEN—No. I've had enough theatre to last a long while.

DAVID—Is that on my account?

ELLEN—No. On mine.

DAVID—You know I wouldn't want you to do anything you don't want to do—just for me, don't you, Gypsy?

ELLEN—I think I'd better stay home and start that set of Cooper.

DAVID—Probably Jerry will be here.

ELLEN—Oh, do you think so?

DAVID—Of course. Didn't you think of it?

ELLEN—It never occurred to me.

DAVID—I thought, may be—

ELLEN—Oh, no.

DAVID—Well, he'll be here, of course.

ELLEN—It wasn't on that account. It was—I think maybe I'd better go after all. Would you rather I did?

DAVID—I wouldn't want to decide, honey. You know how I want things to be with us.—I don't want to be one of those watching husbands—asking questions and making rules. We didn't start out that way and we couldn't live that way. I want it to be so that it doesn't matter where we go or what we do we'll always be secure. I want it to be just our secret, somehow, and we carry it everywhere with us, and the world doesn't know about it. And maybe people think it doesn't exist, some of them, and all the time we can laugh at them. I want you to love me—but I know how you dislike feeling bound and tied down.

ELLEN—But, David—

DAVID—So, darling, you go to the theatre, or you stay home, or you do anything you like—it's all right, isn't it?

ELLEN—I did want to see Cleve again.

DAVID—And you weren't going to, on my account?

ELLEN—Yes.

DAVID—That's not fair, is it? Because then you won't like me, if I keep you from doing things you want to do.

ELLEN—It is all right, isn't it? Even if he is interested in me, and even if I'm—interested in him?

DAVID—Oh, darling—do you have to go?

ELLEN—No, dear.

DAVID—Of course you do. Or I'd be wishing you had.

ELLEN—It's funny—about Jerry coming.

DAVID—So, let's plan it.

ELLEN—What dress shall I wear?

DAVID—The new one, dear; you always feel gay in a new dress.

ELLEN—I know, only it's a little dull, somehow. I wanted something a little more flaming. (*She goes to the closet and opens the door, taking down an armful of dresses. She lays them over the backs of chairs and looks at them.*) I think I'll wear this one.

DAVID—It's hardly a theatre frock, darling.

ELLEN—We may just go for a ride—if we can't get seats.

DAVID—Oh.

ELLEN (*kissing him*)—Is it all right, darling?

DAVID—I think so.

ELLEN—I don't know—I think maybe I'd better wear something else.

The curtain falls.

ACT II

Four months later Ellen and David are having their usual late Sunday morning breakfast in their apartment. David is rather solicitous as to Ellen's state of health. A recent operation and her early return to work before she was entirely convalescent have left her, he fears, a bit weak.

It is Ellen's opinion, however, that she is perfectly well and the reference to the operation reminds her that she does not purpose having David pay the cost of it. That was her own affair. It was she who did not want to have a baby, not David. And he will need all his money if he goes on with his plan to continue his studies.

Ellen's mother is again in town and expecting David to take her to the theatre when he goes. Cleve Christen is also expected over for his usual Sunday afternoon call. Cleve, admits David, is still good company, despite the success of his book. It's a wonder Ellen hasn't fallen in love with him. Women must love a man for what he does as much as for what he is. Cleve is a success and her husband is a failure.

A silly thing for him to worry about, according to Ellen, knowing, as he should, that such things make not the slightest difference. Still David is not satisfied.

"I wish you were the way you used to be," he says. "You used to have fun out of everything. Nobody could have been despondent living with you."

"I guess I'm just growing up. It's a kind of delayed adolesence —merging into weltschmerz. I'm just finding out that life's difficult." . . .

Marilyn and Sylvia come in together and there is more talk of Ellen's condition and her failure to take either her mother or her best friend into her confidence when she planned a thing like an operation.

It isn't a subject that Ellen is either ready to discuss or to argue about. She didn't want her baby largely for fear it might have been a girl and grow to be like her—or her mother. That *has* happened. "If I were the child I'd be eternally grateful for not being born," she says. "I'm thoroughly useless, and if I hadn't been born I wouldn't have to die. You see, when it's gone this far, there's no way out except dying."

They can't understand Ellen's mood. To Sylvia she has everything to live for. Marilyn thinks she should have children to stimulate her interest and her belief in things. And David is hurt because he fears that he is in some way responsible for Ellen's unhappiness. But none of them is able now to arrest the flow of Ellen's tears.

"If it were anybody else," ventures Marilyn, "I'd know what was the matter. I'd think she was in love."

"Marilyn thinks you are in love, darling," repeats David. "That's all right—we're both in love—let's have a good cry!"

"Are you going to let me spoil your day, too?" Ellen demands of him.

"Sure; if you're unhappy, I want to be unhappy, too. And if you don't want to have a baby, we won't have one—and any time you want to commit suicide, why, just call on me and we'll go out together."

"My God, it's a suicide pact!" explodes Sylvia.

"Sure, let's have a suicide pact, kid!" laughs David.

"That's the first cheerful thought I've had to-day," agrees Ellen, smiling through her tears.

But there is nothing to smile at so far as Marilyn is concerned. She doesn't approve of such discussions. First thing they know they'll begin to mean it.

"Don't worry," Ellen reassures her. "I fail at everything. I tried it once and when I got all ready to turn on the gas I found it was shut off because I hadn't paid the bill." . . .

Cleve and Mac arrive. They met at the doorbell, Mac explains, and have been inseparable ever since. They, too, are gradually made aware of Ellen's unhappy state of mind and drawn, in a measure, into the discussion of suicide as a proper release.

It is Marilyn's opinion that Cleve, being a novelist and having, as the reviewers of his book insist, "uncanny insight into feminine psychology," should know exactly how to advise Ellen.

MARILYN—Suppose there were a beautiful girl who had everything her heart could desire, and she insisted upon weeping and discussing suicide—right after breakfast on a sunny Sunday morning—

CLEVE—They all do that.

MARILYN—Wouldn't you say she was in love?

CLEVE—Certainly. They all are.

MARILYN—But she's married.

CLEVE—All the more reason. That makes it legal.

SYLVIA—But difficult—damn difficult.

MARILYN—Well, anyway—what would you prescribe?

CLEVE—Her best plan will probably be to take everything said to her with a grain of salt. Or, as I said before, ask Dr. Cadman.

MARILYN—You're no help at all, and I thought you were an authority.

ELLEN—He's no authority—he's a gentleman.

MARILYN—That's enough to put an end to any conversation. They say a gentleman won't tell.

SYLVIA—Won't tell what?

MARILYN—Anything interesting.

ELLEN—If you're talking about me, what I need is a sea voyage. I prefer the Mediterranean. I want to go all alone and be made love to by the captain.

MAC—Now we're getting at it. She's fed up with home life. Hey, David, Ellen wants to go on a deep sea voyage.

DAVID (*emerging, dressed*)—You can't go.

MAC—So the Mediterranean's all wet.

David is ready to take Marilyn to the theatre. Then it occurs to him that it might be possible to make a date with his wife for dinner. At first Ellen seems agreeable—then she remembers about a previous engagement with Cleve. Cleve, however, is perfectly willing to overlook that engagement.

DAVID (*to* ELLEN)—Good!—come and eat with your husband. You can have dinner with Cleve any time. And of course you do.

CLEVE—We'll let it go, of course.

ELLEN—Oh, no, we won't. How could I do that when I've asked you here?

DAVID—Why not both come on up and eat with me? I think that would be grand.

CLEVE—Certainly.

ELLEN—Well, I don't, so let's not argue about it.

DAVID—You won't do it?

ELLEN—No, dear—I have an engagement.

MARILYN—Well, Ellen—

ELLEN—He shouldn't have reminded me that he's my husband. I don't like the idea of anybody having marital rights over me—and he knows that.

DAVID—Oh, grow up, child. Be your age. Why take offense at a word?

ELLEN—It isn't the word. You meant it.

DAVID—you have some ancient infantile fixation on feminine independence.

ELLEN—It's not very ancient and it's not very infantile and I certainly have it—so you might as well accept it.

DAVID—Why, sure. I was quite wrong. Cleve had a previous engagement with you, so naturally— Only don't fall for her, Cleve. God help the poor unfortunates that fall for Ellen. Coming, Marilyn?

MARILYN—I'm ready.

The situation is not helped a great deal when the janitor comes to inquire about the Hastings' intention of renewing the lease and promptly picks Cleve as the Mr. Hastings to whom he should speak. In view of which situation David flounces out of the door casting back of him the advice that Ellen and Cleve had better decide whether they want to re-rent the apartment or not.

Sylvia and Mac are agreed that Ellen was wrong in hurting David's feelings, but Ellen is convinced she was right. There is no special virtue in being a husband, as David seems to think. He doesn't support her. Nobody supports her, nor ever will.

Now Mac and Sylvia are gone and Cleve and Ellen face each other across the room. Neither is very happy. Cleve feels that he is responsible for David and Ellen's misunderstanding and Ellen is sure it is all due to her being in one of her devastating "not giving a damn about anything" moods.

ELLEN—Why didn't I tell him you'd be here to dinner? You couldn't possibly know I'd lied about that.

CLEVE—But it wasn't clever of me.

ELLEN—It was just because you wanted to be nice to him.

CLEVE—I do want to be nice to him. It's pretty embarrassing to talk to him when he doesn't know. It might be worse if he knew, but at any rate, I wouldn't feel like a scoundrel.

ELLEN—I used to believe in doing what I pleased and not being ashamed of it—and I still believe in that—only I can't hurt him that much. I can't tell him now—now that he's feeling so low about his work—and so I live with him—and despise myself. Cleve, I haven't any respect for myself any more. I—I tell lies. I used to think I'd cut off my hand before I'd tell lies.

CLEVE—It is my doing.

ELLEN—No, it isn't. It's mine. It isn't your affair at all.—Only, if it's hard for you to meet him and talk to him, knowing he doesn't know, imagine how utterly I hate myself, living here—and knowing he doesn't know.

CLEVE—And yet you don't tell him.

ELLEN—I can't. I've tried, honestly—and I can't. I can't

bear to hurt him that much when it seems so unnecessary and he hasn't deserved it. If he'd only do something to hurt me—but he won't. He's in love with me so much he couldn't love anybody else. And sometimes when I'm with him I can't believe I love anybody else. He's so generous and perfect—and I do love him.

CLEVE—I ought to go away. I could now. I could give up my job.

ELLEN—I know, I've thought of it.

CLEVE—Do you want me to?

ELLEN—I've thought of it, and I know how it would be. Everything would seem empty if you went away. Do you want to go?

CLEVE—I'll go if you send me. I don't know what I'd do. I wouldn't care where I was.

ELLEN—I almost did go away—without telling you. I have a chance to go now.

CLEVE—Where?

ELLEN—To England. I think I'd like it there. I've never been abroad.

CLEVE—Do you want to go?

ELLEN—David doesn't want me to. Anyway,—I was afraid I'd write to you—and pretty soon I'd come running back to you —and it wouldn't be any use—so—what's the use? (*She smiles ruefully.*) If we could only—not be together—but just love each other and see each other sometimes.

CLEVE—That would mean we were getting over it,—wouldn't it?

ELLEN—Would it? I'd love you just as much. I might love you better—

CLEVE—But we couldn't touch each other without wanting more—

ELLEN—I know—I know—only some time I'll have to tell David—and how can I tell him, Cleve? It doesn't do any good if I don't tell him everything. You don't know what David's meant to me. We—we almost grew up together—we know each other so well—he's made me over and changed me—and I've changed him—it's almost as if I wouldn't have any background without him—and I can never have him back if he doesn't know all about me. So I'll have to tell him—and if there's too much to tell—I couldn't stay here anyway. Maybe there's too much already.

CLEVE—Oh, God, I wish I'd never met David—so I could hurt him—without caring! Or else that I'd met him before I fell in love with you! Then it never would have happened.

ELLEN—But I knew him before I fell in love with you—and it didn't save me, did it? It wasn't your doing. I must have wanted to be unfaithful. But I thought I'd go on loving him just the same. I just felt that I was too young and too much alive never to be free again.—Don't pay any attention to me to-day—forgive me. (*She buries her head on his shoulder.*)

CLEVE—My dear—my dear—

ELLEN (*raising her head*)—Hello, lover.

CLEVE—Hello, sweetheart.

ELLEN—It's been such an unhappy day—let's not be unhappy any more. Tell me what the new novel's going to be about.

CLEVE—I don't know.

ELLEN—You must know.

CLEVE—Well, it's about some people that lived in Boston.—(*A pause.*)

ELLEN—And then what?

CLEVE—Oh, they just lived there and they didn't like it much—

ELLEN—I shouldn't think they would—

CLEVE—And so,—they didn't like it much, and that goes on for some time—and finally they don't like it at all.

ELLEN—Yes?

CLEVE—And that's the end.

ELLEN—Um—you're sure it's Boston?

CLEVE—I think so. It might have been Chicago.

ELLEN—Yes—that part about their not liking it—or Philadelphia. I think it's going to be a wonderful novel. It has such a thrilling plot.

CLEVE—Yes—hasn't it?

ELLEN—But I think I like your fairy stories better. Tell me one.

CLEVE—I don't know any to-day.

ELLEN—Don't you even know the one about once there wasn't any princess and so her father wasn't a king and he didn't have any castle?

CLEVE—And so there wasn't any fairy God-mother at her christening, because there wasn't any christening and she wasn't born at all—

ELLEN—Fortunate, fortunate girl.

CLEVE—And it wasn't true that a knight came riding over the plain and the dwarf let down the draw-bridge—and it couldn't have been true because there wasn't any knight and there wasn't any dwarf and there wasn't any draw-bridge—and all this never happened, once upon a time, long, long, ago.

ELLEN—And all this never happened—once upon a time, long, long, ago. That's why I love you.

CLEVE—Why?

ELLEN—Because of the way you say things.

CLEVE—Do you know why I love you?

ELLEN—No.

CLEVE—Because you're fey. "Your mother was a leprechaun, your father was a Friar."

ELLEN—It may be true about the friar—I never did trust my mother. Did you have any parents, lover, or did you fall from a star?—I never asked you.

CLEVE—The tide washed me up.

ELLEN—All wet.

CLEVE—All washed up.

Now Cleve has gone to the Players' Club to meet a literary lion of sorts. It's about his book or his career or something. He thinks perhaps he won't go, so long as Ellen wants him not to, but she is immediately sensible again and urges him to keep his promise—both to the lion and to her—but he must also promise that he won't fall in love with anybody else,—that he will come back before six and that he will be a little lonely without her. . . .

David's on the phone. He, too, is unhappy. Worried for fear he has been mean to Ellen and eager to come home and explain. She will be there, of course. Cleve has gone and isn't coming back till dinner time, she tells David.

Now Sylvia and Mac are back. Just driving by and thought perhaps Ellen would go for a ride with them. No, Ellen doesn't think she wants to go. She has been planning a long, splendid afternoon "alone with her fixations."

Truth of the matter is, Sylvia confesses, Mac wants to talk with Ellen. Mac's worried about Cleve. Worried about Ellen's flirting with everybody. Worried about the chances she takes of losing David. But Ellen is in no mood to listen, and they go on.

Now Marilyn is back from the theatre, also worried. The time has come, Marilyn thinks, when she and Ellen should talk some things out. Ellen's apparent contempt for her mother for one thing. Marilyn doesn't feel that she has deserved that. What has she done to deserve it? When Ellen was little they had such good times. Then suddenly Ellen seemed to lose all respect for her mother. Why?

Ellen refuses to say. It was only a childish impression. It is still childish of her to remember it. There is nothing to be done about it.

MARILYN—We'll have to do something about it, Ellen—because I'm your mother—and you need me. If you could only respect me for a little while—maybe I could save you.

ELLEN—From what?

MARILYN—From being the kind of person I am.

ELLEN—Well, I'm not the kind of person you are—and I'm not going to be! I think probably you've done more for me that way than you could ever do by talking to me.

MARILYN—Ellen, tell me—I do deserve that much—tell me what it is that has been between us so long—

ELLEN—No.

MARILYN—Ellen—

ELLEN—You really want to know?

MARILYN—Yes.

ELLEN—I don't want to hurt you. (*There is a silence.*) Do you remember—do you remember one summer before Father died when I was ten or so—that you and I went somewhere to stay for a few months—with some relatives—and it was rather crowded and there was only one room for us? and one bed?

MARILYN—Yes.

ELLEN—And there was a man there I didn't like, but you seemed to like him for some reason?

MARILYN—Who was it?

ELLEN—I don't know his name—I just remember there was an odor about him I didn't like—and one night I woke up shuddering—and that odor was in the room—

MARILYN—Darling, you were wrong. It's not true.

ELLEN—Oh, yes. And then there was something else—about—well—it doesn't matter.

MARILYN—It's not true.

ELLEN—Oh, I knew you'd lie about it. You'd always lie—

MARILYN—I'd lie! You dare tell me I'd lie?

ELLEN—Yes, you'd lie! You'd do it and you'd lie about it! You'd do it over and over again, and lie about it every time! And you have!

MARILYN—What kind of thing do you think I am—?

Ellen—I know what you are, and I wouldn't like to tell you! I have begun to tell you what I know about you! You thought I was a child! It's sickening!

Marilyn—You say that to me, knowing that you're deceiving your husband—living with another man and making David a fool—and you find me sickening! Oh, I know you! I know every breath you draw and every thought you think! Looking like a pure, innocent child, and posing that way—and living like a ——. He's your second lover! and how old are you?

Ellen—Why am I that way? Who put it in my blood? You! You! Do you wonder you make me hate myself?—It's not true about me! I won't have it true!

Marilyn—Do you think I wouldn't know about Cleve, Ellen? I know you so well—everything about you. Do you know why I came back, dear? You don't want to be like me and I don't want you to be. Don't, don't be like me! It's misery, darling, long misery. I had something—like David—and then—there was something in me that couldn't live up to him and now I'm just empty—and you will be—oh, I know so well! Keep David, dear one, and live up to him—even if it isn't in you to live up to him. Keep him and learn to be like him—there's happiness that way—and oh! I hope you never know what's on the other side? (*There is a long silence, and then* Marilyn *goes on speaking.*) Ellen, dear, you see, we do need each other. (Ellen *rises and* Marilyn *embraces her.*)

Ellen—Don't.

Marilyn—You see, one has a child and dreams about it—and then one can't bear to have things go wrong in the same way—

Ellen—Don't, don't, Mother—when this thing happened to you, did you—try not to?

Marilyn—Oh, yes.

Ellen—But it happened anyway?

Marilyn—Yes.

Ellen—Don't you see?

Marilyn—If you only wouldn't hate me, maybe I could help you.

Ellen—I can't hate any one as much as I hate myself.

Marilyn—But you're so cold—you're always so cold.

Ellen—You can't help me.

Marilyn—I'm going now.

Ellen—Yes.

Marilyn—I might as well go back to the theatre. I might as well.

ELLEN—Yes. (MARILYN *kisses her and then turns and goes out.*)

Marilyn has no more than closed the door when Ellen turns to the closet, takes out a suitcase and begins deliberately packing it with her things. Once, during the packing, she stops, takes a book from the bookcase and tries to read. But the call of the first impulse is too strong. Again she takes up the packing and finishes it. Then she goes to the telephone, calls Cleve and tells him not to come to dinner. She will see him later at his house.

Ellen is sitting on her packed suitcase by the door, waiting, when David comes. She is in tears as she throws her arms about him and tells him that she is leaving him.

At first he refuses to take her seriously. He, too, has been unhappy at the thought of his being cruel to her. He had to come back and tell her so, his love for her is so great. Frequently she tries to stop him, but his confession is eager and will not be halted.

"Oh, yes, let me tell you what it's been like, Gypsy," he protests. "I used to call you Gypsy in fun long ago because you were such a funny flibbertygibbet girl, always going a little mad and flying off on some wild tangent—and then coming back to me and laughing about it with me—so it was always just a kind of lark between us—so it didn't matter. And I told you you had a gypsy heart, and you said nobody could be as faithful as a gypsy—and it was true—I was sure it was—and then that thing happened—about Jerry—and it was like lightning striking— It was—you know I said I'd trust you just as much afterward—and I have tried to—only I couldn't—all I know is that you love truth and you'll always tell me— . . . And, about Cleve. I don't know whether you believe it or not—but it's going to be the same as with Jerry if it goes on—and that was why I couldn't help being cruel, because I knew that—and when I went away to-day I knew I was driving you to Cleve—but I couldn't help that, either. I thought if I couldn't trust you I didn't want to trust you. Then when I got to the theatre I had to come home to you and tell you—tell you this— You can be a gypsy if you like, dear—only be my gypsy—Come back to me now—before you give too much to Cleve. I know you came back to me, even after Jerry—and you'd come back to me again—if it were that way with Cleve—but it's too hard, dear—I can't bear it. I know I told you, when we were married, that you could always be free—but Gypsy, Gypsy—I can't bear it!

There are tears in Ellen's voice as she tries haltingly to explain that she must go; that only by going can she save him from further misery. She's a horrible person, insists Ellen; a horrible person, like her mother.

"We're liars, both of us—and I hate her for it, and I hate myself. Just to-day I knew that I was like her—and now I know I'm horrible—and there's no help for me."

Then in the fulness of a further confession she tells him of Cleve and of her disloyalty all the months she has known Cleve; of the lies she told because to tell him the truth would hurt him so. It wasn't Cleve's fault. At least it was her fault as much as Cleve's.

ELLEN—At first I thought if I'd tell you it would be all right again—as it was before—and we'd be back together—and then I saw if I told you—it would be the end. And it is—David—it is.

DAVID—Yes, you'd better go— It isn't you any more—it isn't you standing there—a fiend out of hell couldn't have hurt me more, couldn't have planned it to hurt me more! But—it can't be! We—couldn't live—

ELLEN—You'd hate me some time. I want to go, while there's still beauty to remember—before you quite hate me.

DAVID—It isn't you I hate, Gypsy. It's the whole world, for being like this.

ELLEN—I've been so untrue you'd never believe me again—and—it isn't over—with Cleve. If I lived here it would be a lie. —And—that was why I couldn't take the money from you.

DAVID (*burying his face in his hands*)—Yes, oh, yes. Oh, yes.

ELLEN—Oh, you'll be so much better off without me—David, dear. If only you'd never known me—if you'd loved somebody else—

DAVID—I couldn't. There's never been anybody else. There couldn't be. When you go—all the beauty in the world goes with you. And it won't come again. Never, never. It will never come again. I'll never believe anything again. I've never believed in anything but you—and even now—if you told me—it wasn't true—and you'd come back to me—I think I'd believe you.

ELLEN (*kneeling and taking his hands*)—Oh, it is true, and

I won't come back, my David, and you won't know where I am, and so I needn't hurt you any more—but if I did I'd hurt you again and again and again—till you would hate me—don't you see? (*He takes her in his arms and they kiss passionately.*)

DAVID—Oh, Gypsy, Gypsy, Gypsy! (*She loosens herself from his arms and goes to the door.*) Yes—it's true.

ELLEN—Good-by, David. Please—remember me the way you loved me.

DAVID—Are you going to Cleve?

ELLEN—You're never to know where I am.

DAVID—I must know that. (*A pause.*)

ELLEN—No—I'm not. I couldn't very well go to Cleve, could I? Even I couldn't very well go from one man to another

DAVID—How can I know that?

ELLEN—I've been a bad penny to you, David—and now that you're losing me you'll have all your luck—everything you ever dreamed of. Don't let me hurt you any more!

DAVID—What else have I to live for? Nothing but—just you.

ELLEN—I'm not worth it. Good-by.

DAVID (*rising, smiling at her*)—Do you think I'd ever say good-by to you, Gypsy girl? Don't you know whose girl you are—even now?

ELLEN—I know how hard it is to say good-by. (*He moves a step toward her.*) No, don't come. I think I'll always love you, David. But I've told so many lies—so many lies. I don't want to lie any more. I've told my last lie to you, David. Good-by. (*She goes out.*)

The curtain falls.

ACT III

Two weeks later, in Ellen's one-room furnished apartment on East 41st Street, Cleve Christen is seated at a table writing. It is "a rather dull little place, made lively by one or two spots of color added by Ellen—a bright shawl, perhaps, and futurist draperies at the window."

A moment later, Ellen lets herself in the hall door. She is pleased to find Cleve there. It is nice for him to have a key to her apartment. There is a thrill in thinking all the way home from the office that he will be there waiting for her.

There is a shade of disappointment in her voice, however, when she discovers that in place of finishing the chapter he has promised to deliver to his publishers the following morning Cleve has spent practically the whole day writing a poem. Poetry, Cleve confesses, is a vice with him. He never does it except at such times as he should be doing something else.

Cleve lets Ellen read the poem, though under protest. She is not to think that it's about her. The first of it begins—

"Your love is like a quicksand where men build,
Day after day, bright palaces of years,
Walling them in with music they have willed,
Hanging them with dark tapestries of fears—"

"Whose love is like a quicksand?" The thought troubles Ellen. But Cleve is sure it can't be his love of her. And the poem is so beautiful that she is of a mind to forgive him for having written it instead of the chapter he should have written. Now they will have to stay in for the evening while the chapter is written, even though Cleve is quite doubtful that he would be able to write with Ellen in the room, even if she did sit in the corner and never make a sound, as she promises.

They are both a little troubled about their love. Despite his protestations to the contrary Ellen can't feel quite certain that Cleve loves her "terribly," as he insists. She is still worried a little about the love that is like a quicksand. And it may be her thought is somewhat disturbed by the fact that she has had luncheon with David, who still doesn't know all about Cleve and thinks Ellen is indulging her passion for freedom by living by herself. Perhaps, thinks Ellen, she should go back to David. She doesn't seem to be of much good to Cleve, and David does need her. She still can't bring herself to hurt David by telling him all the truth.

"You see, if he were in my place—if we were still living together and I loved him but he'd fallen in love with some one else—he'd grind that other love out of himself like a devil—he'd put his heel on it and stay with me—and even if he were living alone away from me he'd set his teeth and school himself to live alone, no matter how he was tempted. He can't imagine being any other way. And so he can't imagine that I'd go deliberately from him to any one else. He thinks we're dedicated to each other—that there's something sacred between us. How could I tell him?"

There's a letter from Jerry, too. The dashing Jerry, with the colossal ego. Jerry has heard that Ellen has left David and he thinks she may as well return to him. A silly idea to Ellen. Not so impossible to Cleve. Ellen can understand how she could have fallen in love with Jerry originally. She was living with the staid and sober David and along came Jerry "who dances and knows all the good places to go and all the new songs before anybody else has heard them—" But that is all over. Now she loves being staid and sober with Cleve.

"Sometimes it seems to me that it will be the same with me as with David," says Cleve. "As if—any time I took my hand away from you—you'd be gone. As if—I'd happened to catch a bird in my hand, and the minute I unclasped my fingers—it would leave me—and glad to be free."

And later he says: "I'm not so easily hurt as some people, Ellen. I'm fairly hard-boiled and aware of myself. But if I let myself go as deep in love with you as I could—and then you got tired of being slow and quiet, and drifted away again with somebody like Jerry—well—I'd be pretty near ruined. How much can you promise me, Ellen—and for how long?"

"One can't promise in love," she answers, frankly. "A woman can't. Only—even if I did want excitement for a while, that wouldn't last long, and I'd want you more afterwards."

"It wouldn't do any good then. If there were ever anybody else—even the shadow of anybody else—we'd have to come to an end. I'm not patient that way."

If he could only believe her, Ellen insists, nobody else matters. Neither Jerry—nor Mr. Young—nor Wells— Wells? Whose Wells? Oh, just a man in the office who takes Ellen to lunch occasionally. And makes love to her, the way men do. But that doesn't really matter—

And then Jerry calls. A rather flashy, actor type is Jerry, thoroughly self-poised. He has not come with any thought of staying, he assures both Ellen and Cleve. He'd just found out at the office where Ellen was and he thought he might as well take a chance on calling since she wouldn't answer telephone calls or letters. Of course, if she's all dated up—That's all right with Jerry—

"As the fellow said when he was kicked out of the speakeasy the third time: 'I know what's the matter. They don't want me in there.' "

Still, as he has only two days in town, Jerry thought—

Ellen isn't interested. Even after Cleve has considerately, and a little peevishly, left them alone, Ellen isn't interested. Which isn't easy for Jerry to understand.

"Things like that don't change, darling," Jerry is insisting. "I'm just the same and you're just the same. And as long as I want you the way I do, I know you want me—even if you won't admit it."

"Oh, no, I don't," Ellen answers him. "I don't know anything about you and I care less. I never felt such relief in all my life as when I was able to say to you that last time—that nothing you could say or do would ever move me. I hated myself for loving you, and being a slave to you—and do what you wanted—and I hate to think of it now. And I hope I'll never have to tell you this again. You made me say it. I don't like being cruel."

It's true, Ellen admits, that she has left David, and that she is in love with Cleve. But she's going back to David.

It is all quite mystifying to Jerry, but he accepts the situation gracefully and is gone.

There is a telephone call from the man named Wells—at the office. It's about the possibility of Ellen's going to the theatre with him that evening. She doesn't see how she can—and yet—No, it is all too complicated. She can't tell when she will be free. But everything is all right. She's not angry—

Then David comes. He's awfully lonesome. He's fussed, too, by the people who learn someway that Gypsy has left him. He isn't getting along very well, but he tries not to be too complaining about it. He doesn't want to distress her with his "melancholy Dane stuff." But he does wonder if she feels any freer, now that she doesn't have to go home to a husband every night.

Ellen—Maybe all those old fellows were right when they said there wasn't any freedom.

David—"Husbands do not a prison make, nor marriage life a cage?"

Ellen—Something like that.

David—We've learned something, anyway, haven't we?

Ellen—You, too?

David—I'm learning so fast it makes me dizzy. I walked home with a fellow out of the show last night, and he kept saying—"Christ, I wish something would happen—anything!" I said, "How'd you feel if your wife left you?" and he said, "Well, I'd know I was alive anyway." That's one thing I could never complain of about you. You never gave me much chance to get bored.

Ellen—That's not supposed to be one of the wifely virtues, is it?

David—I guess I don't care much for wifely virtues. Anyhow, you've spoiled me for any one else. You make the run of girls look so damned insipid. They haven't any minds of their own and they wouldn't know how to act if they had. They get on my nerves.

Ellen—I've been thinking if you married some one like that you'd be really happy—for the first time. It would be so peaceful—and you could settle down and get some work done.

David—Oh, to hell with the peaceful ones! I think I probably fell in love with you because you were so much alive nobody could ever count on you. It's better to cause excitement than to be a housewife. I only wish I weren't such a damned good housewife myself. You ought to see the old place. I keep it so clean I don't dare walk across the floor. Very likely I'm hoping all the time you'll come back to it.—Only I know you're in love with Cleve now. I've finally realized that.—No, I haven't either. I don't believe it. I simply can't believe it.

Ellen—I can't either—when I see you and talk to you.

David—Are you ever coming back, Gypsy?

Ellen—Are you sure you want me?

David—I'd give the world for you. If you wanted to come.

Ellen—Wouldn't it matter, about Cleve?

David—You do love him, don't you?

Ellen—Yes.

David—Then—you can't come— How could you?

Ellen—We'd remember Cleve, dear—and you'd be tortured over that sometimes—but I'd get over it. It wouldn't matter in the end. I suppose I'd always be the same bad egg—only I'd try so much harder to live your way. David, I'm so sick of being the kind of person I am. Maybe what I want is for you to save me from myself. I feel so empty here. I wouldn't be doing it for you. If I go on—without you—I'll never know who I am.—If only I could love you—

David—You'll love me again some time if you come to me, Ellen. It isn't too late. If you'd gone to Cleve when you left me it might have been—I'd have felt so deadly estranged and cold—to have you do that deliberately. But we aren't really apart now—and Gypsy, girl, I wish you knew how empty our little place is down town without you. It's the center of all emptiness. There's just nothing there—

Ellen—David!

DAVID—What is it, dear?

ELLEN—Oh, I can't! I can't! I can't!

DAVID—What is it?

ELLEN—I've been living with Cleve! He's been living here with me. (*A pause.*)

DAVID—How can you say that? You don't mean that?

ELLEN—I have to say it!

DAVID—Then—you lied to me—when you said you weren't going to him. In the very moment of your truth-telling, you lied to me.

ELLEN—I thought I'd never see you again! David, it's true—It's true—but it's true, too, that I'm lost without you. I need so much to go back to you—need you more than you need me. —Isn't there any way?

Before David can answer Cleve is at the door. He has come to take Ellen to dinner. Finding David, he senses the need of an explanation.

"I don't know what you think of me, David," he says, "but I guess I'd know what I'd think of you—if we changed places. You'll never forgive me, and I don't blame you. But I do want to say this: I loved Ellen before I knew you. It had all begun before I knew you. It wouldn't have happened if that hadn't been true."

"It doesn't make much difference now," says David, as he walks out the door. Ellen calls after him but he does not turn.

Instinctively she turns to Cleve for comfort. Her mind is confused. She had to tell David the truth, even though Cleve can't understand why. She feels now that she has lost them both. "I've tried telling the truth and I've tried telling lies," she says.

"You don't use discretion, my dear," ventures Cleve. "You throw lies and the truth around like brickbats. Maybe you're essentially a truth-telling person and shouldn't try to lie."

"I'm afraid I'm essentially a liar and never should have tried to tell the truth," she says.

"If you were you'd do it better."

"Something's changed in me, Cleve," she goes on. "I'm all different. I used to have things to be proud of. I did what I wanted to do because I wasn't afraid. There was some kind of character in that, even when I hurt people. But now I'm like a slinking little animal, spitting out the truth when I'm cornered —just like every woman I've ever despised."

Cleve tries to be comforting. There are further assurances of his love, further declarations that he always will love her, knowing her for all that she is.

"Nobody could love me if he didn't make up things to believe about me," insists Ellen. Nor is she satisfied with the repetition of his statement that she is adorable.

ELLEN—No, I want you to know! I want you to know so I can be sure! Tell me what I'm like and call me all the bad names I deserve, so I can be sure you know me and love me anyway.

CLEVE—What bad names do you deserve?

ELLEN—Darling, I hate women who play the game with men, and lead them on when it doesn't mean anything, and scheme to take men away from other women, and play one man off against another! I hate it—and loathe them—and I'm always doing it—oh—without intending to at all—always making myself liked too much, and getting a thrill out of it even while I most despise it. Did you know that about me?

CLEVE—Isn't that perfectly natural?

ELLEN—Well—and I am hard-hearted, Cleve, even with you sometimes—and then again I can't help wanting to be too good to people—to men who seem to want me a lot—it seems so unimportant not to. Oh, no, I can't make you see it.

CLEVE—Dearest, women have been that way since the world began.

ELLEN—All women?

CLEVE—To a certain extent.

ELLEN—So that they were never quite sure of themselves, and they had to fight to be honest and true and faithful—to the person they're in love with?

CLEVE—I don't believe that of you.

ELLEN—Don't you?

CLEVE—There was Jerry, for instance. He wanted you a lot this evening, didn't he? And you weren't overly good to him.

ELLEN—No. But I let him kiss me good-by.

CLEVE—Did you, dear?

ELLEN—Yes. And something in me tells me not to tell you that—never to tell anything like that—only I want so terribly to be honest with somebody, dear—

CLEVE—Well—

ELLEN—Will you mind if I tell you things like that? Don't mind, please. It's all right if I can tell you, but if I can't it goes on eating at me till I'm not sure of myself. And then—

there's another thing. Cleve, you asked me about Wells. Would you think I didn't love you if you knew he'd kissed me? Because I do love you.

CLEVE—Since you've known me?

ELLEN—Yes. But it didn't mean anything, dear. Oh, lover, do you think I ought to be called terrible names? You remember I told you somebody kept me at the office pouring a long story into my ear? It was just Wells trying to argue me into going out with him—and—that's all.

Almost involuntarily Cleve moves away from her, and there is no sympathy in his voice as he questions her. Wasn't it something like this that she told David when she met him? Her despairing admission that it might have been brings fear to his heart. Thus it is always to be with Ellen. "You're like quicksilver, like an image in a mirror," he says; "and the worst of it is you don't want to be that way—but you are—"

"Cleve, you hurt me—so—"

CLEVE—I'd rather—anything else—than have to hurt you—but if I don't you'll hurt me some time—more terribly than anything can ever hurt you. I saw David go out that door. I don't want ever to go out a door that way, beaten—beaten by life, because of you. I wouldn't ever dare pin that much hope on you. I'd never know, and you'd never know, when you'd betrayed me and have to deceive me.

ELLEN—Lover, do you think I'd lie to you?

CLEVE—Some time.

ELLEN—No, no, Cleve. That was why we talked about all this—because I wanted you to know I wouldn't lie to you!—I want so much to be true! I want somebody to make me true! Don't you think I can, Cleve, if you'll help me? (*He glances at her—torn but unable to answer.*) You could have all of me, Cleve! I don't want anything else! I don't even want to live. I wish David had killed me.

CLEVE—Think, dear, and answer this candidly—has anybody ever had all of you? Could you be true to any one—for a lifetime?

ELLEN—No.

CLEVE—You see what that would mean to me? I love you—as I've never loved anybody else—but I'd rather hurt us both now than be broken on the wheel by you.

ELLEN—Do you think you'd—better not see me again?

CLEVE—Yes.

ELLEN—Cleve!

CLEVE—It's not easy for me.

ELLEN—Why?

CLEVE—It's too late. I can't leave you.

ELLEN—Oh, you poor silly. You think it's going to hurt me too much. Do you imagine anybody matters that much to me?

CLEVE—I do.

ELLEN—Pure masculine vanity, darling. They all think that. Anyhow you're a Greek derelict and I refuse to wreck you. I have some respect for literature—

CLEVE—Don't pretend with me, Ellen. If I go now I'm failing you utterly.

ELLEN—Wouldn't you rather fail me now than have me fail you later? Because I assure you I would. I fail everybody in the end. I'm quite certain of that because you told me so yourself.

CLEVE—Ellen!

ELLEN (*angry*)—How could I want you here after what you've said to me? Go—and go quickly! (*He steps toward her.*) No! Never! (*He stops.*) You were quite right about me. I would have betrayed you and lied to you and broken you. I'm perfectly unreliable and indecent! And now that I know it and you know it there's nothing more to say. (*He is silent.*) Is there any other way I can tell you I don't want you here? If there is I'll say it! (CLEVE *looks at her a moment, then takes his hat and goes.* ELLEN *slips down beside the chair where* CLEVE *sat, sobbing quietly. She rises, sees the poem and reads it.*)

> "Your love is like a quicksand where men build,
> Day after day, bright palaces of years,
> Walling them in with music they have willed,
> Hanging them with dark tapestries of fears,
> And finding there when next they see your face
> No tower or image out of all that dream
> They set upon you; only in its place
> Sweet disenchanted laughter, mocking them."

Well, I'm a good poem, anyway. That's something. (*She looks toward the gas-jet on the wall, goes to it, turns it on—then off—goes to the window and closes it, then enters the kitchenette for a moment. Reëntering, she lies on the bed, the manuscript still in her hand. She reads to herself, and sniffs at the gas in annoyance, making childish faces. The telephone rings. She ignores it, but it continues to ring. She finally gets up, takes the receiver off the hook and sets it down on the table. Then she decides to answer, and puts the receiver to her ear.*) Hello. Hello. Who's calling? Yes. (*She reads aloud.*)

"Here, where is nothing, was the first stone laid,
And there, where nothing stands, rose into air
High battlements to hold against the world,
Lest our two souls be lonely and afraid—
And over them the lipless sands have curled,
And I, too, have forgotten that they were."

Hello. Hello, Wells! What did you say, Wells? I didn't hear. No, I'm sorry. I can't go. I know, and it is good of you —only I have something I must do. No, please don't call again. I am. I'm all dressed—and I'm all alone. Just something I must do and it can't be put off. Wells, wait just a minute. (*She presses a hand across her forehead.*) My dear, is this any time to talk about tangoes? Well, I can't explain but it doesn't sound reasonable to me. Yes, I hear you. Dance till midnight, dance till dawn and have breakfast at Narragansett! Oh, an excellent memory! And it's still working. Yes, I know to-morrow's Sunday. Wait a minute, Wells! I think I left a gas-jet open! (*She runs to the window, throws it up, takes a breath of air and goes into the kitchenette, returning immediately. She takes up the phone.*)

"And over them the lipless sands have curled,
And I, too, have forgotten that they were."

Wells! I didn't run away! I was just opening a window! Oh, Wells, darling, you saved my life, you really did—

The curtain falls.

Note—A revised version of the last act ended with Gypsy's reading of the poem. The phone continued to ring as the gas fumes slowly filled the room. This suicide version, during the eight-week run of the play, was most frequently used, but the above ending follows the author's original script.

THE KINGDOM OF GOD

A Drama in Three Acts

By G. Martinez Sierra

(English Version by Helen and Harley Granville-Barker)

AN event of more significance in the theatre than its casual acceptance indicated was the opening, in December, 1928, of the Ethel Barrymore Theatre in New York.

It is the first American theatre to be named for a member of the American theatrical family that stands at the head of our list of native actors, an honor too long deferred and an honor deservedly bestowed. There were no attending ceremonies, and the first play offered, Sierra's "The Kingdom of God," proved no better than a quasi-popular success.

The play grew in favor, however, as the Barrymore following, loyal as usual and pleased to applaud that which their favorite actress chooses to play, found Miss Barrymore rising to one of those inspiring Barrymore moments to which she is so splendidly equal. The last act made the play for her, and in the last act she is probably less the Ethel Barrymore of tradition than she has been before in years.

The Sierra drama ran for ninety-three performances and was followed by "The Love Duel," adapted by Zoe Akins from the original of the Baroness Lili Hatvany of Austria. These were the first two selections for a Barrymore repertoire of plays, and by her choice of them they attain an importance no other American actress could give them.

The first scene of "The Kingdom of God" is in "the garden of a ducal palace that has been converted to a home for poverty-stricken old men. The garden itself is still both stately and charming. We are in a part of it that is walled with clipped hedges of box and myrtle."

"Gabriel, one of the old pensioners, is sitting on a bench cracking pine nuts with a stone. He is a very thin old man, shrunk within his blue uniform. But he is as sharp as a needle and as lively as a lizard."

"Trajano, a still older inmate, is walking backwards and forwards, evidently somewhat out of temper. He has a fine, rather apostolic, head; he limps a little from rheumatism."

They are quarreling, these two. Trajano resents Gabriel and the favors he wins from the sisters. Resents his possession of the pine nuts, though his anger does not prevent his eating more than his share of them, after they are cracked. But Gabriel doesn't care. If the sisters do treat him better than he deserves it is because they recognize him as a man of breeding. A snob? Perhaps. He had much rather be a snob than an anarchist.

Sister Gracia and Sister Juliana come carrying a basket of potatoes between them and laughing like children when some of the potatoes spill over. "Sister Gracia is a girl of 19; pretty, fragile and very gay. Sister Juliana is about the same age, but commonplace to look at, her face high-colored."

It is Sister Gracia who tries to compose the differences of the old men; to gently chide the fiery Trajano for his boasts that he is indeed a Radical, a Freethinker and even a Freemason, as Gabriel charges. What of it? Let the King of England come and cut off all their heads, says Sister Gracia. What will happen then? They will all go to heaven and be very glad to get there. And when the old man explodes again with temper and a little asthma Sister Gracia comforts him.

"Come, now," she says, cheerily, "here's a Marquis's granddaughter wiping your head for you. How much further can your Social Revolution take you?"

It is Sister Manuela, the Mother Superior, whose coming finally quiets the protesting Trajano, and it is Sister Gracia who, by discreet pleading, earns the Reverend Mother's permission for Trajano and Gabriel to go to town.

Sister Manuela is not sure she should let them go. Especially Trajano. The last time he went he came home as drunk as an owl and tried to proclaim a Spanish Republic in the middle of his supper. But with Sister Gracia willing to go bail for them, as it were, taking their promise that they will not drink on this trip, town leave is granted. They must promise that they will be home before dark, and Trajano is to wash his beard before he goes. "There are wild beasts in that jungle," Sister Manuela suspects. . . .

Word has come that Sister Gracia's family is on the way to see her. The news pleases but does not greatly thrill her. It is Sister Juliana who enjoys the thrill. To have lived, as Sister Gracia has lived, in the world; to have known society; to have even danced with a king, and gone to a theatre, and read novels—these present scarifying but fascinating visions to Sister Juliana. She enjoyed no such experiences when she was in the world. She never had read but one novel, even, and that was terribly disturbing. Another girl had sneaked it into the convent. "Claudine's Adventures in Paris" it was called and even now it is terribly hard for Sister Juliana to get Claudine out of her mind. . . .

Now Sister Gracia's family has arrived—Maria Isabel, her rather austere and forbidding mother; Don Lorenzo, her greatly loved father, and Lulu, her younger sister.

Maria Isabel is, as she always has been, quite disgusted with her daughter's determination to join, even probationally, this stupid order. There are others, not of her class or upbringing, to do such work as peeling potatoes. But there is a complete and understanding sympathy between Don Lorenzo and his daughter. These two are walking about the garden now, hand in hand, while Maria Isabel listens to Gabriel, once a valet in her father's family, recount the glories of the old Spanish family that lived in that palace that is now a home for old men.

"All the best gentlemen of Madrid used to come here," Gabriel is saying.

"And the worst women," counters Maria Isabel.

"Well," says Gabriel, "God created the one lot to balance the other, I suppose. And a fine lot they were, I tell you . . . worth staring at. They made the house what it was . . . and what it is. (*He grows confidential and important.*) For when his Grace the Duke went and died . . . his Grace, now in glory . . . probably . . . oh, they say they're not very hard on you up there when it has only been petticoats . . . when his Grace the Duke died here . . . for it was here he came back to die after trapesing all over the world . . . he'd hardly drawn his last breath when his two latest lady friends . . . one was fair and one was dark, and a pretty picture they made, I can tell you . . . they started to fill all the baskets and trunks in the place with whatever they could lay their hands on, . . . clothes, pictures, mirrors, books, china . . . why, they took the very quilt off the poor gentleman's bed, a satin quilt it was, as thick as that, and embroidered in colours with history-pictures two hundred years old! They didn't let the grass grow under their feet . . . the baggages. Why, it was like the day of judgment. And I saw it. For I'd been sent to inquire after the sick man by the Marquis . . . now in glory . . . and he was just at his last gasp when I got here . . . and there was the undertaker driving up at one door and the wagon full of things . . . piled high with them . . . driving off from the other. If they left the walls standing it was only that they shouldn't dirty their pretty hands with the bricks and mortar."

Now Gabriel has gone finally to join Trajano for the trip to town. Sister Gracia, pausing in her visit with her father, has quieted the fears of Lulu, who has seen an aging Cuban, one Liborio, peeping out of the bushes at her. Poor old Liborio is harmless, though a little weak in the head, and is made happy when Don Lorenzo gives him a cigar with a pretty band on it that shows it came from the Cuba that Laborio is wont to mourn as lost.

That gives Sister Gracia an idea. Her father shall send her some cheap cigars and some of the expensive bands from his own brand, and with the two she will keep old Liborio happy for hours at a time.

MARIA ISABEL (*suddenly breaking out*)—What your father will do if he has one ounce of common sense . . . for you haven't . . . is to take you home with him this very minute.

SISTER GRACIA (*startled and grieved*)—Mother!

MARIA ISABEL—My dear child . . . this has been a very pretty whim . . . but it has lasted long enough. Three months in a hospital dressing people's sores and laying them out when they were dead. Six months a probationer . . . making yourself look such a fright with that thing on your head. And now here . . . among these disgusting old men . . . why, they may be lepers! No . . . no more of it. . . . Home you come with us this very minute.

SISTER GRACIA (*her eyes cast down . . . but her voice firm*)—No. . . . I can't do that, Mother.

MARIA ISABEL—Why can't you, pray?

SISTER GRACIA—I have taken a vow.

MARIA ISABEL—Oh, yes . . . for a year.

SISTER GRACIA—In my heart . . . I took it for all my life.

MARIA ISABEL—Don't talk nonsense.

SISTER GRACIA—It's not nonsense, Mother.

MARIA ISABEL—It is ridiculous affectation. You're a spoiled child . . . you've always been given your own way. And now you want to play at being a nun . . . just as you used to play sweethearts.

SISTER GRACIA—Mother!

MARIA ISABEL—But please remember, my dear, that you're

not of age yet. Your father can have something to say to this.

SISTER GRACIA—Father gave his consent.

MARIA ISABEL—He did not . . . and you know that perfectly well. He let you go and said nothing about it . . . which is not the same thing at all. You took very good care to leave the house when he wasn't there. And why? Because you were afraid he'd stop you.

SISTER GRACIA—That wasn't the reason.

MARIA ISABEL—Wasn't it? Then perhaps it was because you hadn't the courage to say good-by to him. Well . . . answer me.

SISTER GRACIA—Yes, that was why.

MARIA ISABEL—Oh, you never found it very hard to get around people. (*Then to her husband.*) Well, here's your spoilt baby . . . Papa's darling . . . always in his pocket . . . crying if her dear father left home without saying good-by to her . . . couldn't go to sleep at night unless he came in to kiss her . . . was to grow up to be the comfort of his old age. Well, here you have it . . . the comfort and happiness she promised you. And because she calls her conduct by a fine sounding name . . .

SISTER GRACIA—But, Mother, I've done nothing wrong.

MARIA ISABEL (*with a final fling of sorrowful wrath*)—And this is what children are given us for!

LORENZO (*quietly intervening*)—Maria Isabel . . . children are not an idle gift.

MARIA ISABEL—What do you mean?

LORENZO—I mean that they are not our own to do as we like with.

MARIA ISABEL—So like a man! Easy to see you don't suffer to bring them into the world.

LORENZO (*gravely*)—We sweat blood though, sometimes, to keep them alive in it. But we owe them more than that. Did we so deliberately plan to bring them into the world? They are ours through our frailty.

MARIA ISABEL—Frailty!

LORENZO—What else? And if they are the fruit of our happiness what right have we to deny them their own . . . unless they seek it in evil ways?

MARIA ISABEL—And you believe she'll find happiness here?

LORENZO—She has made herself believe so. What then can I say?

SISTER GRACIA—But I haven't made myself believe it, Father. . . . I haven't indeed.

MARIA ISABEL—Petted and brought up in luxury as she has been!

LORENZO—You were brought up in just such luxury. You were rich and came of a great family and you were nineteen as she is now. Every sort of pleasure was yours for the asking, and life promised you very many of them. Then you met me . . . a good for nothing, a firebrand . . . so your family told you. And certainly I was a nobody. But you gave up everything to endure privations and persecutions and suffering by my side. Isabel, have you forgotten the courage with which you faced it all . . . just for the sake of the love that we so believed in? Our first child was born in an attic . . . that's twenty-five years ago. Have you forgotten? I've not forgotten my debt to you. (*He kisses her hand.*) Ah, my dear . . . don't give your own nature the lie when you see it again in your daughter.

MARIA ISABEL—What I did, I did because I loved you. That was very different.

SISTER GRACIA—Mother . . . I do this for love.

MARIA ISABEL (*recovering her ill temper*)—Love . . . who for? God! D'you imagine you're Saint Teresa?

SISTER GRACIA—No, Mother . . . I don't imagine any such thing. I know that I'm nobody. But then you don't need to be anybody here . . . for we're all nobodies together. Here, you see, we gather in people that the world has no more use for. . . . No one loves them or wants them . . . they've nowhere to go . . . the poor, the sick, the homeless. Well, then, one needs to be a nobody to be of any use to them . . . it's so much better to be a nobody . . . for the less you count in the world yourself . . . the closer you come to them.

MARIA ISABEL—You need not live among poor people in order to help them.

SISTER GRACIA—Oh, yes, Mother . . . oh, yes, you must.

MARIA ISABEL—Not at all. You can be charitable . . . you can give alms.

SISTER GRACIA (*quite carried away now*)—Give alms! No . . . No . . . oh, no! Where's the good in giving away a little of what you have too much of . . . and keeping the rest. . . . and not caring . . . spending money amusing oneself . . . while they have so much to endure . . . and you do nothing for them, nothing at all. Because giving alms is nothing. . . . oh, I don't mean one shouldn't give alms. But no . . . (*to her father*) oh, isn't this true . . . for you've said so a thousand times . . . that one must give one's life, one's whole life . . . to the last breath and the last drop of blood, if one wants to atone for the wickedness of the world. For misery is wickedness and want is crime . . . because God gave his world to us all alike . . . and our daily bread. And if his children starve and are homeless . . . that's crime, yes, a crime. And the man who keeps more than he needs robs the man who's in need. Turn away your eyes when your brother is dying . . . and you're an accomplice in his death. Oh, Father, Father . . . when I've heard you speak . . . if only I could have been a man, a man like you . . . to speak like that so that people must hear me . . . and plead the cause of the oppressed, stand up for them, make laws that will help them! But of course I'm only an ignorant girl. What can I do? I might stand and shout for ever, and no one would listen. I'm no use. I'm nobody. I've nothing to give but my happiness . . . so I want to give that, you see, to those that have none.

LORENZO—My dear . . . my dear. . . .

SISTER GRACIA—Because no one seems to think of giving that. Food, oh, yes . . . but happiness! Why, if it's only to amuse them a little . . . to joke with them . . . and then to make believe, so that just for a little they may believe that there's still something left for them to hope for . . . that they still count for something in the world . . . that they're human beings still. That's what matters, isn't it, Father?

LORENZO—Yes, you're right. That's to say . . . Ah, yes, my dear . . . believing as you do you are right to be doing what you do.

MARIA ISABEL—And you say that, do you . . . when you believe in nothing at all.

LORENZO—I may not . . . but then she does.

MARIA ISABEL (*to* SISTER GRACIA)—You show great consideration . . . for everybody but us.

SISTER GRACIA—But you don't need me.

MARIA ISABEL—And to think that when you were so high; . . . how I cried and cried when they said you might die of diphtheria . . . and I took a vow to wear a penitent's dress for a year . . . and I cut off all my hair that your father was so fond of . . . and now . . . this is what happens. (*She begins to cry.*) One never does know what one is really asking God to grant.

SISTER GRACIA (*putting her arms round her mother, but smil-*

ing in spite of herself)—Oh, mama, don't say that . . . just because I'm still alive.

It is the opinion of Lulu, who has kept a discreet distance from this family discussion, that mothers are very hard things to understand. "She is angry with you," she says to Sister Gracia, "because you went to be a nun . . . and just as angry with me because I want to get married. The fact is, I suppose, that if older people couldn't amuse themselves by upsetting themselves about nothing they'd be bored to death, poor things!"

Now the Reverend Mother has come to meet Sister Gracia's family and to defend with persuasive argument their daughter's decision to devote her life to the care and happiness of others. But, on the other hand, if Sister Gracia should decide to accede to her mother's wishes she is privileged to return to her home at any time.

"Our order takes no perpetual vows," explains Sister Manuela. "Our sainted founder thought well to account for the weakness of human will. If any one of us finds her chain too heavy she can break it whenever she likes."

Now the family has gone. Sister Juliana has watched them leave and gazed longingly after them from the kitchen door, sighing a little helplessly. "Oh, how pretty they look. And what hats!"

"The dusk is deepening now. After a moment three old men pass along on their way in. The first, leaning heavily on his stick, does not stop. The second pauses at each bench he comes to, and sits down wiping it first very carefully with his handkerchief. The third stops at every other step, gesticulating, talking to himself as if he were addressing some one else. First he argues, hotly, wrathfully. Then he looks at his supposed adversary with pitying condescension and assents ironically to what the fellow has been saying, as if he were humouring a madman. Finally he takes off his hat and bows, as if to let him pass. And then when the phantom has turned his back, he laughs, shrugs, watches him disappear, and then goes on his own way with the greatest complacency. Then a Sister of Charity passes with some flowers in her hand. And then Liborio comes from the kitchens, with his cigar still in his hand, and singing in great content . . . "Far off I see the Cuban mountains. . . ."

Sister Gracia is back and anxious about her two charges, Gabriel and Trajano. They are the last to be accounted for.

Soon Trajano's voice is heard down the road. "He is a little drunk and in high good fellowship with Gabriel, who is very cheery and a little drunk, too, and has his arm protectingly around Trajano's shoulder. Sister Gracia interrupts the song. "Well, this time you've surpassed yourself, Trajano! This is how you keep your word to a lady! Drunk again!"

TRAJANO (*with utmost dignity*)—I . . . drunk! Well . . . let me see now, let me see. Are you drunk, Trajano? Speak the truth, now. Yes, Señor Trajano Fernandez is undoubtedly drunk. But he is a free citizen . . . so what has any one to say to that? And what has the lady-bishop to say to that? Bring her here . . . fetch her right out here . . . the lady-bishop, so that I can drink her health in the name of the most worshipful Republic.

GABRIEL—In the name of her royal highness the Republic. . . . (GABRIEL *laughs foolishly and then pretends to open a carriage door and to bow the lady out.*) Will your royal highness the Republic be pleased to step in? If your royal highness will be good enough to give me your card, I will immediately acquaint the Warden . . . whom God preserve.

TRAJANO—I drink to the lady-bishop! Can't you see that I'm drinking to the lady-bishop?

SISTER GRACIA—Oh . . . for God's sake, Trajano. . . .

TRAJANO (*solemnly*)—For whose sake? Will you please to remember that my god is not the god of Sinai? No, indeed! (*Then to* GABRIEL.) Is there a brotherhood of man, or is there not?

GABRIEL—Brotherhood-a-man? Please to step in, Señor Brotherhood-a-man. If your excellency would be kind enough. . . .

TRAJANO—Is there a brotherhood of man or is there not?

SISTER GRACIA—Yes, by all means . . . only do be quiet or I shall get so scolded.

TRAJANO—Oh, no. . . . I'll not have that. If they attempt to scold you I shall raise an insurrection. . . . I say that I will raise an insurrection.

SISTER GRACIA—Yes, yes . . . but quietly.

TRAJANO—I will raise that insurrection because I wish to raise that insurrection. . . .

SISTER GRACIA—What you'd better do now at once is to go and put your head under the pump and see if cold water won't sober you. Then no one need find out the state you came back in. (*She takes him firmly by the arm and tries to get him away.*)

TRAJANO—Water . . . cold water! Never! Death rather than submission to tyranny.

Sister Gracia finds it a little difficult not to laugh at her charges. And when they are joined by the slightly demented Liborio, robbed of his cigar by the gardeners and still worried about his lost Cuba, her troubles increase. She promises Liborio another cigar and finally finds his Cuba for him in the sky—the lone bright evening star that's his lost country, just as it used to be on his flag. And after a while perhaps they'll all sail away in a boat and go travelling to that star.

The old fellows are grouped like children around her, the slightly rebellious Trajano breaking occasionally into song, when Sister Manuela puts her head out the window.

"Who's that singing?" the Reverend Mother calls.

SISTER GRACIA—It's Trajano. He's here with me, Reverend Mother.

SISTER MANUELA—Is any one missing?

SISTER GRACIA—No, Reverend Mother, . . . they're all back now.

SISTER MANUELA—Bring them in then, or they'll take cold in this night air.

SISTER GRACIA—Yes, Reverend Mother. (SISTER MANUELA *disappears, and the old men breathe again.*)

SISTER GRACIA—Come along now . . . come along. (*She goes first with* LIBORIO. *The two others follow her.* TRAJANO *singing in a whisper and hushing* GABRIEL, *apparently under the impression that it is he.*)

TRAJANO—Democracy's bright sword shall shine. . . .
Sh! . . .
Its dauntless trumpet. . . .
Sh! Sh! . . .

GABRIEL—The most serene lady-bishop is served.

SISTER GRACIA—Come along now . . . quietly.

LIBORIO—The star . . . the star. . . . Cuba not lost.

TRAJANO—The blood of nobles and of priests. . . .
Sh! . . .
Unceasingly shall flow. . . .
The Throne shall be. . . .
Sh! . . . Sh! . . .

They go out by the little kitchen door. It is now quite dark. The curtain falls.

ACT II

The scene is "a large patio which serves as a place of recreation for the inmates of a maternity home (for women who have 'come to grief') which has been established in some old noble mansion in the north of Castile. . . . The center of the patio was once a garden, no doubt; now it is nothing but a jungle of uncared-for shrubs, lilies, celandine, hawthorn and a tree or two."

Three of the inmates of the home are discovered—Candelas, Cecilia and a dumb girl. "Candelas is a swarthy young woman with a bit of the devil about her. She has fine, black-green eyes and looks serpent-like when she moves about. She is poorly dressed. Her voice is harsh. She has put a flower in her hair. She is washing out some handkerchiefs in a trough by a well and she is singing:

"I asked a sick man the complaint
Of which he was to die;
'Of loving you . . . of loving you,'
The sick man made reply."

Candelas, however, is the only one of the three who feels like singing. Cecilia, with her child sleeping in a basket cradle near, is wearied and unhappy. Her troubles press upon her and she mutters her fear of them. But she gets little sympathy from Candelas.

"Oh, Holy Mother . . . what are your troubles, I should like to know?" demands Candelas. "You fell in love and you had a baby. Well . . . what else are women for? Then he deserted you and they took you in here out of charity . . . and your character's gone. . . . But that had gone a bit earlier, hadn't it? What you've got to do, my girl, is to make the best of a bad job . . . there's no help for it now, anyway. Besides . . . things happen because they're meant to . . . and you make them no better by crying about them. The day your mother bore you your steps in this world were all counted . . . from your first to your last one. . . .

"Yes, my girl . . . it's all been settled beforehand, every bit of it . . . and you've only to wait for it to come to pass. And nothing happens to any one that hasn't happened sometime to some one else. I tell you this world's like a road with a lot of inns along it . . . and if you're not cheated in one of them, why, you will be in another . . . and whichever one of them it is some one's always been cheated there before you. But I know . . . once you're all dressed up and ready to start you think you know everything . . . and nobody can advise you!"

Candelas goes back to her washing and her singing, but she quits both when Sister Cristina comes from the house. Sister Cristina, at 45, is head of the home, "a sympathetic, well-bred woman with an unaffected motherly dignity about her. But she thinks of the women under her charge as lost souls, for all that she pities them, as a woman may who knows what life is."

Sister Cristina seeks to bring comfort to the group, but her success is not great. The Dumb Girl, as though frightened, clings more tightly to the infant she holds in her arms as the Sister tries to induce her to hold the child more comfortably. Cecilia is of a mind to continue her weeping and lamenting. Only Candelas is ready to talk, to defend and explain. Candelas is not ashamed of being in the home. It isn't a prison and she isn't a criminal. Merely an unfortunate who went "loving a man far better than he deserved." Candelas would like to know when she is going to be released, too. She has been there four months, her child is dead and she would leave. But she must stay six months in all and she must nurse another's infant, Sister Cristina tells her. That was her bargain. And for those four months, at least, she will live as God meant her to. . . .

Quica is back. Sister Feliciana brings her in. Quica is "a woman from some Castilian village, ugly, dirty, and unkempt," who has been an inmate of the home on four previous occasions. Nor is Quica conscious of shame. Any one can make a mistake so long as men are what they are. Quica likes it at the home. What with nursing her own and others' infants Quica has managed to live for four years and six months for nothing, and been paid for a part of her services as well. But she can't get either Candelas or Cecilia to think of that as a bargain.

Now Sister Gracia comes from the house. She has been directing two of her assistants in the collecting of clothes from a line. She turns to the girls in the patio and smiles pleasantly at them.

"Sister Gracia is now 29. She is pale and evidently tired and overstrained, though she does her best to hide this by her smiles." Now suddenly she leans against a pillar, her eyes closed, and the quick-seeing Candelas is fearful lest she faint.

They bring Sister Gracia a chair and a glass of water. Still she will not admit that she is in need of their help. As she accepts the chair the Dumb Girl, a new light of trustfulness in her eyes, brings her baby and lays it in Sister Gracia's lap.

She is sitting thus, looking, as Candelas whispers, like the Blessed Virgin of Carmen, when the doctor comes. He is Dr. Enrique, "a man of about 35, pleasant, good-looking and dressed in a plain dark suit."

On seeing the doctor Sister Gracia jumps to her feet. She is displeased that the girls have summoned him and overeager, it may be, to assure him there is nothing wrong with her. She had, she admits, spent the whole morning in the laundry, where it is dark, and when she had come suddenly into the bright light of the patio she had felt a momentary dizziness—that was all. . . .

Enrique looks a bit worried, but goes back to the convalescent ward, and Candelas is impudently amused at Sister Gracia's irritation because they had brought the handsome young doctor to attend her. Candelas knows the doctor was glad to come. He's got eyes in his head, that man, says Candelas.

"I've seen him once a day goin' on for two months now . . . and I know he's got eyes in his head. He'll pass near a particular person and be knocked all of a heap, poor thing! Oh, every one's noticed that. (*Then she looks at* SISTER GRACIA *and says coaxingly.*) You've an angel's face . . . that's a fact."

But Sister Gracia will have none of their foolishness and tries persistently to quiet them. Quica is forced to smother her laughter at Candelas' pointed suggestions.

"I tell you, Sister . . . you don't know what you're missing," persists Candelas.

"You don't . . . she's right . . . you don't," chimes in Quica.

"You're talking nonsense," answers Sister Gracia, turning away deliberately.

"Would I be a woman . . . and young and pretty . . . and be shut up here washing other women's babies' faces . . . when I might be having my own? Yes, Señora . . . it's her own babies . . . and their father's, the man she could love and who'd be mad about her . . . that's what a woman wants . . . so I tell you."

"You've nothing more to do here, have you, either of you?" demands Sister Gracia. "So be off now, to the refectory. It is nearly dinner time."

It is not easy to be rid of the girls, but Sister Gracia manages it finally, the voice of Candelas trailing back after she has gone, singing,

> "I have a grief, a grief
> Which if I longer bear . . .
> A coffin and a grave
> For me they can prepare."

"Left alone Sister Gracia leans a moment against the stone trough to rest. Her face is drawn and sad, but after a little she smiles to herself and then goes to a door that has not been opened yet, opens it and disappears and then comes back with Margarita."

"Margarita is a delicately pretty girl of 20. Her dark dress and the large silk scarf of blue and black that she wears stamp her as belonging to the middle classes. The settled look on her face speaks of a medley of shame and anger, and her voice is sometimes sad and sometimes sharp with a sort of despair."

It is Sister Gracia's task of the moment to comfort Margarita, to rouse her from her despair of God's comfort and understanding. Margarita would die if she could, and forget, even with her child unborn.

She will not feel that way once she holds her son in her arms, Sister Gracia insists. "When God sends you a child he offers you pardon for your sin," comforts the nun.

"Pardon—"

"Why, yes. Would you have left sinning if the child had not come to convince you that you were sinning? God puts redemption in your arms. Don't miss the chance of it. Oh, think what it can mean to you to live and suffer for your child . . . and to teach him to be good. God in his mercy is calling to you . . . and you must answer . . . you must turn away. Oh, yes . . . cry if you want to because you repent . . . but not because you're in despair. And in a little while now an angel will come to dry your tears."

It isn't easy to convince Margarita. Stubbornly she nurses her grief and the thought of her misery if she should attempt to return to the world. Her father does not know of her trouble. Only her stepmother. . . .

Sister Feliciana brings in the mail, and again Margarita is plunged into hopeless despair. There is no letter for her from her lover. It is plain that he has deserted her; that he doesn't care; that those other women have taken him away from her.

And now Margarita is wildly hysterical, crying aloud her woe and her defiance, crying her love and blaspheming in the sight of the sisters.

"It's hell! It's like being burnt alive!" shouts the unhappy girl. "It's like having one's heart torn out. . . . Look what I've brought on myself just to please him. And I cried . . . I prayed God I might die . . . and it meant nothing to him. But there was one day . . . yes, just one . . . when he did love me. And I tell you, I'd lose my soul and see him lose his, to have that day over again! . . . I tell lies about it all. . . . I do nothing but lie. For I'm not sorry for the sin and the shame of it. . . . I'm not. If he wants me, what do I care about honour or dishonour . . . he's my life. . . . I've no other."

"Be quiet . . . be quiet, I tell you," commands Sister Gracia. "Are you mad . . . or do you want to lose your last hope of salvation?"

Losing all control of herself Margarita clings desperately, hysterically to Sister Gracia, begging, pleading, demanding that her lover be sent for, until Sister Gracia must call for help, a call that brings both Sister Feliciana and again Dr. Enrique.

Soon Margarita is all right again. And now it is Sister Gracia who seems on the point of a breakdown. The adventure has been trying on her unquiet nerves. Enrique realizes that and feels that he must be professionally firm with her, though she would avoid talking with him if she could. When she would leave a little precipitately, following the others, Enrique calls her back and bids her sit down and close her eyes until she is composed.

She is quite alright, Sister Gracia assures Enrique; she is not going to have hysterics, too. And then in answer to his question she tells him the history he wants to know: That she is 29; that she has been professed since she was 18; that she has been at the maternity home only four and a half years; that before that she was in an asylum for old men—pathetic old things, who came to love her and think of her as a kind of granddaughter. It had made her miserable to leave them.

And then she had come to this home where it seems "all the sorrow in the world is to be found."

"I don't know whether it makes me more wretched to have them suffer so . . . or for them to think nothing of it at all," she says. "And the babies . . . the ones that are born here . . . and those that they bring here . . . outcasts every one . . . with people only thinking how best they can be rid of them . . .

as if they were something unclean and shameful altogether. And . . . oh, my God . . . a month ago, while you were away . . . one night when I was on duty, some one put a dead child into the basket at the gate. That is . . . it hadn't died—its throat was cut. I shall never forget it. With big blue wide open eyes that seemed to be asking . . . But why . . . but why?"

ENRIQUE—This can't go on, you know, Sister Gracia.

SISTER GRACIA—What do you mean?

ENRIQUE—You can't stay on here.

SISTER GRACIA—Where?

ENRIQUE—Surrounded by this misery and pain—misery of the body and of the spirit too. For you're right . . . the whole world's unhappiness is centered here . . . we're at the very heart of its corruption. Vice or cowardice it may be . . . degeneracy, self-will . . . but over it all, despair. For what have they to look forward to . . . any of them?

SISTER GRACIA—I know, I know . . . there's nothing . . . and that's what is so horrible. My poor old men now . . . who cared what became of them? But it was so easy to take them out of themselves . . . why, if I'd promise them the moon to play with, they'd have felt quite sure of getting it . . . because I'd promised. But these wretched souls . . . what vision can one give them? Some of them are callous, and some only wish they were dead, and some just want to be revenged. But there's not one . . . not one that even wants to rise above it all. And, if they did . . . what could we promise them? They leave here . . . and what is waiting for them? More misery . . . more hunger . . . more vice . . . more shame. Do you know, I think sometimes . . . oh, not very often, but sometimes I can't help thinking . . . that if one of these women would only lift up her head, take her child in her arms and outface what the world calls her dishonour . . . why, God at least would forgive her. For he always does forgive us if we call on him. But then . . . they don't know how to call on him. How should they? No one has taught them. They hardly know that he exists. Then how can one sin against a God one doesn't know? And if they've not knowingly sinned . . . how should they feel the shame, and why . . . oh, why . . . should such punishment fall on them? God . . . God . . . but who is to blame then for so much misery?

ENRIQUE—Sister Gracia . . . Sister Gracia!

SISTER GRACIA—What am I saying . . . what have I said?

Oh, forget it, please. And God forgive me . . . blessed Jesus! . . . thy will be done . . . and as you have willed it . . . then so it should be. As it is . . . it is right . . . although we cannot understand. Have pity on us and forgive us all. . . . Lord . . . Lord!

ENRIQUE—But, . . . why are you crying, then?

SISTER GRACIA—Oh, indeed I'm not . . . well . . . no, I'm not quite myself yet. That girl . . . like a mad creature . . . like some fury from another world. You mustn't think I'm generally so impressionable as this. But to-day . . . well, you'll forgive such foolishness . . . and another time. . . . (*She starts to go.*)

ENRIQUE—Wait . . . wait a little.

SISTER GRACIA—No, really . . . there is so much to be done. . . .

ENRIQUE—Wait . . . please . . . just for a minute. I want to speak to you . . . of something that may touch you very nearly.

SISTER GRACIA—That may touch me! . . .

ENRIQUE—Well, then . . . that does touch me very, very nearly . . . that means more to me than anything in the world. (*At a gesture from her.*) No . . . for God's sake don't be offended.

SISTER GRACIA—Let me go, please.

ENRIQUE—You guess what it is?

SISTER GRACIA—No.

ENRIQUE—Ah . . . but you do. (*He is deeply moved for all that he speaks quietly and stands very still; she, trembling rather, stands as still, to listen.*) Sister Gracia . . . you can't go on leading this life. How can you endure to be sunk here in this pit of bitterness and despair? Well, then . . . I can't endure that you should be. For three years now I've been coming here and seeing you every day . . . and from the first day I've cared for you. . . .

SISTER GRACIA—Oh, God in heaven, don't say that . . . hush, hush!

ENRIQUE—Why? I have cared for you . . . felt for you more and more . . . and more deeply. For you are all that I believe a woman should be . . . you are good, you are true, you have sense . . . and you are full of joy . . . you were when I first knew you. And if you're unhappy now . . . why, then, indeed, you are not yourself. You are a sick woman now.

SISTER GRACIA—I! . . .

ENRIQUE—Yes . . . the foul breath of this place has poisoned you. All the tears that you have seen shed are heavy on your heart. And all the suffering you've seen and all the blasphemies you've heard have beaten back into your body and your mind. But you need the bright sky above you and the fresh air to breathe . . . and on your horizon some gleams of hope.

SISTER GRACIA—No, no . . . oh, no!

ENRIQUE—Yes, yes . . . and that's what I bring you when I bring you . . . my love.

SISTER GRACIA—Oh, for God's sake. . . .

ENRIQUE—My love. We must call things by their names.

SISTER GRACIA—And you dare to speak to me of love . . . here . . . where we see how it all ends.

ENRIQUE—It isn't love that came to such an end . . . that has eaten like a cancer into these lives. True love between men and women is health and strength to both.

SISTER GRACIA—That is enough! (*And she turns away determinedly.*)

ENRIQUE—No, don't go away . . . listen . . . there's nothing I'm saying that need offend you. Love that is worthy of the name brings peace of mind and harmony . . . clear thoughts and steadfastness. And work to be done . . . and shared . . . oh, anxious hours enough . . . but with their burden lightened by just half. Day after day of toil and weariness . . . but at the end of each the comfort of a heart that beats near yours. Come out of this prison and learn to laugh again. Take off that habit which is black like death and that coif . . . it's like the cloth that you lay on a dead woman's face . . . and honour me by trusting me to make you happy.

SISTER GRACIA—I am happy. God knows it.

ENRIQUE—But won't you be as happy with me? And I should be so happy with you. Ah . . . forgive that from a man who really isn't used to being selfish. I'm not offering you what's called a life of pleasure . . . mine's austere. I'm not well off, and I'm a doctor and you'd be brought close enough, if you were my wife, to all the ills of mankind. Don't be afraid that you'd have no chance of doing good. I live for my work . . . and though I don't worship science for its own sake . . . I do believe it can help me to help my neighbor. Won't you help me too? You have grown wise in charity. Working together we could give such life to our work . . . won't you try? I'm a free man . . . and you are free . . .

SISTER GRACIA—I . . . free! How can you say that?

ENRIQUE—Why, you wouldn't be the first to leave the hard road you chose when you were young and full of illusions for a simpler way . . . the human way, you know, that love makes easier.

SISTER GRACIA—I have given my love once and for all. I abide by that vow. I live for that love and I will die in it.

ENRIQUE—Sister Gracia. . . .

SISTER GRACIA—Oh, yes, you're right . . . I am unhappy . . . unhappier than you can think. And I'm tired, and perhaps I'm ill . . . poisoned . . . oh, no doubt, as you say. But God, who has my love, is with me. I may not see him, but he is with me. And while I love him he will not leave me. Oh, yes, it's true that just now he has put bitterness in the cup . . . but he has given me so much other happiness . . . that I have so little deserved. And he will again . . . I know that he will. And even if he does not I have given myself forever.

ENRIQUE—Sister Gracia. . . .

SISTER GRACIA—Forever . . . forever! And no one has the right to try and turn me from my way. My love and my sorrow are my God's. No, don't speak and don't come near me. Don't ever speak or ever think of this again.

ENRIQUE—Is that your last word?

SISTER GRACIA—My last . . . and my only one. Good-by. (*She is more than a little shaken by all this, by the violence she is doing herself. Once again she turns to go.*)

ENRIQUE—Well, at least let me as a doctor give you some advice. I really think you are ill . . . you are worn out.

SISTER GRACIA—Don't let that trouble you. The Superior is responsible for my good health. What I need she will order. Good-by.

ENRIQUE—Good-by.

He bows and goes without turning his head. Sister Gracia turns now to go out on the left and so she has to cross the whole patio. She is quite broken with emotion and physical fatigue; she moves very slowly and rests wherever she can, by a tree, a chair, a pillar. Halfway across she can hear the impudent, sensual voice of Candelas singing.

> "I asked a sick man the complaint
> Of which he was to die,
> 'Of loving you . . . of loving you,'
> The sick man made reply."

"Sister Gracia stops to listen and there comes over her like an agony, all the temptation of love and its happiness. She wrings her hands, then crosses them on her breast, and stands there trembling. Then she lets her arms fall and stands for a moment, with closed eyes. Then she pulls herself together, takes the crucifix from her sleeve, looks at it for a little, presses it to her breast and says."

SISTER GRACIA—Jesus . . . beloved saviour . . . do not leave me without help! (*She starts on her way again, and, as she reaches the door, meets the Superior coming out.*)

SISTER GRACIA—Sister Cristina.

SISTER CRISTINA—What is it? Why, what's the matter? You're shaking all over. Are you ill?

SISTER GRACIA—No, indeed. But I want to ask a favour. Will you be so kind as to write to-day . . . to-day, please . . . to the authorities and ask them if they will transfer me. . . .

SISTER CRISTINA—But . . .

SISTER GRACIA—Please . . . please! I want to leave here at once . . . and without any one knowing . . . of knowing where I go! I beg you . . . for the love of God! It is a case of conscience. . . .

The curtain falls.

ACT III

The scene is again changed. This is the kitchen of an orphanage with whitewashed walls. On a sort of platform that raises the rear of the room above the forepart is a great stove with huge saucepans on top of it and large two-handled pots at its base.

In the front of the room are two long tables, and benches, where the big boys eat. And beyond the tables at back there are high windows through which the sky and trees can be seen. Beneath the windows a shrine with the Virgin and Child, adorned with two flower pots and artificial flowers.

The evening meal is being prepared by Sister Dionisia, "a sister of charity aged about 35, a country woman, uneducated and taciturn, but full of common sense and sturdy, practical virtue."

Engracia and Lorenza, inmates of the orphanage, "Engracia pretty and delicate in her movements, Lorenza a rather ugly country girl," bring a large box, with cord handles, filled with hunks of bread for the soup. It isn't very much bread, but it is all there is, and Sister Donisia is forced to slight the pots that are to go to the older children, if the little ones get any at all.

And there are no peppers for the soup. Lorenza notices that. "The drippings are not colored at all," she reports. There's no use making broth without peppers. The big boys won't eat it. They'll go to bed starving first, insists Lorenza. But there are no peppers, so Sister Dionisia can't put any in. They will have to make the best of what they have.

Lorenza and Engracia and Sister Dionisia too can dream of food even if they can't have any. There's the picture of an actress on a matchbox that Engracia finds—one of those lucky ladies who sings and dances and has motor cars and silk clothes and all the lentils she wants to eat. . . . Think of it!

The Innocent, too, furnishes further spur to their appetites. "The Innocent is what is sometimes called a 'natural,' a grown woman with the undeveloped brain of a child. She has, however, an old woman's face, and her hair is gray and bristly."

The Innocent brings in a twist of paper filled with scraps from a banquet—a leg of chicken, a cutlet bone with quite a little meat still on it, a bit of fried fish and a sweet. She is generous with her find, too, and Lorenza is grateful. But Engracia can't eat—not even the sweet. She is so hungry, and has been hungry so long, there's a touch of madness in her craving now.

The banquet, from which the Innocent got the food, is being held in the village in honor of a great event. There is to be a bullfight and, wonder of wonders, the fighter is to be Juan de Dios who used to be in the orphanage. Juan de Dios, who is so grateful for what the home did for him that he is pleased now and proud to advertise his origin. "Juan de Dios Garcia, the Foundling. From the Orphanage of San Vicente de Paolo." That's the way the billing reads and by Juan's orders.

"Fancy flourishing it back at them like that when they meant it as a disgrace," cries Engracia, enviously. "Foundling! And perhaps his father will be watching him fight . . . and he may see him killed! He'll be one of those in a black coat and a high hat who's been at the dinner. Foundling! That's what I'll call myself, Engracia the Foundling . . . and if I'm a success I'll make some of the gentlemen in high hats pay pretty dear for the use of the name. Foundling! Foundling!"

Now there is a disturbance in the yard. Policarpo, a hunchback tailor, a drunken, debased fellow, is beating little Morenito, a boy of 10. And Vicente, one of the orphans, a well set up boy of 16, is taking Morenito's part. Vicente is threatening to break the ugly head of Policarpo when Sister Gracia comes from the garden and stops them.

"Sister Gracia is now an old lady of 70. She supports herself with a stick, suffers from rheumatism and wears spectacles, but she is lively and merry all the same. As a rule she speaks gently enough, but she can get excited and be very angry too."

Sister Gracia demands attention now, and obedience. A report, too, of how the quarrel started, and of what so little a boy as Morenito could do to make Policarpo ill-treat him. Morenito was making faces and laughing and calling him "hunchie," Policarpo reports, like the others. To which Morenito's defense is that the tailor was making him sew with a pointless needle and cuffing him when he failed.

Morenito is sent to stand in the corner with his face to the wall and Policarpo is warned that such a thing is not to happen again on pain of complaint to the Board that he is unfit for his job. Let him boast of his influence. There is also the influence of the church to reckon with, and Sister Gracia commands that.

"So one's to treat these charity brats as if they were the sons of dukes," sneers Policarpo.

"They are the sons of God," answers Sister Gracia, "and that's a higher title still."

And now there is another matter for Sister Gracia to settle. What is Master Vicente doing there fighting with Policarpo? And how did he get there? With a skeleton key? Oh, ho! A key that lets into the patio on the other side of which are the girls' quarters! So Vicente has a sweetheart! And who is this sweetheart Vicente has come to see? Engracia, perhaps? No? Who then? Paca? And which Paca?

"Little Paca . . . that works in the bakery . . . she's his sweetheart," calls out the naughty Morenito from the corner.

So Sister Gracia must send for Paca and investigate this breach of discipline that involves not only the lovers, but the go-betweens, too: The Innocent, who carried letters, and little Morenito who pridefully boasts that he was also a messenger and got a special cake from Paca herself for his reward.

And now, Paquita—Little Paca—has come, a pretty girl of 17, dressed like the others. She evidently is a little troubled, but as evidently has her mind made up. She is not awed by Sister Gracia's tone. She knows why Vicente had let himself through the patio with a skeleton key—it was to see her. It may be courage that prompts her to confess it, but Paquita thinks perhaps it may also be because she loves Vicente better than he loves her. Which Vicente vigorously denies. This becomes so important an issue to them that they quite forget Sister Gracia until, "with a burst of half humorous anger," she interrupts them.

SISTER GRACIA—That's right . . . that's all right, children! Go on sweethearting . . . don't attend to me! Well, this is the last straw!

VICENTE—Oh . . . we don't mean to be rude. But we . . . she . . . you see . . .

SISTER GRACIA—Yes, I see her . . . and I see you . . . and a pretty pair of noodles you are! And what do you think is going to happen now, I should like to know? (*She starts to get up, and with her rheumatism that's not easy, so* PAQUITA *goes to help her. But with all the impatience of an old lady who hates to be reminded of her infirmities she goes on.*)

SISTER GRACIA—Let me be . . . let me be! Well . . . I like your impudence. One little angel of light mentions quite casually that he has made himself a skeleton key . . . and this girl confesses as calmly as you please that it's for clandestine meetings with her! And instead of being ashamed of yourselves and asking forgiveness . . .

PAQUITA—But it isn't a sin to love people.

SISTER GRACIA—But it's hardly a virtue, is it . . . to go making skeleton keys?

VICENTE—Oh . . . she knows I never wanted to.

PAQUITA—No . . . because you haven't the courage of a mouse.

SISTER GRACIA (*banging on the ground with her stick*)—Goodness gracious me . . . what a pair of children! May I ask if I'm to be allowed to get a word in edgeways?

VICENTE—Yes, Señora.

SISTER GRACIA—Much obliged, I'm sure! Well, now . . . how long have you two been romancing like this?

VICENTE—It's since St. James' day . . . that's the Warden's birthday . . . and Paquita went there with the Innocent to wait at table . . . and I was there seeing to the lock of the cupboard. And we started talking and I said to her . . .

SISTER GRACIA—Thank you. I can guess what you said to her . . . and what she answered.

PAQUITA (*with great dignity*)—No, Señora. . . . I didn't answer him at all till the Eve of Our Lady's Day, when I was in the bakehouse with the Innocent . . . and he came in with the chopped wood . . . and then I said . . .

VICENTE—She said I could make a key.

SISTER GRACIA—Excellent! And now what happens?

PAQUITA—We're going to get married.

SISTER GRACIA—At once?

PAQUITA—Yes . . . just as soon as he can get fifty dollars to buy the furniture.

SISTER GRACIA—Oh . . . and then what?

PAQUITA—Then . . . ! We're used to going hungry. It won't be so bad to go hungry together.

VICENTE—And I'm sure I don't know why you need say you'll have to go hungry . . . when you know perfectly well you won't have to with me there to look after you. I can work . . . and though I say it that shouldn't, I know my trade with the best. . . . I'm worth five pesetas a day anywhere. And I'd be earning it now and have the fifty dollars saved if it wasn't . . .

SISTER GRACIA—That's the thing. To-morrow we'll find you some work and we'll get you a lodging.

PAQUITA—What . . . send him away!

SISTER GARCIA—Yes, if you please. It doesn't suit me at all to have such a good locksmith living here.

VICENTE (*to* PAQUITA)—There . . . what have I always told you!

PAQUITA—Send him away! Yes . . . you'll save your fifty dollars right enough . . . but who'll you spend them on then?

VICENTE—Why, whatever should I want fifty dollars for . . . but to spend it on you?

PAQUITA—Oh, you say that now. . . .

VICENTE—I say it now . . . and I always shall . . . and God may strike me dead else.

SISTER GRACIA (*very angrily*)—And we've learnt to swear, have we? I've had enough of this. You be off to the bakehouse again . . . and you (*to* VICENTE) get back to your work. Hurry up. To-morrow I shall have a talk with the Warden about you . . . and that's the end of that.

VICENTE (*meekly*)—You won't tell him about the skeleton key, will you?

SISTER GRACIA (*pretending to be very angry*)—I shall tell him just exactly what I choose. Of all the impudence! Get along with you. (VICENTE *and* PAQUITA *linger, gazing at each other.*)

SISTER GRACIA—Will you both be off . . . when I tell you?

VICENTE (*very meekly*)—Yes, Señora. (*He turns to go and then back to* PAQUITA *with* . . .) Good-by, Paquita.

PAQUITA (*as she turns away unresponsive*)—And a nice mess we've got into! This is what comes of trying to be happy!

Supper is served now, with Sister Dionisia at the ladles and Lorenza and Engracia placing the plates of dripping-bread and broth on the tables.

For the moment Sister Gracia is free and as she sinks upon a bench with a sigh "she crosses herself and says a Paternoster in a low voice. On ending it she takes a little stone from her pocket and throws it out into the patio."

"Eah!" she sighs. "The first Paternoster I've been able to say all day. (*She picks up the crucifix from her side and smiles at it lovingly.*) Ah . . . sweet Saviour, it's little time we get to talk to each other, you and I. But we're an old couple now," she adds, kissing the crucifix in simple affection.

And now Sister Gracia returns to her duties. Did the peppers come? They didn't? And why? Because the Orphanage Board owed the merchant for fourteen bags already, Dionisia reports. He was willing to trust the Sisters, but not the Board.

And the flour? Yes, the flour had come. But it was poor flour: bran and common rye. It was hard to do anything with it, Sister Dionisia reports, and there were cockroaches in some of it.

"Then it must all be sent back at once," storms Sister Gracia.

"But we sent it back last time . . . and it did no good," explains Sister Dionisia. "The contractor's on the Board, you know . . . and, as if that wasn't enough, his brother-in-law's the party chairman."

Sister Gracia would go—that very minute—to the Town Hall and tell those worthies a thing or two, but it would do no good to-day. Everybody is at the bullfight. Even supper must wait for the bullfight, because some of the older boys had permission to go stand by the ring and hear about it. So Sister Gracia sits again to wait, and to pray quietly to herself. . . .

Now there is a great cheering in the streets outside. And above the cheering shouts for Juan de Dios. "Hurrah for Juan de Dios! Hurrah for the Foundling!" Even above the cheering Juan's voice can be heard: "Where's Reverend Mother?"

Now Juan has broken from the crowd that parts to let him through the door and is kneeling at the feet of Sister Gracia with his arms about her waist. And she, "surprised and a little embarrassed, but very pleased, pushes him away."

"Here . . . here! What is all this? Get away!" she cries. But there is no anger in her voice. As Juan sits beside her on the bench she leans on him a little, and he is worried for fear she might be ill. A thin little smile of confidence reassures him.

The girls crowd around Juan admiringly, and the bigger boys push in, still cheering. But Juan de Dios has eyes only for the Reverend Mother. It is she he has come to tell of the wonders that have happened to him.

JUAN DE DIOS—The porter didn't want to let us in. A fine thing to have had the door shut in my face . . . to-day of all others! . . . D'you hear that . . . d'you hear that? "Hurrah for the Foundling!" And in the Bull-ring . . . you should just have heard them shouting it there. They threw me cigars and they threw their hats in . . . and all the beautiful young ladies in the boxes stood up and applauded me . . . they did. And before you can say "knife" I'll have all Spain applauding me . . . and adoring me . . . and shouting . . . every one of them. . . . "Hurrah for the Foundling" . . . and that's me . . . that's me . . . who hadn't any father or a name of his own . . . but went hungry and cold . . . ! Oh, Reverend Mother, I have dreamed of this day . . . and I've kept myself for it . . . yes, I have . . . like one of God's blessed angels.

SISTER GRACIA—Hush, hush . . . don't talk like that.

JUAN DE DIOS (*very seriously*)—But I have . . . I swear it. And look here . . .

(*He now proceeds to show* SISTER GRACIA *by a lively pantomime how he disposed of his bull, the present spectators cheering him at every point with cries of "Ole! Ole!" He pulls out his handkerchief for a muleta—the red cloth by which the bull is distracted.*)

JUAN DE DIOS—The muleta . . . so! One pass . . . over his head to blind him. Then a high one to get my position. That leaves me exposed . . . so four more over his head, quickly, one after another. The one to turn him . . . one from down on my knees right at his horns. And then . . . the thrust! And you should have heard them shout. I tell you . . . they went mad! And if you had only been there too . . . with a white mantilla on . . . and I could have dedicated my bull to you.

SISTER GRACIA—Quiet . . . quiet . . . you heretic!

JUAN DE DIOS—But for all that, I've brought you . . . a present. Give it here . . . give it here. (*One of the boys gives him something that is carefully wrapped up in a silk handkerchief.* SISTER GRACIA *hesitates a moment before she takes it.*) . . . Take it . . . you deserve it . . . better than any one else does. Open it . . . open it. (SISTER GRACIA *undoes the handkerchief, and discloses a bull's ear . . . all bloody still.*)

SISTER GRACIA—Mother of God . . . what's this?

SISTER DIONISIA (*innocently*)—Why . . . it's an ear off a cow!

JUAN DE DIOS (*very offendedly*)—What d'you mean by a cow? It's the bull's ear, Señora . . . my bull that I killed . . . and that is his ear to prove it! (*Once more the whole assemblage bursts into cheers.*) . . . And there were fifty people at least came and asked me for it as a souvenir. But it's for you . . . just for you . . . to hang in your room . . . and every one that sees it there will envy you.

SISTER GRACIA—Thank you . . . my son. (*She cannot think what to do with her present, but* ENGRACIA *takes it and does it up again with the greatest care.*)

JUAN DE DIOS—And look . . . look at the tie-pin his Excellency threw me! Isn't it wonderful . . . isn't it, Sister Dionisia . . . and all of you . . . aren't you proud . . . and happy . . . isn't this a wonderful day for our Orphanage? (*The boys and girls agree enthusiastically.*) . . . But do look happy, Reverend Mother. (*He puts his arm round her and calls to the people in the doorway and out in the patio.*) For she is my mother . . . she is . . . she is! The other one left me in a basket on the doorstep . . . but she took me in and brought me up and cared for me. And Hurrah for our Reverend Mother . . . she's all the mother I ever want. (*Tremendous cheering.*)

SISTER GRACIA—Be quiet now. Tell them all to be quiet.

JUAN DE DIOS—But why don't you look happy? Oh, . . . haven't you made up your mind yet to my being a bull-fighter? I know . . . I know! Oh, wasn't she just set on my staying a carpenter all my life!

SISTER GRACIA—But suppose a bull kills you, my son?

JUAN DE DIOS—Well . . . if a bull kills me after I've done my duty by him, they'll give me a finer funeral than they would the Prime Minister.

SISTER GRACIA—Mother of God!

JUAN DE DIOS—And whether or no. . . . I have a good time and everybody talks about me and all the women go mad about me and I get lots of money . . . yes, I'm going to be rich . . . do you know that? I got nothing for fighting to-day . . . because it was the first time. But I did so well that for next Sunday they're giving me a thousand pesetas . . . one thousand pesetas! (*This creates an enormous sensation. The orphans stare and comment upon the marvel in low, impassioned tones. And* JUAN DE DIOS *adds impulsively.*) . . . And fifty of them for you . . . and then Sister Dionisia can cook you such a dinner. Hurrah, girls, hurrah! Meat for dinner next Sunday! (*They all cheer ecstatically.*) . . . But I must be off . . . they're waiting for me. (*To* SISTER GRACIA.) Oh, . . . come as far as the gate with me, so that everybody can see us together.

SISTER GRACIA—My son . . . I never heard of such a thing!

JUAN DE DIOS—Please . . . please, for it's the happiest day of my life. Good-by, everybody . . . good-by!

They get to the door, Sister Gracia and Juan de Dios, she leaning a little heavily on her cane as he leads her. And there are cheers for both of them. "Hurrah for the Foundling! Hurrah for our Reverend Mother!" These gradually die away, and Sister Dionisia returns to the business of supper.

Now the bigger boys are piling in, "jostling, stepping over each other or crawling even under the tables." There might be some fighting over places if Sister Dionisia did not stop it. Even so it is all she can do to keep them quiet long enough for her to bless the food they are about to receive and ask the Lord to preserve them from the sin of gluttony.

Suddenly above the hubbub protests take form. There are no peppers in the broth. And Felipe, for one, is not going to eat it.

"But, my children, if there's nothing else," pleads the distressed Sister Dionisia, "why, for the love of God, eat this!"

"We don't want it and we won't eat it," answers Felipe, mounting a bench the better to address the crowd. "We've had enough of eating bread and water for the love of God!" And as Sister Dionisia tries to stop him he adds: "Always shaking a crucifix at you whenever they want to cheat you out of something."

Soon the strike is well organized. "The boy who put a spoon in his plate is a coward!" shouts Felipe. "And the boy that sits down to table again is a disgrace to us all!"

It is Felipe's idea that they should go forth and take by force what they can't get by asking nicely.

"You stop interfering or it will be the worse for you," he warns Sister Dionisia. "Come on, boys! They keep us penned up here as if we were brute beasts. We may shout as loud as we like and we shan't be heard . . . they've forgotten us. And we're just starved. Well . . . there's bread outside . . . and there's meat outside . . . and there's wine outside . . . so come outside and get it. If it has to be stolen we'll steal it . . . and if killing's what's needed . . . well, we'll do some killing!"

Despite Sister Dionisia's efforts to control them and hold them back they are forming in line ready to march through the door. As a last defence she rushes to the bellrope and pulls it violently. From the other rooms the girls crowd in and Felipe's appeal is made to them.

"Let's have the whole orphanage out in the streets to demand its rights," he shouts. "If we're nobody's children . . . why, we're everybody's children! Come along, then . . . March!"

Sister Gracia stands in the doorway to face them. At the sound of her voice and the sight of her they pause. Sister Dionisia tries to explain what has happened. It must be that people have been giving wine to the boys who went to the bullfight, they have become suddenly so unmanageable.

Sister Gracia takes charge of the situation. Where are they going? To get their suppers . . . to take them, if necessary! To knock down doors, to break open locks if they have to, they shout.

"And do you think if there were any locked door that would open I shouldn't have been there by this to knock at it for you?" she asks.

"Yes. . . . But you go asking so prettily. We're going to try if a few stones won't make them attend."

The answer to a stone is often a bullet, Sister Gracia warns them, and when they still hold their ground she grows stern and orders them back to their places. Slowly they are cowed by her firmness and return to the tables, Felipe the last to go. And then, as they sullenly accept the rest of the broth, such as it is, Sister Gracia stands over them and quietly and kindly, though masterfully still, talks to them.

SISTER GRACIA—And d'you think you're the only folk in this world who don't get all that they want to eat? No, my children, no. There are people worse off than you . . . some of them so poor that they'd think your plate of supper a luxury. You'll have a roof over your head to-night and a mattress to sleep on and a blanket to cover you. Think of the people who'll sleep in a ditch by the roadside with no roof but the sky, and only the hoarfrost to come down and cover them. Think of the sick people . . . of people without a friend . . . stumbling through the world with not a hand held out to them . . . nobody caring. While you have a home and all the love we can give you. You are sheltered . . . you are taught . . . you are kept in right paths. And then think if you don't owe a few thanks to God after all.

FELIPE—To God . . . to God! There is no God. (*A stir of horror among the children.* SISTER DIONISIA *crosses herself and exclaims, "Blessed Jesus!"*)

SISTER GRACIA—And whatever do you think you mean by that, you little fool?

FELIPE—Because if there were . . . would he think this was all right?

SISTER GRACIA—God does not think this is right. Men break his laws. He made them brothers. Is it his fault if they turn wolves and devour each other? God does not think it right that his children should go hungry . . . and the innocent are not ever disgraced in his eye. It is by no will of His that some are poor and neglected while some are set up in pride. For God is Love and he loves us all and to each one he gives a share in heaven and in this earth.

FELIPE—Don't listen to her . . . she's just preaching lies to you. Nuns have all sold themselves to the rich. Do they ever go hungry? And as long as they can get us to keep up the sham they're let stuff themselves with food in peace.

SISTER GRACIA—I am not lying to you. I am telling you the truth and the whole truth. God does not smile upon the injustice of this world. He endures it . . . for how long? . . . ah, that we do not know. But he does not think it right.

FELIPE—Well, then . . . let's go and break the heads of those that do . . . and God will thank us for that. (*A few of the boys cheer up at this and approve.*)

SISTER GRACIA—Ah, no, no . . . all that can be done for this wicked world is to help to make it good.

FELIPE—And who's going to?

SISTER GRACIA—You. . . . You . . . not by hating but through love. Yes, all of you will help do that. For, when you are men . . . and go away from here, it will be because you have suffered from injustice that you'll know how to make and want to make . . . laws that are just. Oh, yes, my sons, yes . . . the world is yours . . . for you have won it by hunger and by suffering and pain. So when you hold it in your hands make it what it ought to be. God is watching you . . . his hopes are all in you. You suffer now that you may succour his world then. God sees you . . . God hears you. Now say with me, Lord, Lord, we thank thee for this food which is given us in thy name. There is not much of it, it is not very good, and we will not forget the taste of this bitter bread. And by thy precious love we swear that the children on this earth shall eat of it no more . . . say it with me . . . say it. . . . (*The boys repeat after her solemnly and quietly.*) . . . Jesus, Son of God . . . Christ, son of man, by the divine blood that thou didst shed for us we swear to spend our own to the last drop when we are men . . . that children may not be forsaken any more . . . that no more mothers may be wronged and go hungry and be ashamed to carry their children in their arms. My sons . . . my sons, promise me that when you are men you'll try to bring these things to pass . . . that you'll help to build on earth the Kingdom of God. (*Very quietly, very solemnly, they murmur "Yes."*)

SISTER GRACIA—Thank you, my children . . . thank you, And now . . . supper's over . . . go to bed and sleep in peace. (*The boys go slowly out. Only* FELIPE *does not move. He is sitting on his bench, head buried in his arms, and crying.* SISTER GRACIA *goes to him and puts a hand upon his shoulder.*)

SISTER GRACIA—Don't cry . . . for men don't cry, you know. And they don't complain. They suffer . . . but they work and hope.

The curtain falls.

THE PLAYS AND THEIR AUTHORS

"Street Scene." Drama in three acts by Elmer Rice. Copyright, 1928, 1929, by the author. Copyright and published, 1929, by Samuel French, New York.

Elmer Rice, born in New York in 1892, was headed first for a business career, which he did not approve, and later for the law. He passed his bar examinations, took a violent dislike to the profession and turned to playwriting. His first play was "On Trial," a drama that introduced the so-called flashback of the movies to the acted drama. After that he wrote "The Iron Cross" and "The Home of the Free" during the war; "For the Defense" after the war, and followed these plays with "Wake-up, Jonathan," played by Mrs. Fiske, on which he collaborated with Professor Hatcher Hughes of Columbia. The first expressionistic drama with an American background, "The Adding Machine," which the Theatre Guild produced was his, and he followed this with "Close Harmony" (with Dorothy Parker); "Cock Robin" (with Philip Barry); "The Subway" and "Street Scene." He not only wrote "Street Scene," but attended largely to the details of its sale to William A. Brady, after many other managers had refused it, took charge of the casting and did all the directing.

"Journey's End." Drama in three acts by R. C. Sherriff. Copyright, 1929, by the author. Copyright and published, 1929, by Brentano's.

Mr. Sherriff was 17 when he went to war as a lieutenant with the East Surrey regiment. Out of the war he became an inspector of buildings for an insurance company. By way of diversion he played back on the Rosslyn Football club and rowed in the shell of the Kingston Rowing club. The Kingstons wanted to produce a play and Sherriff, who had long had an interest in amateur theatricals, agreed to try and write one for them. He thought to set down as simply as possible certain of his adventures and reactions at the front. The play, when finished, was sent up to London as a sort of speculation. None of the established managers could see anything promising in it. The independent Stage Society, however, agreed by the margin of a single vote to give it a Sunday night hearing. Its dramatic value being then proved, Maurice Browne secured the rights to its professional production. It was a sensational success in London and duplicated this record in New York when imported by Gilbert Miller and Mr. Browne.

"Wings Over Europe." Drama in three acts by Robert Nichols and Maurice Browne. Copyright, 1928, 1929, by the authors. Copyright and published, 1929, by Covici-Friede, New York.

Robert Nichols, in his middle thirties, is one of England's younger modern poets. When they speak of his verse on the other side they link him with Gordon Bottomley, Lascelles Abercrombie and Robert Graves. He comes of a long line of men of letters and is a graduate of Trinity College, Cambridge. Out of college he went to war with the Royal Field Artillery. He was wounded and invalided home the first year out. During his convalesence he wrote a book, "Ardours and Endurances." "Fantastica," "The Smile of the Sphinx" and "Golgotha & Co" are also his. He was professor of English literature in Tokyo University, one of Lafcadio Hearn's successors. He also had a brief experience in Hollywood, helping with Douglas Fairbanks' picture, "The Black Pirate," and writing on his own "Twenty Below Zero."

Maurice Browne, who spent some years in Chicago, is also an Englishman and a graduate of Cambridge. He is generally credited with having affixed the name of Little Theatre to those amateur ventures which resulted finally in a definite artistic movement in the theatre. As an actor he has appeared in support of his wife, Ellen Von Valkenburg, and plans at some future time to play a leading part in his own play, "The Wife of William Flavy." It was he who, among semi-professional producers, first recognized in London the commercial possibilities of "Journey's End." He is associated with Gilbert Miller in the American presentation of that play.

"Holiday." Comedy in three acts by Philip Barry. Copyright, 1928, by the author. Copyright and published, 1929, by Samuel French, New York.

Mr. Barry is frequently included in these volumes. He made his début as a writer of "Best Plays" with "You and I" years ago, followed with "The Youngest" and was represented last year by "Paris Bound." He graduated from Yale in 1918, studied playwriting with Professor Baker at Harvard the year following, went in temporarily for writing advertising copy and has been a successful dramatist ever since. He was born in Rochester, N. Y., 33 years ago.

"The Front Page." Drama in three acts by Charles MacArthur and Ben Hecht. Copyright, 1928, by the authors. Copyright and published, 1928, by Covici-Friede, New York.

Mr. MacArthur, having been born to the church in the sense that he is the son of a Unitarian clergyman and was for two years a student at a theological seminary, escaped at a comparatively early age into journalism. He was a special writer on the Chicago Hearst papers when he was absorbing much of the material that appears in "The Front Page." He went to war with the Rainbow division and wrote about it in the vivid "War Bugs" novel. He has helped write two other plays, "Salvation," with Sidney Howard, and "Lulu Belle," with Edward Sheldon, his uncle. He was born in Scranton, Pa., in 1897.

Ben Hecht also has spent much of his working life in Chicago, though he was born in New York in 1893. He was at one time publisher of the *Literary Times* and has written several novels that have attracted attention, notably "Eric Dorn." His plays include "The Egoist," written for Leo Ditrichstein, and "The Stork," an adaptation. He, too, was a Hearst newspaper man.

"Let Us Be Gay." Comedy in three acts by Rachel Crothers. Copyright, 1928, 1929, by the author. Copyright and published, 1929, by Samuel French, New York.

Miss Crothers was represented in two of the earlier volumes of the "Best Plays," first by "Nice People" (1920-21) and again by "Mary the Third" (1922-23). She was born in Bloomington, Ill., tried her hand at both playwriting and play production in college, and later came east. She was first a student and later an instructor at the Wheatcroft Dramatic school. Her first play, "The Three of Us," was produced in 1906. She has written some twenty or thirty plays, most of which have been produced and many of which have been successful. She was the founder of the Stage Women's War Relief during the war. Her home is in Redding, Conn.

"Little Accident." Comedy in three acts by Floyd Dell and Thomas Mitchell. Copyright, 1928, by the authors.

Mr. Dell, born in Barry, Ill., in 1887, is the author of the story, "An Unmarried Father," from which the play, "Little Accident," was fashioned. He is a writing man whose output has been considerable, his novels including "Moon-Calf," "The Briary Bush" and "Janet March." He was at one time literary editor of the *Chicago Post* and later, in New York, was associate editor of the Socialist papers, *The Masses* and *The Liberator*. He has written many essays, one or two short plays and a biography of Upton Sinclair. He also edited, with Paul Jordan Smith, an edition of Burton's "Anatomy of Melancholy."

Mr. Mitchell is an actor, though he has done considerable writing for the stage as well.

"Machinal." Drama in ten episodes by Sophie Treadwell. Copyright, 1928, by the author.

It has been some time since Sophie Treadwell was a protégée of Mme. Helena Modjeska, but that event is linked so indissolubly with her beginnings as a dramatist that there is no passing it by. She had, from the earlier years of her California childhood, been interested in the theatre and particularly in Mme. Modjeska, who was the first real actress she had ever seen. Miss Treadwell was graduated from the University of California after she had devoted a good part of her junior and senior years to acting in such plays as were given there, notably in the dedicatory drama at the Greek theatre. Out of college she went to Los Angeles, played in stock and made extra dollars singing in vaudeville. It was in vaudeville that Mme. Modjeska heard her and shortly thereafter adopted her as a sort of protégée. Miss Treadwell lived on the Modjeska ranch, recited pieces to the actress and, finally, helped with the compilation of the Modjeska memoirs. After that she tried her hand at playwriting. "Gringo" was her first New York production, and "Oh, Nightingale" followed.

"The Kingdom of God." Drama in three acts by G. Martinez Sierra. Copyright, 1923, 1929, by G. Martinez Sierra.

Copyright and published, 1929, by E. P. Dutton & Co., New York.

Martinez Sierra, the best known of modern Spanish dramatists, has once before appeared in these volumes, with the production the season of 1926-27 of his "Cradle Song" by Eva Le Gallienne and the Civic Repertory company. He was born in Madrid in 1881 and educated at the University of Madrid. His first years out of college were devoted to story writing and the composition of prose poems. His first novel, "The Humble Truth," was published in 1904. He became associated with Jacinto Benevente in the conduct of the Spanish Arts Theatre and later succeeded Benevente as director of the enterprise. Returning to Spain with this company in May, 1927, Señor Sierra stopped over in New York and played a two-week engagement.

"Gypsy." Drama in three acts by Maxwell Anderson. Copyright, 1928, by the author.

Mr. Anderson, who first appeared in these volumes as co-author with Laurence Stallings of the highly successful war play, "What Price Glory," later made a reëntry on his own with "Saturday's Children." He is the son of a Baptist minister, was born in Atlantic, Pa., lived a good share of his life and was educated in the Northwest. He has been on the faculties of the University of North Dakota, Leland Stanford University, and Whittier College in Southern California. He turned later to newspaper work, has been an editorial writer west and east, but has devoted himself rather assiduously to playwriting the last several years. "White Desert," "Outside Looking In," and several collaborations with Mr. Stallings are part of his playwriting record.

PLAYS PRODUCED IN NEW YORK

June 15, 1928—June 15, 1929

(Plays marked with asterisk were still playing June 15, 1929)

PATIENCE

(24 performances)

A comic opera in two acts by W. S. Gilbert and Arthur Sullivan. Produced by The Play-Arts Guild, Inc., at the Masque Theatre, New York, June 25, 1928.

Cast of characters—

Patience....................................Mary Bokee
Reginald Bunthorne..........................Donald Kirkley
Archibald Grosvenor.........................Edmund Leonard
Rapturous Maidens—
The Lady Jane...........................Gertrude M. Gossman
The Lady Saphir.............................Wilma Lanyon
The Lady Angela.............................Nancy Arnold
The Lady Ella...........................Eunice Schramm
The Lady Celia..........................Margaret Gilner
Officers of the Dragoon Guards—
Colonel Calverley.......................Burt B. Royce, Jr.
Major Murgatroyd........................Carroll Robinson
Lieutenant, the Duke of Dunstable...........William Lester
An Ecstatic Dancing Maiden..................Estelle Dennis
Mr. Bunthorne's Solicitor...................Earl Jordan

Rapturous Maidens: Emma Baum, Margaret Brinkley, Eleanor Etheridge, Betty Harriss, Lillian Moore, Dorothy Miller, Carolyn Parker, Gertrude Schanze, Marjorie Springer, Lonah Straw, Beatrice Wilson and Betty Woodall.

Dragoon Guards: Joseph Arnold, Graye Boone, Ellis Farber, John Head, Ralph Hoyt, Arthur Lawder, Stanley Mitten, Henry Miller, Lynn Perkins, Norton Smith, William Randolph and William Wambold.

Soloists in Ensemble: Emma Baum and John Head.

Act I.—Exterior of the Castle Bunthorne. Act II.—A Woodland Glade.

SAY WHEN

(24 performances)

An intimate musical comedy in two acts by Calvin Brown. Produced by Elisabeth Marbury and Carl Reed at the Morosco Theatre, New York, June 26, 1928.

Cast of characters—

Michael Graham	Raymond Guion
Cora	Cora La Redd
Toody Hubbard	Doris Vinton
Sydney Farnham	Jane Alden
Diana Wynne	Dorothy Fitsgibbons
Gregory Farnham	Bartlett Simmons
Comtessa Scaracchi	Alison Skipworth
Colin	Duquesne Miller
Count Scippio Varelli	Joseph Lertora
Joe Turner	Roger Gray
Assistant Radio Announcer	J. Gibbs Penrose
The Four Recorders	Donald Wells, Robert Moody, Alan Ray, William J. Cleary
Miss Jefferson	Mildred Quigley
Miss Lee	Sally Anderson
Miss Jackson	Ann Freshman
Miss Thomas	Patricia McGrath
Miss Gordon	Kathryn Hamill
Miss Brady	Ruth Fallows
Miss Davis	Peggy Fish
Miss Randall	Ruth Altman
Miss Carter	Joyce Arling
Miss Stuart	Josephine Adair
Miss Stean	Dorothy Jones
Miss Scott	Helen Kaiser
Miss Udall	Genevieve Kent
Miss Hewitt	Katherine Hereford
Miss Custis	Mabel Martin
Miss Monroe	Anna Rex
Miss Warrenton	Beverly Maude
Mr. Grant	Archie Thompson
Mr. Meade	Warren Crosby
Mr. McClellan	Harold Williams
Mr. Lincoln	Bradley Cass
Mr. Chase	Harry Kirk

Acts I and II.—The Wynne Home.
Staged by Bertram Harrison and Max Scheck.

Diana Wynne, permitting herself to become engaged to Count Varelli because she does not want to hurt his feelings with a refusal, tries to fib her way out of the situation when called to account by her regular sweetheart, Gregory Farnham. Trouble threatens for two hours. The original play was called "Love in a Mist," was written by Amelie Rives and Gilbert Emery and played by Madge Kennedy and Sidney Blackmer.

GEORGE WHITE'S SCANDALS

(230 performances)

Musical revue in twenty-four scenes by Wm. K. Wells and Mr. White, music by De Sylva, Brown and Henderson. Produced by Mr. White at the Apollo Theatre, New York, July 2, 1928.

Principals engaged—

Willie Howard	Ann Pennington
Harry Richman	Frances Williams

Tom Patricola
Eugene Howard
William O'Neal
Bernice and Emily
Arnol Johnson's band
Hastings Twins
Rose Perfect
Belle Osborne
Frances Lyle
Isabel Mohr
G. White girls
Russell Mackert dancers

Staged by Mr. White.

WANTED

(16 performances)

A comedy in three acts by Don Mullally. Produced at the Wallack's Theatre, New York, July 2, 1928.

Cast of characters—

Skelly	Martin Malloy
Cassidy	George McEntee
O'Brien	H. R. Chase
Lt. Foley	Lloyd Sabine
James Bruce	Ken Cartier
Penelope Merton	Alney Alba
Marie Newton	Irene Shirley
Rena Henry	Teresa Brooks
Daisy Brooks	Inez Clough
Hugh Clark	George Connor
Major Longstreet	Frank Ardrews
Mrs. Robert Trent	Margaret Pitt
Mr. Robert Trent	Charles Angelo

Act I.—Scene 1—Assembly Room at Uptown Police Station. 2—Living Room at Penelope Merton's Apartment. Act II.—The Trent Apartment on Park Avenue. Act III.—Lieutenant's Private Room, Police Station.

Staged by Mr. Mullally.

Penelope Merton, a sweetheart of the South, alone and broke in New York, escapes the snares of a rough New Yorker who means her no good. She takes refuge in the rich home of society people left in charge of her old mammy. The missing family has carelessly left the family jewels behind and when these disappear Penelope is suspected, arrested, rescued by and eventually married to James Bruce.

THE LAWYER'S DILEMMA

(24 performances)

A farce comedy in three acts by Seaman Lewis. Produced by S. L. Simpson at the Belmont Theatre, New York, July 9, 1928.

Cast of characters—

Nettie Ney	Isabel Dawn
John Lawson	Hal Munnis
M. T. Dial	Robert G. Pitkin
Betty Kidder	Mary Mead
Jim Kidder	Robert Toms
I. P. Berry	Lee Beggs
Tony	David Manning

Acts I, II and III.—In the Law Office of M. T. Dial, New York.
Staged by E. J. Bluntcall.

A rewritten version of "Babies a la Carte" in which Nettie and Bettie, hearing that an eccentric uncle has left a million dollars to the first child born to his heirs, enter a stork race hoping to win the money. Their children arrive within an hour of each other, one standard the other daylight saving time. Then a codicil to the will discovers another heir.

THE INTRUDER

(5 performances)

A drama in three acts by Paul Eldridge. Produced by Edward Sargent Brown at the Biltmore Theatre, New York, July 25, 1928.

Cast of characters—

Woman	Vilma Walden
Katy	Viola Frayne
Man	Lon Carter
Young Woman	Millicent Green
Dr. John Weston	Richard Gordon
Mrs. Weston	Anne Sutherland
Nurse	Valerie Hickerson

Acts I, II and III.—Reception Room of Dr. John Weston.
Staged by Edward Sargent Brown.

Katy, left alone with Dr. Weston in his office on a rainy afternoon, learns something of the facts of life. Six years later she returns demanding that the doctor divorce Mrs. Weston, marry her and give their child a name. The doctor tells his wife everything and Katy, having learned that understanding is greater than love, leaves them to stew in the consciousness of their own errors.

VANITIES

(203 performances)

Musical revue in forty-six scenes assembled by Earl Carroll, music by Grace Henry and Morris Hamilton. Produced by Mr.

Earl Carroll at the Earl Carroll Theatre, New York, August 6, 1928.

Principals engaged—

W. C. Fields	Ray Dooley
Joe Frisco	Dorothy Knapp
Gordon Dooley	Martha Morton
Vincent Lopez' band	Ruth Patterson
Ernest Charles	Beryl Halley
Brian Macdonald	Lilian Roth
Edward Graham	Dorothy Lull
Maurice La Pue	Vercell sisters
Joey Ray	Jean Tennyson
Barto and Mann	Naomi Johnson
Ted Bradford	Fay Adler
	Sixteen Vanities girls

Staged by Mr. Carroll.

GUNS

(48 performances)

A story of gangdom, in three acts, by James Hagan. Produced by Jack Kingsberry at Wallack's Theatre, New York, August 6, 1928.

Cast of characters—

Joe	Ralph Hertz
"Wop" Murphy	Dexter Reynolds
Queenie Olson	Marion Haslup
Cora Chase	Suzanne Bennett
The "Halstead Sheik"	Freddie Laberer
Dutch Moeller	Frank Horton
Charlie O'Connor	Jesse Le Roy
"Nick" the Greek Chirkopolis	William Boulia
Hokey Pokey Kid	Rey Stewart
"Jimmy Plankey" "The Colorado Special"	Hugh Thompson
"Stink Foot" Louie	Teddy Hart
The "Blues" Singer	Frances Claire
"Officer"	Arthur Van Slyke

Act I.—A "Speak-easy" on Second Avenue, New York. Act II.—A "Speak-easy" in Chicago. Act III.—Somewhere Along the Mexican Border.

Staged by Jack Kingsberry.

A story of beer runners in Chicago and Chinese runners along the Rio Grande.

ELMER GANTRY

(48 performances)

A play by Patrick Kearney, based on the novel of the same name by Sinclair Lewis. Produced by Joseph E. Shea at the Playhouse, New York, August 7, 1928.

Cast of characters—

Deacon Bains....................................Ernest Pollock
Mrs. Bains....................................Mabel Montgomery
Frank Shallard....................................Robert Harrigan
Lulu Bains....................................Gwendolyn Hathaway
Elmer Gantry....................................Edward Pawley
Floyd Naylor....................................Tom Fadden
Adelbert Shoop....................................Frank Johnson
Lily Anderson....................................Rose Burdick
First Trumpeter....................................Jennie Bradley
Second Trumpeter....................................Marion Sargent Connolly
Third Trumpeter....................................Llewella Lloyd
Fourth Trumpeter....................................Agnes Geraldi
First Choir Singer....................................Betty Donn
Second Choir Singer....................................Ann Meares
Third Choir Singer....................................Mary Anderson
Fourth Choir Singer....................................Alma Chase
Fifth Choir Singer....................................Julia Collier
Sixth Choir Singer....................................Betty Wald
Seventh Choir Singer....................................Hazel Clinger
Eighth Choir Singer....................................Louise Ross
Cecil Ayleston....................................Eustace Wyatt
Sharon Falconer....................................Vera Allen
Hettie Dowling....................................Winifred Barry
Father Harvey....................................Frank Shannon
Rev. Willis Fortune Tata....................................Edward Boralle
Irving Tillish....................................Eustace Wyatt
Rabbi Bernard Amos....................................Arthur Ross
Dr. Hickenlooper....................................Ernest Pollock
Josiah Jessup....................................Eugene Blake
Oscar Dowling....................................Henry Sherwood
T. J. Riggs....................................Lumsden Hare

Act I.—Home of Deacon Bains, Schoenheim, Kansas. Act II.—Scene 1—Sharon Falconer's Revival Meeting, Lincoln, Nebraska. 2—Back of the Platform at Sharon's Atlantic Ocean Tabernacle. Act III.—Study of the Rev. Dr. Gantry, Wellspring Church, Zenith.

Staged by Lumsden Hare.

Elmer Gantry breaks into the religious racket at Schoenheim, Kansas, and seduces the daughter of Deacon Bains. Working eastward, Elmer is saved by Sharon Falconer and joins her troupe of revivalists to help build the tabernacle at Atlantic City. After the tabernacle and Sharon go up in flames Elmer takes on the purification of Zenith.

HE UNDERSTOOD WOMEN

(36 performances)

A continental comedy in three acts by Frances Lynch and Michael Kallesser. Produced by Michael Kallesser at the Belmont Theatre, New York, August 15, 1928.

Cast of characters—

Aline....................................Peggy Allenby
Lieutenant Maurice Lonsaine....................................Allan Devitt
Baroness LeLong....................................Hilda Spong
Baron LeLong....................................William Augustine

Julien Romain....................................Joseph Granby
Auguste Bertrand..................................Frank G. Bond

Act I.—Baroness LeLong's Apartment in Paris. Acts II and III.—Julian's Home in Lamboix.

Staged by Frank G. Bond.

Julian Romain, convinced that the system by which he wins his way with all women should be handed down to a son, marries to have a son, discovers after he has married that all the women who had loved him had done so to win favors from him for their real lovers. Even his wife had had her affairs with other men, for which he casts her from his home—and then calls her back again.

THE SONG WRITER

(56 performances)

A play in three acts by Crane Wilbur. Produced by Alexander Yokel at the 48th Street Theatre, New York, August 13, 1928.

Cast of characters—

Ruth Sabath..Beatrice Blinn
Joe...F. A. Walton
Fanny Kaye..Ethel Wilson
Andy Little..Neil Pratt
David Bernard......................................Georgie Price
Patricia Thayer.....................................Mayo Methot
Willie Abrams.......................................Irving Hirsch
Belle Ryan..Marian Winston
Dolly Ryan..Bea Thrift
Benny Hart.......................................Robert Sinclair
Mrs. Bernard...................................Jennie Moscowitz
J. Rodman Peck....................................Hugh Huntley

Act I.—The Star Rehearsal Room of the Bernstein Music Publishing Co., New York City. Act II.—J. Rodman Peck's Apartment in the Hotel Berwyck. Act III.—The Bernard Apartment.

Staged by Alexander Leftwich.

David Bernard, Jewish song writer, marries Patricia Thayer, daughter of a wealthy gentile family. Both families object. Two months later Patricia, made unhappy by Dave's family, runs away with J. Rodman Peck of her own set. A year in Paris and she is cured. She knows she loves both Dave and his songs, comes home to beg his forgiveness and they start over again.

THE FRONT PAGE

(276 performances)

A play in three acts by Ben Hecht and Chas. MacArthur. Produced by Jed Harris at the Times Square Theatre, New York, August 14, 1928.

Cast of characters—

Wilson, *American*....................Vincent York
Endicott, *Post*....................Allen Jenkins
Murphy, *Journal*....................Willard Robertson
McCue, *City Press*....................William Foran
Schwartz, *Daily News*....................Tammany Young
Kruger, *Journal of Commerce*....................Joseph Spurin-Calleia
Bensinger, *Tribune*....................Walter Baldwin
Mrs. Schlosser....................Violet Barney
Woodenshoes Eichorn....................Jay Wilson
Diamond Louis....................Eduardo Ciannelli
Hildy Johnson, *Herald-Examiner*....................Lee Tracy
Jennie....................Carrie Weller
Mollie Malloy....................Dorothy Stickney
Sheriff Hartman....................Claude Cooper
Peggy Grant....................Frances Fuller
Mrs. Grant....................Jessie Crommette
The Mayor....................George Barbier
Mr. Pincus....................Frank Conlan
Earl Williams....................George Leach
Walter Burns....................Osgood Perkins
Carl, a Deputy....................Matthew Crowley
Frank, a Deputy....................Gene West
A Policeman....................Larry Doyle
A Policeman....................George T. Fleming

Acts I, II and III.—The Press Room of the Criminal Courts Building, Chicago.

Staged by George S. Kaufman.

See page 152.

GANG WAR

(80 performances)

A play in three acts by Willard Mack. Produced by Willard Mack at the Morosco Theatre, New York, August 20, 1928.

Cast of characters—

A Newsboy....................Fred Verdi
Martin Maccarati....................Joseph Skinner
Otto Ludbeck....................True Boardman
Al Castoldi....................Antony Spirella
Officer Mullen....................Earl Redding
Officer Crowley....................Reginald Holden
Charlie Horan....................Walter Gilbert
"Big" Fred....................Charles Henderson
Louie the "Bat"....................Gordon Earle
Tony....................H. Lee Adams
Joe Magelli....................Donald Kirke
Mike Capistero....................Clyde Veaux
Verna....................Arden Benlain
Mazie Dowley....................Anne Forrest
Sheriff Dave Brannagin....................Charles T. Lewis
Hite (Deputy) Ellery....................Albert Moore
Olive Gilmour....................Wilma Lanyon
Lieut. Carl Gorson....................Robert Middlemass
McGee....................John Horan
"Duke" Kelton....................Louis Kimball
Shirley Mayne....................Beatrice Nichols
Mr. Gilmour....................Max Von Mitzel
Charlie Harrison....................Hardie Albright
Bosco....................Jess Romer

Act I.—Scene 1—The Steps and Front Door of St. Dominic's Church. 2—Back Room of the Venetian Cafe. Act II.—Scene 1—Office of Lieut. Gorson. 2—Venetian Cafe. Act III.—The Same.
Staged by Mr. Mack.

Al Castoldi is shot by members of the "Duke" Kelton gang on the steps of St. Dominic's church. Joe Magelli, his lieutenant, takes over his leadership of the Castoldi gang. The Kelton gang continues its attacks, killing Shirley Mayne, Magelli's secret sweetheart. Magelli's men grab Kelton, bring him to their headquarters, which are bombed by Kelton's gang while their leader is there. The Castoldis are planning reprisals at the play's end.

RELATIONS

(104 performances)

A comedy drama in three acts by Edward Clark. Produced by the author at the Masque Theatre, New York, August 20, 1928.

Cast of characters—

Sophie Glass.................................Peggy Coudray
Sidney Weingart..............................Wolfe Barzell
Max Tureck...................................J. A. Curtis
Eva Bergman..................................Barbara Brown
"Uncle Wolfe" Michaels.......................Edward Clark
Mortimer Boasberg............................Dan'l Makarenko
Irving Mintz.................................Bert Scott
David Lubin..................................Horace Braham

Act I.—"Uncle Wolfe's" Millinery Store, East Side, New York. Act II.—Offices of David Lubin's Emporium. Act III.—The Lubin Flat, in the Bronx.
Staged by Edward Clark.

Uncle Wolfe Michaels fires all his relations from his employ. David Lubin, his nephew from Australia, starts a business and takes all the relations in. The relations, including Uncle, swindle David. And then an Australian uncle dies and leaves a legacy with a happy ending.

THE BIG POND

(47 performances)

A play in three acts by George Middleton and A. E. Thomas. Produced by Edwin H. Knopf and William P. Farnsworth, at the Bijou Theatre, New York, August 21, 1928.

Cast of characters—

Francesco....................................Marius Rogati
Ronny Davis....................................Reed Brown, Jr.
Mrs. Billings....................................Marie Curtis
Mrs. Livermore....................................Doris Rankin
Barbara....................................Lucile Nikolas
Pierre DeMirande....................................Kenneth MacKenna
Henry Billings....................................Harlan Briggs
Sarah....................................Virginia Russell
Molly Perkins....................................Penelope Rowland

Act I.—Venice. Acts II and III.—Vernon, Ohio.
Staged by Edwin H. Knopf.

The Henry Billings of Vernon, O., are in Europe for a year. Pierre De Mirande is their courier. Barbara Billings thinks she loves Pierre, Papa Billings hates him. Papa thinks if he could get Pierre to Vernon he could show him up and Barbara would be cured. In Vernon Pierre turns out to be a great success as a rotarian business man. But Barbara liked him best as a poet. So she marries Ronny Davis, a home town boy.

GOIN' HOME

(76 performances)

A drama in three acts by Ransom Rideout. Produced by Brock Pemberton at the Hudson Theatre, New York, August 23, 1928.

Cast of characters—

Slim, U. S. Military Police....................................John Irwin
Bill, U. S. Military Police....................................Ralph Cullinan
Lise....................................Barbara Bulgakov
Sergeant Durant....................................Arvid Paulson
Corporal Picot....................................Alexander Zaroubine
Commandant Juneste....................................Georges Renevant
Israel Du Bois....................................Richard Hale
Tom ....Brevard Burnett
Luke....................................Leo Bailey
Major Edward Powell of the A. E. F....................................Russell Hicks
Samba Saar....................................Clarence Redd
Jake....................................Seifert C. Pyle
Bill....................................F. Barclay Trigg
Spuds....................................Ferdinand J. Accooe
Slick....................................J. William Maxwell
Walt....................................Frederick D. McCoy
Mose....................................Charles H. Brown
Chuck....................................Charles Benjamin
Banjo Eph....................................Fred H. Jennings
Buck....................................Ray Giles
Chip....................................Snippy Mason
Jim....................................Thomas Moseley

Acts I, II and III.—A Cafe in a French Seaport Town After the Signing of the Versailles Treaty.
Staged by Brock Pemberton and Antoinette Perry.

Israel Du Bois, New Orleans Negro shanghaied into the Foreign Legion the first year of the war, comes out a hero and marries Lise, who thinks him a rich American. They open a café in a seaport town through which black American troupes pass on their way home. Major Powell, son of the family that brought Israel up as a servant, finds the boy there, learns of his mixin' with white folks, undertakes to set matters right, gets mixed up with Lise, starts a miniature race war in which his life is saved by Israel and finally gets rid of Lise and takes Israel back to the states.

THE LIDO GIRL

(60 performances)

A play in three acts by Edward Elsner. Produced by Edward Elsner at the Totten Theatre, New York, August 23, 1928.

Cast of characters—

Robert Gordon....................................Frank R. London
Daniel Hamilton....................................Wallace Furie
Richard Towns....................................William Wolfe
Claire Carson....................................Ethel Fisher
Anna Jackson....................................Blanche Collins
Barbara Kingsley....................................Amy Hodges
Isabelle Millard....................................Kathleen Evane
Craig Boyd....................................William De Vaudray
Jack Mitchell....................................Alan Archer

Act I.—Scene 1—At Robert's Apartment in Greenwich Village. Act II.—At Robert and Claire's. Act III.—At Claire's.
Staged by Edward Elsner.

Claire Carson had been very, very wicked and quite promiscuous. Men had killed themselves for her in practically every act. And then she found true love in Robert's duplex apartment.

GENTLEMEN OF THE PRESS

(128 performances)

A play in three acts by Ward Morehouse. Produced by Thos. E. Jackson and H. S. Kraft at the Henry Miller Theatre, New York, August 27, 1928.

Cast of characters—

Braddock....................................Granville Bates
Britt....................................Allan Nagle
Sweezer....................................Elmer Cornell

Wick Snell...John Cromwell
Pansy True...Carlotta Irwin
Charlie Haven......................................Hugh O'Connell
Fitzgerald...Cornelius Vezin
McManahan..Francis Pierlot
Ollie Wilkins....................................J. Hammond Dailey
Copy Boy...Billy Quinn
Night Porter.......................................A. O. Huhan
Dorothy Snell......................................Betty Lancaster
Ted Hanley...Paul Clare
Alonzo...Harry Levian
Myra May...Helen Flint
Abner Pennyfather..................................Duncan Penwarden
Kelly..William Pawley
Cutler...Lawrence Leslie
McBee..Millard Mitchell
Bellflower...Russel Crouse
Branch...Philip Wood
Haley..Harold Grau
First Waiter.......................................Thos. A. Linker
Second Waiter......................................George Humbert
Western Union Messenger............................Louis Halprin
Kenner...J. H. Stoddart, 2nd
Pop Blalock..John Paschall
Riggs..Harry Cronk
Vickery..George Spelvin, Jr.

Act I.—A Section of the City Room, 2.30 A.M. Act II.—An Office With an East River View. Act III.—Scene 1—A Room in a Seventh Avenue Hotel. 2—The City Room.

Staged by George Abbott.

Wick Snell, after a lifetime devoted to newspaper work, takes a position as publicity agent for a big realty firm. His boss goes over Wick's head to call in the newspaper men and give them a silly story. Wick takes the reporters' part, is fired, tries freelancing, fails and is glad to go back to his old rewrite job.

THE MONEY LENDER

(16 performances)

A play in three acts by Roy Horniman. Produced by Ned Jakobs at the Ambassador Theatre, New York, August 27, 1928.

Cast of characters—

Mrs. Luttrell......................................Marion Grey
Maid...Nan Sheldon
Capt. Harry Yarborough.............................Geoffrey Harwood
Colonel Luttrell...................................Charles Esdale
Rev. Henry Luttrell................................Grant Stewart
Lillian Luttrell...................................Katherine Standing
Letitia Lady Ingleby...............................Isabel O'Madigan
Mr. Evan Jones.....................................Horace Pollock
Samuel Levi..Herbert Clark
Miss Tallant.......................................Nina Walker
Willoughby Heriot..................................Fothringham Lysons
Lord Carhampton....................................Guy Standing, Jr.
Sister of Mercy....................................Nan Sheldon
Solomon Levi.......................................Louis Sorin
Rachel Levi..Lulu Mae Hubbard

Jacob Dacosta....................................George Farren
Sarah Levi....................................Genevieve Belasco
Ike Levi....................................Lester Salko

Act I.—A Drawing Room in the Luttrell's Home at Twickenham, England. Act II.—The Money Lender's Office in Saville Row. Act III.—Scene 1—Solomon Levi's Antique and Second-Hand Furniture Store. 2—The Money Lender's Office.

Staged by Edward Clark Lilley.

Colonel Luttrell, Christian, who made his money in business with Simon Levi, Jew, is eager his daughter Lillian shall marry his old partner's son, Samuel. He leaves them 200,000 pounds on condition that they do marry. The young people are willing until they quarrel as to in which faith their children shall be raised. Then Sam marries his Jewish Rose and Lillian her Christian Harry.

EVA THE FIFTH

(63 performances)

A play in three acts by Kenyon Nicholson and John Golden. Produced by John Golden and Edgar Selwyn at the Little Theatre, New York, August 28, 1928.

Cast of characters—

Tracy Boone....................................Al Roberts
Grace Steeple....................................Sheila Trent
Connie Bard....................................Nila Mack
Leon Montrose....................................William Wadsworth
Lorna Montrose....................................May Duryea
Dave Amazon....................................Ross Hertz
Oriole Hartley....................................Lois Shore
Hattie Hartley....................................Claiborne Foster
Mal Thorne....................................Buford Armitage
Ed Bondell....................................Edward M. Favor
Ernest Beaumont....................................William Sellery
Newton Wampler....................................Philip Barrison
Jeff Morgan....................................Julian Noa
Jane Truxton....................................Florence Pendleton
A Flagman....................................Harry Swan
Violet....................................Diana G.

Act I.—Hattie Hartley's Dressing Room in the Opera House at Hiawatha, Kansas. Act II.—The Bondell U. T. C. Troupe Car. Act III.—Scene 1—The Committee Room in the K. of P. Hall, Centralia, Kansas. 2—The Stage of K. of P. Hall.

Staged by John Golden.

Hattie Hartley has played Little Eva with an Uncle Tom show all her stage life. Now she is getting too big for the part and her little sister Oriole is a candidate. The Tom troupe is stranded, Hattie agrees to marry a village hick to save the situation, Oriole takes on the rôle of Eva, Hattie grows jealous and feeds Oriole chocolates which make her sick in front of the audience. Then Hattie goes back to the troupe, her old lover and her old part.

RINGSIDE

(37 performances)

A play in three acts by Edward E. Paramore, Jr., Hyatt Daab and George Abbott. Produced by Gene Buck at the Broadhurst Theatre, New York, August 29, 1928.

Cast of characters—

Huffy	Brian Donlevy
Phil	Harry Cooke
Jim	Frank Verigun
Curley	William Franklin
Artie	Carlo De Angelo
Jake	George J. Williams
Bennie	Ashley Cooper
Peter Murray	John Meehan
Sid Durham	Joseph Crehan
John Zelli	Robert Gleckler
Chauffeur	Warren Colston
Doris O'Connell	Harriet MacGibbon
Bobby Murray	Richard Taber
Paula Vornoff	Suzanne Caubaye
Ed	James Lane
Joe	Charles Wagenheim
Skeeter	Donald Heywood
Buster	William F. Walker
Maxie Kaufman	Craig Williams
Grace	Yvonne Grey
Bunny	Bobbe Weeks
Florence	Kaye Hastings
Ethel	Laurel Adams
Referee	George Spelvin
Radio Announcer	J. Ascher Smith
Fight Announcer	Dan. E. Hanlon
McCabe	Packey O'Gatty
Policeman	James Horgan

Act I.—Bobby Murray's Training Quarters. Act II.—Paula Vornoff's Roof Bungalow in New York. Act III.—Scene 1—Bobby Murray's Dressing Room, Madison Square Garden. 2—Ringside.

Staged by George Abbott.

Bobby Murray, lightweight champion, is training for a title bout under the direction of his manager and father, old Peter Murray. John Zelli, night club racketeer, is trying to undermine Bobby's morals so he can induce him to throw the fight, giving the gamblers a chance to clean up. Zelli lures Bobby with liquor. Paula Vornoff lures him with Paula Vornoff. They almost get him. But old Peter is there at the finish threatening to kill his son rather than see him fight a crooked fight, and Bobby wins.

CARAVAN

(21 performances)

A melodrama of gypsy life in three acts by Clifford Pember and Ralph Cullinan. Produced by Richard Herndon at the Klaw Theatre, New York, August 29, 1928.

Cast of characters—

A Barker.....Michael Rice
Tonio.....Jerome Daly
Concha.....Kate Mayhew
Jaques O'Moil.....Barry Macollum
Fernand.....Michael Rice
Gornez.....Edwin Thompson
Paulette.....Louise Mainland
Irma.....Mildred Byron
Silvio Mazetti.....Leo Kennedy
Alza Gaudet.....Virginia Pemberton
Chiquita.....Elsa Shelley
Julio Layet.....Robert Hyman
Madre Layet.....Katherine Clinton
M. Francois Lambert.....Edmunde Forde
A Stranger.....H. H. McCollum
Sergeant Duluc.....George Neville
Detective Leland.....Jethro Warner
Black Bear.....George Thornton
Cinnamon Bear.....Joseph Casey

Acts I, II and III.—Inside and Outside the Caravan of Madre Layet, Carnival Grounds, Brest, France.
Staged by Rollo Lloyd.

Alza Gaudet, orphan, brought up by Madre Layet, gypsy, is loved by two men, Julio, Madre's son, and Silvio, Chiquita's lover. Silvio and Julio clash one, two, maybe three times. Silvio is killed. Alza is suspected. Julio confesses. But it was Chiquita's husband who really did it.

THE PHANTOM LOVER

(15 performances)

A translation by Herman Bernstein and Adolph E. Meyer from Georg Kaiser's "Oktobertag." Produced by Gustav Blum at the 49th Street Theatre, New York, September 4, 1928.

Cast of characters—

A Servant.....Cameron Clemens
Madame Jattefaux.....Louise Mackintosh
Monsieur Coste.....George MacQuarrie
Lieutenant Jean-Marc Marrien.....David Newell
Mademoiselle Catherine.....Edith Barrett

Leguerche....................................Romney Brent
Acts I, II and III.—Drawing Room of Monsieur Coste's Villa, Outside of Paris.
Staged by Mr. Blum.

Mlle. Catherine, filled with love thoughts, stands alongside Lieutenant Jean-Marc Marrien window shopping and falls strangely in love with him. She follows him to the church, where she reads his name in the lining of his hat. She follows him to the opera and sits next to him. The lieutenant goes his way and Catherine goes home. That evening she forcibly stops the butcher boy on his way to visit a maid. Later a child is born to Mlle. Catherine which she dreams was fathered by Lieutenant Jean-Marc Marrien. Jean-Marc protests his innocence, but, realizing Mlle. Catherine's sad plight and her entire sincerity he kills the butcher boy and marries Catherine.

HEAVY TRAFFIC

(61 performances)

A new comedy in three acts by Arthur Richman. Produced by Charles Frohman at the Empire Theatre, New York, September 5, 1928.

Cast of characters—

Dodd....................................Herbert Belmore
Susan Perry....................................Jean Dixon
Tommy Fairchild....................................Leo G. Carroll
Rosalie West....................................Mary Boland
Wilbur Richardson....................................Robert Strange
Malcolm West....................................Reginald Mason
Isabel Mancini....................................Kay Strozzi
Philip Mancini....................................Edward Crandall
Ralph Corbin....................................A. E. Matthews
Acts I, II and III.—The West Residence, New York City.
Staged by Bertram Harrison.

Rosalie West, maturing and amorous, collects lovers. Malcolm, her husband, is past the age of caring, so long as she is reasonably discreet. But Malcolm himself falls in love with Isabel Mancini, eager but respectable, and offers Rosalie a quarter million to divorce him. She refuses. Malcolm collects evidence against Rosalie and Isabel's brother, Philip. Isabel refuses to take her happiness at the cost of involving Philip in a scandal. So Malcolm has to get new evidence, which the handsome detective who has just met Rosalie agrees to furnish within the week.

GOOD BOY

(253 performances)

A musical play in two acts, book by Otto Harbach, Oscar Hammerstein, 2nd, and Henry Myers; music and lyrics by Herbert Stothart, Bert Kalmar and Harry Ruby. Produced by Arthur Hammerstein at the Hammerstein Theatre, New York, September 5, 1928.

Cast of characters—

Ma Meakin	Effie Shannon
Pa Meakin	Sam Hearn
Elvira Hobbs	Evelyn Bennett
Cicero Meakin	Charles Butterworth
Walter Meakin	Eddie Buzzell
Pansy McManus	Helen Kane
A. A. Stone	Lester Bernard
"New York"	Roy Sedley
Manhattan	Milton Douglass
Betty Summers	Barbara Newberry
Bobby D'Arnell	Dan Healy
Jimmie	Borrah Minevitch
Policeman	Dick Neely
Brakeman	Stan Rock
Ticket Speculator	Joseph Ames
Movie Doorman	Neil Stone
Old Lady	Elsie Percival
A Grafter	Gus Quinlan
Miss Badger	Virginia Case
Hotel Clerk	Jack O'Hare
First Bellboy	Tom Martin
Second Bellboy	Arthur Sullivan
Elevator Boy	Gordon Merrit
Trevor	Austin Clark
Pawnbroker	Morris Tepper
Justice of the Peace	Joseph Ames
License Clerk	Bob Abbott
Landlady	Muriel Greel
Theatre Doorman	Neil Stone
Theatre Treasurer	William Metz
Theatregoer	Phil Daly
His Girl Friend	Louise Blakeley

Act I.—Scene 1—Outside the Meakin Farmhouse, Butlersville, Arkansas. 2—Section 10 of "The Arkansas Flyer." 3—The Bow of the New Jersey-New York Ferry. 4—The Skyline of New York. 5—Broadway. 6—Upper Broadway. 7—Outside of a Boarding House. 8—A Kitchen. 9—Interior of Meakin Home in Butlersville. 10—The Stage of a Theatre. 11—A Taxicab. 12—A Hotel Entrance. 13—Lobby of the Hotel. 14—A Hotel Suite. 15—A Balcony. Act II.—Scene 1—The Meakin Home. 2—Wally's Wedding (as Ma Imagines It). 3—A Country Road. 4—A Pawn Shop. 5—License Bureau. 6—A Justice of the Peace. 7—Betty's Room. 8—Telephone Pay Station. 9—A Street. 10—A Theatre Lobby. 11—The Stage. 12—Cellar of the Boys' Club. 13—The Equity Ball. 14—Peacock Alley. 15—Hotel Lobby. 16—A Hotel Bedroom.

Staged by Reginald Hammerstein and Busby Berkeley.

Walter Meakin starts from Butlersville, Ark., for New York, determined to go on the stage. His first walk up Broadway he bumps into the dream girl in front of the Paramount building. She gets him a job in the chorus with her, but he is a pretty sad chorus boy. The stage director knocks him around and takes his girl away from him. Walter gets her back at 11.10 P.M.

MACHINAL

(91 performances)

A play in two parts by Sophie Treadwell. Produced by Arthur Hopkins at the Plymouth Theatre, New York, September 7, 1928.

Cast of characters—

A Young Woman	Zita Johann
A Telephone Girl	Millicent Green
A Stenographer	Grace Atwell
A Filing Clerk	Leopold Badia
An Adding Clerk	Conway Washburn
A Mother	Jean Adair
A Husband	George Stillwell
A Bellboy	Otto Frederick
A Nurse	Nancy Allen
A Doctor	Monroe Childs
A Young Man	Hal K. Dawson
A Girl	Zenaide Ziegfeld
A Man	Jess Sidney
A Boy	Clyde Stork
A Man	Clark Gable
Another Man	Hugh M. Hite
A Waiter	John Hanley
A Judge	Tom Waters
A Lawyer for Defense	John Connery
A Lawyer for Prosecution	James Macdonald
A Court Reporter	Otto Frederick
A Bailiff	John Hanley
A Reporter	Conway Washburn
Second Reporter	Hugh M. Hite
Third Reporter	Hal K. Dawson
A Jailer	John Hanley
A Matron	Mrs. Chas. Willard
A Priest	Charles Kennedy

Part I.—Episode 1—In an Office. 2—In a Flat. 3—In a Hotel. 4—In a Hospital. 5—In a Speakeasy. 6—In a Furnished Room. 7—In a Drawing Room. Part II.—Episode 8—In a Court Room. 9—In a Prison. 10—In the Dark.

Staged by Arthur Hopkins.

See page 225.

THE HIGH ROAD

(144 performances)

A comedy in three acts by Frederick Lonsdale. Produced by Charles Dillingham at the Fulton Theatre, New York, September 10, 1928.

Cast of characters—

Alex....................Nancy Ryan
Ernest....................Mackenzie Ward
Lady Minster....................Winifred Harris
Lady Trench....................Hilda Spong
Lord Trench....................Frederick Kerr
Sir Reginald Whelby....................Lionel Pape
Lord Crayle....................H. Reeves-Smith
Morton....................Edward Martin
Duke of Warrington....................Herbert Marshall
Lord Teylesmore....................John Williams
Elsie Hilary....................Edna Best
James Hilary....................Alfred Drayton

Acts I, II and III.—At Lord Crayle's.
Staged by Frederick Lonsdale.

Elsie Hilary, actress, is loved enthusiastically by the young Lord Teylesmore. His aristocratic family objects. Elsie defies them. They invite her to visit them, hoping the contact may discourage her. She agrees. In four weeks she is out of love with his lordship and more desperately in love than ever with his cousin, the Duke of Worrington. But the Duke, unfortunately, is honor bound to the wife of an invalid. In the end, when the invalid husband dies, Elsie sends the Duke to his first love and goes back on the stage.

WHITE LILACS

(136 performances)

A romance with music in three acts based on the life of Frederic Chopin from the German original by Sigurd Johannsen. Book and lyrics by Harry B. Smith, music by Karl Hajos from Melodies by Frederic Chopin. Produced by Messrs. Shubert at the Shubert Theatre, New York, September 10, 1928.

Cast of characters—

Countess D'Agoult....................Charlotte Woodruff
Prince Obelenski....................Frank Horn
Delphine Potocka....................Grace Brinkley
Gaston de Flavigny....................Maurice Holland
Heinrich Heine....................Ernest Lawford
Giacomo Meyerbeer....................Charles Croker-King
Dubusson....................De Wolf Hopper
Mme. George Sand....................Odette Myrtil
Frederic Chopin....................Guy Robertson
Luselle....................Allan Rogers
Balzac....................Franklin Van Horn
Mlle. Taglioni....................Eva Mascagno
Louison....................Melba Alter
Franz Liszt....................Vernon Rudolph
Catherine....................Louise Beaudet
Marquise De Mours....................Phyllis Newkirk
Juanita....................Juanita

Paco .... Paco
Trio .... Charlotte Woodruff, Melba Alter, Phyllis Newkirk

Act I.—The Fragonard Room in the Countess D'Agoult's House, Paris. Act II.—The Gardens at George Sand's Villa, on the Island of Majorca. Act III.—Chopin's Studio in Paris. Time—France, 1840.

Staged by J. J. Shubert and George Marion.

George Sand meets Frederic Chopin at the Countess D'Agoult's party. They are mutually attracted and go to live in Mme. Sand's villa on the Island of Majorca. Soon their artistic temperaments clash, there is a separation and Chopin goes back to Paris.

THE GREAT POWER

(23 performances)

A new drama in four acts by Myron C. Fagan. Produced by Myron C. Fagan at the Ritz Theatre, New York, September 11, 1928.

Cast of characters—

Margaret (Peggy) Wray .... Helene Shipman
Hilda .... Eleanor Martin
Judge Ben Forrest .... G. Davidson Clark
Senator (Dick) Wray .... John Anthony
Frank Forrest .... Nelan Jaap
Joan Wray .... Minna Gombell
Bruce Power .... Alan Birmingham
Graves .... Jack Leslie
Jordan .... Walter F. Scott
Senator Charles Davis .... Walter Walker
John Power .... John T. Doyle
Rev. Dr. Elliott .... Conway Wingfield
District Attorney Crane .... Alfred Swenson
Sargeant McQuade .... James O'Brien
Chairman of the Committee .... Hirshell Mayall
Other Members of Committee .... { Joseph Eisner / Robert Ryan }
Doctor .... William Cort
Nurse .... Myrtle Brown

Acts I and IV.—Living Room in the Home of Senator (Dick) Wray, Washington, D. C. Acts II and III.—John Power's Library, New York.

Staged by Myron C. Fagan.

John Power, a man of enormous wealth and ambition, crushes everything that threatens to thwart him until he crashes into Joan Wray. Joan's brother is a Senator and when Power tries to hurt the Senator Joan retaliates by trapping Power's son. Finally it turns out that young Power is an adopted son and that Joan is really Power's own daughter. Follows a scene at the Judgment Seat with Power trying to answer for his crimes.

TRAPPED

(15 performances)

A melodrama in three acts by Samuel Shipman and Max Marcin. Produced by Max Marcin at the National Theatre, New York, September 11, 1928.

Cast of characters—

Vincent Lorrimore	William Ingersoll
James	Alf Helton
Nellie	Florence Arden
Inspector Manning	John Miltern
Helen Lorrimore	Janet McLeay
Guthrie Daniels	Edward Woods
George	Frank Collins
Tom	James T. Morey
Nick	Calvin Thomas
Loony	Natan Sack
Angela	Mary Robinson
Tony	Ralph Locke
Judd	George Larkin
Alex	Felix Krembs
Pete	Clarence Risien
Callahan	John T. Samson
Burke	Harvey Helm
Joe	Louis Rosner

Act I.—The Home of Vincent Lorrimore, New York City. Acts II and III.—Scene 1—Sitting Room of an Old Fashioned Country Mansion in Westchester. 2—An Old Wharf.
Staged by Max Marcin.

Vincent Lorrimore, banker, is warned that his daughter is likely to be kidnaped. He calls the police, and a plan of campaign is outlined. That night Guthrie Daniels, a messenger from father's bank, offers to take Helen to a wedding rehearsal. The two are kidnaped by Sicilians. Helen is threatened with crimes considerably worse than death, Guthrie maneuvers to save her by pretending to join the gang and finally succeeds.

NIGHT HOSTESS

(117 performances)

A dramatic comedy in three acts by Philip Dunning. Produced by John Golden at the Martin Beck Theatre, New York, September 12, 1928.

Cast of characters—

Tish	Porter Hall
Ben Fischer	Maurice Freeman
Hennessy	Francis O'Reiley
Frank Wardell	Harold Woolf

Joe.....Henry Lawrence
Buddy Miles.....Ruth Lyons
Herman.....John L. Kearney
Dot.....Lilian Lyndon
Rita.....Jane Allyn
First Chump.....J. S. Boatsman
Second Chump.....Chester DeWhirst
Chris Miller.....Averell Harris
Cyril Keane.....Graham Velsey
Julia.....Gail DeHart
Peggy.....Louise Kirtland
Rags Conway.....Norman Foster
Tom Hayes.....Charles Laite
Musicians.....Nicholas Nardullo, Carl Alps, Larry Roland, Norman Levene, Ned Norton
Other Hostesses....Peggy Vaughn, Doris Podmore, Barbara Willison, Helen Henderson, Helen McKay, Katherine Burns, Janet Spitzer
Croupiers.....{ Jeff Gaines, Philip Frank, William Cox }
Other Attendants.....{ John Humphrey, George Wright, Jr. }
Winners and Losers....Michael Mack, James G. Morton, Bjorn M. Koefoed, Burleigh Morton, Jacob Frank, George Nolan, Jane Dix, Harry L. Beck, May Rice, Beth Gear, Elsie Hyde
Hoodlums.....Richard Terry, Ellsworth Jones, John LeFevre

Acts I, II and III.—The Lounge Room of the "Little Casino," an Exclusive Gambling Establishment in New York City.
Staged by Winchell Smith.

Buddy Miles, hostess of the "Little Casino" night club, is desired by Chris Miller the manager. Before he can have Buddy, however, Chris feels he must get rid of Julia, his other girl. He chokes Julia and hides her body in a trunk. He is trying to ship the trunk to Chicago when Rags Conway, Buddy's better sweetheart, helps the police uncover the crime.

LUCKEE GIRL

(81 performances)

A musical comedy in prologue and three acts adapted by Gertrude Purcell from the French "Un Bon Garcon"; music by Maurice Yvain and Maurie Rubens, lyrics by Max Lief and Nathaniel Lief. Produced by Messrs. Shubert at the Casino, New York, September 15, 1928.

Cast of characters—

Arlette.....Irene Dunne
Colette.....Flo Perry
Man.....Clifford Smith
Lucien DeGravere.....Irving Fisher
Tampon.....Lou Powers
Lulu.....Gertrude McGushion
Lili.....Dorothy McGushion
Celina.....Dorothy Barber
Pontaves.....Frank Lalor

Hercules	Billy House
Camille	Doris Vinton
Mme. Falloux	Josephine Drake
Jean	Clifford Smith
Paul Pechard	Harry Puck
Mme. Pontaves	Loraine Weimar
DeGravere	Harold Vizard
Four Diplomats	Andy Hamilton Johnny Ferrara Lenny Nelson Hal Saliers

Prologue—Rue Pigalle, Montmartre, Outside Coco's, Paris. Act 1.—Private Room at Coco's. Act II.—Drawing Room in Mme. Falloux's House in the Provinces. Act III.—Garden Outside Mme. Falloux's.

Staged by Lew Morton and Harry Puck.

Arlette, loving Lucien in Paris, discovers that he is bound to marry another girl in his old home town. When Lucien leaves Paris Arlette commandeers a comic waiter to act as her chaperon and follows her love to the provinces. There she manages, after a song or two, to have things pretty much her own way.

THIS THING CALLED LOVE

(136 performances)

A comedy in three acts by Edwin Burke. Produced by Patterson McNutt at the Elliott Theatre, New York, September 17, 1928.

Cast of characters—

Harry Bertrand	Malcolm Duncan
Florence Bertrand	Juliette Day
Ann Marvin	Violet Heming
Dumary	J. H. Brewer
Dolly Garrett	Ruth Garland
Fred Garrett	Bruce Elmore
Tice Collins	Minor Watson
Miss Alvaraz	Enid Romany
Normie De Wit	Henry Whittemore
Marie	Josephine Lewis

Acts I, II and III.—The Apartment of the Bertrands in the East Sixties, New York City.

Staged by Howard Lindsay.

Harry and Florence Bertrand, five years married, quarrel bitterly and agree to separate. Ann Marvin, Florence's sister, hearing and seeing the quarrel, determines never to marry. When Tice Collins proposes and admits that what he most wants is a home Ann suggests that she might marry him but serve him only as his housekeeper. There is no reason she can see why a home organization cannot be perfect as long as love is kept out of it. In three weeks Tice and Ann are desperately in love and ready to break their housekeeping arrangement. Three weeks later they are quarreling and unhappy. The conclusion being that sex love is human but untrustworthy.

CROSS MY HEART

(64 performances)

A musical comedy, in two acts. Lyrics by Joseph McCarthy, music by Harry Tierney, book by Daniel Kusell. Produced by Sammy Lee at the Knickerbocker Theatre, New York, September 17, 1928.

Cast of characters—

Charles Graham....................................Bobby Watson
Mrs. T. Montgomery Gobble......................Lulu McConnell
Elsie Gobble..Doris Eaton
Sally Blake..Mary Lawlor
(By courtesy of Charles B. Dillingham)
The Maharajah of Mah-Ha........................Eddie Conrad
Maxie Squeeze.....................................Harry Evans
Richard Todd................................Clarence Nordstrom
Tommy Fitzgerald..............................Franklyn Ardell
Marie...Arvil Avery
Beatrice Van Ness..............................Amy Atkinson
Cigarette Girl......................................Edith Martin
Bennett...Martin LeRoy
Finnie..Dorothy Bow
Specialty Dancers.......................Bob Gilbert, Arvil Avery
Rialto Trio—
Charles Peters, Ramon Rameau, Martin LeRoy, Edgar Fairchild and Ralph Rainger and Their Brunswick Recording Orchestra
The Ten Little Tappers—Geneva Duker, Topsy Humphrey, Cora Stephens, Ann Brown, Bobbe Campbell, Anna Rex, Frances Stone, Dorothy Patterson, Dorothy Bow, Joey Benton

Acts I and II.—At Mrs. T. Montgomery Gobble's Home, and in the Slave Ship Cafe, Greenwich village.
Staged by Sammy Lee.

Because Mrs. Gobble wants to marry her daughter Elsie to a title Elsie's sweetheart, Charlie Graham, decides to find one for her. He hires a comic Maharajah who helps make Mrs. Gobble ridiculous, and this leads to an agreement that Elsie and Charlie may as well get married.

THE BIG FIGHT

(31 performances)

A drama of New York life by Milton Herbert Gropper and Max Marcin. Produced by Sam H. Harris and Albert Lewis at the Majestic Theatre, New York, September 18, 1928.

Cast of characters—

Steve Logan	Jack Roseleigh
Berrelli	William Ricciardi
Nick	Lewis Shuman
Ross	Jefferson Hall
Reinhart	Henry Phillipi
Dr. Driggs	Harry Stubbs
Winnie	Edna Bennett
Balloon Man	Dave Weinstein
Slim	Victor Kilian
Happy	J. W. Jackson
Jim	Jean Sidney
Shirley	Estelle Taylor
Phil	Harry Mitchell
Henry	George Cole
Pinkie Frye	Owen Martin
George	Carl De Mel
Chuck "Flower" Sloan	Arthur R. Vinton
Billie Moore	Billie McManus
Lester	Roy Hargrave
Sniffy Joyce	Eddie Mann
Lefty Wilson	Gordon Conover
Whitey Lewis	Leo Pardello
Ralph	Shirley Wynne
Jack Dillon, known as The Tiger	Jack Dempsey
Snowball	Henry Clark
Lieutenant Rooney	E. J. Le Saint
Battling Baker	Ralph Smith
Rad	Frank Callahan
Danny	Dan Kelly
Bill	Alan Allyn
Jerry the Greek	Jerry Luvadis
Battler's Second	"Italian Jack" Herman
Battler's Second	Anthony McCauliffe
Messenger Boy	Victor Kilian, Jr.
Messenger Boy	Neil Malloy
Officer Kelly	John Kelly
Referee	Joe Bernstein
Announcer	Joe Humphreys
Radio Announcer	Norman Pearce

Acts I, II and III.—In a Barber Shop, at Chuck Sloan's, and in Madison Square Garden.

Staged by David Belasco.

Both Tiger Dillon, the heavyweight champion, and Steve Logan, his manager, are in love with Shirley the manicurist. Steve tries to doublecross the Tiger, first by lying to Shirley and later by conspiring with Chuck Sloan, the big gambler, to force Shirley to put powders in the Tiger's drinking water. The Tiger remains true to his old alma mater, however, and knocks his opponent's block practically off the night of the big fight.

* THE NEW MOON

(309 performances)

A romantic musical comedy in two acts by Oscar Hammerstein, 2nd, Frank Mandel and Laurence Schwab, music by Sigmund Romberg. Produced by Laurence Schwab and Frank Mandel at the Imperial Theatre, New York, September 19, 1928.

Cast of characters—

Julie	Marie Callahan
Monsieur Beaunoir	Pacie Ripple
Captain Paul Duval	Edward Nell, Jr.
Vicomte Ribaud	Max Figman
Robert	Robert Halliday
Alexander	Gus Shy
Besac	Lyle Evans
Jacques	Earle Mitchell
Marianne	Evelyn Herbert
Proprietor of the Tavern	Daniel Barnes
Flower Girl	Olga Albani
A Spaniard	Herman Belmonte
A Dancer	Edith Sheldon
Phillippe	William O'Neal
Clotilde Lombaste	Esther Howard
Fouchette	Thomas Dale
Captain Dejean	Lester Dorr
The Dancers	Rosita and Ramon
The Musicians	Hernandez Brothers Trio

Act I.—Grand Salon of Monsieur Beaunoir's Mansion Near New Orleans, and at the Chez Creole. Act II.—Scene 1—The Deck of "The New Moon" and on an island.
Musical numbers staged by Bobby Connelly.

Robert, bondman to Monsieur Beaunoir in New Orleans in 1788, is in love with Marianne Beaunoir. Robert is also a nobleman in his own right, but cannot tell because the police of Paris are looking everywhere for him. When the police find Robert they start back to Paris with him. Marianne is on the same boat. There is a mutiny, the bondmen come into power, everybody goes ashore and gets married and a new republic is founded. But Marianne, her pride hurt, at first refuses to marry Robert. It takes him the rest of the evening to convince her.

ELMER THE GREAT

(40 performances)

An American comedy in three acts by Ring Lardner. Produced by George M. Cohan at the Lyceum Theatre, New York, September 24, 1928.

Cast of characters—

Elmer Kane	Walter Huston
Mrs. Kane	Lida MacMillan
Nick	Thomas V. Gillen
Nellie Poole	Nan Sunderland
Sarah	Kate Morgan
Amy Gillan	Edith Luckett
Ben Beeson	Mark Sullivan
Bull Wade	Tom Blake

Evelyn Corey	Katharine Francis
Some of the Regulars of a N. Y. Baseball Club:	
Dave Walker	Harold Healy
Gabby Sutton	Rodney Hildebrand
Kit Graham	Barney Thronton
Kid Crowley	Gordon Hicks
Grouch Stevens	George Sawyer
Bone Bonham	Bill Bender
Johnny Abbott	Henry Shelvey
Nosey Noonan	Dan Carey
Odd Olds	Charles Johnson
Slat Stout	Jack Williams
High Hip Healy	Jack Clifford
Pinky Doyle	Ted Newton
Cy Allen	Fred de Cordova
Ed Murphy	Edgar Eastman
Joe Mullen	Everett Surratt
Oscar	D. J. Hamilton
Mr. Grayson	John Pierson
Mr. Stillman	Arthur Finnegan
Chief Harris	Edwin Walter
Martha	Mary Lohman

Act I.—The Kane Homestead at Gentryville, Indiana. Act II.—A Room in a Hotel—Training Quarters—Fort Gregg, Florida. Act III.—The Club House in St. Louis and back in Indiana.

Staged by Sam Forrest.

Elmer Kane, solid bone above the ears but the best pitcher in the Three-I league, refuses to leave Gentryville, Ind., because secretly he is in love with Nellie Poole, who owns the grocery for which he drives the delivery wagon. Not even an offer from the New York Giants can tempt him. Guessing his secret, Nellie fires Elmer. Then Elmer goes to New York, muddles through a wonderful season, wins most of his games, takes to gambling, retains little besides his shirt and is tempted to throw a deciding game to get himself out of a mess. A way is found for him to come through clean and take Nellie home.

JARNEGAN

(136 performances)

A play in three acts by Charles Beahan and Garrett Fort, based on Jim Tully's novel. Produced by Charles K. Gordon and Paul Streger at the Longacre Theatre, New York, September 24, 1928.

Cast of characters—

Jack Jarnegan	Richard Bennett
Edward Bernard	Robert Cain
Nathan Leedman	Hooper L. Atchley
Daisy Carol	Joan Bennett
Pauline Clare	Wynne Gibson
Alice Toren	Ruthelma Stevens
Dorothy Chester	Margaret Mower
Jimmy Fallon	James H. Bell
Jacob Isaacs	James R. Waters

Patsy Brady....................................Henry O'Neill
Velma....................................Beatrice Kay
Cherry Lindal....................................Edith Arnold
Sally....................................Dennie Moore
Mrs. Crossman....................................Mabel Allyn
Herb....................................Jack Klendon
Nurse....................................Angela Raigh
Watchman....................................Walter Plinge
Maid....................................Betty Jordan
Dancer....................................Lillian Gibson
Guests at Leedman's Party—Mindelle D'Or, Betty James, Polly Peyton, Renee Shepard, Claudia Delys, Eleanor Cabot, Peggy Blair, Velma Forrest, Lucy Dietz, Louise Dear, Helen Nafe, Dorothy Young, Violet Gray, Marian Martin, Elmer Barlab, S. K. Benyon, Moss Fleisig, Guido Alexander, Samuel Levine, Frederick Rudin, Maynard Holmes, Lionel Stander, Ralph Willard, Robert B. Nelson, Eddie Court, Harry Schaefer, Frank Ross, Jack Reiger

Act I.—Outer Office of the Pioneer Studio, Hollywood. Act II.—Jarnegan's Office at the Metropolis Studio. Act III.—Leedman's Home.

Staged by Richard Bennett.

Jack Jarnegan, one of the rougher but better directors of pictures in the Hollywood studios, casually takes under his protection a young girl named Daisy Carol, come to make her fortune on the screen. Daisy is seduced by Edward Bernard, a rival director, and the night she dies from the effects of an illegal operation Jarnegan gets drunk, invades a Hollywood party and violently proclaims his disgust of the game.

THE WAR SONG

(80 performances)

An American play in three acts by The Spewacks and George Jessel. Produced by Albert Lewis and Sam H. Harris at the National Theatre, New York, September 24, 1928.

Cast of characters—

Mrs. Rosen....................................Clara Langsner
Social Worker....................................Eda Heinemann
Emily Rosen....................................Shirley Booth
Sid Swanson....................................Raymond Guion
Sally Moss....................................Lola Lane
Herman Wagner....................................Paul Ker
Eddie Rosen....................................George Jessel
Bob Elkins....................................Edward Leiter
Dr. Hayman....................................Ted Athey
Civilian Officer....................................Frank Spelvin
An M. P....................................Charles Peters
Priv. James Perkins....................................William Gargan
Priv. Harris Winters....................................Joseph Latham
First Sergeant Michael Gilhooley....................................Clyde Franklyn
Captain Conroy....................................Charles Wilson
Priv. Higgenbotham....................................Peter K. Hawley
Mr. King of the Y. M. C. A....................................Edwin Jerome
Corporal Ringling....................................Paul O'Brien
Priv. Chickopopolis....................................H. C. Warren
Priv. Rudy Shorer....................................T. F. Benson

Mrs. James Perkins.................................Patricia Kenny
German Operator...............................Lieut. Paul Schultz
Von Bergen...........................Major S. Albon Rumann
Brinkerhoff...........................Capt. Herman Lehmann
Major Von Stoch...............................Col. Edmund Loewe
German Sergeant...............................Lieut. Hans Golle
First German Guard...............................Harry Von Zynda
Second German Guard...................................Carl Worms
Third German Guard...................................Harry Bass

Act I.—Home of the Rosens, New York. Act II.—Orderly Room, Camp Upton. Act III.—Back of the Lines in France.

Staged by Albert Lewis.

Eddie Rosen, a talented song plugger and the support of his mother, widowed by the Spanish-American war, is drafted in the Great War and grows increasingly rebellious as the trouble goes on in France. Few of the breaks are his and he is a terrible soldier. He loses his girl, his sister gets into trouble, he follows her seducer into the German lines and is taken prisoner the day he hears of his mother's death.

ADVENTURE

(23 performances)

A new play in three acts by John Willard. Produced by Bernard Steele, Inc., at the Republic Theatre, New York, September 25, 1928.

Cast of characters—

Kitty...Ruth Hunter
Porter..Richard Bengal
Clerk..Harold Kennedy
Colonel Stetson.................................Joseph Eggenton
Michael O'Shane...................................John B. Litel
Jane Merwin......................................Helen Mayon
Dolores Hampton.................................Roberta Arnold
"Spider"...Clyde Dilson
First Herder.....................................J. Gordon Kelly
Pedro...Rollo Lloyd
Second Herder....................................Ernie Teele
"Angel" Evans...............................Harry D. Southard
Steve Lane...Leo Kennedy
Jed Hampton.....................................William Ingersoll

Act I.—Lobby of a Small Family Hotel, Uptown, New York City. Act II.—The Grand Hotel, Bitter Creek, Wyoming. Act III.—Sitting Room in the Hampton Ranch House.

Staged by Bernard Steele and Rollo Lloyd.

Michael O'Shane, soldier of fortune after the war, meeting Dolores Hampton under romantic circumstances in New York, follows her to her father's ranch in the west and accepts a job fighting her father's cattlemen to protect the grazing range for the sheep interests. Bad Man Angel Evans tries to get him, but Michael shoots first and Dolores keeps her man.

CHEE-CHEE

(31 performances)

A musical narrative in two acts by Fields, Rodgers and Hart. Produced by Lew Fields at the Lew Fields' (Mansfield) Theatre, New York, September 25, 1928.

Cast of characters—

A Eunuch....................................Ralph Glover
Another....................................Alan Lowe
Prince Tao-Tee....................................Stark Patterson
Li-Li-Wee....................................Betty Starbuck
Li-Pi Siao....................................George Hassell
Miss Smile of a Rose at the Dawning of Spring......Dorothy Roye
Li-Pi Tchou....................................William Williams
Chee-Chee....................................Helen Ford
San Toy....................................George Ali
A Very Narrow-Minded Owl....................William Griffith
Innkeeper....................................Philip Loeb
The Tartar Chief....................................George Houston
Leader of Khonghouses........................Marshall Bradford
Radiance and Felicity..........................William Griffith
Profundity and Meditation............................Philip Loeb
Holy Emperor....................................Ralph Glover
Dancing Idols........................Masa Sanami, Violetta Aoki

Act I.—Scene 1—A Corridor in the Palace of the Holy Emperor. 2—The Road to the Future. 3—A Wayside Tavern. Act II.—Scene 1—A Forest. 2—Visiting Day at the Monastery of Celestial Clouds. 3—The Gallery of Torments. 4—The Palace.

Staged by Alexander Leftwich and Jack Haskell.

Li-Pi Siao, grand eunuch at the court of the Holy Emperor, is eager that his son, Li-Pi Tchou, should succeed him as chief guard of the harem. Both the boy and his bride object. Being banished they take to the road, suffer trying adventures, are returned to the Palace and believe themselves defeated. A way is found, however, for Li-Pi Tchou to keep both the job and his peace of mind.

FAST LIFE

(21 performances)

A melodrama in three acts by Samuel Shipman and John B. Hymer. Produced by A. H. Woods at the Ambassador Theatre New York, September 26, 1928.

Cast of characters—

Mildred Allen....................................Dorothy Payne
Rodney Hall....................................Donald McClelland
Buddy Williams....................................Frank Reyman
Julie Sutherland....................................Anne Tarnoff
Nola Mercer....................................Mabel Williams

Gladys Tucker....................................Muriel Robinson
Charles Percy....................................Walter Tyrrell
Douglas Stratton.................................Donald Dillaway
Patricia Mason...................................Claudette Colbert
Christina Johnson................................Irene Cattell
Donald Bliss.....................................Wells Richardson
Chester Palmer...................................Chester Morris
Jim Taylor, Doorman..............................Robert Toms
Clyde Turner.....................................Frank A. Howson
Richard Palmer...................................William Morris
Bradford Palmer..................................Crane Wilbur
John Holmes......................................Frederick Earle
Willard Halliday.................................Paul Wilson
Andrew Stratton..................................C. Edwin Brandt
Burton Hall......................................Thomas Irwin
Guard..Robert Toms
Press Carroll....................................Adrian Morris
Daniel Coleman...................................Jean Clarendon
Negro..Vincent Gulliver
Wong...Goo Chong
Chaplain...Frank B. Miller
Martin Cobb......................................John Burch
Doctor...Frank Graham

Act I.—Douglas Stratton's Apartment. Act II.—The Executive Mansion. Act III.—Scene 1—Inside the Prison. 2—Electrocution Chamber. 3—Executive Mansion.

Staged by A. H. Van Buren.

Rodney, Douglas and Chester all love Patricia Mason. Patricia prefers Douglas and marries him secretly. When she sneaks back to his apartment after a party Rodney follows. Finding them in bed and refusing to believe their explanation, Rodney becomes abusive. In the hall, as he is leaving, he is shot and killed. Douglas is arrested, tried, convicted and sentenced to the chair. Pleas are made to the governor, who is Chester's father. Everything failing Chester confesses that he is the murderer. Doug is freed and the governor has to see his own son go to jail.

BY REQUEST

(28 performances)

A new comedy in three acts by J. C. Nugent and Elliott Nugent. Produced by George M. Cohan at the Hudson Theatre, New York, September 27, 1928.

Cast of characters—

William Abbott....................................Elliott Nugent
Jean Abbott.......................................Norma Lee
John Hector Henry.................................J. C. Nugent
Claudia Wynn......................................Verree Teasdale
Hal Curtiss.......................................Grant Mills
Judith Swann......................................Eleanor Winslow Williams
Freddie Page......................................Harry McNaughton
Antonio Rini......................................Jules Epailly
Gerald Onglow.....................................Wills Claire
The Pullman Porter................................Charles Halton
A "Red Cap".......................................Milton C. Herman

Acts I and II.—Abbott's Apartment, New York City. Act III.—On the Bar Harbor Express.
Staged by the authors.

William Abbott of Ohio, in New York looking for a correspondent's job, becomes seriously interested in Claudia Wynn and promises to travel companionately with her as far as Bar Harbor. When Mrs. Abbott arrives and learns the truth she frankly requests her husband to go on with his affair and gather experience while he may. But she secretes herself in the same Pullman and when William's courage fails the wife is there to reclaim him.

THE WOULD-BE GENTLEMAN

(34 performances)

A play in three acts by Moliere, adapted by F. Anstey. Produced by the Civic Repertory Theatre, Eva Le Gallienne, Director, at the Civic Repertory Theatre, New York, October 1, 1928.

Cast of characters—

Music Master	John Eldredge
Nicole	Beatrice de Neergaard
Dancing Master	J. Blake Scott
M. Jourdain	Egon Brecher
Baptiste	Walter Beck
Second Lackey	Robert Ross
Music Master's Pupil	Adelle Schuyler
Fencing Master	Paul Leyssac
Professor of Philosophy	Sayre Crawley
Madame Jourdain	Alma Kruger
Dorante, Comte De Chateau-Gaillard	Donald Cameron
Lucile Jourdain	Ria Mooney
Cleonte Dubois	Harold Moulton
Covielle	J. Edward Bromberg
Tailor	Lewis Leverett
His Assistant	Landon Herrick
Dorimene	Mary Morris
Page	Harold Francis
Cook's Assistant	Vernon Jones
Dancers	J. Blake Scott, Jocelyn Gordon
Musicians	Theodore Zarkevich, Constantine Shevtchen, Peter Tcharkovsky, Abraham Batken, Paul Zamulenko
Slaves	Herbert Shapiro, Ted Fetter
Dancing Dervishes	Margaret Love, Glesca Marshall, Jocelyn Gordon, Robert Ross, Lewis Leverett, Landon Herrick
Mufti	John Eldredge
Guests	Agnes McCarthy, Leslie Cooley

Acts I, II and III.—At M. Jourdain's House.
Staged by Miss Le Gallienne.

The ridiculous Jourdain, grown rich, seeks to buy social position and to ape the manners and customs of his betters. He is amusingly exposed but is too ignorant to appreciate the joke.

WHEN CRUMMLES PLAYED

(40 performances)

A satire of the Victorian era arranged by Nigel Playfair. Produced by Charles L. Wagner at the Garrick Theatre, New York, October 1, 1928.

Cast of characters—

THE PROLOGUE

Vincent Crummles....Halliwell Hobbes
Nicholas Nickleby....Mylor Merriam
Smike....Parker Mills
Mrs. Vincent Crummles....Nell Carter
Miss Ninetta Crummles....Maureen O'Moor
Mr. Folair....Harry Hilliard
Mr. Lenville....John Troughton
Mr. Snittle Timberry....Byron Russell
Miss Bravassa....Nancy Bevill
Miss Belvawney....Margaret de Mille
Miss Snevellicci....Nancie B. Marsland
Mrs. Grudden....Hilda Plowright
Mr. Snevellicci....J. P. Wilson
Mr. Fluggers....Lee Elmore
Master Crummles....Hugh Miller
Master P. Crummles....Geoffry Harwood
Scene—The Stage of the Portsmouth Theatre, 1827.

THE PLAY
GEORGE BARNWELL OR
THE LONDON MERCHANT
A Tragedy in Three Acts by Mr. George Lillo
First Played, June, 1731

Thorowgood....Mr. Vincent Crummles
George Barnwell....Master Crummles
Frederic Trueman....Master P. Crummles
Maria....Miss Ninetta Crummles
Mrs. Millwood....Mrs. Vincent Crummles
Lucy (Servant)....Miss Snevellicci
Blun (Servant)....Mr. Snittle Timberry
The Entertainment....Mr. Folair and Miss Bravassa
Uncle Barnwell....Mr. Snevellicci
Officers, Jailers....Mrs. Grudden, Miss Belvawney
Servants, Crowd, etc....Mr. Lenville and Mr. Fluggers

THE HARLEQUINADE

Clown....Mr. Lenville
Plantaloon....Master P. Crummles
Harlequin....Miss Belvawney
Columbine....Miss Ninetta Crummles
Staged by Halliwell Hobbes.

The troupe of players Nicholas Nickleby knew are followed through a performance of "George Barnwell or the London Merchant," an eighteenth century curiosity which at one time was performed by command of the London authorities as a warning to young men of a gay life's temptations.

BILLIE

(112 performances)

A musicalization of "Broadway Jones" by George M. Cohan. Staged by Edward Royce and Sam Harris, at the Erlanger's Theatre, New York, October 1, 1928.

Cast of characters—

Maid....................June O'Dea
Rankin....................Joe Ross
Bob Wallace....................Robinson Newbold
Jackson Jones....................Joseph Wagstaff
Winnie Sheldon....................Marjorie Lane
Mrs. Ambrose Gerard....................Ina Hayward
Peter Pembroke....................Carl Francis
Billie....................Polly Walker
Wilbur Cheatington....................Ernie Stanton
Sir Alfred Huntington....................Val Stanton
Harry Thompson....................David London
Higgins....................Richard Barry
Judge Spotswood....................Joseph Kennedy
Page....................Ethel Allen
Will....................Billy Bradford
Marion....................Marion Hamilton
Charles....................Charles Sabin
Sheriff....................Larry L. Wood
Grover Sheldon....................Albert Froom
Ladies of the Ensemble, Gentleman of the Ensemble
Ballet Specialty Dancers......Anita Avila, Gertrude Stanton, Marie Grimaldi, Eddee Belmont, Elvira Gomez, Ruth Love, Mildred Glasson, Martha Galston

Acts I, II and III.—At the Home of Jackson Jones and in the Business Office of the Gum Plant.

Staged by Edward Royce and Sam Forrest.

Jackson Jones, wasting time and money on Broadway, inherits his uncle's chewing gum factory and is all for selling it quickly to the gum trust until he meets Billie, secretary to the uncle. Billie inspires Jackson with song and story to remain true to his uncle's ambitions as an independent.

PLEASURE MAN

(2 performances)

A comedy drama in three acts by Mae West. Produced by Carl Reed at the Biltmore Theatre, New York, October 1, 1928.

Cast of characters—

Stanley Smith....................Stan Stanley
Rodney Terrill....................Alan Brooks
Tom Randall....................Jay Holly
Steve McAllister....................William Augustin
Dolores....................Camelia Campbell
Ted Arnold....................Edgar Barrier

Mary Ann	Elaine Ivans
The Bird of Paradise	Leo Howe
Lester Queen	Lester Sheehan
Edgar "It" Morton	Wally James
Nell Morton	Martha Vaughn
Toto	Ed Hearn
Fritz Otto	William Selig
Herman Otto	Herman Lenzen
Flo	Julie Childrey
Bobby	Margaret Bragaw
Jewel	Anna Keller
Jane	Jane Rich
Bill	Frank Leslie
Bradley	William Cavanaugh
Peaches	Charles Ordway
Chuck	Chuck Connors, II.
Joe	Fred Dickens
Mother Goddam	Harry Armand
The Cobra	Sylvan Repetti
Bunny	Gene Drew
Rene	Albert Dorando
Ray	Lew Lorraine
Billie	Jo Huddleston
Sonny	Walter MacDonald
Ripley Hetherington	James F. Ayers
Mrs. Hetherington	Augusta E. Boylston
Lizzie	Marguerite Leo
Maggie	Kate Julianne
Tillie	May Davis
Bridget	Mae Russell
Burbank, Chief of Police	Edward Roseman
Pork Chops	Herman Linsterino
Sugarfoot	Robert Cooksey
The Leader	Paul South

Rodney Terrill, actor, is careless with women. Having wronged many the brother of one seeks to incapacitate him for further activities and Terrill dies as a result of the operation. The murder occurs at a party of theatrical people, largely attended by female impersonators. (The police closed the play following the second performance.)

SUNNY DAYS

(32 performances)

A musical comedy in three acts, book and lyrics by Clifford Grey and William Cary Duncan, from the French of Hennequin and Weber. Revived by Montmartre Productions, Inc., at the Century Theatre, New York, October 1, 1928.

Cast of characters—

Victor Duval	Bob Lively
Nanine	Elyse La Deaux
Babette	Elsie Elliott
Georgette	Phœbe Wallace
Angele Larue	Ruth Lockwood
Ginette Bertin	Mildred Keats
Maurice Vane	Jack Sheehan
Leon Dorsay	Douglas Leavitt

Paul Morel....................................Gattison Jones
A Thief....................................Harry Gordon
Bergeot....................................George Clidd
Countess D'Exmore....................................Verenetta Hoots
Madame Dorsay....................................Audrey Maple
Rudolph Max....................................Billy B. Van
Butler....................................Edward Cobham

Act I.—Shop of "Victor Duval et Cie" Florist, Rue de la Paix, Paris. Acts II and III.—At Leon Dorsay's Chateau, Fontainebleau.
Dances staged by Ralph Reader.

See "Best Plays 1927-28"

POSSESSION

(47 performances)

A comedy in three acts by Edgar Selwyn. Produced by Edgar Selwyn at the Booth Theatre, New York, October 2, 1928.

Cast of characters—

Hardy....................................William Postance
George Morrow....................................George Graham
Edward Whiteman....................................Robert Montgomery
Molly Russell....................................Edna Hibbard
J. P. Hassard....................................Pierre Watkin
Mrs. Anne Whiteman....................................Margaret Lawrence
Larry Beagle....................................Robert Craig
Rachael....................................Maude Malcolm
Stanley Whiteman....................................Walter Connolly
Edythe Grange....................................Roberta Beatty
Her Butler....................................Charles Santon
Doctor Graham....................................Joseph Baird
Officer....................................Robert Long

Act I.—Living Room in the Home of Mrs. Anne Whiteman, New York City. Act II.—A Room in Edythe Grange's Apartment. Evening of the Same Day (During This Act the Curtain is Lowered for a Moment to Indicate a Lapse of Time). Act III.—The Same. Three Days Later.
Staged by Edgar Selwyn.

Stanley Whiteman, twenty-five years married to Anne, who is possessively tender of him, decides he can stand the home situation no longer and goes to live with Edythe Grange, who is more understanding of his needs and desires. Anne refuses Stanley a divorce and is eager to be revenged upon his mistress. Complications following, Stanley is wounded in Mrs. Grange's apartment and Anne moves in to nurse him. In the end she recovers her man and takes him home.

THE COMMAND PERFORMANCE

(29 performances)

A comedy in three acts by C. Stafford Dickens. Produced by Herman Shumlin, at the Klaw Theatre, New York, October 3, 1928.

Cast of characters—

Hildred Sabidoff............................William H. Barwald
Paul Masoch....................................Ivan Simpson
Ansche Milosovic...............................Zvee Scooler
Lydia Petrovic.................................Rose Keane
Yana Lodoffski.................................Maria Ziccardi
Peter Kraditch.................................Ian Keith
Count Vellenburg...............................Lee Baker
A Sergeant of Police...........................George Spelvin
Servant..George Haight
Elinor, Queen of Moldavia......................Beatrice Terry
Alexis, Prince of Moldavia.....................Ian Keith
Elizabeth, Queen of Wallachia..................Charlotte Granville
Nicolas, King of Wallachia.....................Hubert Druce
Katerina, Princess of Wallachia................Jessie Royce Landis
Blondel..Robert Clear
Hugo...Walter Soderling

Act I.—Scene 1—Stage of the Municipal Theatre, Baroc, Moldavia. 2—Room at the Royal Palace, Baroc. Act II.—The Royal Palace, Dinikar, Wallachia. Act III.—The Royal Palace, Baroc.

Staged by Clifford Brooke.

Peter Kraditch, actor, attacks a crowd of ruffians who would kidnap the leading woman of his troupe. Later he discovers that one of the ruffians was the Crown Prince. The police take Peter in charge. Later Peter is offered his freedom if he will substitute for the Crown Prince, who is dissolute, and win the hand of a neighboring princess. Peter becomes the Prince, wins the Princess and truly loves her. He is about to be deported when the Crown Prince disappears and Peter must go on substituting.

L'INVITATION AU VOYAGE

(19 performances)

A play in three acts by Jean-Jacques Bernard translated by Ernest Boyd. Produced by Civic Repertory Co., at the Civic Repertory Theatre, New York, October 4, 1928.

Cast of characters—

Olivier Mailly.................................Donald Cameron
Marie-Louise...................................Eva Le Gallienne
Gerard...Vernon Jones
M. Landreau....................................Walter Beck
Jacqueline.....................................Ria Mooney
M. Galais......................................Robert Ross

Acts I, II and III.—In the Apartment of Marie-Louise, France.

Staged by Miss Le Gallienne.

Marie-Louise thinks, when her husband's partner leaves suddenly for the Argentine, that she is in love with him. She dreams of her love and makes much of it until the partner returns. Then she discovers that she was mistaken and returns dutifully to the arms of the husband who bores her.

STRAIGHT THRU THE DOOR

(44 performances)

A mystery comedy in three acts by William Hodge. Produced by Mr. Hodge at the 49th Street Theatre, New York, October 4, 1928.

Cast of characters—

Meyers....................Jack C. Connolly
Arnold....................Abbott Adams
Bushner....................Jack Cheatham
Anna Ashland....................Jeanette Fox-Lee
Artanio....................William De Rosa
Roy Saunders....................John Edwards
Amy Thomas....................Marjorie Lytell
Eugene Thomas, Jr....................Leland Chandler
Wowser....................Arthur Donaldson
Mrs. Harriett Thomas....................Ruth Gates
Abby Thomas....................Ann Roth
Eugene Thomas....................William Hodge
John Witherspoon....................Franklyn Fox
Martin Rollins....................William Cullen
John Finley....................George Harcourt
Frederick Ottman....................Maurice Barrett
Sarah Fernhardt....................Margaret Mullen
Acts I, II and III.—Eugene Thomas' New Home, Thirty Miles from New York.
Staged by Maurice Barrett.

Eugene Thomas, actor, is building a home near New York. Harriet Thomas, his wife, is superintending it and flirting discreetly with the architect. The carpenters and masons gossip about the possibilities. One speaks lightly of Mrs. Thomas and Thomas threatens him. That day the fellow is shot straight thru the door and also the heart. Suspicion falls on Thomas, but it turns out to have been the architect who did the shooting.

FAUST

(48 performances)

A play with prologue and eighteen scenes by Goethe. Music by Wolfgang Zeller. Produced by The Theatre Guild at the Guild Theatre, New York, October 8, 1928.

Cast of characters—

Mephistopheles....................Dudley Digges
Faust....................George Gaul
Wagner....................Walter Vonnegut
Voice of the Earth Spirit....................Martin Wolfson
A Young Peasant....................Edward Hogan
An Old Peasant....................William T. Hays
A Student....................William Challee

Siebel....................Stanley G. Wood
Frosch....................Edward Hogan
Brander....................Martin Wolfson
Altmeyer....................Herbert J. Biberman
She-Ape....................Christine Putnam
He-Ape....................Eric Linden
The Witch....................Gale Sondergaard
Margaret....................Helen Chandler
Martha....................Helen Westley
Elizabeth....................Anna Kostant
Valentine....................Douglas Montgomery
Voice of the Ignis Fatuus....................Rita Vale
Lilith....................Rita Vale
Voices......Douglas Montgomery, Edward Hogan, Martin Wolfson, Rita Vale, Herbert J. Biberman, Maurice Cass
Peasants, Burghers, Witches, Wizards, Singers, Dancers, etc.—Maxine Arnolde, Adelaide George, Marcella Henry, Helen Ann Hughes, Nettie Kittridge, Elza Moses, Helen Steers, Frances Stock, Kathleen Sternberg, Ruth Seward, Mary Ellen Vorse, Kitty Wilson, Anatole Bendukov, Bernard F. Day, George W. Ballard, Leonard Perry, Maurice Soble, Alan Wallace.

Prologue—In Heaven. Scene 2—Faust's Study. 3—Outside the City Gate. 4 and 5—Faust's Study. 6—Auerbach's Cellar. 7—Witch's Kitchen. 8—Outside the Church. 9—Margaret's Chamber. 10—A Street. 11—Room in Martha's House. 12—Martha's Garden. 13—A Forest Glade. 14—Martha's Garden. 15—By the Well. 16—Inside the Church. 17—On the Brocken. 18—A Prison.

Staged by Friederich Holl.

A straightforward translation beginning with a prologue in Heaven with Mephistopheles in boastful controversy with the voice of God. Returning to the earth in search of Dr. Faustus Mephisto makes the contact and the contract, Faustus is transformed, Margaret is ruined and the pure souls are saved in prison.

PARIS

(195 performances)

A musicomedy in three acts by Martin Brown, songs by Cole Porter and E. Ray Goetz. Produced by Gilbert Miller in association with Mr. Goetz, at the Music Box Theatre, New York, October 8, 1928.

Cast of characters—

Andrew Sabot....................Eric Kalkhurst
Harriet....................Florence Edney
Valet....................Reed Hamilton
Brenda Kaley....................Elizabeth Chester
Cora Sabot....................Louise Closser Hale
Guy Pennel....................Arthur Margetson
Vivienne Rolland....................Irene Bordoni
Marcel Prince....................Theodore St. John

Acts I, II and III.—Vivienne Rolland's Hotel.

Staged by W. H. Gilmore.

Vivienne Rolland, actress, is much in love with Andrew Sabot of the New England Sabots, and Cora Sabot, Andrew's aunt, is terribly worried. But Vivienne manages to sing her way into the family.

COURAGE

(280 performances)

A comedy in three acts by Tom Barry. Produced by Lew Cantor at the Ritz Theatre, New York, October 8, 1928.

Cast of characters—

Mary Colebrook....................................Janet Beecher

HER CHILDREN

Reginald...Paul Jones
Muriel...Dulcie Cooper
Gwendolyn...Gertrude Durkin
Vincent..Teddy Jones
Gladys...Charlotte Henry
Richard..Edwin Phillips
Bill...Junior Durkin

THERE COME TO THE HOUSE

Lynn Willard...Gene Gowing
Miss Caroline Colebrook..........................Helen Strickland
Mr. Rudlin...Robert Conness

Prologue—Studio of a Fashionable Boston Photographer. Acts I, II and III.—In the Living Room of an Old Colonial Mansion in Cambridge, Mass.

Staged by Priestly Morrison.

Mary Colebrook, widow and the mother of seven children, brings her brood east from Iowa for the cultural advantages and also to renew financial contact with the Colebrook family. Miss Caroline Colebrook, representing the family, will have nothing to do with Mary because she happens to know that Bill, the seventh child, is not a Colebrook. Miss Caroline also wins the six other children away from their mother. But a flint-souled neighbor loves young Bill and leaves him half a million. Mary takes Bill and goes back west to marry his father.

JUST A MINUTE

(80 performances)

A musical play by H. C. Greene, lyrics by Walter O'Keefe, music by Harry Archer. Produced by Phil Morris and H. C. Greene at the Ambassador Theatre, New York, October 8, 1928.

Cast of characters—

Count Berni Vici and his Symphonic Girls....	(In the Orchestra Pit)
Mandy	Billie Yarbo
Mrs. Callahan	Madeline Grey
Helen	Gypsy Byrne
Carlson	Harry Holbrook
Patricia Callahan	Helen Patterson
Mr. O'Brien	Tommy Havel
Miss Reynolds	Helen Lockhart
Louis Schultz	Sam Sidman
Joe Winston	Arthur Havel
Charlie Winston	Morton Havel
Tom } The Three Recorders / Nifty Three	Dale Jones
May } The Three Recorders / Nifty Three	Helen Lockhart
Dick } The Three Recorders / Nifty Three	Harold Madsen
Jerry Conklin	John Hundley
Policeman	Dave Bender
Bev Johnson	Virginia Smith
Kay Bolton	Brenda Bond
Spike	George Leonard
Kid Gans	Frankie Stevens
Battling Brown	Al Mario
Eddie Frisco	Eddie Frisco
Kid Williams	Arthur Havel
Announcer	Dave Bender
Referee	Flavio Theodore
Stage Director	Burt Harger
Pickings Club Orchestra	Peek-a-Boo Jimmie and His Band
Soubrette	Maude Russell
Waiter	Walter Brogsdale
Specialty Dancers	Walker and Thompson

16 Russell Markert Girls—Ebony Steppers
Helen Howell, Messrs. Harger and Theodore

The Action of the Play Occurs in New York City.
Staged by H. C. Greene.

Vaudeville specialties strung on a thread of story.

UPS-A DAISY

(64 performances)

A musical comedy in two acts, books and lyrics by Clifford Grey and Robert A. Simon, music by Lewis E. Gensler. Produced by Lewis E. Gensler at the Shubert Theatre, New York, October 8, 1928.

Cast of characters—

Jimmy Ridgeway	Russ Brown
Madge Mallory	Joan Carter Waddell
Ethel Billings	Luella Gear
"Pinky" Parks	Buster West
Lurline	Nell Kelly
Montmorency Billings	William Kent
Fletcher	John West
Polly Mallory	Marie Saxon
Roy Lindbrooke	Roy Royston
Oskar	Joseph Caits
Sepp	Louis Caits
Ambrose Wattle	George Paunceforte
Screeves	Bob Hope

Scrams....................Alan Fox
Marigold....................Georgia Moore
Irene....................Mildred Tolle
Mary....................Jocelyn Lyle
Gertrude....................Rita Crane
Freddie....................Fred Maye
Walter....................Billy Neely
A Page....................Alan Crane
At the Pianos....................Muriel Pollock, Constance Mering

Act I.—Drawing Room at Billings' Home in Surrey. Act II.—Scene 1—An Inn in the Alps. 2—A Mountain Road. 3—Garden of the Billings Home in Surrey.

Staged by Edgar MacGregor and Earl Lindsay.

Montmorency Billings pretends to be the author of a book on mountain climbing. His proud wife insists that he take the cast somewhere in the Alps and climb one. The real author of the book, in love with Polly, the Billings' niece, follows after and there are comic complications.

THE LIGHT OF ASIA

(23 performances)

A play in a prologue and four acts by Georgina Jones Walton. Produced by Walter Hampden at Hampden's Theatre, New York, October 9, 1928.

Cast of characters—

Asita....................William Sauter
King of the Sakyas....................Eugene Powers
Shivamangala....................C. Norman Hammond
Kondanna....................Dallas Anderson
Another Astrologer....................Gordon Hart
Visvamitra....................Cecil Yapp
Ormuzd....................Le Roi Operti
Channa....................Ernest Rowan
A Page....................Omar Le Gant
Siddartha, Prince of the Sakyas....................Walter Hampden
Ananda....................Charles Quigley
King of Koli....................Gage Bennett
Devadatta, Prince of Koli....................Louis Polan
Merchants........Joseph Milton, Robert C. Schnitzer, George Cotton
Nobles....................Forrest Gains, Norbert Cameron
An Attendant....................William Thornton
An Old Leper....................S. Thomas Gomez
A Hermit....................Jan Lindermann
Alara....................Edwin Cushman
Mohanna....................William Sauter
Vappa....................Gordon Hart
Bhadya....................Franklin Salisbury
Assaji....................S. Thomas Gomez
Rahula....................Freddie Stange
A Monk....................Joseph Milton
Soldiers....................Francis Dears, Philip C. Jones
A Citizen....................Edwin Ross, Jr.
A Hillman....................M. D'Arcy
Water Bearers....................Stephen Irving, Richard Lawrence
Queen Maya....................Mabel Moore
Prajapati....................Judith Lowry

Yashodara....................................Ingeborg Torrup
Chitra.......................................Eleanor Mish
Gunga..Beatrice Maude
Draupadi.....................................Caroline Meade
Radha..Evelyn Goodrich
Kisogatami...................................Anna Lubow
Nautch Girls..............Sri Ragini, Anne Mitchell, Isabel S. Hill
Harriet Ingersol
Sujata.......................................Mabel Moore
Purna..Evelyn Goodrich
An Outcaste Woman............................Kate Mayhew

The Action Takes Place in Northern India in the 6th Century B.C.

Staged by Mr. Hampden, Dances by Ruth St. Denis.

A review of the life of Prince Siddartha of the Sakyas which begins with his birth, jumps to his twentieth year when his first view of disease and death sent him into the forests for meditation, follows him through his experience with the ascetics and his spiritual triumph over the temptations of the flesh and brings him as the Buddha back to the world.

* LITTLE ACCIDENT

(289 performances)

An American comedy in three acts by Floyd Dell and Thomas Mitchell. Produced by Crosby Gaige at the Morosco Theatre, New York, October 9, 1928.

Cast of characters—

Mrs. Overbeck.................................Susanne Jackson
Doris Overbeck................................Geraldine Wall
Katie...Madelaine Barr
J. J. Overbeck................................Malcolm Williams
Norman Overbeck...............................Thomas Mitchell
Gilbert Rand..................................Fleming Ward
Lucinda Overbeck..............................Katherine Carrington
Janet Parke...................................Florence Brinton
Emily Crane...................................Helen Myrnes
Madge Ferris..................................Elvia Enders
Rev. Doctor Gifford...........................Harry Forsman
Miss Clark....................................Olga Hanson
Hicks...John Butler
Rudolpho Amendelaro...........................Adrian Rosley
Miss Hemingway................................Elizabeth Bruce
Doctor Zernecke...............................Desmond Kelley
Isabel Drury..................................Katherine Alexander
Monica Case...................................Patricia Barcley
Mrs. Case.....................................Clare Woodbury

Act I.—Dining Room in the Overbeck Home in Vickley, Ill.
Act II.—Reception Room in the Ellen Harris Hospital, Chicago.
Act III.—Mrs. Case's Boarding House, Chicago.

Staged by Joseph Graham and Arthur Hurley.

Norman Overbeck discovers just as he is about to marry Madge Ferris that he is the father of Isabel Drury's baby. Isabel is not one to make demands upon him. She is too greatly interested in her career. She plans to give the child up for adoption. Norman objects and kidnaps the infant. At his boarding house the landlady's daughter wants to marry him. So does Madge. But he escapes them and finally makes it up with Isabel.

*HOLD EVERYTHING

(290 performances)

A musical comedy in two acts, book by B. G. DeSylva and John McGowan, songs by Brown, DeSylva and Henderson. Produced by Alex A. Aarons and Vinton Freedley at the Broadhurst Theatre, New York, October 10, 1928.

Cast of characters—

Marty	Buddy Harak
Mack	Harry Locke
"Murf" Levy	Harry Shannon
"Pop" O'Keefe	Edmund Elton
Norine Lloyd	Betty Compton
Betty Dunn	Alice Boulden
Gink Schiner	Bert Lahr
Sue Burke	Ona Munson
"Toots" Breen	Nina Olivette
"Sonny Jim" Brooks	Jack Whiting
Dan Larkin	Frank Allworth
"Nosey" Bartlett	Victor Moore
Bob Morgan	Robert O'Brien
"The Kicker"	Phil Sheridan
Gladys Martin	Anna Locke

Act I.—Scene 1—"Pop" O'Keefe's Training Camp, Long Island.
Act II.—Hotel Wood and Madison Square Garden, New York.
Dances staged by Jack Haskell and Sam Rose.

Sonny Jim Brooks, welterweight champion, is to box for the Milk Fund. Sue Burke, with whom he has been singing duets ever since they were children, thinks he should fight hard and his trainer thinks he should box lightly and not risk his title. When Sue has words with Sonny's opponent and he slaps her, she tells Sonny and at the fight Sonny wins in a punch.

THREE CHEERS

(210 performances)

A musical entertainment in two acts, book by Anne Caldwell and R. H. Burnside, lyrics by Anne Caldwell, music by Raymond Hubbell. Produced by Charles Dillingham at the Globe Theatre, New York, October 15, 1928.

Cast of characters—

George Mullins	Andrew Tombes
Harry Vance	Alan Edwards
Spike	Edward Allan
Prince Josef	William Valentine
The Duke	Oscar Ragland
Malotte	John Lambert
The Mayor	William Torpey
Daphne De Lorne	Janet Velie
Queen Ysobel	Maude Eburne
Bobbie Bird	Patsy Kelly
Audrey Nugent	Evangeline Raleigh
Floria Farleigh	Thea Dore
Ermyntrude	Cynthia Foley
Letty	Florine Phelps
Betty	Irene Phelps
Zazia	Phyllis Rae
Mike	Kathryn Hereford
Wellington Westland	Ralph Thomson
Cameraman	Joseph Shrode
Inn Keeper	William Kerschell
Captain Meurice	James Murray
Princess Sylvia	Dorothy Stone
King Pompanola	Will Rogers

Act I.—In and around the Palace of Itza. Act II.—In Hollywood.
Staged by R. H. Burnside, Dances by Dave Bennett.

A moving picture company invades the territory of Itza hoping to get some shots of castles, kings and things. Princess Sylvia falls in love with Harry Vance, the director, which slows matters up a little but not much.

THE CHERRY ORCHARD

(63 performances)

A play in four acts by Anton Tchekov, translated by Constance Garnett. Produced by Civic Repertory Theatre, Inc., at the Civic Repertory Theatre, New York, October 15, 1928.

Cast of characters—

Lopahin (Yermolay Alexeyevitch)	Donald Cameron
Dunyasha	Beatrice De Neergaard
Epihodov (Semyon Pantaleyevitch)	John Eldredge
Firs	Sayre Crawley
Madame Ranevsky (Lyubov Andreyevna)	Alla Nazimova
Anya	Josephine Hutchinson
Varya	Eva Le Gallienne
Charlotta Ivanovna	Leona Roberts
Gaev (Leonid Andreyevitch)	Paul Leyssac
Semyonov-Pishtchik	Walter Beck
Yasha	J. Edward Bromberg
Trofimov (Pyotr Sergeyevitch)	Harold Moulton
A Tramp	Robert Ross
The Station Master	Leslie Cooley
A Post-Office Clerk	Herbert Shapiro

Acts I, II, III and IV.—On the Estate of Madame Ranevsky.
Staged by Miss Le Gallienne.

The Ranevskys, improvident Russian aristocrats, drift helplessly through a changing social order. Finally everything is lost. Even the old cherry orchard which had been the Ranevsky's home for generations, goes under the auctioneer's hammer and is sold for building lots to one whose ancestors had been slaves to the Ranevsky line.

THE COMMON SIN

(24 performances)

A play in three acts by Willard Mack. Produced by Mr. Mack at the Forrest Theatre, New York, October 15, 1928.

Cast of characters—

Jim Steele	Thurston Hall
Helen Steele	Millicent Hanley
Jans	Kenneth Lawton
"Bobo" Aster	Lee Patrick
Fleming	Frank Joyner
Henry Banloza	Frederic Worlock
George Graham	Harold Elliott
Nellie Baxter	Regina Brown
Donlin	Frank Shannon
Foy	Edward Racey
McCracken	Percival Lennon
Marie	Justine Smith

Act I.—Scene 1—The Home of Jim Steele, New York. 2—The Apartment of Henry Banloza. Act II.—Nellie Baxter's Flat. Act III.—Bobo's Apartment.
Staged by Mr. Mack.

Jim Steele's wife refuses to help him in a crisis. Jim Steele's former mistress, Bobo Aster, offers to give him everything she has accumulated. Jim Steele is found dead after Bobo's visit and the police take her in. Bobo a few months later pretends to get drunk and tricks Jim Steele's wife into a confession that it was she who did for Jim.

THE K GUY

(8 performances)

A comedy in three acts by Walter De Leon and Alethea Luce. Produced by Irving and Charles Yates at the Biltmore Theatre, October 15, 1928.

Cast of characters—

Reggie Manville	George Nolan
Mrs. Stevens	Jessamine Newcombe
Tom Kush	Arthur Jarrett

Sadie Kelly.....................................Jeanne Greene
Jessie May.......................................Myrtle Miller
Jimmy Carrol.....................................Harry Green
Frank Toney......................................Ralph Murphy
Jane Meadow...................................Constance McKay
The Kid...Alan Ward
Priscilla Golden...............................Faye Armstrong
Mr. Sammelberg.................................John H. Dillson
Prince Mohammed Ali..........................Francis Compton
Big Bill Wysell....................................Edward Keane
Tiny..A. Ryder Keane
Curley...Frank McDonald
Acts I, II and III.—Studio Lunchroom in the Idol Film Co., Hollywood, California.
Staged by Melville Burke.

OLYMPIA

(39 performances)

A comedy in three acts by Ferenc Molnar, English text by Sidney Howard. Produced by Gilbert Miller at the Empire Theatre, New York, October 16, 1928.

Cast of characters—

Countess Lina.................................Cora Witherspoon
Count Albert......................................Grant Stewart
Princess Eugenie Plata-Ettingen................Laura Hope Crews
Olympia, Princess Orsolini.........................Fay Compton
Captain Kovacs.......................................Ian Hunter
Colonel Krehl...Richie Ling
Prince Plata-Ettingen..............................Arnold Korff
Acts I, II and III.—In a Fashionable Austrian Watering Place.
Staged by Gilbert Miller.

The Princess Orsolini, in love with Captain Kovacs, a handsome hussar, is bidden by her mother to send the fellow away and do it so brutally that he never will recover from the wound to his pride. The princess bids the captain go back to the peasantry from which he sprung and never dare raise his eyes to her again. Later Kovacs is reported by the police to be a famous criminal. Knowing she has interceded for him with the King, and fearing scandal, both the Princess and her mother seek to buy the hussar's silence. His price is the Princess's submission. Being thus revenged Kovacs admits the report of his criminality was a trick of his to further his vengeance.

MR. MONEYPENNY

(61 performances)

A verbal cartoon in three acts by Channing Pollock. Produced at the Liberty Theatre, New York, October 17, 1928.

Cast of characters—

IN ACT I.

John Jones.......................................Donald Meek
"Junior" Jones.......................................Evan Heflin
Murphy.......................................Charles Slattery
Mr. Moneypenny.......................................Hale Hamilton
Green, the Guard.......................................Lyons Wickland
Black.......................................Edward De Tisne
White.......................................Stanley Zipser
Brown.......................................Donald Campbell
Gray.......................................Robert Vivian
Ivy.......................................Betty Brenska
Violet.......................................Lee Smith
Rose.......................................Helen Spring
Iris.......................................Marion Morehouse
Pansy.......................................Audrey Baird
Harold.......................................Douglas R. Carter
Pat.......................................Frank Sylvester
Mike.......................................Hamilton Mott
Glory.......................................Catherine Dale Owen
Her Maid.......................................Edith Babson
Her Chauffeur.......................................Grover Burgess
David Jones.......................................Albert Hayes

IN ACT II.

Carrie Jones.......................................Margaret Wycherly
Molly Jones.......................................Ruth Nugent
Michael Morn, "The Professor".......................................John D. Seymour
Bee.......................................Hamilton Mott
See.......................................Stanley Zipser
Miss Dee.......................................Lee Smith
Eph.......................................Douglas R. Carter
Queue.......................................James Coyle
The Count.......................................Edward De Tisne
Mr. Peel.......................................James Coyle
Mr. Smudge.......................................Robert Vivian
Mr. Rich.......................................Charles Slattery
Mr. De Lays.......................................Frank Sylvester
Dr. Pugh.......................................Donald Campbell
Miss Goof.......................................Audrey Baird
Mrs. Chaser.......................................Helen Spring
Three More of the Dull Rich.......................................Misses Babson, Mackay and Cameron
Another Three.......................................Misses Ecklund, Griffith and Knapp
The Ballad-Singer.......................................Stanley Zipser
The Hotsy-Totsy Girl.......................................Lee Smith
The Mistress of Ceremonies.......................................Betty Brenska
The Dead Woman.......................................Marion Morehouse
Her Friend.......................................Clara Everett
Her Escort.......................................George Parker
A Drunken Man.......................................Edward De Tisne
A Gigolo.......................................Douglas R. Carter

IN ACT III.

Mr. Light.......................................Lyons Wickland
Mr. Smart.......................................Frank Sylvester
Mr. Wise.......................................Edward De Tisne
Miss Shine.......................................Lee Smith
The End.......................................Charles Slattery

Act I.—Business. Act II.—Pleasure. Act III.—Happiness.
Staged by Richard Boleslavsky.

John Jones, twenty years a clerk in a bank vault, is visited by Mr. Moneypenny and promised untold wealth if he will sell himself to his benefactor. Jones agrees, is transported into scenes of wild extravagance, given everything money can buy, but finds peace of mind is not included. He returns happily in the end to his suburban home and his suburban family.

JEALOUSY

(136 performances)

A play in three acts by Eugene Walter, based on the French of Louis Verneuil. Produced by A. H. Woods at the Maxine Elliott Theatre, New York, October 22, 1928.

Cast of characters—

Maurice....................John Halliday
Valerie....................Fay Bainter
Acts I, II and III.—A Studio in Paris.
Staged by Guthrie McClintic.

Maurice and Valerie, lovers for some time, marry and plan to settle down in Valerie's apartment. Gradually Maurice's jealousy of Valerie's guardian is aroused and he ends by strangling that old man after he has tricked Valerie into a confession that guardy is indeed a beast. Maurice goes to prison, Valerie is desolate, but hopeful.

THE GREY FOX

(88 performances)

A play in three acts by Lemist Esler. Produced by William A. Brady, Jr., and Dwight Deere Wiman at the Playhouse, New York, October 22, 1928.

Cast of characters—

Biagio....................Andrew Lytle
Francesco Vettori....................J. M. Kerrigan
Arturo....................Robert Buckner
Niccolo Machiavelli....................Henry Hull
Jeffro....................Warren Hymer
Caterina Sforza....................Chrystal Herne
Ottaviano....................Martin Berkeley
Da Casale....................Reynolds Evans
Sergeant of the Guard....................George Tobias
First Soldier....................Mike Flanagan
Second Soldier....................Lewis Milne
Pretty Pietro....................Denis Gurney
The Captain Savelli....................Alfred Webster
Don Michelotto....................Nat Pendleton
Oliverotto Da Ferma....................Norman St. Clair Hales

Cesare Borgia	Edward Arnold
A Blond Girl	Lavita Miller
A Nun	Mallory Davis

The Borgia's Women, Assassins, Noblemen, Soldiers

Act I.—Scene 1—An Office of the Second Chancery of Florence. 2—A Room in the Citadel of Forli. 3—Caterina Sforza's Bedroom. Act II.—A Room in the Gravina Palace, Senigalia. Act III.—Scene 1—Machiavelli's Tent in the Florentine Camp Before Pisa. 2—A Room in the Convent of Annalena, Florence. 3—A Room in Machiavelli's House, San Casciano.

Staged by William A. Brady, Jr., and Lemist Esler.

Niccolo Machiavelli, making progress as a young man, meets and is worsted diplomatically by the beautiful Caterina Sforza, giving him cause to grow in craft and cunning until after his rise to power and the establishment of his republic of Florence. His disintegration in character and manhood is gradual but complete.

EXCEEDING SMALL

(72 performances)

A play in three acts by Caroline Francke. Produced by The Actors' Theatre, Inc., at the Comedy Theatre, New York, October 22, 1928.

Cast of characters—

Platz	Eddie Garvie
A Man	Arthur Leonard
Another Man	Robert Hudson
Min	Kathleen Lowry
Bob	Kenneth Dana
Gert	Ruth Easton
Ed	Eric Dressler
A Blonde	Nan Converse
Her Boy Friend	Frank Frayne
A Young Man	Jack Daniels
His Girl Friend	Gertrude Winborne
Bee	Maybelle Beadling
Harry	Walter Speakman
Lou	Gordon McRae
A Girl	Mary Bradbury
Another Girl	Dorothee Nolan
Mrs. Marone	Caroline Morrison
A Doctor	Halliam Bosworth

Act I.—A Chinese Restaurant and Dance Hall. Acts II and III.—Gert's Room.

Staged by Rachel Crothers.

Ed, burning with love for Gert, induces her finally to marry him and try living on $20 a week. The experiment is a failure and when Ed learns that he has a weak heart and cannot live long he, fearful about leaving Gert behind, induces her to die with him. They shut the windows and turn on the gas.

ANIMAL CRACKERS

(191 performances)

A musical comedy in two acts, book by George S. Kaufman and Morrie Ryskind; lyrics and music by Bert Kalmar and Harry Ruby. Produced by Sam H. Harris at the 44th Street Theatre, New York, October 23, 1928.

Cast of characters—

Hives.....Robert Greig
Mrs. Rittenhouse.....Margaret Dumont
M. Doucet.....Arthur Lipson
Arabella Rittenhouse.....Alice Wood
Mrs. Whitehead.....Margaret Irving
Grace Carpenter.....Bobbie Perkins
Wally Winston.....Bert Mathews
John Parker.....Milton Watson
Roscoe W. Chandler.....Louis Sorin
Mary Stewart.....Bernice Ackerman
Jamison.....Zeppo Marx
Captain Spalding.....Groucho Marx
Emanuel Ravelli.....Chico Marx
The Professor.....Harpo Marx

Show Girls; Dancing Girls; The Sixteen Markert Dancers; Gentlemen.

Act I.—Scene 1—The Long Island Home of Mrs. Rittenhouse. 2—The Grounds. 3—The Drawing Room. Act II.—Scene 1—The Breakfast Room. 2—The Grounds. 3—The Garden.

The Marx brothers pose as celebrities and are the guests of Mrs. Rittenhouse, the great celebrity entertainer of Long Island. They manage to rob the guests comically and steal a swell painting.

GODS OF THE LIGHTNING

(29 performances)

A play in three acts by Maxwell Anderson and Harold Hickerson. Produced by Hamilton MacFadden and Kellogg Gary at the Little Theatre, New York, October 24, 1928.

Cast of characters—

Suvorin.....Leo Bulgakov
Pete.....Arthur Pederson
Heine.....Jules Artfield
Rosalie.....Sylvia Sidney
Ward.....Barton MacLane
Macready.....Charles Bickford
Andy.....Thomas Kelly
Ike.....Sam Silverbush
Milkin.....Ian Wolfe
Sowerby.....Sam Coit

Spiker....Morris Ankrum
Bauer....Jules Ferrar
Capraro....Horace Braham
Salvation Lassie....Molly Ricardel
Jerusalem Slim....Moss Fleisig
Police Sergeant....Lloyd Sabine
Policeman....Benjamin Fessenden
Salter....Robert Brister
Haslet....Willard Dashiell
Judge Vail....Douglas Wood
Assistant to District Attorney....Del Cleveland
Mrs. Lubin....Eva Condon
Bartlett....Harry Bliven
Gluckstein....John R. Hamilton
Lubin....Maynard Burgess
Clerk of the Court....Edward Cutler
Sheriff Henry....Henry Engel

Acts I and III.—Lyceum Restaurant. Act II.—Scene 1—District Attorney's Office. 2—Court Room of the Supreme Court.

Staged by Hamilton MacFadden.

Macready and Capraro, the former a fiery leader of the strikers in a milltown walkout, the latter a passive but fervent anarchist, are arrested for the murder of a payroll messenger. Their trial is framed against them and they are sent finally to their electrocution while their comrades look sorrowfully at the bulletins announcing their passing.

SUN-UP

(101 performances)

A play in three acts by Lulu Vollmer. Revived by Lucille La Verne at the Lucille La Verne Theatre, New York, October 22, 1928.

Cast of characters—

Widow Cagel....Lucille LaVerne
Pap Todd....Owen Meech
Emmy....Anne Elstner
Bud....Walter Scott
Sheriff Weeks....G. O. Taylor
Rufe Cagel....Franklin H. Allen
Preacher....Charles MacDonald
The Stranger....Bernard Craven
Bob....James Lee

Act I.—Interior Widow Cagel's Cabin. Act II.—Same as Act I. Act III.—Same as Act I.—Scene 1—Midnight, February. 2—A Few Hours Later.

Staged by Miss LaVerne.

The Widow Cagel is embittered when her son is drafted in the war and openly rebellious when he is killed. She thinks to take reprisal by shooting the son of one of her enemies, but hears the voice of her dead boy pleading with her to embrace the doctrine of love and expel hate from her heart. See "Best Plays 1922-23."

GIRL TROUBLE

(24 performances)

A play in three acts by Barry Conners. Produced by Richard Herndon at the Belmont Theatre, New York, October 25, 1928.

Cast of characters—

Mrs. James Russell Lockhart, Sr.	Lucia Moore
Miss Georgia Robertson	Virginia Howell
Chauffeur	Charles Peterson
A Waiter	Richard N. Gregg
Sutton	Edward Broadley
Bill Carson	Jack MacBryde
Jimmy Lockhart	Allan Dinehart
Dr. Coleman	Wallace Erskine
Professor Erricson	Boyd Davis
Angela Cadwell	Sara Haden
Evelyn Waldron	Dorothy Hall
Cissy Willard	Georgia Lee Hall

Acts I, II and III.—Apartment of Mrs. Lockhart, Sr. Downtown Apartment of Jimmy Lockhart.
Staged by Allan Dinehart.

Jimmy Lockhart, at 17, eloped with a carnival girl, Evelyn Waldron, aged 15. After a three-day honeymoon Mrs. Lockhart had the marriage annulled. Thereafter mother watched Jimmy as closely as possible, but he was usually in some sort of girl trouble. Finally, to save him from a charmer who is about to take him to Havana, Mrs. Lockhart agrees to the remarriage of Jimmy and Evelyn.

THE UNKNOWN WARRIOR

(8 performances)

Cecil Lewis's translation of Paul Raynal's play, "Le Tombeau Sous l'Arc de Triomphe," in three acts. Produced by Charles Hopkins at the Charles Hopkins Theatre, New York, October 29, 1928.

Cast of characters—

A French Soldier	Lester Vail
An Elderly Man	William Morris
Aude, Who Is 20	Beatrix Thomson

The Scenes of the Three Acts Are in Different Rooms of a House in the Country, a Day's Journey from Paris.
Staged by Charles Hopkins.

A French soldier, on limited leave, comes to visit his father and Aude, his sweetheart. He plans to consummate his marriage to Aude and return to the front for a volunteer duty that promises certain death. Aude gives herself to him rather than waste any of the hours of his leave in civil and church ceremonies. She is forced to confess, however, that she has begun to doubt her love. The soldier, disillusioned, embittered by the loathsome business of war, goes back to the line voicing youth's protest against old men who make wars for young men to fight and resenting the gradual detachment of the women's interest in the men at the front.

CRASHING THROUGH

(40 performances)

A play in three acts by Saxon Kling. Produced by Oliver D. Bailey at the Republic Theatre, New York, October 29, 1928.

Cast of characters—

Phillpots..........Alf Helton
Jones..........G. Lester Paul
Consuelo..........Rose Hobart
The Dowager Mrs. Poole..........Henrietta Crosman
Martha..........Marie Haynes
Richard Jefferson..........Robert Harrigan
Christopher Manson..........Gavin Gordon
Another Steel Worker..........Walter W. Shuttleworth
Peter Poole..........Frederick Truesdell
Terese..........Eleanor Woodruff
Adre Da Silva..........Alberto Carillo
Mrs. Harvey Robbins..........Judith Vosselli
The Bishop Frost..........Albert Bruning

Acts I, II and III.—In the Old New York Home of the Dowager Mrs. Poole.

Produced by Oliver D. Bailey.

Consuelo Poole, tired daughter of a long line of Pooles, sees her fate come crashing through the Poole skylight. He is a handsome young riveter working on a near-by building. Immediately Consuelo and the riveter have dreams of reorganizing their section of society, accept each other in companionate marriage and later boast openly of their expected offspring. The proud Pooles rush to the rescue of the family name and insist that Consuelo shall marry her steel man.

YOUNG LOVE

(87 performances)

A comedy in three acts by Samson Raphaelson. Produced by Kenneth MacGowan and Sidney Ross at the Masque Theatre, October 30, 1928.

Cast of characters—

Fay Hilary....................................Dorothy Gish
David Hallowell....................................Tom Douglas
Peter Bird....................................James Rennie
Nancy Bird....................................Catherine Willard

Act I.—A Veranda on the Birds' Long Island Home. Acts II and III.—Peter Bird's Studio, New York.

Staged by George Cukor.

Fay Hilary, engaged to marry David Hallowell, begins to fear for the future of their love if they should find themselves unhappily mated. She proposes an affair as a test of their affection. Following this experiment Fay is still doubtful and suggests further research. Let them experiment with two of their friends, the Peter Birds, who live superficially and are proud of it. Fay and Peter have their adventure, but David rebels. Fay is glad finally to accept him on the usual conventional terms of matrimony.

AMERICANA

(12 performances)

A revue in two parts, book by J. P. McEvoy, music by Roger Wolfe Kahn, lyrics by J. P. McEvoy and Irving Cæsar. Produced by J. P. McEvoy at the Lew Fields' Theatre, New York, October 30, 1928.

Principals engaged—

Douglas Burley
Joe Donahue
Rosamund Johnson
George Stamper
Thomas Burton
John Hamilton
Geo. Tapps
Roger Kahn Orchestra
Batchelor Octette
Stella Seager
Frances Gershwin
Mary Stauber
Wanda Valle
Doris Carson
Olive McClure
Williams Sisters
Harlem Dancers
Baby Banks

Staged by J. P. McEvoy.

HELLO YOURSELF

(87 performances)

A musical comedy in two acts, book by Walter DeLeon, lyrics by Leo Robin. Produced by George Choos at the Casino Theatre, New York, October 30, 1928.

Cast of characters—

"Speed" Warren....................................Blaine Cordner
Polly....................................Evelyn Nair

Nell....................Betty Reddick
"Scotty"....................."Scotty" Bates
Sue Swift....................Dorothy Lee
Isabel Manning....................Peggy Hoover
Professor Sutton....................William Robertson
Chet....................Joseph Fay
Bobby Short....................Al Sexton
Mrs. MacLauren....................Lucy Monroe
Kate Stevens....................Edythe Maye
"Big" Bertha....................Helen Goodhue
Cicero....................George Haggerty
"Tub" Washburn....................Al Nord
Fred....................Fred Waring
Dale Hartley....................Ruth Sennott
Duke....................Walter Reddick
Nimble Westleyans—Jimmy Ray, The Reddicks

Acts I and II.—Gymnasium, Library and Grounds of Westley University.

Staged by Clarke Silvernail.

THE FINAL BALANCE

(28 performances)

A tragi-comedy in four acts by David Pinski. Produced by Provincetown Players at the Provincetown Playhouse, New York, October 30, 1928.

Cast of characters—

A Laborer....................Lionel J. Stander
The Merchant's Wife....................Mary Michael
The Merchant....................E. J. Ballantine
The Roomer....................Berne Lenrow
The Roomer's Wife....................Emily Graham
The Moneylender....................William Franklin
First Agent....................Edward Gruber
Second Agent....................Lee Winter
Third Agent....................George F. Shoemaker
Fourth Agent....................Samuel S. Bonnell
The Minister....................Samuel S. Bonnell
The Mayor....................Warren Winslow
The Cousin....................Virginia Dale
The Water-Carrier....................Alfred D. Brown
People of the town.................... { Jean Kritzer, Albert Angell, Nina Melville, Genevieve Vevey }

Acts I, II, III and IV.—The Merchant's House.
Staged by Theodore Viehman.

A baker dreams that this year's flour will turn people mad and that last year's flour will cure them. He corners the market on the old flour, sets the whole town mad with the new flour and then seeks to win his neighbor's wife by becoming powerful and rich. His love spurned, he gives the woman he loves the last bit of the bread that cures that she may cure her husband. Then he hangs himself.

THESE FEW ASHES

(39 performances)

A comedy in three acts by Leonard Ide. Produced by Shaw-Nathan Productions, Inc., at the Booth Theatre, New York, October 30, 1928.

Cast of characters—

Mme. de Seguin...Ellis Baker
Elsa von Glahn...................................Henrietta Goodwin
Oki...Goo Chong
Edith Major.......................................Natalie Schafer
Olga Bukarov..Leni Stengel
John Whitney..Wallis Clark
Kenneth Vail..Hugh Sinclair
Marcel Bonnard....................................Georges Romain
Pierre de Seguin......................................Ralph J. Locke
Victor Duprees.......................................James Meighan

Prologue and Acts I, II and III.—Kenneth Vail's Apartment in St. Moritz, Switzerland.

Staged by Clifford Brooke.

Kenneth Vail's love conquests become so easy they lose charm. He determines to step out of the picture, announces his demise, and leaves a jar of ashes with his valet to be claimed by the one of four women who can prove her best right to them. The women come, view the ashes and, each finding that she was but one of four, backs out. Vail comes out of hiding to recapture the last of them, who was the one he loved best all the time.

REVOLT

(30 performances)

A play in three acts by Harry Wagstaff Gribble. Produced by William Powell at the Vanderbilt Theatre, New York, October 31, 1928.

Cast of characters—

Faith..Charlotte Denniston
Hope..Elizabeth Allen
Charity...Eunice Stoddard
The Rev. Barnabas Ford............................Hugh Buckler
Mrs. Emily Pasteel................................Helene Lackaye
Edna..Eloise Keeler
Paul..Ackland Powell
Sol Rosenbloom.......................................Eliott Rothe
Dr. Salter...A. G. Andrews
The Rev. John Hammond..........................Paul Guilfoyle

Acts I, II and III.—In the Large Room on the Second Floor of Gethsemane Church Parsonage.

Staged by Harry Wagstaff Gribble.

Rev. Barnabas Ford, widower and churchman, has brought up three daughters, Faith, Hope and Charity, and one son, Paul, with the conventional fundamentalist's stern rod of discipline. Paul goes liberal and unregenerate in college and Hope rebels at home. To add to the Rev. Barnabas' troubles, when he tries to rewaken interest in his church by importing a sensational girl evangelist, Edna Pasteel, she faints at the thought of baptism by immersion. Ordered on a long vacation by the trustees, the Rev. Barnabas shoots himself rather than face the disgrace.

TIN PAN ALLEY

(69 performances)

A play in three acts by Hugh Stanislaus Stange. Produced by Harry Lang and Henry B. Forbes at the Biltmore Theatre, New York, November 1, 1928.

Cast of characters—

Peggy Loree	Constance McKay
Pete	Herbert Heywood
Tony Costero	Curtis Karpe
"Rio Rita Girls"	Grace Walsh, Mildred Waterbury
Escorts	Arnold Goodrow, Henry Hammond
Isadore Marks	Ben Welden
Ruthie Day	Marcia Manning
Jill O'Dare	Claudette Colbert
Joe Prividi	John Wray
Charlie Roseberg	Bert Wilcox
Fred Moran	Norman Foster
Johnny Dolan	Edgar Nelson
Dumb Dora	Charlotte Hunt
Rialto Rounders	Ward Argo, William Truda
Gyp	Horbert Harwood
Small Timers	Claire Farrell, Marion Waters, Arthur Gaby, Melvin Leewood
Billie	Sara Floyd
Georgie Dunn	Ramon Racomar
Nick	Irving Sklar
Wop	Walter Powers
Jake	David Manning
Bull	William Nally
Brakeman	John O. Hewitt
Suburbanites	Marie Preston, Marian Florance, Arline Lloyd, John Graham, Alton Hamilton
Conductor	George M. Lloyd
Mr. and Mrs.	Mortimer Hunt, Marjorie Hubert
Old Lady	Dorothy Farnum
Her Son	Roger Bacon
Three Jolly Good Fellows	George Bleasdale, John Abrams, Richard Finley
Porters	Donald Wynne, Donald Lashley
Sgt. Dillon	William A. Norton
Detective Hogan	George Rogers
Telephone "Troublehunter"	Samuel Levine

The Action of the Play Takes Place in New York City at the Present Time.

Staged by Lester Lonergan.

Fred Moran is a lovable but irresponsible songwriter, Jill O'Dare his unhappy but loyal wife. Joe Prividi, a rotten night-club and bootleg man, tries to get Jill, first by turning her against Fred and later by ordering Fred killed. The gunmen miss and Jill recovers her boy.

AN ENEMY OF THE PEOPLE

(16 performances)

A play in five acts by Henrik Ibsen. Revived by Walter Hampden at the Hampden Theatre, New York, November 5, 1928.

Cast of characters—

Doctor Thomas Stockmann	Walter Hampden
Mrs. Stockmann	Mabel Moore
Petra	Evelyn Goodrich
Eilif	Leroy Wade
Morten	Omar Le Gant
Peter Stockmann	C. Norman Hammond
Morten Kiil	William Sauter
Hovstad	Dallas Anderson
Billing	Gordon Hart
Horster	Ernest Rowan
Aslaksen	Cecil Yapp
AND AT THE MASS-MEETING:	
Mr. Vik	Louis Polan
A Drunken Man	S. Thomas Gomez

Acts I and II.—Dr. Stockmann's Sitting-Room. Act III.—Editor's Room of the "People's Messenger." Act IV.—A Room in Captain Horster's House. Act V.—Dr. Stockmann's Study.
Staged by Walter Hampden.

See "Best Plays of 1927-28."

THIS YEAR OF GRACE

(157 performances)

A revue in two parts by Noel Coward. Produced by Arch Selwyn at the Selwyn Theatre, New York, November 7, 1928.

Principals engaged—

Noel Coward	Beatrice Lillie
Dick Francis	Madeline Gibson
Tommy Hayes	Queenie Leonard
Sonnie Ray	Rita Mackay
Georges Fontanna	Marjorie Moss
Tom Devine	Phyllis Harding
G. P. Huntley, Jr.	Albertina Vitak
Philip Wade	Florence Desmond
Mervyn Pearce	Muriel Montrose
James Cameron	Mimi Hayes

Nelson Welch	Audrey Pointing
James Hepburn	Oriel Ross
William Harn	Nan Hearn
Billy Milton	Sheila Rawle

Staged by Charles B. Cochran.

THE YELLOW JACKET

(69 performances)

A play in three parts by George C. Hazelton and Benrimo. Produced by Mr. and Mrs. Coburn at the Coburn Theatre, New York, November 7, 1928.

Cast of characters—

Property Man.................................Arthur Shaw
Chorus.................................Charles Coburn
Wu Sin Yin (Great Sound Language)................Walter Edwin
Due Jung Fah (Fuchsia Flower)..................Virginia Gordon
Tso (Fancy Beauty)..........................Dorothy Guthern
Tai Fah Min (Great Painted Face)...................Frank Peters
Assistant Property Men.................... David Shesgreen, Wakeman Hartley, Henry Senber, Shepperd Strudwick
Chee Moo (Kind Mother)..........................Mrs. Coburn
Lee Sin.................................N. St. Clair Hales
Suey Sin Fah (Lily Flower)...................Ethel Morrison
Ling Won (Spirit)..........................Henry Stillman
Wu Hoo Git (Young Hero of the Wu Family)...Alexander Kirkland
Wu Fah Din (Daffodil)........................Schuyler Ladd
Yin Suey Gong (Purveyor of Hearts)...............Walter Edwin
See Quoe Fah (Four Season Flower).............Dorothy Guthern
Mow Dan Fah (Peony)........................Marie J. Simpson
Yong Soo Kow (Hydrangea).......................Ruth Marion
Chow Wan (Autumn Cloud).......................Marjorie Dille
Moy Fah Loy (Plum Blossom)..................Mary Hutchinson
See Noi...................................Helen Tilden
Tai Char Shoong............................Henry Stillman
The Widow Ching.............................Eugenie Webb
Maid.....................................Marie J. Simpson
Git Hok Gar..................................Frank Peters
Loy Gong...............................N. St. Clair Hales
Kom Loi.....................................Walter Edwin

Part I.—The Mother's Parting. Part II.—The Story of Love. Part III.—The Conflict.
The Scene Represents the Stage of a Chinese Theatre.
Staged by Benrimo.

Revival of the Chinese fantasy that has been frequently restored to the stage since its first performance the season of 1912-13.

TREASURE GIRL

(68 performances)

A musical comedy in two acts, book by Fred Thompson and Vincent Lawrence, lyrics by Ira Gershwin. Produced by Alex A.

Aarons and Vinton Freedley at the Alvin Theatre, New York, November 8, 1928.

Cast of characters—

Betty	Dorothy Jordan
Madge	Virginia Franck
Kitty	Peggy O'Neill
Arthur	Victor Garland
"Nat" McNally	Clifton Webb
Mary Bird	Gertrude McDonald
Polly Tees	Mary Hay
Jack Wrigley	Charles Barron
Footman	Stephen Francis
Larry Hopkins	Walter Catlett
Ann Wainwright	Gertrude Lawrence
Neil Forrester	Paul Frawley
Mortimer Grimes	Ferris Hartman
Bunce	Norman Curtis
"Slug" Bullard	Frank G. Bond
First Mate	John Dunsmuir
Postman	Edwin Preble

Act I.—Scene 1—The Beach. 2—The Drive. 3—The Garden.
Act II.—Scene 1—The Island. 2—The Drive. 3—The Ballroom.
Staged by Bertram Harrison, Dances by Bobby Connelly.

Mortimer Grimes hides $100,000 on an island and starts a treasure hunt at a pirate's party on his estate. Ann Wainwright, who needs the money desperately if she is to pay for the gowns she wears, makes an active search for the treasure, aided at times and interfered with at other times by Neil Forrester, an independent sort of baritone who loves her but won't confess it.

A MAN WITH RED HAIR

(20 performances)

A play in three acts by Benn W. Levy from the novel by Hugh Walpole. Produced by Charles L. Wagner and the Garrick Players at the Garrick Theatre, New York, November 8, 1928.

Cast of characters—

David Dunbar	Barry O'Neill
Servant	Morris Lee
Charles Percy Harkness	Harold Vermilyea
Hesther Tobin	Mary Kennedy
Mr. Crispin	Edward G. Robinson
Herrick Crispin	Kirby Hawkes
Dr. Tobin	Henry Carvill
Second Servant	William Kim
Third Servant	Meayon Yon Kim

Acts I, II and III.—In an Old Mansion Outside Treliss, in Cornwall, England.
Staged by John D. Williams.

Mr. Crispin, a maniacal saddist, traps in his home Charles Harkness, David Dunbar and Hester Tobin, who is forced into a marriage with young Crispin. Thereafter Crispin proceeds to try various torture tests on his victims, assisted by Japanese servants whose tongues have been cut out. The imprisoned victims escape and Crispin is threatened by his abused servants with proper punishment.

HOTBED

(19 performances)

A comedy drama in three acts by Paul Osborn. Produced by Brock Pemberton at the Klaw Theatre, New York, November 8, 1928.

Cast of characters—

Reverend David Rushbrook	William Ingersoll
Hattie	Josephine Hull
Lila	Alison Bradshaw
John	Richard Spencer
Lawrence Binnings	Preston Sturges
Prof. Clark	Carl Anthony
Louis Willard	William Faversham, Jr.
George Courtenay	Walter Greenough
Dean Slawson	Paul Gilmore
Prof. Kimball	Leigh Lovel
Prof. Staton	Charles Abbe

Acts I and III.—The Study of the Reverend Rushbrook. Act II.—Louis Willard's Room and Dean Slawson's Private Office.
Staged by Brock Pemberton and Antoinette Perry.

Rev. David Rushbrook is determined to stop the spread of immorality among the undergraduates of the large university town in which he lives. He is hard and bigoted, ruling his family with the usual rod of iron. Before the university faculty he makes charges against Louis Willard, a young instructor and a liberal, who has been accused of receiving a girl coed in his rooms. Willard's dismissal is forced by the dean to save a scandal. He refuses to name the girl, but she names herself. She is Lila Rushbrook and a little relieved at being thrown out of her father's house.

ON CALL

(67 performances)

A dramatic comedy in three acts by Roland Oliver. Produced by Jules J. Leventhal at the Waldorf Theatre, New York, November 9, 1928.

Cast of characters—

Jane Smith	Emily Ross
Robert Gray	Charles Dosch
John Q. Smith	Ray Collins
Mary Randall	Eleanor Z. Audley
George Pierpont	Raymond Walburn
Margie	Dorothea Chard
Private Detective	Selwyn Goddard
Rosie LaTour	Ann Chase

Acts I, II and III.—In the Smith Apartment.
Staged by Frank McCoy.

John Q. Smith discovers his wife entertaining Robert Gray, an innocent from Ohio, in the Smith apartment. Smith determines on divorce, but being a gentleman prefers his wife should name him as defendant. They send to Mme. Rosie LaTour for a professional corespondent and it just happens that Margie Gray, Robert's also innocent sister, is sent over. It is her first case. The Grays and Mr. Smith go back to Ohio.

THE DARK MIRROR

(32 performances)

An American saga in a prologue and five acts by Irving Stone. Produced by The Lenox Hill Players at the Cherry Lane Theatre, New York, November 9, 1928.

Cast of characters—

John Atkins	Jerome Seplow
Alvin Atkins, His Son: The Boy	Milton Gendel
Alvin Atkins, His Son: The Man	Louis John Latzer / Mitchell Padraic Marcus
Ma Atkins, His Wife	Adeline Ruby
Harry Cosgrove, A Friend	A. J. Field
Estelle Cosgrove, His Daughter	Mary Hallett
Helen Atkins, Alvin's Daughter	Syd Brenner
Jerry West, A Friend of Alvin	Ben Nelson
Elsie West, His Wife	Lillian Azair
Robert Belcher	Mitchell Padraic Marcus / Louis John Latzer
Margery Belcher, His Wife	Fanny Shack
Doctor	Jesse Loewenthal
Nurse	Evah Schwab
Minister	Harold Smith

Prologue—First Decade, 1910. Act I.—Second Decade, 1920. Act II.—Third Decade, 1930. Act III.—Fourth Decade, 1940. Act IV.—Fifth Decade, 1950. Act V.—Sixth Decade, 1960.
Staged by Adele Gutman Nathan.

Ma Atkins is a dominant and terrific figure. Pa Atkins is a procrastinator. Ma runs the show and in a prologue and five acts sees most of her kin slide out from under her wrath to gain their reward, if any, in heaven.

THESE DAYS

(8 performances)

A play in three acts by Katharine Clugston. Produced by Arthur Hopkins at the Cort Theatre, New York, November 12, 1928.

Cast of characters—

ACTS I AND II

Rosilla Dow	Mary Hall
Virginia MacRae	Mildred McCoy
Pansy, Larue Mott	Gertrude Moran
Veronica Sims	Katharine Hepburn
Miss Guadaloupe Gorham	Gladys Hopeton
"Chippy" Davis	Bruce Evans
Dwight Elbridge	William Johnstone
Stephen MacRae	Edwin Philips
Frannie MacRae	Elaine Koch
Mrs. MacRae	May Buckley
Mr. MacRae	George MacQuarrie
Miss Dorothea Utterback	Marie Bruce
Stephanie Bliss	Ruth Reed
Miss Signhild Valdemir VanAlstyne	Helen Freeman
Miss Cleo Almeda Young	Ada Potter
Winifred Black	Suzanne Freeman
Miss Wilda Hall	Mary Hubbard
Miss Serena Lash	Nellie Malcolm

ACT III

Virginia	Mildred McCoy
Dolly	Marian Lee
Marjory	Ruth Wilton
Richard	Francis Corbin Burke
Guy	Willard S. Robertson
Philip	Henri Lase
Puss	Ruth Wilcox

Act I.—Scene 1—A Pullman Car in Train Going West at Christmas Time. 2—Virginia's Home in a Large Mid-Western City. Act II.—Scene 1—Anteroom in Miss VanAlstyne's Finishing School. 2—The Room of "Silly" and Virginia in the School. Act III.—Parlor of a Hotel Suite, on the Riviera.

Staged by Arthur Hopkins.

Virginia MacRae, unhappy daughter of an alcoholic millionaire father and a shallow, hair-dyed mother, is disgusted with her life both at home and at Miss VanAlstyne's fashionable finishing school. In a mood of depression she elopes with Dwight Elbridge, poor but eloquent son of an actor. Two years later Virginia is a Paris divorcée and still unhappy.

THE SQUEALER

(64 performances)

A melodrama in three acts by Mark Linder. Produced by Jack Linder at the Forrest Theatre, New York, November 12, 1928.

Cast of characters—

Hi Loo	George Neville
Wing Lee	Gaylord B. Kingston
Sam Woo	J. Kunihari
"Flippy" Sadie	Goldie Pemberton
Flora	Lois Jesson
Molly	Dorothy Brown
Charlie Wong	Robert Harrison
Slick	Fred Monti
Dora Deane	Ruth Shepley
"Slippery" Jimmy	Robert Bentley
"Gimpty" Kelly	Guy Harrington
Doorman	Mang Long
Luigi	Victor Adams
Detective Logan	William Jeffrey
Officer Sullivan	E. M. Johnstone
Officer Kelly	George C. Mack
"Red" Harrigan	Tom Fadden
Ike Morris	Ben Bernard
Leslie Dobbs	Clark Hundley
Flower Girl	Soo Yong
Cigarette Girl	Rae Kasten
Carrie	Carlotta Davies
Hattie	Lillian Martin
Becky	Natalie Kessler
Head Waiter	Joe Cogert
Police Inspector	Martin A. Somers

Act I.—Charlie Wong's Oriental Palace. Act II.—Apartment of Jimmy and Dora. Act III.—Wong's Oriental Palace.
Staged by Clarke Silvernail.

Slippery Jimmy, dope peddler, and Dora Deane, cabaret entertainer, want to go straight before Dora's baby is born. Evil forces, directed for the most part by Charlie Wong and helped along by a bribed detective named Logan, make it practically impossible. Jimmie's friend, "Gimpty" Kelly, turns out to be a plain clothes fellow, however, and everything is fine, even if the last curtain does usher in the San Francisco earthquake.

"TO-NIGHT AT 12"

(60 performances)

A play in three acts by Owen Davis. Produced by Herman Shumlin at the Hudson Theatre, New York, November 13, 1928.

Cast of characters—

Nan Stoddard	Diane Esmonde
Barbara Warren	Spring Byington
Dora Eldridge	Florence Rittenhouse
Alice Keith	Anne Shoemaker
Jane Eldridge	Patricia Barclay
Tony Keith	Owen Davis, Jr.
John Keith	William Roselle
Professor Eldridge	Moffat Johnston
Bill Warren	William David
Tom Stoddard	Edward H. Wever
Ellen	Florence Short
Mary	Viola Frayne
Joe	Gerald Cornell

Acts I and III.—The Keiths' Living Room. Act II.—Professor Eldridge's Library.
Staged by Melville Burke.

Mrs. Keith has seen Mr. Keith put a note in a cloisonné box on the mantel. The note reads "To-night at 12" and during the assembling of a dinner party disappears. Mrs. Keith thereupon concludes that one of her lady guests is her husband's mistress, and declares an intention of ferreting her out before any one goes home that night. Tony Keith, at a signal from his father, insists the note was written to him, but Mrs. Keith is not satisfied. Circumstances pick out each of the women in turn as suspects, Tony all but loses his fiancée and then a compromise is made possible by the confession of Mary, the maid, who knows a lot about the note and all the husbands, too. They pay her not to tell.

MACBETH

(64 performances)

A tragedy in four acts by William Shakespeare. Revived by George C. Tyler at the Knickerbocker Theatre, New York, November 19, 1928.

Cast of characters—

Duncan, King of Scotland	Douglas Ross
Malcolm	(1st part) Burford Hampden
Malcolm	(2nd part) George Macready
Donalbain	Moliclare Oliphant
Macbeth	Lyn Harding
Banquo	William Farnum
Macduff	Basil Gill
Lennox	Leonard Mudie
Ross	William P. Carleton
Montieth	Frank Holman
Angus	Edwin Lawson
Caithness	Bryan Hughes
Fleance	Gloria Kelly
Siward	Douglas Ross
Young Siward	Burford Hampden
Seyton	Harold Hartsell
A Lord	Alfred Dickens
An English Doctor	Stephen Parker
A Porter	Percival Vivian
An Old Man	Leopold Lane
Lady Macbeth	Florence Reed
Gentlewoman	Olive Oliver
First Witch	Leonard Mudie
Second Witch	Gerald Lindgard
Third Witch	Arthur Barry
First Apparition	Clayton Fielding
Second Apparition	Evelyn Ross
Third Apparition	Mary Rose
First Murderer	Bernard Savage
Second Murderer	Harold Thomas
A Singer	Evelyn Ross
A Piper	Alex Stewart

First Messenger....................Thomas Rutherford
Second Messenger....................Frank Raymond

Act I.—Scene 1—A Place Near Forres. 2—Forres. King Duncan's Palace. 3—Inverness. Macbeth's Castle. 4—Before Macbeth's Castle. Act II.—Macbeth's Castle. Act III.—Scene 1—Forres. The Palace. 2—Near the Palace. 3—Hall in the Palace. 4—Cavern. Act IV.—Scene 1—England. Near the King's Palace. 2—Dunsinane, Part of the Castle. 3—The Castle. 4—Near Birnam Wood. 5—The Castle. 6—Before the Castle. 7—The Castle.

Staged by Douglas Ross.

The Shakespearean tragedy with a Gordon Craig "designment."

THE SACRED FLAME

(24 performances)

A play in three acts by Somerset Maugham. Produced by Messmore Kendall and Gilbert Miller at the Henry Miller Theatre, New York, November 19, 1928.

Cast of characters—

Maurice Tabret....................Robert Harris
Dr. Harvester....................Stanley Logan
Mrs. Tabret....................Mary Jerrold
Nurse Wayland....................Clare Eames
Alice....................Eva Leonard Boyne
Major Liconda....................Hubert Harben
Stella Tabret....................Casha Pringle
Colin Tabret....................Anthony Bushell

Acts I, II and III.—Drawing Room at Gatley House, Mrs. Tabret's Residence, Near London.

Staged by Gilbert Miller.

Maurice and Stella Tabret have been married five years, during all of which time Maurice has been a helpless paralytic as the result of an airplane crash. During the last year Colin, Maurice's brother, has been home and he and Stella have fallen in love with each other. Maurice is found dead in bed. His nurse insists he has been murdered. Suspicion points ominously at Stella, the wife, who confesses she is to become the mother of Colin's child. Mrs. Tabret, the boy's mother, confesses that it was she who had given her poor son release from unhappiness by doubling his sleeping potion.

MAJOR BARBARA

(84 performances)

A play in four acts by George Bernard Shaw. Revived by The Theatre Guild at the Guild Theatre, New York, November 19, 1928.

Cast of characters—

Stephen Undershaft..................................Maurice Wells
Lady Britomart Undershaft..........................Helen Westley
Barbara Undershaft...............................Winifred Lenihan
Sarah Undershaft...............................Gale Sondergaard
Adolphus Cusins.....................................Elliot Cabot
Charles Lomax..............................Charles Courtneidge
Morrison..Isidore Marcil
Andrew Undershaft..................................Dudley Digges
Rummy Mitchens..............................Alice Cooper Cliffe
Snobby Price...Edgar Kent
Jenny...Phyllis Connard
Peter Shirley...A. P. Kaye
Bill Walker...Percy Waram
Mrs. Baines..Edythe Tressider
Bilton...Ralph Sumpter

Act I.—Library in Lady Britomart Undershaft's House in Wilton Crescent. Act II.—Yard of the West Ham Shelter. Act III.—Same as Act I. Act IV.—Foundry of Undershaft and Lazarus at Perivale St. Andrews.

Staged by Philip Moeller.

Barbara Undershaft is distressed by the state of society. She joins the Salvation Army to help counteract the spiritually devastating influences of the capitalists as represented by her father, Andrew Undershaft, manufacturer of cannon and ammunition. In the Army, at the peak of her enthusiasm, Barbara discovers that even the charity organizations are beholden to the capitalists and comes to agree partly with her pater that poverty is the only crime as well as the greatest incitement to crime.

REDEMPTION

(20 performances)

A play in two acts by Leo N. Tolstoi adapted by August Scholz. Revived by Morris Gest in association with Edgar Selwyn at the Ambassador Theatre, New York, November 19, 1928.

Cast of characters—

Nurse...Margaret Schmied
Anna Pavlovna.......................................Emilie Unda
Sasha...Irmgard Richter
Karenin...Karl Ludwig Diehl
Lisa..Charlotte Schultz
Afremoff..Rudolf Amendt
Fedya (Fyodor Protasoff).....................Alexander Moissi
Ivan Makarovitsch..............................Willy Schmieder
Natasya Ivanova.....................................Emilie Unda
Masha...Lydia Li
Officer..Othmar Biegler
Musician...G. H. Schnell
Physician.......................................Friedrich Kuhne
Servant to Afremoff..............................Othmar Biegler
Servant to Karenin..............................Anton Daneborg
Anna Dimitrievna...............................Johanna Terwin

Prince Abreskoff.................................G. H. Schnell
Waiter.................................Josef Zeislmeier
Alexandroff.................................Wilhelm Diegelmann
Vosnessenskiy.................................Dietrich Jenke
Pyotushkoff.................................Rudolf Amendt
Artyomyeff.................................Friedrich Kuhne
Examining Magistrate.................................Friedrich Kuhne
Magistrate's Secretary.................................Anton Daneborg
Bailiff.................................Othmar Biegler
Petruschin.................................Willy Schmieder
A Lady.................................Margaret Schmied

Act I.—Scene 1—Dining Room of Fyodor Protasoff's Flat in Moscow. 2—The Gypsy's House. 3—Dining Room. 4—Afremo's House. 5—Anna Dimitrievna's House. 6—Fedya's Room. Act II.—Scene 1—Private Room in a Restaurant. 2—Protasoff's Flat. 3—A Restaurant. 4—A Bungalow in the Country. 5—A Courtroom.

Staged by Max Reinhardt.

Fedya, unhappy at home, leaves Lisa, his wife, and is believed to be dead. Lisa marries again. Discovered in the midst of the social depths to which he sinks, Fedya kills himself rather than have Lisa arrested and tried on a charge of having committed bigamy.

THE WILD DUCK

(80 performances)

A play in five acts by Henrik Ibsen. Translated by William Archer. Revived by The Actors' Theatre, Inc., at the 49th Street Theatre, New York, November 19, 1928.

Cast of characters—

Pettersen.................................George Bratt
Jensen.................................Jack Daniels
Old Ekdal.................................John Daly Murphy
Mrs. Sorby.................................Claire Townshend
Chamberlain Flor.................................Orrin Burke
Chamberlain Balli.................................Frank Howson
Chamberlain Kasperson.................................Frank I. Frayne
Werle.................................Reginald Goode
Gregers Werle.................................Ralph Roeder
Hialmar Ekdal.................................Dallas Anderson
Graberg.................................Richard Skinner
Gina.................................Blanche Yurka
Hedvig.................................Linda Watkins
Relling.................................Frank Monroe
Molvik.................................Cecil Clovelly
Guests.........Edward Hudson, William Dupont, Arthur Leonard, Douglas Rowland, Harold Hecht, Thomas Cox
Waiter.................................Thomas Hayes

Act I.—Werle's House. Acts II, III, IV and V.—Hialmar Ekdal's Studio.

Staged by Blanche Yurka.

See "Best Plays 1924-25."

CAPONSACCHI

(16 performances)

A play in three acts, prologue and epilogue by Arthur Goodrich and Rose A. Palmer. Based on Robert Browning's poem, "The Ring and the Book." Revived by Walter Hampden at the Hampden Theatre, New York, November 19, 1928.

Cast of characters—

Giotti.......................................Joseph Milton
Melchior.....................................Stephen Irving
Andrea.......................................Francis Dears
Montini......................................Jan Lindermann
Pope Innocent XII............................William Sauter
Guido Franceschini...........................Ernest Rowan
Caponsacchi..................................Walter Hampden
Tommati......................................Gage Bennett
Venturini....................................Louis Polan
Scalchi......................................Gordon Hart
Gherardi.....................................Charles Quigley
Pietro Comparini.............................Franklin Salisbury
Violante Comparini...........................Caroline Meade
Pompilia.....................................Ingeborg Torrup
Canon Conti..................................Cecil Yapp
Governor of Arezzo...........................C. Norman Hammond
Archbishop of Arezzo.........................Edwin Cushman
Margherita...................................Mabel Moore
Salvatore....................................Robert C. Schnitzer
Peppina......................................Anne Lubow
Innkeeper at Castelnuovo.....................S. Thomas Gomez
His Servant..................................Le Roi Operti
Marinetta....................................Evelyn Goodrich
Guard at Castelnuovo.........................Eric Wetherly
Duchesses........Evelyn Goodrich, Harriet Ingersoll, Isabel S. Hill
Messenger....................................William Thornton

Prologue—A Court of Justice at the Vatican. Act I.—The Carnival, Arezzo. Act II.—Scene 1—Caponsacchi's Cell, Arezzo. 2—Street Outside Guido's Palace. 3—Inn at Castelnuovo. Act III.—Scene 1—A Court of Justice at the Vatican. 2—Pietro's Villa. Epilogue—A Court of Justice at the Vatican.

Staged by Walter Hampden.

See "Best Plays 1926-27."

THE JEALOUS MOON

(71 performances)

In a prologue, a dream in three parts, and epilogue by Theodore Charles and Jane Cowl. Produced by William A. Brady, Jr., and Dwight Deere Wiman, at the Majestic Theatre, New York, November 20, 1928.

Cast of characters—

Peter Parrot.................................Philip Merivale
Desti..Guy Standing

Judy.....Jane Cowl
Papa Louis.....Harry Davenport

THE PUPPETS

Harlequin.....Guy Standing
Pantaloon.....Harry Davenport
Pierrot.....Philip Merivale
Columbine.....Jane Cowl
Scaramouche.....Hale Norcross
Ophelia.....Marion Evensen
Hamlet.....Richard Nicholls
Punch.....Leo Stark
Vermilia.....Joyce Carey
Grimaldi.....William Randall
Joey.....Robert Lowe
Young Flunkey.....Ben Lackland
Gown-Boy.....Ben W. Barnett
Gondolier.....Garner Weed
Horatio.....Coburn Goodwin
Principessa Guilio di Caravodossi.....Esther Stockton
Principe Guilio di Caravodossi.....Robert Lowe
Duchessa di Carlione.....Lionel Hogarth
Contessa Flora.....Marion Evensen
Doge of Venice.....William Randall

The Prologue—Scene 1—The Marionette Show. 2—The Marionette Work Shop. In Peter's Dream. Part I.—Pierrot's Sitting Room. Part II.—Harlequin's House in Venice. Part III.—Pierrot's Sitting Room. The Epilogue—The Marionette Work Shop.

Staged by Priestly Morrison.

Peter Parrot, the Pierrot of a puppet show, neglects Judy, the Columbine. When Judy goes to dinner with Desti, the Harlequin, Peter dreams the love tragedy that was Pierrot's in the play and wakes to make it up with Judy.

THE ROYAL BOX

(39 performances)

A comedy romance in four acts by Charles Coghlan adapted from Alexandre Dumas' play "Kean." Produced by Walter Whiteside at the Belmont Theatre, New York, November 20, 1928.

Cast of characters—

Ebba.....Don Currie
Footman.....A. Syms
Countess Felsen.....Lulu Mae Hubbard
Lady Robert.....Catherine Proctor
Lord Bassett.....Charles Penman
Count Felsen.....Manart Kippen
H. R. H., The Prince of Wales.....Hugh Huntley
James Clarence.....Walker Whiteside
Davis.....Alexander F. Frank
Tommy Widgetts.....Frank Henderson
Mrs. Barker.....Daisy Belmore
Celia Pryse.....Franc Hale
Bailiff Tips.....Elwyn Eaton
Stage Manager.....Richard Ranier
Call Boy.....Carl Vose
Rickards.....William Dunne

Act I.—Reception Room at the Swedish Embassy, London. Act

II.—Lodgings of James Clarence, Actor. Act III.—Scene 1—James Clarence's Dressing Room at Drury Lane. 2—Stage of Drury Lane. Act IV.—James Clarence's Lodgings.
Staged by Walter Whiteside.

James Clarence, a popular and temperamental actor, fascinates the pretty débutante, Celia Pryse, gives her a chance as a player in his company, despite the opposition of the jealous Countess Felsen. After a scene in which Clarence gives offense to the Prince of Wales seated in the royal box, he accepts Celia as his leading lady for life.

RAINBOW

(29 performances)

A romantic musical play of California in the days of '49, by Laurence Stallings and Oscar Hammerstein II. Produced by Philip Goodman at the Gallo Theatre, New York, November 21, 1928.

Cast of characters—

Major Davolo	Rupert Lucas
Mess Sergeant	Ned McGurn
Sergeant Major	Harland Dixon
Penny	Helen Lynd
Colonel Brown	Henry Pemberton
"Nasty" Howell	Charles Ruggles
Captain Robert Singleton	Brian Donlevy
Virginia Brown	Louise Brown
Fanny	Herself
Harry Stanton	Allan Prior
Lotta	Libby Holman
Corporal	Leo Mack
First Private	Stewart Edwards
Second Private	Leo Dugan
Third Private	Ward Arnold
Rookie	Randall Fryer
Bartender	Frank King
Senora Mendoza	Mary Carney
Peon	Leo Nash
Servant	Charles Ralph
Spanish Girl	Valla Valentinova
Hattie	Sadie Black
Frenchie	George Magis
Mr. Jackson	Chester Bree
Egg	Edward Nemo
Tough	Ralph Walker
Kitty	Kitty Coleman

Staged by Oscar Hammerstein II. Dances by Bushy Berkeley.

Major Davolo and Captain Stanton quarrel over a woman. Stanton whips Davolo and avoids arrest by flight. Later the men meet again and Stanton kills Davolo. This time he escapes disguised as a parson with the army, falls in love with the Colonel's daughter, takes her out of the army, marries her, supports her by gambling and is finally restored to his uniform and command.

A PLAY WITHOUT A NAME

(48 performances)

A play in two acts by Austin Strong. Produced by Frank C. Reilly at the Booth Theatre, New York, November 26, 1928.

Cast of characters—

John Russell	Kenneth MacKenna
Anne Russell	Peggy Wood
Billy Neuman	Katherine Wilson
Adolph	William H. Jones
Endicott	Percy Moore
Harry	Scott Welsh
Kitty	Helen Stewart
Fusi	Hiroji Yano
Hole	Herbert Dawley
Grant	Ben Hoagland
Kennedy	James C. Lane
Harjes	Bernard Thornton
Tolhurst	Ernest Hunter
Anderson	Dwight Bridge
Crinks	John Buckler
Uncle Oliver	A. G. Andrews
Theodore	Jean Del Val
Central Control	Percy Moore

Act I.—Scene 1—John's Flat. 2—In John's Brain. 3—John's Flat.
Act II.—Scene 1—Kitty's Apartment. 2—General Headquarters. 3—John's Flat.
Staged by Austin Strong.

John and Anne Russell, happily married and still ambitious after leaving college, are trying to boost John's chances for a foreign appointment by taking Columbia extention courses. The coveted appointment goes to another and John, disheartened, goes on a sort of a bust with Billy Neuman, a beautiful girl and an old friend. But John (the workings of his brain being mechanically exposed) can only go so far with Billy. Then visions of Anne intervene and send him home conscience-stricken. Anne is awaiting him, happy in the knowledge that the reason he missed the appointment is because the firm had something better for him.

HOLIDAY

(229 performances)

A comedy in three acts by Philip Barry. Produced by Arthur Hopkins at the Plymouth Theatre, New York, November 26, 1928.

Cast of characters—

Linda Seton	Hope Williams
Johnny Case	Ben Smith
Julia Seton	Dorothy Tree
Ned Seton	Monroe Owsley
Susan Potter	Barbara White
Nick Potter	Donald Ogden Stewart
Edward Seton	Walter Walker
Laura Cram	Rosalie Norman
Seton Cram	Thaddeus Clancy
Henry	Cameron Clemens
Charles	J. Ascher Smith
Delia	Beatrice Ames

Act I.—Room on Third Floor of Edward Seton's House in New York. Act II.—Room on the Top Floor. Act III.—Room on the Third Floor.

Staged by Arthur Hopkins.

See page 120.

PETER PAN

(48 performances)

A play by J. M. Barrie. Produced by the Civic Repertory Theatre, Inc., at the Civic Repertory Theatre, New York, November 26, 1928.

Cast of characters—

Liza	Beatrice de Neergaard
Nana	J. Edward Bromberg
Michael Nicholas Darling	Vernon Jones
Mrs. Darling	Mary Ward
Wendy Moira Angela Darling	Josephine Hutchinson
John Napoleon Darling	Charles McCarthy
Mr. Darling	Donald Cameron
Tinker Bell	Herself
Peter Pan	Eva Le Gallienne
First Twin	David Vivian
Slightly	Landon Herrick
Ostrich	Harold Moulton
Tootles	Glesca Marshall
Curley	Alfred Corn
Second Twin	Henry Melvin
Nibs	Lester Salko
Captain Hook	Egon Brecher
Starkey	Sayre Crawley
Smee	John Eldridge
Blackman	Ted Fetter
Cecco	Harold Moulton
Cookson	Robert Ross
Tiger Lily	Jocelyn Gordon
Great Big Little Panther	J. Blake Scott
Mullins	Robert H. Gordon
Noodles	Walter Beck
Pirate	Lewis Leverett
A Tramp	Robert H. Gordon
A Cabman	Robert Ross

Staged by Eva Le Gallienne and J. Blake Scott.

The first revival of the Barrie classic since that in which Marilyn Miller appeared during the season of 1924-25.

A MOST IMMORAL LADY

(160 performances)

A comedy in three acts by Townsend Martin. Produced by William A. Brady, Jr., and Dwight Deere Wiman at the Cort Theatre, New York, November 26, 1928.

Cast of characters—

Hoskins	Harry Barfoot
Humphrey Sargent	Austin Fairman
John Williams	Robert Strange
Alec Pryor	Sydney Booth
Tony Williams	Guido Nadzo
Laura Sargent	Alice Brady
Joan Porter	Blyth Daly
Natalie Davis	Pauline Denton
Ned	Kirk Ames
Nancy	Helen Brooks
Maitre d'Hotel	Lawrence Adams
Pedro	Ernest R. Sharpe
Dancer	Inger Ghika
Violinist	Michael Hoffman

Acts I and II.—The Sargent Apartment in New York. Act III.—The Restaurant Muscovite, Paris.

Staged by Dwight Deere Wiman and Townsend Martin.

Laura and Humphrey Sargent, reduced to living by their wits, fall into the habit of blackmailing rich old men by the badger game formula. Laura traps them and Humphrey takes a check to ease his wounded feelings. But when Laura falls really in love with Tony Williams, Humphrey's refusal to believe she did not intend him to be a victim leads to complications which are finally solved by divorces and Laura's determination to go straight with Tony.

THE LADY LIES

(24 performances)

A play in three acts by John Meehan. Produced by Joseph Santley, Theodore Barter and John McGowan at the Little Theatre, New York, November 26, 1928.

Cast of characters—

Bob Rossiter	Charles Cromer
Josephine Rossiter	Anna Thomas
Tyler	Robert Barratt
Robert Rossiter	William Boyd
Henry Tuttle	James Seeley
Amelia Tuttle	Cordelia McDonald
Berenice Tuttle	Cara Gould
Ann Gardner	Anita Damrosch

Florence Rossiter....Betty Lawford
Alex Huntington....Henry Wadsworth
Joyce Roamer....Shirley Warde
Hilda Pearson....Nan Sunderland
Thomas....Harry Lillford
Maid....Olive Burgoyne

Acts I and III.—Rossiters' Library. Act II.—Joyce Roamer's Apartment.

Staged by David Burton.

For the seven years Robert Rossiter has been a widower he has lived with Joyce Roamer. Now that his three children are grown he feels having a mistress does not become him. When he tries to throw Joyce over, however, he discovers that he loves her and finally the children themselves come to plead for the loyal lady love.

BACK HERE

(8 performances)

A play in three acts by Olga Printzlau. Produced by William A. Brady, in association with I. H. Herk at the Klaw Theatre, New York, November 26, 1928.

Cast of characters—

Slim....Bryan Lycan
Kelly....Phillip Heege
Peter Linden....George Meeker
Goofy....William Holly
Ruth....Emily Hamill
Sergeant "Terry" O'Brien....Melvyn Douglas
Jimmy Martin....Joseph Lee
Kitty....Jeanne Greene
Melba....June Webster
Winnie....Kitty Kelly
Margie....Kathleen Terry
Sally....Peggy Shannon
"Breezy" Eason....Donald McClelland
Sam Short....John Cambridge
Polly....Florence McGee
Vera (Madame Delane)....Jane Houston
Tibby....Ernest Pollock
Rose Cady....Jean Dixon
Rudy Renaldo....Edward Pawley
Mrs. Duane Hanford....Marza La Rubia

Acts I and III.—Recreation Room in a Soldiers' Hospital. Act II.—One of the Lounging Rooms at "The Arbour," a Taxi Dancehall.

Staged by Victor Morley.

Peter Linden, out of the war and badly battered, gets the faith and tries to pass it on. Tough Terry O'Brien, a buddy with a steel chest and other artificial aids to life, will have none of this religious bunk until his steel breastplate saves his life when he tries to save Peter's girl in a dance hall mess. Terry even finds his own girl in the dance hall and everybody is happy in the end.

THE AGE OF INNOCENCE

(207 performances)

A dramatization of Edith Wharton's novel in five scenes, by Margaret Ayer Barnes. Produced by Gilbert Miller at the Empire Theatre, New York, November 27, 1928.

Cast of characters—

Alice Fordyce....................................Margaret Barker
Tom Hamilton....................................Henry Richard
Lucy Duane...Jean Howard
Harry Delancy....................................Stanley Gilkey
Sillerton Jackson...............................William Podmore
Jessie Lefferts.....................................Nora Stirling
Mrs. Henry van der Luyden.......................Isabel Irving
Mrs. Manson Mingott.........................Katharine Stewart
Mr. Henry van der Luyden.........................Frazer Coulter
Julius Beaufort.....................................Arnold Korff
May van der Luyden...................................Eden Gray
Newland Archer.......................................Rollo Peters
Ellen Olenska.....................................Katharine Cornell
The Duke of St. Austrey............................Peter Spencer
Anastasia...Giannina Gatti
Stephen Letterblair..............................Albert Tavernier
Carlos Saramonte..............................Edouard La Roche
Jean..Pierre Soupault
Newland Archer, Jr...............................Franchot Tone

Scene 1—The Conservatory of Mrs. van der Luyden's House on Astor Place. 2—Madame Olenska's Little House on West Twenty-third Street. 3—Mr. Letterblair's Law Office on Lower Broadway. 4—At Madame Olenska's. 5—Madame Olenska's Apartment on the Rue de Varenne, Paris.

Staged by Guthrie McClintic.

Countess Olenska, an American girl returned from an unhappy experience as the wife of a Polish count, falls in love with Newland Archer, who is engaged to marry May van der Luyden, her cousin. Newland and the Countess fight nobly against their passion in the old New York way, fall briefly and then make the higher sacrifice. The Countess returns to her beastly husband, Newland marries May. Forty years after Newland takes his oldest son to Paris but does not stop to see the Countess. He prefers to keep his memory of her as she was.

CONGAI

(135 performances)

A play in three acts by Harry Hervey and Carleton Hildreth from the novel by Harry Hervey. Produced by Sam H. Harris at the Harris Theatre, New York, November 27, 1928.

Cast of characters—

Thi-Linh.......................................Helen Menken
Kim Khouan.....................................Theodore Hecht
Mama Thi-Bao...................................Vera G. Hurst
Annamite Woman.................................Josephine Wehn
Shopkeeper.....................................Camille Lanier
First French Soldier...........................William Boren
Second French Soldier..........................Robert Toms
Father Mehry...................................John T. Dwyer
Cambodian Dancer...............................Helen Kim
Native Soldier.................................M. Aki
Laotian Girl...................................Catherine Taylor
First Street Woman.............................Blanche Collins
Second Street Woman............................Korena Rove
High Priest....................................J. Marshall De Silva
Col. Urban Chauvet.............................Felix Krembs
Justin Batteur.................................Charles Trowbridge
Capt. Paul Lehrisson...........................Maurice Burke
House Boy......................................Frank De Silva
Nanette..Ara Gerald
Thao...Valerie Bergere
Orderly..M. Aki
Lieut. Lavergne................................Harry Nelson
Major de Brissac...............................Harold Woolf
The Governor...................................H. Dudley Hawley
Major Michaud..................................Robert Toms
Capt. Baudoin..................................William Boren
Lieut. Karcher.................................James Pall
Quyen..Alan Campbell
Native Secretary...............................W. W. Singh

Act I.—Scene 1—The Pool. 2—The Street. Stung Treng. 3—The Bungalow. Act II.—The Barracks. Act III.—Scene 1—The House. 2—The Governor's Office. Saigon.
Staged by Rouben Mamoulian.

Thi-Linh, half-cast daughter of a native Annamite mother and a French father, loves Kim Khouan, also a native, who deserts her. Thereafter Thi-Linh defiantly lives the life of a congai, or courtesan, and manages, through a succession of experiences, to be a little revenged on life and the French officers in Indo-China.

* THE PERFECT ALIBI

(250 performances)

A detective comedy in three acts by A. A. Milne. Produced by Charles Hopkins assisted by William Keighley at the Charles Hopkins Theatre, New York, November 27, 1928.

Cast of characters—

Jimmy Ludgrove.................................Alan Bunce
Susan Cunningham...............................Vivian Tobin
Edward Laverick................................Ivan Simpson
Edward P. Carter...............................Richie Ling
Major Fothergill...............................H. Langdon Bruce
Jane West......................................Mary Newnham-Davis
Mrs. Fulverton-Fane............................Catharine Calhoun Doucet

Arthur Ludgrove....................................Ernest Stallard
Adams....................................Carson Davenport
P. C. Mallet....................................Harry Beresford
"Sergeant" Mallet....................................Leo G. Carrol
Acts I, II and III.—Arthur Ludgrove's Room at Heron Place.
Staged by Charles Hopkins assisted by William Keighley.

Jimmy Ludgrove and Susan Cunningham are living with a retired jurist, Arthur Ludgrove, who is Jimmy's uncle and Susan's guardian. Ludgrove is found dead with all evidence pointing to suicide. Susan, who has read many detective stories, is not convinced. With Jimmy's help she begins piecing together certain suspicions and finally succeeds in breaking what appears to be the perfect alibi of two guests in the house. One was a criminal sentenced by Judge Ludgrove twenty-seven years before and the other a friend of another convict.

ANGELA

(40 performances)

A comedy with music in three acts adapted by Fanny Todd Mitchell, based on "A Royal Family" by Captain Robert Marshall. Produced by the Messrs. Shubert at the Ambassador Theatre, New York, December 3, 1928.

Cast of characters—

Duke of Berascon....................................Gattison Jones
Louis VII, King of Arcacia....................................Eric Blore
Margaret, Queen Consort of Arcacia....................Audrey Maple
Queen Ferdinande....................................Alison Skipworth
Countess Carini....................................Peggy Cornell
Baron Von Holdenson....................................Oscar Figman
Grand Duke Hubert....................................Florenz Ames
Princess Alestine Victorine Angela..............Jeanette MacDonald
Bijou....................................Katherine Gallimore
Servant....................................James Ray
Count Bernadine....................................Roy Hoyer
Phileon Button....................................Gus Alexander
Mr. Sneckkenberger....................................Arthur Cole
The Girl from London....................................Jane Manners
At the Pianos....................Ralph Rainger and Adam Carroll
Act I.—The Ante-Room of the Royal Palace at Caron, Capital of Arcacia. Act II.—The Palace Garden. Act III.—Scene 1—A Room in the Palace. 2—The Throne Room.
Staged by George Marion.

Louis VII of Arcacia is about to force the Princess Angela into an unwelcome marriage to save the country. Angela, in love with a certain Count Bernadine, rebels, but agrees to make the sacrifice. Then, to the surprise of practically no one except the cast, Bernadine turns out to be the prince.

* WHOOPEE

(223 performances)

A musical comedy in two acts and twelve scenes by William Anthony McGuire, based on "The Nervous Wreck" by Owen Davis. Produced by Florenz Ziegfeld at the New Amsterdam Theatre, New York, December 4, 1928.

Cast of characters—

Leslie Daw	Ruth Etting
Betty	Gladys Glad
Mable	Josephine Adair
Estelle	Jean Ackerman
Alice	Adele Smith
Irene	Katherine Burke
Virginia	Myrna Darby
Lucille	Muriel Finley
Vivian	Freda Mierse
Judson Morgan	Louis Morrell
The Padre	Jethro Warner
Jim Carson	Jack Shaw
Pete	Frank Frey
Joe	Bob Rice
Jack	Jack Gifford
Mary Custer	Ethel Shutta
Sheriff Bob Wells	Jack Rutherford
Sally Morgan	Frances Upton
"Brand Iron" Edwards	James P. Houston
Henry Williams	Eddie Cantor
Wanenis	Paul Gregory
Black Eagle	Chief Caupolican
Jerome Underwood	Spencer Charters
Chester Underwood	Albert Hackett
Timothy Sloane	Jack Shaw
Harriet Underwood	Mary Jane
Andy Nab	Will H. Philbrick
Morton	Bob Rice
Yvonne	Bernice Manners
Ma-Ta-Pe	Sylvia Adam
Comulo	James P. Houston
An Indian	Edouard Grobe
Tejou	Jack Shaw
Yolandi	Tamara Geva
Eleanor	Olive Brady

Acts I and II.—On and around the Bar M Ranch, Mission Rest, California.

Staged by Wm. Anthony McGuire and Seymour Felix.

Henry Williams is in California for his health, Henry being a hypochondriac and awfully funny about it. Sally Morgan, in love with Wanenis, supposed to be a half-breed Indian, and not wanting to marry Sheriff Bob Wells, forces Henry to elope with her. They are pursued to an Indian camp by the sheriff and the chorus and finally it is revealed that Wanenis isn't an Indian at all.

SINGING JAILBIRDS

(79 performances)

Drama in three acts by Upton Sinclair. Produced at Provincetown Playhouse, December 6, 1928.

Cast of characters—

Red Adams	Grover Burgess
District Attorney	Edmund Forde
Joe Gunther	Herbert T. Bergman
Matt	Donal Harrington
Gil	Samuel Schneider
Jerry	Douglas Krantzor
Pete	Lionel Stander
Sapper	Fred Boardley
The Dominie	Charles Kuhn
Jake Apperson	Lionel Ferrend
One Lung	Samuel Schneider
Nell	Nellie Gray
A Voice	Doris E. Troutman
Muriel	Charlotte Buchwald
The Bailiff	Lionel Ferrend

Staged by Em Jo Basshe.

Red Adams, an organizer for the I.W.W., is jailed in Los Angeles during a strike and placed in solitary confinement on bread and water. He gradually loses his reason and in his delirium sees his trial as a mockery of justice and all the parade of capitalistic sins that are undermining the country. He dies tragically to the accompaniment of I.W.W. hymns.

WINGS OVER EUROPE

(90 performances)

A play by Robert Nichols and Maurice Browne. Produced by The Theatre Guild at the Martin Beck Theatre, New York, December 10, 1928.

Cast of characters—

Grantby	Ernest Lawford
Arthur	Frank Conroy
Lightfoot	Alexander Kirkland
Stapp	Hugh Buckler
Dedham	Frank Elliot
Dunn	Gordon Richards
Haliburton	Nicholas Joy
Grindle	Joseph Kilgour
Sunningdale	John Dunn
Blount	Grant Stewart
Faulkiner	Charles Francis
Cossington	Thomas Braidon

Vere..Robert Rendel
Hand..Edward Lester
Taggert...Charles Carden
Rummel..A. P. Kaye
Plimsoll..Wheeler Dryden
Pascoe..George Graham
St. Man...Lionel Bevans

Acts I, II and III.—Scene—A Room at No. 10 Downing Street, London.

Staged by Rouben Mamoulian.

See page 88.

SIGN OF THE LEOPARD

(39 performances)

A Scotland Yard drama in four acts by Edgar Wallace. Produced by Messrs. Shubert and Edgar Wallace at the National Theatre, December 11, 1928.

Cast of characters—

Field...Colin Hunter
First Sub-Editor..Henry Jamieson
Second Sub-Editor.......................................Guy Phillips
Third Sub-Editor..Harry Gordon
Tape Boy..Howard Stevens
Lilley..Kenneth Lawton
Billman...James Kennedy
Electrician...Jack Rigo
Carr..C. Haviland Chappell
Halford...Otto Turnby
Collie..Campbell Gullan
Mr. Butler..Agnew Horine
Millie..Elsa Shelley
Tillman...James Jolley
Captain Leslie..Warren William
Sutton..Murray Kinnell
Beryl...Flora Sheffield
Fenton..Thurston Hall
Sgt. Weaver...Perry Norman
Taylor..Florence Turner
Bill Annerley...Ralph J. Locke
Female Guest..Sara Allen
Second Female Guest.....................................Nina Gore
Lord Frenburn...Donald Hargraves
Jim Annerley..Geoffrey Harwood
Zona..Kathleen Evans
Alphonse..George Hartley
Walters...Kenneth Davis
Weatherly...Wilson Crozier
Guest...Leslie Briggs
Guest...Mary Jane
Giovanni..Roy Pierce
Lena O'Brien..Maureen O'Moor
Kalgrew...Norman MacDonald

Act I.—Scene 1—Sub-Editors' Room of *The Post Courier*. 2—Sutton's Office in Victoria Street, London. Act II.—The Drawing Room of "The Kloof" Wimbledon. Act III.—The Leopard Club. Act IV.—Scene 1—Sutton's Office. 2—The Fire Escape. 3—Sub-Editors' Room of *The Post Courier*.

Staged by Campbell Cullan.

Collie, a Scotch reporter on a London paper, arrives at the office of his paper hours late and begins to dictate the story of his round-up of a notorious criminal, "The Squeaker," for whom all Scotland Yard has been searching for ever so long. The account is acted and shows the pursuit to the Sign of the Leopard, a night club, where murder is done by the man you don't suspect and Collie finally gets the dope.

MIMA

(180 performances)

A play in three acts adapted by David Belasco from "The Red Mill" of Ferenc Molnar. Produced by David Belasco at the Belasco Theatre, New York, December 12, 1928.

Cast of characters—

HUMAN BEINGS	
The Schoolmaster	Philip Bishop
Etel	Madeleine King
Palmyra	Ruth Dayton
The Poet	Eugene Donovan
A Member of Parliament	William Boag
Janos	Sidney Blackmer
Ilonka	Vivienne Giesen
MANIKINS	
Mima	Lenore Ulric
Alfons	Dwight Frye
The Husband	Arthur Stuart Hull
The Maid	Jane Ferrell
Baccarat Scene	
A Croupier	Armand Cortes
An Ogling Man	Maurice Sturez
An Old Gambler	Logan Paul
A Young Gambler	George Ryan
A Woman with a Lorgnette	Helen Withers
A Banker's Wife	Charlcie Hedge
A French Noblewoman	Eva Barcay
A Parisian Merchant	Najeeb Assaf
A Princess	Florence Golden
A Rich Heiress	Loretto Shea
A Letter-Carrier	Bernard Susman
Monte Carlo Scene	
An Old Woman Selling Newspapers	Jane Ferrell
A Gendarme	Andre Dumont
M. Topandy	H. Percy Woodley
A Cocotte	Myra Florian
Cabaret Scene	
A Waiter	H. Percy Woodley
His Serene Highness	Ali Ilma Yousoff
A Gypsy Fiddler	Jah Misko
Vocal Soloist	Kitty Gray

DEVILS

The Laboratory of Magister

Magister	A. E. Anson
Malacoda	Romaine Callender
Rubicante	Lionel Braham
Draghignazzo	Anthony J. Sansome
Alichino	Eduardo Abdo
Calcabrina	Schuyler MacGuffin
Cagnazzo	Jerome Jordan
Scarmiglione	Arthur MacArthur
Libicocco	Richard Lambart
Farfarello	Allan Hale
Barbariccia	Frank Lengel
Chief Stoker	Douglas F. Swanson
Green Imp	Fred Nelson

SATAN AND HIS COURT

His Majesty, the King of Hell	Reginald Carrington
The Adjutant	Lennox Pawle
Secretary to the Adjutant	Harold Seton
The Prime Minister	Charles H. Martin
First Arch-Devil	George Gardon
Second Arch-Devil	Ben Probst
Third Arch-Devil	Kraft Walton
Fourth Arch-Devil	Normand Constantin
Fifth Arch-Devil	W. Gordon Craig
Sixth Arch-Devil	Frederick Raymond

Acts I, II and III.—The Laboratory and "Red Mill," Invention of Magister in Hell.

Staged by David Belasco.

Magister, Satan's chief efficiency man, invents a Red Mill, a soul-corrupter, that is guaranteed to debase the soul of the purest man within the space of an hour. He calls Satan and his cabinet to witness a demonstration, brings down Janos, a young forester, from earth; introduces Janos to Mima, the most fascinating female unit of the Red Mill, and Mima makes of Janos a liar, a thief, a blackmailer and a murderer in record time. But when Mima asks Janos to forgive her in the name of his sainted mother Janos is glad. Thrice Magister tries to force him to say "No!" But he goes on saying "Yes!" At which triumph for the forces of good the white light of grace breaks through and the Red Mill is completely wrecked.

THE LADY OF THE ORCHIDS

(20 performances)

A play of Parisian life in three acts by E. Ray Goetz from the French of Jacques Natanson. Produced by E. Ray Goetz at the Henry Miller Theatre, New York, December 13, 1928.

Cast of characters—

Henri	Edward Crandall
Simone	Peggy Hopkins Joyce

Michel..Kenneth Hunter
Claire..Virginia Chauvenet
Emile..Hugh Sinclair
A Decorator..Wm. Postance

Act I.—Bedroom of Simone's Apartment in Paris. Acts II and III.—Simone's Drawing-Room.
Staged by Wm. H. Gilmore.

Simone is living with Michel, who is rich, and cheating with Emile, who is an actor. She meets Henri, who is young and honorable, and thinks she loves him. Henri takes Emile's place, Michel discovers him, but in place of making a scene determines to save him. He will trade places with Henri. He, Michel, will be the lover and let Henri think himself the protector. And when Henri is cured of his passion Simone can resume her old status.

THE KINGDOM OF GOD

(92 performances)

A play in three acts by G. Martinez Sierra, English version by Helen and Harley Granville Barker. Produced by Lee Shubert at the Ethel Barrymore Theatre, New York, December 20, 1928.

Cast of characters—

ACT I

Sister Gracia..Ethel Barrymore
Sister Juliana..Phyllis Blake
Sister Manuela..Anita Rothe
Maria Isabela..Lenore Chippendale
Lula..Susan Blake
Don Lorenzo..George Alison
Trajano..Harry Plimmer
Gabriel..Ralph Roberts
Liborio..William B. Mack

ACT II

Sister Gracia..Ethel Barrymore
Margarita..Madeline Delmar
Candelas..Ernestine Gaines
Quica..Georgia Harvey
Cecilia..Phyllis Blake
The Dumb Girl..Patrice Amati
Sister Cristina..Gertrude Maitland
Sister Feliciana..Lenore Chippendale
Enrique..McKay Morris

ACT III

Sister Gracia..Ethel Barrymore
Sister Dionisia..Jeannette Sherwin
Engracia..Jane Towneley
The Innocent..Georgie Drew Mendum
Paquita..Eleanor Powers
Lorenza..Joan Carvel
Morenito..Charles Powers
Felipe..Elisha Cook, Jr.
Juan de Dios..J. Warren Lyons

Vincente....................................Marcel Dill
Policarpo....................................Ralph Roberts
Victor....................................Bernard Max
Ramon....................................Leslie Orleans
Alphonse....................................Edward Teene
Jose....................................Lionel Dante

The First Act Takes Place in an Asylum for Poor Old Men; the Second in a Maternity Home; the Third in an Orphanage.

In the First Act Sister Gracia Is 19, in the Second 29, and in the Third Act She is 70.

Staged by E. M. Blythe.

See page 316.

THAT FERGUSON FAMILY

(129 performances)

A comedy drama in three acts by Howard Chenery. Produced by Gustav Blum at the Little Theatre, New York, December 22, 1928.

Cast of characters—

Mertie Ferguson....................................Jean Adair
Fred Ferguson....................................Halliam Bosworth
Tavie Ferguson....................................Marienne Francks
Joe Ferguson....................................Alan Ward
Rupert Striker....................................Arthur Kohl
Laura Connelly....................................Rita Paige
Bert Connelly....................................Spencer Binyon
Mrs. Sarah Thorne....................................Doro Matthews
Bill Fleming....................................George N. Price
Mary Fleming....................................Thelma Paige

Acts I, II and III.—The Living Room at the Fergusons.

Staged by Gustav Blum.

Rebelling against the dominancy of their mother, the three Ferguson children, Tavie, Joe and Laura, determine to live their own lives. Laura elopes with Bert Connelly, Joe elopes with Mary Fleming. Tavie steals gowns from her employer, but is forgiven and marries Rupert Striker. All three marriages turn out much better than Mother Ferguson thought possible. She resigns herself to a lonesome life until her grandchildren are born.

POTIPHAR'S WIFE

(16 performances)

A play in three acts by Edgar C. Middleton. Produced by Whitbar Co., Inc., at the Craig Theatre, New York, December 24, 1928.

Cast of characters—

Allen	Barry O'Neill
Charles, Earl of Aylesbrough	J. P. Wilson
Lady Sylvia Cardington	Ann Delafield
Major Tony Barlow	Roland Hogue
Diana, Countess of Aylesbrough	Frances Carson
Stevens	Harry Lilford
Hon. Mabel Worthington	May Ediss
Rosita Barlow	Audrey Ridgwell
Hon. Maurice Worthington	Colin Campbell
Geoffrey Hayes	George Thorpe
Therese	Juliette Velty
Detective Sergeant Rogers	Marshall Vincent
Mr. Justice Henry	Arthur Lewis
William West, K. C.	Henry Warwick
Geoffrey Stanforth	Jerome Collamore
Clerk of the Court	C. E. Ashley
Aubrey Matthews	F. H. Day
George Hanson	Douglas Barrington

Act I.—Scene 1—The Hall, Maidham Towers, Kent, England. 2—Lady Diana's Boudoir. Act II.—The Hall, Maidham Towers, Kent, England. Act III.—Scene 1—The Chatstone Assize Court. 2—Same as Act II.

Staged by Horace Sinclair.

The Countess of Aylesbrough, desiring Allen, her chauffeur, is incensed when he spurns her advances. Raising great hue and cry, she alarms the family and the neighbors and swears Allen has attacked her. The jury, however, refuses to convict Allen and her ladyship has to engage another chauffeur.

POPPA

(96 performances)

A comedy in three acts by Bella and Samuel Spewack. Produced by H. S. Kraft at the Biltmore Theatre, New York, December 24, 1928.

Cast of characters—

Herbert Schwitzky	Harold Waldrige
Mrs. Schwitzky	Anna Apple
Marjorie	Sylvia Hoffman
Ruth Schwitzky	Mary Ricard
Philip Rosenthal	Edward Shaw
Mrs. Rosenthal	Mara Keval
Pincus Schwitzky	Sam Jaffe
Mr. Finkel	Wilton C. Herman
Jake Harris	William E. Morris
"Big Boy" Shapiro	Raymond O'Brien
Mrs. Finkel	Paula Walter
Fifi	Lillian Toller
Mr. Schlossberg	Martin Malloy
Detective	Morris J. Ward
Flannery	George Sawyer

Acts I and II.—Schwitzky Home. Act III.—Scene 1—A Cell in an East Side Jail. 2—The Schwitzky Home.

Staged by George Abbott.

Poppa Schwitzky, mixing in politics and neglecting his insurance business, is elected alderman and then framed on a bribery charge by Jake Harris. They get Poppa pretty close to jail, but a dictaphone hidden by son Herbert clears him and convicts Harris.

ONE WAY STREET

(56 performances)

A mystery drama in three acts by Beulah Poynter. Produced by George Leffler at the George M. Cohan Theatre, New York, December 24, 1928.

Cast of characters—

Peters.....Ross Hertz
Wilson Garret.....John R. Hamilton
Ned Jenkins.....Thos. B. Carnahan, Jr.
John Stevens.....William Crimans
Terry McConnell.....Alfred Swenson
Jane Gallaway.....Gertrude Hitz
Milton Fleming.....Sherling Oliver
Joe Diamonde.....Bert Wilcox
Jim Burley.....Jean Clarendon
Ching.....J. Harry Jenkins
Sheldon Colby.....Robert Hudson
Limpy Mike.....Walton Butterfield
Elaine Dorrance.....Beatrice Nichols
Policeman.....Thomas Jordan
George Carter.....Maynard Burgess
Madge Garret.....Wilhelmina Morris

Act I.—Bedroom in the Carrington Hotel. Act II.—Sheldon Colby's Home. Act III.—Lobby and Ladies' Room of the Carrington Hotel.

Staged by Hamilton MacFadden.

Sheldon Colby, in the dope business, hires a girl to bring in his drug supplies from Canada. She is murdered and her body stuffed in a trunk. Investigation of many suspected murderers reveals the killing to have been done by a brother whose sister had been led into the dope habit by the dead girl.

CYRANO DE BERGERAC

A poetic drama in five acts by Edmond Rostand, put into English by Brian Hooker. Revived by Walter Hampden at the Hampden Theatre, New York, December 25, 1928.

Cast of characters—

Cyrano de Bergerac.....Walter Hampden
Christian de Neuvillette.....Charles Quigley
Comte de Guiche.....Louis Polan

Ragueneau	Cecil Yapp
Le Bret	Ernest Rowan
Ligniere	William Sauter
Carbon de Castel-Jaloux	C. Norman Hammond
Vicomte de Valvert	Gordon Hart
A Marquis	Franklin Salisbury
Another Marquis	Robert C. Schnitzer
Montfleury	C. Norman Hammond
Bellerose	Antonio Salerno
Jodelet	William Thornton
Cuigy	Francis Dears
Brissaille	Albert G. West
A Busybody	S. Thomas Gomez
A Musketeer	Robert Norton
D'Artagnan	Jan Lindermann
A Spanish Officer	Howard Galt
Cavaliers	Harold Williams O. C. Helming
A Porter	Gage Bennett
A Man	Edmund Voisin
Another Man	Murray D'Arcy
A Guardsman	Stephen Irving
A Citizen	Joseph Milton
His Son	Omar Le Gant
A Pickpocket	Phillip C. Jones
Betrandou	Franklin Salisbury
A Capuchin	Edwin Cushman
Pages	Alvin Proctor Egisto Visser Richard Jack
Lackeys	Edwin S. Ross, Jr. Richard Lawrence
Roxane	Ingeborg Torrup
Her Duenna	Anne Tonetti
Lise	Caroline Meade
An Orange Girl	Mabel Moore
A Flower Girl	Evelyn Goodrich
A Soubrette	Anna Lubow
A Comedienne	Harriet Ingersoll
Another Comedienne	Anne Mitchell
Mother Marguerite de Jesus	Caroline Meade
Sister Marthe	Mabel Moore
Sister Claire	Evelyn Goodrich
A Nun	Anna Lubow
A Little Girl	Stella Kinsley

Act I.—A Performance at the Hotel de Bourgoyne. Act II.—The Bakery of the Poets. Act III.—Roxane's Kiss. Act IV.—The Cadets of Gascoyne. Act V.—Cyrano's Gazette.

Staged by Mr. Hampden.

FALSTAFF

(15 performances)

A comedy in three acts by James Plaisted Webber based on Shakespeare's immortal character. Produced by Mr. and Mrs. Coburn at the Coburn Theatre, New York, December 25, 1928.

Cast of characters—

Prince Hal, Later King Henry the Fifth	John D. Seymour
Duke of Exeter	N. St. Clair Hales
Sir John Falstaff	Charles Coburn
Pistol	Walter Edwin
Robin	Marie Simpson

Bardolph....Francis Tyler
Nym....Arthur Shaw
Poins....Paul Parks
Robert Shallow....Frank Peters
Justice Silence....Harry Thomas
Ford....Lawrence H. Cecil
Sheriff....N. St. Clair Hales
A Sheriff's Officer....Henry Senber
A Trader....Sheppard Strudwick
Another Trader....Donald Black
Mouldy....Jack Shannon
Shadow....Sheppard Strudwick
Wart....Ernest Coan
Feeble....Roger A. Nye
Bullcalf....Romney Fell
A Herald....Sheppard Strudwick
Francis....Frank Howard
Mistress Ford....Mrs. Coburn
Mistress Page....Marjorie Marquis
Anne Page....Kathryn Reece
Mistress Quickly....Ethel Morrison
Doll....Helen Tilden
Cicely Hacket....Ruth Marion
Joan....Virginia Gordon
Jane Smile....Margaret Solley
Helen....Elizabeth Quay
Audrey....Roma Gaskell
Marian....Edith Gwenn
Dorcas....Marjorie Palmer
Mopsa....Grace Hornby
Kate....Marcella Henry
Meg....Helen Anderson
Peter Turph....Donald Black
Henry Pimpernell....David Shesgreen
John Naps....Kenneth Curtis
Nicholas Sugarsop....Garland Brunton

Act I.—Scene 1—Courtyard of The Garter Inn. 2—Before the Inn. 3—The Courtyard. Act II.—Scene 1—A Road Through a Forest. 2—Interior of the Garter Inn. Act III.—Scene 1—A Room in Ford's House. 2—Outside the Inn. 3—The Courtyard.

Staged by Richard Boleslavsky and Henry Stillman.

Falstaff interludes from the Shakespeare dramas woven into a connected tale with several songs added.

THE RED ROBE

(167 performances)

A romantic play with music from the novel by Stanley Weyman, in three acts. Produced by Messrs. Shubert at the Shubert Theatre, New York, December 25, 1928.

Cast of characters—

Nanette....Marjorie Peterson
Lieut. Roland De Brissac....George Dobbs
Captain La Rolle....Barnett Parker
Hercule....Barry Lupino
Jacques....Ivan Arbuckle
A Lady....Peggy Dolan
Marquis De Pombal....Roy Gordon

De Fargis....................Gerald Gehlert
Gil De Berault....................Walter Woolf
Marie....................Violet Carlson
Renee De Cocheforet....................Helen Gilliland
Sir John Blunt....................John H. Goldsworthy
His Eminence, Cardinal Richelieu....................Jose Ruben
Friar Joseph....................Lee Beggs
Sergeant Corbeau....................Edward Orchard
Maids in Cafe Zaton....................Sally Coakley, Alice Kennedy
Nell Moran, Grace Driggs
Elaine, Countess De Cocheforet....................Manila Powers
Henri, Count De Cocheforet....................S. Herbert Bragiotti
Lieutenant Manet....................Charles Carver
Francois....................Hugh Chilvers
Sergeant Malpas....................Fred Von Golisch
An Abbe....................Charles Froom
A Courtier....................Ernest Goodhart
The King's Chamberlain....................Ivan Arbuckle
Louis XIII....................Edward Marshall

Act I.—Cafe Zaton. Act II.—Scene 1—Room in the Chateau De Cocheforet. 2—Park of the Chateau. 3—Garden of the Chateau. Act III.—Salon in the Palais de Richelieu.
Staged by Stanley Logan.

Gil de Berault, soldier of fortune, pardoned by the Cardinal after his arrest and conviction on a duelling charge, undertakes the arrest of Henri de Cocheforet, leader of the Cardinal's enemies. He manages the capture of De Cocheforet and for romantic reasons lets him go. De Berault is properly rewarded.

* BROTHERS

(199 performances)

A play in three acts by Herbert Ashton, Jr. Produced by John Henry Mears at the 48th St. Theatre, New York, December 25, 1928.

Cast of characters—

Dr. Gene Holden....................Ben McQuarrie
Dr. Calvin Moore....................William Ingersoll
Dr. Leslie Stevens....................William J. Kelly
Judge Naughton....................James Seeley
Bess Naughton....................Clara Palmer
Roma Moore....................Grace Menken
"Oily" Joe....................Matt Briggs
Pete....................Ashley Cooper
Marguerite....................Rita Carlyle
Sponge....................Lloyd Carleton
Blutch....................Gene Byram
Bill....................Russell Rockwell
Anne Wolcott....................Irene Shirley
May....................Alyce Dera
Maude....................Rosemary King
Jigger....................Eugene Williams
Officer Mike....................Luke Conness
Robert Naughton }
Eddie Connelly }....................Bert Lytell

Prologue.—Corner of a City Club. Acts I and III.—Judge

Naughton's Home. Act II.—"Oily" Joe's Place, Along the Waterfront.
Staged by Arthur Hurley.

To test their theories respecting the effect of environment on character building three physicians take identical twins and place one for adoption in a cultured family and the other in the slums. The boys grow up, the sheltered one to be a lawyer and dope fiend, the other a friendly east side boy with ambitions and ideals. Murder is done, the east side twin is accused, the west side twin serves as his lawyer and effects his release. The west side twin is put in a sanitarium to take the drug cure, the east side boy takes his place in the cultured family and wins his sweetheart. Fortunately the drug addict dies.

SAKURA

(7 performances)

A play in three acts by Atherton Brownell. Produced by Walker Whiteside at the Belmont Theatre, New York, December 25, 1928.

Cast of characters—

Motsu	Michael Rale
Martha Carlton	Lulu Mae Hubbard
Taizo	Carl H. Vose
Sada Ko	Franc Hale
Alexei Ivanoff	Hugh Huntley
George Stillman	Charles Penman
Robert Carlton	Alexander F. Frank
Yusu	William Dunne
Daisuke	Richard Ranier
Prince Sanetomo Hagane	Walker Whiteside
Tetsujo	Frank Henderson
O'Susume	Catherine Proctor
Tora	Daisy Belmore
Hisa	Don Currie
Goro	Elwyn Eaton
Ivan Ivanow	Manart Kippen

Act I.—Verandah of the American Embassy, in Tokio, Japan. Act II.—Wura Zashiki. Act III.—Omote Zashiki. Act IV.—Garden of the American Embassy, Tokio.
Staged by Walter Whiteside.

Prince Hagane, upholding the honor of old Japan, uncovers the plots of a Russian under-cover man, Alexei Ivanoff, retrieves a secret treaty and prevents Ivanoff from running away with one of Japan's fairest daughters, Onda Sada, who is thus left to give her love to the Prince.

HOUSEBOAT ON THE STYX

(103 performances)

A play in two acts by Kenneth Webb and John E. Hazzard. Produced by Ned Jakobs at the Liberty Theatre, New York, December 25, 1928.

Cast of characters—

Charon, Ferryman of the River Styx	Bertram Peacock
Ponce de Leon	Sam Ash
Queen Elizabeth	Blanche Ring
Salome	Virginia Watts
Mrs. Noah	Jessie Graham
Sappho	Millicent Bancroft
Lucretia Borgia	Mary McDonald
Queen of Sheba	Pauline Dee
Delilah	Helene Arden
Helen of Troy	Georgia Gwynne
Josephine	Marion Stuart
Sir Walter Raleigh	Hal Forde
Catherine of Aragon	Dorothy Humphreys
Anne Boleyn	Edith Britton
Jane Seymour	Grace Cantrelle
Anne of Cleves	Gloria Clare
Katherine Howard	Myrtle Arnette
Katherine Parr	Katharine Porter
Henry VIII	William Danforth
A Servant	Richard MacAleese
Captain William Kidd	John E. Hazzard
Cleopatra	Alice MacKenzie
George Washington	Cliff Heckinger
Adam Eva	Maurine and Norva
Napoleon	Johnny Fields
P. T. Barnum	Harry Bates
Nero	Harry Hermsen
Shakespeare	John Osborne Clemson
Morgan	Richard MacAleese
Captain of Police	Dorothy Humphreys
Columbus	Johnny Fields
Noah	Cliff Heckinger
Sherlock Holmes	Charles Gibney
Specialty Dancers	Al. Jordan, Vera Clarke, Petra Olsen, Dorothy Humphreys

Act I.—Scene 1—Charon's Ferry on the River Styx. 2—Grand Hall in Henry VIII's Castle. 3—Tree of Knowledge. 4—Snuggery of the Houseboat. 5—Houseboat at the Dock. Act II.—Scene 1—Deck of the Houseboat. 2—Street in Hades. 3—Snuggery of the Houseboat. 4—Lookout of the "Gehenna." 5—Wheel of the Houseboat. 6—Fog. 7—Houseboat, Ladies' Day.

Staged by Oscar Eagle.

The ladies of Hades, including Sappho, Queen Elizabeth, Delilah, Cleopatra and the Queen of Sheba, are curious about the houseboat where the men hold their stag parties. Investigating, they find it rather a jolly place, but soon tire of it and are glad to get back home.

BACK SEAT DRIVERS

(15 performances)

A farce-comedy in three acts by Larry E. Johnson. Produced by Roy Walling at the Wallack's Theatre, New York, December 25, 1928.

Cast of characters—

John Wilson.....John Litel
Mrs. Wilson.....Sylva Farnese
Peter Simms.....Len D. Hollister
Mrs. Moffet.....Tabatha Goodwin
Cuthbert Moffet.....Hugh Cameron
Austin Spence.....Cyril Ring
Mrs. Webb-Stephens.....Grace Huff
Mrs. Simms.....Olga Krolow

Acts I, II and III.—The Living-Room of John Wilson Apartment.

Staged by Len D. Hollister.

Mrs. Wilson and Mrs. Moffet, believing their husbands are unwisely led in investments, organize a fake company into which the family savings are put. Their fake partners, however, turn out to be crooks who would have run away with the money if the husbands had not been clever enough to stop them.

HELLO DADDY

(198 performances)

A musical comedy in two acts, book by Herbert Fields, lyrics by Dorothy Fields. Produced by Lew Fields at the Lew Fields' Theatre, New York, December 26, 1928.

Cast of characters—

Miss Prichard.....Florence Earle
Betty Hauser.....Betty Starbuck
Grace.....Marjorie-May Martin
Dot.....Dorothy Roy
Eloise.....Ethel Allen
Ellen.....Elizabeth Crandall
Edna.....Dorothy Croyle
Anthony Bennett.....Wilfred Clark
Lawrence Tucker.....Allen Kearns
Connie Block.....Mary Lawlor
Henry Block.....Lew Fields
Emma Block.....Alice Fischer
Helen.....Wanda Gall
Noel Burnham.....Billy Taylor
Edward Hauser.....George Hassell
Mathilde Burnham.....Madeline Grey
Godfrey Burnham.....Carroll Glucas

Helene }
Gertrude } .... Giersdorf Sisters
Marguerite }

Act I.—Scene 1—Before the Cedarhurst School for Girls. 2—Club Car of a Local Train. 3—Reception Room at Block's. Act II.—Sun Parlor at Block's.

Staged by John Murray Anderson.

Henry Block, Edward Hauser and Anthony Bennett whose wives run the Purity League, discover that all three have been paying a dancer they had known in their youth a weekly allowance for the support of a child she told each of them he had fathered. A sappy boy visiting the town is mistaken for the unhappy offspring to the embarrassment of everybody.

TO-MORROW

(11 performances)

A play in two acts by Hull Gould and Saxon Kling. Produced by John Ashley, Ltd., at the Lyceum Theatre, New York, December 28, 1928.

Cast of characters—

Grace .... Jessie Busley
Herbert .... Clyde Fillmore
Helen .... Mary Loane
Charles .... Harold Elliott
Tommy .... Bruce Evans
Prof. Withers .... Walter Allen
Mary .... Kathleen Mulqueen
A Broker .... Carroll Ashburn
Teddy .... Fred Irving Lewis
Radio Operator .... Joseph Parry
Aunt Ada .... Margaret Arrow
Spanish Singer .... Joan Sudlow

Acts I and II.—New York Home of the Brown Family.

Staged by Philip Bartholomae.

In 1982 the Browns are living on the roof of Excelsior Towers in New York, communicating with their friends by television and radiovision and doing all their traveling by air bus. Charles, a friend, tries to steal an electrical patent from Prof. Withers and elope with the Brown daughter, Helen. He is defeated in both projects.

CAPRICE

(186 performances)

A play by Sil-Vara, translated and adapted by Philip Moeller. Produced by The Theatre Guild at the Guild Theatre, New York, December 31, 1928.

Cast of characters—

Counselor Albert Von Echardt........................Alfred Lunt
A Delicate Lady..................................Geneva Harrison
Minna..Caroline Newcomb
The Doctor.......................................Ernest Cossart
Clerk..Leonard Loan
Amalia...Lily Cahill
Ilsa Von Ilsen.....................................Lynn Fontanne
Robert...............................Douglass Montgomery
Acts I, II and III.—Counselor Von Echardt's Study in Vienna.
Staged by Philip Moeller.

Albert von Echardt, hearing from a former mistress, Amalia, that their son Robert has reached the age of 16 and is in need of a father's counsel, is moved by curiosity and the paternal urge to take his son into his home. There is, however, the objection of his current mistress, Ilsa von Ilsen, to reckon with. Amalia and Robert come, Ilsa runs away to the Bavarian mountains. Two weeks later Ilsa is back and solves Albert's difficulties by permitting Robert to make love to her and then telling him of her relations with his father. Robert and Amalia leave in high dudgeon.

LADY DEDLOCK

(40 performances)

A romantic melodrama in four acts by Paul Kester, founded on the novel "Bleak House" by Charles Dickens. Produced by Murray Phillips and J. J. Leventhal at the Ambassador Theatre, New York, December 31, 1928.

Cast of characters—

Inspector Bucket...................................Hubert Druce
Mr. Guppy...Francis Compton
Volumnia Dedlock...................................Ethel Griffies
William...Robert Vivian
Mary, Lady Woodcourt..........................Katherine Lorimer
Allan Dedlock.....................................Robert Harrigan
Sir Leicester Dedlock..........................St. Clair Bayfield
James...William Eville
Second Footman....................................Frances Moran
Third Footman...................................Charles Campbell
Lady Dedlock......................................Margaret Anglin
Hortense..Margaret Anglin
Mr. Tulkinghorn..................................John Ivancowich
Harold Skimpole...................................Edward Cooper
Jahn Jarndyce....................................Thomas Holding
Esther Summerson..............................Margaret Shackleford
Jo...Charles Cromer
The Duchess of Lincolnshire..........................Esta Rollo
The Duke of Lincolnshire.....................Patrick J. MacMahn
Sir George Barberry...............................Charles O'Neil
Constable Neckert..................................Edward Cooper
Constable Gregory................................Francis Compton
A Link Boy...Charles Dill

Act I.—Ghost's Walk, Chesney Wold. Act II.—Scene 1—Street Scene in the Slums. 2—Drawing Room at Chesney Wold. Act III.—Drawing Room at Chesney Wold. Act IV.—Scene 1—Outside the Church Yard Gate. 2—Street. 3—Park of Chesney Wold.
Staged by Margaret Anglin.

At Chesney Wold Lady Dedlock is faced by the discovery of her husband's solicitor, Mr. Tulkinghorn, that she is the mother of Esther Summerson, the fiancée of Allan Dedlock. She had thought her child dead. Mr. Tulkinghorn is murdered mysteriously, suspicion points to Lady Dedlock, and, though innocent, rather than face the disgrace of a trial, she kills herself on the grave of Esther's father, Geoffrey Hawdon.

THE STREET WOLF

(8 performances)

A melodramatic comedy in three acts by Hyman Adler and Edward Paulton. Produced by Hyman Adler, at the Garrick Theatre, New York, December 31, 1928.

Cast of characters—

Chick Lollipop	Eddie O'Connor
Waiter	Jack Byrne
Mike Sullivan	Walter Jay Wilson
Abe Fitzpatrick	Jacob Frank
Mary Taylor	Katherine Raynore
Florence Wainwright	Mabel Bunyea
Monk Lester	Cornelius Roddy
Gilbert Taylor	Richard Beach
Minnie Wilton	Grace E. Durkin
Dorothy Hansen (Tuffie)	Peggy O'Connor
Chief Edwards	Edward Roseman
Mr. Wilton	Max Von Mitzel
Officer Riordan	Robert Blake

Acts I, II and III.—Lounging Room of a Rathskeller in the Village.
Staged by Hyman Adler.

THE MARRIAGE BED

(72 performances)

Ernest Pascal's dramatization of his novel in three acts. Produced by Sam H. Harris, at the Booth Theatre, New York, January 7, 1929.

Cast of characters—

Gilbert Reid	Edward Emery
Mary Boyd	Ann Davis
Cecily Reid	Helen Chandler
Andrew Trask	Edwin Stanley
Caroline Reid	Elizabeth Patterson

Mollie Saunders.............................Harriet MacGibbon
Clyde Saunders.............................Ernest Wood
George Boyd.............................Allan Dinehart
Christine Kennedy.............................Helen Flint
Acts I, II and III.—The Home of the George Boyds.
Staged by Robert Milton.

Mary Boyd, knowing that George, her husband, has been having an affair with Christine Kennedy, refuses to let the knowledge blind her to her contract as homemaker and mother. She refuses to give George a divorce until she discovers that her own sister Cecily is also carrying on with a married man and cannot marry him because of an equally stubborn wife. By the time Mary is ready to grant the divorce George is back home pleading to be forgiven.

THE GUINEA PIG

(64 performances)

Comedy in three acts by Preston Sturges. Produced by Mr. Sturges at the President Theatre, New York, January 7, 1929.

Cast of characters—

Miss Snitkin.............................Rhoda Cross
Seth Fellows.............................Robert Robson
Sam Small.............................Alexander Carr
Wilton Smith.............................John Ferguson
Helen Reading.............................Ruth Thomas
Robert Fleming.............................John Vosburgh
Catherine Howard.............................Mary Carroll
Natalie.............................Andree Corday
Act I.—Office of Sam Small. Acts II and III.—Mrs. Howard's Living Room.
Staged by Walter Greenough.

Sam Small, play producer, tells Catherine Howard, playwright, that her dramas will never be convincing until she herself has experienced the emotions of which she writes. Catherine decides to practice a little and grabs Wilton Smith as her "guinea pig" or laboratory material. By the time she has her emotions catalogued Catherine is in love with Wilton.

DEEP HARLEM

(8 performances)

A musical comedy in two acts, book by Whitney and Tutt, lyrics by Homer Tutt and Henry Creamer, music by Joe Jordan. Produced at the Biltmore Theatre, New York, January 7, 1929.

Principals engaged—

Andrew Bishop	Rosa White
Chappie Chappelle	Juanita Stinnette
Salem Whitney	Mabel Ridley
Homer Tutt	Neeka Shaw
Columbus Jackson	Marietta Warren
Sterling Grant	Mary Welch
John Mason	Louise Williams
William Edmondson	Mary King
Billy Andrews	Alice Gorgas
Howard Elmore	Carrie Huff
Cutout and Leonard	Inez Glover
Ivy Black	Gertrude Gardeen
Virginia Branum	Lena Wilson

Staged by Henry Creamer.

VERMONT

(15 performances)

A play in a prologue and four acts by A. E. Thomas. Produced by George M. Cohan, at the Erlanger Theatre, New York, January 7, 1929.

Cast of characters—

James Belden	Allyn Joslyn
Henry Carter	John T. Doyle
Jane Selden	Kate Mayhew
Ann Carter	Phyllis Povah
John Carter	Thomas V. Gillen
William Burr	Harold Healy
Hanson	Theodore Newton
Donovan	Jack Williams
Charles Carter	Frank Rowan
Al Farley	Mark Sullivan
Robert Walker	Ring Thomas

Acts I, II and III.—At the Carter Homestead in Vermont.
Staged by Sam Forrest.

For generations the Carters have been honest and law-abiding citizens of Vermont. When prohibition starts rum running across the Canadian border Henry Carter is sorely tempted to shut his eyes and open his old barn as a daylight hideout for the bootleggers. He finally takes a bribe of $50 a week, thinking it will help him pay for medical treatment for his oldest son, who has been blinded by bad liquor, and send his youngest son through college. Ann Carter, daughter, induces her father to give back the bribe and recover some shred of his self-respect. Before he can do it he is killed in a fight between hi-jackers and bootleggers and his young son is jailed.

POLLY

(15 performances)

A musical version of David Belasco's "Polly with a Past," in two acts, book by Guy Bolton and George Middleton, music and lyrics by Herbert Stothart, Philip Charig and Irving Cæsar. Produced by Arthur Hammerstein, at the Lyric Theatre, New York, January 8, 1929.

Cast of characters—

Clay Cullen.................................William Seabury
Sue..Marion Saki
Betty...Inez Courtney
Harry Richards..........................Harry K. Morton
Polly Shannon..June
Bill Collector.................................Alonzo Price
Addie Stiles......................................Fred Allen
Rex Van Zile................................John Hundley
Myrtle Grant....................................Lucy Monroe
Mrs. Van Zile.............................Isabel O'Madigan
Prentice Van Zile........................Charles Esdale
Arturo..Tudor Penrose

Act I.—Scene 1—Aba Daba Night Club. 2—Editorial Room, Hampton Bee. 3—Southampton Golf Club. Act II.—Scene 1—Garden of Mrs. Van Zile's Home in Southampton. 2—Railroad Station. 3—Spanish Inn.

Staged by Jack Haskell.

Polly Shannon, an honest chorus girl in love with Rex Van Zile, a swell polo player of Southampton, L. I., agrees to pose as a naughty French actress and friend of Van Zile to arouse the jealousy of Myrtle Grant, with whom Van Zile fancies himself in love. During the working out of the conspiracy Polly and Van Zile discover that they are in love with each other.

* FOLLOW THRU

(181 performances)

A musical slice of country club life in two acts by Laurence Schwab and B. G. DeSylva. Produced by Laurence Schwab and Frank Mandel, at the 46th Street Theatre, January 9, 1929.

Cast of characters—

"Mac" Moore.............................Arthur Aylesworth
Thomas Darcy "Dinty" Moore....................Don Tomkins
Lora Moore.......................................Irene Delroy
Angie Howard....................................Zelma O'Neal
Martin Bascomb...............................Frank Kingdon
Babs Bascomb..................................Margaret Lee
J. C. Effingham.................................John Sheehan

Jerry Downs.......................................John Barker
Jack Martin.......................................Jack Haley
Ruth Van Horn.......................................Madeline Cameron
Mrs. Bascomb.......................................Edith Campbell
Mr. Manning.......................................Al Downing
Molly.......................................Eleanor Powell
Steve.......................................Paul Howard
Olive.......................................Dorothy Christie
Glenna.......................................Yvonne Grey
Virginia.......................................Constance Lane
The Country Club Boys—Carrick Douglas, Jack Lawrence, W. E. Critzer, Oscar Ellinger, John Hammond, Fred Kuhnly, Arthur Bryan, Maurice Siegel

Act I.—Scene 1—The Bound Brook Country Club. 2—Golf Course. 3—Sun Porch. 4—Behind the First Tee. 5—In Front of the Club House. Act II.—Scene 1—In Front of Club House. 2—Near Club House. 3—Ladies' Dressing Room. 4—Fourteenth Hole. 5—Eighteenth Green. 6—Behind First Tee. 7—The Gate.

Staged by Edgar MacGregor and Donald Oenslager.

Lora Moore, daughter of a golf club professional, and Ruth Van Horn are rivals for the championship of the club and likewise the smiles and songs of Jerry Downs, an amateur champion turned professional. Lora wins.

S. S. GLENCAIRN

(90 performances)

Four episodes of the sea by Eugene O'Neill. Revived at the Provincetown Theatre, New York, January 9, 1929.

Cast of characters—

The Crew of the British Tramp Steamer Glencairn:
Yank.......................................Lionel J. Stander
Driscoll.......................................Byron Russell
Olson.......................................Walter Abel
Davis.......................................Harold McGee
Cocky.......................................George Tawde
Smitty.......................................E. J. Ballantine
Ivan.......................................George Tobias
Scotty.......................................Archie Sinclair
Paul.......................................Richard Gaines
Old Tom.......................................Harold McGee
Big Frank.......................................Charles A. Wagner
Paddy.......................................H. L. Remsten
The Captain.......................................Robert Lucius Cook
The First Mate.......................................Max Essin
West Indian Negresses:
Bella.......................................Mary Johns
Susie.......................................Louise Bradley
Violet.......................................Barbara Benedict
Pearl.......................................Christine Cooper
Londoners:
Joe.......................................Robert Lucius Cook
Nick.......................................A. Montague Ash
Mag.......................................Barbara Benedict
Freda.......................................Dorothee Nolan
Kate.......................................Christine Cooper
First Rough.......................................H. L. Remsten
Second Rough.......................................Max Essin

Singers.............................Ena Hourwich, Evelyn Hill, Madeline Ray, Lucienne Schreve

First Episode—"The Moon of the Caribbees." The Forward Deck of the S. S. Glencairn, at Anchor Off an Island in the West Indies in 1913. Second Episode—"In the Zone." Forecastle of the S. S. Glencairn During the Great War. Third Episode—"Bound East for Cardiff." Forecastle of the S. S. Glencairn During a Voyage from New York to Cardiff Some Years Later. Fourth Episode—"The Long Voyage Home." A Bar of a Dive on the London Waterfront.

Staged by E. J. Ballantine.

Four one-act Eugene O'Neill plays first combined in the form of a four-act play in 1924.

* STREET SCENE

(180 performances)

A play in three acts by Elmer Rice. Produced by William A. Brady, Ltd., at the Playhouse, New York, January 10, 1929.

Cast of characters—

Abraham Kaplan...................................Leo Bulgakov
Greta Fiorentino.............................Eleanor Wesselhoeft
Emma Jones..Beulah Bondi
Olga Olsen...Hilda Bruce
Willie Moran....................................Russell Griffin
Anna Moran.......................................Mary Servoss
Daniel Buchanan...........................Conway Washburne
Frank Moran.......................................Robert Kelly
George Jones.....................................T. H. Manning
Steve Sankey.....................................Joseph Baird
Agnes Cushing...................................Jane Corcoran
Carl Olsen.....................................John M. Qualen
Shirley Kaplan....................................Anna Kostant
Filippo Fiorentino............................George Humbert
Alice Simpson......................................Emily Hamill
Laura Hildebrand.............................Frederica Going
Mary Hildebrand..................................Eileen Smith
Charlie Hildebrand...........................Alexander Lewis
Samuel Kaplan....................................Horace Braham
Rose Moran.....................................Erin O'Brien-Moore
Harry Easter.......................................Glenn Coulter
Mae Jones...Millicent Green
Dick McGann...Joseph Lee
Vincent Jones..................................Matthew McHugh
Dr. John Wilson....................................John Crump
Officer Harry Murphy.........................Edward Downes
A Milkman..Ralph Willard
A Letter-Carrier.............................Herbert Lindholm
An Ice-Man....................................Samuel S. Bonnell
Two College Girls............................Rose Lerner, Astrid Alwynn
A Music Student..................................Mary Emerson
Marshall James Henry........................Ellsworth Jones
Fred Cullen..Jean Sidney
An Old-Clothes Man.................................Joe Cogert
An Interne.....................................Samuel S. Bonnell
An Ambulance Driver..........................Anthony Pawley
A Furniture Mover..............................Ed. A. McHugh
Two Nurse-Maids...............................Astrid Alwynn, Nelly Neil

Policemen	Carl C. Milter John Kelly Anthony Pawley
Two Apartment Hunters	Frances F. Golden Otto Frederick

Acts I, II and III.—A Night in June, and on the Morning and Afternoon of the Following Day, New York.
Staged by Elmer Rice.

See page 26.

SKYROCKET

(11 performances)

A play in three acts by Mark Reed. Produced by Gilbert Miller in association with Guthrie McClintic, at the Lyceum Theatre, New York, January 11, 1929.

Cast of characters—

Del Ewing	Mary Phillips
Mr. Ewing	J. C. Nugent
Vic. Ewing	Humphrey Bogart
Mrs. Ewing	Clara Blandick
Mrs. Bemis	Lotta Linthicum
Homer Bemis	Howard Freeman
Oishi	Morris Lee
Frank Greer	Ian Wolfe
Reggie MacSweeney	William Broussard
Kitty Marsh	Dorothie Bigelow
Lillian	Gwyneth Gordon

Act I.—The Ewing Home. Acts II and III.—An Apartment on Park Avenue.
Staged by Guthrie McClintic.

Vic Ewing, boastful but likeable in spite of the fault, patents a novelty, makes a lot of money within a few months, moves to Park Avenue and proceeds to go the Park Avenue pace. That excitement waning Vic takes on a musical comedy blonde. Del Ewing, Vic's thrifty wife, resents the blonde and tries to get Vic back to normal living and thinking. She succeeds—after he has lost all his money.

PRECIOUS

(24 performances)

A farcical comedy in a prologue and three acts by James Forbes. Produced by Rosalie Stewart, at the Royale Theatre, New York, January 14, 1929.

Cast of characters—

Andrew Hoyt	John Cumberland
Jepson	Howard Benton

Luke Radcliffe....Hale Hamilton
Stella Peck....Cora Witherspoon
Eva Mills....Dorothy Hall
Alice....Frances McHugh
Alvarez....Jules Epailly
Oliver Denton....Edward Leiter
Sonia....Verree Teasdale
Prologue and Act I.—Home of Andrew Hoyt. Act II and III.—A Suite at a New York Hotel.
Staged by Melville Burke.

Fighting the laws of nature and the advice of his best friends, Andrew Hoyt marries Eva Mills, young enough to be his daughter. Realizing a month later that he has been duped by Eva and her designing sister, Stella, Andrew schemes to force Eva to elope with a young and handsome architect, Oliver Denton.

GYPSY

(64 performances)

A play in three acts by Maxwell Anderson. Produced by Richard Herndon, at the Klaw Theatre, New York, January 14, 1929.

Cast of characters—

Ellen....Claiborne Foster
Cleve....Louis Calhern
Janitor....Jefferson Hall
David....Lester Vail
Mac....Wallace Ford
Sylvia....Ruth Findlay
Marilyn....Mary Young
Acts I and II.—Hastings Apartment, New York City. Act III.—Ellen's One-Room Apartment, New York City.
Staged by George Cukor.

See page 283.

THE LADY FROM ALFAQUEQUE

(17 performances)

A comedy in two acts translated by Helen and Harley Granville-Barker. Produced by the Civic Repertory Theatre, Inc., at the Civic Repertory Theatre, New York, January 14, 1929.

Cast of characters—

Don Pascual....Donald Cameron
Rosita....Beatrice De Neergaard
Alberta....Francis Williams
Realito....J. Edward Bromberg
Fernandita....Alma Kruger
Blanca....Jocelyn Gordon

Neblejas.......................................Paul Leyssac
Nicelas.......................................Robert H. Gordon
Adoracien.......................................Leona Roberts
Felipe Rivas.......................................Lewis Leverett
Paloma.......................................Ria Mooney
Staged by Miss Le Gallienne.

Fernandita, having lived her youth in Alfaqueque, has a sentimental urge to be kind to all other natives of the village. As a result she has many visitors, most of them fakers, who sponge upon her. Chief of these is Felipe Rivas, a rascal but fascinating. Complications follow Felipe's appearances, but they are later adjusted.

ZEPPELIN

(72 performances)

A mystery drama in three acts by McElbert Moore, Earle Crooker and Lowell Brentano. Produced by Jimmie Cooper, at the National Theatre, New York, January 14, 1929.

Cast of characters—

Hans.......................................John Gruenwald
Chief Mech. Heinrich.......................................Bjorn Koefoed
Steward.......................................Alfred A. Hesse
Lt. Sobel.......................................Edward Powell
Prof. Alexander MacKenzie.......................................Julian Noa
Dr. Donald Vail.......................................C. W. Van Voorhis
Connie Vail.......................................Joan Marion
Ed Totten.......................................Raymond Walburn
John Clayton.......................................Paul Guilfoyle
Karl.......................................Frederick Rudin
Lola Bartel.......................................Zolya Talma
Mrs. Burnham.......................................Priscilla Knowles
Del Rodman.......................................Edward Woods
Roger Bates.......................................Alden Chase
Wynne Madison.......................................Rose Hobart
Prof. Philip Keene.......................................Charles Abbe
Capt. Koll.......................................Wallis Clark
Otto.......................................John M. James
Radio Operator.......................................Milton Krimes
Boatman.......................................Gordon Hawthorne
Act I.—Cabins Along the Cat-Walk. Inside the Bag. Acts II and III.—Forward Cabin in the Observation Gondola, Under the Bag.
Staged by Frank Merlin.

Prof. Keene, having invented a gas so powerful that it will spread the curse of leprosy over any community in which it is released, starts with it for a peace conference abroad. By turning it over to a peace league he hopes to prevent war forever. On board the Zeppelin which is carrying the professor and his formula is a leprosy-stricken stowaway seeking to be revenged on the professor. The formula is stolen and re-stolen to the accompaniment of chills and fever both sides of the footlights.

HOUSE UNGUARDED

(39 performances)

A play in three acts by Len D. Hollister and Lester Lonergan. Produced by Bernard Steele, at the Little Theatre, New York, January 15, 1929.

Cast of characters—

Anderson	Jerome Daley
Elliot	Frank Knight
May Wong	Soo Yong
Laura	Shirley Warde
Sam Lee	Goo Chong
Col. James Thorne	Lester Lonergan
Lieut. Harley	John Marston
Mabel Carter	Leila Frost
Higgins	Raymond Bramley
Capt. Clark	Philip Wood
Corp. Dunn	Henry Crossen

Acts I, II and III.—Alternately on the Veranda of a Middle Class Cafe in Balboa, Panama Canal Zone, and in the Living Room of Col. Thorne's Quarters at the U. S. Army Post of That Territory.
Staged by Bernard Steele.

Anderson from New York and Elliot of the Canal Zone, newspaper men, meet in a café in Balboa when both are working on a murder story. Col. Thorne, married to a young wife, has been killed and a young naval lieutenant known to have been visiting Mrs. Thorne is suspected. Anderson relates his own particular love-nest version of the story, which is acted out. Then Elliot begins his version and that is the second act. Finally the fugitive naval lieutenant interrupts them and tells the true story, which is the last act. The colonel was killed by his orderly, who had been blackmailing Mrs. Thorne and the lieutenant.

NED WAYBURN'S GAMBOLS

(31 performances)

In two acts and twenty-eight scenes, lyrics by Morrie Ryskind, music by Walter G. Samuels. Produced by Ned Wayburn, at the Knickerbocker Theatre, New York, January 15, 1929.

Principals engaged—

Charles Irwin
Wm. Holbrook
Roger Gray
Lew Hearn
Fuzzy Knight
Charles Elbey

Libby Holman
Ann Pritchard
Shirley Richards
Olive McClure
Grace Bowman
Virginia Alexander

Butler and Parker	Patricia McGrath
Jack Randall	Frances Cole
John Byam	Eileen Healy

Staged by Ned Wayburn.

CAFE DE DANSE

(31 performances)

A play in three acts, adapted by Leontrovitch Mitchell and Clarke Silvernail from the French play, "Le Maison De Danse." Produced by Ben Bernie and Phil Baker, at the Forrest Theatre, New York, January 14, 1929.

Cast of characters—

Estrellita	Trini
Tomasa	Alison Skipworth
Ramon	Leonard Ceeley
Luisito	Martin Burton
Dolores	Enid Romany
Rinkleman	Gregory Ratoff
Concha	Mary Robinson
Elena	Eileen Culshaw
Mercedes	Pearl Ramoy
Trinidad	Minnie Stanley
Ampara	Isobel Vernon
Chico	Pierre Mario
Rositta	Harriet Donovan
The Guitarist	Bert Melville
Pedro	Mel. A. Buser
1st Sailor	Frank Collins

Acts I, II and III.—In a Cafe de Danse, Barcelona, Spain.
Staged by Gregory Ratoff.

Estrellita is poor but fearfully ambitious. Hoping Tomasa, proprietress of the Café de Danse, will teach her to dance Estrellita is willing to do odd jobs about the place. She even agrees to accept Ramon Tomasa, the beast, if he will help her get her chance. Fiesta night Dolores, the favorite, disappears and Estrellita takes her place. She wins a great success and eludes Ramon, the dog.

THE PARSON'S BRIDE

A melodrama in three acts. Author anonymous. Produced by the Princess Floating Theatre, Norman Thom, director, at the Belmont Theatre, New York, January 21, 1929.

Cast of characters—

Rev. Fred Thorpe	Norman F. Thom
Harry Thorpe	B. H. Buhler
Bill Hicks	Earl Williams

Jared Bumble..Roy F. Burn
Hinky Dink..Willard Cole
Ellen Blake...Queen Marlowe
Sadie Bese..Pansy Mason
Mary Brown..Grace Neill
Acts I, II and III.—On board a river show boat.

A genuine Mississippi river show boat troupe enacts the story of the pretty school teacher with a past she refuses to reveal. Fired from school she finds refuge in the home of a bachelor parson whose brother seeks to seduce her. He fails and she is offered marriage by the parson. She can't marry because her husband, an ex-convict, is still alive. The complication is cleared in time for a happy ending.

The Thom company also presented "Shadow of the Rockies" during this engagement.

MERRY ANDREW

(24 performances)

A comedy in three acts by Lewis Beach. Produced by Laurence Rivers, Inc., at the Henry Miller Theatre, New York, January 21, 1929.

Cast of characters—

Andrew Aiken..Walter Connolly
Ernestine Aiken.....................................Effie Shannon
Janet Aiken...Nedda Harrigan
Sue Aiken...Ellen Dorr
Richard Milburn.....................................Grant Mills
Terry Ellis...Reed Brown, Jr.
Rufus Norcross......................................Joseph Crehan
Bart Pickman..John C. King
Karl Bowker...J. Hammond Dailey
Glenn Nash..Edward Hodge
Katie...Mary Marble
Pearl...Virginia Williams
A Salesman..Orville Harris
Acts I, II and III.—The Drugstore and Later the Home of Andrew Aiken in a City of a Hundred Thousand in the Middle West.
Staged by John Hayden assisted by the author.

Andrew Aiken, village druggist, has worked all his life. On his 60th birth anniversary his wife induces him to sell the store and retire. In three months Andrew is restless and more or less impossible around the house. The maid quits; one daughter quarrels with her fiancé because he insists on devoting his life to work as enthusiastically as did her father; another daughter elopes with a rich young idler who sees no sense in working if you don't have to, and finally Mrs. Aiken schemes to buy back the drug stone and get Andrew out of the house.

HOT WATER

(32 performances)

A play in three acts by Helena Dayton and Louise Bascom Baratt. Produced at the Lucille La Verne Theatre, New York, January 21, 1929.

Cast of characters—

Plumie Gussett	Sara Haden
Clare Bennett	Marga Waldron
Barney McCosh	John M. James
Mrs. Schuyler Grant	Harriet Keehn
Hampton Curtis	Boyd Marshall
Duckie (Also known as Jessica Dale)	Lucille La Verne
Mrs. Binney	Augusta E. Boylston
Lee Carter	Blaine McKendrick
Jack O'Brien	James Orr Ryan
Elain Dumont	Florence Auer
Paul Harding	Charles MacDonald
Peter Gerard	G. O. Taylor

Act I.—Duckie's Basement Quarters. Act II.—Gerard Theatre. Act III.—Scene 1—A Park Bench. 2—A Factory.
Staged by Miss La Verne.

Duckie, an old-time actress, is the janitress of an apartment building and the main support of a house filled with spongers. She invents an umbrella called the "showersal," loses her money, tries to return to the stage, fails and disappears. A lodger successfully puts the showersal umbrella on the market and finds Duckie on a park bench. He tells her the good news, proposes marriage and she agrees to keep him in hot water the rest of his life.

BALIEFF'S CHAUVE-SOURIS

(47 performances)

A revue in the Russian manner. Produced by Morris Gest, at the Jolson Theatre, New York, January 22, 1929.

The following sketches featured—

Blind Street Musicians
Romance of the Toys
Russian Folk Songs
Billeting of the Hussars
Russian Folk Rhymes
Midnight Revue
Knife Grinder
In a Little French Cafe
Boublitchki
Popoff's Porcelains
Doorman at Maxim's
Les Amours de Jean-Pierre
An Etruscan Vase
In the Square
Russian Cossacks
Organ Grinder
You Ought to Hear Olaf Laugh

Staged by Nakita Balieff.

SERENA BLANDISH

(93 performances)

A fabulous comedy in two acts by S. N. Behrman, based on the novel of that name by "A Lady of Quality." Produced by Jed Harris, at the Morosco Theatre, New York, January 23, 1929.

Cast of characters—

Nikkie	Tyrrell Davis
Serena Blandish	Ruth Gordon
Sigmund Traub	Clarence Derwent
Head Waiter	Harold White
Mrs. Blandish	Alice John
A Chauffeur	Derex Hume
Countess Flor di Folio	Constance Collier
Edgar Malleson	Hugh Sinclair
Martin	A. E. Matthews
A Lady of Refined Appearance	Julia Hoyt
Lord Ivor Cream	Henry Daniell
A Gushing Mama	Marion Grey
A Marriageable Daughter	Eileen Byron
Sir Everard Pycheon	Wallace Erskine
Michael	Douglas Garden
A Poet	Alfred Shirley
A Bus Conductor	John Gray
A Musician	Juan Varro

Act I.—Scene 1—A Fashionable Restaurant in London. 2—At Mrs. Blandish's. 3—In the Countess' Limousine. 4—At the Countess'. Act II.—Scene 1—At the Countess'. 2 and 3—At Lord Ivor Cream's. 4—Top of a London Bus. 5—At the Countess'. 6—At the Countess'.

Serena, left with an unpaid check in a restaurant, is rescued by the jeweler Traub who proposes that she permit him to deck her with diamonds and serve as an advertisement in aristocratic London society. He places her under the chaperonage of the Countess Flor di Folio who tries to arrange a rich marriage for her. Serena does her best to get a husband, but not being amorous, though weak, the men elude her. She elopes finally with Edgar Malleson, the least important, socially and financially, of her new acquaintances.

JUDAS

(12 performances)

A play in three acts by Walter Ferris and Basil Rathbone. Produced by William A. Brady, Jr., and Dwight Deere Wiman, at the Longacre Theatre, New York, January 24, 1929.

Cast of characters—

Simon Ish Kerioth....William Courtleigh
Rebekah....Jennie Eustace
Naomi....Dorothy Cumming
Judas....Basil Rathbone
Flavius....Charles Henderson
Marcus....Doan Borup
Thomas....Lyons Wickland
Andrew....Harold Moffet
James....William D. Post
Matthew....Charles Halton
John....William Challee
Peter....Doan Borup
First Priest....John O'Meara
Second Priest....Tom Hayes
Third Priest....A. Lymmborn
Fourth Priest....Ralph Thomas
Caiphas....William Courtleigh
A Priest of the Guard....Joseph Redalieu
Akiba....Charles Halton
Joseph of Arimathea....Robert Barrat

Act I.—The Courtyard of the House of Simon: Kerioth—Judea. Act II.—A House in Bethany, Near Jerusalem. Act III.—The Temple—Jerusalem.

Staged by Richard Boleslavsky.

A defense of the betrayer in which Judas is shown as the most devoted of Jesus' desciples but determined to arouse the Savior as a militant rather than as a spiritual redeemer of the Jewish people. The betrayal is a part of Judas' plan to inspire Jesus' rebellion.

THE SUBWAY

(35 performances)

An episodic play in nine scenes by Elmer Rice. Produced by The Lenox Hill Players, Inc., at the Cherry Lane Theatre, New York, January 25, 1929.

Cast of characters—

Sophie Smith....Jane Hamilton
Mr. Smith....E. Brooks Dascomb
Mrs. Smith....Adeline Ruby
Annie Smith....Evah Schwab
Tom Smith....Herman Bandes
Eugene Bohm....Louis John Latzer
George Clark....Harry Jay Marks
James Bradley....Mitchell Padraic Marcus
Maxwell Hurst....Ben Nelson
Robert Anderson....Peter Gwyn

Nine Scenes Carrying Sophie Smith to Work, to Her Home, to the Movies, to a Young Artist's Studio and to Her Death.

Staged by Adele Gutman Nathan.

Sophie Smith, pursuing beauty and happiness through a series of drab experiences, meets Eugene Bohm in the office in which she works. She is thrown into disturbing contact with him in the subway, and again at the movies, goes with him to his studio, becomes his mistress, fears the resulting disgrace and returns to the subway to throw herself under the wheels of a passing train.

BOOM BOOM

(72 performances)

A musical comedy in prologue and two acts, book by Fanny Todd Mitchell (adapted from the play "Mlle. Ma Mere," by Louis Verneuil), lyrics by Mann Holiner and J. Keirn Brennan, music by Werner Janssen. Produced by Messrs. Shubert, at the Casino Theatre, New York, January 28, 1929.

Cast of characters—

Jean	Jeanette MacDonald
Tony Smith	Stanley Ridges
Skippy Carr	Kendall Capps
Texas	Eddie Nelson
Gussie	Laurette Adams
Tilly McGuire	Nell Kelly
Worthington Smith	Frank McIntyre
Sigmund Squnk	Richard Lee
Reggie Phipps	Archie Leach
Maybella La Tour	Marcella Swanson
Head Waiter	Harry Welsh
Cortez	Cortez
Peggy	Peggy
Four Nightingales	Evelyn Sayres Loretta Sayres Doreen Glover Jessie Payne
Friend of Tilly	Jackie Hurlbert

Prologue—On Deck of S.S. *Argentine*. Act I.—Scene 1—Roof Garden of Worthington Smith's Penthouse. 2—Smith's Living Room. Act II.—Scene 1—Frolic Farms. 2—Sun Parlor, Smith's Apartment.

Staged by George Marion.

Jean, meeting Tony Smith on shipboard, bids him good-by with the hope that they will meet again. A year later Jean is practically forced into marrying Worthington Smith and is sentimentally disturbed to discover that he is Tony's father. A way is later found to abrogate the first marriage.

LADY FINGERS

(132 performances)

A musical comedy in two acts based on the comedy "Easy Come, Easy Go," by Owen Davis, adapted by Eddie Buzzell, music by Joseph Meyer, lyrics by Edward Eliscu. Produced by

Lyle D. Andrews, at the Vanderbilt Theatre, New York, January 31, 1929.

Cast of characters—

Mortimer Quayle	Herbert Waterous
Horace Winfield	Al Sexton
Hope Quayle	Louise Brown
Ruth	Ruth Gordon
Red	Red Harnden
Jim Bailey	Eddie Buzzell
Dick Tain	John Price Jones
Policeman	Jack Dugan
Policeman	James Curran
A Porter	John Bragg
Nash	Edwin Walter
Masters	Robert Fleming
Molly Maloney	Marjorie White
Shadow Martin	Jim Diamond
Dr. Jasper	William Griffith
Barbara Stanford	Gertrude MacDonald
Margie	Dorothy McCarthy
Betty	Margaret McCarthy
Mrs. Wright	Esther Muir

Act I.—Pennsylvania Station, New York. 2—En Route. 3—Dr. Jasper's Health Farm. Act II.—At the Farm.
Staged by Lew Levenson.

Dick Tain, son of a good family, falls in with Jim Bailey, a likable crook, and takes care of him through a fever. Jim, seeking to reward Dick, makes him party to a bank robbery. In trying to elude the law until the theft is straightened out Dick and Jim find themselves at a health farm where the banker they have robbed is also a guest. Dick, in love with the banker's daughter, manages an adjustment of the robbery and an engagement with the daughter.

HEDDA GABLER

(25 performances)

A play in four acts by Henrik Ibsen. Produced by The Actors' Theatre, Inc., at the 49th Street Theatre, New York, February 2, 1929.

Cast of characters—

George Tesman	Dallas Anderson
Hedda Tesman	Blanche Yurka
Miss Juliana Tesman	Claire Townshend
Mrs. Elvsted	Linda Watkins
Judge Brack	Frederic Worlock
Eilbert Lovborg	Ralph Roeder
Berta	Genevieve Williams

Acts I, II and III.—Drawing Room of Tesmans' Villa, in the West End of Christiania.
Staged by Blanche Yurka.

"Best Plays, 1927-28."

ALL THE KING'S MEN

(32 performances)

A comedy drama in three acts by Fulton Oursler. Produced by Lew Cantor, at the Fulton Theatre, New York, February 4, 1929.

Cast of characters—

Mrs. Rhodes..........Mrs. Jacques Martin
Junior Fairchild..........Bobby Mullin
Walter Fairchild..........Grant Mitchell
Florence Wendell..........Mayo Methot
Gilbert Saylor..........Hugh Huntley
Act I.—Home of a Widower. Act II.—Home of a Bridegroom. Act III.—Home of a Married Man.
Staged by Priestly Morrison.

Walter Fairchild, a one-year widower with a 9-year-old son, decides to marry a second time. Florence Wendell, the second Mrs. Fairchild, insists on a home relieved of all memories of the first Mrs. Fairchild. A year later Florence is to bear Fairchild a second child. A few days before the second accouchement Fairchild hears his son, who has been sent to Switzerland to school, is desperately ill. He decides to sail immediately. His decision angers Florence. A year after her own daughter is born Florence decides to elope with another man. The other man refuses to take her baby with them. Florence then realizes her unfairness to Walter because of his interest in his firstborn and a reconciliation follows.

BE YOUR AGE

(32 performances)

A play in three acts by Thomas P. Robinson and Esther Willard Bates. Produced by Richard Herndon, at the Belmont Theatre, New York, February 4, 1929.

Cast of characters—

Elinor Merriam..........Mary Stills
Forbes..........Edward Broadley
Bishop Bradford..........Holliwell Hobbes
Dr. Gage..........Romney Brent
Mrs. Merriam..........Spring Byington
Philip Latimer..........John Miltern
Acts I, II and III.—Living Room in Mrs. Merriam's House.
Staged by Ira Hards.

Mrs. Merriam, a grandmother, becomes enthused over young Dr. Gage's belief in the rejuvenation treatment and submits to the operation. Dropping thirty years from her age she becomes enamored of Dr. Gage and loses interest in her elderly admirers. Later she becomes convinced that she will be happier being her age and renounces her new found youth.

FIORETTA

(111 performances)

A romantic Venetian musical comedy in two acts, music and lyrics by George Babgy and G. Romilli, book by Earl Carroll, adapted by Charlton Andrews. Produced by Earl Carroll, at the Earl Carroll Theatre, New York, February 5, 1929.

Cast of characters—

Duke of Venice	Theo Karle
Duchess of Venice	Ethel Jane Walker
Jester	Clement Taylor
Sergeant	Martin Sheppard
Count Matteo Di Brozzo	Lionel Atwill
Ugo	Leo Pardello
Lady from Rome	Blanche Stachel
Spanish Ambassador's Daughter	Carol Kingsbury
Lady from Milan	Margaret Manners
Lady from Pisa	Elsie Pedrick
Lady from Naples	Irma Philbin
Dancer from Paris	Evelyn Crowell
Captain of the Guard	G. Davison Clark
Guiseppa	Rita Crane
Julio Pepoli	Leon Errol
A Herald	Alphonso Mullarkey
Pietro	Leonard Trion
Enrico	Frank Fiore
Giacomo	Frank Cullen
Fioretta Pepoli	Dorothy Knapp
Roberto	August Lindauer
Rosamanda	Lillian Bond
Silvia	Vivian Wilson
Lucetta	Louise Brooks
Beatrice	Elsie Connor
Orsino (Count di Rovani)	George Houston
Tito	Harry Goldberg
Luigi	Giovanni Guerreri
Marco	Sidney Schlesser
Marchesa Vera Di Livio	Fannie Brice
Caponetti	Jay Brennan
Marquis Filippo Di Livio	Charles Howard
Harlequin	Nelson Snow
Harlequin	Charles Columbus
Soldier	Vic Banks
Corporal	Stuart N. Farrington
Rosa	Peggy Taylor
Bishop	Gean Greenwald
Bishop	Wallace Magill
Turnkey	Jackson Fairchild
Paulo	David Gerry
Geranium	Himself

Acts I and II.—In and Around Venice, 18th Century.
Staged by Earl Carroll.

Fioretta Pepoli, the prettiest girl in Venice, is admired by the Duke, who plans to have her married to the young Count di Rovani, fugitive from justice. Following the marriage Di Rovani is to be executed and Fioretta delivered to the Duke. Through the aid of Fioretta's father, Julio, Di Rovani escapes, rescues Fioretta and there is dancing along the canals.

DYNAMO

(50 performances)

A play in three acts by Eugene O'Neill. Produced by The Theatre Guild, at the Martin Beck Theatre, New York, February 11, 1929.

Cast of characters—

Rev. Light	George Gaul
Mrs. Light	Helen Westley
Reuben Light	Glenn Anders
Ramsay Fife	Dudley Digges
May Fife	Catherine Doucet
Ada Fife	Claudette Colbert
Jennings	Hugh Forrester
Rocco	Edgar Kent

Acts I and II.—The Light and Fife Houses in a Small Town in Connecticut. Act III.—Interior of the Light and Power Company's Hydro-Electric Plant.
Staged by Philip Moeller.

The Rev. Light has been a hard and fast Christian, fearing the Lord but not walking any too humbly. Ramsay Fife has slipped gradually into atheism. They live next door to each other and there is rivalry between them and contempt in their hearts. Reuben Light falls in love with Ada Fife, daughter of the atheist. Ada and her father seek to test Rueben's faith by playing a joke on him. Reuben takes the joke seriously, and when he is upbraided by his father, forswears religion and goes in search of knowledge and understanding. Years later he returns convinced Electricity is the only god. Again he is tempted by Ada, falls, and in expiation of his sin, kills Ada and throws himself upon the Dynamo and is executed.

THE WHISPERING GALLERY

(79 performances)

A comedy mystery in a prologue and three acts by Percy Robinson and Terence de Marney. Produced by E. E. Clive, at the Forrest Theatre, New York, February 11, 1929.

Cast of characters—

Martin Condell....................................Hugh Miller
Morgan....................................Charles Warburton
Jim Stowell....................................Harry McNaughton
Frances Arnott....................................Gwineth Gordon
Tom Arnott....................................Edmund George
Lady Elliott....................................Bertha Belmore
Sir Hugh Elliott....................................Charles Esdale
Jim Stowell....................................Olga Katzin
Robert Condell....................................Hugh Miller
Abraham Lincoln Johnson....................................Frank Frayne
Bird....................................A. B. Kaye
Prologue—Martin Condell's Studio, Odmondthorpe, Cornwall.
Acts I, II and III.—Robert Condell's Studio.

Martin Condell, a mad artist, hears voices telling him his wife is unfaithful. He strangles her in his gallery studio. Thirty years later Robert Condell, Martin's son, visits the whispering gallery but brings a lot of London friends with him, including a representative of the police. Robert is afraid. Lights out and Robert is stabbed. Lights out again and the body disappears. There are weird mutterings back of the gallery. Closing time finds Martin Condell, still a mad artist, escaped from an asylum and hiding in the house.

* MY GIRL FRIDAY

(135 performances)

A play in three acts by William A. Grew. Produced by Schnebbe-Bacon, Inc., at the Republic Theatre, New York, February 12, 1929.

Cast of characters—

Martins....................................Judson Langill
Frances Mordaunt....................................Lucila Mendez
Shirley Winters....................................Alice Weaver
Harvey Travers....................................William Carey
Paul Manger....................................Bernard Randall
Jean Marcel....................................Esther Muir
John Hartwell....................................William A. Grew
Zazu....................................Sam Kim
Albert Whelan....................................Richard Sterling
Sidney Fallon....................................Robert Bentley
Marcel the Great....................................Nat Pendelton
Elizabeth Hartwell....................................Mabel Acker
Josephine Whelan....................................Louise Kelley
Act I—Stage, Frolic Theatre. Acts II and III.—John Hartwell's Summer Home.
Staged by Mr. Grew.

Frances Mordaunt, Shirley Winters and Jean Marcel, chorus girls, are ordered by the stage manager of their show to go to the home of John Hartwell, backer of the show, and entertain his guests. The girls protest, but go. Apparently agreeing to all the advances of the men they meet Jean dopes their wine, the girls leave their underthings in their beds and next day accuse their would-be seducers of an attack. Two of the men's wives and the sweetheart of one of the girls appear and the befuddled men are glad to settle out of court.

PLEASURE BOUND

(136 performances)

A revue in two acts, music by Muriel Pollock, book and lyrics by Harold Atteridge, Max and Nathaniel Lief. Produced by Messrs. Shubert, at the Majestic Theatre, New York, February 18, 1929.

Principals engaged—

Phil Baker	Aileen Stanley
Jack Pearl	Grace Brinkley
Al Shaw	Pepita
Sam Lee	Yolanda
Fred Hillebrand	Virginia Barrett
Ralph Locke	Rosita Morena
William Bonelli	Betty Bowman
Roy Hoyer	Dorothy Drum
Tito	Rosalind Wishon

Staged by Lew Morton, dances by Busby Berkeley.

KIBITZER

(120 performances)

A comedy in three acts by Jo Swerling and Edward G. Robinson. Produced by Patterson McNutt, at the Royale Theatre, New York, February 18, 1929.

Cast of characters—

Lazarus	Edward G. Robinson
Josie	Jeanne Greene
Emil Schmidt	Hobart Cavanaugh
Meyer	Arthur S. Ross
Kikoupoupoulous	Alexis Polianov
Sarnov	Louis La Bey
Marks	Al Roberts
Loomis	Tom Fadden
Mullins	Walter F. Scott
Wescott	C. J. Williams
Customer	George Spelvin, Jr.
Bill Livingston	Nelan Jaap
James Livingston	Eugene Powers
Hanson	Charles Hammond
An Officer	George Spelvin, Sr.
Briggs	Samuel T. Godfrey

Yankel.......................................Jacob Katzman
Phillips.......................................Stanley G. Wood
Nolan.......................................James Whittaker
Michaels.......................................Michael Porter
Photographer.......................................Hunter Kaufman
Reporter.......................................Vincent Strain
1st Kibitzer.......................................Henry Howard
2nd Kibitzer.......................................Rex Boyd
1st Customer.......................................Lloyd Russell
2nd Customer.......................................Agnew T. Horine
A Butcher.......................................Fred M. Mitchell
A Barometer Salesman.......................Travis "Weather" Hoke
1st Neighbor.......................................Martha Edwards
2nd Neighbor.......................................Beatrice Bayard
Acts I and III.—Cigar Store of I. Lazarus. Act II.—Library in the Home of James Livingston.
Staged by Patterson McNutt.

Lazarus runs a cigar store in Amsterdam Avenue. He is chief adviser to the neighborhood, instructing everybody, from the pinochle players to the followers of the ponies and the stock market, how to place their wagers. He befriends accidentally James Livingston, a millionaire, and is given his choice between a bunch of stock and a cash reward. He takes the stock, installs a ticker in the cigar store and becomes in his own mind a heavy operator on the market. The stock soars ten points. Lazarus refuses to sell. The stock slides back and Lazarus thinks he is wiped out. But a daffy cousin has given the order to sell when the stock was at its peak.

FLIGHT

(40 performances)

A comedy in three acts by Susan Meriwether and Victor Victor. Produced by Laura D. Wilck, at the Longacre Theatre, New York, February 18, 1929.

Cast of characters—

Mrs. Camilla Bradford.......................................Marion Lee
Arthur Larrimore (Larry).......................George MacQuarrie
Margaret Larrimore.......................................Eleanor Woodruff
Cynthia Larrimore.......................................Miriam Hopkins
Terry Hamilton.......................................John D. Seymour
Stephen Fairbank.......................................Ernest Glendinning
Virginia Watson.......................................Pauline Drake
Patricia Delevan.......................................Joan Blair
Richard Scofield (Scoofy).......................Henry Wadsworth
Frederika Jordan.......................................Gertrude Bryan
John Hill.......................................Donald Dillaway
Gates.......................................Henry Vincent
Acts I, II and III.—A Room at the Larrimore Country Place.
Staged by Lemist Esler.

Cynthia Larrimore has been reared in an unhappy family atmosphere. Her father and mother, living their own lives, have avoided divorce for her sake. Growing up a free child, Cynthia is of a mind to experiment with life. She takes a lover, Terry. The next week she meets a young aviator, John Hill, and falls desperately in love with him. They, too, forget the conventions. John wants to marry Cynthia. She confesses the affair with Terry. John flies away, but comes back. Cynthia is forced to a second confession. She is to become a mother and is not sure of the parentage of her expected child. John flies away again but again returns and is content to accept Cynthia as technically Terry's widow.

LET US BE GAY

(132 performances)

A comedy in a prologue and three acts by Rachel Crothers. Produced by John Golden, at the Little Theatre, New York, February 19, 1929.

Cast of characters—

Kitty Brown....Francine Larrimore
Bob Brown....Warren William
Mrs. Boucicault....Charlotte Granville
Dierdre Lessing....Rita Vale
Townley Town....Kenneth Hunter
Bruce Keen....Ross Alexander
Madge Livingston....Adele Klaer
Wallace Grainger....Gilbert Douglas
Whitman....George Wright, Jr.
Struthers....James C. Lane
Perkins....Natalie Potter

Prologue—Kitty Brown's Bedroom. Acts I, II and III.—Mrs. Boucicault's Home in Westchester.

Staged by Rachel Crothers.

See page 195.

THE BROKEN CHAIN

(29 performances)

A drama in three acts by William J. Perlman. Produced by Jacob A. Weiser, at the Maxine Elliott Theatre, New York, February 19, 1929.

Cast of characters—

Shifra....Angela Jacobs
Stranger....John Pote
Razele....Sarah Biala
A Woman....Dorothy Raymond
A Young Wife....Sara Floyd

A Young Husband	Walter Geer
Second Stranger	Martin Noble
Samuel	Jess Sidney
Gabriel	Edgar Barrier
Esther	Mary Fowler
Benjamin	Alan Lowe
First Batlon	Max von Mitzel
Second Batlon	Ralph Adams
Third Batlon	Douglas Krantzor
Fourth Batlon	George Bratt
Reb Velvele Slomner	Frank McGlynn
Beryl	Seldon Bennet
Noah	Maurice Cass
Isaac	Eugene Ordway
Daniel	J. Carrol Nash
Mordecai	Eduard Franz
Joseph	Harry Moss
Emanuel Sutro	Geoffrey Wardwell
A Hassid	John Pote
An Old Woman	Virginia Gregori
Second Woman	Elaine Fay
A Girl	Estelle Kamins
A Mother	Joy Douglas
An Old Man	Martin Noble

Acts I, II and III.—Living Room of Reb Velvele in New York City.

Staged by Mark Schweid.

Reb Velvele, a rabbi, is eager that his son shall follow him in the church. The son takes to prize fighting instead. Reb turns to his daughter, Esther, hoping she will marry an orthodox Jew and bear a son to carry on the family tradition. Esther deserts her husband and goes to live with her unorthodox lover.

HARLEM

(93 performances)

Drama in three acts by W. J. Rapp and Wallace Thurman. Produced by Edward A. Blatt at the Apollo Theatre, New York, February 20, 1929.

Cast of characters—

George Williams	Clarence Taylor
Mazie Williams	Elise Thomas
Arabella Williams	Edna Wise Barr
Ma Williams	Inez Clough
Pa Williams	Lew Payton
Cordelia Williams	Isabell Washington
Basil Venerable	Richard Landers
Jasper Williams	Emory S. Richardson
Effie	Lillian Fairley
Jimmie	Hemsley Winfield
Thaddeus Jenkins	Collington Hayes
Ippy Jones	Hillis Walters
Mary Lou	Carmen Marshall
Roy Crowe	Billy Andrews
Briggs	Frank Badham
Will	A. B. Walker

Others in the Cast were—Joseph Slocum, Mary Jane Watkins, Mae

Morrison, George Thomas, Rita Weldon, Albert W. Patrick, Cora Parkes, William McFarland, Jenney Roe, Daisy Pilgram, Robert Corbin, Irene Temple, Ernest De Sharpe, Lillian Maxwell, Lorenze E. Graham, George Grissom, Aline Lewis, Grace Burke, Emory Bonner, Stanley Wolcott, Roy De Coverly, Gertie Chambers, Thula Ortiz, Rex Goreleigh, Emma Maitland, Larri Lorear, A. Wheedlin, Suzanne Cartier, Mary Daniels, Alec Archer, Phœbe Roe, Ray Coleman, Harry Long, Robert Bramlett, Rosette Brown, Alberta Foster, Jimmy Young, Bud Allen, Ernest R. Whitman, F. Barclay Trigg, Arthur Hughes, Nat Cash, Ardelle Dabney, Malvina Dabney

Acts I and III.—Living Room of the Williams' Railroad Flat in Harlem. Act II.—Roy's Apartment.

Staged by Chester Erskin.

The Williams family, Negroes, have come to Harlem from South Carolina. Their experiences are unhappy. Cordelia Williams becomes a loose woman. The family is reduced to giving rent parties to raise the landlord's money. Cordelia refuses to marry her West Indian lover and takes up with a Harlem gambler. The gambler is killed and the West Indian accused of the crime. The police free the West Indian and Cordelia continues her wild life.

KATERINA

(19 performances)

A play in four acts by Leonid Andreyev, translated by Herman Bernstein. Produced by Civic Repertory Theatre, Inc., at the Civic Repertory Theatre, New York, February 25, 1929.

Cast of characters—

Katerina Ivanovna	Alla Nazimova
George Stibelev	Walter Beck
Alexey	Robert Ross
Fomin	John Eldredge
Maid	Francoise Du Moulin
Vera Ignatyevna	Leona Roberts
Governess	Frances Williams
Nurse	Agnes McCarthy
Paul Koromisslov	Donald Cameron
Arcady Mentikov	Robert H. Gordon
Tatyana Andreyevna	Alma Kruger
Liza	Ria Mooney
Maid	Paula Miller
Jacob Teplovsky	Harold Moulton
Toropets	J. Edward Bromberg
Ludwig	J. Blake Scott
Zhura	Glesca Marshall

Act I.—Dining Room of Stibelev's House. Act II.—Living Room in the House of Tatyana Andreyevna. Acts III and IV.—Koromisslov's Studio.

Staged by Miss Le Gallienne.

Katerina Ivanovna, suspected by her husband because she innocently spends an hour or two in a gentleman friend's room, is shot at and missed. The shots, however, kill her soul and thereafter, brooding over the unjust accusation, she feels an inexplicable urge to do all the things of which he has suspected her. She takes numerous lovers while the husband, feeling to blame, sits supinely by and observes her descent in the general direction of hell.

MEET THE PRINCE

(96 performances)

A comedy in three acts by A. A. Milne. Produced at the Lyceum Theatre, New York, February 25, 1929.

Cast of characters—

Simon Battersby.................................Moffat Johnston
Angela.................................Cecile Dixon
Jennifer.................................Mary Ellis
Emily.................................Lillian Brennard Tonge
Capt. Robert Holt.................................Eric Blore
Ethel Holt.................................Ester Mitchell
Mrs. Faithfull.................................Alice Belmore Cliffe
Imogene Faithfull.................................Eunice Stoddard
Dr. Ainslie.................................J. M. Kerrigan
Prince Michael.................................Basil Sydney
James Oiiver.................................Donald Blackwell

Acts I, II and III.—Living Room in Battersby's Cottage in Wych Trentham, Outside of London, England.

Staged by Basil Sydney.

Michael and Jennifer quarreled and parted after Michael came back from the war. Michael went adventuring and pretended (along the Riviera) he was a prince of one of the newer Balkan countries. Jennifer changed her name to Bulger and pretended to be the widow of a great general. Michael, hearing his wife is visiting in England, gets himself invited to the same house. There he amusingly continues his deception but finally induces Jennifer to forgive him.

INDISCRETION

(40 performances)

A play in four acts by Myron C. Fagan. Produced by Myron C. Fagan, at the Mansfield Theatre, New York, March 4, 1929.

Cast of characters—

Margaret.................................Minna Gombell
Bob Burton.................................Harland Tucker
Billy Noel.................................Louis Kimball
Walter Davenport.................................Arthur R. Vinton
Sally.................................Lora Rogers

Helen Morse....................................Diantha Pattison
Betty...Betty Lancaster
Don Dudley....................................Harold Elliott
Act I.—Venice. Act II.—Scene 1—Frances Ainsley's Dressing Room. 2—Balconnade of Residence of Helen Morse. Acts III and IV.—Frances Ainsley's Hotel Suite.
Staged by Myron C. Fagan.

Margaret and Bob, denied marriage by Bob's millionaire father, are living together in Venice. Bob suddenly is recalled to his father's bedside and Margaret reads of his engagement to another girl. Eighteen years later Bob is a senator and Margaret is Frances Ainsley, a great actress. Walter Davenport, who wants Margaret for himself, keeps them apart. Finally Margaret learns that Bob has been true all these years. And Bob learns that Margaret never, never, lived with that Italian count.

SHE GOT WHAT SHE WANTED

(120 performances)

A farcical comedy in three acts by George Rosener. Produced by George E. Wintz, at the Wallack's Theatre, New York, March 4, 1929.

Cast of characters—

Mahnya...Galina Kopernak
Boris..Alan Brooks
Dave...William Pike
Eddie..Franklyn Ardell
Dugan..Aubrey Beattie
Acts I, II and III.—Home of Mahnya and Boris.
Staged by Edward Elsner.

Mahnya married Boris, who became philosophic and detached. Mahnya, lonesome, agrees to go with Dave, her boarder, and also Eddie, of the vaudevilles. She settles on Dave and Boris, her husband, becomes the boarder. After which it is practically no time at all before Mahnya realizes it is Boris she really loved after all.

TROIS JEUNES FILLES NUES

(40 performances of repertoire)

A musical comedy in three acts, book and lyrics by Yves Mirande and Albert Willemetz, music by Raoul. Produced by J. A. Gauvin and his modern French musical comedy company, at the Jolson Theatre, New York, March 4, 1929.

Cast of characters—

Hegesippe	Mr. Servatius
Patara	Mr. Fadeuilhe
Jacques	George Foix
The Commander	Mr. Pazzi-Preval
Marcel	Mr. Garchery
The Director	Mr. Daufy
Maurice	Mr. Laurenzo
The Author	Mr. Decart
Lord Cresson	Mr. Jose
The Compere	Mr. Luguet
The Gardner	Mr. Darcey
The Mailman	Mr. Jules
The Delivery Man	Mr. Gardet
First Sailor	Mr. Henri
Second Sailor	Mr. Georges
Lotte	Sonia Alny
Lilette	Ginia Barty
Mrs. Ducros	Jane De Poumayrac
Tapsy	Marion Gaillard
Lola	Yvette Herbaux
Lulu	Alice Penven
The Lobster Woman	Mado Thys
The Opener	Luce Lucior
A Girl	Henriette
Girls From the Folies Bergere	The Terry Girls

Four young girls from the country run away to Paris to join the Folies Bergere Company. They find four sweethearts and sing songs to them. The sweethearts sing back.

Also included in the repertoire were, "Passionnément," "Comte Obligado," and "Ta Bouche."

THE EARTH BETWEEN

(27 performances)

A play in two acts by Vergil Geddes. Produced at the Provincetown Theatre, New York, March 5, 1929.

Cast of characters—

Jake	William Challee
Mrs. Nelson	Janne Burbie
Mr. Nelson	Warren Colston
Nat Jennings	Carl Ashburn
Floy Jennings	Bette Davis
Wilbur	Grover Burgess

Act I.—Scene 1—The Sitting Room in the Nelson Farmhouse. 2—A Section of Pasture Land on the Jennings Farm. 3—The Parlor in Nat Jennings' Home. 4—The Hayloft in the Jennings Barn. Act II.—Scene 1—Sitting Room in the Nelson Farmhouse. 2—The Rear Part of the Jennings Farmhouse. 3—The Dooryard of the Jennings Farmhouse. 4—A Wheatfield.

Staged by James Light.

Nat Jennings, widower, has brought his daughter Floy up from babyhood and become possessively selfish in his determination to keep her. Every farmhand in the neighborhood is viewed with distrust and suspicion as Floy reaches womanhood. Jake, the boy in whom she takes the most interest, is sent to the barn to sleep. Floy follows but Jake gently spurns her advances and catches cold instead. He dies of pneumonia. It is charged that Nat Jennings kept Jake's medicine away from him. Nat is content. He still has Floy.

BEFORE BREAKFAST

By Eugene O'Neill

Mrs. Rowland..Mary Blair

O'Neill's "Before Breakfast" is a monologue for Mrs. Rowland, a young woman married to a no-good artist in Greenwich Village. As he shaves in the adjoining room she upbraids him for his treatment of her and he cuts his throat with a razor.

CONFLICT

(37 performances)

A play in three acts by Warren F. Lawrence. Produced by Spad Producing Co., Inc., at the Fulton Theatre, New York, March 6, 1929.

Cast of characters—

Roger Winship....................................Edward Arnold
Chet Touteen....................................George Meeker
Ruth Winship....................................Peggy Allenby
A Maid..Lois Arnold
Mary Bishop....................................Dennie Moore
Richard Banks..................................Spencer Tracy
A Batman...Charles Scott
Lieut. "Pop" Touso..............................Seth Arnold
Sgt. "Chink" Burt..............................Frank McHugh
Lieut. Scott......................................Joseph Boland
Lieut. Anderson..................................David Mann
Lieut. Williams...................................Jack Mead
Baron Von Mueller.........................Albert Van Dekker
A Bartender.....................................Jack Bennett
Daisy Hall...Mabel Allyn

Act I.—Scenes 1 and 3—A Room in Ruth Winship's Home. 2—Sleeping Quarters of the Flight Commander of the 361st Aero Squadron. Act II.—Scene 1—A Speakeasy. 2—Ruth Winship's Home. Act III.—Ruth Winship's Home.

Staged by Edward Clarke Lilley.

Richard Banks is a clerk who waits for the draft. Before the war he meets his employer's niece, Ruth Winship, who is obviously patronizing. During the war Richard makes the aviation service, becomes a flight commander and earns many decorations. After the war, loaded with honors, he is much sought after. Now Ruth Winship is willing to break her engagement to another man to marry Richard. They are married and happy through the honeymoon. After that the readjustment convinces Ruth she has made a mistake. Richard realizes how she feels, agrees to divorce her and goes back to his own kind, getting a job as a commercial flyer.

SPRING IS HERE

(104 performances)

A musical comedy in two acts, book by Owen Davis, music by Richard Rodgers, lyrics by Lorenz Hart. Produced by Alex A. Aarons and Vinton Freedley at the Alvin Theatre, New York, March 11, 1929.

Cast of characters—

Emily Braley....................Maidel Turner
Maude Osgood....................Thelma White
Mary Jane....................Inez Courtney
Steve Alden....................Dick Keene
Willie Slade....................Gil Squires
Peter Braley....................Charles Ruggles
Betty....................Lillian Taiz
Stacy Haydon....................John Hundley
Terry Clayton....................Glenn Hunter
Rita Conway....................Joyce Barbour
Ebens....................Cy Landry
Jennings....................Lewis Parker
Policeman....................Frank Gagen
Victor Arden and Phil Ohman at the Pianos
Act I.—The Garden. Act II.—Scene 1—Osgood's Barn Dance. 2—Betty's Bed Room. 3—Morning Room at Maude Braleys.
Staged by Alexander Leftwich. Dances by Bobby Connelly.

Terry Clayton is deeply in love with Betty Braley, who believes she loves Stacy Haydon. Stacy and Betty are preparing to elope when her father interferes and after several false starts Terry proves that he is a man after all, even if he can't sing.

THE TOWN'S WOMAN

(16 performances)

A play in three acts by Martin Mooney and Thomson Burtis. Produced by Martin Mooney and Thomson Burtis, at the Craig Theatre, New York, March 11, 1929.

Cast of characters—

Shirley Hudson....................Gladys Griswold
Clara....................Pearl Hight
Peter Vorhees....................Don Darcy
William Hudson....................Frank Monroe

Jaeger....................Joseph Granby
Robert Hudson....................Jack McKee
Dr. Gordon Lee....................Edward Keane
Nancy North....................Helen Baxter
Chuck....................Bill Cox
Harry....................Jerry Kennedy
Peggy....................Mary Hutchinson
Charlie Curry....................Ross Hertz
Chrystal Waters....................Astrid Jason
Stewart Sands....................Norman V. Pearce
Lowell Gardner....................Charles O'Donnell

Acts I and III.—The Home of William Hudson. Act II.—Nancy North's Tearoom.

Staged by Ralph Murphy.

Nancy North, former actress, quits Broadway to run a tearoom near a race track. Certain of the noisier villagers, particularly William Hudson, suspect the tearoom of being a speakeasy and try to make it unpleasant for Nancy, who has attracted and held the attention of Hudson's boy, Robert. Robert gambles his last cent on Nancy's tip and loses, Nancy sells the tearoom to give him back his money and in the end he makes a man and an aviator of himself and a happy wife of her.

THE OCTOROON

A melodrama in five acts by Dion Boucicault. Revived by John Leffler at the Maxine Elliott Theatre, New York, March 12, 1929.

Cast of characters—

Salem Scudder....................Herbert Corthell
Wahnotee....................Maurice Freeman
Jacob McClosky....................David Landau
Old Pete....................William Nunn
Captain Ratts....................Burke Clarke
Colonel Pointdexter....................Herbert Haywood
Mr. Sunnyside....................John E. Henshaw
George Peyton....................James Meighan
La Fouche....................Frank Andrews
Jules Thibodeaux....................Charles Bunnell
Judge Caillou....................William Marble
Jackson....................Arthur P. Hoyt
Zoe....................Inez Plummer
Dora Sunnyside....................Marjorie Dille
Paul (a Boy Slave)....................Margaret Bayers
Mrs. Peyton....................Luella Morey
Grace....................Emma Hayner

Act I.—A View of the Plantation Terrebonne, Louisiana. Acts II and IV.—The Wharf. Act III.—A Room in Mrs. Peyton's House. Act V.—Scene 1—Negroes' Quarters on the Plantation. 2—Cane-Break Bayou.

Directed by Frank Hatch.

The pathetic story of Zoe, the octoroon, and her love for George Peyton, sacrificed in the cause of race standards and a better understanding of the slavery issue.

YOUNG ALEXANDER

(7 performances)

A play in three acts by Hardwick Nevin. Produced at the Biltmore Theatre, New York, March 12, 1929.

Cast of characters—

Aristotle	A. E. Anson
Parmenio	Edward Donnelly
Clitus	Doan Borup
Aristandos	A. E. Anson
A Courtesan	Gladys Lloyd
Another Courtesan	Cleo Coil
Alexander	Henry Hull
Themakales	Bernard Thornton
Philotas	Peter Parke
Statira	Jessie Royce Landis
Darius III	Charles Dalton
Persian Captains	Francis Moran, Don Goss
A Young Greek Boy	Ben Starkie
Macedonian Soldiers	William Wallack James B. Devereaux
Spithrides	Edward Rigby
Coenus	Lawrence Zavell
Slaves	A. McWaith, Henry Davis
Persian Soldier	Arthur West

Acts I, II and III.—In the Camps of Alexander and Darius on the Banks of a River in Persia.
Staged by Ira Hards.

Alexander of Macedon is 22 and convinced that he is a god. As a god he decides to forswear the intimate friendships of the fair sex. He also would like to force his armies to take a similar oath of chastity. The men are disinclined to approve Alexander's decision. His generals and his friend, Aristandos, both urge him to modify his decree. Meeting Darius of Persia and defeating him Alexander also meets Mrs. Darius, disguised as a Greek soldier, in the enemy camp. That night he dreams that Mrs. Darius, who has dropped her disguise, is Helen of Troy. Temporarily Alexander becomes a human of humans. Next morning he returns to his battles, and even Aristandos, who turns out to be Aristotle, is unable to change his thought.

BUCKAROO

(9 performances)

A melodramatic comedy in three acts by A. W. and E. L. Barker and Charles Beahan. Produced by Hamilton MacFadden, at the Erlanger Theatre, New York, March 16, 1929.

Cast of characters—

Eddie Margolis....................................Dell Cleveland
Skippit..Lois Shore
Nosebag...Harold Moffatt
Shorty Scott (Ocmulgee, Oklahoma)...................Fred Miller
Homer Creed (Ismay, Montana).....................William Lowe
Ben Bishop (Swan River, Canada)...................Edward Allen
Dot Farley (Kirkland, Arizona)......................Ruth Holden
Goldie Burns (Bar C Ranch, Texas)................Eileen Douglas
Sam Sundown (Mexico City, Mexico)................Augie Gomez
Derby Dan (Chugwater, Texas)....................Slim Cavanaugh
Pecos Kid (Indian Hill, Wyoming).................J. S. Boatsman
Lee Irwin (Cowbell Canyon, Idaho)................Nydia Westman
Maxine Madison.....................................Ruth Easton
Whitey..Frank Henry
Colonel Johns (Director of Rodeo)...............William Balfour
Dolly Shukas..................................Mary Alice Collins
Stray Murfee (Cowbell Canyon, Idaho)..................James Bell
Ernestine Boswell..................................Peggy Boland
Madge Duval....................................Frances Halliday
Gink..Paul Nugent
Benny Morris......................................Clyde Dilson
Swaggerty.......................................Morris Ankrum
Rita Arnaldo (Taos, New Mexico)....................Violet Dunn
Eva Bishop (Swan River, Canada)....................Bobby Allen
Knife Thrower's Partner.........................Ethel McConnell
Finkelstein...Bert Wilcox
Chick Hannan.......................................By Himself

Other Cowboys and Cowgirls, Spectators, etc.

Acts I, II and III.—Under the Stadium at Soldier Field, Grant Park, Chicago.

Staged by Hamilton MacFadden.

Lee Irwin, cowgirl, is determined to protect Stray Murfee, a champion broncho buster but otherwise a dull-witted youth of the cow country, when Maxine Madison, one of the Chicago girls, tries to gyp him at the rodeo. Stray doesn't much want to be protected until after Benny Morris, Maxine's friend, shoots him in the arm. Then he tries to ride, faints and is happy in Lee's arms.

LADY FROM THE SEA

(24 performances)

A play in four acts by Henrik Ibsen. Produced by the Actors' Theatre, Inc., at the Bijou Theatre, New York, March 18, 1929.

Cast of characters—

Doctor Wangel...................................Edward Fielding
Ellida Wangel.....................................Blanche Yurka
Bolette...Linda Watkins
Hilda..Florida Friebus
Arnholm...Dallas Anderson
Lyngstrand......................................Walter Speakman
Ballested.......................................John Daly Murphy
A Stranger...G. Pat Collins

Act I.—Dr. Wangel's Garden. Act II.—Lookout Point. Acts III and IV.—A Remote Corner of Dr. Wangel's Garden.

Staged by Cecil Clovelly.

Ellida Wangel, daughter of a lighthouse keeper, marries Dr. Wangel and moves far up the fjord. The call of the sea is still upon her and a memory of meeting a Stranger who announced her wedding to him when he took a ring from her finger, placed it on a keyring with one of his own and threw them both into the sea, is an obscession she cannot clear from her mind. The Stranger returns to claim her, Dr. Wangel releases her from all her obligations toward him and the possession of her freedom clears Ellida's mind.

A TRIP TO SCARBOROUGH

(30 performances)

A play with music in three acts by Richard Brinsley Sheridan. Produced by the Jitney players, at the Cherry Lane Theatre, New York, March 18, 1929.

Cast of characters—

Tom Fashion	William Lovejoy
Lory	Jack Rennick
Lieutenant Townley	Bushnell Cheney Ralph W. Shattuck
Lord Foppington	David Elliott
La Varole	Ferris Hartman
Mendlegs	Robert R. Parsons
Mrs. Calico	Julia Parlow
Mrs. Coupler	Elizabeth Zachary
Loveless	Harrison Dowd
Amanda	Frances Simpson
Berinthia	Alice B. Keating
Probe	Ferris Hartman
Sir Tunbelly Clumsy	Robert R. Parsons
Servant	Ferris Hartman
Miss Hoyden	Gene Magnus
Nurse	Elizabeth Zachary

Acts I, II and III.—Scarborough and Its Neighborhood.
Staged by Bushnell Cheney.

An early play by Richard Brinsley Sheridan retailing an adventure of the fashionables of the day.

* JOURNEY'S END

(99 performances)

A play in three acts by R. C. Sherriff. Produced by Gilbert Miller (by arrangement with Maurice Browne) at the Henry Miller Theatre, New York, March 22, 1929.

Cast of characters—

Captain Hardy	Evelyn Roberts
Lieut. Osborne	Leon Quartermaine
Private Mason	Victor Stanley
2nd Lieut. Raleigh	Derek Williams
Captain Stanhope	Colin Keith Johnson
2nd Lieut. Trotter	Henry Wenman
2nd Lieut. Hibbert	Jack Hawkins
Company Sergeant Major	Sidney Seaward
The Colonel	Eric Stanley
German Soldier	———

Acts I, II and III.—Dugout in the British Trench Before St. Quentin, March, 1918.
Staged by James Whale.

See page 54.

THE DRAGON

(5 performances)

A play in three acts by Lady Gregory. Produced by the Jitney Players, at the Cherry Lane Theatre, New York, March 25, 1929.

Cast of characters—

The Dall Glic	Jack Rennick
The King	Harrison Dowd
The Queen	Alice B. Keating
The Princess Nuala	Frances Simpson
The Nurse	Elizabeth Zachary
Gatekeeper	Ferris Hartman
The Prince of the Marshes	David Elliott
Two Aunts of the Prince of the Marshes	Gene Magnus Juliette Phillips
Fintan, the Astrologer	Bushnell Cheney Ralph W. Shattuck
Manus, King of Sorcha	William Lovejoy
Taig	Robert R. Parsons
The Dragon	———

Acts I, II and III.—A Room in the King's House at Burren.
Staged by David Elliott.

There is a fear that the Princess will indeed be eaten by the Dragon on a certain birth anniversary unless the King and Queen can manage to marry her off meantime. The Dragon doesn't care particularly for married girls. The King, in some desperation, seeks to speed the market by offering to give his daughter to the first man who enters the palace. This one turns out to be a cook looking for a job. The King tries to back out of his bargain, but the cook also turns out to be a Prince in disguise, so that's all right.

SECURITY

(24 performances)

A play in three acts by Esme Wynne-Tyson. Produced by Lee Shubert, at the Maxine Elliott Theatre, New York, March 28, 1929.

Cast of characters—

Jane Mapleson....................................Margaret Anglin
Lillith Chartres.................................Marjorie Gateson
Delia..Florence Wessels
Lacey..Eva Leonard Boyne
Wells..Howard Benton
Eda Mapleson.....................................Irene Brown
Ronnie Newton....................................Reginald Mason
Rosanne..Anita Kerry
George Merrall...................................Robert Harrigan
James Mapleson...................................Thurston Hall
Muriel...Hope Drown
Sir Daniel Marchant..............................Charles Millward

Acts I, II and III.—Jane Mapleson's Sitting Room, Regent's Park, London.

Staged by Stanley Logan.

Jane Mapleson has known for years that James, her husband, is a liar and a cheat so far as other women are concerned, but she accepts the security of the lie for her children's sake. When James seduces his stenographer and scandal threatens, Jane not only refuses to believe but also helps James lie himself out of a coroner's inquest when the stenographer kills herself. When James confesses the truth to her, however, Jane can no longer go on pretending and threatens to leave him. James kills himself and shortly after Jane agrees to marry another man against her will merely to guarantee her son-in-law's security in the diplomatic service.

PAOLO AND FRANCESCA

(16 performances)

A play in four acts by Stephen Phillips. Produced by William A. Brady, Jr., and Dwight Deere Wiman, at the Forrest Theatre, New York, April 1, 1929.

Cast of characters—

Giovanni...Guy Standing
Francesca..Jane Cowl
Paolo..Philip Merivale
Lucrezia...Katherine Emmet
Nita...Joyce Carey

Costanza.................................Helen Wilson
Carlo.................................Ben Lackland
Angela.................................Jessie Ralph
Marco.................................Lewis Martin
Mirra.................................Virginia Norton
Sergeant.................................George Graves
First Soldier.................................Coburn Goodwin
Second Soldier.................................Franc C. Strang
First Peasant Girl.................................Maren Evensen
Second Peasant Girl.................................Helen Wilson
Inn Keeper.................................D. M. Bishop
Corrado.................................Hale Norcross
Luigi.................................Robert Lowe
Valentino.................................William Randall
Tessa.................................Maren Evensen
Pulci.................................Lionel Hogarth
First Courier.................................Lewis Martin
Second Courier.................................George Graves
Messenger.................................Coburn Goodwin

Acts I, II, III and IV.—In and Near the Malatesta Castle in 13th Century Italy.

Staged by Miss Cowl.

The Stephen Phillips version of the "Francesca di Rimini" legend, first shown in America by Laurence Irving in 1906.

MAN'S ESTATE

(48 performances)

A play in three acts by Bruce Gould and Beatrice Blackmar. Produced by The Theatre Guild, at the Biltmore Theatre, New York, April 1, 1929.

Cast of characters—

Joseph Jordan.................................Edward Favor
William P. Jordan.................................Dudley Digges
Caroline Jordan.................................Florence Gerould
Minnie Jordan.................................Elizabeth Patterson
Jerry Jordan.................................Earle Larimore
Emily Bender.................................Armina Marshall
Dr. Frank Bender.................................Edward Pawley
Sesaly Blaine.................................Margalo Gillmore
Rev. Dr. Eustace Potter.................................Louis Veda
Cousin Grace.................................Maria Ziccardi

Act I.—Terrace and Lawn of the Jordan Home. Acts II and III.—Living Room in the Jordan Home.

Staged by Dudley Digges.

Jerry Jordan and Sesaly Blaine love each other. Jerry, having won a scholarship in college, is eager to pursue his career as an architect. Father Jordan thinks Jerry ought to go to work. Jerry and Sesaly succumb to their love and the lure of the moon, but although Sesaly, as a result, expects a baby she is eager that Jerry should not be hampered by responsibilities and therefore declares their marriage non-effective until her husband has embraced his career. Jerry weakens and accepts a job in a hardware store. For the moment he had rather be a husband than an architect.

MRS. BUMPSTEAD-LEIGH

(72 performances)

A farcical comedy in three acts by Harry James Smith. Produced by George C. Tyler, at the Klaw Theatre, New York, April 1, 1929.

Cast of characters—

Justin Rawson....................Fuller Mellish
Miss Rawson....................Jennie A. Eustace
Geoffrey Rawson....................Edmund George
Anthony Rawson....................John Anthony
Stephen Leavitt....................William Lorenz
Mrs. Leavitt....................Valerie Valaire
Peter Swallow....................Sidney Toler
Kitson....................Dallas Welford
Mrs. De Salle....................Stella Mayhew
Mrs. Bumpstead-Leigh....................Mrs. Fiske
Violet De Salle....................Eleanor Griffith
Nina....................Doris Freeman

Acts I, II and III.—Living Room in Mrs. Rawson's Long Island Country House.
Staged by Harrison Grey Fiske.

Della Sales, daughter of old Jim Sales, herb doctor, is socially ambitious. After her father's death she takes her mother and sister to Europe, changes her name to De Salle and returns to conquer the snobs of Long Island. Peter Swallow, her Iowa sweetheart, would expose her but Della talks him down. Then the younger sister tells the truth, annexes a socially important younger son and Della is for the time nonplussed.

MUSIC IN MAY

(80 performances)

A musical play in three acts, book by Fanny Todd Mitchell; adapted from the original by Heinz Merley and Kurt Breuer; music by Emile Berte and Maury Rubens; lyrics by J. Kiern Brennan. Produced by the Messrs. Shubert, at the Casino Theatre, New York, April 1, 1929.

Cast of characters—

Hans....................Joseph Toner
Vita....................Gertrude Lang

Karl Von Dorn....................................Greek Evans
Popkin....................................Charles Lawrence
Zenzi....................................Marie Dayne
Rausenbach....................................Solly Ward
Baron Metternich....................................Joseph Lertora
Prince Stephan....................................Bartlett Simmons
Comtesse Olga....................................Gladys Baxter
Lisa....................................Edith Scott
Alois....................................George Offerman, Jr.
Kranz....................................Charles Chesney
Loibner....................................Francis Lyman
Kuhmeier....................................James Norris
Prinz....................................Peter Petraitis
Butler....................................Earl Plummer
Courier....................................Francis Lyman
Officers....................................Charles Chesney, Francis Lyman
James Norris, Peter Petraitis
Officer....................................Frazer McMahon
Lintchy....................................Julia Lane
Footmen.............Messrs. Plummer, Spiro, Hertel and St. John

Act I.—A Garden. Act II.—A Drinking Place. Act III.—A Garden and a Studio.

Staged by Lou Morton and Stanley Logan.

Vita, village belle, is undecided between two suitors when Prince Stephan appears. Vita and Stephan fall desperately in love but the Prince is ordered home. He finds a way in the last act, however, to make Vita a baroness and marry her.

APPEARANCES

(24 performances)

A comedy-drama with prologue, epilogue and three acts by Garland Anderson. Produced by C. Mischell Picard, at the Hudson Theatre, New York, April 1, 1929.

Cast of characters—

Frank Thompson....................................Norvell Thompson
Carl Sanderson....................................James LaCurto
Mrs. Thompson....................................Donna Pasdeloup
Fred Kellard....................................Lee Millar
Elsie Benton....................................Verna A. Felton
Louise Thornton....................................Martina Martin
Judge Thornton....................................Thaddeus Gray
Rufus Jones....................................Doe Doe Green
Ella Buford....................................Sally Rutter
Jack Wilson....................................Rupert LaBelle
Police Officer....................................Delmar Nightingale
Judge Robinson....................................Robert W. Smiley
Clerk of Court....................................Jerome Wise
Court Stenographer....................................Hazel Gray
Gerald Saunders....................................Stanley Ruhland
Hiram Mathews....................................Harry Davis
Bailiff....................................Willie Meehan
A. A. Andrews....................................Harry Bond
Prologue.................................... James LaCurto, Thaddeus Gray, Robert W. Smiley

Prologue and Acts I and III.—Lobby of Hotel Shasta, San Francisco. Act II.—A Court Room.
Staged by Lee Miller.

"Best Plays, 1925-26."

UNDER THE GASLIGHT

(23 performances)

A play in five acts by Augustin Daly. Produced by Larry Fay and Alex Yokel, at the Fay's Bowery Theatre, New York, April 2, 1929.

Cast of characters—

Ray Trafford	James Meighan
Snorkey	John Ferguson
Byke	Earl Mitchell
Ed. Demilt	J. Martiny
Windel	W. Richardson
Justice Bowling	H. Bledsoe
Counsellor Splinter	Norman Stewart
Bermudas	Robert Griffith
Peanuts	J. Donohue
Lillywhite	J. Worden
Sam	Eddie Mann
Rafferdi	John Burkell
The Sergeant	S. Mansfield
Policeman 999	J. Rogers
Martin	H. Perkins
Peter Rich	A. Wilson
The Signal Man	William Corbett
Laura Cortlandt	Helene Dumas
Pearl Cortlandt	Vera Loday
Peachblossom	Ella F. Houghton
Old Judas	Lizzie McCall
Mrs. Van Dam	Lois Ross
Sue Earlie	Mabel Kern
Lizzie Liston	Sarah Carey

Act I.—Scene 1—Home of the Cortlandts' on the Avenue. 2—The Hat Room of the Tuesday Sociable. 3—Delmonico's Ball Room. Act II.—Basement in Rivington Street. Act III.—Scene 1—Tombs Police Court. 2—Exterior of the Tombs. 3—The Piers of the City. Act IV.—Scene 1—Villa at Long Branch. 2—Hedge near Shrewsbury Station. 3—Station Shed by Shrewsbury Bend! Act V.—Pearl's Boudoir at Long Branch.
Staged by Mr. Frank Hatch.

Laura Cortlandt, a belle of society, is in love with Ray Trafford, "a New York blood." Before they can marry Laura's past arises to smite her in the person of Byke, her foster father and a frightful villain. Laura is the deserted daughter of rich and idle parents, but before she can prove it she suffers many hardships and a ducking in the river.

HE WALKED IN HER SLEEP

(21 performances)

A farce comedy in three acts by Norman Cannon. Produced by Superb Plays Corporation, at the Princess Theatre, New York, April 4, 1929.

Cast of characters—

Marie....................................Margaret Paige
Andrew Tankers................................Ralph Roberts
Henrietta Tankers...........................Beatrice Nichols
June Tankers...................................Clare Stratton
Jeffery Deacon..............................Antony Stanford
Robert Donovan..............................Reed Brown, Jr.
Acts I and II.—Living Room of the Tankers. Act III.—Scene 1—The Tankers' Bedroom. 2—Living Room.

Andrew Tankers, being advised that if he will give his wife some cause for suspicion he will succeed in diverting her mind from a certain person in whom he suspects she is interested, seeks to disappear from one twin bed while Mrs. Tankers is asleep in another alongside. He makes the excursion successfully and then learns his suspicions were groundless.

* BIRD IN HAND

(84 performances)

A comedy in three acts by John Drinkwater. Produced by Lee Shubert, at the Booth Theatre, New York, April 4, 1929.

Cast of characters—

Joan Greenleaf..............................Jill Esmond Moore
Alice Greenleaf...................................Amy Veness
Thomas Greenleaf.............................Herbert Lomas
Gerald Arnwood..............................Charles Hickman
Mr. Blanquet.....................................Ivor Barnard
Cyril Beverley..............................Charles Maunsell
Ambrose Godolphin, K.C..........................Frank Petley
Sir Robert Arnwood............................Roddy Hughes
Acts I and III.—The Bar Parlor. Act II.—Beverley's Bedroom.
Staged by John Drinkwater.

Thomas Greenleaf, at seventy-five, is the last Greenleaf to carry on the Bird in Hand Inn after three hundred years. His daughter, Joan, at twenty, takes to walking and riding out with Gerald Arnwood, the son of the squire. Thomas believes firmly that when a young man of station steps out of his class to be nice to a girl socially his inferior he does so for no good purpose. Joan, being modern, considers her father's attitude ridiculous. One night her father chases Joan home and the inn is aroused. Three guests agree to sit in the family conference and help the old man solve his problem. In the end the squire himself asks Joan to marry Gerald.

MYSTERY SQUARE

(44 performances)

A play in prologue and three acts by Hugh A. Anderson and George Bamman (by arrangement with Constance Collier), based on Robert Louis Stevenson's "Suicide Club" and "The Rajah's Diamond." Produced by Murray Phillips, at the Longacre Theatre, New York, April 4, 1929.

Cast of characters—

Prince Florizel	Gavin Muir
Colonel Geraldine	Thomas Holding
Newsboy	Eddie Edwards
Sporting Gent	Knox Herold
Fast Young Lady	Winifred Carter
Waiter	Kenneth Lawton
Carolyn Vandeleur	Marie Adels
Eileen O'Shea	Daphne Warren Wilson
Dr. Noel	John Ivancovich
Harry Hartley	Frank Hearn
Kyn	John Brewster
Roland Tenby	Robert Vivian
Algernon Clive	Kenneth Lawton
Mr. Malthus	Edgar Stehli
The President	Hubert Druce
Teresa Valdevia	Patricia Otis
Desborough Carrom	Knox Herold
Charlie Pendragon	Milton Roberts
Madame Mendizabel	Joan Blaine
Miss Sorcerlel	Laura Carpenter
Mrs. Malder	Francelia Waterbury
Miss Miles	Winifred Carter

Prologue—Act I.—Scene 1—In a Hansom Cab. 2—Oyster Bar. Act II.—Scene 1—President's Cabinet at Rochester House. 2—Drawing Room at Rochester House. Act III.—Scene 1—In a Hansom Cab. 2—Assembly Room of the Suicide Club.

Staged by Murray Phillips.

Prince Florizel and Colonel Geraldine, thrill hunters of another day, are in search of adventure when fate leads them into a meeting of the Suicide Club. They are elected members, the Prince is given the death card and his assassin appointed. The club is run by the three villains, Dr. Noel, Mr. Malthus and the President, and they are after the Rajah's diamond, which the Prince has taken from Harry Hartley. In the end, by a narrow margin, royalty's life is saved and the villains apprehended.

THE SEAGULL

(31 performances)

A play in four acts by Anton Chekov. Produced by A Co-operative Company, at the Comedy Theatre, New York, April 9, 1929.

Cast of characters—

Masha	Dorothy Yockel
Semyon Semyonovitch Medvedenko	Ian M. Wolfe
Konstantin Gavrilovitch Treplev	Lewis Leverett
Pyotr Nikolayevitch Sorin	E. J. Ballantine
Yakov	Maynard Burgess
Nina Mihaillovna Zaretchny	Barbara Bulgakova
Polina Andreyevna	Barbara Benedict
Yevgeny Sergeyevitch Dorn	Carroll Ashburn
Irina Nikolayevna Arkadin	Dorothy Sands
Ilya Afanasyevitch Shamraev	William Challee
Boris Alexeyevitch Trigorin	Walter Abel
Housemaid	Ruth Nelson

Act I.—Park on Sorin's Estate. Act II.—Lawn in Front of Sorin's House. Act III.—Dining Room of Sorin's House. Act IV.—Sitting Room in Sorin's House.

Staged by Leo Bulgakov.

Irina, a popular actress, has taken her lover, Trigorin, a popular novelist, to visit her father's home. There Trigorin meets and is fascinated by Nina, loved by Ilya. Nina later follows Trigorin to Moscow. Trigorin and Nina share experiences, Nina becomes a mother, her child dies, Trigorin leaves her to return to Irina. Nina goes back home unhappily wiser. Ilya kills himself.

* JONESY

(79 performances)

A comedy of youth by Anne Morrison and John Peter Toohey. Produced by Earle Boothe, at the Bijou Theatre, New York, April 9, 1929.

Cast of characters—

Anne Jones	Eloise Keeler
Mildred Ellis	Nydia Westman
Mrs. Henry Jones	Spring Byington

A Plumber....................Robert Crozier
Another Plumber....................Edward Racey
Henry Jones....................Donald Meek
Wilbur Jones....................Raymond Guion
Billy Morgan....................Jack Mead
Katie....................Kate Mayhew
Diana Devereaux....................Helen Brooks
Stanley Jackson....................Percy Moore
Mr. Silverberg....................Selden Bennett
A Policeman....................Edward Racey

Acts I, II and III.—The Jones Living Room.
Staged by Earle Boothe.

Wilbur Jones, home from college on vacation, forms an attachment for Diana, the ingenue of the local stock company. His father and mother proceed ruthlessly in breaking up the attachment, only to discover that Diana is the niece of the town's richest citizen and the man from whom Mr. Jones expects to get a job. The Joneses then try to undo what they have done and bring Diana and Wilbur together again. In the end Wilbur takes a job on the town sprinkling cart to prove his manhood and pay his debts.

THE VEGETABLE

(13 performances)

A fantasy in three acts by F. Scott Fitzgerald. Produced by Lenox Hill Players, Inc., at the Cherry Lane Theatre, New York, April 10, 1929.

Cast of characters—

Jerry Frost....................Jerome Seplow
Charlotte....................Eve Saxer
Dada....................Louis John Latzer
Doris....................Fanny Shack
Snooks....................Mitchell Padriac Marcus
Mr. Jones....................Harold Smith
Gen. Pushing....................Herman Bandes
Mr. Fish....................Harry Jay Marks
Judge Fossile....................David Kerman
Detective....................Martin K. Altman
Senators....................{ Harry J. Marks / David Kerman / Harold Smith }
Chorus....................{ Syd Brenner / Lilya Slotnikov / Mildred P. Seplow }

Acts I, II and III.—In the Home of Jerry Frost.
Staged by Lee Strasberg.

Satirical fantasy in which a poor man drinks gin and dreams that he is president. His adventures in the White House convince him that he had rather be a postman.

* CAMEL THROUGH THE NEEDLE'S EYE

(72 performances)

A play in three acts by Frantisek Langer, adapted by Philip Moeller. Produced by The Theatre Guild, Inc., at the Martin Beck Theatre, New York, April 15, 1929.

Cast of characters—

Mr. Pesta	Henry Travers
Mrs. Pesta	Helen Westley
Susi Pesta	Miriam Hopkins
Boy	Norman Williams
Bezchyba	Joseph Kilgour
Andrejs	Morris Carnovsky
Lady	Catherine Doucet
Lady's Daughter	Mary Kennedy
Alik	Elliot Cabot
Joe Vilim	Claude Rains

Act I.—Cellar Residence of the Pesta Family. Act II.—Living Room of Alik's Home. Act III.—The Dairy.
Staged by Philip Moeller.

Susi, illegitimate daughter of Mrs. Pesta, a beggar, meets Alik Vilim, the none too bright son of a rich father. Alik, fascinated, proposes making Susi his mistress, and she, knowing her mother's story, concludes that she, too, is entitled to her romance. She goes to live with Alik and makes a man of him. When Alik's father tries to buy her off she leaves Alik but he follows her. Together they open a model dairy lunch, achieve success, and Alik definitely refuses to return to his father's house. He marries Susi and acknowledges her child.

* THE LOVE DUEL

(72 performances)

A modern play in three acts by Lili Hatvany, adapted by Zoe Akins. Produced by Lee Shubert (in association with Gilbert Miller), at the Ethel Barrymore Theatre, New York, April 15, 1929.

Cast of characters—

He	Louis Calhern
An Attache	Martin Burton
A Footman	Marcel Dill
She	Ethel Barrymore
The Herr Professor	Henry Stephenson
His Excellency, an Ambassador	Ferdinand Gottschalk
An Extra Young Man	Leslie Barrie
Baby	Dorothy Hall

Marie..Anita Rothe
A Cook..Gertrude Maitland
A Kitchen Maid...................................Carol March
A Young Widow...............................Jeannette Sherwin

Act I.—An Occasional Room in a Palace. Act II.—A Drawing Room. Act III.—A Principal Room in a Small Swiss Chalet.
Staged by E. M. Blyth.

She has lived fully and freely, having had many lovers. He has lived fully and freely, having known many women. Irresistibly drawn together and each accepting the other as a worthy adversary they agree to test their power to make each other either happy or miserable. Soon each is desperately in love with the other but neither will acknowledge defeat. He lets her believe he is to marry another. She lets him believe she is in love with another. He searches her out in Switzerland, where she has borne him a child. The duel a draw, reconcilation and marriage follow.

BEFORE YOU'RE 25

(23 performances)

A gay comedy in three acts by Kenyon Nicholson. Produced by Lawrence Boyd, at the Maxine Elliott Theatre, New York, April 16, 1929.

Cast of characters—

Mary Ellen...Harriet Donovan
Gibbons...William Eville
Marabeth Downing...............................Carolyn Ferriday
Miss Mumfort...Mary Hubbard
Cornelia Corbin......................................Josephine Hull
Jeffery A. Corbin.....................................Fritz Williams
Leonard Corbin......................................Donald McKee
Clement Corbin..Eric Dressler
Murphy...F. Cecil Butler
Joan Abbott...Mildred McCoy
The Rev. Dwight Simpson...................Edward Broadley
Norman Philbrick..............................Ernest Glendinning
Giuseppe Bellini.................................Federico Conzona
Norina Bellini...Lola Vanni

Acts I, II and III.—The Corbins' Residence.

Clement Corbin, young and rebellious, quits his father's home in Chicago rather than go into the furniture business. In New York he becomes the editor and proprietor of a radical monthly. Government authorities drive him out of New York and he starts with his companionate wife for California. On the train she gives birth to a son. They stop off at Clement's Chicago home for her convalescence. At the end of a month which Clement has spent in jail the companionate wife has gone conservative and favors marrying Clement and bringing up their child in security. She urges his taking the furniture business seriously. He rebels but is won over.

ROCKBOUND

(19 performances)

Drama by Amy Wales and Michael Kallesser. Produced by Michael Kallesser, at the Cort Theatre, New York, April 19, 1929.

Cast of characters—

Ellen Higgins................................Emily Ann Wellman
Jed Higgins......................................Willard Bowman
Maudie May Higgins................................Gene Paul
Dave Higgins...............................Ricardo de Angelis
Amos Higgins...................................John F. Hamilton
Lucy..Renita Randolph

Ellen Higgins, married to a brute of a man in a fishing village on the Maine coast, is forced by circumstances to take Lucy. She tells the family Lucy is her niece. Lucy is really her daughter born out of wedlock before she married. The truth comes out when Lucy falls in love and wants to marry her half brother, Amos. Lucy and her mother are turned out of the house, but Ellen, a slave to her family obligations, comes back to take care of her husband and her sons.

THE COME-ON MAN

(24 performances)

A play in three acts by Herbert Ashton, Jr. Produced by Roy Walling at the 49th Street Theatre, New York, April 22, 1929.

Cast of characters—

William Strange..............................George MacQuarrie
Marguerite Strange...............................Jane Marbury
Betty Strange.......................................Mary Wall
Rodney Stewart..............................Donald Campbell
Maria Stewart.......................................Teresa Dale
Rodney Stewart, Jr.........................Anthony Stanford
Stevens..................................Robert W. Lawrence
Jeff...Herbert Ashton
Jimmie McGuire............................Herbert Ashton, Jr.
Jack Harold....................................Harold Webster
Mrs. Schaeffer..................................Leona Hollister

Acts I, II and III.—William Strange's Home.
Staged by Herbert Ashton.

William Strange, crook of high degree, engages Jimmie McGuire as a handsome lure to attract wealthy and bejewelled women into the Strange home, where they can be robbed of their possessions. Jimmie, falling in love with Betty, Strange's daughter, manages a consistent sort of reformation.

MARRY THE MAN

(8 performances)

A companionate comedy in three acts by Jean Archibald. Produced by Clyde Elliott, at the Fulton Theatre, New York, April 22, 1929.

Cast of characters—

Kate	Fay Warren
Wm. Leland	J. Anthony Hughes
Timothy	Richard Ward
Mrs. Jeffries	Ann Dere
John Jeffries	Lew J. Welsh
Lillian Jeffries	Joan Peers
Jack Hanno	Jerry Bowman
Mollie Jeffries	Vivian Martin
Gregory Martin	Lester Vail
Mary	Florence McGee

Acts I, II and III.—New York Suburban Home of Mollie Jeffries.
Staged by Priestly Morrison.

Mollie Jeffries, convinced that marriages would be happier without the binding forces of the ceremony with ring and book, induces Gregory Martin to sign a contract and go to live with her in a bungalow. Gregory, deeply in love with Mollie, is haunted by a fear of losing her and wants to make the union legal. Mollie holds him to his bargain—until she suspects he is preparing to marry some one else.

MESSIN' AROUND

(33 performances)

A modern musical novelty in two parts, lyrics by Perry Bradford, music by Jimmy Johnson. Produced by Louis Isquith, at the Hudson Theatre, New York, April 22, 1929.

Principals engaged—

Sterling Grant	Monette Moore
Paul Floyd	Cora La Redd
Billy McLaurin	Audrey Thomas
James Thompson	Freda Jackson

Walter Brogsdale	Queenie Price
Arthur Porter	Hilda Perleno
James Dyer	Lena Shadney
Bamboo McCarver	Susie Wroten
Frank Lloyd	Emma Maitland
William McKelvey	Aurelia Wheeldin

Staged by Louis Isquith and Eddie Rector.

CARNIVAL

(24 performances)

A drama in three acts by William R. Doyle. Produced by Irving Lande, at the Forrest Theatre, New York, April 24, 1929.

Cast of characters—

Mrs. Spencer............................Virginia True Boardman
Lillian.................................Agnes Young
Mr. Spencer.............................Frank G. Bond
Bobbie Spencer..........................Norman Foster
Fred Spalding...........................Antrim Short
Helen Herbert...........................Anne Forrest
Mildred Connors.........................Josephine Evans
Blackie.................................Walter Fenner
Babe....................................Esther Keefe
Liz.....................................Ramona Kogan
Kitty...................................Sybil Larayne
Fifi....................................Germaine Giroux
Ju Ju...................................Bee Jackson
Shorty..................................Frank Horton
Billie..................................Adele Gilbert

Act I.—Living Room of the Spencer Home. Act II.—Scene 1—Helen's Room. 2—Living Room. 3—The "Smoker." Act III.—Dressing Tent.

Bobbie Spencer picks up and falls desperately in love with Helen Herbert, a "cooch" dancer in a street carnival passing through his town. For days the romance flourishes in a "hide-away," at the end of which time Bobbie wants to marry Helen, but Helen loves him too much to ruin his life. She lets him see her as a dancer at a stag party, hoping to disgust him. When this doesn't work she substitutes for the parachute jumper and does not open the chute.

THE PASSION PLAY

(48 performances)

The Freiburg Passion Play, produced by Morris Guest, at the Hippodrome Theatre, New York, April 29, 1929.

Cast of characters—

The Christus............................Adolph Fassnacht
Judas...................................Georg Fassnacht

Mary	Amalie Fassnacht
Mary Magdalene	Elsa Fassnacht
Johannes	Georg Fassnacht, Jr.
The Blind Woman	Augusta Fassnacht
Pontius Pilate	Lothar Mayring
Caiphas	Fritz Schoeller
Dathan	Willie Ehrhardt
Annas	Joseph Danner
Nathaniel	Otto Ludwig
Ezekiel	Joseph Meier
Rabbi	Joseph Langer
Joseph of Arimathæa	Waldemar Schoenstein
Simon of Cyrene	Fritz Helger
Nicodemus	Heinrich Knopper
Veronica	Helen Heikamph
Kleopha	Betty Hofstaetter
Baruch	C. Kurz
Rachel	Anna Miller
Quintus	J. Moses
Longinus	Emil Krautter
Selpho	John Strehlow
Japhet	A. Shaefer
Abrion	K. Knopp
Barabbas	Alfred Hacker
First Murderer	Carl Schneider
Second Murderer	Fritz Schmitt
King Herod	Adam Schoenfeld
Peter	Heinrich Hauk

Staged by David Belasco.

This German version of the life of Christ beginning with the Entrance into Jerusalem and ending with the Crucifixion, has been periodically produced in Freiburg, Germany, every three years since 1760, members of the Fassnacht families taking the principal rôles.

THE LITTLE SHOW

(55 performances)

A musical revue in two acts, lyrics mostly by Howard Dietz, music mostly by Arthur Schwartz. Produced by William A. Brady, Jr., and Dwight Deere Wiman, in association with Tom Weatherly, at the Music Box Theatre, New York, April 30, 1929.

Principals engaged—

Clifton Webb	Libby Holman
Fred Allen	Helen Lynd
Romney Brent	Peggy Conklin
John McCauley	Kay Lazell
Ernest Sharpe	Bettina Hall
Harold Moffat	Joan Carter-Waddell
Paul Bissinger	Dorothy Humphreys
Adam Carroll	Portland Hoffa

Staged by Dwight Deere Wiman, dances by Danny Dare.

CONGRATULATIONS

(39 performances)

A new comedy in three acts by Morgan Wallace. Produced by Lawrence Shubert Lawrence, at the National Theatre, New York, April 30, 1929.

Cast of characters—

Caldwell	Herbert Yost
Jack Rogers	Freddy Larimer
Andrea Darnell	Blenche Benton
Mary Sutton	Laurette Bullivant
Arthur Scott	Robert Farrell
Wilmer Farrell	Max Von Mitzel
Bert	Preston Foster
Madge Wells	Leneta Lane
Morgan Wallace	Henry Hull
S. L. Richardson	John A. Butler
Tim Murry	John T. Doyle
Hal Conklin	Charles F. McCarthy
Susie Curtis	Virginia Howell
Irene Johnson	Joan Bourdelle
Peter Johnson	Robert Cummings
Tony Sicardo	George Anderson
Frank Mann	Halliam Bosworth

Act I.—Scene 1—The Stage of the Grand Opera House. 2—Back Stage. Act II.—Scene 1—Wallace's Room. 2—Stage. 3—Richardson's Room. 4—Stage. Act III.—An Office.

Staged by Edward Clarke Lilley.

Morgan Wallace, leading man and part proprietor of a stock company in a mid-western town, is facing bankruptcy when the town's political boss offers him a chance to run for mayor. The actor is to represent the reform element and get enough votes to make election easy for the machine candidate. By a fluke Wallace is elected and decides to give the town an honest administration for a change.

* GRAND STREET FOLLIES OF 1929

(53 performances)

An annual satirical revue, book and lyrics by Agnes Morgan, music by Arthur Schwartz and Max Ewing, additional numbers by William Irwin and Serge Walter. Produced by The Actor-Managers, Inc., in association with Paul Moss, at the Booth Theatre, New York, May 1, 1929.

Principals engaged—

Albert Carroll
Otto Hulett
Marc Loebell
Dorothy Dands
Paula Trueman
Edla Frankau

James Cagney
Junius Matthews
Hal Brogan
Blaine Cordner
George Heller
Mary Williams
Mae Noble
Kathleen Kidd
Katherine Gauthier

Staged by Agnes Morgan, dances by Dave Gould.

LITTLE THEATRE TOURNAMENT

(7 performances)

Conducted by Walter Hartwig, in coöperation with the Manhattan Little Theatre Club, Inc., for the David Belasco Trophy, at the Waldorf Theatre, New York, the week of May 6, 1929.

MONDAY EVENING, MAY 6

The Mimes and Mummers of Fordham University, New York City, in "The Rhythm of the City," by Donald J. Ryan.

The Cast—
Jack Merry....................John P. King
Hughes....................James P. Casey
Canby....................Bernard J. Lane
Reporter....................William J. Flanagan
Mr. Williams....................James E. Higgins
Scene—A New York Night Club.

The Monticello Players of Manhattan in "The Father Returns," by Kiruchi Kwan.

The Cast—
Kenichiro, aged 28....................Ted DeCorsia
Otaka, His Mother....................Alice Normandeau
Shinjiro, His Younger Brother....................William Stillwagon
Otane, His Young Sister....................Marilyn Kaltman
Sotaro, His Father....................Thomas Keenan
A Passerby....................Harry Sacks
Scene—A Six-mat Room in a Middle-class Home—a Small Town in the Nankaido, Japan.
The play adapted and directed by Conrad V. Norman.

The Fonnesbeck Players of Manhattan in "Joint Owners in Spain," by Alice Brown.

The Cast—
Mrs. Mitchell, Director of the Old Ladies' Home....Helen Thackrey
Miss Dyer } Inmates of the Home............ { Tracy Aylwin
Mrs. Blair } Inmates of the Home............ { Mary Jane Roberts
Scene—A Room in the Home.
Staged and Directed by Lydia Fonnesbeck.

Old Fort Club of Brooklyn in "Another Room for Rent," by John Kanaley.

The Cast—
Jerry Strange....................Lawrence McManus
Bob Wallace....................Frederick Thurston
Miss Lambert....................Elizabeth Watters
Mr. McMahon....................Edwin S. Parker
Mrs. McMahon....................Bessie Duncan
Directed by Hans Axel Wolleen.

TUESDAY EVENING, MAY 7

The Argonaut Players of Manhattan in "Sightseers," by Bernice Breen.

The Cast—
Christopher, a Guide....................Thomas V. Caulkins
Madeleine, John, The Old Woman, The Old Man } Party of Sightseers........ { Elizabeth Carlton, Leslie G. Anderson, Violet Jones, William Forst
Scene—A Remote Part of the Crystal Caverns.
Produced Under the Personal Direction of the Author.

League of American Pen Women of New York City Branch in "The Aristocrat," by Teja Werbing.
The Cast—
Herman Osterman (Americanized "Harvey Easter")..James Metcalfe
Muriel Vanderveldt....................Verna Carleton
Hedwig Osterman....................Lillian W. Browne
The Unexpected....................Ernest Howard
Scene—Living Room of Harvey Easter's Apartment, New York City.
Play Directed by Lillian W. Browne.

The Association Players Stock Company of the Y.M.H.A. of 92nd St., Manhattan, in "The Man in the Stalls," by Alfred Sutro.
The Cast—
Hector....................Saul Trochman
Walter....................Pat Feil
Betty....................Eve Lynn
Maid....................June White
Scene—The Drawing Room of Hector's Apartment.
Produced Under the Direction of Myron E. Sattler.

The Dramatic Union of Our Lady of Lourdes of Manhattan in "The House With the Twisty Windows," by Mary Parkington.
The Cast—
James Roper, K. C....................Nicholas Healy
Charles Clive....................Adrian Powers
Teresa, Lady Ponting....................Anne Hamilton Slattery
Heather Sorrell....................Gloria Russ
Anne Sorrell....................Madeleine Killalea
Derrick Moore....................John Hiro
Stepan....................William Brennan
Scene—The Cellar of a House in Petrograd, During the "Red Terror."
Produced Under the Direction of Gertrude Wainwright.

WEDNESDAY EVENING, MAY 8

Community Players of South County of Peace Dale, Rhode Island, in "Fancy Free," by Stanley Houghton.
The Cast—
Fancy....................Bertha Taft
Alfred....................Richard C. Taft
Ethelbert....................T. Pierrepont Hazard
Delia....................Nathalie F. Pierce
Scene—A Corner of the Writing Room of the Hotel Cosmopolitan, Babylon-on-Sea.
Directed by Bertha Taft.

The Sunnyside Playhouse of Sunnyside, L. I., in "The Severed Cord," by Maxine Finsterwald.
The Cast—
Anna....................Helen Cross
Karl....................Robert Sangster
Jake....................Frank Sangster
Scene—The Kitchen in a Shack in a Small Manufacturing Town near Boston.
Produced Under the Direction of Maxine Finsterwald.

The Gardens Players of Forest Hills, L. I., in "Shall We Join the Ladies," by Sir James M. Barrie.

The Cast—
Sam Smith....John B. Bruns
Lady Jane Raye....Loretta Howson
Sir Joseph Wrathie....Frederick Kiendl
Lady Wrathie....Arlene Greening
Mr. Preen....Walter Claypoole
Mrs. Preen....Agnes Kiendl
Mr. Valie....C. E. Silcox
Miss Valie....Irma Wagner
Mr. Gourlay....Edward Moir
Mrs. Castro....Rose Schulze-Berge
Captain Jennings....Harper Canaday
Miss Isit....G. Marian Burton
Mrs. Bland....Helen Clevenger
Dolphin....Otto Berman
Lucy (the Maid)....Mabel Claypoole
Policeman....Harry Foskett
Scene—Dining Room of Sam Smith's Home.
The Play Directed by Albert S. Howson.

The Derry Association Players of New York City in "Rachel Cowan," by Shane Conway.
The Cast—
Bredin Hewitt, a "Small" Farmer....Shane Conway
Martha Hewitt, His Wife....Belle Butler
Rachel Cowan, Adopted by the Hewitts....Tessie MacFarlane
Jack Guildford, the Son of a Neighboring Farmer...Chas. McElhone
Scene—A Kitchen in the Home of the Hewitts, Situated in the Innishowen Peninsula Section of the North of Ireland.
Play Directed by Shane Conway.

THURSDAY EVENING, MAY 9

Columbia Players of the Community Drama Guild of Washington, D. C., in "The Monkey's Paw," by W. W. Jacobs.
The Cast—
Mr. White....George Odell
Mrs. White....Elizabeth Dyer
Herbert, Their Son....Paul Alexander
Sergeant-Major Morris....Harry Westcott
Mr. Sampson....Bauk Hage
Scene—The Living Room of An Old-fashioned Cottage in a London Suburb.
Director—Aurora M. Poston.

The Chaminade Players of Dayton, Ohio, in "The Yellow Triangle," by George W. Sutton, Jr.
The Cast—
Henderson, a Trader....D. C. Ashton
Helen, His Wife....Rose Marie Abel
Dorand, Chief of Police....Maurice Costello
Bardow, American Consul....Jack Janszen
Alidini Viseram, Arab Ivory Agent....Cletus Robbeloth
Ali, Head House Boy....Robert Schields
Mabruki, Swohili Servant....Richard Zenni
Scene—Zanzibar, East Africa; Office in Henderson's House.
D. C. Ashton, Director.

The Little Theatre of St. Augustine, Florida in "Poor Old Jim," by Wm. C. De Mille.
The Cast—
Jim....Chas. F. Hopkins, Jr.
Marie, His Wife....Hazel Hopkins
Paul, the Doctor....Fred A. Henderich
Scene—Sitting Room in Jim's Apartment—New York City.
Directed by Chas. F. Hopkins, Jr.

The Hearthstone Players of Denver, Colorado, in "Thirst," by Eugene O'Neill.

The Cast—
A Dancer....................................Lucille Ferry
A Gentleman....................................Noble Laesch
A Negro Sailor....................................Eugene Beuerman
Scene—A Brine Washed Steamer's Life Raft, Afloat on a Tropic Sea, at Midnight.
Katharine Anne Ommanney, Director.

FRIDAY EVENING, MAY 10

The Anniston Little Theatre of Anniston, Alabama, in "The End of the Dance," by Hudson Strode.
The Cast—
Madeline Marsden....................................Edel Ayers
Dr. Stanley Gregg....................................Raymond Wheeler
Nurse Trewin....................................Carrie Knox
Gerald Marsden....................................Knox Ide
Scene—Up-stairs Sitting Room in the Home of Dr. Gregg.
Directed by Donald Marye.

The Temple Arts Club of Cincinnati, Ohio, in "Edna," by Ralph C. Zimmerman and Robert F. Chester.
The Cast—
Edna Schmidt....................................Katherine Gray
"Mom" Schmidt....................................Dolly Britten
Fred Schmidt....................................Ralph Zimmerman
"Dad" Schmidt....................................Clarence Frohliger
Clif Akers, Newspaperman....................................Darvin Mueller
Scene—The Second Floor Flat of the Schmidts' in the Suburb of Evanston, Cincinnati.
Directed by Ralph C. Zimmerman.

The Morgan College Dramatic Club of Baltimore, Maryland in "The Man Who Died at Twelve O'Clock," by Paul Green.
The Cast—
Sallie Evans....................................Allien F. Koger
Charlie....................................James D. Carr
January Evans....................................Osborne B. Dixon
Scene—A Room in the Home of January Evans on a Farm in Eastern North Carolina.
Randolph Edmonds, Director.

The Guild Play Shop of Denver, Colorado in "Rain," by Dana Burnett.
The Cast—
Jim Baird....................................John Stapp
Allie Baird....................................Giana Regamey
"Worthy"....................................Richard Henson
Scene—A Village Hut on the Coast of Maine.
Lucille Langdon, Director-Manager.

At the conclusion of the tournament prizes were awarded the Gardens Players of Forest Hills, L. I.; The Guild Play Shop of Denver, Colorado; The Anniston Little Theatre of Anniston, Alabama; The Sunnyside Playhouse of Sunnyside, L. I. The Belasco trophy was awarded The Gardens Players for their performance of Sir James M. Barrie's "Shall We Join the Ladies."

THE FIRST LAW

(8 performances)

A drama in three acts by Dmitry Scheglov, adapted from the Russian by Herman Bernstein and Leonid Snegoff. Produced by

N. S. R. Productions, Inc., at the Masque Theatre, New York, May 6, 1929.

Cast of characters—

Ollan Stevens....................................Frances Carson
Henry Woodhouse..................................Reginald Goode
Vladimir...Leonid Snegoff
Uleiga...Samuel Schneider
Eugene Hunter....................................Wilfred Seagram
Acts I, II and III.—An Abandoned Hut in Siberia.
Staged by Leonid Snegoff.

Ollan Stevens, daughter of a mines manager in Siberia, and Henry Woodhouse, her aristocratic fiancé, are escaping the revolutionists when they are pursued by wolves and take refuge in a hut in the forest. Into the same hut stumbles Vladimir, Bolshevist engineer. Vladimir proves the stronger of the two men and wins Ollan's love away from Woodhouse. The men fight; Woodhouse is killed; Vladimir and Ollan are happy until relief comes. Then Ollan is torn between giving up her class and giving up Vladimir. She gives up Vladimir.

THE JADE GOD

(40 performances)

Mystery drama in three acts by William E. Barry, from the novel of Alan Sullivan. Produced by Ben Stein at the Cort Theatre, New York, May 13, 1929.

Cast of characters—

Perkins..Margaret Wycherly
John Millicent...................................Ronald Dexter
Jack Derrick.....................................Richard Nicholls
Edith Derrick....................................Gwyneth Gordon
Mrs. Thursby.....................................Phyllis Joyce
John Martin......................................H. H. McCollum
Jean Millicent...................................Lyle Stackpole
Inspector Burke..................................Stanley Harrison
Blunt..Leslie King
Peters...Oscar Serlin
Acts I, II and III.—The Study, Beech Lodge, Bamberly, Sussex, England.
Staged by Walter Greenough.

John Millicent is found murdered, his throat cut with a Malay creese. Jack Derrick, a novelist in love with Jean Millicent, takes over the Millicent house with his sister and swears he will solve the mystery. His investigations involve most of the servants and an itinerant peddlar from the Orient. He also discovers a jade idol which Millicent picked up in an India temple, and which carries a curse, to be the cause of the crime. The reënactment of the murder impells Perkins, the housemaid, to confess.

PANSY

(3 performances)

All-colored musical revue in two acts, book by Alex Belledna, music by Maceo Pinkard. Produced by Maceo Pinkard at the Belmont Theatre, New York, May 14, 1929.

Cast of characters—

Dean Liggett....................................Ralph Harris
James..Al Frisco
Campus "Cut Ups"................Tom and Austin—Cole Brothers
Miss Wright.....................................Ida Anderson
Bill (Proposition Kid)...........................Alfred Chester
Miss Merritt...................................Elizabeth Taylor
Pansy...Pearl McCormack
Ulysses Grant Green (Father of Pansy)..............Speedy Wilson
Mrs. Green.......................................Amon Davis
Bob..Billy Andrews
Sadie..Jackie Young
Penn Comedy Four.............................{ W. Crumbley, L. Randall, H. Mattingly, D. Davis }
Bessie Smith.....................................Bessie Smith
Acts I and II.—On and around the campus of a Southern university on commencement day.

A hit and miss revue, considerably more miss than hit.

STEPPING OUT

(24 performances)

Farce in three acts by Elmer Harris. Produced by Charles Dillingham in association with Eddie Dowling and Edgar MacGregor at the Fulton Theatre, New York, May 20, 1929.

Cast of characters—

Sally Smith....................................Jobyna Howland
Tubby Smith...................................Herbert Corthell
Tom Martin.....................................Walter Connoly
Parker...Audrey Davis
Eve Martin......................................Grace La Rue
Davis...Allen Fagan
Cleo Del Rio.....................................Lillian Bond
Madge Horton..................................Martha Sleeper
Charles Miller..................................Hale Hamilton
Paul Puff...Charles Dill
Harold Huggin...................................Kim Peacock
Porter...Jere McAuliffe
Act I.—Martin's Home in Hollywood. Act II and III.—Eve's Cabin Near Yosemite Valley, Calif.

Tubby Smith and Tom Martin, having invested in the motion picture business and met some of the actresses, decide on a bit of a fling to test their hope that they may not be as old as their years indicate. With their wives away they invite two young gold diggers, Cleo and Madge, for a party at Mr. Martin's home. The wives return, threaten to divorce their husbands and to be even run away to the mountains and flirt with a couple of college boys. The husbands, contrite but consistent, manage to force a reconciliation upon their mates.

*A NIGHT IN VENICE

(31 performances)

Revue in two acts; music by Lee Davis and Maury Rubens, lyrics by J. Keirn Brennan and Moe Jaffe. Produced by the Messrs. Shubert at the Shubert Theatre, New York, May 21, 1929.

Principals engaged—

Ted Healy	Dodge Sisters
Arthur Havel	Laura Lee
Morton Havel	Betsy Rees
Joe Michon	Ann Seymour
Peter Michon	Anita Case
Halfred Young	Sarah Granzow
Stanley Rogers	Florence Powell
John Byams	Fodi Brown
Ferral and Paul	The Johnsons
Shemp Howard	Walter Armin
Dudley Clements	Stevens Brothers
Chester Hale Girls	Allen Foster Girls

Staged by Lew Morton and Thomas A. Hart; dances by Busby Berkeley.

CHINESE O'NEILL

(13 performances)

Melodrama in three acts, by Capt. Cushing Donnell. Produced by the author at the Forrest Theatre, New York, May 22, 1929.

Cast of characters—

Captain Fowler	George Buzante
Fong Li	Gustave Rolland
Soy Yong	Howard Hall
Executioner	Al. Boucari
Hsi San	Frank G. Bond
Millie	Josephine Evans
Frenchy	John Buckler, Jr.

"Chinese" O'Neill.......................... Douglass R. Dumbrille
Louisiana.. Frank De Silva
Mississippi.. Arthur Rossman
Gerson St. George.................................... Hugh Buckler
Lady Agatha Beresford......................... Lenore Chippendale
The Hon. Nancy Beresford..................... Audrey Ridgwell
Lord Herbert Lenox................................ Edward Rigby
Captain Clarkson.............................. Frederick B. Manatt
Coolie in White................................. Gordon Conover
Coolie in Black.. Sigh Alti
Malays........................ Frank De Silva, Arthur Rossman
Chinese.................. Sang Ti, Fah Lo, Fuen Wah, Wong Foo
Prologue—The Justice of Chang Kai Chang. Acts I and II.—The Inn of the Honest Sailors. Act III.—The House of Chang Kai Chang. Time—1925. The Port of Hainan on the China Coast.

"Chinese" O'Neill, adventurous Yankee who fought in the great war with the Canadians, is running a couple of gunboat convoys for the English along the China coast. In the port of Hainan he finds Gerson St. George and party in jeopardy. Chang Kai Chang, "master of the China sea," has sworn to be even with St. George for having offered a reward for the capture of Chang. O'Neill, falling in love with the girl St. George is forcing to marry him, takes charge of the situation and manages finally to outwit and defeat Chang and save the girl.

UNCLE VANYA

(2 performances)

Drama in three acts by Anton Chekov. Produced by Irma Kraft at the Morosco Theatre, New York, May 24, 1929.

Cast of characters—

Marina.. Ludmilla Toretzka
Mikhail Lvovitch................................... Franchot Tone
Ivan Petrovitch (Uncle Vanya).................. Morris Carnovsky
Alexander Vladimirovitch.......................... Hubert Druce
Helena Andreievna..................................... Ara Gerald
Sonya.. Rose Keane
Ilya Ilyitch... Jules Artfield
Maria Vassilievna................................ Marjorie Dalton
Workman.. Anton Bundsman
Acts I, II and III.—On the Estate of the Voinetskoy in Russia.

Uncle Vanya, at 47, is embittered and disillusioned. For years he and his relatives have slaved to support and educate Alexander Vladimirovitch and now Alexander turns out a pompous and shallow professor of literature. Uncle Vanya also suffers a deep-seated love attack, being enamored of Alexander's second wife, the beautiful Helena. Helena does not return his love, but hungers instead after Mikhail, who, in turn, is loved hopelessly by Sonya. Uncle Vanya, in desperation, tries to kill Alexander but is even a failure at that. After which life settles back into a somewhat distressing normalcy.

* DECISION

(24 performances)

Comedy in three acts by Carl Henkle. Produced by Robert Sterling at the 49th Street Theatre, New York, May 27, 1929.

Cast of characters—

Nancy Lane....................................Margaret Barnstead
Mrs. Mack..Nellie Gill
John Grey......................................George Neville
Mr. Mack.......................................Francis Keeley
Jim Curtis......................................Edward Martin
George Lane....................................Buddy Schubert
Kate Lane..Frances Hess
Bill Young...Paul Martin
Mabel Lane..Wilva Davis
Margaret Pendleton.............................Ruby Blackburn
Archie Pendleton...................................Roy Bucklee
Judge Crosby.............................George H. Weiseman
Acts I, II and III.—Nancy Lane's Home. A Suburb of Worcester, Mass.

Nancy Lane, having taken the two children of her dead sister when their mother died, finds herself ten years later the beneficiary of a rich relative who leaves her a quarter million and her foster children three times as much. Immediately Nancy and the children are hounded by scheming relatives who try to prove Nancy's legal claim upon the children defective. The judge decides in Nancy's favor and she marries Jim Curtis, an honest green grocer who has loved her for a long time.

CHIPPIES

(5 performances)

Comedy drama in three acts by Luther Yantis. Produced by F. A. D. Productions, Inc., at the Belmont Theatre, New York, May 29, 1929.

Cast of characters—

Beth Ramsey...Maud Brooks
Mrs. Emma Ramsey..................................Maude Dayton
Ruby Stone...Klar Magnus
Clay Maxwell.......................................Warren Colt
Tony Perrotta......................................Cullen Landis
Sammy Marcus....................................Saul Z. Martell
Charley Hicks......................................Omar Glover
Eddie Mack.......................................Thomas Swift

Jack Olmstead....................................Fred Ardath
Officer Dukes....................................Lynn Root

Act I.—Living Room of the Ramsey Home. Painsville, Ohio. Act II.—Charley's Beer Flat. Cleveland, Ohio. Act III.—Scene 1—Beth's Boudoir. 2—Ramsey Home.

Beth Ramsey, a small town girl expecting to marry Clay Maxwell, is lured away to Cleveland, Ohio, by her tough chum, Ruby Stone, and becomes the mistress of Tony Perotta, a more or less noble bootlegger. In the end she sees the evil of her ways, and though Tony marries her, she gets back home just in time for her mother's funeral.

BECKY SHARP

(8 performances)

Comedy in four acts by Langdon Mitchell, based on Thackeray's "Vanity Fair." Revived by the Players' Club at the Knickerbocker Theatre, New York, June 3, 1929.

Cast of characters—

Becky Sharp....................................Mary Ellis
Amelia Sedley....................................Patricia Collinge
Miss Crawley....................................Cecilia Loftus
Marchioness of Steyne....................................Lillian Brennard Tonge
Lady Bareacres....................................Marguerite St. John
Lady Blanche....................................Haroldine Humphreys
Lady Jane Crawley....................................Mary Hone
Duchess of Richmond....................................Helen Freeman
Duchess of Buccleugh....................................Ida Mulle
Briggs....................................Mrs. Tom Wise
Fifine....................................Nedda Harrigan
Lady Stafford....................................Edith Barrett
Lady Rose of Kilrarock....................................Julia McMahan
Honorable Miss Greville....................................Erna Rowan
Miss Lamb....................................Cecily Work
Vi Countess St. Maur....................................Genevieve Williams
Lady Dukinfield....................................Agnes Brady
Hon. Miss Sybil Hampsheer....................................Pam Sweeny
Hon. Miss Wilton....................................Alice Papo
Miss Valida St. Gray....................................Adele Walker
Miss Zenobia Green....................................Elsie Keene
Honorable Miss Charteris....................................Evelyn Goodrich
The Marquis of Steyne....................................Moffat Johnston
Sir Pitt Crawley....................................James T. Powers
Pitt Crawley....................................Arthur Hohl
Rawdon Crawley....................................Basil Sydney
William Dobbin....................................Leonard Willey
George Osborne....................................Donald Brian
Joseph Sedley....................................Ernest Cossart
Major Loder....................................Henry Mortimer
Lord Bareacres....................................Etienne Girardot
Lord Tarquin....................................Herbert Ranson
Lord Southdown....................................Frazer Coulter
The Duke Brunswick....................................Ernest Rowan
Prince Peterwaradin....................................Wright Kramer
Tommy Baikes....................................Gerald Hamer
General Tufto....................................A. G. Andrews

Lieut. Ranlagh....................................John D. Seymour
Major Blenkinsop....................................Jay Fassett
Fritz....................................Jay Fassett
Max....................................Roland Hogue
Bowles....................................Doan Borup
Raggles....................................Clifford Walker
Landlord....................................Owen Meech
Lord Cheshire of Cherrington....................................Roland Hogue
Lieut. Ballard....................................Gordon Hart
Capt. McGregor....................................William Sams
Sir Roger Cameron....................................Jack O'Donnell
Lieut. Kinsale....................................Thomas Gomez
Lord Anglesey....................................J. Walter Smith
Lord Hereford....................................Loren Stout
Lieut. John Campbell....................................Bruce Bairnsfather
Admiral Sir John Hollingshead, K.C.B.........Edward MacNamara
Lieut. Blake....................................Raymond Thayer

Act I.—Miss Crawley's Residence, Park Lane, London. Act II.—Duchess of Richmond's Ball, Brussels. Act III.—Becky's House in Curzon Street, London. Act IV.—Becky's Lodgings in Pumpernickel.

Staged by Dudley Digges.

The familiar version staged originally by Minnie Maddern Fiske in 1899. Becky Sharp is introduced as Miss Crawley's companion in London and Rawdon Crawley's charmer. She is next seen at the Duchess of Richmond's ball in Brussels on the eve of Waterloo. Back in London she flirts with Lord Steyne and is discovered by the jealous Rawdon. Lastly she is in lodgings in Pumpernickel, bringing Amelia and Dobbin together and managing the affair with Joseph Sedley.

* TIRED BUSINESS MAN

(16 performances)

Comedy in three acts by Lyle Weaver Hall. Produced by Regent Productions, Inc., at the Waldorf Theatre, New York, June 3, 1929.

Cast of characters—

Henry Gilbert....................................Harlan Briggs
Josephine Gilbert....................................Frances McGrath
Archibald White....................................Harold Kennedy
Sidney Grund....................................Lawrence C. O'Brien
Mittie....................................Mary Vance
Roy Clarke....................................Eddie Kaspar
Tod Williams....................................Thomas Carnahan
Miss Matilda Weatherspoon....................................Isabel Vernon
Cora....................................Hilda Manners
George Quincy Pringle....................................Jack Byrne
Juanita....................................Ollie Burgoyne
Stub....................................A. Roberts
Dan....................................John Howard
Messenger Boy....................................George Hart

Acts I, II and III.—Henry Gilbert's Flat.

Staged by Marion Gering.

Henry and Josephine Gilbert agree to live in separate residences. Henry, newspaper proprietor, seeking diversion, takes Mittie, a manicurist, to Topeka's Coney Island and brings her home to his apartment at 3 in the morning, to rest on the couch while he sleeps in the arm chair. A rival newspaper photographer gets a picture of Henry and Mittie and schemes are laid to run Henry for mayor and then hold the picture evidence over him for no good purpose. Henry is elected but outwits the conspirators and he and Josephine are reconciled.

* NICE WOMEN

(8 performances)

Comedy in three acts by William A. Grew. Produced by L. Lawrence Weber at the Longacre Theatre, New York, June 10, 1929.

Cast of characters—

Elizabeth Girard.................................Sylvia Sidney
John Girard.................................Warren McCollum
Mary..Helen Joy
Geraldine Girard.................................Hope Drown
William Wells.....................................Albert Hayes
Martha Girard.................................Lotta Linthicum
James Girard.................................George Barbier
Mark Chandler.................................Robert Warwick
Conners.....................................Edward Broadley
Dorothy Drew.....................................Verree Teasdale

Act I.—Girard Apartment, New York. Acts II and III.—Mark Chandler's Apartment.
Staged by W. B. Friedlander.

Mark Chandler, rich and ready to settle down, decides to marry Geraldine Girard, daughter of an employé. Geraldine, being engaged to William Wells, does not want to marry the aging Chandler, but is ready to sacrifice herself for her family. Discovering the situation, Chandler decides to release Geraldine, give up thought of marrying and return to his favorite mistress, when in bursts Elizabeth Girard, Geraldine's younger and more advanced sister. She convinces Chandler that she is really the girl for him.

* ADAM'S APPLE

(8 performances)

Farce comedy in three acts by Test Dalton. Produced by John J. Kelly at the Princess Theatre, New York, June 10, 1929.

Cast of characters—

Billy Aldrich	Kenneth Lane
Cecily Tennant	Dorothy Severns
Casper	Richard Thornton
Riggs	Percy Kilbride
Uncle John	Charles Kennedy
Maggie	Loraine Lally
Eve Van Alstyne	Helen Holmes
Adam Van Alstyne	Stanley Price

Acts I, II and III.—Drawing Room of the Van Alstynes. New York City.

Staged by Charles D. Pitt.

Adam Van Alstyne explains his absences when he is stepping out by inventing an Uncle John. He is overheard by a burglar telling his friend Casper of Uncle John. When caught, the burglar declares he is the mythical Uncle John. With Adam in chains the burglar enjoys the freedom of the Van Alstyne house and flirts with Eva, the wife, until at 10.45 he is forced to confess that he is only an eccentric financier who has disappeared for a stock ticker purpose.

STATISTICAL SUMMARY

(LAST SEASON PLAYS WHICH ENDED RUNS AFTER JUNE 15, 1928.)

Plays	*Number Performances*	*Plays*	*Number Performances*
Bachelor Father	263	Married and How	36
Blackbirds	518	Paris Bound	234
Burlesque	372	Porgy	367
Connecticut Yankee	418	Present Arms	155
Coquette	366	Rain or Shine	356
Cyclone Lover	31	Road to Rome	440
Diamond Lil	176	Rosalie	335
Diplomacy	40	The Royal Family	345
Excess Baggage	216	Show Boat	572
Funny Face	244	Silent House	277
Get Me in the Movies	32	Skidding	448
Good News	551	The Skull	96
Grand Street Follies	144	Strange Interlude	426
Greenwich Village Follies	158	Ten Nights in a Barroom	111
Happy Husband	72	Three Musketeers	318
Here's Howe	71	Trial of Mary Dugan	437
The Ladder	789		

PLAYS THAT HAVE RUN OVER 500 PERFORMANCES ON BROADWAY

To June 15, 1929

Plays	*Number Performances*	*Plays*	*Number Performances*
Abie's Irish Rose	2,532	Adonis	603
Lightnin'	1,291	Kiki	600
The Bat	867	Blossom Time	592
The Ladder	789	Show Boat	572
The First Year	760	The Show-off	571
Seventh Heaven	704	Sally	570
Peg o' My Heart	692	Good News	551
East Is West	680	The Music Master	540
Irene	670	The Boomerang	522
A Trip to Chinatown	657	Blackbirds	518
Rain	648	Sunny	517
Is Zat So	618	The Vagabond King	511
Student Prince	608	Shuffle Along	504
Broadway	603		

WHERE AND WHEN THEY WERE BORN

Abbott, George	Hamburg, N. Y.	1895
Adams, Maude	Salt Lake City, Utah	1872
Allen, Viola	Huntsville, Ala.	1869
Ames, Robert	Hartford, Conn.	1893
Ames, Winthrop	North Easton, Mass.	1871
Andrews, Ann	Los Angeles, Cal.	1895
Anglin, Margaret	Ottawa, Canada	1876
Anson, A. E.	England	1879
Arbuckle, Maclyn	San Antonio, Texas	1866
Arliss, George	London, England	1868
Arthur, Julia	Hamilton, Ont.	1869
Astaire, Adele	Omaha, Neb.	1900
Astaire, Fred	Omaha, Neb.	1899
Atwell, Roy	Syracuse, N. Y.	1880
Atwill, Lionel	London, England	1885
Bacon, Frank	California	1864
Bainter, Fay	Los Angeles, Cal.	1892
Barbee, Richard	Lafayette, Ind.	1887
Barrie, James Matthew	Kirriemuir, N. B.	1860
Barrymore, Ethel	Philadelphia, Pa.	1879
Barrymore, John	Philadelphia, Pa.	1882
Barrymore, Lionel	London, England	1878
Bates, Blanche	Portland, Ore.	1873
Bayes, Nora	Milwaukee, Wis.	1880
Beban, George	San Francisco, Cal.	1873
Beckley, Beatrice	Roedean, England	1885
Best, Edna	England	1901
Beecher, Janet	Chicago, Ill.	1884
Belasco, David	San Francisco, Cal.	1853
Ben-Ami, Jacob	Minsk, Russia	1890
Bennett, Richard	Cass County, Ind.	1873
Bennett, Wilda	Asbury Park, N. J.	1894
Berlin, Irving	Russia	1888
Bernard, Barney	Rochester, N. Y.	1877
Bernard, Sam	Birmingham, England	1863

Bernhardt, Sarah	Paris, France	1844
Bingham, Amelia	Hickville, Ohio	1869
Binney, Constance	Philadelphia, Pa.	1900
Blackmer, Sidney	Salisbury, N. C.	1896
Blinn, Holbrook	San Francisco, Cal.	1872
Boland, Mary	Detroit, Mich.	1880
Bordoni, Irene	Paris, France	1895
Brady, Alice	New York	1892
Brady, William A.	San Francisco, Cal.	1863
Breese, Edmund	Brooklyn, N. Y.	1871
Brian, Donald	St. John's, N. F.	1871
Broadhurst, George H.	England	1866
Bryant, Charles	England	1879
Buchanan, Jack	England	1892
Buchanan, Thompson	Louisville, Ky.	1877
Burke, Billie	Washington, D. C.	1885
Burton, Frederick	Indiana	1871
Byron, Arthur	Brooklyn, N. Y.	1872
Cahill, Marie	Brooklyn, N. Y.	1871
Cantor, Eddie	New York	1894
Campbell, Mrs. Patrick	England	1865
Carle, Richard	Somerville, Mass.	1871
Carlisle, Alexandra	Yorkshire, England	1886
Carr, Alexander	Russia	1878
Carter, Mrs. Leslie	Lexington, Ky.	1862
Catlett, Walter	San Francisco, Cal.	1889
Cawthorne, Joseph	New York	1868
Chaplin, Charles Spencer	London	1889
Chatterton, Ruth	New York	1893
Cherry, Charles	England	1872
Churchill, Burton	Toronto, Can.	1876
Claire, Ina	Washington, D. C.	1892
Clarke, Marguerite	Cincinnati, Ohio	1887
Cliffe, H. Cooper	England	1862
Clifford, Kathleen	Charlottesville, Va.	1887
Coburn, Charles	Macon, Ga.	1877
Coghlan, Gertrude	England	1879
Coghlan, Rose	Petersborough, England	1850
Cohan, George M.	Providence, R. I.	1878
Cohan, Georgette	Los Angeles, Cal.	1900
Colbert, Claudette	Paris	1905
Collier, Constance	Windsor, England	1882
Collier, William	New York	1866

Collinge, Patricia	Dublin, Ireland	1894
Collins, José	London, England	1896
Conroy, Frank	London, England	1885
Cooper, Violet Kemble	London, England	1890
Cornell, Katharine	Buffalo, N. Y.	1900
Corrigan, Emmett	Amsterdam, Holland	1871
Corthell, Herbert	Boston, Mass.	1875
Courtenay, William	Worcester, Mass.	1875
Courtleigh, William	Guelph, Ont.	1869
Coward, Noel	England	1899
Cowl, Jane	Boston, Mass.	1887
Crane, William H.	Leicester, Mass.	1845
Craven, Frank	Boston, Mass.	1880
Crews, Laura Hope	San Francisco, Cal.	1880
Crosman, Henrietta	Wheeling, W. Va.	1865
Crothers, Rachel	Bloomington, Ill.	1878
Cumberland, John	St. John, N. B.	1880
Dale, Margaret	Philadelphia, Pa.	1880
Dalton, Charles	England	1864
Daly, Arnold	New York	1875
Daniels, Frank	Dayton, Ohio	1860
Dawn, Hazel	Ogden, Utah	1891
Day, Edith	Minneapolis, Minn.	1896
De Angelis, Jefferson	San Francisco, Cal.	1859
Dean, Julia	St. Paul, Minn.	1880
De Cordoba, Pedro	New York	1881
Dillingham, Charles B.	Hartford, Conn.	1868
Dinehart, Allan	Missoula, Mont.	1889
Ditrichstein, Leo	Temesbar, Hungary	1865
Dixey, Henry E.	Boston, Mass.	1859
Dodson, John E.	London, England	1857
Dolly, Rosy	Hungary	1892
Dolly, Jennie	Hungary	1892
Doro, Marie	Duncannon, Pa.	1882
D'Orsay, Lawrence	England	1860
Dressler, Marie	Cobourg, Canada	1869
Drew, John	Philadelphia, Pa.	1853
Drew, Louise	New York	1884
Druce, Herbert	England	1870
Dunn, Emma	England	1875
Dupree, Minnie	San Francisco, Cal.	1875
Duse, Eleanora	Vigerano, Italy	1859

Eagels, Jeanne	Kansas City, Mo.	1894
Eames, Clare	Hartford, Conn.	1896
Edeson, Robert	Baltimore, Md.	1868
Eldridge, Florence	Brooklyn, N. Y.	1901
Ellis, Mary	New York	1900
Elliston, Grace	Wheeling, W. Va.	1881
Ellinger, Desirée	Manchester, Vt.	1895
Elliott, Gertrude	Rockland, Me.	1874
Elliott, Maxine	Rockland, Me.	1871
Ellsler, Effie	Philadelphia, Pa.	1898
Eltinge, Julian	Boston, Mass.	1883
Emerson, John	Sandusky, Ohio	1874
Errol, Leon	Sydney, Australia	1881
Fairbanks, Douglas	Denver, Colo.	1883
Farnum, Dustin	Hampton Beach, N. H.	1874
Farnum, William	Boston, Mass.	1876
Farrar, Geraldine	Melrose, Mass.	1883
Faversham, William	Warwickshire, England	1868
Fealy, Maude	Memphis, Tenn.	1883
Fenwick, Irene	Chicago, Ill.	1887
Ferguson, Elsie	New York	1883
Fields, Lew	New York	1867
Fields, W. C.	Philadelphia, Pa.	1883
Fischer, Alice	Indiana	1869
Fiske, Minnie Maddern	New Orleans, La.	1867
Fontanne, Lynn	London, England	1892
Forbes, Robertson, Sir J.	London, England	1853
Foster, Claiborne	Shreveport, La.	1899
Foy, Edward Fitzgerald	New York	1854
Frederick, Pauline	Boston, Mass.	1884
Friganza, Trixie	Cincinnati, Ohio	1870
Frohman, Daniel	Sandusky, Ohio	1850
Garden, Mary	Scotland	1876
Gaythorne, Pamela	England	1882
George, Grace	New York	1879
Gillette, William	Hartford, Conn.	1856
Gillmore, Frank	New York	1884
Gillmore, Margalo	England	1901
Gleason, James	New York	1885
Glendinning, Ernest	Ulverston, England	1884
Gottschalk, Ferdinand	London, England	1869

Grey, Jane	Middlebury, Vt.	1883
Grey, Katherine	San Francisco, Cal.	1873
Haines, Robert T.	Muncie, Ind.	1870
Hale, Louise Closser	Chicago, Ill.	1872
Hall, Laura Nelson	Philadelphia, Pa.	1876
Hamilton, Hale	Topeka, Kansas	1880
Hampden, Walter	Brooklyn, N. Y.	1879
Harding, Lyn	Newport	1867
Harris, Sam H.	New York	1872
Hawtrey, Charles	Eton, England	1858
Hayes, Helen	Washington, D. C.	1900
Hazzard, John E.	New York	1881
Hedman, Martha	Sweden	1888
Heggie, O. P.	Australia	1879
Heming, Violet	Leeds, England	1893
Herbert, Evelyn	Brooklyn, N. Y.	1900
Herbert, Victor	Dublin, Ireland	1859
Herne, Chrystal	Dorchester, Mass.	1883
Hitchcock, Raymond	Auburn, N. Y.	1870
Hodge, William	Albion, N. Y.	1874
Hopper, DeWolf	New York	1858
Hopper, Edna Wallace	San Francisco, Cal.	1874
Holmes, Taylor	Newark, N. J.	1872
Howard, Leslie	London, England	1890
Hull, Henry	Louisville, Ky.	1893
Huston, Walter	Toronto	1884
Illington, Margaret	Bloomington, Ill.	1881
Irving, Isabel	Bridgeport, Conn.	1871
Irwin, May	Whitby, Ont.	1862
Janis, Elsie	Delaware, Ohio	1889
Joel, Clara	Jersey City, N. J.	1890
Jolson, Al.	Washington, D. C.	1883
Keane, Doris	Michigan	1885
Keenan, Frank	Dubuque, Ia.	1858
Keightley, Cyril	New South Wales, Aus.	1875
Kennedy, Madge	Chicago, Ill.	1890
Kerrigan, J. M.	Dublin, Ireland	1885
Kerr, Geoffrey	London, England	1895
Kershaw, Willette	Clifton Heights, Mo.	1890

Kosta, Tessa	Chicago, Ill.	1893
Kruger, Otto	Toledo, Ohio	1895
Lackaye, Wilton	Virginia	1862
Larrimore, Francine	Russia	1888
La Rue, Grace	Kansas City, Mo.	1882
Lauder, Harry	Portobello, England	1870
Lawton, Thais	Louisville, Ky.	1881
Lawrence, Gertrude	London	1898
Lawrence, Margaret	Trenton, N. J.	1890
Lean, Cecil	Illinois	1878
Le Gallienne, Eva	London, England	1900
Levey, Ethel	San Francisco, Cal.	1881
Lewis, Ada	New York	1871
Lewis, Mabel Terry	London, England	1872
Logan, Stanley	Earlsfield, England	1885
Loraine, Robert	England	1876
Lord, Pauline	Hanford, Cal.	1890
Lorraine, Lillian	San Francisco, Cal.	1892
Lou-Tellegen	Holland	1881
Lunt, Alfred	Milwaukee, Wis.	1893
Mack, Andrew	Boston, Mass.	1863
Mack, Willard	Ontario, Canada	1873
Mackay, Elsie	London, England	1894
MacKellar, Helen	Canada	1896
Mann, Louis	New York	1865
Mantell, Robert B.	Ayrshire, Scotland	1854
Merivale, Philip	India	1886
Marlowe, Julia	Caldbeck, England	1870
Matthews, A. E.	Bridlington, England	1869
Matthison, Edith Wynne	England	1875
Maude, Cyril	London, England	1862
McIntyre, Frank	Ann Arbor, Mich.	1879
McRae, Bruce	India	1867
Meighan, Thomas	Pittsburgh	1879
Melba, Nellie	Melbourne, Australia	1866
Mellish, Fuller	England	1865
Mercer, Beryl	Seville, Spain	1882
Miller, Marilyn	Findlay, Ohio	1898
Mitchell, Grant	Columbus, Ohio	1874
Mitzi (Hajos)	Budapest	1891
Moores, Clara	Omaha, Neb.	1897

Morgan, Helen	Danville, Ill.	1900
Murphy, Tim	Rupert, Vt.	1860
Nash, Florence	Troy, N. Y.	1888
Nash, Mary	Troy, N. Y.	1885
Nazimova, Alla	Crimea, Russia	1879
Nielsen, Alice	Nashville, Tenn.	1876
Nugent, J. C.	Miles, O.	1875
Nugent, Elliott	Dover, O.	1900
Olcott, Chauncey	Providence, R. I.	1862
O'Neill, Eugene Gladstone	New York	1888
O'Neil, Nance	Oakland, Cal.	1875
O'Ramey, Georgia	Mansfield, Ohio	1886
Painter, Eleanor	Iowa	1890
Pawle, Lenox	London, England	1872
Pennington, Ann	Philadelphia, Pa.	1898
Perkins, Osgood	Boston, Mass.	1892
Pickford, Mary	Toronto	1893
Post, Guy Bates	Seattle, Wash.	1875
Powers, James T.	New York	1862
Power, Tyrone	London, England	1869
Rambeau, Marjorie	San Francisco, Cal.	1889
Rathbone, Basil	Johannesburg	1892
Reed, Florence	Philadelphia, Pa.	1883
Rennie, James	Toronto, Canada	1890
Revelle, Hamilton	Gibraltar	1872
Rickard, Amy	Boston, Mass.	1880
Richman, Charles	Chicago, Ill.	1870
Ring, Blanche	Boston, Mass.	1876
Ring, Frances	New York	1882
Roberts, Theodore	San Francisco, Cal.	1861
Robson, May	Australia	1868
Ross, Thomas W.	Boston, Mass.	1875
Ruben, José	Belgium	1886
Russell, Annie	Liverpool, England	1864
Russell, Lillian	Clinton, Iowa	1860
Ryan, Mary	New York	1885
Sanderson, Julia	Springfield, Mass.	1887
Santley, Joseph	Salt Lake City	1889

Sawyer, Ivy	London, England	1897
Scheff, Fritzi	Vienna, Austria	1879
Scott, Cyril	Ireland	1866
Sears, Zelda	Brockway, Mich.	1873
Segal, Vivienne	Philadelphia, Pa.	1897
Selwyn, Edgar	Cincinnati, Ohio	1875
Serrano, Vincent	New York	1870
Shannon, Effie	Cambridge, Mass.	1867
Shepley, Ruth	New York	1889
Schildkraut, Joseph	Bucharest, Roumania	1896
Sherman, Lowell	San Francisco, Cal.	1885
Sidney, George	New York	1876
Sitgreaves, Beverly	Charleston, S. C.	1867
Skelly, Hal	Allegheny, Pa.	1891
Skinner, Otis	Cambridgeport, Mass.	1857
Sothern, Edward H.	New Orleans, La.	1859
Spong, Hilda	Australia	1875
Stahl, Rose	Montreal, Canada	1872
Standing, Sir Guy	London	1873
Starr, Frances	Oneonta, N. Y.	1886
Stevens, Emily	New York	1882
Stone, Fred	Denver, Colo.	1873
Stone, Dorothy	New York	1905
Sydney, Basil	London	1894
Taliaferro, Edith	New York	1892
Taliaferro, Mabel	New York	1887
Tanguay, Eva	Middletown, Conn.	1878
Taylor, Laurette	New York	1884
Tell, Alma	New York	1892
Tell, Olive	New York	1894
Terry, Ellen	Coventry, England	1848
Thomas, Augustus	St. Louis, Mo.	1859
Thomas, John Charles	Baltimore, Md.	1887
Tobin, Genevieve	New York	1901
Tobin, Vivian	New York	1903
Toler, Sidney	Warrensburg, Mo.	1874
Trevor, Norman	Calcutta	1877
Truex, Ernest	Denver, Colo.	1890
Tynan, Brandon	Dublin, Ireland	1879
Ulric, Lenore	New Ulm, Minn.	1897

Varesi, Gilda .... Milan, Italy 1887
Victor, Josephine .... Hungary 1891

Wainwright, Marie .... Philadelphia, Pa. 1853
Walker, June .... New York 1904
Walker, Charlotte .... Galveston, Texas 1878
Warfield, David .... San Francisco, Cal. 1866
Warwick, Robert .... Sacramento, Cal. 1878
Ware, Helen .... San Francisco, Cal. 1877
Weber, Joseph .... New York 1867
Welford, Dallas .... Liverpool, England 1874
Westley, Helen .... Brooklyn, N. Y. 1879
Westman, Nydia .... White Plains, N. Y. 1906
Whiffen, Mrs. Thomas ...... London, England 1845
Whiteside, Walker .... Logansport, Ind. 1869
Wilson, Francis .... Philadelphia, Pa. 1854
Winwood, Estelle .... England 1883
Wise, Thomas A. .... England 1865
Wood, Peggy .... Brooklyn, N. Y. 1894
Wright, Haidee .... London, England 1868
Wycherly, Margaret .... England 1883
Wyndham, Olive .... Chicago, Ill. 1886
Wynn, Ed. .... Philadelphia, Pa. 1886

Ziegfeld, Florenz, Jr. .... Chicago, Ill. 1867

NECROLOGY

June 15, 1928—June 15, 1929

Johnny Dooley, comedian, 41. Born Glasgow, Scotland; family name Dool. Came to America as his father's helper in the pantry of a United Fruit steamer. Followed his brother William into vaudeville and was followed by brother Gordon and sister Ray. Specialized in acrobatic comedy. Later prominent in several Ziegfeld revues and in "Listen Lester," "The Girl in the Spotlight" and Carroll's "Vanities." Died New York, June 7, 1928.

Holbrook Blinn, actor, 56. Born San Francisco, Cal. Did some acting as a boy before enrolling in Stanford University. Back to the stage, played many parts and became prominent as a leading man. Was interested in the establishment of an American Grand Guignol at the Princess Theatre in New York. With the failure of this enterprise owing to war conditions he returned to leading rôles and his recent successes included "The Famous Mrs. Fair," "The Bad Man," "The Dove" and "The Play's the Thing." Succeeded Henry Miller as president of the Actors' Fidelity League. Died Croton, N. Y., June 24, 1928.

Leo Ditrichstein, actor, 63. Born Tomesbar, Hungary. Made his début as an actor in Berlin and was later engaged by Gustav Amberg to play with the German company at the Irving Place Theatre, New York. After he had conquered English went with Charles Frohman and scored his first hit in "Trilby." Later devoted much time to the writing and adapting of plays. These included one he wrote with Clyde Fitch called "Gossip," the familiar farces, "Are You a Mason?," "Mlle. Fifi," "Vivienne's Papas," etc. With Belasco he scored a personal hit in his own adaptation of "The Concert" and later in "The Great Lover." Retired a few years ago and was living abroad at the time of his death. Died Vienna, Austria, June 28, 1928.

Robert Bruce Mantell, actor, 74. Born Ayrshire, Scotland. Educated in Belfast, Ireland, and became an English actor. Came to America in support of Helena Modjeska, the Polish

actress, playing Romeo to her Juliet. Returned to England but came back in 1882 to support Fanny Davenport in repertoire. Became a star four years later, playing "Tangled Lives," "A Marble Heart," "Monbars," and notably "The Corsican Brothers." Turning to the Shakespearean repertoire his rôles included Othello, Hamlet, King Lear, Macbeth, Iago, and several of the comedy parts. Died Atlantic Highlands, N. J., June 27, 1928.

Avery Hopwood, playwright, 46. Born Cleveland, Ohio. Educated at the University of Michigan. Took up newspaper work and came to New York as a correspondent of the Cleveland *Leader*. Wrote "Clothes" with Channing Pollock and never went back to newspaper work. One of his earlier successes was the farce "Seven Days," written with Mary Roberts Rinehart, with whom he later collaborated on "The Bat," a second success. Wrote innumerable farces of the French school, including "Fair and Warmer," "Nobody's Widow," "Naughty Cinderella," "Why Men Leave Home," "Mr. Bluebeard" and "The Harem." Died by drowning at Juan-les-Pines, France, July 1, 1928.

Will A. Page, press agent, 55. Active for years, after leaving a newspaper job in Washington, as a herald for the attractions of all the bigger managers, including the Frohmans, the Shuberts, Ziegfeld and finally Dillingham. Had done a considerable amount of writing for the magazines, was author of one or two books, the last "Broadway Beauty Trust," and extensively known in theatrical circles. Died New York, July 20, 1928.

Ellen Terry, actress, 80. Born Coventry, England, 1848. The child of strolling players, became an actress about the time she was learning to walk, though her official début was twelve years later in "The Winter's Tale." Toured the provinces for years. Made a hit in London in 1866 in "Still Waters Run Deep." Joined Henry Irving shortly thereafter and for the next twenty-five years was practically co-starred with that illustrious player. Irving and Terry made numerous American tours, and were as popular in America as in England. Miss Terry lived in retirement the last several years of her life. Died Kent, England, July 21, 1928.

Rex Cherryman, actor, 30. Born California. Had played many stock rôles in the west and was just making his way on Broadway, having scored first in "The Noose" and last season in "The Trial of Mary Dugan." Feeling ill, had retired from the cast and sailed for a European vacation. Taken off the boat at Cherbourg he died in the hospital at Havre, August 10, 1928.

Helen Costigan Cohan, actress, 74. Mother of George M. and Josephine Cohan. Starred for many years with her husband, Jere Cohan, and her children. Died Monroe, N. Y., August 26, 1928.

Sedley Brown, actor and director, 72. For many years a director of stock companies. First husband of Henrietta Crosman. Died Los Angeles, September 29, 1928.

Dixie Hines, press agent, 56. Prominent many years as an international representative. Organizer of the Theatrical Press Representatives of America. Died New York, Oct. 1, 1928.

George Beban, actor, 55. Born San Francisco. Advanced through minstrelsy to musical comedy and the Weberfields revues. Prominent in cast of "Nancy Brown," "Fantana," and "The American Idea." His last years devoted to pictures. Died Los Angeles, California, October 5, 1928.

Edward Connelly, actor, 73. Born New York. Prominent in the casts of "Shore Acres," "The Belle of New York," and "Babette" with Fritzi Scheff. Played with Nazimova in "The Wild Duck" and was starred in "Marse Covington." Last years in pictures. Died Hollywood, California, November 21, 1928.

Theodore Roberts, actor, 67. Played many important rôles in the drama, making his début with James O'Neill in "Richelieu." Later played in "Uncle Tom's Cabin," "The Squaw Man," and "Trilby." Was one of the first legitimate actors to turn to the movies, scoring many major successes in that field. Died Hollywood, Cal., December 14, 1928.

Thomas J. Ryan, comedian, 73. Played in the Cohan comedies but was best known in vaudeville as a member of the team of Ryan and Richfield. A veteran of the Tony Pastor Theatre. Died Lake Charles, La., December, 1928.

J. Hartley Manners, playwright, 58. Born London, England. Wrote many successful plays, in most of which his wife, Laurette Taylor, was starred. His biggest success was "Peg-o'-My Heart." Other plays were "The Indiscretion of Youth," "The House Next Door," "The Girl in Waiting," "The Wooing of Eve," "Out There" and "The Harp of Life." Died New York, December 19, 1928.

Fred Wright, comedian, 57. Born England. Scored many successes at the London Gaiety. Played in America, most recently in an Ames revival of "The Mikado." Brother of Haidee Wright and member of an old stage family in England. Died New York, December 12, 1928.

Wallace Eddinger, actor, 47. Born Albany, N. Y. Son of Lawrence and May Eddinger, both of the stage. Made his début as a boy and was the original Little Lord Fauntleroy. Prominent in the casts of "The Third Degree," "Officer 666," "Seven Keys to Baldpate," "The Boomerang," "Captain Applejack," "Wedding Bells" and "So to Bed." Married Margaret Lawrence. Died Pittsburgh, Pa., January 8, 1929.

Tim Murphy, actor, 67. Born Rupert, Vt. His first successes were scored in the Charles Hoyt comedies, notably "A Texas Steer," in which he was starred for years. In his early days was famous as an imitator of actors in vaudeville. Died New York, January 11, 1928.

Walter Kingsley, press agent, 52. Well known and popular publicity man; with Albee vaudeville interests for fifteen years; with Florenz Ziegfeld 1928-29. Died New York, February 14, 1929.

Frank Keenan, actor, 70. Popular leading man, notably in "The Girl of the Golden West," "The Warrens of Virginia," and a revival of "Julius Cæsar" in which he played Cassius. Born Dubuque, Ia.; died New York, February 24, 1929.

William Norris, actor, 57. Played prominently in "Children of the Ghetto," "Babes in Toyland," "Madame Sherry," "Francesco di Rimini" and "A Connecticut Yankee." Born New York; died New York, March 20, 1929.

Florence Rittenhouse, actress, 35. Philadelphia amateur who achieved success professionally, playing notably in "The Shame Woman." President of the Twelfth Night Club at the time of her death. Born Philadelphia; died New York, March 28, 1929.

Paul Ker, actor and singer, 54. One of the early members of Henry W. Savage's operatic ventures; sang in "Blossom Time," acted in "The Constant Nymph" and "Twin Beds." Born Germany; died New York.

Albert Bruning, actor, 70. Prominent character actor, advised to come to America by Edwin Booth; played notably with Booth and Barrett; played the Ghost to Booth's Hamlet on the occasion of Booth's last performance; later years prominent in Belasco repertoire, with Mrs. Carter in "Zaza," with Blanche Bates in "The Darling of the Gods"; lastly with Theatre Guild, playing in "Back to Methuselah"; was rehearsing with "Camel Through the Needle's Eye" at the time of his death. Born Berlin; died New York, April 9, 1929.

Paul Gordon, actor, 43. Family name Thomas Achelis; played prominently in "Prunella," "Kitty Mackaye," "Merry Wives of Windsor." Retired from stage, lived in Florence, Italy. Born Brooklyn, N. Y., died Florence, Italy, May 3, 1929.

Mary Shaw, actress, 69. Began with the Boston Museum; later supported Helena Modjeska, Julia Marlowe and Mrs. Fiske; played prominently in "Ben Hur" and "Polygamy"; later years devoted principally to Shaw and Ibsen; to "Ghosts," "Hedda Gabler" and "Mrs. Warren's Profession"; played with Civic Repertory in "The Cradle Song" en tour. Born Boston; died New York, May 18, 1929.

Harry H. Frazee, manager, 49. From a start as an usher in a theatre in his home town of Peoria, Ill., ambition carried him to a place among the most successful showmen. He produced, with George W. Lederer, "Mme. Sherry," and later "A Pair of Sixes," "My Lady Friends" and "No, No, Nanette." He had a hand in building the Cort Theatre, Chicago, and the Longacre Theatre, New York. Born Peoria, Ill.; died New York, June 4, 1929.

John E. Kellerd, actor, 67. Was leading man in support of many early American players, including W. J. Florence, Frederick Warde, Helena Modjeska and Joseph Jefferson. First American engagement was played at the Boston Museum in 1883. Achieved a run of 100 performances of "Hamlet" on Broadway. Born London; died New York, June 8, 1929.

Margaret Lawrence, actress, 40. Went on the stage in 1910, made her first hit in "Over Night" the following season, married Orson D. Munn in 1911 and retired. Returned to the stage seven years later in "Tea for Three," again gained prominence as a leading woman, notably in "Wedding Bells" and "Lawful Larceny." Born Philadelphia, Pa.; died New York, June 9, 1929.

Louis Bennison, actor, 46. Started as a super at the Alcazar Theatre, San Francisco; toured with various wagon and rail troupes; became leading man for Robert Downing in legitimate repertoire; went back to Alcazar stock; came east in 1915 to play in "The Unchastened Woman." Played many unimportant leads after that, finished in vaudeville. Born San Francisco; died New York, June 9, 1929.

INDEX OF AUTHORS

Abbott, George, 365
Adler, Hyman, 448
Akins, Zoe, 316, 493
Anderson, Garland, 11, 487
Anderson, Hugh A., 490
Anderson, Maxwell, 8, 283, 351, 402, 455
Andrews, Charlton, 466
Andreyev, Leonid, 473
Ansky, S., 24
Anstey, F., 383
Archer, Harry, 391
Archer, William, 420
Archibald, Jean, 496
Asch, Sholom, 15
Ashton, Herbert, Jr., 442, 495
Atteridge, Harold, 469

Bagby, George, 466
Bamman, George, 490
Baratt, Louise Bascom, 460
Barker, A. W., 480
Barker, E. L., 480
Barnes, Margaret Ayer, 8, 428
Barrie, J. M., 5, 10, 12, 24, 425
Barry, Philip, 8, 25, 121, 347, 348, 424
Barry, Tom, 8, 19, 24, 391
Barry, William E., 504
Bates, Esther Willard, 465
Beach, Lewis, 9, 459
Beahan, Charles, 24, 378, 480
Behrman, S. N., 9, 22, 461
Belasco, David, 9, 434, 451
Belledna, Alex, 505
Benrimo, J. H., 411
Bernard, Jean-Jacques, 388
Bernstein, Herman, 366, 473, 503
Berte, Emile, 486
Blackmer, Beatrice, 10, 485
Bolton, Guy, 451
Boucicault, Dion, 6, 24, 479
Boyd, Ernest, 388
Bradford, Perry, 496
Brennan, J. Kiern, 463, 486, 506
Brentano, Lowell, 456
Breuer, Kurt, 486
Brown, Calvin, 352
Brown, Lew, 353, 395
Brown, Martin, 390
Browne, Maurice, 9, 88, 348, 432
Brownell, Atherton, 443
Browning, Robert, 421
Burke, Edwin, 374
Burnside, R. H., 395
Burtis, Thomson, 478
Buzzell, Eddie, 463

Cæsar, Irving, 406, 451
Caldwell, Anne, 395
Cannon, Norman, 489
Capek Brothers, 22
Carroll, Earl, 7, 355, 466
Charig, Philip, 451
Charles, Theodore, 421
Chekov, Anton, 491, 507
Chenery, Howard, 437
Chiarelli, Luigi, 20
Clark, Edward, 360
Clugston, Katharine, 415
Coghlan, Charles, 422
Cohan, George M., 8, 385
Collier, Constance, 490
Conners, Barry, 404
Coward, Noel, 8, 410
Cowl, Jane, 421
Craig, Gordon, 13
Creamer, Henry, 449
Crooker, Earle, 456
Crothers, Rachel, 9, 195, 349, 471
Cullinan, Ralph, 366

Daab, Hyatt, 365
Daly, Augustin, 488
Dalton, Test, 511
Davis, Lee, 506
Davis, Owen, 10, 416, 431, 463, 478
Dayton, Helena, 460
De Leon, Walter, 397, 406
Dell, Floyd, 8, 252, 350, 394
de Marney, Terence, 467
De Sylva, B. G., 353, 395, 451

Dickens, C. Stafford, 387
Dickens, Charles, 447
Dickson, Sam, 19
Dietz, Howard, 498
Dijon, Pierre, 19
Donnell, Capt. Cushing, 506
Dostoievsky, 24
Doyle, William R., 497
Drinkwater, John, 489
Dubois, William, 24
Dumas, Alexandre, 422
Duncan, William Cary, 386
Dunning, Philip, 7, 372

Eldridge, Paul, 355
Eliscu, Edward, 463
Elsner, Edward, 362
Esler, Lemist, 400
Ewing, Max, 499

Fagan, Myron C., 371, 474
Fagin, James B., 14
Ferris, Walter, 461
Fields, Dorothy, 9, 445
Fields, Herbert, 9, 445
Fields, Lew, 381
Fitzgerald, F. Scott, 492
Forbes, James, 454
Fort, Garrett, 378
Francke, Caroline, 401

Galsworthy, John, 22
Garnett, Constance, 396
Gawthorn, Peter, 23
Geddes, Vergil, 476
Gensler, Lewis E., 392
Gershwin, Ira, 411
Gilbert, W. S., 7, 14, 18, 22, 352
Goethe, 389
Goetz, E. Ray, 390, 435
Golden, John, 364
Goldsmith, Oliver, 20
Goodrich, Arthur, 421
Gould, Bruce, 10, 485
Gould, Hull, 446
Granville-Barker, Harley and Helen, 12, 316, 436, 455
Greene, H. C., 391
Gregory, Lady, 483
Grew, William A., 468, 511
Grey, Clifford, 386, 392
Gribble, Harry Wagstaffe, 5, 408
Gropper, Milton Herbert, 375

Hagan, James, 356
Hajos, Karl, 370
Hall, Lyle Weaver, 510
Hamilton, Morris, 355
Hammerstein, Oscar, 2nd, 368, 376, 423
Harbach, Otto, 368
Harris, Elmer, 505
Hart, Lorenz, 381, 478
Hatvany, Baroness Lili, 316, 493
Hazelton, George C., 411
Hazzard, John E., 444
Hecht, Ben, 7, 152, 349, 358
Henderson, Ray, 353, 395
Henkle, Carl, 508
Hennequin and Weber, 386
Henry, Grace, 355
Hervey, Harry, 428
Hickerson, Harold, 8, 402
Hicks, Seymour, 24
Hildreth, Carleton, 428
Hodge, William, 389
Holiner, Mann, 463
Hollister, Len D., 457
Hooker, Brian, 439
Horniman, Roy, 363
Howard, Sidney, 22, 349, 398
Hubbell, Raymond, 395
Hughes, Hatcher, 347
Hymer, John B., 381

Ibsen, Henrik, 24, 410, 420, 464, 481
Ide, Leonard, 408
Irvine, St. John, 22
Irwin, William, 499

Jaffe, Moe, 506
Janssen, Werner, 463
Jessel, George, 379
Johannsen, Sigurd, 370
Johnson, Jimmy, 496
Johnson, Larry E., 445
Jordan, Joe, 449

Kahn, Roger Wolfe, 406
Kaiser, Georg, 366
Kallesser, Michael, 357, 495
Kalmar, Bert, 368, 402
Kaufman, George S., 8, 402
Kearney, Patrick, 356
Kester, Paul, 447
Kirkland, Frank, 14

Kling, Saxon, 405, 446
Kusell, Daniel, 375

Lady of Quality, A. (Pseud.), 461
Lane, Lupino, 23
Langer, Frantisek, 493
Lardner, Ring, 377
Lawrence, Vincent, 411
Lawrence, Warren F., 477
Levy, Benn W., 412
Lewis, Cecil, 404
Lewis, Seaman, 354
Lewis, Sinclair, 7, 356
Lief, Max, 373, 469
Lief, Nathaniel, 373, 469
Linder, Mark, 415
Lindsay, Howard, 12
Lonergan, Lester, 457
Lonsdale, Frederick, 7, 25, 252, 369
Luce, Alethea, 397
Lynch, Francis, 357

MacArthur, Charles, 7, 152, 349, 358
Mack, Willard, 359, 397
Mandel, Frank, 376
Marcin, Max, 372, 375
Marshall, Capt. Robert, 430
Martin, Townsend, 426
Maugham, W. Somerset, 8, 418
McCarthy, Joseph, 375
McDermott, John, 24
McEvoy, J. P., 406
McGowan, John, 395
McGroarty, John Steven, 24, 25
McGuire, William Anthony, 431
Meehan, John, 426
Meriwether, Susan, 470
Merley, Heinz, 486
Meyer, Adolph E., 366
Meyer, Joseph, 463
Middleton, Edgar C., 437
Middleton, George, 360, 451
Milne, A. A., 8, 9, 429, 474
Mirande, Yves, 475
Mitchell, Fanny Todd, 430, 463, 486
Mitchell, Langdon, 509
Mitchell, Leontrovitch, 458
Mitchell, Thomas, 8, 252, 394
Moeller, Philip, 10, 446, 493
Molière, 383
Molnar, Ferenc, 398, 434
Mooney, Martin, 478
Moore, McElbert, 456
Morehouse, Ward, 362
Morgan, Agnes, 499
Morrison, Anne, 491
Mullally, Don, 354
Myers, Henry, 368

Natanson, Jacques, 435
Nevin, Hardwick, 480
Newing, DeWitt, 19
Nichols, Robert, 9, 88, 348, 432
Nicholson, Kenyon, 364, 494
Nugent, Elliott, 382
Nugent, J. C., 382

O'Casey, Sean, 12
O'Keefe, Walter, 391
Older, Mrs. Fremont, 19
Oliver, Roland, 413
O'Neill, Eugene, 5, 9, 22, 452, 467, 477
Osborn, Paul, 413
Oursler, Fulton, 465

Palmer, Rose A., 421
Paramore, Edward E., Jr., 365
Parker, Dorothy, 347
Pascal, Ernest, 24, 448
Paulton, Edward, 448
Pember, Clifford, 366
Perlman, William J., 471
Phillips, Stephen, 484
Pinero, Arthur W., 24
Pinkard, Maceo, 505
Pinski, David, 407
Pirandello, Luigi, 12, 24
Playfair, Nigel, 384
Pollock, Channing, 8, 398
Pollock, Muriel, 469
Porter, Cole, 390
Poynter, Beulah, 439
Printzlau, Olga, 24, 427
Purcell, Gertrude, 373

Quinteros, Serafin and Joaquin, 13

Raphaelson, Samson, 405
Rapp, W. J., 472
Rathbone, Basil, 461
Raynal, Paul, 404
Reed, Mark, 454
Rice, Elmer, 9, 26, 347, 453, 462
Richman, Arthur, 367
Rideout, Ransom, 7, 361
Robin, Leo, 406

Robinson, Bertrand, 12
Robinson, Edward G., 469
Robinson, Percy, 467
Robinson, Thomas P., 465
Rodgers, Richard, 381, 478
Rolland, Romaine, 24
Romberg, Sigmund, 377
Romilli, G., 466
Rosener, George, 475
Rostand, Edmond, 439
Rubens, Maury, 373, 486, 506
Ruby, Harry, 368, 402
Ryskind, Morrie, 402, 451

Samuels, Walter G., 457
Scheglov, Dmitry, 503
Scholz, August, 15, 419
Schwab, Laurence, 376, 451
Schwartz, Arthur, 498, 499
Selwyn, Edgar, 387
Shakespeare, 13, 18, 20, 417, 440
Shaw, George Bernard, 8, 20, 22, 24, 418
Sheldon, Edward, 349
Sheridan, 11, 482
Sherriff, R. C., 10, 54, 347, 482
Shipman, Samuel, 372, 381
Sierra, G. Martinez, 9, 315, 350, 351, 436
Sil-Vara, 446
Silvernail, Clarke, 458
Simon, Robert A., 392
Sinclair, Upton, 432
Smith, Harry B., 370
Smith, Harry James, 486
Snegoff, Leonid, 503
Spewack, Belle and Samuel, 379, 438
Stallings, Laurence, 351, 423
Stange, Hugh Stanislaus, 409
Stevenson, R. L., 490
Stone, Irving, 414
Stothart, Herbert, 368, 451
Strong, Austin, 424
Sturges, Preston, 449
Sullivan, Alan, 504
Sullivan, A. S., 7, 14, 18, 22, 352
Swerling, Jo, 469

Tchekov, Anton, 5, 396
Thackeray, W. M., 509
Thomas, A. E., 360, 450
Thompson, Fred, 411
Thurman, Wallace, 472
Tierney, Harry, 375
Tolstoi, Leo N., 419
Toohey, John Peter, 491
Treadwell, Sophie, 7, 225, 350, 369
Tully, Jim, 8, 15, 378
Tutt, Homer, 449

Van Loan, H. H., 19
Verneuil, Louis, 400, 463
Victor, Victor, 470
Vollmer, Lulu, 403

Wales, Amy, 495
Wallace, Edgar, 433
Wallace, Morgan, 499
Walpole, Hugh, 412
Walter, Eugene, 400
Walter, Serge, 499
Walton, Georgina Jones, 393
Waters, Harley, 24
Wayburn, Ned, 457
Webb, Kenneth, 444
Webber, James Plaisted, 440
Weber and Hennequin, 386
Wells, Wm. K., 353
West, Mae, 8, 14, 385
Weyman, Stanley, 441
Wharton, Edith, 428
White, George, 7, 353
Whitney and Tutt, 449
Wilbur, Crane, 19, 357
Willard, John, 380
Willametz, Albert, 475
Wynne-Tyson, Esme, 484

Yantis, Luther, 508
Yvain, Maurice, 373

Zeller, Wolfgang, 389

INDEX OF PLAYS AND CASTS

Abie's Irish Rose, 513
Adam's Apple, 511
Adding Machine, The, 26, 347
Adonis, 513
Adventure, 380
After Dark, 6, 11
Age of Innocence, The, 8, 428
All the King's Men, 465
Americana, 406
And So to Bed, 14
Angela, 430
Animal Crackers, 8, 402
Appearances, 11, 487
Arms and the Man, 13

Baby Cyclone, The, 23
Bachelor Father, The, 15, 17, 513
Back Here, 427
Back Seat Drivers, 445
Bad Man, The, 23, 24
Bat, The, 513
Becky Sharp, 509
Before Breakfast, 477
Before You're 25, 494
Beggar's Opera, The, 22, 23
Be Your Age, 465
Big Fight, The, 375
Big Pond, The, 360
Billie, 8, 385
Bird in Hand, 489
Blackbirds, 513, 514
Black Crook, The, 6
Bleak House, 447
Blossom Time, 513
Bon Garcon, Un, 373
Boom Boom, 463
Boomerang, The, 514
Broadway, 25, 513
Broadway Jones, 385
Broken Chain, The, 471
Brothers, 9, 442
Buckaroo, 480
Burlesque, 15, 23, 513
By Request, 382

Café de Danse, 458
Camel Through the Needle's Eye, The, 10, 493
Caponsacchi, 421
Caprice, 9, 13, 446
Captive, The, 18
Caravan, 366
Carnival, 497
Chauve-Souris, 460
Chee-Chee, 381
Cherry Orchard, The, 5, 396
Chinese O'Neill, 506
Chippies, 508
Clarence, 24
Close Harmony, 347
Cock Robin, 347
Come-On Man, The, 495
Command Performance, The, 387
Command to Love, The, 15, 17
Common Sin, The, 397
Conflict, 477
Congai, 8, 428
Congratulations, 499
Connecticut Yankee, A, 513
Coquette, 14, 17, 513
Courage, 8, 391
Cradle Song, 351
Crashing Through, 405
Critic, The, 12
Cross My Heart, 375
Cyclone Lover, 513
Cyrano de Bergerac, 9, 439

Dancing Mothers, 24
Danger, 24
Dark Mirror, The, 414
Dear Brutus, 12
Decision, 508
Deep Harlem, 449
Desert Song, The, 23
Diamond Lil, 14, 15, 513
Diplomacy, 513
Doctor's Dilemma, 22
Dracula, 15, 23, 25

Dragon, The, 483
Dybbuk, The, 24
Dynamo, 5, 9, 467

Earth Between, The, 476
East Is West, 514
East Lynne, 24
Easy Come, Easy Go, 463
Easy for Zee Zee, 19
Egoist, The, 349
Elmer Gantry, 7, 356
Elmer the Great, 377
Envoy of the People, An, 410
Escape, 22
Eva the Fifth, 364
Exceeding Small, 401
Excess Baggage, 513

Falstaff, 440
Fast Life, 381
Faust, 389
Final Balance, The, 407
Fioretta, 9, 466
First Law, The, 503
First Year, The, 514
Flight, 470
Follow Thru, 9, 451
For the Defense, 347
Frankie and Johnnie, 14, 15
Freiburg Passion Play, 497
Front Page, The, 7, 14, 23, 152, 252, 349, 358
Funny Face, 513

Gang War, 15, 359
Gay Paree, 23
Gentlemen of the Press, 7, 362
George Barnwell, or The London Merchant, 384
George White's Scandals, 8, 353
Get Me in the Movies, 513
Ghost Train, The, 24
Girl Trouble, 404
Gods of the Lightning, 8, 402
Goin' Home, 7, 361
Golem, The, 12
Gondoliers, The, 14, 18
Good Boy, 7, 368
Good Natured Man, The, 20
Good News, 513, 514
Grand Street Follies, The, 10, 499, 513
Great Power, The, 371
Greenwich Village Follies, 513
Grey Fox, The, 400
Gringo, 350
Guardsman, The, 22, 24
Guinea Pig, The, 449
Guns, 356
Gypsy, 283, 351, 455

Hamlet, 14, 18, 25
Happy Husband, 513
Harlem, 9, 16, 472
Hazel Kirke, 20
Heavy Traffic, 367
Hedda Gabler, 464
Hello, Daddy, 9, 445
Hello Yourself, 406
Henry IV, 18
Her Cardboard Lover, 23
Here's Howe, 513
He Understood Women, 357
He Walked in Her Sleep, 489
High Road, The, 7, 14, 25, 252, 369
Hold Everything, 8, 395
Holiday, 8, 25, 120, 348, 424
Home of the Free, The, 347
Hotbed, 413
Hot Water, 460
Houseboat on the Styx, 444
House Unguarded, 457
Hundred Years Old, A, 13

In Abraham's Bosom, 15
Indiscretion, 474
Intruder, The, 355
Invitation au Voyage, L', 388
Iolanthe, 14, 18
Irene, 514
Iron Cross, The, 347
Is Zat So, 514

Jade God, The, 504
Jarnegan, 7, 8, 15, 378
Jealous Moon, The, 421
Jealousy, 8, 14, 400
John Ferguson, 22
Jonesy, 491
Joseph and His Brethren, 25
Journey's End, 10, 12, 54, 347, 348, 482
Judas, 461
Julius Cæsar, 14
Just a Minute, 391

Katerina, 473
Kean, 422

K Guy, The, 397
Kibitzer, 9, 469
Kiddus Hashem, 15
Kiki, 513
Kingdom of God, The, 9, 10, 316, 350, 436

Ladder, The, 513, 514
Lady Dedlock, 447
Lady Fingers, 463
Lady from Alfaqueque, 455
Lady from the Sea, 481
Lady Lies, The, 426
Lady of the Orchids, The, 435
Lawyer's Dilemma, The, 354
Lazarus Laughed, 24
Let Us Be Gay, 9, 23, 195, 349, 471
Lido Girl, The, 362
Lightnin', 513
Light of Asia, 393
Little Accident, 8, 252, 350, 394
Little Orchid Annie, 24
Little Show, The, 10, 498
Little Theatre Tournament, 10, 500-503
Lombardi, Ltd., 17
Love Duel, The, 10, 317, 493
Luckee Girl, 373
Lulu Belle, 349
Lupino Lane's Review, 23

Macbeth, 8, 13, 417
Machinal, 225, 252, 350, 369
Maison de Danse, La, 458
Major Barbara, 8, 13, 418
Maniac, The, 19
Man's Estate, 10, 485
Man with Red Hair, A, 412
Marche Indienne, La, 20
Marco Millions, 13
Marriage Bed, The, 23, 24, 448
Married and How, 513
Marry the Man, 496
Mary the Third, 349
Meet the Prince, 9, 474
Merchant of Venice, The, 13, 23
Merry Andrew, 9, 459
Merry Wives of Windsor, The, 14, 18
Messin' Around, 496
Mid-Channel, 24
Mikado, The, 14, 18
Mima, 9, 434
Mission Play, The, 23, 24, 25
Mlle. Ma Mere, 463
Money Lender, 363
Most Immoral Lady, A, 8, 426
Mr. Moneypenny, 8, 398
Mr. Pim Passes By, 22
Mrs. Bumpstead-Leigh, 486
Music in May, 486
Music Master, The, 514
My Girl Friday, 468
Mystery Square, 490

Ned McCobb's Daughter, 22
Ned Wayburn's Gambols, 457
Nervous Wreck, The, 431
New Moon, The, 7, 376
Nice People, 349
Nice Women, 511
Nicholas Nickleby, 384
Night Hostess, 7, 372
Night in Venice, A, 506
Nineteenth Hole, The, 17, 23

Octoroon, The, 479
Oh, Nightingale, 350
Oktobertag, 366
Olympia, 398
On Call, 413
One Way Street, 439
On Trial, 26, 347
Osceola, 24
Outside Looking In, 351

Pair O' Docs, A, 23
Pansy, 505
Paola and Francesco, 484
Paris, 8, 120, 390
Paris Bound, 14, 25, 349, 513
Parson's Bride, The, 458
Passion Play, The, 10, 497
Patience, 7, 352
Peg O' My Heart, 514
Perfect Alibi, The, 8, 429
Peter Pan, 5, 425
Phantom Lover, 366
Pilgrimage Play, The, 25
Pirate, The, 24
Pirates of Penzance, 14, 18
Play Without a Name, A, 424
Pleasure Bound, 469
Pleasure Man, 8, 385
Polly, 451
Polly with a Past, 451
Poppa, 438

Porgy, 13, 15, 513
Possession, 387
Potiphar's Wife, 437
Precious, 454
Present Arms, 513

Queen's Husband, The, 14

Rain, 514
Rainbow, 423
Rain or Shine, 513
Rajah's Diamond, 490
Redemption, 15, 419
Red Mill, The, 434
Red Robe, The, 441
Relations, 360
Revolt, 408
Richard III, 18
Right You Are If You Think You Are, 24
Ring and the Book, The, 421
Ringside, 365
Rio Rita, 13
Road to Rome, The, 17, 23, 513
Rockbound, 495
Romance, 24
Romance, Inc., 19
Rosalie, 513
Royal Box, 422
Royal Family, The, 14, 23, 430, 513
Ruddigore, 18
R.U.R., 13

Sacred Flame, The, 8, 418
Sakura, 443
Sally, 514
Salvation, 349
Saturday's Children, 283, 351
Say When, 352
Scandals, 7, 353
Seagull, The, 491
Second Man, The, 22
Security, 484
Serena Blandish, 9, 461
Seventh Heaven, 514
Shadow of a Gunman, 12
Shall We Join the Ladies?, 10
Shannons of Broadway, The, 23
She Got What She Wanted, 475
Show Boat, 513, 514
Show-off, The, 514
Shuffle Along, 514
Sign of the Leopard, 433
Silent House, The, 17, 513
Silver Cord, The, 22
Singing Jailbirds, 432
Six Characters in Search of an Author, 12
Skidding, 513
Skull, The, 23, 513
Skyrocket, 454
Some One in White, 19
Song Writer, The, 358
So This Is London, 23
Souriante Mme. Bendet, La, 20
Spider, The, 17, 23
Spring Is Here, 10, 478
Squawk, 24
Squealer, The, 415
S. S. Glencairn, 452
Stepping Out, 505
Stork, The, 349
Straight Thru the Door, 23, 389
Strange Interlude, 5, 13, 22, 23, 513
Street Scene, 9, 26, 347, 453
Streets of New York, The, 23, 24
Street Wolf, The, 448
Student Prince, 514
Subway, The, 347, 462
Suicide Club, 490
Sunny, 514
Sunny Days, 386
Sun-Up, 403
Swan, The, 23, 24

Taming of the Shrew, The, 14
Ten Nights in a Barroom, 24, 513
That Ferguson Family, 437
These Days, 415
These Few Ashes, 408
This Thing Called Love, 7, 374
This Year of Grace, 8, 410
Torchbearers, The, 24
Three Cheers, 8, 395
Three Musketeers, 513
Three of Us, The, 349
Tin Pan Alley, 409
Tired Business Man, 510
Tombeau Sous l'Arc de Triomphe, Le, 404
To-Morrow, 446
To-Night at Twelve, 416
Town's Woman, The, 478
Trapped, 15, 372
Treasure Girl, 411
Trial by Jury, 14, 18
Trial of Mary Dugan, The, 14, 513

Trip to Chinatown, A, 514
Trip to Scarborough, A, 482
Trois Jeunes Filles Nues, 475

Uncle Vanya, 507
Under the Gaslight, 488
Unknown Warrior, The, 404
Ups-a Daisy, 392

Vagabond King, 514
Vanities, 7, 355
Vanity Fair, 509
Vegetable, The, 492
Vermont, 450
Vignes du Seigneur, Les, 20
Volpone, 13

Wake up, Jonathan, 347
Wanted, 354
War Song, The, 379
What a Man, 24
What a Woman Wants, 19
What Price Glory, 351
When Crummles Played, 384
Whispering Gallery, The, 467
White Desert, 351
White Lilacs, 370
Whoopee, 9, 431
Why Men Leave Home, 23
Wife of William Flavy, The, 348
Wild Duck, The, 420
Window Panes, 24
Wings Over Europe, 9, 13, 88, 348, 432
Wishing Well, The, 23
Wolves, The, 24
World We Live In, The, 22
Would-Be Gentleman, The, 383

Yellow Jacket, The, 8, 411
You and I, 349
Young Alexander, 480
Youngest, The, 349
Young Love, 405
Your Uncle Dudley, 12

Zeppelin, 456

Ref.
PN6112
.B45
1928-1929

The Best plays of 1928-1929.